Utilitarianism with Critical Essays

Utilitarianism

John Stuart Mill

with Critical Essays

Edited by

Samuel Gorovitz

THE BOBBS-MERRILL COMPANY, INC.
INDIANAPOLIS NEW YORK

The Bobbs-Merrill

Text and Commentary

Series / Harold Weisberg,

General Editor

FIRST PRINTING

PRINTED IN THE UNITED STATES OF AMERICA
Library of Congress Catalog Card Number 74-132935

Contents

Selected Bibliography

Preface

The articles reprinted here constitute a small portion of those which—by their very numbers, by the distinction of their authors, and by their continued persistent appearance—give testament to the monumental importance of Mill's *Utilitarianism* as a treatise in ethical theory. This limited selection reflects, as any such selection must, a definite bias. I shall not attempt to justify that bias, but I do wish to make clear what I take it to be.

The objective of the *Text and Commentary* series is to provide in a single volume an important classical work and a selection of critical commentaries relevant to that work. Despite the brevity of *Utilitarianism,* the variety of issues it raises makes impossible discussion in depth of the bulk of them within a single volume. The choice, then, seemed to me to be between a survey of the relevant issues on the one hand, and a sustained treatment of some closely clustered issues on the other. I have opted for the latter.

In choosing the particular issues and the articles which discuss them, I have used a number of criteria, and not always consistently. Accessability to advanced undergraduate readers has been of paramount importance in the choice of articles, and the choice of issues reflects my own sense of what such readers find most compelling. Thus, I have emphasized questions of punishment, justice, and political and social issues, and have excluded such issues, in spite of their importance, as interpersonal utility comparisons and, indeed, sustained attempts to clarify the notion of utility itself. Basically, I have tried to provide an honest picture of current work in the areas in question, and hence have tried to select the most significant recent works and to include the prior works on which an understanding of them depends. I abandoned early any attempt to separate the articles into distinct sections. There is far too much overlap in content for that. Rather, I have ordered them approximately chronologically, which seems to me to add some sense of the historical development of the discussions. I have in some cases included short and sharply focused discussions, which provide useful foils for student criticism. Finally, I have excluded the important discussions in such classical books as those by Bentham, Ross, Moore, and Sidgwick, in order to maximize the space available for articles, and on the ground that such materials are readily enough available elsewhere.

It is my belief that, as the editor of a collection, I ought not to receive royalties from the scholarship of my colleagues in the profession. I therefore proposed that the royalties from that portion of the book which includes works for which permission was granted be assigned to the Council for Philosophical Studies, to further its work in encouraging teaching and scholarship in philosophy. I am grateful to the authors, who all agreed, and to those journals which agreed, for waiving permission fees and otherwise cooperating in the implementation of that arrangement. I wish to express special appreciation to Professor John Rawls for permission to include the previously unpublished underground classic "Justice as Reciprocity." I am indebted to Professors Rolf Sartorius, John O'Connor, and Jan Narveson for their most helpful guidance, and to Professor Charles Lemmen for meticulous bibliographical work. Finally, I wish to thank Barbara Von Eckardt Klein for her excellent editorial assistance.

S.G.

Introduction

1. Mill. The life of John Stuart Mill has been a source of fascination to philosophers and non-philosophers alike, and there is no shortage of reference material concerning it. Born in 1806, J. S. Mill was the son of James Mill, an ardent student and supporter of the philosopher Jeremy Bentham. Bentham's utilitarian principles were ingrained in the young Mill by his father during the course of one of the most intense and structured educations on record. As a young man, Mill showed the strains of the extreme intellectual pressure to which he was subjected as a child. Yet his literary and philosophical accomplishments stand deserving of the highest admiration, the more so since Mill was a full-time employee of the East India Company until its nationalization in 1858, and thus for most of his adult life he wrote only in his spare time.

The *Autobiography* of J. S. Mill provides a sensitive documentation of the author's life, including his education and the mental crises occasioned by it; the importance of John Austin's influence in his life; his intense and enduring relationship with Harriet Taylor; his years as a Member of Parliament, and the overall course of his intellectual and psychological development. Many other works about Mill, long and short, are readily available. Some of them are listed separately in the bibliography of this volume, which also cites more comprehensive bibliographical works.

2. *Utilitarianism.* Mill so grossly underestimated the importance of *Utilitarianism* that in his autobiography he devoted but a single sentence to it:

> Soon after this time [1861] I took from their repository a portion of the unpublished papers which I had written during the last years of our married life, and shaped them, with some additional matter, into the little work entitled

> "Utilitarianism"; which was first published, in three parts, in successive numbers of *Fraser's Magazine*, and afterward reprinted in a volume.

But the primary thesis of the work is so compelling, and its discussion by Mill so engaging, that it has since come to be described by J. O. Urmson as "a work which every undergraduate is set to read." Urmson makes his remark in the context of lamenting what he describes as "the almost universal misconstruction placed upon Mill's ethical doctrines" (see p. 168 this volume). Whether or not misunderstanding of Mill is as widespread as Urmson suggests, it is incontestable that his ethical writings have stimulated one of the liveliest and most sustained discussions in philosophical literature. It is in the interest of facilitating access to this discussion, as well as in the interest of promoting accurate understanding of Mill, that this anthology has been prepared.

In the last chapter of the last book of Mill's *A System of Logic* (1843) he argues that:

> There must be some standard by which to determine the goodness or badness, absolute and comparative, of ends or objects of desire. And whatever that standard is, there can be but one . . .

He goes on to "declare," without argument:

> That the general principle to which all rules of practice ought to conform, and the test by which they should be tried, is that of conduciveness to the happiness of mankind, or rather, of all sentient beings.

Utilitarianism constitutes Mill's subsequent attempt to explain and defend the conviction thus declared. He explicitly grants that questions of ultimate ends are not amenable to proof in "the ordinary and popular meaning of the term," and that in the case of an ethical doctrine such as utilitarianism the equivalent of proof consists in the presentation of considerations capable of "determining the intellect" to give assent to the doctrine (7; p. 15 below). After making such general introductory remarks, Mill moves to a discussion of what utilitarianism is. In one sense, the question is easily answered. It is the doctrine that "actions are right in proportion as they tend to promote happiness; wrong as they tend to produce the reverse of happiness." Happiness is then characterized as pleasure and the absence of pain; its reverse as pain and the privation of pleasure (10; p. 18 below). But it soon becomes unclear whether the principle thus stated is put forth as a description of human motivation or as exhortation to utilitarian behavior. Mill writes that the pursuit of pleasure and the avoidance of pain are the "end of human action" (16; p. 21 below) and, later, that it is "psychologically true" that "human nature is so constituted as to desire nothing which is not either a part of happiness or a means of happiness" (48; p. 40 below). If this is the case, then we are all utilitarians of one sort or another, and it is pointless to consider the utilitarian principle to be advice one might choose or decline to follow. Yet Mill suggests that he is discussing "the directive rule of human conduct"—a principle the adoption of which might guide people to do what they otherwise might not. But if the principle is to be recommended as a guide to behavior, it can hardly be defended on the ground that it is a psychological truth.

As a normative principle, the principle of utilitarianism has an enormous intuitive appeal. It calls for an agent to perform that action which will do more good for more people than any other, and it is hard to imagine how such an action could fail to be the right thing to do. Even though many objections to utilitarianism as a moral theory have been raised, this basic appeal remains for many people, who are more inclined to try to meet the objections than to abandon what is initially such a plausible moral theory.

However the principle of utilitarianism is taken, the notion of utility is central to it, and a cluster of questions arises as soon as one focuses on that notion. Mill seems to identify utility with pleasure; but his discussion of the verdict of the morally competent judges, from which, he writes, "there can be no appeal," suggests that the right choice among an array of alternative actions is the one that reflects a certain kind of informed rational preference (15; p. 20 below). How such informed preference can be explained is unclear. If the morally competent judge is defined simply as one whose preferences are utilitarian, then recourse to the notion of a judge is unilluminating and, indeed, misleading. But if the judge is described in terms of other characteristics, it remains to be seen how and why those characteristics relate to the standard of utility.

The question of how utility is to be construed is only the beginning. If maximization of utility is the ultimate criterion, it then becomes essential that an agent seeking to make a utilitarian choice must compare the estimated utilities which would most likely result from each of the alternatives he considers. Bentham believed that such comparisons were possible, and he proposed a hedonistic calculus to facilitate comparison among pleasures by identifying such relevant factors as the intensity, duration, certainty, propinquity, fecundity, and purity of the pleasures being compared. But even if it were possible to rank one's own prospective pleasures according to some such calculus, it does not follow that it would be possible to compare one man's pleasure with another man's. Such a comparison, however, is required if the utilitarian is to maximize the pleasure of all those who stand to be influenced by his action. Once this problem—that of estimating the happiness-producing potential of an agent's alternatives—is recognized, additional questions immediately arise. What are the consequences of an action? Do they extend without limit into the future? If so, a man may never rest, no matter how much good he has seen flow from his endeavors, secure that subsequent undesirable consequences will not show his action to have been wrong after all. Yet any attempt to clarify the notion of the consequences of an action leads to a morass of philosophical difficulty.

Further, we must be clear about whose utility counts. The directive to seek the greatest happiness of the greatest number is unclear as to what it is the greatest number of which we should seek to please. Is it, as Mill writes, "the whole sentient creation" the happiness of which determines moral value? Then how do we balance human desires against those of non-human species? And in any case, the question remains as to whether it is merely actual creatures who count, or possible creatures as well. We would judge it wrong to purify our water with a chemical that would destroy life two centuries hence, yet none of us would suffer the undesirable consequences. Our judgment then must be accounted for in terms of some obligation to future generations. Then how do we weigh their interests against our own?

The question of future generations poses another problem as well. If we are to maximize the happiness of the greatest number, does it follow that as a means to that end the utilitarian ought to maximize the number of sentient creatures? Or, less generally, if you have reason to believe that an additional child would be a happy one, are you morally obliged to have one? Are you morally barred from having a child if the odds favor his being unhappy? These considerations suggest that it is perhaps not merely the total amount of happiness that matters, but how it is distributed as well. If we may speak quantitatively at all of happiness, it seems plausible that a world with a billion people in it with five units of happiness each is a better world than one with six billion people, half of whose happiness level is zero and half of whose happiness level has fallen, as a result of the overpopulation, to two units each. Yet there is greater total happiness of a greater number of people in the second world.

Such questions of distribution give rise to a major source of criticism of utilitarian ethics generally. It is argued that the utilitarian principle in no way directs men to act justly, and that the principle therefore is at best an articulation of one major moral sentiment that needs to be tempered by others. Unjust distributions of goods or pleasures are, of course, merely one species of injustice. One can imagine a situation in which the punishment or victimization of an innocent person seems to have generally desirable consequences. A classic example is from *Crime and Punishment:*

> ". . . look here; on one side we have a stupid, senseless, worthless, spiteful, ailing, horrid old woman, not simply useless, but doing actual mischief, who has not an idea what she is living for herself, and who will die in a day or two in any case. . . . On the other side, fresh young lives thrown away for want of help, and by thousands, on every side. A hundred thousand good deeds could be done and helped, on that old woman's money which will be buried in a monastery! Hundreds, thousands perhaps, might be set on the right path; dozens of families saved from destitution, from ruin, from vice, from the lock hospitals—and all with her money. Kill her, take her money and with the help of it devote oneself to the service of humanity and the good of all. What do you think, would not one tiny crime be wiped out by thousands of good deeds? For one life thousands would be saved from corruption and decay. One death, and a hundred lives in exchange—it's simple arithmetic!"

We resist the claim that the act is right; the anti-utilitarian arguing that it is wrong and thus is a counter-example to the utilitarian principle, and the utilitarian denying that his principle entails that the action is right. But how can the utilitarian hold to such a defense, when the case seems so clear cut?

Mill points out that the utilitarian principle has as corollaries a number of secondary moral rules. These secondary rules include such common moral precepts as the prohibition of murder. It is by invoking such a rule that the utilitarian can condemn the action in question. He remains a utilitarian, since the rule he invokes is itself defended on utilitarian grounds—that is, on the basis of the empirical fact that murder tends to be injurious to the general welfare, and it is thus in the interest of the greatest happiness of the greatest number to prohibit it.

Such a move seems at first to save the day—to avoid the particular counter-example, and more generally, to pave the way for an account of how utilitarianism can be defended as honoring our conceptions of justice. For if justice can be viewed as embodied in principles which can in turn be defended as utilitarian, then Mill's claim can be vindicated:

> That justice is a name for certain moral requirements which, regarded collectively, stand higher in the scale of social utility, and are therefore of more paramount obligation, than any others. . . . (78; pp. 56–57 below.)

But celebration would be premature. For the role of the utilitarian principle has now changed drastically. Originally, it was a principle for the evaluation of actions. Now it seems to be offered as a principle which is used to evaluate rules or maxims which are then used to evaluate actions (hence, under this interpretation, it is called rule utilitarianism). It no longer seems to apply to actions directly. But moral dilemmas arise when maxims conflict. And a maxim that is usually honored may have to be overruled in the face of a weightier one in some instances. Thus, as Mill recognizes:

> To save a life, it may not only be allowable, but a duty, to steal or take by force the necessary food or medicine, or to kidnap and compel to officiate the only qualified medical practitioner (78; p. 57 below).

If we could put the secondary moral maxims in an ordered list so that each one had a unique weighting in a hierarchy of moral importance, then the possibility of conflict between maxims could be readily resolved. For then the maxim that dominates in any such conflict situation would simply be the one with the greater moral weight. But no such ranking seems possible. We agree that one ought not to lie and that one ought to keep one's promises. But sometimes one must lie in order to keep a promise. Yet neither moral principle always dominates in such conflicts. In one situation it might be better to lie and keep the promise; in another the morally preferable act might be to break the promise and avoid the lie. Mill recognizes that such conflicts between moral principles can occur, and he writes that the principle of utility:

> May be invoked to decide between them when their demands are incompatible (33; p. 30 below).

So now the principle of utility again applies to particular acts, but "only in these cases of conflict between secondary principles" (33, p. 30 below). We then have a ready solution, the direct application of the one relevant secondary moral principle, in just those cases wherein we have no significant moral problem. In all the morally interesting cases, however, wherein moral principles conflict, we must resort to the primary principle for resolution.

But now the purported counter-example reappears. Of course one ought not to murder. On the other hand, we surely ought to save lives, do good deeds, and serve humanity. Moral principles thus clash over this case, and we must appeal to the principle of utility for resolution. But then it seems that we are back where we started, with a case wherein the principle of utility directs us to approve what we know to be wrong.

Such problems have engendered efforts among moral philosophers to distinguish two species of utilitarianism—act utilitarianism, whereby the utility principle is used to evaluate specific actions, and rule utilitarianism, whereby it is used to evaluate moral rules. But critics of utilitarianism argue either that no such distinction will bear scrutiny, or else that such a distinction, though tenable, still cannot save utilitarianism from the basic objection to it—that objection being that there are morally relevant considerations in the evaluation of an act that are independent of the consequences of that act. Such is the force of the purported counter-example from *Crime and Punishment.* For if we grant both that on balance the consequences of the action would maximize utility and that they are therefore good, our condemnation of the act must be based on considerations independent of consequences.

A non-utilitarian approach to such an example might be to condemn the proposed action simply on the grounds that it is prohibited by law. To take such a position, to the effect that any illegal action is therefore wrong, is to suggest that in any situation the right thing to do is necessarily legal. But that is an extreme position. Though men of good will disagree strongly about what circumstances justify action in violation of law, most men agree that there are some cases at least where right action requires violation of law. If that is the case, then the relationship between law and morality is called into question. We may grant that one has an obligation to obey the law. If we also admit that sometimes a law ought to be violated, for example, in cases of justified civil disobedience, then we must acknowledge that the obligation to obey the law is not inviolable, but rather may be overridden on the basis of judgments about what is right—the law to the contrary notwithstanding. Any adequate moral theory must then be able to account both for our conviction that obeying the law is for the most part right, and also for our willingness to relinquish that conviction in particular situations. Whether the utilitarian can provide such an account is a disputed point.

Questions of law are, like questions of justice, closely linked to questions of government. Bentham's doctrine of utilitarianism, in fact, was developed largely in the interest of providing a framework for legislation. Mill, also, both as a private citizen and as a Member of Parliament, maintained a deep and active concern with questions of government and legislation. Critics and proponents of utilitarianism often have been concerned to examine the consequences of the theory both for particular issues related to law, such as questions of punishment, civil disobedience, and the protection of minority rights, and also for more general questions, such as the compatability of utilitarianism with basic principles of democracy and social change. A thorough defense of utilitarianism against the purported counter-example thus leads beyond questions of ethics into issues in social philosophy and philosophy of law, well illustrating the tenuousness of such philosophical classifications.

Two other classic cases offered in support of an anti-utilitarian view are those of promising and punishment. The utilitarian holds that one's obligation to keep a promise can be accounted for entirely in terms of the consequences either of the act in question or of such actions generally. The anti-utilitarian denies it, claiming that cases can be described that clearly show the existence of morally valid reasons for keeping a promise that have no dependence on consequences at all. Similarly, the utilitarian justifies the imposition of punishment on the grounds that its consequences have social utility. The retributionist argues, on the other hand, that punishment is justified by the fact that someone has done something wrong.

The principle of utilitarianism thus presents us with an ethical theory at once enchanting and enigmatic. Its surface clarity quickly gives way as we are drawn by an attempt to understand the theory into vigorously contested philosophical disputes. But the theory will not go away. For the notion of the right action being that action which will do more good for more people than any other accords so well with such a substantial portion of our moral intuitions that the defenders of utilitarianism remain dedicated to the attempt to clarify and rework it until it accounts for them all.

The articles that follow are addressed to most of the issues raised above. They do not contain every interesting position; they do not cover every important question. But they do provide a representative sampling of the best efforts in the on-going debate, and in so doing they invite the reader to enter into the controversy himself.

3. The Commentary. Twenty-eight critical articles follow. It is obviously inappropriate to recount the arguments in them here. Rather, a brief description of each is included to provide the reader with some initial direction as to the issues treated in the various discussions, and how they relate.

The reprinted articles begin with three early discussions that have received substantial attention since their appearance. Professor Prichard, in his classical article "Does Moral Philosophy Rest on a Mistake?", attacks utilitarianism by arguing more generally that any theory is wrong which holds that one's obligation to perform or abstain from performing an act is dependent on what the consequences would be of performing it. Prichard, espousing an intuitionist position, holds that moral truths "can only be apprehended directly by an act of moral thinking"—a species of thought which he contrasts with the sort of empirical inquiry into consequences that Mill's view makes a part of moral judgment. Professor Harrod, in "Utilitarianism Revised," attempts to restate the utilitarian view in a way that escapes the objections that were raised in criticism of it. In Part I, Harrod accepts the position of Prichard, that moral value cannot be attached to states of affairs, and hence, to consequences. But he argues that utilitarianism has no dependence on such a claim. In Part II, he turns to the notion of obligation. Prichard had argued that utilitarianism cannot account for moral obligation;

Harrod holds that, revised and clarified as he suggests, it can. Professor Mabbott, in "Punishment," takes a different tack in opposing utilitarianism. He considers the problem of justifying the imposition of punishment on one who has done wrong, and he concludes that utilitarian considerations must be rejected absolutely from such justification. If, as he argues, punishment is justified on other grounds, then utilitarianism fails to provide a general criterion for moral justification.

Professor Hall's article "The 'Proof' of Utility in Bentham and Mill" provides a sustained reaction to the barrage of criticism that was engendered by Mill's discussion of the possibility of proving his position to be correct. Hall reiterates Mill's statement that moral theory does not admit of deductive proof and he concludes with the contention that a sympathetic reading of Mill's remarks about proof will render the criticisms inappropriate. Professor Melden, in "Two Comments on Utilitarianism," resumes the attack, arguing that utilitarianism simply cannot account adequately for the rights that people have to the goods which experience can provide. He further argues that an examination of the special case of promising shows utilitarianism to be inadequate as an account of such obligations as those incurred by promise-making. Professor Brown also addresses this question, arguing in "Duty and the Production of Good" that utilitarianism cannot adequately account for moral obligations.

Professor Aiken's article on "Definitions, Factual Premises, and Ethical Conclusions," is not on the face of it primarily about utilitarianism. His concern is with moral reasoning generally, and he illustrates with a consideration of Mill's hedonistic doctrine that pleasure is the sole desirable end. He concludes, in the course of his discussion, that the nature of moral reasoning is such as to exempt Mill's position from some of the objections that critics, misunderstanding *Utilitarianism,* have raised.

Professor Harrison introduces a new concern in "Utilitarianism, Universalisation, and Our Duty to be Just." It is often regarded as a significant moral point that if the consequences would be undesirable, were everyone in circumstances C to perform an act of kind A, then I, in particular, ought not to perform an act of kind A in circumstances C, even if my performance of the act would not in itself be detrimental. Harrison examines the relationship between this principle and the principle of utilitarianism. In the end, he holds that the utilitarian principle as originally proposed could not justifiably be included in a system of universal legislation, whereas a modified utilitarian principle could.

Many commentators on *Utilitarianism* argue that misunderstanding of Mill's writing underlies much of the criticism of it. One might have expected, given the amount of attention focused on *Utilitarianism,* that some common understanding of his position would emerge. But as recently as 1953, in his widely read essay, "The Interpretation of the Moral Philosophy of J. S. Mill," Professor Urmson has argued, at least with respect to Mill's views about the place in moral philosophy of a supreme good, "that the current interpretations of Mill's *Utilitarianism* are so unsympathetic and so incorrect that the majority of criticisms which have in fact been based on them are irrelevant and worthless." Urmson goes on to offer an interpretation which he takes to be accurate.

In "Two Concepts of Rules," a highly regarded and often reprinted essay, Professor Rawls offers a defense of utilitarianism "against those objections which have traditionally been made against it in connection with punishment and the obligation to keep promises." His defense rests on the distinction between justifying a practice and justifying a particular action which is an instance of the practice. The essay then attempts to explain the relationship between the general utilitarian principle and the secondary moral rules in a way that accords well with our moral intuitions. Rawls' suggestion that the utilitarian principle is properly cited in justification of practices rather than of their instances is not entirely new; in fact, Urmson claimed that Mill is properly interpreted as making the same suggestion. There thus seem to be two main species of utilitarianism available for consideration, one in which use of the principle is restricted to the justification of rules, practices, or secondary principles, and the other in which it justifies particular actions. Professor Smart, in "Extreme and Restricted Utilitarianism," designates the former version as restricted utilitarianism (subsequently called *rule* utilitarianism) and the latter as extreme utilitarianism (subsequently called *act* utilitarianism). But Smart goes on to examine the distinction in greater detail, and calls into serious question the contention that a rational restricted utilitarianism is substantively different from extreme utilitarianism. On balance, Smart's discussion constitutes a defense of the extreme utilitarian position.

Professor McCloskey's "An Examination of Restricted Utilitarianism" is just that. He discusses the earlier articles by Smart, Urmson, and Rawls ("Two Concepts of Rules"), and defends the thesis "that *restricted utilitarianism* is no more tenable as an ethical theory than is the better known *extreme utilitarianism* which it is intended to supercede." He concludes that "Utilitarianism, therefore, breaks down as an account of our moral obligations" because of an inability to account for activities which are intrinsically obligatory.

Professor Benn returns to the question of punishment, and defends an essentially utilitarian position against the retributionist theory generally, and Professor Mabbott's arguments in particular. His discussion, "An Approach to the Problems of Punishment," reflects the growing interest in the notion of a practice or institution, and his position may be described as a modified restricted utilitarianism.

In "Desire as Proof of Desirability," Professor Kretzmann applauds Professor Hall's discussion of Mill's proof, and goes on to discuss the implications of Mill's remarks for social and political ethics. He argues that Mill's discussion, sympathetically read, properly interpreted, and somewhat extended, implies a democratic thesis, presumably the implication of which lends credence to utilitarianism itself. The social dimensions of ethical issues are also of primary concern in "Justice as Reciprocity," by Professor Rawls. (This article, previously unpublished, is an expanded version of "Justice as Fairness" which appeared in 1958.) He considers justice primarily as the notion applies to institutions or practices, and he argues that both justice and fairness are properly understood in terms of the notion of reciprocity. Rawls then argues that classical utilitarianism is unable to account for those aspects of justice which he has considered. He concludes that it is possible to include his conception of justice within a utilitarian framework, but only at the cost of admitting non-utilitarian principles of justice as constraints on social utility functions. To do so, however, is to relinquish the sole supremacy of the utilitarian principle as a moral principle.

"Utilitarianism and Democracy" by Professor Burns is a direct reply to Professor Kretzmann's remarks about democracy and Mill's attitude toward it. He argues that the political ideal embodied in Mill's works "is one to which the term 'democracy' has only the vaguest and most unhelpful application."

Professor Kaplan, in "Some Problems of the Extreme Utilitarian Position," argues, in direct reply to Smart, that no rational man can follow extreme utilitarianism. Kaplan then suggests that the most fruitful use of the utilitarian principle is not as a standard in the general conduct of one's life, but rather as "an evaluative yardstick" for determining which moral rules are best for society.

Professor Narveson's short essay "The Desert Island Problem" concerns the anti-utilitarian charge that some obligations are independent of any considerations of consequences. Narveson considers a classical example offered in support of such a view, and contends that the example itself, properly understood, shows that the obligations in question do depend on consequences in precisely the way that classical utilitarianism specifies. The brief note by Professor Cargile, "Utilitarianism and the Desert Island Problem," is a response to Narveson in which Cargile invokes the distinction between judging actions and judging men, and supports Narveson's claim, though in a different way, that the desert island problem is no real problem for utilitarianism.

The discussion of the utilitarian theory has centered to a large degree, in one way or another, on the compatability of that theory with moral maxims that we are inclined to accept. Thus Mill attempted to show that principles of justice, to which we attach great importance, follow from utilitarianism, and McClosky argued that certain principles regarding obligation are independent of utilitarian considerations. Another widely accepted moral maxim is that one ought to obey the law, although disobedience of the law is justified in certain very special kinds of cases. Professor Wasserstrom addresses this issue in "The Obligation to Obey the Law" and discusses its relation to issues in the dispute about the coherence of utilitarianism as a moral theory. He defends utilitarianism against certain critics, and rejects as fallacies certain arguments against the justifiability of civil disobedience.

Professor Diggs, in "Rules and Utilitarianism," returns to the question of the nature of moral rules, and points out that the concept of a rule is much less clear than it has often been taken to be. He distinguishes various kinds of rules, often confused but importantly different from one another, and he argues that when one is clear about the differences, "rule utilitarianism loses much of its initial appeal." In the course of the essay, Diggs explicitly discusses the articles by Rawls, Urmson, Smart, and McClosky. Professor Brandt, on the other hand, finds substantial appeal in rule utilitarianism. In "Some Merits of One Form of Rule-Utilitarianism," he argues that utilitarianism cannot be fully understood without reliance on a prior notion of morality. Brandt then distinguishes various forms of utilitarianism, and opts "for an 'ideal' rule utilitarianism, of the 'maximum utility' variety." He argues that the theory he then discusses under the name "the Ideal Moral Code Theory" is very similar to the view put forward by Mill. But he points out certain differences, rejects the claim that such a theory collapses into act utilitarianism, and concludes by raising some questions which his defense of rule utilitarianism leaves unanswered.

The task of understanding utilitarianism in detail includes the task of understanding just what is to count as utility. Critics of the theory have claimed that the utilitarian must value each man's pleasures as equally valuable, and this has been cited as an objection, on the ground that the pleasures of malevolence are somehow plainly inferior to the pleasures, say, of benevolence. Professor Ten, in "Mill on Self-Regarding Actions," argues that Mill did not hold all pleasures as relevant to determinations of utility. He further argues that Mill's defense of individual freedom in *On Liberty* is not a strictly utilitarian defense. Professor Narveson addresses the related question of whose utility is to count, in his essay "Utilitarianism and New Generations." He is particularly concerned with the question of whether or not one has, on utilitarian grounds, an obligation to produce children. He concludes that no such obligation follows from the utilitarian position.

Professor McClosky returns once again to the question of punishment in "Utilitarian and Retributive Punishment." He responds to critics of his earlier paper, arguing again that utilitarianism cannot provide an acceptable account of the morality of punishment. He illustrates his position with a consideration of such classic cases as the Tait Case, the Great Train Robbery, and the Eichmann Case.

Professor Margolis, in "Mill's Utilitarianism Again," holds that much of the disputation about Mill's "desirability" proof is of little interest because that proof is "an absolute anomoly"—a purported proof which, in spite of its appearance in *Utilitarianism*, is one of which "Mill actually does not avail himself . . . and says a great many things which conclusively show that he never subscribed to it." Professor Mandelbaum continues the debate on interpretation of Mill. His essay "On Interpreting Mill's Utilitarianism" is an attempt to clarify certain obscure portions of the book by drawing "on the whole corpus of Mill's writings, rather than attempting to deal with *Utilitarianism* in isolation." Mandelbaum discusses the relationship between Mill and Bentham and the connection, in Mill, between virtue and utility. The synoptic view of Mill's work that he brings to bear on the questions he considers is a good example of the best in Mill scholarship.

The final essay, "Utilitarian Ethics and Social Change," by Professor MacRae, is a fitting selection with which to conclude the anthology since it emphasizes the same kind of concern with social issues that was so much a part of early English utilitarianism. The emphasis of the article is not on legislation specifically, but on structure and change of social norms more broadly construed. MacRae offers a critique of rule utilitarianism and the generalization principle "from a sociological perspective," and he concludes by calling for continued sociological research into problems of social norms and social change.

We end, then, with a sense that utilitarianism as a moral theory is too trouble-ridden to accept and too attractive to reject—too trouble-ridden because of the many objections to it that point out non-utilitarian features of our value structure, and too attractive because of the basic appeal of a standard that selects as right the action which maximizes happiness. But if we demand of a moral theory that it yield, for each action considered, a univocal moral evaluation that corresponds with our moral intuitions insofar as we have them, perhaps we demand too much. If Mill was right in his judgment that human values are grounded in human psychology—and the position is a most plausible one—then it should be no surprise that no single moral principle adequately captures the entire substance of human values. For human desires are diverse and often inconsistent, and ambivalence is a pervasive feature of the human scene. The detailed discussions of utilitarianism that follow show that it accounts for enough of our evaluative judgments to qualify as an insightful and important moral theory. The conviction that it requires tempering with considerations of justice, individual rights, and social change may be no more than a reflection of the human realities with which philosophy must deal.

Textual Note

Chapter XII from ON THE LOGIC OF THE MORAL SCIENCES *(Book VI of Mill's* A SYSTEM OF LOGIC*), is reprinted from Bobbs-Merrill's Library of Liberal Arts edition (New York, 1965). The text of* UTILITARIANISM *is also from the Library of Liberal Arts (1957).*

The commentary consists of articles reprinted in full from the sources cited, with the exception of "Justice as Reciprocity" by John Rawls, which is published for the first time in this volume. "Extreme and Restricted Utilitarianism" has been revised by the author, J. J. C. Smart, and a number of minor corrections have been made in several other articles. Footnotes throughout are those of the authors unless bracketed and designated as editor's notes.

A System of Logic Book VI Chapter XII

Of the logic of practice, or art; including morality and policy

1. In the preceding chapters we have endeavoured to characterise the present state of those among the branches of knowledge called Moral which are sciences in the only proper sense of the term, that is, inquiries into the course of nature. It is customary, however, to include under the term Moral Knowledge, and even (though improperly) under that of Moral Science, an inquiry the results of which do not express themselves in the indicative, but in the imperative mood, or in periphrases equivalent to it; what is called the knowledge of duties, practical ethics, or morality.

Now, the imperative mood is the characteristic of art, as distinguished from science. Whatever speaks in rules or precepts, not in assertions respecting matters of fact, is art; and ethics or morality is properly a portion of the art corresponding to the sciences of human nature and society.[1]

The Method, therefore, of Ethics, can be no other than that of Art, or Practice, in general: and the portion yet uncompleted, of the task which we proposed to ourselves in the concluding Book is to characterise the general Method of Art, as distinguished from Science.

2. In all branches of practical business, there are cases in which individuals are bound to conform their practice to a pre-established rule, while there are others in which it is part of their task to find or construct the rule by which they are to govern their conduct. The first, for example, is the case of a judge under a definite written code. The judge is not called upon to determine what course would be intrinsically the most advisable in the particular case in hand, but only within what rule of law it falls; what the legislature has ordained to be done in the kind of case, and

[1] It is almost superfluous to observe, that there is another meaning of the word Art, in which it may be said to denote the poetical department or aspect of things in general, in contradistinction to the scientific. In the text, the word is used in its older, and, I hope, not yet obsolete sense.

[This final chapter of Mill's monumental treatise on logic is reprinted here because it contains an early presentation of his point of view about moral action. *Utilitarianism* may be viewed as Mill's subsequent attempt to explain and defend the convictions expressed here. Ed.]

must therefore be presumed to have intended in the individual case. The method must here be wholly and exclusively one of ratiocination or syllogism; and the process is obviously what in our analysis of the syllogism we showed that all ratiocination is, namely, the interpretation of a formula.

In order that our illustration of the opposite case may be taken from the same class of subjects as the former, we will suppose, in contrast with the situation of the judge, the position of the legislator. As the judge has laws for his guidance, so the legislator has rules and maxims of policy; but it would be a manifest error to suppose that the legislator is bound by these maxims in the same manner as the judge is bound by the laws, and that all he has to do is to argue down from them to the particular case, as the judge does from the laws. The legislator is bound to take into consideration the reasons or grounds of the maxim; the judge has nothing to do with those of the law, except so far as a consideration of them may throw light upon the intention of the lawmaker, where his words have left it doubtful. To the judge, the rule, once positively ascertained, is final; but the legislator, or other practitioner, who goes by rules rather than by their reasons, like the old-fashioned German tacticians who were vanquished by Napoleon, or the physician who preferred that his patients should die by rule rather than recover contrary to it, is rightly judged to be a mere pedant, and the slave of his formulas.

Now, the reasons of a maxim of policy, or of any other rule of art, can be no more than the theorems of the corresponding science.

The relation in which rules of art stand to doctrines of science may be thus characterised. The art proposes to itself an end to be attained, defines the end, and hands it over to the science. The science receives it, considers it as a phenomenon or effect to be studied, and having investigated its causes and conditions, sends it back to art with a theorem of the combination of circumstances by which it could be produced. Art then examines these combinations of circumstances, and according as any of them are or are not in human power, pronounces the end attainable or not. The only one of the premises, therefore, which Art supplies is the original major premise, which asserts that the attainment of the given end is desirable. Science then lends to Art the proposition (obtained by a series of inductions or of deductions) that the performance of certain actions will attain the end. From these premises Art concludes that the performance of these actions is desirable, and finding it also practicable, converts the theorem into a rule or precept.

3. It deserves particular notice that the theorem or speculative truth is not ripe for being turned into a precept until the whole, and not a part merely, of the operation which belongs to science has been performed. Suppose that we have completed the scientific process only up to a certain point; have discovered that a particular cause will produce the desired effect, but have not ascertained all the negative conditions which are necessary, that is, all the circumstances which, if present, would prevent its production. If, in this imperfect state of the scientific theory, we attempt to frame a rule of art, we perform that operation prematurely. Whenever any counteracting cause, overlooked by the theorem, takes place, the rule will be at fault; we shall employ the means, and the end will not follow. No arguing from or about the rule itself will help us through the difficulty; there is nothing for it but to turn back and finish the scientific process which should have preceded the formation of the rule. We must reopen the investigation to inquire into the remainder of the conditions on which the effect depends; and only after we have ascertained the whole of these are we prepared to

transform the completed law of the effect into a precept, in which those circumstances or combinations of circumstances which the science exhibits as conditions are prescribed as means.

It is true that, for the sake of convenience, rules must be formed from something less than this ideally perfect theory; in the first place, because the theory can seldom be made ideally perfect; and next, because, if all the counteracting contingencies, whether of frequent or of rare occurrence, were included, the rules would be too cumbrous to be apprehended and remembered by ordinary capacities, on the common occasions of life. The rules of art do not attempt to comprise more conditions than require to be attended to in ordinary cases; and are therefore always imperfect. In the manual arts, where the requisite conditions are not numerous, and where those which the rules do not specify are generally either plain to common observation or speedily learnt from practice, rules may often be safely acted on by persons who know nothing more than the rule. But in the complicated affairs of life, and still more in those of states and societies, rules cannot be relied on, without constantly referring back to the scientific laws on which they are founded. To know what are the practical contingencies which require a modification of the rule, or which are altogether exceptions to it, is to know what combinations of circumstances would interfere with, or entirely counteract, the consequences of those laws: and this can only be learnt by a reference to the theoretic grounds of the rule.

By a wise practitioner, therefore, rules of conduct will only be considered as provisional. Being made for the most numerous cases, or for those of most ordinary occurrence, they point out the manner in which it will be least perilous to act, where time or means do not exist for analysing the actual circumstances of the case, or where we cannot trust our judgment in estimating them. But they do not at all supersede the propriety of going through (when circumstances permit) the scientific process requisite for framing a rule from the data of the particular case before us. At the same time, the common rule may very properly serve as an admonition that a certain mode of action has been found by ourselves and others to be well adapted to the cases of most common occurrence; so that if it be unsuitable to the case in hand, the reason of its being so will be likely to arise from some unusual circumstance.

4. The error is therefore apparent of those who would deduce the line of conduct proper to particular cases from supposed universal practical maxims, overlooking the necessity of constantly referring back to the principles of the speculative science, in order to be sure of attaining even the specific end which the rules have in view. How much greater still, then, must the error be of setting up such unbending principles, not merely as universal rules for attaining a given end, but as rules of conduct generally; without regard to the possibility, not only that some modifying cause may prevent the attainment of the given end by the means which the rule prescribes, but that success itself may conflict with some other end, which may possibly chance to be more desirable.

This is the habitual error of many of the political speculators whom I have characterised as the geometrical school; especially in France, where ratiocination from rules of practice forms the staple commodity of journalism and political oratory; a misapprehension of the functions of Deduction which has brought much discredit, in the estimation of other countries, upon the spirit of generalisation so honourably characteristic of the French mind. The commonplaces of politics, in France, are large and sweeping practical maxims, from which, as ultimate premises, men reason downwards to particular applications, and this they call being logical and consistent. For instance, they are perpetually arguing that such and such a measure ought to be adopted, because it is a consequence of the principle on which the form of government is founded; of the principle of legitimacy, or the principle of the sovereignty of the people. To which it may be answered, that if these be really practical principles, they must rest on speculative grounds; the sovereignty of the people (for example) must be a right foundation for government, because a government thus constituted tends to produce certain beneficial effects. Inasmuch, however, as no government produces all possible beneficial effects, but all are attended with more or fewer inconveniences, and since these cannot usually be combated by means drawn from the very causes which produce them, it would be often a much stronger recommendation of some practical arrangement that it does not follow from what is called the general principle of the government, than that it does. Under a government of legitimacy, the presumption is far rather in favour of institutions of popular origin; and in a democracy, in favour of arrangements tending to check the impetus of popular will. The line of argumentation so commonly mistaken in France for political philosophy tends to the practical conclusion that we should exert our utmost efforts to aggravate, instead of alleviating, whatever are the characteristic imperfections of the system of institutions which we prefer, or under which we happen to live.

5. The grounds, then, of every rule of art are to be found in theorems of science. An art, or a body of art, consists of the rules, together with as much of the speculative propositions as comprises the justification of those rules. The complete art of any matter includes a selection of such a portion from the science as is necessary to show on what conditions the effects which the art aims at producing depend. And Art in general consists of the truths of science, arranged in the most convenient order for practice, instead of the order which is the most convenient for thought. Science groups and arranges its truths so as to enable us to take in at one view as much as possible of the general order of the universe. Art, though it must assume the same general laws, follows them only into such of their detailed consequences as have led to the formation of rules of conduct, and brings together from parts of the field of science most remote from one another the truths relating to the production of the different and heterogeneous conditions necessary to each effect which the exigencies of practical life require to be produced.[2]

Science, therefore, following one cause to its various effects, while art traces one effect to its multiplied and diversified causes and conditions, there is need of a set of intermediate scientific truths, derived from the higher generalities of science, and destined to serve as the generalia or first principles of the various arts. The scientific operation of framing these intermediate principles, M. Comte characterises as one of those results of philosophy which are reserved for futurity. The only complete example which he points out as actually realised. and which can be held up as a type to be imitated in more important matters, is the general theory of the art of Descriptive Geometry, as conceived by M. Monge. It is not, however, difficult to understand what the nature of these intermediate principles must generally be. After framing the most comprehensive possible conception of the end to be aimed at, that is, of the effect to be produced, and determining in the same comprehensive manner the set of conditions on which the effect depends, there remains to be taken

[2] Professor Bain and others call the selection from the truths of science made for the purposes of an art, a Practical Science; and confine the same Art to the actual rules.

a general survey of the resources which can be commanded for realising this set of conditions; and when the result of this survey has been embodied in the fewest and most extensive propositions possible, those propositions will express the general relation between the available means and the end, and will constitute the general scientific theory of the art, from which its practical methods will follow as corollaries.

6. But though the reasonings which connect the end or purpose of every art with its means belong to the domain of Science, the definition of the end itself belongs exclusively to Art, and forms its peculiar province. Every art has one first principle, or general major premise, not borrowed from science; that which enunciates the object aimed at, and affirms it to be a desirable object. The builder's art assumes that it is desirable to have buildings; architecture, (as one of the fine arts,) that it is desirable to have them beautiful or imposing. The hygienic and medical arts assume, the one that the preservation of health, the other that the cure of disease, are fitting and desirable ends. These are not propositions of science. Propositions of science assert a matter of fact: an existence, a co-existence, a succession, or a resemblance. The propositions now spoken of do not assert that anything is, but enjoin or recommend that something should be. They are a class by themselves. A proposition of which the predicate is expressed by the words *ought* or *should be,* is generically different from one which is expressed by *is* or *will be.* It is true that, in the largest sense of the words, even these propositions assert something as a matter of fact. The fact affirmed in them is, that the conduct recommended excites in the speaker's mind the feeling of approbation. This, however, does not go to the bottom of the matter, for the speaker's approbation is no sufficient reason why other people should approve; nor ought it to be a conclusive reason even with himself. For the purposes of practice, every one must be required to justify his approbation; and for this there is need of general premises, determining what are the proper objects of approbation, and what the proper order of precedence among those objects.

These general premises, together with the principal conclusions which may be deduced from them, form (or rather might form) a body of doctrine, which is properly the Art of Life, in its three departments, Morality, Prudence or Policy, and Aesthetics; the Right, the Expedient, and the Beautiful or Noble, in human conduct and works. To this art (which, in the main, is unfortunately still to be created) all other arts are subordinate; since its principles are those which must determine whether the special aim of any particular art is worthy and desirable, and what is its place in the scale of desirable things. Every art is thus a joint result of laws of nature disclosed by science, and of the general principles of what has been called Teleology, or the Doctrine of Ends;[3] which, borrowing the language of the German metaphysicians, may also be termed, not improperly, the principles of Practical Reason.

A scientific observer or reasoner, merely as such, is not an adviser for practice. His part is only to show that certain consequences follow from certain causes, and that to obtain certain ends, certain means are the most effectual. Whether the ends themselves are such as ought to be pursued, and if so, in what cases and to how great a length, it is no part of his business as a cultivator of science to decide, and science alone will never qualify him for the decision. In purely physical science there is not much temptation to assume this

[3] The word Teleology is also, but inconveniently and improperly, employed by some writers as a name for the attempt to explain the phenomena of the universe from final causes.

ulterior office; but those who treat of human nature and society invariably claim it; they always undertake to say, not merely what is, but what ought to be. To entitle them to do this, a complete doctrine of Teleology is indispensable. A scientific theory, however perfect, of the subject-matter, considered merely as part of the order of nature, can in no degree serve as a substitute. In this respect the various subordinate arts afford a misleading analogy. In them there is seldom any visible necessity for justifying the end, since in general its desirableness is denied by nobody, and it is only when the question of precedence is to be decided between that end and some other, that the general principles of Teleology have to be called in; but a writer on Morals and Politics requires those principles at every step. The most elaborate and well-digested exposition of the laws of succession and co-existence among mental or social phenomena, and of their relation to one another as causes and effects, will be of no avail towards the art of Life or of Society, if the ends to be aimed at by that art are left to the vague suggestions of the *intellectus sibi permissus* [the intellect permitting itself], or are taken for granted without analysis or questioning.

7. There is, then, a *Philosophia Prima* peculiar to Art, as there is one which belongs to Science. There are not only first principles of Knowledge, but first principles of Conduct. There must be some standard by which to determine the goodness or badness, absolute and comparative, of ends or objects of desire. And whatever that standard is, there can be but one: for if there were several ultimate principles of conduct, the same conduct might be approved by one of those principles and condemned by another; and there would be needed some more general principle as umpire between them.

Accordingly, writers on moral philosophy have mostly felt the necessity not only of referring all rules of conduct, and all judgments of praise and blame, to principles, but of referring them to some one principle; some rule or standard, with which all other rules of conduct were required to be consistent, and from which by ultimate consequence they could all be deduced. Those who have dispensed with the assumption of such an universal standard have only been enabled to do so by supposing that a moral sense, or instinct, inherent in our constitution, informs us, both what principles of conduct we are bound to observe, and also in what order these should be subordinated to one another.

The theory of the foundations of morality is a subject which it would be out of place, in a work like this, to discuss at large, and which could not to any useful purpose be treated incidentally. I shall content myself therefore with saying, that the doctrine of intuitive moral principles, even if true, would provide only for that portion of the field of conduct which is properly called moral. For the remainder of the practice of life some general principle, or standard, must still be sought; and if that principle be rightly chosen, it will be found, I apprehend, to serve quite as well for the ultimate principle of Morality, as for that of Prudence, Policy, or Taste.

Without attempting in this place to justify my opinion, or even to define the kind of justification which it admits of, I merely declare my conviction, that the general principle to which all rules of practice ought to conform, and the test by which they should be tried, is that of conduciveness to the happiness of mankind, or rather, of all sentient beings: in other words, that the promotion of happiness is the ultimate principle of Teleology.[4]

I do not mean to assert that the pro-

[4] For an express discussion and vindication of this principle, see the little volume entitled *Utilitarianism* [1861].

motion of happiness should be itself the end of all actions, or even of all rules of action. It is the justification, and ought to be the controller, of all ends, but is not itself the sole end. There are many virtuous actions, and even virtuous modes of action, (though the cases are, I think, less frequent than is often supposed,) by which happiness in the particular instance is sacrificed, more pain being produced than pleasure. But conduct of which this can be truly asserted admits of justification only because it can be shown that on the whole more happiness will exist in the world if feelings are cultivated which will make people, in certain cases, regardless of happiness. I fully admit that this is true: that the cultivation of an ideal nobleness of will and conduct should be to individual human beings an end, to which the specific pursuit either of their own happiness or of that of others (except so far as included in that idea) should, in any case of conflict, give way. But I hold that the very question, what constitutes this elevation of character, is itself to be decided by a reference to happiness as the standard. The character itself should be, to the individual, a paramount end, simply because the existence of this ideal nobleness of character, or of a near approach to it, in any abundance, would go further than all things else towards making human life happy, both in the comparatively humble sense of pleasure and freedom from pain, and in the higher meaning of rendering life, not what it now is almost universally, puerile and insignificant, but such as human beings with highly developed faculties can care to have.

8. With these remarks we must close this summary view of the application of the general logic of scientific inquiry to the moral and social departments of science. Notwithstanding the extreme generality of the principles of method which I have laid down, (a generality which, I trust, is not in this instance synonymous with vagueness,) I have indulged the hope that to some of those on whom the task will devolve of bringing those most important of all sciences into a more satisfactory state these observations may be useful, both in removing erroneous and in clearing up the true conceptions of the means by which, on subjects of so high a degree of complication, truth can be attained. Should this hope be realised, what is probably destined to be the great intellectual achievement of the next two or three generations of European thinkers will have been in some degree forwarded.

Utilitarianism

Chapter I / General remarks

There are few circumstances among those which make up the present condition of human knowledge more unlike what might have been expected, or more significant of the backward state in which speculation on the most important subjects still lingers, than the little progress which has been made in the decision of the controversy respecting the criterion of right and wrong. From the dawn of philosophy, the question concerning the *summum bonum,* or, what is the same thing, concerning the foundation of morality, has been accounted the main problem in speculative thought, has occupied the most gifted intellects and divided them into sects and schools carrying on a vigorous warfare against one another. And after more than two thousand years the same discussions continue, philosophers are still ranged under the same contending banners, and neither thinkers nor mankind at large seem nearer to being unanimous on the subject than when the youth Socrates listened to the old Protagoras and asserted (if Plato's dialogue be grounded on a real conversation) the theory of utilitarianism against the popular morality of the so-called sophist.

It is true that similar confusion and uncertainty and, in some cases, similar discordance exist respecting the first principles of all the sciences, not excepting that which is deemed the most certain of them —mathematics, without much impairing, generally indeed without impairing at all, the trustworthiness of the conclusions of those sciences. An apparent anomaly, the explanation of which is that the detailed doctrines of a science are not usually deduced from, nor depend for their evidence upon, what are called its first principles. Were it not so, there would be no science more precarious, or whose conclusions were more insufficiently made out, than algebra, which derives none of its certainty from what are commonly taught to learners as its elements, since these, as laid down by some of its most eminent teachers, are as full of fictions as English law, and of mysteries as theology. The truths which are ultimately accepted as the first principles of a science are really the last results of metaphysical analysis practiced on the elementary notions with which the science is conversant; and their relation to the science is not that of foundations to an edifice, but of roots to a tree, which may perform their office equally well though they be never dug down to and exposed to light. But though in science the particular truths precede the general theory, the contrary might be expected to be the case with a practical art, such as morals or legislation. All action is for the sake of some end, and rules of action, it seems natural to suppose, must take their whole character and color from the end to which they are subservient. When we engage in a pursuit, a clear and precise conception of what we are pursuing would seem to be the first thing we need, instead of the last we are to look forward to. A test of right and wrong must be the means, one would think, of ascertaining what is right or wrong, and not a consequence of having already ascertained it.

The difficulty is not avoided by having recourse to the popular theory of a natural faculty, a sense of instinct, informing us of right and wrong. For—besides that the existence of such a moral instinct is itself one of the matters in dispute—those believers in it who have any pretensions to philosophy have been obliged to abandon the idea that it discerns what is right or wrong in the particular case in hand, as our other senses discern the sight or sound actually present. Our moral faculty, according to all those of its interpreters who are entitled to the name of thinkers, supplies us only with the general principles of moral judgments; it is a branch of our reason, not of our sensitive faculty, and must be looked to for the abstract doctrines of morality, not for perception of it in the concrete. The intuitive, no less than what may be termed the inductive, school of ethics insists on the necessity of general laws. They both agree that the morality of an individual action is not a question of direct perception, but of the application of a law to an individual case. They recognize also, to a great extent, the same moral laws, but differ as to their evidence and the source from which they derive their authority. According to the one opinion, the principles of morals are evident *a priori*, requiring nothing to command assent except that the meaning of the terms be understood. According to the other doctrine, right and wrong, as well as truth and falsehood, are questions of observation and experience. But both hold equally that morality must be deduced from principles; and the intuitive school affirm as strongly as the inductive that there is a science of morals. Yet they seldom attempt to make out a list of the *a priori* principles which are to serve as the premises of the science; still more rarely do they make any effort to reduce those various principles to one first principle or common ground of obligation. They either assume the ordinary precepts of morals as of *a priori* authority, or they lay down as the common groundwork of those maxims some generality much less obviously authoritative than the maxims themselves, and which has never succeeded in gaining popular acceptance. Yet to support their pretensions there ought either to be some one fundamental principle or law at the root of all morality, or, if there be several, there should be a determinate order of precedence among them; and the one principle, or the rule for deciding between the various principles when they conflict, ought to be self-evident.

To inquire how far the bad effects of this deficiency have been mitigated in practice, or to what extent the moral beliefs of mankind have been vitiated or made uncertain by the absence of any distinct recognition of an ultimate standard, would imply a complete survey and criticism of past and present ethical doctrine. It would, however, be easy to show that whatever steadiness or consistency these moral beliefs have attained has been mainly due to the tacit influence of a standard not recognized. Although the nonexistence of an acknowledged first principle has made ethics not so much a guide as a consecration of men's actual sentiments, still, as men's sentiments, both of favor and of aversion, are greatly influenced by what they suppose to be the effects of things upon their happiness, the principle of utility, or, as Bentham latterly called it, the greatest happiness principle, has had a large share in forming the moral doctrines even of those who most scornfully reject its authority. Nor is there any school of thought which refuses to admit that the influence of actions on happiness is a most material and even predominant consideration in many of the details of morals, however unwilling to acknowledge it as the fundamental principle of morality and the source of moral obligation. I might go much further and say that to all those *a priori* moralists who deem it necessary to argue at all, utilitarian arguments are indispensable. It is not my present purpose to criticize these thinkers; but I cannot help referring, for illustration, to a systematic treatise by one of the most illustrious of them, the *Metaphysics of Ethics* by Kant. This remarkable man, whose system of thought will long remain one of the landmarks in the history of philosophical speculation, does, in the treatise in question, lay down a universal first principle as the origin and ground of moral obligation; it is this: "So act that the rule on which thou actest would admit of being adopted as a law by all rational beings." But when he begins to deduce from this precept any of the actual duties of morality, he fails, almost grotesquely, to show that there would be any contradiction, any logical (not to say physical) impossibility, in the adoption by all rational beings of the most outrageously immoral rules of conduct. All he shows is that the *consequences* of their universal adoption would be such as no one would choose to incur.

On the present occasion, I shall, without further discussion of the other theories, attempt to contribute something toward the understanding and appreciation of the "utilitarian" or "happiness" theory, and toward such proof as it is susceptible of. It is evident that this cannot be proof in the ordinary and popular meaning of the term. Questions of ultimate ends are not amenable to direct proof. Whatever can be proved to be good must be so by being shown to be a means to something admitted to be good without proof. The medical art is proved to be good by its conducing to health; but how is it possible to prove that health is good? The art of music is good, for the reason, among others, that it produces pleasure; but what proof is it possible to give that pleasure is good? If, then, it is asserted that there is a comprehensive formula, including all things which are in themselves good, and that whatever else is good is not so as an end but as a means, the formula may be accepted or rejected, but is not a subject of what is commonly understood by proof. We are not, however, to infer that its acceptance or rejection must depend on blind impulse or arbitrary choice. There is a larger meaning of the word "proof," in which this question is as amenable to it as any other of the disputed questions of philosophy. The subject is within the cognizance of the rational faculty; and neither does that faculty deal with it solely in the way of intuition. Considerations may be presented capable of determining the intellect either to give or withhold its assent to the doctrine; and this is equivalent to proof.

We shall examine presently of what nature are these considerations; in what manner they apply to the case, and what rational grounds, therefore, can be given for accepting or rejecting the utilitarian formula. But it is a preliminary condition of rational acceptance or rejection that the formula should be correctly understood. I believe that the very imperfect notion ordinarily formed of its meaning is the chief obstacle which impedes its reception, and that, could it be cleared even from only the grosser misconceptions, the question would be greatly simplified and a large proportion of its difficulties removed. Before, therefore, I attempt to enter into the philosophical grounds which can be given for assenting to the utilitarian standard, I shall offer some illustrations of the doctrine itself, with the view of showing more clearly what it is, distinguishing it from what it is not, and disposing of such of the practical objections to it as either originate in, or are closely connected with, mistaken interpretations of its meaning. Having thus prepared the ground, I shall afterwards endeavor to throw such light as I can call upon the question considered as one of philosophical theory.

Chapter II / What utilitarianism is

A passing remark is all that needs be given to the ignorant blunder of supposing that those who stand up for utility as the test of right and wrong use the term in that restricted and merely colloquial sense in which utility is opposed to pleasure. An apology is due to the philosophical opponents of utilitarianism for even the momentary appearance of confounding them with anyone capable of so absurd a misconception; which is the more extraordinary, inasmuch as the contrary accusation, of referring everything to pleasure, and that, too, in its grossest form, is another of the common charges against utilitarianism: and, as has been pointedly remarked by an able writer, the same sort of persons, and often the very same persons, denounce the theory "as impracticably dry when the word 'utility' precedes the word 'pleasure,' and as too practicably voluptuous when the word 'pleasure' precedes the word 'utility.' " Those who know anything about the matter are aware that every writer, from Epicurus to Bentham, who maintained the theory of utility meant by it, not something to be contradistinguished from pleasure, but pleasure itself, together with exemption from pain; and instead of opposing the useful to the agreeable or the ornamental, have always declared that the useful means these, among other things. Yet the common herd, including the herd of writers, not only in newspapers and periodicals, but in books of weight and pretension, are perpetually falling into this shallow mistake. Having caught up the word "utilitarian," while knowing nothing whatever about it but its sound, they habitually express by it the rejection or the neglect of pleasure in some of its forms: of beauty, of ornament, or of amusement. Nor is the term thus ignorantly misapplied solely in disparagement, but occasionally in compliment, as though it implied superiority to frivolity and the mere pleasures of the moment. And this perverted use is the only one in which the word is popularly known, and the one from which the new generation are acquiring their sole notion of its meaning. Those who introduced the word, but who had for many years discontinued it as a distinctive appellation, may well feel themselves called upon to resume it if by doing so they can hope to contribute anything toward rescuing it from this utter degradation.[1]

The creed which accepts as the foundation of morals "utility" or the "greatest happiness principle" holds that actions are right in proportion as they tend to promote happiness; wrong as they tend to produce the reverse of happiness. By happiness is intended pleasure and the absence of pain; by unhappiness, pain and the privation of pleasure. To give a clear view of the moral standard set up by the theory, much more requires to be said; in particular, what things it includes in the ideas of pain and pleasure, and to what extent this is left an open question. But these supplementary explanations do not affect the theory of life on which this theory of morality is grounded—namely, that pleasure and freedom from pain are the only things desirable as ends; and that all desirable things (which are as numerous in the utilitarian as in any other scheme) are desirable either for pleasure inherent in themselves or as means to the promotion of pleasure and the prevention of pain.

Now such a theory of life excites in many minds, and among them in some of the most estimable in feeling and purpose, inveterate dislike. To suppose that life has (as they express it) no higher end than pleasure—no better and nobler object of desire and pursuit—they designate as utterly mean and groveling, as a doctrine worthy only of swine, to whom the followers of Epicurus were, at a very early period, contemptuously likened; and modern holders of the doctrine are occasionally made the subject of equally polite comparisons by its German, French, and English assailants.

When thus attacked, the Epicureans have always answered that it is not they, but their accusers, who represent human nature in a degrading light, since the accusation supposes human beings to be capable of no pleasures except those of which swine are capable. If this supposition were true, the charge could not be gainsaid, but would then be no longer an imputation; for if the sources of pleasure were precisely the same to human beings and to swine, the rule of life which is good enough for the one would be good enough for the other. The comparison of the Epicurean life to that of beasts is felt as degrading, precisely because a beast's pleasures do not satisfy a human being's conceptions of happiness. Human beings have faculties more elevated than the animal appetites and, when once made conscious of them, do not regard anything as happiness which does not include their gratification. I do not, indeed, consider the Epicureans to have been by any means faultless in drawing out their scheme of consequences from the utilitarian principle. To do this in any sufficient manner, many Stoic, as well as Christian, elements require to be included. But there is no known Epicurean theory of life which does not assign to the pleasures of the intellect, of the feelings and imagination, and of the moral sentiments a much higher value as pleasures than to those of mere sensation. It must be admitted, however, that utilitarian writers in general have placed the superiority of mental over bodily pleasures chiefly in the greater permanency, safety, uncostliness, etc., of the former—that is, in their circumstantial advantages rather than in their intrinsic na-

[1] The author of this essay has reason for believing himself to be the first person who brought the word "utilitarian" into use. He did not invent it, but adopted it from a passing expression in Mr. Galt's *Annals of the Parish.* After using it as a designation for several years, he and others abandoned it from a growing dislike to anything resembling a badge or watchword of sectarian distinction. But as a name for one single opinion, not a set of opinions—to denote the recognition of utility as a standard, not any particular way of applying it—the term supplies a want in the language, and offers, in many cases, a convenient mode of avoiding tiresome circumlocution.

ture. And on all these points utilitarians have fully proved their case; but they might have taken the other and, as it may be called, higher ground with entire consistency. It is quite compatible with the principle of utility to recognize the fact that some kinds of pleasure are more desirable and more valuable than others. It would be absurd that, while in estimating all other things quality is considered as well as quantity, the estimation of pleasure should be supposed to depend on quantity alone.

If I am asked what I mean by difference of quality in pleasures, or what makes one pleasure more valuable than another, merely as a pleasure, except its being greater in amount, there is but one possible answer. Of two pleasures, if there be one to which all or almost all who have experience of both give a decided preference, irrespective of any feeling of moral obligation to prefer it, that is the more desirable pleasure. If one of the two is, by those who are competently acquainted with both, placed so far above the other that they prefer it, even though knowing it to be attended with a greater amount of discontent, and would not resign it for any quantity of the other pleasure which their nature is capable of, we are justified in ascribing to the preferred enjoyment a superiority in quality so far outweighing quantity as to render it, in comparison, of small account.

Now it is an unquestionable fact that those who are equally acquainted with and equally capable of appreciating and enjoying both do give a most marked preference to the manner of existence which employs their higher faculties. Few human creatures would consent to be changed into any of the lower animals for a promise of the fullest allowance of a beast's pleasures; no intelligent human being would consent to be a fool, no instructed person would be an ignoramus, no person of feeling and conscience would be selfish and base, even though they should be persuaded that the fool, the dunce, or the rascal is better satisfied with his lot than they are with theirs. They would not resign what they possess more than he for the most complete satisfaction of all the desires which they have in common with him. If they ever fancy they would, it is only in cases of unhappiness so extreme that to escape from it they would exchange their lot for almost any other, however undesirable in their own eyes. A being of higher faculties requires more to make him happy, is capable probably of more acute suffering, and certainly accessible to it at more points, than one of an inferior type; but in spite of these liabilities, he can never really wish to sink into what he feels to be a lower grade of existence. We may give what explanation we please of this unwillingness; we may attribute it to pride, a name which is given indiscriminately to some of the most and to some of the least estimable feelings of which mankind are capable; we may refer it to the love of liberty and personal independence, an appeal to which was with the Stoics one of the most effective means for the inculcation of it; to the love of power or to the love of excitement, both of which do really enter into and contribute to it; but its most appropriate appellation is a sense of dignity, which all human beings possess in one form or other, and in some, though by no means in exact, proportion to their higher faculties, and which is so essential a part of the happiness of those in whom it is strong that nothing which conflicts with it could be otherwise than momentarily an object of desire to them. Whoever supposes that this preference takes place at a sacrifice of happiness—that the superior being, in anything like equal circumstances, is not happier than the inferior—confounds the two very different ideas of happiness and content. It is indisputable that the being whose capacities of enjoyment are low has the greatest chance of having them fully satisfied; and a highly endowed being will always feel that any happiness which he can look for, as the world is constituted, is imperfect. But he can learn to bear its imperfections, if they are at all bearable; and they will not make him envy the being who is indeed unconscious of the imperfections, but only because he feels not at all the good which those imperfections qualify. It is better to be a human being dissatisfied than a pig satisfied; better to be Socrates dissatisfied than a fool satisfied. And if the fool, or the pig, are of a different opinion, it is because they only know their own side of the question. The other party to the comparison knows both sides.

It may be objected that many who are capable of the higher pleasures occasionally, under the influence of temptation, postpone them to the lower. But this is quite compatible with a full appreciation of the intrinsic superiority of the higher. Men often, from infirmity of character, make their election for the nearer good, though they know it to be the less valuable; and this no less when the choice is between two bodily pleasures than when it is between bodily and mental. They pursue sensual indulgences to the injury of health, though perfectly aware that health is the greater good. It may be further objected that many who begin with youthful enthusiasm for everything noble, as they advance in years, sink into indolence and selfishness. But I do not believe that those who undergo this very common change voluntarily choose the lower description of pleasures in preference to the higher. I believe that, before they devote themselves exclusively to the one, they have already become incapable of the other. Capacity for the nobler feelings is in most natures a very tender plant, easily killed, not only by hostile influences, but by mere want of sustenance; and in the majority of young persons it speedily dies away if the occupations to which their position in life has devoted them, and the society into which it has thrown them, are not favorable to keeping that higher capacity in exercise. Men lose their high aspirations as they lose their intellectual tastes, because they have not time or opportunity for indulging them; and they addict themselves to inferior pleasures, not because they deliberately prefer them, but because they are either the only ones to which they have access or the only ones which they are any longer capable of enjoying. It may be questioned whether anyone who has remained equally susceptible to both classes of pleasures ever knowingly and calmly preferred the lower, though many, in all ages, have broken down in an ineffectual attempt to combine both.

From this verdict of the only competent judges, I apprehend there can be no appeal. On a question which is the best worth having of two pleasures, or which of two modes of existence is the most grateful to the feelings, apart from its moral attributes and from its consequences, the judgment of those who are qualified by knowledge of both, or, if they differ, that of the majority among them, must be admitted as final. And there needs be the less hesitation to accept this judgment respecting the quality of pleasures, since there is no other tribunal to be referred to even on the question of quantity. What means are there of determining which is the acutest of two pains, or the intensest of two pleasurable sensations, except the general suffrage of those who are familiar with both? Neither pains nor pleasures are homogeneous, and pain is always heterogeneous with pleasure. What is there to decide whether a particular pleasure is worth purchasing at the cost of a particular pain, except the feelings and judgment of the experienced? When, therefore, those feelings and judgment declare the pleasures derived from the higher faculties to be preferable *in kind*, apart from the question of intensity, to those of which the animal nature, disjoined from the higher faculties, is susceptible, they are entitled on this subject to the same regard.

I have dwelt on this point as being a necessary part of a perfectly just conception of utility or happiness considered as the directive rule of human conduct. But it is by no means an indispensable condition to the acceptance of the utilitarian standard; for that standard is not the agent's own greatest happiness, but the greatest amount of happiness altogether; and if it may possibly be doubted whether a noble character is always the happier for its nobleness, there can be no doubt that it makes other people happier, and that the world in general is immensely a gainer by it. Utilitarianism, therefore, could only attain its end by the general cultivation of nobleness of character, even if each individual were only benefited by the nobleness of others, and his own, so far as happiness is concerned, were a sheer deduction from the benefit. But the bare enunciation of such an absurdity as this last renders refutation superfluous.

According to the greatest happiness principle, as above explained, the ultimate end, with reference to and for the sake of which all other things are desirable—whether we are considering our own good or that of other people—is an existence exempt as far as possible from pain, and as rich as possible in enjoyments, both in point of quantity and quality; the test of quality and the rule for measuring it against quantity being the preference felt by those who, in their opportunities of experience, to which must be added their habits of self-consciousness and self-observation, are best furnished with the means of comparison. This, being according to the utilitarian opinion the end of human action, is necessarily also the standard of morality, which may accordingly be defined "the rules and precepts for human conduct," by the observance of which an existence such as has been described might be, to the greatest extent possible, secured to all mankind; and not to them only, but, so far as the nature of things admits, to the whole sentient creation.

Against this doctrine, however, arises another class of objectors who say that happiness, in any form, cannot be the rational purpose of human life and action; because, in the first place, it is unattainable; and they contemptuously ask, What right hast thou to be happy?—a question which Mr. Carlyle clinches by the addition, What right, a short time ago, hadst thou even *to be*? Next they say that men can do *without* happiness; that all noble human beings have felt this, and could not have become noble but by learning the lesson of *Entsagen*, or renunciation; which lesson, thoroughly learned and submitted to, they affirm to be the beginning and necessary condition of all virtue.

The first of these objections would go to the root of the matter were it well founded; for if no happiness is to be had at all by human beings, the attainment of it cannot be the end of morality or of any rational conduct. Though, even in that case, something might still be said for the utilitarian theory, since utility includes not solely the pursuit of happiness, but the prevention or mitigation of unhappiness; and if the former aim be chimerical, there will be all the greater scope and more imperative need for the latter, so long at least as mankind think fit to live and do not take refuge in the simultaneous act of suicide recommended under certain conditions by Novalis.[2] When, however, it is thus positively asserted to be impossible that human life should be happy, the assertion, if not something like a verbal quibble, is at least an exaggeration. If by happiness be meant a continuity of highly pleasurable excitement, it is evident enough

[2] [Pseudonym of Friedrich Leopold Freiherr von Hardenberg (1772–1801), German poet and leader of early German Romanticism.]

that this is impossible. A state of exalted pleasure lasts only moments or in some cases, and with some intermissions, hours or days, and is the occasional brilliant flash of enjoyment, not its permanent and steady flame. Of this the philosophers who have taught that happiness is the end of life were as fully aware as those who taunt them. The happiness which they meant was not a life of rapture, but moments of such, in an existence made up of few and transitory pains, many and various pleasures, with a decided predominance of the active over the passive, and having as the foundation of the whole not to expect more from life than it is capable of bestowing. A life thus composed, to those who have been fortunate enough to obtain it, has always appeared worthy of the name of happiness. And such an existence is even now the lot of many during some considerable portion of their lives. The present wretched education and wretched social arrangements are the only real hindrance to its being attainable by almost all.

The objectors perhaps may doubt whether human beings, if taught to consider happiness as the end of life, would be satisfied with such a moderate share of it. But great numbers of mankind have been satisfied with much less. The main constituents of a satisfied life appear to be two, either of which by itself is often found sufficient for the purpose: tranquillity and excitement. With much tranquillity, many find that they can be content with very little pleasure; with much excitement, many can reconcile themselves to a considerable quantity of pain. There is assuredly no inherent impossibility of enabling even the mass of mankind to unite both, since the two are so far from being incompatible that they are in natural alliance, the prolongation of either being a preparation for, and exciting a wish for, the other. It is only those in whom indolence amounts to a vice that do not desire excitement after an interval of repose; it is only those in whom the need of excitement is a disease that feel the tranquillity which follows excitement dull and insipid, instead of pleasurable in direct proportion to the excitement which preceded it. When people who are tolerably fortunate in their outward lot do not find in life sufficient enjoyment to make it valuable to them, the cause generally is caring for nobody but themselves. To those who have neither public nor private affections, the excitements of life are much curtailed, and in any case dwindle in value as the time approaches when all selfish interests must be terminated by death; while those who leave after them objects of personal affection, and especially those who have also cultivated a fellow-feeling with the collective interests of mankind, retain as lively an interest in life on the eve of death as in the vigor of youth and health. Next to selfishness, the principal cause which makes life unsatisfactory is want of mental cultivation. A cultivated mind—I do not mean that of a philosopher, but any mind to which the fountains of knowledge have been opened, and which has been taught, in any tolerable degree, to exercise its faculties—finds sources of inexhaustible interest in all that surrounds it: in the objects of nature, the achievements of art, the imaginations of poetry, the incidents of history, the ways of mankind, past and present, and their prospects in the future. It is possible, indeed, to become indifferent to all this, and that too without having exhausted a thousandth part of it, but only when one has had from the beginning no moral or human interest in these things and has sought in them only the gratification of curiosity.

Now there is absolutely no reason in the nature of things why an amount of mental culture sufficient to give an intelligent interest in these objects of contemplation should not be the inheritance of everyone born in a civilized country. As little is there an inherent necessity that any human being should be a selfish egotist, devoid of every feeling or care but those which center in his own miserable individuality. Something far superior to this is sufficiently common even now, to give ample earnest of what the human species may be made. Genuine private affections and a sincere interest in the public good are possible, though in unequal degrees, to every rightly brought up human being. In a world in which there is so much to interest, so much to enjoy, and so much also to correct and improve, everyone who has this moderate amount of moral and intellectual requisites is capable of an existence which may be called enviable; and unless such a person, through bad laws or subjection to the will of others, is denied the liberty to use the sources of happiness within his reach, he will not fail to find this enviable existence, if he escape the positive evils of life, the great sources of physical and mental suffering—such as indigence, disease, and the unkindness, worthlessness, or premature loss of objects of affection. The main stress of the problem lies, therefore, in the contest with these calamities from which it is a rare good fortune entirely to escape; which, as things now are, cannot be obviated, and often cannot be in any material degree mitigated. Yet no one whose opinion deserves a moment's consideration can doubt that most of the great positive evils of the world are in themselves removable, and will, if human affairs continue to improve, be in the end reduced within narrow limits. Poverty, in any sense implying suffering, may be completely extinguished by the wisdom of society combined with the good sense and providence of individuals. Even that most intractable of enemies, disease, may be indefinitely reduced in dimensions by good physical and moral education and proper control of noxious influences, while the progress of science holds out a promise for the future of still more direct conquests over this detestable foe. And every advance in that direction relieves us from some, not only of the chances which cut short our own lives, but, what concerns us still more, which deprive us of those in whom our happiness is wrapt up. As for vicissitudes of fortune and other disappointments connected with worldly circumstances, these are principally the effect either of gross imprudence, of ill-regulated desires, or of bad or imperfect social institutions. All the grand sources, in short, of human suffering are in a great degree, many of them almost entirely, conquerable by human care and effort; and though their removal is grievously slow—though a long succession of generations will perish in the breach before the conquest is completed, and this world becomes all that, if will and knowledge were not wanting, it might easily be made—yet every mind sufficiently intelligent and generous to bear a part, however small and inconspicious, in the endeavor will draw a noble enjoyment from the contest itself, which he would not for any bribe in the form of selfish indulgence consent to be without.

And this leads to the true estimation of what is said by the objectors concerning the possibility and the obligation of learning to do without happiness. Unquestionably it is possible to do without happiness; it is done involuntarily by nineteen-twentieths of mankind, even in those parts of our present world which are least deep in barbarism; and it often has to be done voluntarily by the hero or the martyr, for the sake of something which he prizes more than his individual happiness. But this something, what is it, unless the happiness of others or some of the requisites of happiness? It is noble to be capable of resigning entirely one's own portion of happiness, or chances of it; but, after all, this self-sacrifice must be for some end; it is not its own end; and if we are told that its end is not happiness but virtue, which is better than happiness, I ask, would the sacrifice be made if the hero or martyr did not believe that it would earn for others immunity from similar sacrifices? Would it be made if he thought that his renunciation of happiness for himself would produce no fruit for any of his fellow creatures, but to make their lot like his and place them also in the condition of persons who have renounced happiness? All honor to those who can abnegate for themselves the personal enjoyment of life when by such renunciation they contribute worthily to increase the amount of happiness in the world; but he who does it or professes to do it for any other purpose is no more deserving of admiration than the ascetic mounted on his pillar. He may be an inspiriting proof of what men *can* do, but assuredly not an example of what they *should.*

Though it is only in a very imperfect state of the world's arrangements that anyone can best serve the happiness of others by the absolute sacrifice of his own, yet, so long as the world is in that imperfect state, I fully acknowledge that the readiness to make such a sacrifice is the highest virture which can be found in man. I will add that in this condition of the world, paradoxical as the assertion may be, the conscious ability to do without happiness gives the best prospect of realizing such happiness as is attainable. For nothing except that consciousness can raise a person above the chances of life by making him feel that, let fate and fortune do their worst, they have not power to subdue him; which, once felt, frees him from excess of anxiety concerning the evils of life and enables him, like many a Stoic in the worst times of the Roman Empire, to cultivate in tranquillity the sources of satisfaction accessible to him, without concerning himself about the uncertainty of their duration any more than about their inevitable end.

Meanwhile, let utilitarians never cease to claim the morality of self-devotion as a possession which belongs by as good a right to them as either to the Stoic or to the Transcendentalist. The utilitarian morality does recognize in human beings the power of sacrificing their own greatest good for the good of others. It only refuses to admit that the sacrifice is itself a good. A sacrifice which does not increase or tend to increase the sum total of happiness, it considers as wasted. The only self-renunciation which it applauds is devotion to the happiness, or to some of the means of happiness, of others, either of mankind collectively or of individuals within the limits imposed by the collective interests of mankind.

I must again repeat what the assailants of utilitarianism seldom have the justice to acknowledge, that the happiness which forms the utilitarian standard of what is right in conduct is not the agent's own happiness but that of all concerned. As between his own happiness and that of others, utilitarianism requires him to be as strictly impartial as a disinterested and benevolent spectator. In the golden rule of Jesus of Nazareth, we read the complete spirit of the ethics of utility. "To do as you would be done by," and "to love your neighbor as yourself," constitute the ideal perfection of utilitarian morality. As the means of making the nearest approach to this ideal, utility would enjoin, first, that laws and social arrangements should place the happiness or (as, speaking practically, it may be called) the interest of every individual as nearly as possible in harmony with the interest of the whole; and, secondly, that education and opinion, which have so vast a power over human character, should so use that power as to establish in the mind of every individual an indissoluble association between his own happiness and the good of the whole, especially between his own happiness and the practice of such modes of conduct, negative and positive, as regard for the universal happiness prescribes; so that not only he may be unable to conceive the possibility of happiness to himself, consistently with conduct opposed to the general good, but also that a direct impulse to promote the general good may be in every individual one of the habitual motives of action, and the sentiments connected therewith may fill a large and prominent place in every human being's sentient existence. If the impugners of the utilitarian morality represented it to their own minds in this its true character, I know not what recommendation possessed by any other morality they could possibly affirm to be wanting to it; what more beautiful or more exalted developments of human nature any other ethical system can be supposed to foster, or what springs of action, not accessible to the utilitarian, such systems rely on for giving effect to their mandates.

The objectors to utilitarianism cannot always be charged with representing it in a discreditable light. On the contrary, those among them who entertain anything like a just idea of its disinterested character sometimes find fault with its standard as being too high for humanity. They say it is exacting too much to require that people shall always act from the inducement of promoting the general interests of society. But this is to mistake the very meaning of a standard of morals and confound the rule of action with the motive of it. It is the business of ethics to tell us what are our duties, or by what test we may know them; but no system of ethics requires that the sole motive of all we do shall be a feeling of duty; on the contrary, ninety-nine hundredths of all our actions are done from other motives, and rightly so done if the rule of duty does not condemn them. It is the more unjust to utilitarianism that this particular misapprehension should be made a ground of objection to it, inasmuch as utilitarian moralists have gone beyond almost all others in affirming that the motive has nothing to do with the morality of the action, though much with the worth of the agent. He who saves a fellow creature from drowning does what is morally right, whether his motive be duty or the hope of being paid for his trouble; he who betrays the friend that trusts him is guilty of a crime, even if his object be to serve another friend to whom he is under greater obligations.[3] But to speak only of actions done from the motive of duty, and in direct obedience

[3] An opponent, whose intellectual and moral fairness it is a pleasure to acknowledge (the Rev. J. Llewellyn Davies), has objected to this passage, saying, "Surely the rightness or wrongness of saving a man from drowning does depend very much upon the motive with which it is done. Suppose that a tyrant, when his enemy jumped into the sea to escape from him, saved him from drowning simply in order that he might inflict upon him more exquisite tortures, would it tend to clearness to speak of that rescue as 'a morally right action'? Or suppose again, according to one of the stock illustrations of ethical inquiries, that a man betrayed a trust received from a friend, because the discharge of it would fatally injure that friend himself or someone belonging to him, would utilitarianism compel one to call the betrayal 'a crime' as much as if it had been done from the meanest motive?"

I submit that he who saves another from drowning in order to kill him by torture afterwards does not differ only in motive from him who does the same thing from duty or benevolence; the act itself is different. The rescue of the man is, in the case supposed, only the necessary first step of an act far more atrocious than leaving him to drown would have been. Had Mr. Davies said, "The rightness or wrongness of saving a man from drowning does depend very much"—not upon the motive, but—"upon the *intention*," no utilitarian would have differed from him. Mr. Davies, by an oversight too common not to be quite venial, has in this case confounded the very different ideas of Motive and Intention. There is no point which utilitarian thinkers (and Bentham preeminently) have taken more pains to illustrate than this. The morality of the action depends entirely upon the intention—that is, upon what the agent *wills to do*. But the motive, that is, the feeling which makes him will so to do, if it makes no difference in the act, makes none in the morality: though it makes a great difference in our moral estimation of the agent, especially if it indicates a good or a bad habitual *disposition*—a bent of character from which useful, or from which hurtful actions are likely to arise.

[The foregoing note appeared in the second (1864) edition of Utilitarianism *but was dropped in succeeding ones.]*

to principle: it is a misapprehension of the utilitarian mode of thought to conceive it as implying that people should fix their minds upon so wide a generality as the world, or society at large. The great majority of good actions are intended not for the benefit of the world, but for that of individuals, of which the good of the world is made up; and the thoughts of the most virtuous man need not on these occasions travel beyond the particular persons concerned, except so far as is necessary to assure himself that in benefiting them he is not violating the rights, that is, the legitimate and authorized expectations, of anyone else. The multiplication of happiness is, according to the utilitarian ethics, the object of virtue: the occasions on which any person (except one in a thousand) has it in his power to do this on an extended scale—in other words, to be a public benefactor—are but exceptional; and on these occasions alone is he called on to consider public utility; in every other case, private utility, the interest or happiness of some few persons, is all he has to attend to. Those alone the influence of whose actions extends to society in general need concern themselves habitually about so large an object. In the case of abstinences indeed—of things which people forbear to do from moral considerations, though the consequences in the particular case might be beneficial—it would be unworthy of an intelligent agent not to be consciously aware that the action is of a class which, if practiced generally, would be generally injurious, and that this is the ground of the obligation to abstain from it. The amount of regard for the public interest implied in this recognition is no greater than is demanded by every system of morals, for they all enjoin to abstain from whatever is manifestly pernicious to society.

The same considerations dispose of another reproach against the doctrine of utility, founded on a still grosser misconception of the purpose of a standard of morality and of the very meaning of the words "right" and "wrong." It is often affirmed that utilitarianism renders men cold and unsympathizing; that it chills their moral feelings toward individuals; that it makes them regard only the dry and hard consideration of the consequences of actions, not taking into their moral estimate the qualities from which those actions emanate. If the assertion means that they do not allow their judgment respecting the rightness or wrongness of an action to be influenced by their opinion of the qualities of the person who does it, this is a complaint not against utilitarianism, but against any standard of morality at all; for certainly no known ethical standard decides an action to be good or bad because it is done by a good or a bad man, still less because done by an amiable, a brave, or a benevolent man, or the contrary. These considerations are relevant, not to the estimation of actions, but of persons; and there is nothing in the utilitarian theory inconsistent with the fact that there are other things which interest us in persons besides the rightness and wrongness of their actions. The Stoics, indeed, with the paradoxical misuse of language which was part of their system, and by which they strove to raise themselves above all concern about anything but virtue, were fond of saying that he who has that has everything; that he, and only he, is rich, is beautiful, is a king. But no claim of this description is made for the virtuous man by the utilitarian doctrine. Utilitarians are quite aware that there are other desirable possessions and qualities besides virtue, and are perfectly willing to allow to all of them their full worth. They are also aware that a right action does not necessarily indicate a virtuous character, and that actions which are blamable often proceed from qualities entitled to praise. When this is apparent in any particular case, it modifies their estimation, not certainly of the act, but of the agent. I grant that they are, notwithstanding, of opinion that in the long run the best proof of a good character is good actions; and resolutely refuse to consider any mental disposition as good of which the predominant tendency is to produce bad conduct. This makes them unpopular with many people, but it is an unpopularity which they must share with everyone who regards the distinction between right and wrong in a serious light; and the reproach is not one which a conscientious utilitarian need be anxious to repel.

If no more be meant by the objection than that many utilitarians look on the morality of actions, as measured by the utilitarian standards, with too exclusive a regard, and do not lay sufficient stress upon the other beauties of character which go toward making a human being lovable or admirable, this may be admitted. Utilitarians who have cultivated their moral feelings, but not their sympathies, nor their artistic perceptions, do fall into this mistake; and so do all other moralists under the same conditions. What can be said in excuse for other moralists is equally available for them, namely, that, if there is to be any error, it is better that it should be on that side. As a matter of fact, we may affirm that among utilitarians, as among adherents of other systems, there is every imaginable degree of rigidity and of laxity in the application of their standard; some are even puritanically rigorous, while others are as indulgent as can possibly be desired by sinner or by sentimentalist. But on the whole, a doctrine which brings prominently forward the interest that mankind have in the repression and prevention of conduct which violates the moral law is likely to be inferior to no other in turning the sanctions of opinion against such violations. It is true, the question "What does violate the moral law?" is one on which those who recognize different standards of morality are likely now and then to differ. But difference of opinion on moral questions was not first introduced into the world by utilitarianism, while that doctrine does supply, if not always an easy, at all events a tangible and intelligible, mode of deciding such differences.

It may not be superfluous to notice a few more of the common misapprehensions of utilitarian ethics, even those which are so obvious and gross that it might appear impossible for any person of candor and intelligence to fall into them; since persons, even of considerable mental endowment, often give themselves so little trouble to understand the bearings of any opinion against which they entertain a prejudice, and men are in general so little conscious of this voluntary ignorance as a defect that the vulgarest misunderstandings of ethical doctrines are continually met with in the deliberate writings of persons of the greatest pretensions both to high principle and to philosophy. We not uncommonly hear the doctrine of utility inveighed against as a *godless* doctrine. If it be necessary to say anything at all against so mere an assumption, we may say that the question depends upon what idea we have formed of the moral character of the Deity. If it be a true belief that God desires, above all things, the happiness of his creatures, and that this was his purpose in their creation, utility is not only not a godless doctrine, but more profoundly religious than any other. If it be meant that utilitarianism does not recognize the revealed will of God as the supreme law of morals, I answer that a utilitarian who believes in the perfect goodness and wisdom of *God* necessarily believes that whatever God has thought fit to reveal on the subject of morals must fulfill the requirements of utility in a supreme degree. But others besides utilitarians have been of opinion that the Christian revelation was intended, and is fitted, to inform the hearts and minds of mankind with a spirit which should enable them to find for themselves what is right, and incline them to do it when found, rather than to tell them, except in a very general way, what it is; and that we need a doctrine of ethics, carefully followed out, to *interpret* to us the will of God. Whether this opinion is correct or not, it is superfluous here to discuss; since whatever aid religion, either natural or revealed, can afford to ethical investigation is as open to the utilitarian moralist as to any other. He can use it as the testimony of God to the usefulness or hurtfulness of any given course of action by as good a right as others can use it for the indication of a transcendental law having no connection with usefulness or with happiness.

Again, utility is often summarily stigmatized as an immoral doctrine by giving it the name of "expediency," and taking advantage of the popular use of that term to contrast it with principle. But the expedient, in the sense in which it is opposed to the right, generally means that which is expedient for the particular interest of the agent himself; as when a minister sacrifices the interests of his country to keep himself in place. When it means anything better than this, it means that which is expedient for some immediate object, some temporary purpose, but which violates a rule whose observance is expedient in a much higher degree. The expedient, in this sense, instead of being the same thing with the useful, is a branch of the hurtful. Thus it would often be expedient, for the purpose of getting over some momentary embarrassment, or attaining some object immediately useful to ourselves or others, to tell a lie. But inasmuch as the cultivation in ourselves of a sensitive feeling on the subject of veracity is one of the most useful, and the enfeeblement of that feeling one of the most hurtful, things to which our conduct can be instrumental; and inasmuch as any, even unintentional, deviation from truth does that much toward weakening the trustworthiness of human assertion, which is not only the principal support of all present social well-being, but the insufficiency of which does more than any one thing that can be named to keep back civilization, virtue, everything on which human happiness on the largest scale depends—we feel that the violation, for a present advantage, of a rule of such transcendent expediency is not expedient, and that he who, for the sake of convenience to himself or to some other individual, does what depends on him to deprive mankind of the good, and inflict upon them the evil, involved in the greater or less reliance which they can place in each other's word, acts the part of one of their worst enemies. Yet that even this rule, sacred as it is, admits of possible exceptions is acknowledged by all moralists; the chief of which is when the withholding of some fact (as of information from a malefactor, or of bad news from a person dangerously ill) would save an individual (especially an individual other than oneself) from great and unmerited evil, and when the withholding can only be effected by denial. But in order that the exception may not extend itself beyond the need, and may have the least possible effect in weakening reliance on veracity, it ought to be recognized and, if possible, its limits defined; and, if the principle of utility is good for anything, it must be good for weighing these conflicting utilities against one another and marking out the region within which one or the other preponderates.

Again, defenders of utility often find themselves called upon to reply to such objections as this—that there is not time, previous to action, for calculating and weighing the effects of any line of conduct on the general happiness. This is exactly as if anyone were to say that it is impossible to guide our conduct by Christianity because there is not time, on every occasion on which anything has to be done, to read through the Old and New Testaments. The answer to the objection is that there has been ample time, namely, the whole past duration of the human species. During all that time mankind have been learning by experience the tendencies of actions; on which experience all the prudence as well as all the morality of life are dependent. People talk as if the commencement of this course of experience had hitherto been put off, and as if, at the moment when some man feels tempted to meddle with the property or life of another, he had to begin considering for the first time whether murder and theft are injurious to human happiness. Even then I do not think that he would find the question very puzzling; but, at all events, the matter is now done to his hand. It is truly a whimsical supposition that, if mankind were agreed in considering utility to be the test of morality, they would remain without any agreement as to what *is* useful, and would take no measures for having their notions on the subject taught to the young and enforced by law and opinion. There is no difficulty in proving any ethical standard whatever to work ill if we suppose universal idiocy to be conjoined with it; but on any hypothesis short of that, mankind must by this time have acquired positive beliefs as to the effects of some actions on their happiness; and the beliefs which have thus come down are the rules of morality for the multitude, and for the philosopher until he has succeeded in finding better. That philosophers might easily do this, even now, on many subjects; that the received code of ethics is by no means of divine right; and that mankind have still much to learn as to the effects of actions on the general happiness, I admit or rather earnestly maintain. The corollaries from the principle of utility, like the precepts of every practical art, admit of indefinite improvement, and, in a progressive state of the human mind, their improvement is perpetually going on. But to consider the rules of morality as improvable is one thing; to pass over the intermediate generalization entirely and endeavor to test each individual action directly by the first principle is another. It is a strange notion that the acknowledgment of a first principle is inconsistent with the admission of secondary ones. To inform a traveler respecting the place of his ultimate destination is not to forbid the use of landmarks and direction-posts on the way. The proposition that happiness is the end and aim of morality does not mean that no road ought to be laid down to that goal, or that persons going thither should not be advised to take one direction rather than another. Men really ought to leave off talking a kind of nonsense on this subject, which they would neither talk nor listen to on other matters of practical concernment. Nobody argues that the art of navigation is not founded on astronomy because sailors cannot wait to calculate the Nautical Almanac. Being rational creatures, they go to sea with it ready calculated; and all rational creatures go out upon the sea of life with their minds made up on the common questions of right and wrong, as well as on many of the far more difficult questions of wise and foolish. And this, as long as foresight is a human quality, it is to be presumed they will continue to do. Whatever we adopt as the fundamental principle of morality, we require subordinate principles to apply it by; the impossibility of doing without them, being common to all systems, can afford no argument against any one in particular; but gravely to argue as if no such secondary principles could be had, and as if mankind had remained till now, and always must remain, without drawing any general conclusions from the experience of human life is as high a pitch, I think, as absurdity has ever reached in philosophical controversy.

The remainder of the stock arguments against utilitarianism mostly consist in laying to its charge the common infirmities of human nature, and the general difficulties which embarrass conscientious persons in shaping their course through life. We are told that a utilitarian will be apt to make his own particular case an exception to moral rules, and, when under temptation, will see a utility in the breach of a rule, greater than he will see in its observance. But is utility the only creed which is able to furnish us with excuses for evil-doing and means of cheating our own conscience? They are afforded in abundance by all doctrines which recognize as a fact in morals the existence of conflicting considerations, which all doctrines do that have been believed by sane persons. It is not the fault of any creed, but of the complicated nature of human affairs, that rules of conduct cannot be so framed as to require no exceptions, and that hardly any kind of action can safely be laid down as either always obligatory or always condemnable. There is no ethical creed which does not temper the rigidity of its laws by giving a certain latitude, under the moral responsibility of the agent, for accommodation to peculiarities of circumstances; and under every creed, at the opening thus made, self-deception and dishonest casuistry get in. There exists no moral system under which there do not arise unequivocal cases of conflicting obligation. These are the real difficulties, the knotty points both in the theory of ethics and in the conscientious guidance of personal conduct. They are overcome practically, with greater or with less success, according to the intellect and virtue of the individual; but it can hardly be pretended that anyone will be the less qualified for dealing with them, from possessing an ultimate standard to which conflicting rights and duties can be referred. If utility is the ultimate source of moral obligations, utility may be invoked to decide between them when their demands are incompatible. Though the application of the standard may be difficult, it is better than none at all; while in other systems, the moral laws all claiming independent authority, there is no common umpire entitled to interfere between them; their claims to precedence one over another rest on little better than sophistry, and, unless determined, as they generally are, by the unacknowledged influence of consideration of utility, afford a free scope for the action of personal desires and partialities. We must remember that only in these cases of conflict between secondary principles is it requisite that first principles should be appealed to. There is no case of moral obligation in which some secondary principle is not involved; and if only one, there can seldom be any real doubt which one it is, in the mind of any person by whom the principle itself is recognized.

Chapter III / Of the ultimate sanction of the principle of utility

The question is often asked, and properly so, in regard to any supposed moral standard—What is its sanction? what are the motives to obey? or, more specifically, what is the source of its obligation? whence does it derive its binding force? It is a necessary part of moral philosophy to provide the answer to this question, which, though frequently assuming the shape of an objection to the utilitarian morality, as if it had some special applicability to that above others, really arises in regard to all standards. It arises, in fact, whenever a person is called on to *adopt* a standard, or refer morality to any basis on which he has not been accustomed to rest it. For the customary morality, that which education and opinion have consecrated, is the only one which presents itself to the mind with the feeling of being *in itself* obligatory; and when a person is asked to believe that this morality *derives* its obligation from some general principle round which custom has not thrown the same halo, the assertion is to him a paradox; the supposed corollaries seem to have a more binding force than the original theorem; the superstructure seems to stand better without than with what is represented as its foundation. He says to himself, I feel that I am bound not to rob or murder, betray or deceive; but why am I bound to promote the general happiness? If my own happiness lies in something else, why may I not give that the preference?

If the view adopted by the utilitarian philosophy of the nature of the moral sense be correct, this difficulty will always present itself until the influences which form moral character have taken the same hold of the principle which they have taken of some of the consequences—until, by the improvement of education, the feeling of unity with our fellow creatures shall be (what it cannot be denied that Christ intended it to be) as deeply rooted in our character, and to our own consciousness as completely a part of our nature, as the horror of crime is in an ordinarily well-brought-up young person. In the meantime, however, the difficulty has no peculiar application to the doctrine of utility, but is inherent in every attempt to analyze morality and reduce it to principles; which, unless the principle is already in men's minds invested with as much sacredness as any of its applications, always seems to divest them of a part of their sanctity.

The principle of utility either has, or there is no reason why it might not have, all the sanctions which belong to any other system of morals. Those sanctions are either external or internal. Of the external sanctions it is not necessary to speak at any length. They are the hope of favor and the fear of displeasure from our fellow creatures or from the Ruler of the universe, along with whatever we may have of sympathy or affection for them, or of love and awe of Him, inclining us to do His will independently of selfish consequences. There is evidently no reason why all these motives for observance should not attach themselves to the utilitarian morality as completely and as powerfully as to any other. Indeed, those of them which refer to our fellow creatures are sure to do so, in proportion to the amount of general intelligence; for whether there be any other ground of moral obligation than the general happiness or not, men do desire happiness; and however imperfect may be their own practice, they desire and commend all conduct in others toward themselves by which they think their happiness is promoted. With regard to the religious motive, if men believe, as most profess to do, in the goodness of God, those who think that conduciveness to the general happiness is the essence or even only the criterion of good must necessarily believe that it is also that which God approves. The whole force therefore of external reward and punishment, whether physical or moral, and whether proceeding from God or from our fellow men, together with all that the capacities of human nature admit of disinterested devotion to either, become available to enforce the utilitarian morality, in proportion as that morality is recognized; and the more powerfully, the more the appliances of education and general cultivation are bent to the purpose.

So far as to external sanctions. The internal sanction of duty, whatever our standard of duty may be, is one and the same—a feeling in our own mind; a pain, more or less intense, attendant on violation of duty, which in properly cultivated moral natures rises, in the more serious cases, into shrinking from it as an impossibility. This feeling, when disinterested and connecting itself with the pure idea of duty, and not with some particular form of it, or with any of the merely accessory circumstances, is the essence of conscience; though in that complex phenomenon as it actually exists, the simple fact is in general all encrusted over with collateral associations derived from sympathy, from love, and still more from fear; from all the forms of religious feeling; from the recollections of childhood and of all our past life; from self-esteem, desire of the esteem of others, and occasionally even self-abasement. This extreme complication is, I apprehend, the origin of the sort of mystical character which, by a tendency of the human mind of which there are many other examples, is apt to be attributed to the idea of moral obligation, and which leads people to believe that the idea cannot possibly attach itself to any other objects than those which, by a supposed mysterious law, are found in our present experience to excite it. Its binding force, however, consists in the existence of a mass of feeling which must be broken through in order to do what violates our standard of right, and which, if we do nevertheless violate that standard, will probably have to be encountered afterwards in the form of remorse. Whatever theory we have of the nature or origin of conscience, this is what essentially constitutes it.

The ultimate sanction, therefore, of all morality (external motives apart) being a subjective feeling in our own minds, I see nothing embarrassing to those whose standard is utility in the question, What is the sanction of that particular standard? We may answer, the same as of all other moral standards—the conscientious feelings of mankind. Undoubtedly this sanction has no binding efficacy on those who do not possess the feelings it appeals to; but neither will these persons be more obedient to any other moral principle than to the utilitarian one. On them morality of any kind has no hold but through the external sanctions. Meanwhile the feelings exist, a fact in human nature, the reality of which, and the great power with which they are capable of acting on those in whom they have been duly cultivated, are proved by experience. No reason has ever been shown why they may not be cultivated to as great intensity in connection with the utilitarian as with any other rule of morals.

There is, I am aware, a disposition to believe that a person who sees in moral obligation a transcendental fact, an objective reality belonging to the province of "things in themselves," is likely to be more obedient to it than one who believes it to be entirely subjective, having its seat in human consciousness only. But whatever a person's opinion may be on this point of ontology, the force he is really urged by is his own subjective feeling, and is exactly measured by its strength. No one's belief that duty is an objective reality is stronger than the belief that God is so; yet the belief in God, apart from the expectation of actual reward and punishment, only operates on conduct through, and in proportion to, the subjective religious feeling. The sanction, so far as it is disinterested, is always in the mind itself; and the notion, therefore, of the transcendental moralists must be that this sanction will not exist *in* the mind unless it is believed to have its root out of the mind; and that if a person is able to say to himself, "That which is restraining me and which is called my conscience is only a feeling in my own mind," he may possibly draw the conclusion that when the feeling ceases the obligation ceases, and that if he find the feeling inconvenient, he may disregard it and endeavor to get rid of it. But is this danger confined to the utilitarian morality? Does the belief that moral obligation has its seat outside the mind make the feeling of it too strong to be got rid of? The fact is so far otherwise that all moralists admit and lament the ease with which, in the generality of minds, conscience can be silenced or stifled. The question, "Need I obey my conscience?" is quite as often put to themselves by persons who never heard of the principle of utility as by its adherents. Those whose conscientious feelings are so weak as to allow of their asking this question, if they answer it affirmatively, will not do so because they believe in the transcendental theory, but because of the external sanctions.

It is not necessary, for the present purpose, to decide whether the feeling of duty is innate or implanted. Assuming it to be innate, it is an open question to what objects it naturally attaches itself; for the philosophic supporters of that theory are now agreed that the intuitive perception is of principles of morality and not of the details. If there be anything innate in the matter, I see no reason why the feeling which is innate should not be that of regard to the pleasures and pains of others. If there is any principle of morals which is intuitively obligatory, I should say it must be that. If so, the intuitive ethics would coincide with the utilitarian, and there would be no further quarrel between them. Even as it is, the intuitive moralists, though they believe that there are other intuitive moral obligations, do already believe this to be one; for they unanimously hold that a large *portion* of morality turns upon the consideration due to the interests of our fellow creatures. Therefore, if the belief in the transcendental origin of moral obligation gives any additional efficacy to the internal sanction, it appears to me that the utilitarian principle has already the benefit of it.

On the other hand, if, as is my own belief, the moral feelings are not innate but acquired, they are not for that reason the less natural. It is natural to man to speak, to reason, to build cities, to cultivate the ground, though these are acquired faculties. The moral feelings are not indeed a part of our nature in the sense of being in any perceptible degree present in all of us; but this, unhappily, is a fact admitted by those who believe the most strenuously in their transcendental origin. Like the other acquired capacities above referred to, the moral faculty, if not a part of our nature, is a natural outgrowth from it; capable, like them, in a certain small degree, of springing up spontaneously; and susceptible of being brought by cultivation to a high degree of development. Unhappily it is also susceptible, by a sufficient use of the external sanctions and of the force of early impressions, of being cultivated in almost any direction, so that there is hardly anything so absurd or so mischievous that it may not, by means of these influences, be made to act on the human mind with all the authority of conscience. To doubt that the same potency might be given by the same means to the principle of utility, even if it had no foundation in human nature, would be flying in the face of all experience.

But moral associations which are wholly of artificial creation, when the intellectual culture goes on, yield by degrees to the dissolving force of analysis; and if the feeling of duty, when associated with utility, would appear equally arbitrary; if there were no leading department of our nature, no powerful class of sentiments, with which that association would harmonize, which would make us feel it congenial and incline us not only to foster it in others (for which we have abundant interested motives), but also to cherish it in ourselves—if there were not, in short, a natural basis of sentiment for utilitarian morality, it might well happen that this association also, even after it had been implanted by education, might be analyzed away.

But there *is* this basis of powerful natural sentiment; and this it is which, when once the general happiness is recognized as the ethical standard, will constitute the strength of the utilitarian morality. This firm foundation is that of the social feelings of mankind—the desire to be in unity with our fellow creatures, which is already a powerful principle in human nature, and happily one of those which tend to become stronger, even without express inculcation, from the influences of advancing civilization. The social state is at once so natural, so necessary, and so habitual to man, that, except in some unusual circumstances or by an effort of voluntary abstraction, he never conceives himself otherwise than as a member of a body; and this association is riveted more and more, as mankind are further removed from the state of savage independence. Any condition, therefore, which is essential to a state of society becomes more and more an inseparable part of every person's conception of the state of things which he is born into, and which is the destiny of a human being. Now society between human beings, except in the relation of master and slave, is manifestly impossible on any other footing than that the interests of all are to be consulted. Society between equals can only exist on the understanding that the interests of all are to be regarded equally. And since in all states of civilization, every person, except an absolute monarch, has equals, everyone is obliged to live on these terms with somebody; and in every age some advance is made toward a state in which it will be impossible to live permanently on other terms with anybody. In this way people grow up unable to conceive as possible to them a state of total disregard of other people's interests. They are under a necessity of conceiving themselves as at least abstaining from all the grosser injuries, and (if only for their own protection) living in a state of constant protest against them. They are also familiar with the fact of co-operating with others and proposing to themselves a collective, not an individual, interest as the aim (at least for the time being) of their actions. So long as they are co-operating, their ends are identified with those of others; there is at least a temporary feeling that the interests of others are their own interests. Not only does all strengthening of social ties, and all healthy growth of society, give to each individual a stronger personal interest in practically consulting the welfare of others, it also leads him to identify his *feelings* more and more with their good, or at least with an even greater degree of practical consideration for it. He comes, as though instinctively, to be conscious of himself as a being who *of course* pays regard to others. The good of others becomes to him a thing naturally and necessarily to be attended to, like any of the physical conditions of our existence. Now, whatever amount of this feeling a person has, he is urged by the strongest motives both of interest and of sympathy to demonstrate it, and to the utmost of his power encourage it in others; and even if he has none of it himself, he is as greatly interested as anyone else that others should have it. Consequently, the smallest germs of the feeling are laid hold of and nourished by the contagion of sympathy and the influences of education; and a complete web of corroborative association is woven round it by the powerful agency of the external sanctions. This mode of conceiving ourselves and human life, as civilization goes on, is felt to be more and more natural. Every step in political improvement renders it more so, by removing the sources of opposition of interest and leveling those inequalities of legal privilege between individuals or classes, owing to which there are large portions of mankind whose happiness it is still practicable to disregard. In an improving state of the human mind, the influences are constantly on the increase which tend to generate in each individual a feeling of unity with all the rest; which, if perfect, would make him never think of, or desire, any beneficial condition for himself in the benefits of which they are not included. If we now suppose this feeling of unity to be taught as a religion, and the whole force of education, of institutions, and of opinion directed, as it once was in the case of religion, to make every person grow up from infancy surrounded on all sides both by the profession and the practice of it, I think that no one who can realize this conception will feel any misgiving about the sufficiency of the ultimate sanction for the happiness morality. To any ethical student who finds the realization difficult, I recommend, as a means of facilitating it, the second of M. Comte's two principal works, the *Traité de politique positive.* I entertain the strongest objections to the system of politics and morals set forth in that treatise, but I think it has superabundantly shown the possibility of giving to the service of humanity, even without the aid of belief in a Providence, both the psychological power and the social efficacy of a religion, making it take hold of human life, and color all thought, feeling, and action in a manner of which the greatest ascendancy ever exercised by any religion may be but a type and foretaste; and of which the danger is, not that it should be insufficient, but that it should be so excessive as to interfere unduly with human freedom and individuality.

Neither is it necessary to the feeling which constitutes the binding force of the utilitarian morality on those who recognize it to wait for those social influences which would make its obligation felt by mankind at large. In the comparatively early state of human advancement in which we now live, a person cannot, indeed, feel that entireness of sympathy with all others which would make any real discordance in the general direction of their conduct in life impossible, but already a person in whom the social feeling is at all developed cannot bring himself to think of the rest of his fellow creatures as struggling rivals with him for the means of happiness, whom he must desire to see defeated in their object in order that he may succeed in his. The deeply rooted conception which every individual even now has of himself as a social being tends to make him feel it one of his natural wants that there should be harmony between his feelings and aims and those of his fellow creatures. If differences of opinion and of mental culture make it impossible for him to share many of their actual feelings—perhaps make him denounce and defy those feelings—he still needs to be conscious that his real aim and theirs do not conflict; that he is not opposing himself to what they really wish for, namely, their own good, but is, on the contrary, promoting it. This feeling in most individuals is much inferior in strength to their selfish feelings, and is often wanting altogether. But to those who have it, it possesses all the characters of a natural feeling. It does not present itself to their minds as a superstition of education or a law despotically imposed by the power of society, but as an attribute which it would not be well for them to be without. This conviction is the ultimate sanction of the greatest happiness morality. This it is which makes any mind of well-developed feelings work with, and not against, the outward motives to care for others, afforded by what I have called the external sanctions; and, when those sanctions are wanting or act in an opposite direction, constitutes in itself a powerful internal binding force, in proportion to the sensitiveness and thoughtfulness of the character, since few but those whose mind is a moral blank could bear to lay out their course of life on the plan of paying no regard to others except so far as their own private interest compels.

Chapter IV / Of what sort of proof the principle of utility is susceptible

It has already been remarked that questions of ultimate ends do not admit of proof, in the ordinary acceptation of the term. To be incapable of proof by reasoning is common to all first principles, to the first premises of our knowledge, as well as to those of our conduct. But the former, being matters of fact, may be the subject of a direct appeal to the faculties which judge of fact—namely, our senses and our internal consciousness. Can an appeal be made to the same faculties on questions of practical ends? Or by what other faculty is cognizance taken of them?

Questions about ends are, in other words, questions what things are desirable. The utilitarian doctrine is that happiness is desirable, and the only thing desirable, as an end; all other things being only desirable as means to that end. What ought to be required of this doctrine, what conditions is it requisite that the doctrine should fulfill—to make good its claim to be believed?

The only proof capable of being given that an object is visible is that people actually see it. The only proof that a sound is audible is that people hear it; and so of the other sources of our experience. In like manner, I apprehend, the sole evidence it is possible to produce that anything is desirable is that people do actually desire it. If the end which the utilitarian doctrine proposes to itself were not, in theory and in practice, acknowledged to be an end, nothing could ever convince any person that it was so. No reason can be given why the general happiness is desirable, except that each person, so far as he believes it to be attainable, desires his own happiness. This, however, being a fact, we have not only all the proof which the case admits of, but all which it is possible to require, that happiness is a good, that each person's happiness is a good to that person, and the general happiness, therefore, a good to the aggregate of all persons. Happiness has made out its title as *one* of the ends of conduct and, consequently, one of the criteria of morality.

But it has not, by this alone, proved itself to be the sole criterion. To do that, it would seem, by the same rule, necessary to show, not only that people desire happiness, but that they never desire anything else. Now it is palpable that they do desire things which, in common language, are decidedly distinguished from happiness. They desire, for example, virtue and the absence of vice no less really than pleasure and the absence of pain. The desire of virtue is not as universal, but it is as authentic a fact as the desire of happiness. And hence the opponents of the utilitarian standard deem that they have a right to infer that there are other ends of human action besides happiness, and that happiness is not the standard of approbation and disapprobation.

But does the utilitarian doctrine deny that people desire virtue, or maintain that virtue is not a thing to be desired? The very reverse. It maintains not only that virtue is to be desired, but that it is to be desired disinterestedly, for itself. Whatever may be the opinion of utilitarian moralists as to the original conditions by which virtue is made virtue, however they may believe (as they do) that actions and dispositions are only virtuous because they promote another end than virtue, yet this being granted, and it having been decided, from considerations of this description, what *is* virtuous, they not only place virtue at the very head of the things which are good as means to the ultimate end, but they also recognize as a psychological fact the possibility of its being, to the individual, a good in itself, without looking to any end beyond it; and hold that the mind is not in a right state, not in a state conformable to utility, not in the state most conducive to the general happiness, unless it does love virtue in this manner—as a thing desirable in itself, even although, in the individual instance, it should not produce those other desirable consequences which it tends to produce, and on account of which it is held to be virtue. This opinion is not, in the smallest degree, a departure from the happiness principle. The ingredients of happiness are very various, and each of them is desirable in itself, and not merely when considered as swelling an aggregate. The principle of utility does not mean that any given pleasure, as music, for instance, or any given exemption from pain, as for example health, is to be looked upon as means to a collective something termed happiness, and to be desired on that account. They are desired and desirable in and for themselves; besides being means, they are a part of the end. Virtue, according to the utilitarian doctrine, is not naturally and originally part of the end, but it is capable of becoming so; and in those who live it disinterestedly it has become so, and is desired and cherished, not as a means to happiness, but as a part of their happiness.

To illustrate this further, we may remember that virtue is not the only thing originally a means, and which if it were not a means to anything else would be and remain indifferent, but which by association with what it is a means to comes to be desired for itself, and that too with the utmost intensity. What, for example, shall we say of the love of money? There is nothing originally more desirable about money than about any heap of glittering pebbles. Its worth is solely that of the things which it will buy; the desires for other things than itself, which it is a means of gratifying. Yet the love of money is not only one of the strongest moving forces of human life, but money is, in many cases, desired in and for itself; the desire to possess it is often stronger than the desire to use it, and goes on increasing when all the desires which point to ends beyond it, to be compassed by it, are falling off. It may, then, be said truly that money is desired not for the sake of an end, but as part of the end. From being a means to happiness, it has come to be itself a principal ingredient of the individual's conception of happiness. The same may be said of the majority of the great objects of human life: power, for example, or fame, except that to each of these there is a certain amount of immediate pleasure annexed, which has at least the semblance of being naturally inherent in them—a thing which cannot be said of money. Still, however, the strongest natural attraction, both of power and of fame, is the immense aid they give to the attainment of our other wishes; and it is the strong association thus generated between them and all our objects of desire which gives to the direct desire of them the intensity it often assumes, so as in some characters to surpass in strength all other desires. In these cases the means have become a part of the end, and a more important part of it than any of the things which they are means to. What was once desired as an instrument for the attainment of happiness has come to be desired for its own sake. In being desired for its own sake it is, however, desired as *part* of happiness. The person is made, or thinks he would be made, happy by its mere possession; and is made unhappy by failure to obtain it. The desire of it is not a different thing from the desire of happiness any more than the love of music or the desire of health. They are included in happiness. They are some of the elements of which the desire of happiness is made up. Happiness is not an abstract idea but a concrete whole; and these are some of its parts. And the utilitarian standard sanctions and approves their being so. Life would be a poor thing, very ill provided with sources of happiness, if there were not this provision of nature by which things originally indifferent, but conducive to, or otherwise associated with, the satisfaction of our primitive desires, become in themselves sources of pleasure more valuable than the primitive pleasures, both in permanency, in the space of human existence that they are capable of covering, and even in intensity.

Virtue, according to the utilitarian conception, is a good of this description. There was no original desire of it, or motive to it, save its conduciveness to pleasure, and especially to protection from pain. But through the association thus formed it may be felt a good in itself, and desired as such with as great intensity as any other good; and with this difference between it and the love of money, of power, or of fame—that all of these may, and often do, render the individual noxious to the other members of the society to which he belongs, whereas there is nothing which makes him so much a blessing to them as the cultivation of the disinterested love of virtue. And consequently, the utilitarian standard, while it tolerates and approves those other acquired desires, up to the point beyond which they would be more injurious to the general happiness than promotive of it, enjoins and requires the cultivation of the love of virtue up to the greatest strength possible, as being above all things important to the general happiness.

It results from the preceding considerations that there is in reality nothing desired except happiness. Whatever is desired otherwise than as a means to some end beyond itself, and ultimately to happiness, is desired as itself a part of happiness, and is not desired for itself until it has become so. Those who desire virtue for its own sake desire it either because the consciousness of it is a pleasure, or because the consciousness of being without it is a pain, or for both reasons united; as in truth the pleasure and pain seldom exist separately, but almost always together—the same person feeling pleasure in the degree of virtue attained, and pain in not having attained more. If one of these gave him no pleasure, and the other no pain, he would not love or desire virtue, or would desire it only for the other benefits which it might produce to himself or to persons whom he cared for.

We have now, then, an answer to the question, of what sort of proof the principle of utility is susceptible. If the opinion which I have now stated is psychologically true—if human nature is so constituted as to desire nothing which is not either a part of happiness or a means of happiness—we can have no other proof, and we require no other, that these are the only things desirable. If so, happiness is the sole end of human action, and the promotion of it the test by which to judge of all human conduct; from whence it necessarily follows that it must be the criterion of morality, since a part is included in the whole.

And now to decide whether this is really so, whether mankind do desire nothing for itself but that which is a pleasure to them, or of which the absence is a pain, we have evidently arrived at a question of fact and experience, dependent, like all similar questions, upon evidence. It can only be determined by practiced self-consciousness and self-observation, assisted by observation of others. I believe that these sources of evidence, impartially consulted, will declare that desiring a thing and finding it pleasant, aversion to it and thinking of it as painful, are phenomena entirely inseparable or, rather, two parts of the same phenomenon—in strictness of language, two different modes of naming the same psychological fact; that to think of an object as desirable (unless for the sake of its consequences) and to think of it as pleasant are one and the same thing; and that to desire anything except in proportion as the idea of it is pleasant is a physical and metaphysical impossibility.

So obvious does this appear to me that I expect it will hardly be disputed; and the objection made will be, not that desire can possibly be directed to anything ultimately except pleasure and exemption from pain, but that the will is a different thing from desire; that a person of confirmed virtue or any other person whose purposes are fixed carries out his purposes without any thought of the pleasure he has in contemplating them or expects to derive from their fulfillment, and persists in acting on them, even though these pleasures are much diminished by changes in his character or decay of his passive sensibilities, or are outweighed by the pains which the pursuit of the purposes may bring upon him. All this I fully admit and have stated it elsewhere as positively and emphatically as anyone. Will, the active phenomenon, is a different thing from desire, the state of passive sensibility, and, though originally an offshoot from it, may in time take root and detach itself from the parent stock, so much so that in the case of a habitual purpose, instead of willing the thing because we desire it, we often desire it only because we will it. This, however, is but an instance of that familiar fact, the power of habit, and is nowise confined to the case of virtuous actions. Many indifferent things which men originally did from a motive of some sort they continue to do from habit. Sometimes this is done unconsciously, the consciousness coming only after the action; at other times with conscious volition, but volition which has become habitual and is put in operation by the force of habit, in opposition perhaps to the deliberate preference, as often happens with those who have contracted habits of vicious or hurtful indulgence. Third and last comes the case in which the habitual act of will in the individual instance is not in contradiction to the general intention prevailing at other times, but in fulfillment of it, as in the case of the person of confirmed virtue and of all who pursue deliberately and consistently any determinate end. The distinction between will and desire thus understood is an authentic and highly important psychological fact; but the fact consists solely in this—that will, like all other parts of our constitution, is amenable to habit, and that we may will from habit what we no longer desire for itself, or desire only because we will it. It is not the less true that will, in the beginning, is entirely produced by desire, including in that term the repelling influence of pain as well as the attractive one of pleasure. Let us take into consideration no longer the person who has a confirmed will to do right, but him in whom that virtuous will is still feeble, conquerable by temptation, and not to be fully relied on; by what means can it be strengthened? How can the will to be virtuous, where it does not exist in sufficient force, be implanted or awakened? Only by making the person *desire* virtue—by making him think of it in a pleasurable light, or of its absence in a painful one. It is by associating the doing right with pleasure, or the wrong with pain, or by eliciting and impressing and bringing home to the person's experience the pleasure naturally involved in the one or the pain in the other, that it is possible to call forth that will to be virtuous which, when confirmed, acts without any thought of either pleasure or pain. Will is the child of desire, and passes out of the dominion of its parent only to come under that of habit. That which is the result of habit affords no presumption of being intrinsically good; and there would be no reason for wishing that the purpose of virtue should become independent of pleasure and pain were it not that the influence of the pleasurable and painful associations which prompt to virtue is not sufficiently to be depended on for unerring constancy of action until it has acquired the support of habit. Both in feeling and in conduct, habit is the only thing which imparts certainty; and it is because of the importance to others of being able to rely absolutely on one's feelings and conduct, and to oneself of being able to rely on one's own, that the will to do right ought to be cultivated into this habitual independence. In other words, this state of the will is a means to good, not intrinsically a good; and does not contradict the doctrine that nothing is a good to human beings but in so far as it is either itself pleasurable or a means of attaining pleasure or averting pain.

But if this doctrine be true, the principle of utility is proved. Whether it is so or not must now be left to the consideration of the thoughtful reader.

Chapter V / On the connection between justice and utility

In all ages of speculation one of the strongest obstacles to the reception of the doctrine that utility or happiness is the criterion of right and wrong has been drawn from the idea of justice. The powerful sentiment and apparently clear perception which that word recalls with a rapidity and certainty resembling an instinct have seemed to the majority of thinkers to point to an inherent quality in things; to show that the just must have an existence in nature as something absolute, generically distinct from every variety of the expedient and, in idea, opposed to it, though (as is commonly acknowledged) never, in the long run, disjoined from it in fact.

In the case of this, as of our other moral sentiments, there is no necessary connection between the question of its origin and that of its binding force. That a feeling is bestowed on us by nature does not necessarily legitimate all its promptings. The feeling of justice might be a peculiar instinct, and might yet require, like our other instincts, to be controlled and enlightened by a higher reason. If we have intellectual instincts leading us to judge in a particular way, as well as animal instincts that prompt us to act in a particular way, there is no necessity that the former should be more infallible in their sphere than the latter in theirs; it may as well happen that wrong judgments are occasionally suggested by those, as wrong actions by these. But though it is one thing to believe that we have natural feelings of justice, and another to acknowledge them as an ultimate criterion of conduct, these two opinions are very closely connected in point of fact. Mankind are always predisposed to believe that any subjective feeling, not otherwise accounted for, is a revelation of some objective reality. Our present object is to determine whether the reality to which the feeling of justice corresponds is one which needs any such special revelation, whether the justice or injustice of an action is a thing intrinsically peculiar and distinct from all its other qualities or only a combination of certain of those qualities presented under a peculiar aspect. For the purpose of this inquiry it is practically important to consider whether the feeling itself, of justice and injustice, is *sui generis* like our sensations of color and taste or a derivative feeling formed by a combination of others. And this it is the more essential to examine, as people are in general willing enough to allow that objectively the dictates of justice coincide with a part of the field of general expediency; but inasmuch as the subjective mental feeling of justice is different from that which commonly attaches to simple expediency, and, except in the extreme cases of the latter, is far more imperative in its demands, people find it difficult to see in justice only a particular kind or branch of general utility, and think that its superior binding force requires a totally different origin.

To throw light upon this question, it is necessary to attempt to ascertain what is the distinguishing character of justice, or of injustice; what is the quality, or whether there is any quality, attributed in common to all modes of conduct designated as unjust (for justice, like many other moral attributes, is best defined by its opposite), and distinguishing them from such modes of conduct as are disapproved, but without having that particular epithet of disapprobation applied to them. If in everything which men are accustomed to characterize as just or unjust some one common attribute or collection of attributes is always present, we may judge whether this particular attribute or combination of attributes would be capable of gathering round it a sentiment of that peculiar character and intensity by virtue of the general laws of our emotional constitution, or whether the sentiment is inexplicable and requires to be regarded as a special provision of nature. If we find the former to be the case, we shall, in resolving this question, have resolved also the main problem; if the latter, we shall have to seek for some other mode of investigating it.

To find the common attributes of a variety of objects, it is necessary to begin by surveying the objects themselves in the concrete. Let us therefore advert successively to the various modes of action and arrangements of human affairs which are classed, by universal or widely spread opinion, as just or as unjust. The things well known to excite the sentiments associated with those names are of a very multifarious character. I shall pass them rapidly in review, without studying any particular arrangement.

In the first place, it is mostly considered unjust to deprive anyone of his personal liberty, his property, or any other thing which belongs to him by law. Here, therefore, is one instance of the application of the terms "just" and "unjust" in a perfectly definite sense, namely, that it is just to respect, unjust to violate, the *legal rights* of anyone. But this judgment admits of several exceptions, arising from the other forms in which the notions of justice and injustice present themselves. For example, the person who suffers the deprivation may (as the phrase is) have *forfeited* the rights which he is so deprived of—a case to which we shall return presently. But also—

Secondly, the legal rights of which he is deprived may be rights which *ought* not to have belonged to him; in other words, the law which confers on him these rights may be a bad law. When it is so or when (which is the same thing for our purpose) it is supposed to be so, opinions will differ as to the justice or injustice of infringing it. Some maintain that no law, however bad, ought to be disobeyed by an individual citizen; that his opposition to it, if shown at all, should only be shown in endeavoring to get it altered by competent authority. This opinion (which condemns many of the most illustrious benefactors of mankind, and would often protect pernicious institutions against the only weapons which, in the state of things existing at the time, have any chance of succeeding against them) is defended by those who hold it on grounds of expediency, principally on that of the importance to the common interest of mankind, of maintaining inviolate the sentiment of submission to law. Other persons, again, hold the directly contrary opinion that any law, judged to be bad, may blamelessly be disobeyed, even though it be not judged to be unjust but only inexpedient, while others would confine the license of disobedience to the case of unjust laws; but, again, some say that all laws which are inexpedient are unjust, since every law imposes some restriction on the natural liberty of mankind, which restriction is an injustice unless legitimated by tending to their good. Among these diversities of opinion it seems to be universally admitted that there may be unjust laws, and that law, consequently, is not the ultimate criterion of justice, but may give to one person a benefit, or impose on another an evil, which justice condemns. When, however, a law is thought to be unjust, it seems always to be regarded as being so in the same way in which a breach of law is unjust, namely, by infringing somebody's right, which, as it cannot in this case be a legal right, receives a different appellation and is called a moral right. We may say, therefore, that a second case of injustice consists in taking or withholding from any person that to which he has a *moral right.*

Thirdly, it is universally considered just that each person should obtain that (whether good or evil) which he *deserves,* and unjust that he should obtain a good or be made to undergo an evil which he does not deserve. This is, perhaps, the clearest and most emphatic form in which the idea of justice is conceived by the general mind. As it involves the notion of desert, the question arises what constitutes desert? Speaking in a general way, a person is understood to deserve good if he does right, evil if he does wrong; and in a more particular sense, to deserve good from those to whom he does or has done good, and evil from those to whom he does or has done evil. The precept of returning good for evil has never been regarded as a case of the fulfillment of justice, but as one in which the claims of justice are waived, in obedience to other considerations.

Fourthly, it is confessedly unjust to *break faith* with anyone: to violate an engagement, either express or implied, or disappoint expectations raised by our own conduct, at least if we have raised those expectations knowingly and voluntarily. Like the other obligations of justice already spoken of, this one is not regarded as absolute, but as capable of being overruled by a stronger obligation of justice on the other side, or by such conduct on the part of the person concerned as is deemed to absolve us from our obligation to him and to constitute a *forfeiture* of the benefit which he has been led to expect.

Fifthly, it is, by universal admission, inconsistent with justice to be *partial*—to show favor or preference to one person over another in matters to which favor and preference do not properly apply. Impartiality, however, does not seem to be regarded as a duty in itself, but rather as instrumental to some other duty; for it is admitted that favor and preference are not always censurable, and, indeed, the cases in which they are condemned are rather the exception than the rule. A person would be more likely to be blamed than applauded for giving his family or friends no superiority in good offices over strangers when he could do so without violating any other duty; and no one thinks it unjust to seek one person in preference to another as a friend, connection, or companion. Impartiality where rights are concerned is of course obligatory, but this is involved in the more general obligations of giving to everyone his right. A tribunal, for example, must be impartial because it is bound to award, without regard to any other consideration, a disputed object to the one of two parties who has the right to it. There are other cases in which impartiality means being solely influenced by desert, as with those who, in the capacity of judges, preceptors, or parents, administer reward and punishment as such. There are cases, again, in which it means being solely influenced by considerations for the public interest, as in making a selection among candidates for a government employment. Impartiality, in short, as an obligation of justice, may be said to mean being exclusively influenced by the considerations which it is supposed ought to influence the particular case in hand, and resisting solicitation of any motives which prompt to conduct different from what those considerations would dictate.

Nearly allied to the idea of impartiality is that of *equality,* which often enters as a component part both into the conception of justice and into the practice of it, and, in the eyes of many persons, constitutes its essence. But in this, still more than in any other case, the notion of justice varies in different persons, and always conforms in its variations to their notion of utility. Each person maintains that equality is the dictate of justice, except where he thinks that expediency requires inequality. The justice of giving equal protection to the rights of all is maintained by those who support the most outrageous inequality in the rights themselves. Even in slave countries it is theoretically admitted that the rights of the slave, such as they are, ought to be as sacred as those of the master, and that a tribunal which fails to enforce them with equal strictness is wanting in justice; while, at the same time, institutions which leave to the slave scarcely any rights to enforce are not deemed unjust because they are not deemed inexpedient. Those who think that utility requires distinctions of rank do not consider it unjust that riches and social privileges should be unequally dispensed; but those who think this inequality inexpedient think it unjust also. Whoever thinks that government is necessary sees no injustice in as much inequality as is constituted by giving to the magistrate powers not granted to other people. Even among those who hold leveling doctrines, there are differences of opinion about expediency. Some communists consider it unjust that the produce of the labor of the community should be shared on any other principle than that of exact equality; others think it just that those should receive most whose wants are greatest; while others hold that those who work harder, or who produce more, or whose services are more valuable to the community, may justly claim a larger quota in the division of the produce. And the sense of natural justice may be plausibly appealed to in behalf of every one of these opinions.

Among so many diverse applications of the term "justice," which yet is not regarded as ambiguous, it is a matter of some difficulty to seize the mental link which holds them together, and on which the moral sentiment adhering to the term essentially depends. Perhaps, in this embarrassment, some help may be derived from the history of the word, as indicated by its etymology.

In most if not all languages, the etymology of the word which corresponds to "just" points distinctly to an origin connected with the ordinances of law. *Justum* is a form of *jussum,* that which has been ordered. *Dikaion* comes directly from *dike,* a suit at law. *Recht,* from which came *right* and *righteous,* is synonymous with law. The courts of justice, the administration of justice, are the courts and the administration of law. *La justice,* in French, is the established term for judicature. I am not committing the fallacy, imputed with some show of truth to Horne

Tooke,[4] of assuming that a word must still continue to mean what it originally meant. Etymology is slight evidence of what the idea now signified is, but the very best evidence of how it sprang up. There can, I think, be no doubt that the *idée mère,* the primitive element, in the formation of the notion of justice was conformity to law. It constituted the entire idea among the Hebrews, up to the birth of Christianity; as might be expected in the case of a people whose laws attempted to embrace all subjects on which precepts were required, and who believed those laws to be a direct emanation from the Supreme Being. But other nations, and in particular the Greeks and Romans, who knew that their laws had been made originally, and still continued to be made, by men, were not afraid to admit that those men might make bad laws; might do, by law, the same things, and from the same motives, which if done by individuals without the sanction of law would be called unjust. And hence the sentiment of injustice came to be attached, not to all violations of law, but only to violations of such laws as *ought* to exist, including such as ought to exist but do not, and to laws themselves if supposed to be contrary to what ought to be law. In this manner the idea of law and of its injunctions was still predominant in the notion of justice, even when the laws actually in force ceased to be accepted as the standard of it.

It is true that mankind consider the idea of justice and its obligations as applicable to many things which neither are, nor is it desired that they should be, regulated by law. Nobody desires that laws should interfere with the whole detail of private life; yet everyone allows that in all daily conduct a person may and does show himself to be either just or unjust. But even here, the idea of the breach of what ought to be law still lingers in a modified shape. It would always give us pleasure, and chime in with our feelings of fitness, that acts which we deem unjust should be punished, though we do not always think it expedient that this should be done by the tribunals. We forego that gratification on account of incidental inconveniences. We should be glad to see just conduct enforced and injustice repressed, even in the minutest details, if we were not, with reason, afraid of trusting the magistrate with so unlimited an amount of power over individuals. When we think that a person is bound in justice to do a thing, it is an ordinary form of language to say that he ought to be compelled to do it. We should be gratified to see the obligation enforced by anybody who had the power. If we see that its enforcement by law would be inexpedient, we lament the impossibility, we consider the impunity given to injustice as an evil and strive to make amends for it by bringing a strong expression of our own and the public disapprobation to bear upon the offender. Thus the idea of legal constraint is still the generating idea of the notion of justice, though undergoing several transformations before that notion as it exists in an advanced state of society becomes complete.

The above is, I think, a true account, as far as it goes, of the origin and progressive growth of the idea of justice. But we must observe that it contains as yet nothing to distinguish that obligation from moral obligation in general. For the truth is that the idea of penal sanction, which is the essence of law, enters not only into the conception of injustice, but into that of any kind of wrong. We do not call anything wrong unless we mean to imply that

[4] [Reference is to John Horne (1736–1812), who in 1782 adopted the name of his friend, William Tooke. He was cofounder of the Constitutional Society, a club of radical writers whose endorsement of the French Revolution, incidentally, was severely criticized by Burke in his *Reflections on the Revolution in France.* In his later years he was a close friend of Bentham, Coleridge, and Tom Paine.]

a person ought to be punished in some way or other for doing it—if not by law, by the opinion of his fellow creatures; if not by opinion, by the reproaches of his own conscience. This seems the real turning point of the distinction between morality and simple expediency. It is a part of the notion of duty in every one of its forms that a person may rightfully be compelled to fulfill it. Duty is a thing which may be *exacted* from a person, as one exacts a debt. Unless we think that it may be exacted from him, we do not call it his duty. Reasons of prudence, or the interest of other people, may militate against actually exacting it, but the person himself, it is clearly understood, would not be entitled to complain. There are other things, on the contrary, which we wish that people should do, which we like or admire them for doing, perhaps dislike or despise them for not doing, but yet admit that they are not bound to do; it is not a case of moral obligation; we do not blame them, that is, we do not think that they are proper objects of punishment. How we come by these ideas of deserving and not deserving punishment will appear, perhaps, in the sequel; but I think there is no doubt that this distinction lies at the bottom of the notions of right and wrong; that we call any conduct wrong, or employ, instead, some other term of dislike or disparagement, according as we think that the person ought, or ought not, to be punished for it; and we say it would be right to do so and so, or merely that it would be desirable or laudable, according as we would wish to see the person whom it concerns compelled, or only persuaded and exhorted, to act in that manner.[5]

[5] See this point enforced and illustrated by Professor Bain, in an admirable chapter (entitled "The Ethical Emotions, or the Moral Sense"), of the second of the two treatises composing his elaborate and profound work on the Mind [*The Emotions and the Will*, 1859].

This, therefore, being the characteristic difference which marks off, not justice, but morality in general from the remaining provinces of expediency and worthiness, the character is still to be sought which distinguishes justice from other branches of morality. Now it is known that ethical writers divide moral duties into two classes, denoted by the ill-chosen expressions, duties of perfect and of imperfect obligation; the latter being those in which, though the act is obligatory, the particular occasions of performing it are left to our choice, as in the case of charity or beneficence, which we are indeed bound to practice but not toward any definite person, nor at any prescribed time. In the more precise language of philosophic jurists, duties of perfect obligation are those duties in virtue of which a correlative *right* resides in some person or persons; duties of imperfect obligation are those moral obligations which do not give birth to any right. I think it will be found that this distinction exactly coincides with that which exists between justice and the other obligations of morality. In our survey of the various popular acceptations of justice, the term appeared generally to involve the idea of a personal right—a claim on the part of one or more individuals, like that which the law gives when it confers a proprietary or other legal right. Whether the injustice consists in depriving a person of a possession, or in breaking faith with him, or in treating him worse than he deserves, or worse than other people who have no greater claims—in each case the supposition implies two things: a wrong done, and some assignable person who is wronged. Injustice may also be done by treating a person better than others; but the wrong in this case is to his competitors, who are also assignable persons. It seems to me that this feature in the case—a right in some person, correlative to the moral obligation—constitutes the specific difference between justice and generosity or beneficence. Justice implies something which it is not only right to do, and wrong not to do, but which some individual person can claim from us as his moral right. No one has a moral right to our generosity or beneficence because we are not morally bound to practice those virtues toward any given individual. And it will be found with respect to this as to every correct definition that the instances which seem to conflict with it are those which most confirm it. For if a moralist attempts, as some have done, to make out that mankind generally, though not any given individual, have a right to all the good we can do them, he at once, by that thesis, includes generosity and beneficence within the category of justice. He is obliged to say that our utmost exertions are *due* to our fellow creatures, thus assimilating them to a debt; or that nothing less can be a sufficient *return* for what society does for us, thus classing the case as one of gratitude; both of which are acknowledged cases of justice, and not of the virtue of beneficence; and whoever does not place the distinction between justice and morality in general, where we have now placed it, will be found to make no distinction between them at all, but to merge all morality in justice.

Having thus endeavored to determine the distinctive elements which enter into the composition of the idea of justice, we are ready to enter on the inquiry whether the feeling which accompanies the idea is attached to it by a special dispensation of nature, or whether it could have grown up, by any known laws, out of the idea itself; and, in particular, whether it can have originated in considerations of general expediency.

I conceive that the sentiment itself does not arise from anything which would commonly or correctly be termed an idea of expediency, but that, though the sentiment does not, whatever is moral in it does.

We have seen that the two essential ingredients in the sentiment of justice are the desire to punish a person who has done harm and the knowledge or belief that there is some definite individual or individuals to whom harm has been done.

Now it appears to me that the desire to punish a person who has done harm to some individual is a spontaneous outgrowth from two sentiments, both in the highest degree natural and which either are or resemble instincts: the impulse of self-defense and the feeling of sympathy.

It is natural to resent and to repel or retaliate any harm done or attempted against ourselves or against those with whom we sympathize. The origin of this sentiment it is not necessary here to discuss. Whether it be an instinct or a result of intelligence, it is, we know, common to all animal nature; for every animal tries to hurt those who have hurt, or who it thinks are about to hurt, itself or its young. Human beings, on this point, only differ from other animals in two particulars. First, in being capable of sympathizing, not solely with their offspring, or, like some of the more noble animals, with some superior animal who is kind to them, but with all human, and even with all sentient, beings; secondly, in having a more developed intelligence, which gives a wider range to the whole of their sentiments, whether self-regarding or sympathetic. By virtue of his superior intelligence, even apart from his superior range of sympathy, a human being is capable of apprehending a community of interest between himself and the human society of which he forms a part, such that any conduct which threatens the security of the society generally is threatening to his own, and calls forth his instinct (if instinct it be) of self-defense. The same superiority of intelligence, joined to the power of sympathizing with human beings generally, enables him to attach himself to the collective idea of his tribe, his country, or mankind in such a manner that any act hurtful to them raises his instinct of sympathy and urges him to resistance.

The sentiment of justice, in that one of its elements which consists of the desire to punish, is thus, I conceive, the natural feeling of retaliation or vengeance, rendered by intellect and sympathy applicable to those injuries, that is, to those hurts, which wound us through, or in common with, society at large. This sentiment, in itself, has nothing moral in it; what is moral is the exclusive subordination of it to the social sympathies, so as to wait on and obey their call. For the natural feeling would make us resent indiscriminately whatever anyone does that is disagreeable to us; but, when moralized by the social feeling, it only acts in the directions conformable to the general good: just persons resenting a hurt to society, though not otherwise a hurt to themselves, and not resenting a hurt to themselves, however painful, unless it be of the kind which society has a common interest with them in the repression of.

It is no objection against this doctrine to say that, when we feel our sentiment of justice outraged, we are not thinking of society at large or of any collective interest, but only of the individual case. It is common enough, certainly, though the reverse of commendable, to feel resentment merely because we have suffered pain; but a person whose resentment is really a moral feeling, that is, who considers whether an act is blamable before he allows himself to resent it—such a person, though he may not say expressly to himself that he is standing up for the interest of society, certainly does feel that he is asserting a rule which is for the benefit of others as well as for his own. If he is not feeling this, if he is regarding the act solely as it affects him individually, he is not consciously just; he is not concerning himself about the justice of his actions. This is admitted even by anti-utilitarian moralists. When Kant (as before remarked) propounds as the fundamental principle of morals, "So act that thy rule of conduct might be adopted as a law by all rational beings," he virtually acknowledges that the interest of mankind collectively, or at least of mankind indiscriminately, must be in the mind of the agent when conscientiously deciding on the morality of the act. Otherwise he uses words without a meaning; for that a rule even of utter selfishness could not *possibly* be adopted by all rational beings—that there is any insuperable obstacle in the nature of things to its adoption—cannot be even plausibly maintained. To give any meaning to Kant's principle, the sense put upon it must be that we ought to shape our conduct by a rule which all rational beings might adopt *with benefit to their collective interest.*

To recapitulate: the idea of justice supposes two things—a rule of conduct and a sentiment which sanctions the rule. The first must be supposed common to all mankind and intended for their good. The other (the sentiment) is a desire that punishment may be suffered by those who infringe the rule. There is involved, in addition, the conception of some definite person who suffers by the infringement, whose rights (to use the expression appropriated to the case) are violated by it. And the sentiment of justice appears to me to be the animal desire to repel or retaliate a hurt or damage to oneself or to those with whom one sympathizes, widened so as to include all persons, by the human capacity of enlarged sympathy and the human conception of intelligent self-interest. From the latter elements the feeling derives its morality; from the former, its peculiar impressiveness and energy of self-assertion.

I have, throughout, treated the idea of a *right* residing in the injured person and violated by the injury, not as a separate element in the composition of the idea and sentiment, but as one of the forms in which the other two elements clothe themselves. Those elements are a hurt to some assignable person or persons, on the one hand, and a demand for punishment, on the other. An examination of our own minds, I think, will show that these two things include all that we mean when we speak of violation of a right. When we call anything a person's right, we mean that he has a valid claim on society to protect him in the possession of it, either by the force of law or by that of education and opinion. If he has what we consider a sufficient claim, on whatever account, to have something guaranteed to him by society, we say that he has a right to it. If we desire to prove that anything does not belong to him by right, we think this done as soon as it is admitted that society ought not to take measures for securing it to him, but should leave him to chance or to his own exertions. Thus a person is said to have a right to what he can earn in fair professional competition, because society ought not to allow any other person to hinder him from endeavoring to earn in that manner as much as he can. But he has not a right to three hundred a year, though he may happen to be earning it; because society is not called on to provide that he shall earn that sum. On the contrary, if he owns ten thousand pounds three-per-cent stock, he *has* a right to three hundred a year because society has come under an obligation to provide him with an income of that amount.

To have a right, then, is, I conceive, to have something which society ought to defend me in the possession of. If the objector goes on to ask why it ought, I can give him no other reason than general utility. If that expression does not seem to convey a sufficient feeling of the strength of the obligation, nor to account for the peculiar energy of the feeling, it is because there goes to the composition of the sentiment, not a rational only but also an animal element—the thirst for retaliation; and this thirst derives its intensity, as well as its moral justification, from the extraordinarily important and impressive kind of utility which is concerned. The interest involved is that of security, to everyone's feelings the most vital of all interests. All other earthly benefits are needed by one person, not needed by another; and many of them can, if necessary, be cheerfully foregone or replaced by something else; but security no human being can possibly do without; on it we depend for all our immunity from evil and for the whole value of all and every good, beyond the passing moment, since nothing but the gratification of the instant could be of any worth to us if we could be deprived of everything the next instant by whoever was momentarily stronger than ourselves. Now this most indispensable of all necessaries, after physical nutriment, cannot be had unless the machinery for providing it is kept unintermittedly in active play. Our notion, therefore, of the claim we have on our fellow creatures to join in making safe for us the very groundwork of our existence gathers feelings around it so much more intense than those concerned in any of the more common cases of utility that the difference in degree (as is often the case in psychology) becomes a real difference in kind. The claim assumes that character of absoluteness, that apparent infinity and incommensurability with all other considerations which constitute the distinction between the feeling of right and wrong and that of ordinary expediency and inexpediency. The feelings concerned are so powerful, and we count so positively on finding a responsive feeling in others (all being alike interested) that *ought* and *should* grow into *must*, and recognized indispensability becomes a moral necessity, analogous to physical, and often not inferior to it in binding force.

If the preceding analysis, or something resembling it, be not the correct account of the notion of justice—if justice be totally independent of utility, and be a standard *per se,* which the mind can recognize by simple introspection of itself—it is hard to understand why that internal oracle is so ambiguous, and why so many things appear either just or unjust, according to the light in which they are regarded.

We are continually informed that utility is an uncertain standard, which every different person interprets differently, and that there is no safety but in the immutable, ineffaceable, and unmistakable dictates of justice, which carry their evidence in themselves and are independent of the fluctuations of opinion. One would suppose from this that on questions of justice there could be no controversy; that, if we take that for our rule, its application to any given case could leave us in as little doubt as a mathematical demonstration. So far is this from being the fact that there is as much difference of opinion, and as much discussion, about what is just as about what is useful to society. Not only have different nations and individuals different notions of justice, but in the mind of one and the same individual, justice is not some one rule, principle, or maxim, but many which do not always coincide in their dictates, and, in choosing between which, he is guided either by some extraneous standard or by his own personal predilections.

For instance, there are some who say that it is unjust to punish anyone for the sake of example to others, that punishment is just only when intended for the good of the sufferer himself. Others maintain the extreme reverse, contending that to punish persons who have attained years of discretion, for their own benefit, is despotism and injustice, since, if the matter at issue is solely their own good, no one has a right to control their own judgment of it; but that they may justly be punished to prevent evil to others, this being the exercise of the legitimate right of self-defense. Mr. Owen,[6] again, affirms that it is unjust to punish at all, for the criminal did not make his own character; his education and the circumstances which surrounded him have made him a criminal, and for these he is not responsible. All these opinions are extremely plausible; and so long as the question is argued as one of justice simply, without going down to the principles which lie under justice and are the source of its authority, I am unable to see how any of these reasoners can be refuted. For in truth every one of the three builds upon rules of justice confessedly true. The first appeals to the acknowledged injustice of singling out an individual and making him a sacrifice, without his consent, for other people's benefit. The second relies on the acknowledged justice of self-defense and the admitted injustice of forcing one person to conform to another's notions of what constitutes his good. The Owenite invokes the admitted principle that it is unjust to punish anyone for what he cannot help. Each is triumphant so long as he is not compelled to take into consideration any other maxims of justice than the one he has selected; but as soon as their several maxims are brought face to face, each disputant seems to have exactly as much to say for himself as the others. No one of them

[6] [Reference is to Robert Owen (1771–1858), British reformer and a pioneer of the co-operative movement in Great Britain and the United States. His major work, *A New View of Society, or Essay on the Principle of the Formation of the Human Character,* expounds the theory that man's character is wholly determined by environment.]

can carry out his own notion of justice without trampling upon another equally binding. These are difficulties; they have always been felt to be such; and many devices have been invented to turn rather than to overcome them. As a refuge from the last of the three, men imagined what they called the freedom of the will—fancying that they could not justify punishing a man whose will is in a thoroughly hateful state unless it be supposed to have come into that state through no influence of anterior circumstances. To escape from the other difficulties, a favorite contrivance has been the fiction of a contract whereby at some unknown period all the members of society engaged to obey the laws and consented to be punished for any disobedience to them, thereby giving to their legislators the right, which it is assumed they would not otherwise have had, of punishing them, either for their own good or for that of society. This happy thought was considered to get rid of the whole difficulty and to legitimate the infliction of punishment, in virtue of another received maxim of justice, *volenti non fit injuria*—that is not unjust which is done with the consent of the person who is supposed to be hurt by it. I need hardly remark that, even if the consent were not a mere fiction, this maxim is not superior in authority to the others which it is brought in to supersede. It is, on the contrary, an instructive specimen of the loose and irregular manner in which supposed principles of justice grow up. This particular one evidently came into use as a help to the coarse exigencies of courts of law, which are sometimes obliged to be content with very uncertain presumptions, on account of the greater evils which would often arise from any attempt on their part to cut finer. But even courts of law are not able to adhere consistently to the maxim, for they allow voluntary engagements to be set aside on the ground of fraud, and sometimes on that of mere mistake or misinformation.

Again, when the legitimacy of inflicting punishment is admitted, how many conflicting conceptions of justice come to light in discussing the proper apportionment of punishments to offenses. No rule on the subject recommends itself so strongly to the primitive and spontaneous sentiment of justice as the *lex talionis,* an eye for an eye and a tooth for a tooth. Though this principle of the Jewish and of the Mohammedan law has been generally abandoned in Europe as a practical maxim, there is, I suspect, in most minds, a secret hankering after it; and when retribution accidentally falls on an offender in that precise shape, the general feeling of satisfaction evinced bears witness how natural is the sentiment to which this repayment in kind is acceptable. With many, the test of justice in penal infliction is that the punishment should be proportioned to the offense, meaning that it should be exactly measured by the moral guilt of the culprit (whatever be their standard for measuring moral guilt), the consideration what amount of punishment is necessary to deter from the offense having nothing to do with the question of justice, in their estimation; while there are others to whom that consideration is all in all, who maintain that it is not just, at least for man, to inflict on a fellow creature, whatever may be his offenses, any amount of suffering beyond the least that will suffice to prevent him from repeating, and others from imitating, his misconduct.

To take another example from a subject already once referred to. In co-operative industrial association, is it just or not that talent or skill should give a title to superior remuneration? On the negative side of the question it is argued that whoever does the best he can deserves equally well, and ought not in justice to be put in a position of inferiority for no fault of his own; that superior abilities have already advantages more than enough, in the admiration they excite, the personal influence they command, and the internal sources of satisfaction attending them, without adding to these a superior share of the world's goods; and that society is bound in justice rather to make compensation to the less favored for this unmerited inequality of advantages than to aggravate it. On the contrary side it is contended that society receives more from the more efficient laborer; that, his services being more useful, society owes him a larger return for them; that a greater share of the joint result is actually his work, and not to allow his claim to it is a kind of robbery; that, if he is only to receive as much as others, he can only be justly required to produce as much, and to give a smaller amount of time and exertion, proportioned to his superior efficiency. Who shall decide between these appeals to conflicting principles of justice? Justice has in this case two sides to it, which it is impossible to bring into harmony, and the two disputants have chosen opposite sides; the one looks to what it is just that the individual should receive, the other to what it is just that the community should give. Each, from his own point of view, is unanswerable; and any choice between them, on grounds of justice, must be perfectly arbitrary. Social utility alone can decide the preference.

How many, again, and how irreconcilable are the standards of justice to which reference is made in discussing the repartition of taxation. One opinion is that payment to the state should be in numerical proportion to pecuniary means. Others think that justice dictates what they term graduated taxation—taking a higher percentage from those who have more to spare. In point of natural justice a strong case might be made for disregarding means altogether, and taking the same absolute sum (whenever it could be got) from everyone; as the subscribers to a mess or to a club all pay the same sum for the same privileges, whether they can all equally afford it or not. Since the protection (it might be said) of law and government is afforded to and is equally required by all, there is no injustice in making all buy it at the same price. It is reckoned justice, not injustice, that a dealer should charge to all customers the same price for the same article, not a price varying according to their means of payment. This doctrine, as applied to taxation, finds no advocates because it conflicts so strongly with man's feelings of humanity and of social expediency; but the principle of justice which it invokes is as true and as binding as those which can be appealed to against it. Accordingly it exerts a tacit influence on the line of defense employed for other modes of assessing taxation. People feel obliged to argue that the state does more for the rich man than for the poor, as a justification for its taking more from them, though this is in reality not true, for the rich would be far better able to protect themselves, in the absence of law or government, than the poor, and indeed would probably be successful in converting the poor into their slaves. Others, again, so far defer to the same conception of justice as to maintain that all should pay an equal capitation tax for the protection of their persons (these being of equal value to all), and an unequal tax for the protection of their property, which is unequal. To this others reply that the all of one man is as valuable to him as the all of another. From these confusions there is no other mode of extrication than the utilitarian.

Is, then, the difference between the just and the expedient a merely imaginary distinction? Have mankind been under a delusion in thinking that justice is a more sacred thing than policy, and that the latter ought only to be listened to after the former has been satisfied? By no means. The exposition we have given of the nature and origin of the sentiment recognizes a real distinction; and no one of those who profess the most sublime contempt for the consequences of actions as an element in their morality attaches more importance to the distinction than I do. While I dispute the pretensions of any theory which sets up an imaginary standard of justice not grounded on utility, I account the justice which is grounded on utility to be the chief part, and incomparably the most sacred and binding part, of all morality. Justice is a name for certain classes of moral rules which concern the essentials of human well-being more nearly, and are therefore of more absolute obligation, than any other rules for the guidance of life; and the notion which we have found to be of the essence of the idea of justice—that of a right residing in an individual—implies and testifies to this more binding obligation.

The moral rules which forbid mankind to hurt one another (in which we must never forget to include wrongful interference with each other's freedom) are more vital to human well-being than any maxims, however important, which only point out the best mode of managing some department of human affairs. They have also the peculiarity that they are the main element in determining the whole of the social feelings of mankind. It is their observance which alone preserves peace among human beings; if obedience to them were not the rule, and disobedience the exception, everyone would see in everyone else an enemy against whom he must be perpetually guarding himself. What is hardly less important, these are the precepts which mankind have the strongest and the most direct inducements for impressing upon one another. By merely giving to each other prudential instruction or exhortation, they may gain, or think they gain, nothing; in inculcating on each other the duty of positive beneficence, they have an unmistakable interest, but far less in degree; a person may possibly not need the benefits of others, but he always needs that they should not do him hurt. Thus the moralities which protect every individual from being harmed by others, either directly or by being hindered in his freedom of pursuing his own good, are at once those which he himself has most at heart and those which he has the strongest interest in publishing and enforcing by word and deed. It is by a person's observance of these that his fitness to exist as one of the fellowship of human beings is tested and decided; for on that depends his being a nuisance or not to those with whom he is in contact. Now it is these moralities primarily which compose the obligations of justice. The most marked cases of injustice, and those which give the tone to the feeling of repugnance which characterizes the sentiment, are acts of wrongful aggression or wrongful exercise of power over someone; the next are those which consist in wrongfully withholding from him something which is his due—in both cases inflicting on him a positive hurt, either in the form of direct suffering or of the privation of some good which he had reasonable ground, either of a physical or of a social kind, for counting upon.

The same powerful motives which command the observance of these primary moralities enjoin the punishment of those who violate them; and as the impulses of self-defense, of defense of others, and of vengeance are all called forth against such persons, retribution, or evil for evil, becomes closely connected with the sentiment of justice, and is universally included in the idea. Good for good is also one of the dictates of justice; and this, though its social utility is evident, and though it carries with it a natural human feeling, has not at first sight that obvious connection with hurt or injury which, existing in the most elementary cases of just and unjust, is the source of the characteristic intensity of the sentiment. But the connection, though less obvious, is not less real. He who accepts benefits and denies a return of them when needed inflicts a real hurt by disappointing one of the most natural and reasonable of expectations, and one which he must at least tacitly have encouraged, otherwise the benefits would seldom have been conferred. The important rank, among human evils and wrongs, of the disappointment of expectation is shown in the fact that it constitutes the principal criminality of two such highly immoral acts as a breach of friendship and a breach of promise. Few hurts which human beings can sustain are greater, and none wound more, than when that on which they habitually and with full assurance relied fails them in the hour of need; and few wrongs are greater than this mere withholding of good; none excite more resentment, either in the person suffering or in a sympathizing spectator. The principle, therefore, of giving to each what they deserve, that is, good for good as well as evil for evil, is not only included within the idea of justice as we have defined it, but is a proper object of that intensity of sentiment which places the just in human estimation above the simply expedient.

Most of the maxims of justice current in the world, and commonly appealed to in its transactions, are simply instrumental to carrying into effect the principles of justice which we have now spoken of. That a person is only responsible for what he has done voluntarily, or could voluntarily have avoided, that it is unjust to condemn any person unheard; that the punishment ought to be proportioned to the offense, and the like, are maxims intended to prevent the just principle of evil for evil from being perverted to the infliction of evil without that justification. The greater part of these common maxims have come into use from the practice of courts of justice, which have been naturally led to a more complete recognition and elaboration than was likely to suggest itself to others, of the rules necessary to enable them to fulfill their double function—of inflicting punishment when due, and of awarding to each person his right.

That first of judicial virtues, impartiality, is an obligation of justice, partly for the reason last mentioned, as being a necessary condition of the fulfillment of other obligations of justice. But this is not the only source of the exalted rank, among human obligations, of those maxims of equality and impartiality, which, both in popular estimation and in that of the most enlightened, are included among the precepts of justice. In one point of view, they may be considered as corollaries from the principles already laid down. If it is a duty to do to each according to his deserts, returning good for good, as well as repressing evil by evil, it necessarily follows that we should treat all equally well (when no higher duty forbids) who have deserved equally well of *us,* and that society should treat all equally well who have deserved equally well of *it,* that is, who have deserved equally well absolutely. This is the highest abstract standard of social and distributive justice, toward which all institutions and the efforts of all virtuous citizens should be made in the utmost possible degree to converge. But this great moral duty rests upon a still deeper foundation, being a direct emanation from the first principle of morals, and not a mere logical corollary from secondary or derivative doctrines. It is involved in the very meaning of utility, or the greatest happiness principle. That principle is a mere form of words without rational signification unless one person's happiness, supposed equal in degree (with the proper allowance made for kind), is counted for exactly as much as another's. Those conditions being supplied, Bentham's dictum, "everybody to count for one, nobody for more than one," might be written under the principle of utility as an explanatory commentary.[7] The equal claim of everybody to happiness, in the estimation of the moralist and of the legislator, involves an equal claim to all the means of happiness except in so far as the inevitable conditions of human life and the general interest in which that of every individual is included set limits to the maxim; and those limits ought to be strictly construed. As every other maxim of justice, so this is by no means applied or held applicable universally; on the contrary, as I have already remarked, it bends to every person's ideas of social expediency. But in whatever case it is deemed applicable at all, it is held to be the dictate of justice. All persons are deemed to have a *right* to equality of treatment, except when some recognized social expediency requires the reverse. And hence all social inequalities which have ceased to be considered expedient assume the character, not of simple inexpediency, but of injustice, and appear so tyrannical that people are apt to wonder how they ever could have been tolerated—forgetful that they themselves, perhaps, tolerate other inequalities under an equally mistaken notion of expediency, the correction of which would make that which they approve seem quite as monstrous as what they have at last learned to condemn. The entire history of social improvement has been a series of transitions by which one custom or institution after another, from being a supposed primary necessity of social existence, has passed into the rank of a universally stigmatized injustice and tyranny. So it has been with the distinctions of slaves and freemen, nobles and serfs, patricians and plebeians; and so it will be, and in part already is, with the aristocracies of color, race, and sex.

It appears from what has been said that justice is a name for certain moral requirements which, regarded collectively,

[7] This implication, in the first principle of the utilitarian scheme, of perfect impartiality between persons is regarded by Mr. Herbert Spencer (in his *Social Statics*) as a disproof of the pretensions of utility to be a sufficient guide to right; since (he says) the principle of utility presupposes the anterior principle that everybody has an equal right to happiness. It may be more correctly described as supposing that equal amounts of happiness are equally desirable, whether felt by the same or different persons. This, however, is not a *pre*supposition, not a premise needful to support the principle of utility, but the very principle itself; for what is the principle of utility if it be not that "happiness" and "desirable" are synonymous terms? If there is any anterior principle implied, it can be no other than this, that the truths of arithmetic are applicable to the valuation of happiness, as of all other measurable quantities.

(Mr. Herbert Spencer, in a private communication on the subject of the preceding note, objects to being considered an opponent of utilitarianism and states that he regards happiness as the ultimate end of morality; but deems that end only partially attainable by empirical generalizations from the observed results of conduct, and completely attainable only by deducing, from the laws of life and the conditions of existence, what kinds of action necessarily tend to produce happiness, and what kinds to produce unhappiness. With the exception of the word "necessarily," I have no dissent to express from this doctrine; and (omitting that word) I am not aware that any modern advocate of utilitarianism is of a different opinion. Bentham, certainly, to whom in the *Social Statics* Mr. Spencer particularly referred, is, least of all writers, chargeable with unwillingness to deduce the effect of actions on happiness from the laws of human nature and the universal conditions of human life. The common charge against him is of relying too exclusively upon such deductions and declining altogether to be bound by the generalizations from specific experience which Mr. Spencer thinks that utilitarians generally confine themselves to. My own opinion (and, as I collect, Mr. Spencer's) is that in ethics, as in all other branches of scientific study, the consilience of the results of both these processes, each corroborating and verifying the other, is requisite to give to any general proposition the kind and degree of evidence which constitutes scientific proof.)

stand higher in the scale of social utility, and are therefore of more paramount obligation, than any others, though particular cases may occur in which some other social duty is so important as to overrule any one of the general maxims of justice. Thus, to save a life, it may not only be allowable, but a duty, to steal or take by force the necessary food or medicine, or to kidnap and compel to officiate the only qualified medical practitioner. In such cases, as we do not call anything justice which is not a virtue, we usually say, not that justice must give way to some other moral principle, but that what is just in ordinary cases is, by reason of that other principle, not just in the particular case. By this useful accommodation of language, the character of indefeasibility attributed to justice is kept up, and we are saved from the necessity of maintaining that there can be laudable injustice.

The considerations which have now been adduced resolve, I conceive, the only real difficulty in the utilitarian theory of morals. It has always been evident that all cases of justice are also cases of expediency; the difference is in the peculiar sentiment which attaches to the former, as contradistinguished from the latter. If this characteristic sentiment has been sufficiently accounted for; if there is no necessity to assume for it any peculiarity of origin; if it is simply the natural feeling of resentment, moralized by being made co-existensive with the demands of social good; and if this feeling not only does but ought to exist in all the classes of cases to which the idea of justice corresponds—that idea no longer presents itself as a stumbling block to the utilitarian ethics. Justice remains the appropriate name for certain social utilities which are vastly more important, and therefore more absolute and imperative, than any others are as a class (though not more so than others may be in particular cases); and which, therefore, ought to be, as well as naturally are, guarded by a sentiment, not only different in degree, but also in kind; distinguished from the milder feeling which attaches to the mere idea of promoting human pleasure or convenience at once by the more definite nature of its commands and by the sterner character of its sanctions.

Critical

essays

Harold Arthur Prichard / Does moral philosophy rest on a mistake?

Probably to most students of Moral Philosophy there comes a time when they feel a vague sense of dissatisfaction with the whole subject. And the sense of dissatisfaction tends to grow rather than to diminish. It is not so much that the positions, and still more the arguments, of particular thinkers seem unconvincing, though this is true. It is rather that the aim of the subject becomes increasingly obscure. "What," it is asked, "are we really going to learn by Moral Philosophy?" "What are books on Moral Philosophy really trying to show, and when their aim is clear, why are they so unconvincing and artificial?" And again: "Why is it so difficult to substitute anything better?" Personally, I have been led by growing dissatisfaction of this kind to wonder whether the reason may not be that the subject, at any rate as usually understood, consists in the attempt to answer an improper question. And in this article I shall venture to contend that the existence of the whole subject, as usually understood, rests on a mistake, and on a mistake parallel to that on which rests, as I think, the subject usually called the Theory of Knowledge.

If we reflect on our own mental history or on the history of the subject, we feel no doubt about the nature of the demand which originates the subject. Any one who, stimulated by education, has come to feel the force of the various obligations in life, at some time or other comes to feel the irksomeness of carrying them out, and to recognize the sacrifice of interest involved; and, if thoughtful, he inevitably puts to himself the question: "Is there really a reason why I should act in the ways in which hitherto I have thought I ought to act? May I not have been all the time under an illusion in so thinking? Should not I really be justified in simply trying to have a good time?" Yet, like Glaucon, feeling that somehow he ought after all to act in these ways, he asks for a *proof* that this feeling is justified. In other words, he asks "*Why* should I do these things?" and his and other people's moral philosophizing is an attempt to supply the answer, i.e., to supply by a process of re-

Reprinted from MIND, *vol. 21, no. 81 (January 1912), pp. 21–37 by permission of the editor and Marjorie M. L. Prichard.*

flection a proof of the truth of what he and they have prior to reflection believed immediately or without proof. This frame of mind seems to present a close parallel to the frame of mind which originates the Theory of Knowledge. Just as the recognition that the doing of our duty often vitally interferes with the satisfaction of our inclinations leads us to wonder whether we really ought to do what we usually call our duty, so the recognition that we and others are liable to mistakes in knowledge generally leads us, as it did Descartes, to wonder whether hitherto we may not have been always mistaken. And just as we try to find a proof, based on the general consideration of action and of human life, that we ought to act in the ways usually called moral, so we, like Descartes, propose by a process of reflection on our thinking to find a test of knowledge, i.e., a principle by applying which we can show that a certain condition of mind was really knowledge, a condition which *ex hypothesi* existed independently of the process of reflection.

Now, how has the moral question been answered? So far as I can see, the answers all fall, and fall from the necessities of the case, into one of two species. *Either* they state that we ought to do so and so, because, as we see when we fully apprehend the facts, doing so will be for our good, i.e., really, as I would rather say, for our advantage, or, better still, for our happiness; *or* they state that we ought to do so and so, because something realized either in or by the action is good. In other words, the reason 'why' is stated in terms either of the agent's happiness or of the goodness of something involved in the action.

To see the prevalence of the former species of answer, we have only to consider the history of Moral Philosophy. To take obvious instances, Plato, Butler, Hutcheson, Paley, Mill, each in his own way seeks at bottom to convince the individual that he ought to act in so-called moral ways by showing that to do so will really be for his happiness. Plato is perhaps the most significant instance because of all philosophers he is the one to whom we are least willing to ascribe a mistake on such matters, and a mistake on his part would be evidence of the deep-rootedness of the tendency to make it. To show that Plato really justifies morality by its profitableness, it is only necessary to point out (1) that the very formulation of the thesis to be met, viz., that justice is ἀλλότριον ἀγαθόν [someone else's good] implies that any refutation must consist in showing that justice is οἰχεῖον ἀγαθόν [one's own good], i.e., really, as the context shows, one's own advantage, and (2) that the term λυσιτελεῖν [to be profitable] supplies the key not only to the problem but also to its solution.

The tendency to justify acting on moral rules in this way is natural. For if, as often happens, we put to ourselves the question "Why should we do so and so?", we are satisfied by being convinced either that the doing so will lead to something which we want (e.g., that taking certain medicine will heal our disease), or that the doing so itself, as we see when we appreciate its nature, is something that we want or should like, e.g., playing golf. The formulation of the question implies a state of unwillingness or indifference towards the action, and we are brought into a condition of willingness by the answer. And this process seems to be precisely what we desire when we ask, e.g., "Why should we keep our engagements to our own loss?"; for it is just the fact that the keeping of our engagements runs counter to the satisfaction of our desires which produced the question.

The answer is, of course, not an answer, for it fails to convince us that we ought to keep our engagements; even if successful on its own lines, it only makes us *want* to keep them. And Kant was really only pointing out this fact when he distinguished hypothetical and categorical imperatives, even though he obscured the nature of the fact by wrongly describing his so-called "hypothetical imperatives" as imperatives. But if this answer be no answer, what other can be offered? Only, it seems, an answer which bases the obligation to do something on the *goodness* either of something to which the act leads or of the act itself. Suppose, when wondering whether we really ought to act in the ways usually called moral, we are told as a means of resolving our doubt that those acts are right which produce happiness. We at once ask: "Whose happiness?" If we are told "Our own happiness," then, though we shall lose our hesitation to act in these ways, we shall not recover our sense that we ought to do so. But how can this result be avoided? Apparently, only by being told one of two things; *either* that anyone's happiness is a thing good in itself, and that *therefore* we ought to do whatever will produce it, *or* that working for happiness is itself good, and that the intrinsic goodness of such an action is the reason why we ought to do it. The advantage of this appeal to the goodness of something consists in the fact that it avoids reference to desire, and, instead, refers to something impersonal and objective. In this way it seems possible to avoid the resolution of obligation into inclination. But just for this reason it is of the essence of the answer, that to be effective it must neither include nor involve the view that the apprehension of the goodness of anything necessarily arouses the desire for it. Otherwise the answer resolves itself into a form of the former answer by substituting desire or inclination for the sense of obligation, and in this way it loses what seems its special advantage.

Now it seems to me that both forms of this answer break down, though each for a different reason.

Consider the first form. It is what may be called Utilitarianism in the generic sense, in which what is good is not limited to pleasure. It takes its stand upon the distinction between something which is not itself an action, but which can be produced by an action, and the action which will produce it, and contends that if something which is not an action is good, then *we ought* to undertake the action which will, directly or indirectly, originate it.[1]

But this argument, if it is to restore the sense of obligation to act, must presuppose an intermediate link, viz., the further thesis that what is good ought to be.[2] The necessity of this link is obvious. An "ought," if it is to be derived at all, can only be derived from another "ought." Moreover, this link tacitly presupposes another, viz., that the apprehension that something good which is not an action ought to be, involves just the feeling of imperativeness or obligation which is to be aroused by the thought of the action which will originate it. Otherwise the argument will not lead us to feel the obligation to produce it by the action. And, surely, both this link and its implication are false.[3] The word "ought" refers to actions and to actions alone. The proper language is never "So and so ought to be," but "I ought to do so and so." Even if we are sometimes moved to say that the world or something in it is not what it ought to be, what we really mean is that God or some human being has not made something what he ought to have made it. And it is merely stating another side of this fact to urge that we can only feel the imperativeness upon us of something which

[1] Cf. Dr. Rashdall's *Theory of Good and Evil* (Oxford: Clarendon Press, 1907), 1: 138.

[2] Dr. Rashdall, if I understand him rightly, supplies this link (cf. ibid., pp. 135–36).

[3] When we speak of anything, e.g., of some emotion or of some quality of a human being, as good, we never dream in our ordinary consciousness of going on to say that therefore it ought to be.

is in our power; for it is actions and actions alone which, directly at least, are in our power.

Perhaps, however, the best way to see the failure of this view is to see its failure to correspond to our actual moral convictions. Suppose we ask ourselves whether our sense that we ought to pay our debts or to tell the truth arises from our recognition that in doing so we should be originating something good, e.g., material comfort in *A* or true belief in *B*, i.e., suppose we ask ourselves whether it is this aspect of the action which leads to our recognition that we ought to do it. We at once and without hesitation answer "No." Again, if we take as our illustration our sense that we ought to act justly as between two parties, we have, if possible, even less hesitation in giving a similar answer; for the balance of resulting good may be, and often is, not on the side of justice.

At best it can only be maintained that there is this element of truth in the Utilitarian view, that unless we recognize that something which an act will originate is good, we should not recognize that we ought to do the action. Unless we thought knowledge a good thing, it may be urged, we should not think that we ought to tell the truth; unless we thought pain a bad thing, we should not think the infliction of it, without special reason, wrong. But this is not to imply that the badness of error is the reason why it is wrong to lie, or the badness of pain the reason why we ought not to inflict it without special cause.[4]

It is, I think, just because this form of the view is so plainly at variance with our moral consciousness that we are driven to adopt the other form of the view, viz., that the act is good in itself and that its intrinsic goodness is the reason why it ought to be done. It is this form which has always made the most serious appeal; for the goodness of the act itself seems more closely related to the obligation to do it than that of its mere consequences or results, and, therefore, if obligation is to be based on the goodness of something, it would seem that this goodness should be that of the act itself. Moreover, the view gains plausibility from the fact that moral actions are most conspicuously those to which the term "intrinsically good" is applicable.

Nevertheless this view, though perhaps less superficial, is equally untenable. For it leads to precisely the dilemma which faces everyone who tries to solve the problem raised by Kant's theory of the good will. To see this, we need only consider the nature of the acts to which we apply the term "intrinsically good."

There is, of course, no doubt that we approve and even admire certain actions, and also that we should describe them as good, and as good in themselves. But it is, I think, equally unquestionable that our approval and our use of the term "good" is always in respect of the motive and refers to actions which have been actually done and of which we think we know the motive. Further, the actions of which we approve and which we should describe as intrinsically good are of two and only two kinds. They are either actions in which the agent did what he did because he thought he ought to do it, or actions of which the motive was a desire prompted by some good emotion, such as gratitude, affection, family feeling, or public spirit, the most prominent of such desires in books on Moral Philosophy being that ascribed to what is vaguely called benevolence. For the sake of simplicity I omit the case of actions done partly from some such desire and partly from a sense of duty; for even if all good actions are done from a combination of these motives, the argument will not be affected. The dilemma is

[4] It may be noted that if the badness of pain were the reason why we ought not to inflict pain on another, it would equally be a reason why we ought not to inflict pain on ourselves; yet, though we should allow the wanton infliction of pain on ourselves to be foolish, we should not think of describing it as wrong.

this. If the motive in respect of which we think an action good is the sense of obligation, then so far from the sense that we ought to do it being derived from our apprehension of its goodness, our apprehension of its goodness will presuppose the sense that we ought to do it. In other words, in this case the recognition that the act is good will plainly *presuppose* the recognition that the act is right, whereas the view under consideration is that the recognition of the goodness of the act *gives rise* to the recognition of its rightness. On the other hand, if the motive in respect of which we think an action good is some intrinsically good desire, such as the desire to help a friend, the recognition of the goodness of the act will equally fail to give rise to the sense of obligation to do it. For we cannot feel that we ought to do that the doing of which is *ex hypothesi* prompted solely by the desire to do it.[5]

The fallacy underlying the view is that while to base the rightness of an act upon its intrinsic goodness implies that the goodness in question is that of the motive, in reality the rightness or wrongness of an act has nothing to do with any question of motives at all. For, as any instance will show, the rightness of an action concerns an action not in the fuller sense of the term in which we include the motive in the action, but in the narrower and commoner sense in which we distinguish an action from its motive and mean by an action merely the conscious origination of something, an origination which on different occasions or in different people may be prompted by different motives. The question "Ought I to pay my bills?" really means simply "Ought I to bring about my tradesmen's possession of what by my previous acts I explicitly or implicitly promised them?" There is, and can be, no question of whether I ought to pay my debts from a particular motive. No doubt we know that if we pay our bills we shall pay them with a motive, but in considering whether we ought to pay them we inevitably think of the act in abstraction from the motive. Even if we knew what our motive would be if we did the act, we should not be any nearer an answer to the question.

Moreover, if we eventually pay our bills from fear of the county court, we shall still have done *what* we ought, even though we shall not have done it *as* we ought. The attempt to bring in the motive involves a mistake similar to that involved in supposing that we can will to will. To feel that I ought to pay my bills is to be *moved towards* paying them. But what I can be moved towards must always be an action and not an action in which I am moved in a particular way, i.e., an action from a particular motive; otherwise I should be moved towards being moved, which is impossible. Yet the view under consideration involves this impossibility, for it really resolves the sense that I ought to do so and so, into the sense that I ought to be moved to do it in a particular way.[6]

So far my contentions have been mainly negative, but they form, I think, a useful, if not a necessary, introduction to what I take to be the truth. This I will now endeavour to state, first formulating what, as I think, is the real nature of our apprehension or appreciation of moral obligations, and then applying the result to elucidate the question of the existence of Moral Philosophy.

The sense of obligation to do, or of the rightness of, an action of a particular kind is absolutely underivative or immediate. The rightness of an action consists in its being the origination of something

[5] It is, I think, on this latter horn of the dilemma that Martineau's view falls; cf. *Types of Ethical Theory*, part ii, book i.

[6] It is of course not denied here that an action done from a particular motive may be *good;* it is only denied that the *rightness* of an action depends on its being done with a particular motive.

of a certain kind *A* in a situation of a certain kind, a situation consisting in a certain relation *B* of the agent to others or to his own nature. To appreciate its rightness two preliminaries may be necessary. We may have to follow out the consequences of the proposed action more fully than we have hitherto done, in order to realize that in the action we should originate *A*. Thus we may not appreciate the wrongness of telling a certain story until we realize that we should thereby be hurting the feelings of one of our audience. Again, we may have to take into account the relation *B* involved in the situation, which we had hitherto failed to notice. For instance, we may not appreciate the obligation to give *X* a present, until we remember that he has done us an act of kindness. But, given that by a process which is, of course, merely a process of general and not of moral thinking we come to recognize that the proposed act is one by which we shall originate *A* in a relation *B*, then we appreciate the obligation immediately or directly, the appreciation being an activity of *moral* thinking. We recognize, for instance, that this performance of a service to *X*, who has done us a service, just in virtue of its being the performance of a service to one who has rendered a service to the would-be agent, ought to be done by us. This apprehension is immediate, in precisely the sense in which a mathematical apprehension is immediate, e.g., the apprehension that this three-sided figure, in virtue of its being three-sided, must have three angles. Both apprehensions are immediate in the sense that, in both, insight into the nature of the subject directly leads us to recognize its possession of the predicate; and it is only stating this fact from the other side to say that in both cases the fact apprehended is self-evident.

The plausibility of the view that obligations are not self-evident but need proof lies in the fact that an act which is referred to as an obligation may be incompletely stated, what I have called the preliminaries to appreciating the obligation being incomplete. If, e.g., we refer to the act of repaying *X* by a present merely as giving *X* a present, it appears, and indeed is, necessary to give a reason. In other words, wherever a moral act is regarded in this incomplete way the question "*Why* should I do it?" is perfectly legitimate. This fact suggests, but suggests wrongly, that even if the nature of the act is completely stated, it is still necessary to give a reason, or, in other words, to supply a proof.

The relations involved in obligations of various kinds are, of course, very different. The relation in certain cases is a relation to others due to a past act of theirs or ours. The obligation to repay a benefit involves a relation due to a past act of the benefactor. The obligation to pay a bill involves a relation due to a past act of ours in which we have either said or implied that we would make a certain return for something which we have asked for and received. On the other hand, the obligation to speak the truth implies no such definite act; it involves a relation consisting in the fact that others are trusting us to speak the truth, a relation the apprehension of which gives rise to the sense that communication of the truth is something owing by us to them. Again, the obligation not to hurt the feelings of another involves no special relation of us to that other, i.e., no relation other than that involved in our both being men, and men in one and the same world. Moreover, it seems that the relation involved in an obligation need not be a relation to another at all. Thus we should admit that there is an obligation to overcome our natural timidity or greediness, and that this involves no relations to others. Still there is a relation involved, viz., a relation to our own disposition. It is simply because we can and because others cannot directly modify our disposition that it is our business to improve it, and that it is not theirs, or, at least, not theirs to the same extent.

The negative side of all this is, of course, that we do not come to appreciate an obligation by an *argument*, i.e., by a process of non-moral thinking, and that, in particular, we do not do so by an argument of which a premise is the ethical but not moral activity of appreciating the goodness either of the act or of a consequence of the act; i.e., that our sense of the rightness of an act is not a conclusion from our appreciation of the goodness either of it or of anything else.

It will probably be urged that on this view our various obligations form, like Aristotle's categories, an unrelated chaos in which it is impossible to acquiesce. For, according to it, the obligation to repay a benefit, or to pay a debt, or to keep a promise, presupposes a previous act of another; whereas the obligation to speak the truth or not to harm another does not; and, again, the obligation to remove our timidity involves no relations to others at all. Yet, at any rate, an effective *argumentum ad hominem* is at hand in the fact that the various qualities which we recognize as good are equally unrelated; e.g. courage, humility, and interest in knowledge. If, as is plainly the case, *ἀγαθά* differ *ᾗ ἀγαθά*,[7] why should not obligations equally differ *qua* their obligatoriness? Moreover, if this were not so there could in the end be only one obligation, which is palpably contrary to fact.[8]

Certain observations will help to make the view clearer.

In the first place, it may seem that the view, being—as it is—avowedly put forward in opposition to the view that what is right is derived from what is good, must itself involve the opposite of this, viz., the Kantian position that what is good is based upon what is right, i.e., that an act, if it be good, is good because it is right. But this is not so. For, on the view put forward, the rightness of a right action lies solely in the origination in which the act consists, whereas the intrinsic goodness of an action lies solely in its motive; and this implies that a morally good action is morally good not simply because it is a right action but because it is a right action done because it is right, i.e., from a sense of obligation. And this implication, it may be remarked incidentally, seems plainly true.

In the second place, the view involves that when, or rather so far as, we act from a sense of obligation, we have no purpose or end. By a "purpose" or "end" we really mean something the existence of which we desire, and desire of the existence of which leads us to act. Usually our purpose is something in which the act will originate, as when we turn round in order to look at a picture. But it may be the action itself, i.e., the origination of something, as when we hit a golfball into a hole or kill someone

[7] [Goods differ *qua* goods.]

[8] Two other objections may be anticipated: (1) that obligations cannot be self-evident, since many actions regarded as obligations by some are not so regarded by others, and (2) that if obligations are self-evident, the problem of how we ought to act in the presence of conflicting obligations is insoluble.

To the first I should reply:

(*a*) That the appreciation of an obligation is, of course, only possible for a developed moral being, and that different degrees of development are possible.

(*b*) That the failure to recognize some particular obligation is usually due to the fact that, owing to a lack of thoughtfulness, what I have called the preliminaries to this recognition are incomplete.

(*c*) That the view put forward is consistent with the admission that, owing to a lack of thoughtfulness, even the best men are blind to many of their obligations, and that in the end our obligations are seen to be co-extensive with almost the whole of our life.

To the second objection I should reply that obligation admits of degrees, and that where obligations conflict, the decision of what we ought to do turns not on the question "Which of the alternative courses of action will originate the greater good?" but on the question "Which is the greater obligation?"

out of revenge.[9] Now if by a purpose we mean something the existence of which we desire and desire for which leads us to act, then plainly, so far as we act from a sense of obligation, we have no purpose, consisting either in the action or in anything which it will produce. This is so obvious that it scarcely seems worth pointing out. But I do so for two reasons. (1) If we fail to scrutinize the meaning of the terms "end" and "purpose," we are apt to assume uncritically that all deliberate action, i.e., action proper, must have a purpose; we then become puzzled both when we look for the purpose of an action done from a sense of obligation, and also when we try to apply to such an action the distinction of means and end, the truth all the time being that since there is no end, there is no means either. (2) The attempt to base the sense of obligation on the recognition of the goodness of something is really an attempt to find a purpose in a moral action in the shape of something good which, as good, we want. And the expectation that the goodness of something underlies an obligation disappears as soon as we cease to look for a purpose.

The thesis, however, that, so far as we act from a sense of obligation, we have no purpose must not be misunderstood. It must not be taken either to mean or to imply that so far as we so act we have no *motive*. No doubt in ordinary speech the words "motive" and "purpose" are usually treated as correlatives, "motive" standing for the desire which induces us to act, and "purpose" standing for the object of this desire. But this is only because, when we are looking for the motive of the action, say, of some crime, we are usually presupposing that the act in question is prompted by a desire and not by the sense of obligation. At bottom, however, we mean by a motive what moves us to act; a sense of obligation does sometimes move us to act; and in our ordinary consciousness we should not hesitate to allow that the action we were considering might have had as its motive a sense of obligation. Desire and the sense of obligation are co-ordinate forms or species of motive.

In the third place, if the view put forward be right, we must sharply distinguish morality and virtue as independent, though related, species of goodness, neither being an aspect of something of which the other is an aspect, nor again a form or species of the other, nor again something deducible from the other; and we must at the same time allow that it is possible to do the same act either virtuously or morally or in both ways at once. And surely this is true. An act, to be virtuous, must, as Aristotle saw, be done willingly or with pleasure; as such it is just not done from a sense of obligation but from some desire which is intrinsically good, as arising from some intrinsically good emotion. Thus, in an act of generosity the motive is the desire to help another arising from sympathy with that other; in an act which is courageous and no more, i.e., in an act which is not at the same time an act of public spirit or family affection or the like, we prevent ourselves from being dominated by a feeling of terror, desiring to do so from a sense of shame at being terrified. The goodness of such an act is different from the goodness of an act to which we apply the term moral in the strict and narrow sense, viz., an act done from a sense of obligation. Its goodness lies in the intrinsic goodness of the emotion and of the consequent desire under which we act, the goodness of this motive being different from the goodness of the moral motive proper, viz., the sense of duty or obligation. Nevertheless, at any rate in certain cases, an act can be done

[9] It is no objection to urge that an action cannot be its own purpose, since the purpose of something cannot be the thing itself. For, speaking strictly, the purpose is not the *action's* purpose but *our* purpose, and there is no contradiction in holding that our purpose in acting may be the action.

either virtuously or morally or in both ways at once. It is possible to repay a benefit either from desire to repay it, or from the feeling that we ought to do so, or from both motives combined. A doctor may tend his patients either from a desire arising out of interest in his patients or in the exercise of skill, or from a sense of duty, or from a desire and a sense of duty combined. Further, although we recognize that in each case the act possesses an intrinsic goodness, we regard that action as the best in which both motives are combined; in other words, we regard as the really best man the man in which virtue and morality are united.

It may be objected that the distinction between the two kinds of motive is untenable, on the ground that the *desire* to repay a benefit, for example, is only the manifestation of that which manifests itself as the *sense of obligation* to repay whenever we think of something in the action which is other than the repayment and which we should not like, such as the loss or pain involved. Yet the distinction can, I think, easily be shown to be tenable. For, in the analogous case of revenge, the desire to return the injury and the sense that we ought not to do so, leading, as they do, in opposite directions, are plainly distinct; and the obviousness of the distinction here seems to remove any difficulty in admitting the existence of a parallel distinction between the desire to return a benefit and the sense that we ought to return it.[10]

Further, the view implies that an obligation can no more be based on or derived from a virtue than a virtue can be derived from an obligation, in which latter case a virtue would consist in carrying out an obligation. And the implication is surely true and important. Take the case of courage. It is untrue to urge that, since courage is a virtue, we ought to act courageously. It is and must be untrue, because, as we see in the end, to feel an obligation to act courageously would involve a contradiction. For, as I have urged before, we can only feel an obligation to *act*; we cannot feel an obligation to *act from a certain desire*, in this case the desire to conquer one's feelings of terror arising from the sense of shame which they arouse. Moreover, if the sense of obligation to act in a particular way leads to an action, the action will be an action done from a sense of obligation, and therefore not, if the above analysis of virtue be right, an act of courage.

The mistake of supposing that there can be an obligation to act courageously seems to arise from two causes. In the first place, there is often an obligation to do that which involves the conquering or controlling of our fear in the doing of it, e.g., the obligation to walk along the side of a precipice to fetch a doctor for a member of our family. Here the acting on the obligation is externally, though only externally, the same as an act of courage proper. In the second place there is an obligation to acquire courage, i.e., to do such things as will enable us afterwards to act courageously, and this may be mistaken for an obligation to act courageously. The same considerations can, of course, be applied, *mutatis mutandis*, to the other virtues.

[10] This sharp distinction of virtue and morality as co-ordinate and independent forms of goodness will explain a fact which otherwise it is difficult to account for. If we turn from books on Moral Philosophy to any vivid account of human life and action such as we find in Shakespeare, nothing strikes us more than the comparative remoteness of the discussions of Moral Philosophy from the facts of actual life. Is not this largely because, while Moral Philosophy has, quite rightly, concentrated its attention on the fact of obligation, in the case of many of those whom we admire most and whose lives are of the greatest interest, the sense of obligation, though it may be an important, is not a dominating factor in their lives?

The fact, if it be a fact, that virtue is no basis for morality will explain what otherwise it is difficult to account for, viz., the extreme sense of dissatisfaction produced by a close reading of Aristotle's *Ethics*. Why is the *Ethics* so disappointing? Not, I think, because it really answers two radically different questions as if they were one: (1) "What is the happy life?" (2) "What is the virtuous life?" It is, rather, because Aristotle does not do what we as moral philosophers want him to do, viz., to convince us that we really ought to do what in our nonreflective consciousness we have hitherto believed we ought to do, or if not, to tell us what, if any, are the other things which we really ought to do, and to prove to us that he is right. Now, if what I have just been contending is true, a systematic account of the virtuous character cannot possibly satisfy this demand. At best it can only make clear to us the details of one of our obligations, viz., the obligation to make ourselves better men; but the achievement of this does not help us to discover what we ought to do in life as a whole, and why; to think that it did would be to think that our only business in life was self-improvement. Hence it is not surprising that Aristotle's account of the good man strikes us as almost wholly of academic value, with little relation to our real demand, which is formulated in Plato's words: οὐ γὰρ περὶ τοῦ ἐπιτυχόντος ὁ λόγος, ἀλλὰ περὶ τοῦ ὅντινα τρόπον χρὴ ζῆν.[11]

I am not, of course, *criticizing* Aristotle for failing to satisfy this demand, except so far as here and there he leads us to think that he intends to satisfy it. For my main contention is that the demand cannot be satisfied, and cannot be satisfied because it is illegitimate. Thus we are brought to the question: "Is there really such a thing as Moral Philosophy, and, if there is, in what sense?"

[11] [We are not discussing trivialities but how we ought to live.]

We should first consider the parallel case—as it appears to be—of the Theory of Knowledge. As I urged before, at some time or other in the history of all of us, if we are thoughtful, the frequency of our own and of others' mistakes is bound to lead to the reflection that possibly we and others have *always* been mistaken in consequence of some radical defect of our faculties. In consequence, certain things which previously we should have said without hesitation that we *knew*, as, e.g., that $4 \times 7 = 28$, become subject to doubt; we become able only to say that we thought we knew these things. We inevitably go on to look for some general procedure by which we can ascertain that a given condition of mind is really one of knowledge. And this involves the search for a criterion of knowledge, i.e., for a principle by applying which we can settle that a given state of mind is really knowledge. The search for this criterion and the application of it, when found, is what is called the Theory of Knowledge. The search implies that instead of its being the fact that the knowledge that *A* is *B* is obtained directly by consideration of the nature of *A* and *B*, the knowledge that *A* is *B*, in the full or complete sense, can only be obtained by first knowing that *A* is *B*, and then knowing that we knew it by applying a criterion, such as Descartes' principle that what we clearly and distinctly conceive is true.

Now it is easy to show that the doubt whether *A* is *B*, based on this speculative or general ground, could, if genuine, never be set at rest. For if, in order really to know that *A* is *B*, we must first know that we knew it, then really, to know that we knew it, we must first know that we knew that we knew it. But—what is more important—it is also easy to show that this doubt is not a genuine doubt but rests on a confusion the exposure of which removes the doubt. For when we *say* we doubt whether our previous condition was one of knowledge, what we *mean,* if we mean anything at all, is that we doubt whether our previous *belief* was *true,* a belief which we should express as the *thinking* that *A* is *B*. For in order to doubt whether our previous condition was one of knowledge, we have to think of it not as knowledge but as only belief, and our only question can be "Was this belief true?" But as soon as we see that we are thinking of our previous condition as only one of belief, we see that what we are now doubting is not what we first *said* we were doubting, viz., whether a previous condition of knowledge was really knowledge. Hence, to remove the doubt, it is only necessary to appreciate the real nature of our consciousness in apprehending, e.g., that $7 \times 4 = 28$, and thereby see that it was no mere condition of believing but a condition of knowing, and then to notice that in our subsequent doubt what we are really doubting is not whether this consciousness was really knowledge, but whether a consciousness of another kind, viz., a belief that $7 \times 4 = 28$, was true. We thereby see that though a doubt based on speculative grounds is possible, it is not a doubt concerning what we believed the doubt concerned, and that a doubt concerning this latter is impossible.

Two results follow. In the first place, if, as is usually the case, we mean by the "Theory of Knowledge" the knowledge which supplies the answer to the question "Is what we have hitherto thought knowledge really knowledge?," there is and can be no such thing, and the supposition that there can is simply due to a confusion. There can be no answer to an illegitimate question, except that the question is illegitimate. Nevertheless the question is one which we continue to put until we realize the inevitable immediacy of knowledge. And it is positive knowledge that knowledge is immediate and neither can be, nor needs to be, improved or vindicated by the further knowledge that it was knowledge. This positive knowledge sets at rest the inevitable doubt, and, so far as by the "Theory of Knowledge" is meant this knowledge, then even though this knowledge be the knowledge that there is no Theory of Knowledge in the former sense, to that extent the Theory of Knowledge exists.

In the second place, suppose we come genuinely to doubt whether, e.g., $7 \times 4 = 28$ owing to a genuine doubt whether we were right in believing yesterday that $7 \times 4 = 28$, a doubt which can in fact only arise if we have lost our hold of, i.e., no longer remember, the real nature of our consciousness of yesterday, and so think of it as consisting in believing. Plainly, the only remedy is to do the sum again. Or, to put the matter generally, if we do come to doubt whether it is true that *A* is *B*, as we once thought, the remedy lies not in any process of reflection but in such a reconsideration of the nature of *A* and *B* as leads to the knowledge that *A* is *B*.

With these considerations in mind, consider the parallel which, as it seems to me, is presented—though with certain differences—by Moral Philosophy. The sense that we ought to do certain things arises in our unreflective consciousness, being an activity of moral thinking occasioned by the various situations in which we find ourselves. At this stage our attitude to these obligations is one of unquestioning confidence. But inevitably the appreciation of the degree to which the execution of these obligations is contrary to our interest raises the doubt whether after all these obligations are really obligatory, i.e., whether our sense that we ought not to do certain things is not illusion. We then want to have it *proved* to us that we ought to do so, i.e., to be convinced of this by a process which, as an argument, is different in kind from our original and unreflective appreciation of it. This demand is, as I have argued, illegitimate.

Hence, in the first place, if, as is almost

universally the case, by Moral Philosophy is meant the knowledge which would satisfy this demand, there is no such knowledge, and all attempts to attain it are doomed to failure because they rest on a mistake, the mistake of supposing the possibility of proving what can only be apprehended directly by an act of moral thinking. Nevertheless the demand, though illegitimate, is inevitable until we have carried the process of reflection far enough to realize the self-evidence of our obligations, i.e., the immediacy of our apprehension of them. This realization of their self-evidence is positive knowledge, and so far, and so far only, as the term Moral Philosophy is confined to this knowledge and to the knowledge of the parallel immediacy of the apprehension of the goodness of the various virtues and of good dispositions generally, is there such a thing as Moral Philosophy. But since this knowledge may allay doubts which often affect the whole conduct of life, it is, though not extensive, important and even vitally important.

In the second place, suppose we come genuinely to doubt whether we ought, for example, to pay our debts, owing to a genuine doubt whether our previous conviction that we ought to do so is true, a doubt which can, in fact, only arise if we fail to remember the real nature of what we now call our past conviction. The only remedy lies in actually getting into a situation which occasions the obligation, or—if our imagination be strong enough—in imagining ourselves in that situation, and then letting our moral capacities of thinking do their work. Or, to put the matter generally, if we do doubt whether there is really an obligation to originate *A* in a situation *B*, the remedy lies not in any process of general thinking, but in getting face to face with a particular instance of the situation *B*, and then directly appreciating the obligation to originate *A* in that situation.

R.F. Harrod /

Utilitarianism revised

This paper is divided into two parts. In the first an attempt is made to state in bare outline a system of moral philosophy, which should probably be classified as utilitarian. The second provides a theory of the nature of moral obligation, which is consistent with the system, but in closer conformity with the ordinary view of obligation than those usually associated with the utilitarian position. The special contribution of this paper lies in part 2, and part 1 may be regarded as a necessary propaedeutic. Some general restatement of the utilitarian position, however, seems desirable, in view of the cogent criticisms which have been advanced against traditional utilitarianism.

A word about method. There is in existence a great body of opinion about moral questions. I conceive it to be the task of the moral philosopher to determine and explain the subject matter of that body of opinion. This is in accordance with Aristotle's teaching that moral philosophers should concern themselves with δόξαι. It is not enough to erect an abstract system of thought. It is required that the system should make sense of what may be called the common moral consciousness. There are, no doubt, serious difficulties. Moral opinion comprises many elements of dogmatism, survivals of the past, and prejudices due to the accidents of history. Moreover most men are content to remain in a condition of incomplete clarity. In resorting to a process of cross-examination with a view to isolating and elucidating what is essential and what makes sense in common moral thought, one is often perforce driven to a self-examination consisting in an effort to think very clearly about the matter oneself. But there is all the difference between attempting to reinterpret in clear terms the essential nature of the δόξαι and constructing an arbitrary system *de novo*.

I

1. The first proposition is that the terms, good and right, well known to moral consciousness, are not indefinable; more broadly, that the fundamental concepts of

Reprinted from MIND, *vol. 45 (April 1936), pp. 137–156 by permission of the author and editors.*

moral philosophy are not indefinable, but on the contrary can be defined in terms belonging to studies outside moral philosophy. When I say this, I do not merely mean that I propose to use good, right, etc., for characters that may be defined, but I mean that in the common moral consciousness they are so used. And though there may in the universe be many indefinable characteristics, known or unknown to us, to which they could be applied by an arbitrary allocation of meaning, any such application would involve a break with the past and an abuse of the language which we inherit, and would fail to interpret correctly the essential nature of the common moral consciousness.

It must be recognised that these words challenge what is probably now the prevailing view among moral philosophers, that in particular they involve a position which Mr. Moore has called the "naturalistic fallacy." In defence of them I shall seek to stand or fall mainly by my success in propounding a system which does correspond to the concepts of the common moral consciousness. Criticism of the opposite view will be very brief.

Mr. Moore's *Principia Ethica* made such a profound impression on the philosophical world and has been cited so frequently as establishing the indefinability of good with success, that it may well be taken as a representative statement. Despite his serried array of devastating arguments, brevity is possible, for the greater part of them are concerned with showing the inconsistency of various views *on the assumption that the good is indefinable.* Arguments addressed to establishing that proposition itself occupy less space. There are, in fact, two.[1] The first is that good clearly stands for something simple and not a complex. But this in itself requires justification. And justification Mr. Moore does not give. I do not believe that the plain man would agree. If you ask him, "Now tell me what exactly do you mean by good, morally good," he would say, "That is a long story; it could be explained, but the explanation would be a complicated one; I do not think I could give it myself, you must ask a philosopher." If you then said, "Oh, well, really my question was a booby-trap, because good is something quite simple like the feeling of cold or pain, which cannot be defined except in terms that presuppose an understanding of it," he would be genuinely surprised, and, indeed, sceptical.

Secondly, Mr. Moore adduces the disagreement of those who have sought to define it. Surely if we mean, every time we use a word, to denote a complex, we ought to be able to say what the elements of the complex are. So the disagreements are attributed to an attempt to do the impossible, to the failure to recognise that the thing is in principle indefinable. But such an argument may be turned against Mr. Moore with as much or as little force. If when we use the word we know what we mean by it and that that is something indefinable, how has it come about that there have been all these attempts to define it? And that by men of philosophical disposition? If the thing was simple and known to be simple, are not these attempts passing strange? There should have been agreements about its simplicity. If there are disagreements about the meaning of a word, is it not more likely that it stands for something complex?

It is true that there have been attempts to define indefinable qualities. Mr. Moore very properly gives the sensation of yellow as an example of this. Any attempt to define this in terms, for instance, of the concepts of physics is fallacious. Agreement among persons of philosophical aptitude that this is fallacious is usually easy to secure. Unfortunately Mr. Moore ad-

[1] See G. E. Moore, *Principia Ethica* (Cambridge: The University Press, 1929), pp. 6–17.

mits that the analogy is imperfect since yellow belongs, and in his view good does not, to the world of nature.

I should prefer to compare good to the term circular, while freely admitting that the analogy is in many ways imperfect. Circular resembles good in being a character that is readily recognised in particular instances. From remote times men have probably recognised particular instances of circularity and have known quite well what they meant in using the word circle. When it comes to definition, it is a very different matter. Those not versed in the elements of geometry would be quite unable to proceed. Does it follow that what they have meant by circle is something indefinable? Our forebears may well have disputed hotly about the definition or urged that no definition was possible. It is possible indeed that a modern philosopher might argue that the circle *can* be taken as an indefinable, and other mathematical concepts, line, point, etc., defined in terms of the circle. This may be so. I do not argue it. But it is very different to say that a thing *may* be taken as indefinable and, as Mr. Moore would say of good, that it *must* be. It is possible that good may, in this sense, be taken as indefinable; but that would involve defining concepts, such as man, sentient being, other, etc., in terms of good. As these concepts are used also in branches of study other than moral philosophy, the procedure would be inconvenient.

Mainly, however, I must rely on my own inability, when trying to be clear and honest with myself (and I can only appeal to others to share my experience), to apprehend any indefinable concept of the kind supposed. When I attempt to do so, it evaporates, so to speak, into thin air, and I am left empty-handed. An attempt will presently be made to sketch out a definition.

Before leaving the negative part I will only say this. It is possibly true, and, if so, we may be beguiled by the fact that contemplation of instances of good gives rise to an emotion which is unique and unanalysable. I am not quite clear that this is so, but it does not seem unlikely. We may be able to isolate this feeling. But though the feeling may be indefinable, it would be fallacious to argue that what gives rise to it is. Just as it would be fallacious to argue that because the sensation of yellow is unanalysable, the physical state of affairs required for the presence of that sensation cannot be defined in terms of other physical magnitudes. There is danger that the presence of peculiar moral feelings, perhaps different in kind from all other feelings, may lead us to argue, wrongly, that the objects, the contemplation of which gives rise to those feelings, are indefinable.

2. The next point appears superficially to be in conflict with the major premise of utilitarianism. It is arguable, however, that it conflicts not with essential doctrine but only with misleading terminology.[2] The proposition is that the term good is not properly applicable to states of affairs but only to conduct considered in relation to states of affairs.

The view that states of affairs may be regarded as good, in an ethical sense, is associated with but not entailed by the view, that an act must be regarded as including the sum of its probable consequences. This last view is stressed in utilitarian philosophy and I regard it as wholly sound. It does not appear to be justifiable to draw a line at any point between the probable physical consequences of an act of volition which belong to the act and those which do not. But from the view that an act should be regarded as including the whole state of affairs expected to result

[2] This point, however, would entail detailed examination of the views, not necessarily mutually consistent, of the various writers.

from a volition, and that the goodness of an act depends essentially on what that state of affairs is, it does not follow that the state of affairs may itself be regarded as good.

May I give a very simple and obvious example? Suppose that the whole consequence of a volition is to cause pleasure to a friend. The act may be judged morally good. The friend might have done the act himself. Suppose the whole sum of consequences the same. Yet the act would not be judged a morally good one. This anyhow is the view of the common moral consciousness.

It is desirable to clear up one point in passing. Mr. W. D. Ross's terminology of act and action appears to be a convenient way of indicating a correct distinction. Moral attributes may apply to both, but not to the states of affairs considered apart from the volition. The act comprises the state of affairs brought about together with the situation of the agent objectively considered. The giving of pleasure to a friend is an act. And it is a good act. The quality of the action depends upon the motive. If the motive is anticipation of reciprocal favours, the action is not necessarily good, though the act is good. To the state of affairs brought about, viz., the friend's pleasure considered by itself, the attribute good is not properly applicable.

Before leaving this topic, I want to draw support for my view from linguistic considerations. Outside moral philosophy I believe the word good is mainly used of means, e.g., a good way of getting to a place, of opening a tin. Or when applied to craftsmanship, it denotes approximation to a perfect model, that perfection being relative to purpose. A good car, a good dinner, are adapted to serving the purposes required of them. In economics the term goods is used for material commodities that serve as means to ends, e.g., articles of food, clothing, etc. But to the acts of consuming these commodities, that is to the ends towards which the commodities are means, the word goods is not applied. Food, cars and books are called goods, but never eating, joy-riding or reading.

In moral philosophy good does not, of course, mean *any* act well adapted to an end; it has a specialised sense. But I believe it to be quite inappropriate in any circumstances to use it of ends. This is often done in philosophy with resulting violence to literary sense. Is knowledge a good, the philosopher asks? But the plain man or the scholar with ear finely adjusted to the proper use of language "have never heard such nonsense." Equally unnatural is the expression, the good. The fact that this usage has an ancient and honourable lineage in philosophical writing strengthens my argument. For the fact that, though present in philosophical writing, waiting to be taken over into general literature and common speech, it never has been taken over, is an indication that it is repugnant to common sense.

3. Definition. *Acts are morally significant when they affect the ends of other people and they are morally good when they promote those ends.* These are not meant to be synthetic propositions but to define the words moral and good. Before elaborating this, it is necessary to deal with two objections which may be urged at the outset.

i. It may be held that certain purely self-regarding actions fall within the common sense view of morality, specifically, long-sighted actions which imply conquest of conflicting impulses. It is possible that such actions are regarded as moral, only instrumentally, as the ὧν ἄνευ οὐ of a moral life. It is the subject's duty to keep himself alive and efficient. But it is not necessary to quarrel with the opposite view. The actions in question have certain attributes in common with many altruistic actions, namely those connected with self-control, the overcoming of natural inclinations.

And for certain purposes it may be useful to group them with certain types of altruistic action and bring them within the sphere of moral consideration. I accept this view as a legitimate one though I shall make no further reference to it. I only note in passing that it has no bearing on the indefinability of good, for this class of actions may readily be defined in terms of natural inclination, the long-period, etc., which are concepts *not* presupposing a knowledge of an indefinable good. The proposition bringing them within the sphere of morality and goodness may be regarded as a definition.

ii. A more important objection may be made to this demarcation of morality. It may be urged that no individual is so self-contained as not to be concerned with the affairs of others, and, further, that in so far as he does take the cares of humanity upon his shoulders, their affairs become a not unimportant part of the content of his consciousness and his life. This comprehensive generalisation that whatever a man concerns himself with becomes in a certain sense a part of himself is no doubt true, and may be of great importance in the psychological problem of how altruistic conduct is possible—anyhow for the kind of determinist who believes that there is such a problem. But for the purpose of demarcating the sphere of morality, a valid distinction may be upheld. Morality begins when the interests of others are considered from *the point of view of their interests,* i.e., as a Kantian kingdom of ends. This demarcates morality even if the interests of others are also the interests of the agent.

To elaborate, acts are good when they promote the ends or interests of others, bad when they frustrate them. Of the special nature of a moral obligation much will be said presently.

Now it may be at once objected that good acts must not be regarded as those which promote any ends of others but only good ends, so that good remains to be defined. It is necessary, of course, to deny this. It is true that the end of another person B may be bad if it conflicts with or frustrates the ends of yet another C. That is already covered by the original definition. A in promoting B's end would thus be frustrating C's and his action might then be a bad one. Ends may be good or bad according as they promote or frustrate the ends of others, but in this aspect they have the characteristic of means. Ends as such are neither good nor bad, in the sense intended in moral philosophy.

I hold that the common moral consciousness takes the good man to be one who concerns himself with promoting the ends of others and that that is what is meant by calling him good. What others? The family or nation? In its crude form moral consciousness may consider limited units only and be regardless of the repercussions of the interests of a limited group on the outer world and, as will be explained in the section on obligation, even a more refined form may have to give special consideration to limited units. But, generally, the moral consciousness which takes a broader view, considering the interests of all sentient beings integrated over future time, is rightly regarded as the higher one.

But, the subtle objector will urge, if you speak of the higher and lower morality are you not committing Mill's fallacy with regard to pleasures, of adopting an external criterion for assessing these conflicting notions of morality? This objection may be met. The broader view may be regarded as better simply because it carries the principle implicit in any moral view to its logical conclusion. The essence of morality being regard for the interests of persons not oneself, extending the purview of persons is simply bringing the principle more fully into operation. The essence of morality is that the end considered should be that of others. If the group of persons included is one more or less closely associated with the self, the moral principle is still cloyed with egoism.

It may be objected that this wide view of all sentient beings, considered throughout future time, is too cold, and pays too little regard to the virtues of love and affection, is too much biassed, for instance, in favour of the disinterested seeker after truth. This is a misconception. Human nature differs, a division of labour is desirable, and various types of virtue must be recognised. It is true that the discoverer of truth may make a boundless contribution to the promotion of human ends; on the other hand the chances that he will are not so great. What the more homely virtues lack in scope of benefit aimed at, they gain in the higher probability that some contribution will actually be made. The happiness conferred by human affection is assured and visible. It is desirable that each should develop the faculties he has. To do this may itself be counted a virtue, for by it the greatest promotion of the common interest will be realised.

A last objection must be met. Granted, it may be said, that the scope of virtuous action has been correctly described. Nonetheless it must be recognised that to call it virtuous is to make a synthetic proposition; otherwise all the proposition amounts to is that promoting the greatest common interest is promoting the greatest common interest. This is not very illuminating and leaves us without any reason for doing so or for praising such conduct.

I can only meet this objection by persisting in my ways. I have only risen to this extent above tautology, in that I hold that when people use the terms good, right, virtue, etc., promotion of the common interest is what they mean. I have given no reason for promoting the common interest. It is beyond the power of reason to prescribe ends. Give unto Caesar the things that are Caesar's. Reason can determine means to ends, and the mutual consistency of different ends. Of ends as such it is altogether beyond its scope and capacity to say, "choose this, reject that." As for praising virtue, I have indeed given no reason for praising virtue. For to do that too would be fallacious. But let us praise virtue!

I hold that when people say that this or that is morally good, they mean that this or that is what, properly considered, promotes the common interest, and that if they say that promoting the common interest is good, the proposition is either a definition or means nothing. It is possible that men do sometimes slip into this tautologous method of speech. I give two reasons why that might naturally happen. (1) Much of what we seek to bring about, many of our proximate ends, are really means—for example, the preservation of the human race and of an ordered society. The preservation of the human race is a means to the maximum realisation of ends integrated through time. The word good is rightly used of these proximate ends, which may indeed be very remote. Constant use of the word of these remote proximate ends may naturally, through force of habit, though fallaciously, lead us to slip over to using the term of true ends. (2) It is possible that the proposition "promotion of the common interest is good" may have a synthetic meaning, the word good now being used in a slightly different sense. It may be used for "what I stand for, what I intend to encourage by my praise, discouraging the opposite by blame and censure." If it be then suggested that I praise it because I think it good, that would be again fallacious. There is no ultimate, as opposed to proximate, reason for doing or praising anything. Ultimate ends are a matter of pure choice. The view that the reason or intellect is able to discern an objective imperative residing in the nature of things is in my judgment fallacious and might well be called, borrowing Mr. Moore's catching rhythm, the rationalistic fallacy.

4. I now come to the question—what are the ends of sentient beings? This question, I think, can only be answered by introspection and observation. These ends are directly given. It is not that we recognise things to have a certain quality and therefore judge them to be ends. They are directly presented to us as ends. It would not, I think, take one far from the meaning I seek to convey if I defined end as the desired. Ends might then be bad, not as such, but because they conflicted with the ends of others. An object of desire which does not conflict with the desires of others considered through time is not bad.

But though the desired is a useful concept in that it may bring home what I mean by directly given, I am not quite happy about identifying end with the desired. I am not merely thinking of foolish desires. A man's desire is foolish if its satisfaction generates a state of affairs which he then desires not to be in. This difficulty is met by identifying the end with the least amount of outstanding unsatisfied desire, considered through time. But I suspect that there may be a deeper difficulty, which may perhaps be solved by a suitable definition of desire. Desire as commonly understood is especially associated with congenital impulse and with well-known types of emotional malaise, e.g., Prof. Watson's palpitating stomach.

I take end to be whatever is found by experience to be capable of acting as a motive to action. But, of course, many of our motives are proximate ends and these must be excluded. To discover what ultimate ends are capable of acting as motives requires very careful scrutiny.

The Utilitarians attempted a great generalisation and affirmed that the sole ultimate end is pleasure. It is not clear that they were successful. Compare pleasure with the desired. It is true that if foolish desires are eliminated by the process I have called integration through time, there may be a much greater measure of consilience between pleasure and the desired than appears at first sight. There may be complete consilience, but I think it is over-dogmatic to assert that there is. Pleasure is certainly an end, but I am not clear that there may not be a conflict between pleasure and desire, even when desires are integrated.

Nor am I clear that pleasure and desire cover the whole field of ultimate motive. If a conflict between pleasure and desire is possible on principle, why not between desire and other things which experience shows to be capable of acting as a motive? The prospect of discovery may certainly act as a motive; it may also evoke desire. But is the strength of the desire always in proportion to the strength of the motive? No doubt on a certain definition of desire, they would always be proportional. If the definition of desire required for that is correct, *cadit quaestio*. But it is possible that such a definition would conflict with that required for certain branches of psychological investigation.

An end, then, is defined as that which is de facto found in and by itself to constitute a motive for sentient beings. And since conflicts of ends are not only possible but rife, to determine morality the ends must be ranked in importance. They must be ranked according to the strength of the motive. A calculus is necessary. A host of subsidiary problems will no doubt arise. I mention one. It is possible that certain ends, though not themselves bad (i.e., conflicting with the ends of other people), usually present themselves to people, by some inner psychological law, many of whose ends are bad. When a detailed system of casuistry is developed, it is possible that these ends should not be given the full status, which the de facto strength of the motive entitles them to.

It may be objected that this philosophy does not generate a very clear system of casuistry, since strength of motive is not easily measurable. The objection lies against ordinary utilitarianism and all systems involving a calculus. Is this definition of good really consistent with the common moral consciousness, with its hard and fast notions? It is doubtful if this objection really is as strong as it seems. Many of the rigid rules are explained by the theory of obligation (vide infra). And for the rest is the plain man always so very sure where the path of goodness lies? Furthermore the great proximate ends, preservation of the human race and of an ordered civilization, are justified with a very high degree of probability without nice measurement of particular motives. Given clearly defined proximate ends, the casuist has considerable scope.

II

I now come to the special nature of obligations. The quite correct view, as I hold it, of the common moral consciousness that certain types of act are obligations has given rise to much erroneous speculation. Prima facie it might appear that the morality of the common interest is inimical to this notion of obligation, that in any situation there are various alternatives shading off into one another, each contributing more or less to the common interest. It is best to choose that which contributes most, better to choose that which contributes more than that which contributes less, and so on. Where is the hard and fast obligation?

Objection to the common interest philosophy can be carried further along these lines. For simplicity suppose the common interest philosophy to be identical with utilitarianism. There may be circumstances in which common moral consciousness would hold it to be obligatory to speak the truth, though no increment of pleasure could be foreseen as a result and certain pain would be caused. No doubt there are also cases, if the pain is very severe and no good served, when the common consciousness would justify a lie. But I think it must be admitted that there are cases when there is a seeming conflict between the common consciousness and the utilitarian principle.

Now to this problem I believe that Kant made a contribution, which is a vital and essential part of any moral system, but he mistook the significance of his own discovery and put it in a setting of fallacy. I refer to his proposition that morality requires action on a maxim that may be made a general law. At first sight this may seem to have no relation to utilitarian philosophy; but I believe it to be indispensable to it.

The Utilitarian says "always choose that action which will contribute to the greatest happiness." Such a maxim is general enough. Its fault is that it is on too high a plane of generality. It is necessary to look in greater detail into human arrangements. Take the case of the lie. The Utilitarian, it would seem, should say, always lie when the probable consequences including the speaker's loss of credit and the possible general loss of confidence in the spoken word involve more happiness than those produced by the truth. If everyone lied in those circumstances and in those circumstances only, all would apparently go well. But as a matter of fact this is not the case.

Communication by language is a notable invention of man for the furtherance of his ends. It is of great importance that communications should be reliable for their truthfulness. Now if the utilitarian rule of life in its crude form, as set out above, were adopted, they would become markedly less reliable and great consequential damage might ensue. But it might be pleaded that the loss of confidence is allowed for in the crude utilitarian maxim —and *some* loss of confidence *is* allowed for. The plea nevertheless is fallacious.

If this plea were correct the consequences indicated by the crude utilitarian principle would always be identical with the consequences deduced by the application of Kant's principle. The consequences of the act considered in and by itself would not be different from the consequences of such an act when always performed in precisely similar relevant circumstances. This brings us to the essence of the matter. *There are certain acts which when performed on* n *similar occasions have consequences more than* n *times as great as those resulting from one performance.* And it is in this class of cases that obligations arise. It is in this class of cases that generalising the act yields a different balance of advantage from the sum of the balances of advantage issuing from each individual act. For example, it may well happen that the loss of confidence due to a million lies uttered within certain limits of time and space is much more than a million times as great as the loss due to any one in particular. Consequently, even if on each and every occasion taken separately it can be shown that there is a gain of advantage (the avoidance of direct pain, let us say, exceeding the disadvantages due to the consequential loss of confidence), yet in the sum of all cases the disadvantage due to the aggregate loss of confidence might be far greater than the sum of pain caused by truth-telling.

He who wishes people so to act that the ends of sentient beings should be best served, must wish them to act in accordance with the Kantian and not the crude utilitarian principle. He will find it necessary to refine the crude utilitarian principle by applying the process of generalisation in all relevant cases, that is in all cases where the consequences of n similar acts exceed n times the consequences of any one.

In constructing a system of morality, it is necessary, then, to choose between the crude utilitarian principle and the Kantian principle, between the lie of expediency and the obligation of truthfulness. A more refined utilitarianism will decide in favour of the obligation, owing to the greater loss of advantage when the lie is generalised. Of course this may not be true in the case of the particular illustration given: the loss of confidence due to the universal lie of expediency may not be so great as the gain of advantage. This is a question of fact. The experience of generations, crystallized in moral consciousness, appears to be against the lie. But whichever side is right in the case of the lie, the point of principle has been established that an act which is expedient in the circumstances but would be inexpedient when done by all in precisely relevant circumstances must be judged to be wrong by a more refined utilitarian system. Thus the Kantian principle is embodied in utilitarian philosophy.[3]

It should be noted in passing that what I call the Kantian principle does not condemn all lies. A lie is justified when the balance of pain or loss of pleasure is such that, if a lie was told in all circumstances when there was no less a balance of pain or loss of pleasure, the harm due to the total loss of confidence did not exceed the sum of harm due to truthfulness in every case. This doctrine, which I believe to be conformable to the common moral consciousness, puts the human interlocutor

[3] It should be noted that approval is only given to Kant's principle, and not to the grounds on which he sought to base it. He defended it not by reference to the advantages of its adoption, but as required by logic, e.g., so that human conduct should not be "self-contradictory." The notion that action may be self-contradictory is found also in Hobbes (cf. *Leviathan*, ed. W. G. Pogson-Smith [Oxford: Clarendon Press, 1909], p. 101). It is doubtful if any such notion can be defended. The defence of Kant's principle in the text has no relation to it. But a *code* of action may be self-contradictory. And it is pointed out below that utilitarian casuistry, unchecked by the Kantian principle, might easily tend to develop a self-contradictory code.

into a much stricter strait-jacket with regard to truthfulness than the crude utilitarian principle quoted at the outset.

Along with lies must be reckoned breaches of promises, of the law, of many, though not all, current standards of morality. The test is always—Would this action if done by all in similar relevant circumstances lead to the breakdown of some established method of society for securing its ends? I believe it will be found that this principle lies at the root of all so-called obligations. Their rigidity is precisely due to the fact that the relevant considerations are not the consequences of the particular act, but the consequences of the act when generalised.

I believe that whereas Kant was wrong in supposing his principle to be at the basis of all morality, it is at the basis of those particular moral acts which are usually thought of as obligations. If the act is of a sort to which the Kantian principle is applicable, it is much more likely that there will turn out to be a balance of advantage in its favour. Hence the rigidity with which we regard those acts commonly called obligations. If there is a question of helping some one, this and that consideration are taken into account, and it is quite likely to turn out on balance even from a purely moral point of view to be not worth doing. But if it is a question of speaking the truth, it is considered very improbable that this should not be done—and this, even though the positive advantage that flows from this particular piece of truthfulness is not greater than that which flows from the particular act of kindness. The difference is due to the fact that in one case the Kantian principle does and in the other does not make a difference to the crude utilitarian principle.

This account explains the prima facie view that there is something in the recognised nature of an obligation that conflicts with any philosophy of ends. The conflict, we have seen, is apparent only. It also accounts for the fact that the quasi-instinctive emotions of disgust, which such actions evoke, often seem unreasonably strong. Only those societies could attain stability in which they were strong, because it is precisely in the case of these actions that the individual not understanding the Kantian principle might, if left unmolested, be most tempted to say—"Well, why on earth should I?" One may even add that it is the subtlety and difficulty of the principle, which cannot be explained to the average man, that has made an arbitrary and authoritarian element in the moral sphere necessary to the evolution of stable society. This enlightened age has its dangers. Perhaps the philosophers of indefinable obligation still have their part to play, and it may be inexpedient that they should be put to public shame by the votaries of expedience.

It is interesting to notice that the system of free competition does not allow for the application of the Kantian principle in the purely economic or katallactic field. And it is precisely the phenomena of "Increasing Returns"—analogous to those requiring the application of the Kantian principle in everyday conduct—which have given one of the strongest arguments in justification of the demand for "economic planning."

Now it is not to be expected that the humble man in the street will be quick to jump spontaneously to what I for brevity call the Kantian point of view. Pessimism about him should not indeed be overdone. "Well, if everyone behaved in that sort of way" is a familiar phrase of condemnation. It will be found, however, that it is most frequently used for breaches of established conventions. It is owing to this weakness of the average man that types of acts to which the Kantian principle is applicable are often associated with *recognized practices and institutions.* In the process by which stable society—temporarily stable society at least!—has evolved, those systems have survived which have established recognised practices and institutions giving effect to the Kantian principle, and allowing members to reap the additional advantages which adherence to it can yield. I am thinking of codes of honour, truthfulness, honesty, discharge of debt, performance of promises, etc., and of states with systems of law and recognised obligations of loyalty.

First consider *practices*. The Kantian principle is applicable if the loss due to n infringements is greater than n times the loss due to one. But suppose that in fact it is generally infringed. Suppose that I live in a society in which the spoken word is seldom to be relied on or men go about in constant fear of their lives. The community is not in fact reaping the benefit which could be reaped by the application of the Kantian principle. What is my obligation? It appears to be doubtful whether it is appropriate in these circumstances to apply the refining process to the crude utilitarian principle. Of course the example of an upright or peacefully minded man may be potent. But the direct effect of example is, it will be remembered, allowed for in the crude utilitarian principle. I think the common moral consciousness would judge the refining process to be inappropriate.

But it ought to be possible to put a finer point upon the argument. The common moral consciousness having endorsed the doctrine of common interest, it ought to be a question of fact whether the application of the refining process will in any case subserve it. Now when the process is applied there will be loss of advantage in particular instances; but there is a gain if it is applied in a large number of instances. The Utilitarian must wish it applied widely. I believe that, where the practice is not general, a second refining process is required. Will the gain due to its application by all conscientious, i.e., moral, people *only* be sufficient to offset the loss which the crude utilitarian principle registers? It may be objected to this that there are no moral people, but only more or less moral people. To meet this, for the word moral in the second refining principle, say people sufficiently moral to act disinterestedly in this kind of case. It may be noticed that the second refining principle introduces some complicated mathematics into moral philosophy. This must not be held as an objection, if the facts demand it! It is needless to say that in practice the calculation will only be implicit and the roughest approximations possible. The game of refined calculation would not be worth the candle, and, anyhow, precise data are lacking.

The point is this. The double set of considerations are interlocked. When the practice is not generally observed, the conscientious man has to take into account not only the amount of crude utilitarian loss due to his particular act but also the amount of conquest of counteracting impulse which observance of the practice in his type of case entails. He may not observe the practice *either* because the direct loss is too severe *or* because the temptation to do the opposite in this case is so great that there would not be sufficient upright men overcoming it in similar circumstances to secure a net gain through wider performance of the practice. He has not only to write down a function showing in the case of various contingencies the relation of gross gain when the action is generalised to the amount of crude loss, but also one for a different but overlapping variety of contingencies showing the relation of the number of people prepared to overcome temptation (and the consequent net gain) to the intensity of the temptation, and he has to study the interaction of the functions. I will refrain from pursuing this line of thought further, and only state my belief that implicit calculations of this kind are actually carried out in the most ordinary affairs of everyday life by moral men.

It may be of greater interest to draw attention to the fact that a properly conceived utilitarianism does involve that the obligatoriness of a certain practice depends on the degree to which it is observed by others and that that in turn partly depends on the prevalence of sanctions embodied in the moral sentiment of disapprobation. Hobbes was substantially right when he held that there are no obligations in a state of nature, i.e., when none of these practices is generally observed, and in the reasons which he gave for that proposition. He was probably right in holding that without sanctions of force one cannot proceed far in getting practices sufficiently widely established to make, in my language, the two refining principles taken together yield much result. But he was wrong to hold that there can be no morality in a state of nature. For even then the crude utilitarian principle is applicable and will be applied by virtuous people.

Before leaving the topic of practices, I may refer to a principle which occupies a central position in the common moral consciousness, which I will call the Principle of Publicity. It has been seen that the obligatoriness of certain acts depends on a (reasonably) wide observance of the practice in question. In a large class of cases the gain of advantage is due to the maintenance of confidence, e.g., in the reliability of informative utterance for truthfulness, of promises for being kept, etc. It might appear that if defalcation could be kept secret, as in the case of lies which could never be discovered, then, since no loss of confidence could ensue, the obligation would lapse and certain gain should not be sacrificed in the interest of truthfulness. Yet in fact common moral consciousness regards secret as more rather than less odious than public defalcations—and rightly. For if it can be shown that undiscovered lies are wrong, severer blame is required to overcome the greater temptation to commit those that will probably be undiscovered, and is therefore justified.

Take the case when the lie can never be discovered. The liar then has no debit due to loss of confidence to set against the interests served by the lie. If, in every case when there was a general balance of advantage and the lie could never be discovered, lies were told, there would be a sensible loss of confidence. Not, it will again be pleaded, if the lies are always to be kept secret. But what is this secrecy? If virtuous men are known to be acting on the crude utilitarian principle when secrecy is possible in the particular case, then it will be known that lies in this case will be told even by the most conscientious and there will be loss of confidence. What presumably is required is that all men should utterly forswear the crude utilitarian principle and at the same time act upon it when secrecy can be maintained. What doctrine is to be preached? The crude utilitarian principle because it is desired that all men should act upon it. Some anti-utilitarian principle because it is desired that all men should believe that no one is acting upon it. To such a system it almost seems that Kant was right to apply the much-abused expression, self-contradictory.

It may be that the common interest would in fact be best served by each man acting on the principle of crude expediency himself and believing that others were following certain arbitrary rules. Such a system would certainly be an interesting one. But it is not one which the word morality is used to denote. This may seem to be an appeal to brute fact. Such an appeal is highly salutary. The words moral obligation have always been used and can conveniently be used to apply to a system of behaviour which is commonly recognised by the participants. Now the system just outlined could not of its nature be commonly recognised. Moreover for a system of moral obligations to be workable—and this is an appeal to a different kind of brute fact—it is necessary that it should be closely connected with the emotion and expression of approbation and disapprobation. This again would be impossible. Thus the utilitarian who wishes the advantages yielded by embodying the Kantian principle in publicly recognised practices to be reaped, must wish them observed whether or not defalcation can be kept secret.

One further point regarding practices. We have found one reason why the common moral consciousness regards obligations as relatively rigid, namely that their force does not spring from the consequences of the act in the particular case, but from wider considerations. There may well be another reason. To get certain practices generally recognised and enforced has not been an easy task. It is probable therefore that among all possible practices, the trouble requisite for their establishment and maintenance has only been taken in cases where the gain was clear and overwhelming. It is possible that in a highly refined society many other practices yielding a smaller advantage may be erected into recognised obligations. But there is danger in too much haste. For if there was too great a proliferation of obligatory practice, the sanctions with which they could rationally be upheld would be weaker and the exceptions recognised as admissible more numerous. Such a state of affairs might become unstable. For, human nature being what it is, there is a strong pull of common sense, on the part of those who simply cannot understand the Kantian principle, towards infringing obligations in the interest of direct advantage. This has no necessary connection with moral failure; for the motive may be purely altruistic, the visible advantages accruing to another. This being the state of affairs, it is well to delimit the sphere of obligatory practices, so that the quasi-sacrosanct character of those there are may be rationally defended.

It is not necessary for me to add much about *institutions.* They may impose sanctions where moral sentiment is insufficient to get a practice established. But, of course, they do much more. They supply machinery for devising practices by which the advantages of the Kantian principle may be reaped, e.g., systems of commercial law. Some of these practices and the consequent mutual obligations will be coterminous with the sphere of influence of the institution.

The state is not the only institution which generates obligations. There is the family, the trade union, the university, etc. The question whether an individual ought to come out on strike in obedience to orders is clearly one, like the question whether to enlist in a war, to which the Kantian principle applies. I now discharge a promise, which I made earlier in this paper, to speak of morality as affecting *particular* groups of others, as distinguished from *all* sentient beings including posterity in general. Application of the Kantian principle may secure net advantage; this advantage is sometimes only possible if recognised institutions exist to define a system of obligations. These institutions only spread their net over a section of the sentient world. The particular system of obligations only applies to their mutual dealings. It follows that morality may make definite claims on the individual in his treatment of the interests of others within limited groups that are absent in his treatment of sentient beings in general.

Of course his obligation is governed by the utility of the institution and of the system of rules which it sets up. Some might hold, for instance, that the family, whatever its services in the past, is in the modern world an outworn institution and not worth preserving at a sacrifice of other interests. The obligations which it imposes are *pro tanto* weakened. This can hardly be said of the state until its many functions are taken over by an actual and effective international institution.

To conclude, it may be well to draw attention to my points of agreement and difference with the traditional utilitarian position.

1. The utilitarians were anxious to establish that the content of any system of moral behaviour is determined by the ends sought and must therefore vary if the most appropriate methods of achieving those ends vary. They would not countenance a system of obligations considered as binding on their own account without reference to the results of the behaviour prescribed. But this position, sound in itself, led them, on my view, to a serious error. Since the system of conduct characterised as good is generated by the ends sought, whatever is good in the conduct, they tended to argue, must spring from some good residing in the ends, and the ends must therefore be regarded as good. This at once gave a twist to their system which strikes the common moral consciousness as a-moral, i.e., not genuinely expressing what is understood by that consciousness. Thus, according to their system no distinction of moral significance can be drawn between an act designed to secure a certain quantum of pleasure for the agent and an act designed to secure an equal quantum of pleasure for someone else. Thus they lost sight of the point that altruism is essential to the ordinary notion of moral goodness (but for a proviso about self-regarding moral acts, vide supra). On the ordinary view, it cannot be that the goodness of virtuous conduct is derived from goodness in the end, for an end ("state of affairs") indistinguishable in all respects from one which would make an altruistic act good would not make a selfish act good.

The introduction of altruism, however, as essential to virtue, is not inconsistent with the utilitarian view that the content of virtuous behaviour must be determined by the end and must be adapted from time to time as appropriate means vary. It is not inconsistent with the general principle of expediency.

2. I am in agreement with the inductive method by which the Utilitarians sought to establish the ends to which a system of moral conduct should be directed. This method consists in distinguishing by observation the ultimate from the proximate ends of conscious endeavour. It is in radical opposition to the view that there is some unanalysable quality, goodness, which can be detected as residing in some, but not in other, ultimate ends. In effect it rescues moral philosophy from the toils of mysticism and from the personal predilections of its practitioners. But I regard the generalization that pleasure is the sole ultimate end as non-proven.

3. Traditional utilitarianism strikes the common moral consciousness as unsatisfactory, also, for lack of a well-defined theory of obligation. It may be held that the substantial point presented in the second part of this paper was appreciated by the best writers. But the point was not argued with precision. Thus it may be claimed that a gap has been filled.

4. The common interest has been presented as the end of moral conduct. But I hold that no reason can be given for pursuing this or any ultimate end. The attempt to give a rational justification for morality, so that the decision to be moral appears to be inferred as a conclusion from premises, can but lead to confusion. Here Hume, right as usual, was on surer ground. He recognised that in this sphere reason is the servant and not the master.

Only in one way, I think, can reason assist in establishing the common interest as the end. The philosopher is shown the spectacle of striving, discordant humanity and is asked to make some observations. If he says that some of their ultimate aims are good and others bad, he is uttering an unjustifiable impertinence. But he can and should express neutrality as between one individual and another. It is not for him to favour any particular person. And by his neutrality the common interest with its consequential system of morality is established. He may indeed have a personal interest in a particular nation, but world philosophical opinion has not. And, since the philosopher expects no immediate recognition, the opinion to which he appeals has no personal interest in the present generation.

J. D. Mabbott /

Punishment

I propose in this paper to defend a retributive theory of punishment and to reject absolutely all utilitarian considerations from its justification. I feel sure that this enterprise must arouse deep suspicion and hostility both among philosophers (who must have felt that the retributive view is the only moral theory except perhaps psychological hedonism which has been definitely destroyed by criticism) and among practical men (who have welcomed its steady decline in our penal practice).

The question I am asking is this. Under what circumstances is the punishment of some particular person justified and why? The theories of reform and deterrence which are usually considered to be the only alternatives to retribution involve well-known difficulties. These are considered fully and fairly in Dr. Ewing's book, *The Morality of Punishment,* and I need not spend long over them.[1] The central difficulty is that both would on occasion justify the punishment of an innocent man, the deterrent theory if he were believed to have been guilty by those likely to commit the crime in future, and the reformatory theory if he were a bad man though not a criminal. To this may be added the point against the deterrent theory that it is the threat of punishment and not punishment itself which deters, and that when deterrence seems to depend on actual punishment, to implement the threat, it really depends on publication and may be achieved if men believe that punishment has occurred even if in fact it has not. As Bentham saw, for a Utilitarian apparent justice is everything, real justice is irrelevant.

Dr. Ewing and other moralists would be inclined to compromise with retribution in the face of the above difficulties. They would admit that one fact and one fact only can justify the punishment of this man, and that is a *past* fact, that he has committed a crime. To this extent reform and deterrence theories, which look only to the consequences, are wrong. But they would add that retribution can determine only *that* a man should be punished. It cannot determine how or how much, and

[1] Alfred Cyril Ewing, *The Morality of Punishment* (London: K. Paul, Trench, Trubner and Co., Ltd., 1929).

Reprinted from MIND, *vol. 48, no. 190 (April 1939), pp. 152–167 by permission of the author and editors.*

here reform and deterrence may come in. Even Bradley, the fiercest retributionist of modern times, says "Having once the right to punish we may modify the punishment according to the useful and the pleasant, but these are external to the matter; they cannot give us a right to punish and nothing can do that but criminal desert." Dr. Ewing would maintain that the whole estimate of the amount and nature of a punishment may be effected by considerations of reform and deterrence. It seems to me that this is a surrender which the upholders of retribution dare not make. As I said above, it is publicity and not punishment which deters, and the publicity though often spoken of as "part of a man's punishment" is no more part of it than his arrest or his detention prior to trial, though both these may be also unpleasant and bring him into disrepute. A judge sentences a man to three years' imprisonment not to three years *plus* three columns in the press. Similarly with reform. The visit of the prison chaplain is not part of a man's punishment nor is the visit of Miss Fields or Mickey Mouse.

The truth is that while punishing a man and punishing him justly, it is possible to deter others and also to attempt to reform him, and if these additional goods are achieved the total state of affairs is better than it would be with the just punishment alone. But reform and deterrence are not modifications of the punishment, still less reasons for it. A parallel may be found in the case of tact and truth. If you have to tell a friend an unpleasant truth you may do all you can to put him at his ease and spare his feelings as much as possible, while still making sure that he understands your meaning. In such a case no one would say that your offer of a cigarette beforehand or your apology afterwards are modifications of the truth, still less, reasons for telling it. You do not tell the truth in order to spare his feelings, but having to tell the truth you also spare his feelings. So Bradley was right when he said that reform and deterrence were "external to the matter" but therefore wrong when he said that they may "modify the punishment." Reporters are admitted to our trials so that punishments may become public and help to deter others. But the punishment would be no less just were reporters excluded and deterrence not achieved. Prison authorities may make it possible that a convict may become physically or morally better. They cannot ensure either result; and the punishment would still be just if the criminal took no advantage of their arrangements and their efforts failed. Some moralists see this and exclude these "extra" arrangements for deterrence and reform. They say that it must be the punishment *itself* which reforms and deters. But it is just my point that the punishment *itself* seldom reforms the criminal and never deters others. It is only "extra" arrangements which have any chance of achieving either result. As this is the central point of my paper, at the cost of laboured repetition I would ask the upholders of reform and deterrence two questions. Suppose it could be shown that a particular criminal had not been improved by a punishment and also that no other would-be criminal had been deterred by it, would that prove that the punishment was unjust? Suppose it were discovered that a particular criminal had lived a much better life after his release and that many would-be criminals believing him to have been guilty were influenced by his fate, but yet that the "criminal" was punished for something he had never done, would these excellent results prove the punishment just?

It will be observed that I have throughout treated punishment as a purely legal matter. A "criminal" means a man who has broken a law, not a bad man; an "innocent" man is a man who has not broken the law in connection with which he is being punished, though he may be a bad man and have broken other laws. Here I dissent from most upholders of the retributive theory—from Hegel, from Bradley, and from Dr. Ross. They maintain that the essential connection is one between punishment and moral or social wrong-doing.

My fundamental difficulty with their theory is the question of *status.* It takes two to make a punishment, and for a moral or social wrong I can find no punisher. We may be tempted to say when we hear of some brutal action, "That ought to be punished"; but I cannot see how there can be duties which are nobody's duties. If I see a man ill-treating a horse in a country where cruelty to animals is not a legal offence, and I say to him, "I shall now punish you," he will reply, rightly, "What has it to do with you? Who made you a judge and a ruler over me?" I may have a duty to try to stop him and one way of stopping him may be to hit him, but another way may be to buy the horse. Neither the blow nor the price is a punishment. For a moral offence, God alone has the *status* necessary to punish the offender; and the theologians are becoming more and more doubtful whether even God has a duty to punish wrong-doing.

Dr. Ross would hold that not all wrong-doing is punishable, but only invasion of the rights of others; and in such a case it might be thought that the injured party had a right to punish. His right, however, is rather a right to reparation, and should not be confused with punishment proper.

This connection, on which I insist, between punishment and crime, not between punishment and moral or social wrong, alone accounts for some of our beliefs about punishment, and also meets many objections to the retributive theory as stated in its ordinary form. The first point on which it helps us is with regard to retrospective legislation. Our objection to this practice is unaccountable on reform and deterrence theories. For a man who commits a wrong before the date on which a law against it is passed, is as much in need of reform as a man who commits it afterwards; nor is deterrence likely to suffer because of additional punishments for the same offence. But the orthodox retributive theory is equally at a loss here, for if punishment is given for moral wrong-doing or for invasion of the rights of others, that immorality or invasion existed as certainly before the passing of the law as after it.

My theory also explains, where it seems to me all others do not, the case of punishment imposed by an authority who believes the law in question is a bad law. I was myself for some time disciplinary officer of a college whose rules included a rule compelling attendance at chapel. Many of those who broke this rule broke it on principle. I punished them. I certainly did not want to reform them; I respected their characters and their views. I certainly did not want to drive others into chapel through fear of penalties. Nor did I think there had been a wrong done which merited retribution. I wished I could have believed that I would have done the same myself. My position was clear. They had broken a rule; they knew it and I knew it. Nothing more was necessary to make punishment proper.

I know that the usual answer to this is that the judge enforces a bad law because otherwise law in general would suffer and good laws would be broken. The effect of punishing good men for breaking bad laws is that fewer bad men break good laws.

[*Excursus on Indirect Utilitarianism.* The above argument is a particular instance of a general utilitarian solution of all similar problems. When I am in funds and consider whether I should pay my debts or give the same amount to charity, I must choose the former because repayment not only benefits my creditor (for the benefit to him might be less than the good done through charity) but also upholds the general credit system. I tell the truth when a lie might do more good to the parties directly concerned, because I thus increase general trust and confidence. I keep a promise when it might do more immediate good to break it, because indirectly I bring it about that promises will be more readily made in the future and this will outweigh the immediate loss involved. Dr. Ross has pointed out that the effect on the credit system of my refusal to pay a debt is greatly exaggerated. But I have a more serious objection of principle. It is that in all these cases the indirect effects do not result from my wrong action—my lie or defalcation or bad faith—but from the publication of these actions. If in any instance the breaking of the rule were to remain unknown then I could consider only the direct or immediate consequences. Thus in my "compulsory chapel" case I could have considered which of my culprits were "law-abiding men generally and unlikely to break any other college rule. Then I could have sent for each of these separately and said, "I shall let you off if you will tell no one I have done so." By these means the general keeping of rules would not have suffered. Would this course have been correct? It must be remembered that the proceedings need not deceive everybody. So long as they deceive would-be law-breakers the good is achieved.

As this point is of crucial importance and as it has an interest beyond the immediate issue, and gives a clue to what I regard as the true general nature of law and punishment, I may be excused for expanding and illustrating it by an example or two from other fields. Dr. Ross says that two men dying on a desert island would have duties to keep promises to each other even though their breaking them would not affect the future general confidence in promises at all. Here is certainly the same point. But as I find that desert-island morality always rouses suspicion among ordinary men I should like to quote two instances from my own experience which also illustrate the problem.

(i) A man alone with his father at his death promises him a private and quiet funeral. He finds later that both directly and indirectly the keeping of this promise will cause pain and misunderstanding. He can see no particular positive good that the quiet funeral will achieve. No one yet knows that he has made the promise nor need anyone ever know. Should he therefore act as though it had never been made?

(ii) A college has a fund given to it for the encouragement of a subject which is now expiring. Other expanding subjects are in great need of endowment. Should the authorities divert the money? Those who oppose the diversion have previously stood on the past, the promise. But one day one of them discovers the "real reason" for this slavery to a dead donor. He says, "We must consider not only the value of this money for these purposes, since on all direct consequences it should be diverted at once. We must remember the effect of this diversion on the general system of benefactions. We know that benefactors like to endow special objects, and this act of ours would discourage such benefactors in future and leave learning worse off." Here again is the indirect utilitarian reason for choosing the alternative which direct utilitarianism would reject. But the immediate answer to this from the most ingenious member of the opposition was crushing and final. He said, "Divert the money but keep it dark." This is obviously correct. It is not the act of diversion which would diminish the stream of benefactions but the news of it reaching the ears of benefactors. Provided that no possible benefactor got to hear of it no indirect loss would result. But the justification of our action would depend entirely on the success of the measures for "keeping it dark." I remember how I felt and how others felt that whatever answer was right this result was certainly wrong. But it follows that indirect utilitarianism is wrong in all such cases. For its argument can always be met by "Keep it dark."]

The view, then, that a judge upholds a bad law in order that law in general should not suffer is indefensible. He upholds it simply because he has no right to dispense from punishment.

The connection of punishment with law-breaking and not with wrong-doing also escapes moral objections to the retributive theory as held by Kant and Hegel or by Bradley and Ross. It is asked how we can measure moral wrong or balance it with pain, and how pain can wipe out moral wrong. Retributivists have been pushed into holding that pain *ipso facto* represses the worse self and frees the better, when this is contrary to the vast majority of observed cases. But if punishment is not intended to measure or balance or negate moral wrong then all this is beside the mark. There is the further difficulty of reconciling punishment with repentance and with forgiveness. Repentance is the reaction morally appropriate to moral wrong and punishment added to remorse is an unnecessary evil. But if punishment is associated with law-breaking and not with moral evil the punisher is not entitled to consider whether the criminal is penitent any more than he may consider whether the law is good. So, too, with forgiveness. Forgiveness is not appropriate to law-breaking. (It is noteworthy that when, in divorce cases, the law has to recognize forgiveness it calls it "condonation," which is symptomatic of the difference of attitude.) Nor is forgiveness appropriate to moral evil. It is appropriate to personal injury. No one has any right to forgive me except the person I have injured. No judge or jury can do so. But the person I have injured has no right to punish me. Therefore there is no clash between punishment and forgiveness since these two duties do not fall on the same person nor in connection with the same characteristic of my act. (It is the weakness of vendetta that it tends to confuse this clear line, though even there it is only by personifying the family that the injured party and the avenger are identified. Similarly we must guard against the plausible fallacy of personifying society and regarding the criminal as "injuring society," for then once more the old dilemma about forgiveness would be insoluble.) A clergyman friend of mine catching a burglar red-handed was puzzled about his duty. In the end he ensured the man's punishment by information and evidence, and at the same time showed his own forgiveness by visiting the man in prison and employing him when he came out. I believe any "good Christian" would accept this as representing his duty. But obviously if the punishment is thought of as imposed *by* the victim or *for* the injury or immorality then the contradiction with forgiveness is hopeless.

So far as the question of the actual punishment of any individual is concerned this paper could stop here. No punishment is morally retributive or reformative or deterrent. Any criminal punished for any one of these reasons is certainly unjustly punished. The only justification for punishing any man is that he has broken a law.

In a book which has already left its mark on prison administration I have found a criminal himself confirming these views. *Walls Have Mouths*, by W. F. R. Macartney, is prefaced, and provided with appendices to each chapter, by Compton Mackenzie. It is interesting to notice how the novelist maintains that the proper object of penal servitude should be reformation,[2] whereas the prisoner himself accepts

[2] W. F. R. Macartney, *Walls Have Mouths*, ed. Compton MacKenzie (London: V. Gollancz, Ltd., 1936), p. 97.

the view I have set out above. Macartney says, "To punish a man is to treat him as an equal. To be punished *for an offence against rules* is a sane man's right."[3] It is striking also that he never uses "injustice" to describe the brutality or provocation which he experienced. He makes it clear that there were only two types of prisoner who were *unjustly* imprisoned, those who were insane and not responsible for the acts for which they were punished[4] and those who were innocent and had broken no law.[5] It is irrelevant, as he rightly observes, that some of these innocent men were, like Steinie Morrison, dangerous and violent characters, who on utilitarian grounds might well have been restrained. That made their punishment no whit less unjust.[6] To these general types may be added two specific instances of injustice. First, the sentences on the Dartmoor mutineers. "The Penal Servitude Act . . . lays down specific punishments for mutiny and incitement to mutiny, which include flogging. . . . Yet on the occasion of the only big mutiny in an English prison, men are not dealt with by the Act specially passed to meet mutiny in prison, but are taken out of gaol and tried under an Act expressly passed to curb and curtail the Chartists—a revolutionary movement."[7] Here again the injustice does not lie in the actual effect the sentences are likely to have on the prisoners (though Macartney has some searching suggestions about that also) but in condemning men for breaking a law they did not break and not for breaking the law they did break. The second specific instance is that of Coulton, who served his twenty years and then was brought back to prison to do another eight years and to die. This is due to the "unjust order that no lifer shall be released unless he has either a job or relations to whom he can go: and it is actually suggested that this is really for the lifer's own good. Just fancy, you admit that the man in doing years upon years in prison had expiated his crime: but, instead of releasing him, you keep him a further time—perhaps another three years—because you say he has nowhere to go. Better a ditch and hedge than prison! True, there are abnormal cases who want to stay in prison; but Lawrence wanted to be a private soldier, and men go into monasteries. Because occasionally a man wants to stay in prison, must every lifer who has lost his family during his sentence (I was doing only ten years and I lost all my family) be kept indefinitely in gaol after he has paid his debt?"[8] Why is it unjust? Because he has paid his debt. When that is over it is for the man himself to decide what is for his own good. Once again the reform and utilitarian arguments are summarily swept aside. Injustice lies not in bad treatment or treatment which is not in the man's own interest, but in restriction which, according to the law, he has not merited.

It is true that Macartney writes, in one place, a paragraph of general reflection on punishment in which he confuses, as does Compton Mackenzie, retribution with revenge and in which he seems to hold that the retributive theory has some peculiar connection with private property. "Indeed it is difficult to see how, in society as it is today constituted, a humane prison system could function. All property is sacred, although the proceeds of property may well be reprehensible, therefore any offence against property is sacrilege and must be punished. Till a system eventuates which is based not on exploitation of man by man and class by class, prisons must be

[3] Ibid., p. 165. My italics.

[4] Ibid., pp. 165–166.

[5] Ibid., p. 298.

[6] Ibid., p. 301.

[7] Ibid., p. 255.

[8] Ibid., p. 400.

dreadful places, but at least there might be an effort to ameliorate the more savage side of the retaliation, and this could be done very easily."[9] The alternative system of which no doubt he is thinking is the Russian system described in his quotations from *A Physician's Tour in Soviet Russia,* by Sir James Purves-Stewart, the system of "correctional colonies" providing curative "treatment" for the different types of criminal.[10] There are two confusions here, to one of which we shall return later. First, Macartney confuses the retributive system with the punishment of one particular type of crime, offences against property, when he must have known that the majority of offenders against property do not find themselves in Dartmoor or even in Wandsworth. After all his own offence was not one against property—it was traffic with a foreign Power—and it was one for which in the classless society of Russia the punishment is death. It is surely clear that a retributive system may be adopted for any class of crime. Secondly, Macartney confuses injustice within a penal system with the wrongfulness of a penal system. When he pleads for "humane prisons" as if the essence of the prison should be humanity, or when Compton Mackenzie says the object of penal servitude should be reform, both of them are giving up punishment altogether, not altering it. A Russian "correctional colony," if its real object is curative treatment, is no more a "prison" than is an isolation hospital or a lunatic asylum. To this distinction between abolishing injustice in punishment and abolishing punishment altogether we must now turn.

It will be objected that my original question, "Why ought X to be punished?" is an illegitimate isolation of the issue. I have treated the whole set of circumstances as determined. X is a citizen of a state. About his citizenship, whether willing or unwilling, I have asked no questions. About the government, whether it is good or bad, I do not enquire. X has broken a law. Concerning the law, whether it is well-devised or not, I have not asked. Yet all these questions are surely relevant before it can be decided whether a particular punishment is just. It is the essence of my position that none of these questions is relevant. Punishment is a corollary of law-breaking by a member of the society whose law is broken. This is a static and an abstract view but I see no escape from it. Considerations of utility come in on two quite different issues. Should there be laws, and what laws should there be? As a legislator I may ask what general types of action would benefit the community, and, among these, which can be "standardized" without loss, or should be standardized to achieve their full value. This, however, is not the primary question since particular laws may be altered or repealed. The choice which is the essential *prius* of punishment is the choice that there should be laws. This choice is not Hobson's. Other methods may be considered. A government might attempt to standardize certain modes of action by means of advice. It might proclaim its view and say "Citizens are requested" to follow this or that procedure. Or again it might decide to deal with each case as it arose in the manner most effective for the common welfare. Anarchists have wavered between these two alternatives and a third—that of doing nothing to enforce a standard of behaviour but merely giving arbitrational decisions between conflicting parties, decisions binding only by consent.

I think it can be seen without detailed examination of particular laws that the method of law-making has its own advantages. Its orders are explicit and general. It makes behaviour reliable and predictable. Its threat of punishment may be so

[9] Ibid., pp. 166, 167.

[10] Ibid., p. 229.

effective as to make punishment unnecessary. It promises to the good citizen a certain security in his life. When I have talked to business men about some inequity in the law of liability they have usually said, "Better a bad law than no law, for then we know where we are."

Someone may say I am drawing an impossible line. I deny that punishment is utilitarian; yet now I say that punishment is a corollary of law and we decide whether to have laws and which laws to have on utilitarian grounds. And surely it is only this corollary which distinguishes law from good advice or exhortation. This is a misunderstanding. Punishment is a corollary not of law but of law-breaking. Legislators do not *choose* to punish. They hope no punishment will be needed. Their laws would succeed even if no punishment occurred. The criminal makes the essential choice; he "brings it on himself." Other men obey the law because they see its order is reasonable, because of inertia, because of fear. In this whole area, and it may be the major part of the state, law achieves its ends without punishment. Clearly, then, punishment is not a corollary of law.

We may return for a moment to the question of amount and nature of punishment. It may be thought that this also is automatic. The law will include its own penalties and the judge will have no option. This, however, is again an initial choice of principle. If the laws do include their own penalties then the judge has no option. But the legislature might adopt a system which left complete or partial freedom to the judge, as we do except in the case of murder. Once again, what are the merits (regardless of particular laws, still more of particular cases) of fixed penalties? At first sight it would seem that all the advantages are with the variable penalties; for men who have broken the same law differ widely in degree of wickedness and responsibility. When, however, we remember that punishment is not an attempt to balance moral guilt this advantage is diminished. But there are still degrees of responsibility; I do not mean degrees of freedom of will but, for instance, degrees of complicity in a crime. The danger of allowing complete freedom to the judicature in fixing penalties is not merely that it lays too heavy a tax on human nature but that it would lead to the judge expressing in his penalty the degree of his own moral aversion to the crime. Or he might tend on deterrent grounds to punish more heavily a crime which was spreading and for which temptation and opportunity were frequent. Or again on deterrent grounds he might "make examples" by punishing ten times as heavily those criminals who are detected in cases in which nine out of ten evade detection. Yet we should revolt from all such punishments if they involved punishing theft more heavily than blackmail or negligence more heavily than premeditated assault. The death penalty for sheep-stealing might have been defended on such deterrent grounds. But we should dislike equating sheep-stealing with murder. Fixed penalties enable us to draw these distinctions between crimes. It is not that we can say how much imprisonment is right for a sheep-stealer. But we can grade crimes in a rough scale and penalties in a rough scale, and keep our heaviest penalties for what are socially the most serious wrongs regardless of whether these penalties will reform the criminal or whether they are exactly what deterrence would require. The compromise of laying down maximum penalties and allowing judges freedom below these limits allows for the arguments on both sides.

To return to the main issue, the position I am defending is that it is essential to a legal system that the infliction of a particular punishment should *not* be determined by the good *that particular punishment* will do either to the criminal or to "society." In exactly the same way it is essential to a credit system that the repayment of a particular debt should not be determined by the good that particular payment will do. One may consider the merits of a legal system or of a credit system, but the acceptance of either involves the surrender of the utilitarian considerations in particular cases as they arise. This is in effect admitted by Ewing in one place where he says, "It is the penal system as a whole which deters and not the punishment of any individual offender."[11]

To show that the choice between a legal system and its alternatives is one we do and must make, I may quote an early work of Lenin in which he was defending the Marxist tenet that the state is bound to "wither away" with the establishment of a classless society. He considers the possible objection that some wrongs by man are not economic and therefore that the abolition of classes would not ipso facto eliminate crime. But he sticks to the thesis that these surviving crimes should not be dealt with by law and judicature. "We are not Utopians and do not in the least deny the possibility and inevitability of excesses by *individual persons,* and equally the need to suppress such excesses. But for this no special machine, no special instrument of repression is needed. This will be done by the armed nation itself as simply and as readily as any crowd of civilized people even in modern society parts a pair of combatants or does not allow a woman to be outraged."[12] This alternative to law and punishment has obvious demerits. Any injury not committed in the presence of the crowd, any wrong which required skill to detect or pertinacity to bring home would go untouched. The lynching mob, which is Lenin's instrument of justice, is liable to error and easily deflected from its purpose or driven to extremes. It must be a mob, for there is to be no "machine." I do not say that no alternative machine to ours could be devised but it does seem certain that the absence of all "machines" would be intolerable. An alternative machine might be based on the view that "society" is responsible for all criminality, and a curative and protective system developed. This is the system of Butler's "Erewhon" and something like it seems to be growing up in Russia except for cases of "sedition."

We choose, then, or we acquiesce in and adopt the choice of others of, a legal system as one of our instruments for the establishment of the conditions of a good life. This choice is logically prior to and independent of the actual punishment of any particular persons or the passing of any particular laws. The legislators choose particular laws within the framework of this predetermined system. Once again a small society may illustrate the reality of these choices and the distinction between them. A Headmaster launching a new school must explicitly make both decisions. First, shall he have any rules at all? Second, what rules shall he have? The first decision is a genuine one and one of great importance. Would it not be better to have an "honour" system, by which public opinion in each house or form dealt with any offence? (This is the Lenin method.) Or would complete freedom be better? Or should he issue appeals and advice? Or should he personally deal with each malefactor individually, as the case arises, in the way most likely to improve his conduct? I can well imagine an idealistic Headmaster attempting to run a school with one of these methods or with a combination of several of them and therefore without punishment. I can even imagine that with a small school of, say, twenty pupils all open to direct personal psycho-

[11] Ewing, *The Morality of Punishment*, p. 66.

[12] Lenin, *The State and Revolution* (Eng. Trans.) (London, Glasgow: British Socialist Party and the Socialist Labor Press, 1919), p. 93. Original italics.

logical pressure from authority and from each other, these methods involving no "rules" would work. The pupils would of course grow up without two very useful habits, the habit of having some regular habits and the habit of obeying rules. But I suspect that most Headmasters, especially those of large schools, would either decide at once or quickly be driven to realize that some rules were necessary. This decision would be "utilitarian" in the sense that it would be determined by consideration of consequences. The question "what rules?" would then arise and again the issue is utilitarian. What action must be regularized for the school to work efficiently? The hours of arrival and departure, for instance, in a day school. But the one choice which is now no longer open to the Headmaster is whether he shall punish those who break the rules. For if he were to try to avoid this he would in fact simply be returning to the discarded method of appeals and good advice. Yet the Headmaster does not decide to punish. The pupils make the decision there. He decides actually to have rules and to threaten, but only hypothetically, to punish. The one essential condition which makes actual punishment just is a condition he *cannot* fulfil—namely that a rule should be broken.

I shall add a final word of consolation to the practical reformer. Nothing that I have said is meant to counter any movement for "penal reform" but only to insist that none of these reforms have anything to do with punishment. The only type of reformer who can claim to be reforming the system of punishment is a follower of Lenin or of Samuel Butler who is genuinely attacking the *system* and who believes there should be no laws and no punishments. But our great British reformers have been concerned not with punishment but with its accessories. When a man is sentenced to imprisonment he is not sentenced also to partial starvation, to physical brutality, to pneumonia from damp cells and so on. And any movement which makes his food sufficient to sustain health, which counters the permanent tendency to brutality on the part of his warders, which gives him a dry or even a light and well-aired cell, is pure gain and does not touch the theory of punishment. Reformatory influences and prisoners' aid arrangements are also entirely unaffected by what I have said. I believe myself that it would be best if all such arrangements were made optional for the prisoner, so as to leave him in these cases a freedom of choice which would make it clear that they are not part of his punishment. If it is said that every such reform lessens a man's punishment, I think that is simply muddled thinking which, if it were clear, would be mere brutality. For instance, a prisoners' aid society is said to lighten his punishment, because otherwise he would suffer not merely imprisonment but also unemployment on release. But he was sentenced to imprisonment, not imprisonment *plus* unemployment. If I promise to help a friend and through special circumstances I find that keeping my promise will involve upsetting my day's work, I do not say that I really promised to help him and to ruin my day's work. And if another friend carries on my work for me I do not regard him as carrying out part of my promise, nor as stopping me from carrying it out myself. He merely removes an indirect and regrettable consequence of my keeping my promise. So with punishment. The Prisoner's Aid Society does not alter a man's punishment nor diminish it, but merely removes an indirect and regrettable consequence of it. And anyone who thinks that a criminal cannot make this distinction and will regard all the inconvenience that comes to him as punishment, need only talk to a prisoner or two to find how sharply they resent these wanton additions to a punishment which by itself they will accept as just. Macartney's chapter on "Food" in the book quoted above is a good illustration of this point, as are also his comments on Clayton's administration. "To keep a man in prison for many years at considerable expense and then to free him charged to the eyes with uncontrollable venom and hatred generated by the treatment he has received in gaol, does not appear to be sensible." Clayton "endeavoured to send a man out of prison in a reasonable state of mind. 'Well, I've done my time. They were not too bad to me. Prison is prison and not a bed of roses. Still they didn't rub it in. . . .' "[13] This "reasonable state of mind" is one in which a prisoner on release feels he has been punished but not *additionally* insulted or ill-treated. I feel convinced that penal reformers would meet with even more support if they were clear that they were *not* attempting to alter the system of punishment but to give its victims "fair play." We have no more right to starve a convict than to starve an animal. We have no more right to keep a convict in a Dartmoor cell "down which the water trickles night and day"[14] than we have to keep a child in such a place. If our reformers really want to alter the system of punishment, let them come out clearly with their alternative and preach, for instance, that no human being is responsible for any wrong-doing, that all the blame is on society, that curative or protective measures should be adopted, forcibly if necessary, as they are with infection or insanity. Short of this let them admit that the essence of prison is deprivation of liberty for the breaking of law, and that deprivation of food or of health or of books is unjust. And if our sentimentalists cry "coddling of prisoners," let us ask them also to come out clearly into the open and incorporate whatever starvation and disease and brutality they think necessary *into the sentences they propose.*[15] If it is said that some prisoners will prefer such reformed prisons, with adequate food and aired cells, to the outer world, we may retort that their numbers are probably not greater than those of the masochists who like to be flogged. Yet we do not hear the same "coddling" critics suggest abolition of the lash on the grounds that some criminals may like it. Even if the abolition from our prisons of all maltreatment other than that imposed by law results in a few down-and-outs breaking a window (as O. Henry's hero did) to get a night's lodging, the country will lose less than she does by her present method of sending out her discharged convicts "charged with venom and hatred" because of the additional and unconvenanted "rubbing it in" which they have received.

I hope I have established both the theoretical importance and the practical value of distinguishing between penal reform as we know and approve it—that reform which alters the accompaniments of punishment without touching its essence—and those attacks on punishment itself which are made not only by reformers who regard criminals as irresponsible and in need of treatment, but also by every judge who announces that he is punishing a man to deter others or to protect society, and by every juryman who is moved to his decision by the moral baseness of the accused rather than by his legal guilt.

[13] Macartney, p. 152.

[14] Ibid., p. 258.

[15] "One of the minor curiosities of jail life was that they quickly provided you with a hundred worries which left you no time or energy for worrying about your sentence, long or short. . . . Rather as if you were thrown into a fire with spikes in it, and the spikes hurt you so badly that you forget about the fire. But then your punishment would *be* the spikes not the fire. Why did they pretend it was only the fire, when they knew very well about the spikes?" (From *Lifer*, by Jim Phelan [London: P. Davies, 1938], p. 40.)

Everett W. Hall / The "proof" of utility in Bentham and Mill

The ostensible object of the present paper is to correct an interpretation that, in the author's estimation, involves a grave historical injustice. Frankly, however, this would never have been undertaken had there not been a supporting motivation—the desire to bring to the attention of contemporary ethicists a basic, yet simple, methodological distinction, a distinction imbedded, so it will be contended, in the writings of Bentham and Mill but almost completely neglected up to the present.

One need not be a worshiper at the shrine of one's intellectual ancestors to feel a slight sense of distaste at the sight of every author of an elementary textbook in logic or ethics scurrying to chapter iv of Mill's *Utilitarianism,* "Of What Sort of Proof the Principle of Utility Is Susceptible," for examples of fallacies sufficiently blatant to be grasped at a glance by the untrained mind. It is just too obvious that the relation of "desirable" to "desired" is only suffixally similar to the relation of "audible" to "heard" ("audited"). And who cannot spot the error of deriving "everyone desires the general happiness" from "each desires his own happiness"? And so we might go down through the traditional list. But were we to try to understand Mill's argument as a whole and in the simple and obvious sense in which, when viewed as a whole, it seems only fair to take it, we might find a core worth serious consideration.

We must charge this tendency to force Mill's proof of the principle of utility into a set of the most patent fallacies to really first line philosophers. For example, F. H. Bradley, in *Ethical Studies,*[1] excuses himself for taking time to point out the tissue of inconsistencies that, so he claims, is Mill's argument. "I am ashamed," he writes, "to have to examine such reasoning, but it is necessary to do so, since it is common enough."[2] I shall, however, be mainly concerned to scrutinize the criticisms of another first-line philosopher, partly because I think he is probably the

[1] (2nd ed.; Oxford: The University Press, 1927), pp. 113–124.

[2] Ibid., p. 115*n*.

Reprinted from ETHICS, *vol. 60 (October 1949), pp. 1–18 by permission of the University of Chicago Press.*

most influential source of the traditional disparagement of Mill's argument and partly because he has stated the supposed case against Mill's proof most clearly and cogently. I refer to G. E. Moore, and specifically to chapter iii of *Principia Ethica*. Moore here admits, candidly enough, that his analysis derives from Sidgwick. This is entirely true, but the tone is quite different, for Sidgwick believed he was simply explicating certain hidden, but necessary, intuitionistic assumptions in utilitarianism, whereas Moore is an avowed, even an aggressive, opponent of that position.

Let us see what Moore's criticism is. For purposes of analysis it is well to have Mill's argument before us, familiar as that argument is. For the moment we shall note only what Moore calls the "first step" and, in fact, only the first half of the first step, which I shall designate "1A":

> 1*A*. "The only proof capable of being given that a thing is visible, is that people actually see it. The only proof that a sound is audible, is that people hear it; and so of the other sources of our experience. In like manner, I apprehend, the sole evidence it is possible to produce that anything is desirable, is that people do actually desire it. If the end which the utilitarian doctrine proposes to itself were not, in theory and in practice, acknowledged to be an end, nothing could ever convince any person that it was so."[3]

Of this, Moore says: "Well, the fallacy in this step is so obvious, that it is quite wonderful how Mill failed to see it."[4] What fallacy? A fallacy Moore calls "the naturalistic fallacy." "Mill has made as naïve and artless a use of the naturalistic fallacy as anybody could desire. 'Good,' he tells us, means 'desirable,' and you can only find out what is desirable by seeking to find out what is actually desired. . . . The important step for Ethics is this one just taken, the step which pretends to prove that 'good' means 'desired.' "[5]

And just what is this naturalistic fallacy that Mill committed so naïvely and artlessly? Let me quote one or two passages, as I fear I cannot find a single straightforward answer:

> It may be true that all things which are good are *also* something else, just as it is true that all things which are yellow produce a certain kind of vibration in the light. And it is a fact, that Ethics aims at discovering what are those other properties belonging to all things which are good. But far too many philosophers have thought that when they named those other properties they were actually defining good; that these properties, in fact, were simply not "other," but absolutely and entirely the same with goodness. This view I propose to call the "naturalistic fallacy" and of it I shall now endeavour to dispose.[6]
>
> If I were to imagine that when I said "I am pleased," I meant that I was exactly the same thing as "pleased," I should not indeed call that a naturalistic fallacy, although it would be the same fallacy as I have called naturalistic with reference to Ethics.[7]
>
> It is a very simple fallacy indeed. When we say that an orange is yellow, we do not think our statement binds us to hold that "orange" means nothing else than "yellow," or that nothing can be yellow but an orange. Supposing the orange is also sweet! Does that bind us to say that "sweet" is exactly the same thing as "yellow," that "sweet" must be defined as "yellow"?[8]
>
> . . . There is no meaning in saying that pleasure is good, unless good is something different from pleasure.[9]

Professor Frankena, in an article on "The Naturalistic Fallacy,"[10] has taken these and similar passages in *Principia Ethica* to mean that the naturalistic fallacy

[3] Quoted by Moore, *Principia Ethica*, p. 66.
[4] Ibid., p. 67.
[5] Ibid., p. 66.
[6] Ibid., p. 10.
[7] Ibid., p. 13.
[8] Ibid., p. 14.
[9] Ibid., p. 14.
[10] *Mind* 48 (new ser., 1939), 464–477.

is a species of the definist fallacy, which "is the process of confusing or identifying two properties."[11] Mr. Frankena rightly points out that this fallacy can occur only within a system that distinguishes the properties said (by him who claims a commission of the naturalistic fallacy) to be confused or identified. Thus a naturalist who denies any property of goodness or desirableness as different from desiredness has not committed the definist fallacy in saying, "The desirable just is the desired." This seems so obviously correct that one wonders how Moore could have failed to see it or how he could have made the equivalent error, "that 'good is indefinable,' and that to deny this involves a fallacy, is a point capable of strict proof: for to deny it involves contradictions."[12]

I think the truth is that Moore had in mind, as well as the definist fallacy, and confused therewith, two others, which *are* strictly fallacies and which, if committed, would involve one in the commission of the definist fallacy or would easily lead to it. The passages already quoted seem to bear this out. First, there is the confusion of the predicative with the identity "is." Let us call this the "predicative fallacy." To go from "the orange is yellow" to "the orange is nothing but yellow," or from "I am pleased" to "I am identical with having pleasure" would be to commit the predicative fallacy. Second, there is what, for lack of a recognized name, I might call the "extensionalist fallacy." This goes from the extensional equivalence of two predicate terms (whenever either is truly predicated of a particular, the other is also) to their identity (they designate the same property). Of course, an extensional language could be set up such that this implication holds. But it does not hold in ordinary language. Moore makes frequent appeal to its invalidity. To go from "Properties A and B always accompany goodness" to "Goodness just is A and B" would be to commit the extensionalist fallacy.

Now to return to the issue. When Moore says that Mill, in step 1*A*, has committed the naturalistic fallacy, what does he accuse him of? I think it is the definist fallacy. In any case, he does nothing to show that Mill committed the extensionalist fallacy. For example, he does not accuse Mill of going from "Whatever is desirable is desired and *vice versa*" to "'Desirableness' and 'desiredness' designate the same property." And, were he to do so, Mill's actual statement would not bear him out; for that statement simply is that the *sole evidence* that anything is desirable is that it is desired. This does not claim extensional equivalence of "*x* is desirable" and "*x* is desired," nor does it go from this to an identification of the two predicates. Nor does Moore show that Mill has committed the predicative fallacy, that, for example, he has gone from "Desirableness is desired" to "Desirableness just is desiredness." So I think that Moore simply means to accuse Mill of identifying two properties that are different, viz., desirableness and desiredness, and this, perhaps, as a step toward identifying goodness with pleasure.

Now we have seen that the definist fallacy is no fallacy unless the predicates definitionally identified are also taken to refer to different properties. So here, if Mill is saying that there is no property of desirableness or goodness different from the property of desiredness, that it is consonant with common usage to suppose that the word "desirableness" just refers to desiredness, he has committed no fallacy whatsoever. I happen to believe, however, that Mill does mean to accept desirableness and desiredness as different properties and that his argument makes this clear and

[11] Ibid., p. 471.

[12] Moore, op. cit., p. 77.

that he does not commit the definist fallacy.

Turning back to step 1*A*, we find Mill saying: "The sole evidence it is possible to produce that anything is desirable is that people actually do desire it." Moore himself correctly paraphrases this in one place: ". . . you can only find out what is desirable by seeking to find out what is actually desired." But then, later, he makes the astounding assertion, without any foundation, that Mill has pretended "to prove that 'good' means 'desired' "! I can only account for this flagrant reading into Mill of the definist fallacy by supposing Moore could not grasp any other sense to Mill's argument and so thought that Mill *must* have committed this fallacy. But *there is* another and an obvious sense to any interpreter not debauched with verbal casuistry, as I hope to show.

To proceed: Moore continues his attack as follows:

> The fact is that "desirable" does not mean "able to be desired" as "visible" means "able to be seen." The desirable means simply what *ought* to be desired or *deserves* to be desired; just as the detestable means not what can be but what ought to be detested and the damnable what deserves to be damned. Mill has, then, smuggled in, under cover of the word "desirable," the very notion about which he ought to be quite clear. "Desirable" does indeed mean "what it is good to desire"; but when this is understood, it is no longer plausible to say that our only test of *that*, is what is actually desired.[13]

This passage is a classic. Does it not show the complete bankruptcy of Mill's proof of utility? But there is one small question. What reason is there to suppose that Mill was not perfectly aware that "desirable" does not mean "able to be desired" and so, in *this* respect, was not at all analogous to "visible"? Could there be no other way in which the evidence for desirability must be like the evidence for visibility than in the suffixes of the adjectival designations? I think a glance at the whole argument shows that there is. And on what grounds does Moore so peremptorily continue: " 'Desirable' does indeed mean 'what it is good to desire'; but when this is understood, it is no longer plausible to say that our only test of *that* is what is actually desired"? Does he mean to make the astounding assertion which he seems to make, that anyone who says that the only test of the occurrence of A is the occurrence of B must be identifying A with B? This would force everyone who admits the extensional equivalence of two properties into a commission of the extensionalist fallacy!

Let us continue with Moore's criticism:

> Is it merely a tautology when the Prayer Book talks of *good* desires? Are not *bad* desires also possible? Nay, we find Mill himself talking of a "better and nobler object of desire," . . . as if, after all, what is desired were not *ipso facto* good, and good in proportion to the amount it is desired.[14]

Heaven forbid that any English philosopher should espouse a position that makes anything in the prayer-book a trivial tautology! I shall not undertake to defend Mill in general against such a serious charge, but on the particular point at issue I think I can clear his name. Apparently Moore's argument (which is here mostly suppressed, which perhaps accounts for its mounting vehemence) is that, since the desirable just is the desired for Mill, every desire must be good (desirable). Note, first, that this again assumes that Mill has committed the definist fallacy. Now, even supposing that he had, Moore's argument breaks down; for this fallacy would identify the desirable with the desired, not with desire. A desirable desire would be a desired desire, and not every desire is desired (in fact, even if it were, to state this would require a synthetic sentence). And,

13 Ibid., p. 67.

14 Ibid.

still on the assumption that the definist fallacy has been committed, it would be appropriate to define "bad" as "being the object of an aversion," so that it could be plausibly held that there are bad desires. However, all this is out of the whole utilitarian framework of ideas. That framework requires that a motive be judged good or bad not by the goodness or badness of its object but by the goodness or badness of its tendency, that is, of its total probable consequences if its object be realized. It is true that Mill rejects the hedonic calculus of Bentham (if that means that the morally good man must calculate the probable effects of every alternative in every choice-situation) in favor of living by traditional moral rules in most situations, but this is only a concession as to a tool for ascertaining probable consequences and does not entail giving up the position that desires can be judged good or bad only by the test of their total probable consequences.

This leads immediately into a consideration of Moore's next thrust:

> Moreover, if the desired is *ipso facto* the good; then the good is *ipso facto* the motive of our actions, and there can be no question of finding motives for doing it, as Mill is at such pains to do. If Mill's explanation of "desirable" be *true*, then his statement . . . that the rule of action may be *confounded* with the motive of it is untrue: for the motive of action will then be according to him *ipso facto* its rule; there can be no distinction between the two, and therefore no confusion, and thus he has contradicted himself flatly.[15]

The reference here is to the following passage from chapter ii of *Utilitarianism:* Some objectors to utilitarianism

> . . . say it is exacting too much to require that people shall always act from the inducement of promoting the general interests of society. But this is to mistake the very meaning of a standard of morals, and confound the rule of action with the motive of it. It is the business of ethics to tell us what are our duties, or by what test we may know them; but no system of ethics requires that the sole motive of all we do shall be a feeling of duty; on the contrary, ninety-nine hundredths of all our actions are done from other motives, and rightly so done, if the rule of duty does not condemn them.[16]

This is in manifest contradiction with the definist fallacy of identifying good with desired (on the assumption, probably correct, that "motive of action" refers to the object desired)—so much so, in fact, that it should have at least raised the suspicion that Mill's argument for the principle of utility does not reduce to a commission of that fallacy.

Finally, Moore formulates his criticism of Mill's step 1*A* in the form of an accusation that Mill has committed the fallacy of ambiguous middle:

> Well, then, the first step by which Mill has attempted to establish his Hedonism is simply fallacious. He has attempted to establish the identity of the good with the desired, by confusing the proper sense of "desirable," in which it denotes that which it is good to desire, with the sense which it would bear if it were analogous to such words as "visible." If "desirable" is to be identical with "good," then it must bear one sense; and if it is to be identical with "desired," then it must bear quite another sense. And yet to Mill's contention that the desired is necessarily good, it is quite essential that these two senses of "desirable" should be the same.[17]

I take it Moore is saying that Mill's argument can be formulated as a syllogism in *Barbara:*

> The good is identical with the desirable.
> The desirable is identical with the desired.
> Therefore, the good is identical with the desired.

And in this syllogism, says Moore, the middle term, "desirable," is ambiguous.

15 Ibid.

16 *Utilitarianism* (Everyman's ed.), p. 17 [p. 25 above].

17 Moore, op. cit., pp. 67–68.

Here the definist fallacy would appear as the conclusion of a fallacious line of proof. But what evidence is there that Mill meant to use such a syllogism? I find none. Of the whole syllogism, it is clear only that Mill would accept the minor premise, that the desirable and the good are identical.

It is now time to turn to the second half of Mill's first step, which I shall name "1*B*":

> 1*B*. "No reason can be given why the general happiness is desirable, except that each person, so far as he believes it to be attainable, desires his own happiness. This, however, being the fact, we have not only all the proof which the case admits of, but all which it is possible to require, that happiness is a good: that each person's happiness is a good to that person, and the general happiness, therefore, a good to the aggregate of all persons. Happiness has made out its title as *one* of the ends of conduct, and consequently one of the criteria of morality."[18]

Moore does not specifically criticize this passage, though it is easy to guess how he would criticize it by reference to his method of dealing with step 1*A* and his discussion (without special reference to this passage) of egoistic hedonism.[19] But there is no need to construct a hypothetical criticism; we can fill in the lacuna in Moore by turning to Bradley, who, in this particular conflict, is clearly an ally. Referring to step 1*B*, Bradley writes:

> Whether our "great modern logician" thought that by this he had proved that the happiness of all was desirable for each, I will not undertake to say. He either meant to prove this, or has proved what he started with, viz., that each desires his own pleasure. And yet there is a certain plausibility about it. If many pigs are fed at one trough, each desires his own food, and somehow as a consequence does seem to desire the food of all; and by parity of reasoning it should follow that each pig, desiring his own pleasure, desires also the pleasure of all.[20]

And in a footnote he adds:

> Either Mill meant to argue, "*Because* everybody desires his own pleasure, *therefore* everybody desires his own pleasure"; or "Because everybody desires his own pleasure, *therefore* everybody desires the pleasure of everybody else." Disciples may take their choice.[21]

Somehow the warning that Mill put right into step 1*B*—"all the proof that the case admits of"—did not make any impression. Bradley, like Moore, is assuming that our "great modern logician," as he derisively characterizes Mill, *must* be presenting in his "proof" of the principle of utility a strict logical deduction. It is high time that this whole interpretation be fundamentally and decisively challenged.

If we turn back to chapter i of *Utilitarianism,* we find Mill unequivocally rejecting any such interpretation:

> On the present occasion, I shall, without further discussion of the other theories, attempt to contribute something towards the understanding and appreciation of the Utilitarian or Happiness theory, and towards such proof as it is susceptible of. It is evident that this cannot be proof in the ordinary and popular meaning of the term. Questions of ultimate ends are not amenable to direct proof. Whatever can be proved to be good, must be so by being shown to be a means to something admitted to be good without proof. . . . If, then, it is asserted that there is a comprehensive formula, including all things which are in themselves good, and that whatever else is good, is not so as an end, but as a mean, the formula may be accepted or rejected, but is not a subject of what is commonly understood by proof.[22]

And the very first sentence of chapter iv reverts to this disavowal of any strict proof of the principle of utility: "It has already been remarked, that questions of

[18] Quoted by Moore (ibid., p. 66).

[19] Cf. ibid., pp. 96–105. His object of condemnation here is Sidgwick.

[20] *Ethical Studies* (2d ed., 1927), p. 113.

[21] Ibid., pp. 113–114*n*.

[22] Mill, p. 4 [p. 15 above].

ultimate ends do not admit of proof, in the ordinary acceptation of the term."[23] Not only does Mill thus explicitly disavow any attempt to give a strict proof of the principle of utility, but he makes it clear that the "proof" which he offers is quite another sort of thing. Returning to chapter i, we find him continuing:

> We are not, however, to infer that its acceptance or rejection must depend on blind impulse, or arbitrary choice. There is a larger meaning of the word "proof," in which this question is as amenable to it as any other of the disputed questions of philosophy. The subject is within the cognisance of the rational faculty; and neither does that faculty deal with it solely in the way of intuition. Considerations may be presented capable of determining the intellect either to give or withhold its assent to the doctrine; and this is equivalent to proof.
>
> We shall examine presently of what nature are these considerations; in what manner they apply to the case, and what rational grounds, therefore, can be given for accepting or rejecting the utilitarian formula.[24]

The very title of chapter iv is illuminating, "Of What Sort of Proof the Principle of Utility Is Susceptible." Apparently, Mill considered that he was not so much giving a proof of the principle of utility as discussing the question of the meaning of "proof" when applied to an ethical first principle. So we find him asking, concerning the principle of utility, "What ought to be required of this doctrine—what conditions is it requisite that the doctrine should fulfill—to make good its claim to be believed?"[25]

So much, then, is obvious. Mill utterly disavows any attempt to give a strict proof of the principle of utility. Thus steps 1*A* and 1*B* cannot be interpreted as Moore and Bradley have interpreted them; for then they would be simply attempted strict deductions that, unfortunately, are failures because of the commission of fallacies that any schoolboy can detect.[26]

This result is final and quite unassailable. We now come to the more interesting and hazardous task of trying to ascertain just what is the nature of those considerations which, Mill thinks, are capable of determining the intellect to give assent to the principle of utility. And first let us call to mind the well-known, but not on that account wholly irrelevant, fact that Mill was an empiricist, an opponent of all forms of intuitionism and a priorism. That Mill himself thought this relevant is clear from chapter i of *Utilitarianism*, which is devoted precisely to its reiteration in application to ethics:

> According to the one opinion, the principles of morals are evident *a priori*, requiring nothing to command assent, except that the meaning of the terms be understood. According to the other doctrine, right and wrong, as well as truth and falsehood, are questions of observation and experience.[27]

Yet Mill is clear that a peculiar problem marks off ethical questions from factual. It is not possible to determine what is right or wrong in individual cases by direct perception. It is necessary, in making ethical judgments, to apply general principles that go back to an ethical first principle: ". . . the morality of an individual action is not a question of direct perception, but of the application of a law to an individual case."[28] Thus this serious ques-

[23] Ibid., p. 32 [p. 37 above].

[24] Ibid., p. 4 [p. 15 above].

[25] Ibid., p. 32 [p. 37 above].

[26] It would do no good were the critic of Mill to say that Mill's disavowal of strict proof applies only to his whole proof, that this latter includes step 2, which is inductive, and that therefore it is permissible to treat steps 1*A* and 1*B* as attempts at strict deduction. First, Mill would call such a combination of deduction and induction a strict proof "in the ordinary acceptation of the term." Second, his disavowal of strict proof is re-emphasized within both step 1*A* and step 1*B*.

[27] Ibid., p. 2 [p. 14 above].

[28] Ibid.

tion faces the ethical empiricist: How can one's ethical first principle (such as the principle of utility) be established? Self-evidence is not available, for appeal to it would be an embracing of intuitionism; nor is inductive generalization, since the rightness or wrongness of individual acts is not open to direct perception.

In this situation Mill makes use of two considerations, both of which he got from Bentham, not to *prove* the principle of utility but to *make it acceptable* to reasonable men. One of these is essentially an appeal to men's honesty. When ordinary men try to justify their moral judgments rationally, they do so by the tacit use of the principle of utility. When an ethicist attempts to show why his ethical first principle (if it differs from that of utility) should be accepted, he does so by utilitarian arguments.[29] This is not, I am convinced, the old *consensus gentium* argument, nor does it rest on a social-agreement theory of truth. If it were, a strict proof of utility would be possible. It is rather, as I have said, an appeal to intellectual honesty. It says: "My dear ethicist, whenever you are caught off guard, either in everyday situations or in arguing for some ethical principle, you find your reasons go back to a tacit assumption of utility as the first principle of ethics. What more does the utilitarian need to do than to bring this clearly to your attention?"

I do not, however, think that this was the main consideration that Mill wished to present in developing a favorable attitude toward the principle of utility. In the first place, it is not in any special sense empirical. In the second place, he adverts to it briefly in chapter i, but not at all in chapter iv, which, as we have seen, is devoted to the task of showing "of what sort of proof the principle of utility is susceptible." Chapter iv is, I wish to urge, simply an explication of a certain sort of consideration that an empiricist can use to gain acceptance for an ethical first principle, the first principle in this instance (though it is not used as a mere illustration, for Mill does wish to get his readers to accept it) being, of course, that of utility.

Let us recall that an empiricist cannot hold that we directly perceive ethical attributes of particular actions. Thus he cannot establish his ethical first principle by an inductive generalization. This, however, is true of any first principle.[30]

> To be incapable of proof by reasoning is common to all first principles; to the first premises of our knowledge, as well as to those of our conduct. But the former, being matters of fact may be the subject of a direct appeal to the faculties which judge of fact—namely, our senses, and our internal consciousness. Can an appeal be made to the same faculties on questions of practical ends? Or by what other faculty is cognisance taken of them?[31]

It is in answer to this question that Mill gives us step 1*A*. Now just what is the analogy that he wishes to urge upon us between visible and seen, on the one hand, and desirable and desired, on the other? I submit the following as an interpretation that at least makes sense of Mill's argument as a whole.

In the area of knowledge the empiricist cannot strictly prove his first principle. He cannot prove, by induction or by deduction from any more ultimate principle, that there are no unobserved entities, that there are no visible things never seen, audible occurrences never heard, and so on. But he can set it up as a plausible principle (as a "meaning criterion," as a later positivist put it) that any epistemological theory that requires visible or audible en-

[29] Cf. ibid., pp. 3–4 [pp. 15–16 above].

[30] The critic can rightly urge that this does not square with the traditional interpretation of Mill's justification of induction (by the use of induction). On this point the critic has, I fear, firmer ground to stand on.

[31] Mill, p. 32 [p. 37 above].

tities that are never seen or heard is talking nonsense. The only test anyone can seriously propose that a thing is visible is that it actually is seen. A theory that conflicts with this requirement will just not be accepted by reasonable people. Similarly in ethical theory. A theory that sets up, as ends desirable in themselves (i.e., good, *not* simply capable of being desired), states of affairs that nobody ever desires is just being academic and unrealistic. "If the end which the utilitarian doctrine proposes to itself were not, in theory and practice, acknowledged to be an end, nothing could ever convince any person that it was so." That is, if no one appealed to the greatest happiness to justify ethical judgments or ever in practice desired the greatest happiness, no considerations capable of getting reasonable people to accept that principle as ethically ultimate could be presented. Let us call this the requirement, directed toward any ethical first principle, of "psychological realism." Since a first principle is incapable of proof, anyone could arbitrarily set up any ethical first principle he chose, and there would be no basis for deciding between this and any other (if we eschew the intuitionist's self-evidence) unless some such requirement as that of psychological realism were set up.

Step 1*B* is to be interpreted in similar fashion, with the addition that Mill is here assuming the truth of psychological hedonism. Now, whatever one's opinion as to this latter doctrine (I believe it to be false), the design of Mill's argument is not affected. "No reason can be given why the general happiness is desirable, except that each person, so far as he believes it to be attainable, desires his own happiness." Let us remember that, for Mill, the desirability of the general happiness is a first principle that cannot be proved. The sentence just quoted, therefore, sets down no requirement as to strict proof. It rather shows what sort of consideration must be presented to lead to the acceptance of this first principle. One cannot sensibly present general happiness as desirable if it is completely unrelated to what individual people actually desire. Mill cannot and does not argue that each seeks the general happiness or that society as a whole somehow has its own motives, over and above those of its members, and that these are directed toward the general happiness. Rather, Mill simply says (anticipating the outcome of step 2 and the acceptance of the pleasure of each individual as a good) that, since the pleasure of each is a good, the sum of these must be a good: "each person's happiness is a good to that person, and the general happiness, therefore, a good to the aggregate of all persons."[32] Or, as he explains in a letter: "I merely meant in this particular sentence to argue that, since A's happiness is a good, B's a good, C's a good, &c., the sum of all these goods must be a good."[33] This may be incorrect; it may be that goods cannot be added, though surely it is not just obvious that Mill is mistaken in this matter. However that may be, Mill is clearly *not* trying to prove that "*because* everybody desired his own pleasure, *therefore* everybody desires the pleasure of everybody else."[34] He is not (if the reader will tolerate another reiteration) trying to *prove* anything. He is attempting simply to present the general-happiness principle in a way that will make it seem acceptable as an ethical first principle to people who, rejecting self-evidence in this matter, still wish to be intelligent.

The test of psychological realism condemns any ethical theory that would set up as good in themselves ends which no one actually ever seeks. The principle of utility comes through this test, in Mill's first step, unscathed. Now comes the sec-

[32] Ibid., p. 33 [p. 37 above].

[33] Hugh S. R. Elliott, *The Letters of John Stuart Mill* (1910), II, 116.

[34] Bradley, op. cit., p. 114*n*.

ond step as a clincher. No other ethical theory can pass this test successfully, since the only thing people ever desire is happiness. Suppose, now, for a moment, that Mill does make this out. Then, clearly, the principle of utility holds the field alone. Any acceptable ethical first principle must meet the test of psychological realism. Only the principle of utility can meet this test. When and as this is shown, utilitarianism will, as a matter of fact, be accepted. No other kind of proof is required or possible.

Mill himself admits that people do desire as ends many things besides pleasure. He tries to square this with his contention that "there is in reality nothing desired except happiness" by appeal to the sort of associationist account that goes back to John Gay. Frequent association of these other things (e.g., money or moral virtue) with pleasures to which they give rise has set up an inseparable association. Whenever we think of these things, we think of them as pleasant, and so we seek *them*, not some pleasant effect. This line of thought bears different possible interpretations. It may mean simply that, though we do desire other things than pleasure, (associated) pleasure is the cause of our doing so. This is a plausible account of motivation, but it does not show that only pleasure is desired; it shows only that pleasure is the cause of our desiring whatever we do desire. Thus it is not to the point, for psychological realism does not require of an ethical theory that what it posits as good must be the cause of our desires but rather that it be something actually desired. And it is clear that Mill wants to show that only pleasure is desired for its own sake. Again Mill may mean to say that we are mistaken, we think we seek other things, but we really seek the pleasure so indissolubly associated with them that we do not, consciously, separate it. It seems, however, rather obvious that this is not what he means, as he reiterates that we do seek these other things than pleasure for their own sakes. Moreover, he says that we seek them as parts of happiness. Tentatively, then, I suggest the following: Only that which is experienced as pleasant is sought for its own sake. Many things originally not themselves experienced as pleasant come to be so through association with pleasant effects. Thus money or virtue really are desired as ends, but only so far as they are experienced as pleasant. This can then be expressed loosely by saying only pleasure is desired, yet other things are also—as concrete parts of it. It would be better to say: Only things experienced as pleasant are desired for their own sakes. Now, if this be accepted, then what does it involve if we are to suppose that the principle of utility successfully passes the test of psychological realism? It requires that that principle, when it says that happiness is the sole good, mean not that pleasantness is good but that things experienced as pleasant, and they alone, are good. Pleasure, as a property, is not good, and certainly not the sole good. Is this a tenable interpretation? I think it is. But this carries us away from the question of the proof of the principle of utility to the nature of that principle, and that will be dealt with at a later point in this paper and only very briefly.

One last word, and I am done with my criticism of the traditional way of disposing with Mill's argument. Moore finishes off his criticism of Mill's step 2 as follows:

> Mill, then, has nothing better to say for himself than this. His two fundamental propositions are, in his own words, "that to think of an object as desirable (unless for the sake of its consequences), and to think of it as pleasant, are one and the same thing; and that to desire anything except in proportion as the idea of it is pleasant, is a physical and metaphysical impossibility." Both of these statements are, we have seen, merely supported by fallacies. The first seems to rest on the naturalistic fallacy; the second rests partly on this, partly on the

> fallacy of confusing ends and means, and partly on the fallacy of confusing a pleasant thought with the thought of a pleasure.[35]

It is clear again that Moore is thinking of Mill's argument as a strict proof. Had he read it in context, even going back one paragraph, he would have had to give up this whole interpretation. Let me set down the paragraph that immediately precedes the passage Moore quotes:

> We have now, then, an answer to the question, of what sort of proof the principle of utility is susceptible. If the opinion which I have now stated is psychologically true—if human nature is so constituted as to desire nothing which is not either a part of happiness or a means of happiness, we can have no other proof, and we require no other, that these are the only things desirable. If so, happiness is the sole end of human action, and the promotion of it the test by which to judge of all human conduct; from whence it necessarily follows that it must be the criterion of morality, since a part is included in the whole.[36]

This, so it seems to me, is just a summary of what step 2 purports to do. It says that, if there is only one sort of thing that is ever desired, then psychological realism requires one's ethical theory to square with this. This sort of plausibility is all that can be required of any ethical theory.

Turning, now, to the paragraph which is the immediate context of the passage that Moore quotes, we find that Mill simply summarizes his contention that there is only one sort of thing ever desired, that this is happiness, that utilitarianism alone, therefore, is acceptable to ethicists who are honestly realistic. However, he does fall into a loose manner of speaking, upon which a casuist is able to capitalize. He writes, "to think of an object as desirable," when the context makes clear that he meant "to desire an object." He has just written, in an earlier part of the same sentence, "desiring a thing and finding it pleasant . . . are phenomena entirely inseparable," which he then reiterates in different words, "to think of a thing as desirable . . . and to think of it as pleasant, are one and the same thing." All this means is that any object desired (for its own sake) is inseparably associated with pleasure. I find no evidence that this commits the naturalistic fallacy in any of its three senses. Mill does use the infelicitous term "desirable" here. But he could have used "good" in the same loose and colloquial sense; i.e., he could have said, in accordance with frequent popular usage, "to think of an object as good" when he meant "to desire an object."

In summary, the argument of chapter iv of Mill's *Utilitarianism* is extremely simple and (in the main) sensible. To an empiricist who eschews all intuitive self-evidence, no ethical first principle can be strictly proved. All that one can do is to present considerations that will lead honest and reasonable people to accept such a principle. These considerations, for an empiricist, must turn on what people actually desire. Each person desires his own happiness. Therefore, a first principle that makes happiness good will prove acceptable to honest men when they consider it. And if the happiness of each is good, then the sum of happiness of all is good. Thus the principle of utility is something that men, constituted as they are, can honestly accept. But no other ethical first principle can meet this simple test of psychological realism; for (and here the reasoning is not too clear) the only thing people seek (for its own sake) is happiness. At least a plausible interpretation of this last consideration is that happiness is not a sum of pleasures in the sense of an amount of sheer pleasantness but is a sum of things experienced (whether by one's original nature or through long association) as pleasant.

It must be admitted that this whole interpretation presupposes a fundamental

[35] *Principia*, p. 72.

[36] Mill, *Utilitarianism*, p. 36 [pp. 39–40 above].

distinction, a distinction which intuitionists[37] like Moore and Sidgwick, thinking they can rest their case on the self-evidence of their first principles, apparently ignore. I refer to the distinction between a statement in a theory and a statement about a theory, which here takes the form of the distinction between a proof within an ethical system and a proof of an ethical system. A first principle in an ethical system (or in an epistemological or ontological system) obviously cannot be proved in that system. It is possible to deal with an ethical system whose first principles are, within that system, self-evident, as a whole, and to ask, "Of what proof is it susceptible?" But this would put it on all fours with other systems and would lose for it the advantage of the supposed certainty which its self-evident first principles give it. In fact, to say that a principle is self-evident may mean just that it is a first principle; in *that* system in which it is self-evident it is not to be questioned; the possibility of its falsehood would just be the possibility of a contradiction in the system. In any other sense the self-evidence of a first principle takes us outside the system. But that brings up the serious question of how a whole ethical system can be established, a question that such an intuitionist as Moore never clearly faced just because he never saw this ambiguity in the concept of self-evidence.

It may, indeed, be contended that Moore meant by "self-evident" simply being a first principle in a system. In fact, Moore explicitly says: "When I call [propositions asserting that something is good in itself] 'intuitions' I mean *merely* to assert that they are incapable of proof; I imply nothing whatever as to the manner or origin of our cognition of them."[38] And again, he says:

> The expression "self-evident" means properly that the proposition so called is evident or true, *by itself* alone; that it is not an inference from some proposition other than *itself*. The expression does *not* mean that the proposition is true, because it is evident to you or me or all mankind, because in other words it appears to be true. That a proposition appears to be true can never be a valid argument that true it really is.[39]

I am not sure that in his later writings Moore so clearly distinguished self-evidence from psychological conviction. His frequent contention that he could be certain about the truth of such propositions as "This is a hand" and that philosophical analysis must start with such indubitable propositions seems to indicate that he did come to confuse first principles and propositions that are psychologically indubitable. But for the present purpose I need only point out that he was not aware in *Principia Ethica* that to be a first principle is always relative to a system. He assumes that self-evident propositions just are true. He does not see that the fact that they are not, in a given system, deduced from other propositions but serve as ultimate premises indicates nothing whatever as to their truth save as that is an intra-systemic matter. Whether the system in which their truth is fundamental to all else is as a whole true or is more acceptable than rival systems is a question he completely fails to see. That is, he fails to distinguish between the question of how a whole ethical system, with its first principles, can in any way be established, and the question of proof within such a system. Mill, in his loose, common-sensical way, is trying to state this distinction and to answer the

[37] Sometimes by "intuitionistic ethics" is meant not an ethics whose first principles are taken to be self-evident but simply an ethics that claims that there is some value term (such as "good") whose reference is uniquely nondescriptive. In this sense, I claim, both Bentham and Mill are intuitionists.

[38] *Principia*, p. x.

[39] Ibid., p. 143.

question, "What kind of proof of an ethical system is possible?" He is saying that an ethical system as a whole cannot be established in any other way than by making it acceptable to reasonable men; and this is done just by showing that it and it alone (in its first principles, though not as theoretically elaborated) is actually accepted by men when outside the philosopher's closet. Mill simply asks ethicists to square their professionally elaborated ethics with the common-sense ethics of every man, including themselves. His statement of his problem and his answer are not too clear-cut; but what, in essentials, he was trying to do should be obvious to any sympathetic reader. All the more so because, in the main, he is just following Bentham, and Bentham did the same thing very clearly.

Having made a case that Mill is arguing *about* his system, not *in* it, and that his argument amounts to an appeal to the honesty of his readers in admitting that only utilitarianism squares with their actual motives, I need not take the space necessary to argue for a similar interpretation of Bentham. I need only point out some passages which show that, particularly in chapter i of *An Introduction to the Principles of Morals and Legislation,* Bentham was doing quite clearly what Mill did somewhat more blunderingly.

"Is the principle of utility susceptible of any direct proof?" asks Bentham. "It should seem not: for that which is used to prove everything else, cannot itself be proved: a chain of proofs must have their commencement somewhere. To give such proof is as impossible as it is needless."[40] However, there are those who do not accept utility as their ethical first principle. To such a one Bentham says: "If he thinks the settling of his opinions on such a subject worth the trouble, let him take the following steps, and at length, perhaps, he may reconcile himself to it."[41] If his alternative is the absence of all first principles whatever, then, in all consistency, he must admit that his ethical judgments are without foundation. If his first principle be merely an expression of some sentiment or approbation of his own, will not his whole system be founded on caprice? Can he claim objectivity for it? Does he give the like right to everyone else to found his ethics on an individual feeling? If so, let him ask himself

> whether it is not anarchial, and whether at this rate there are not as many different standards of right and wrong as there are men? and whether even to the same man, the same thing, which is right today, may not (without the least change in its nature) be wrong tomorrow? and whether the same thing is not right and wrong in the same place at the same time? and in either case, whether all argument is not at an end? and whether, when two men have said, "I like this" and "I don't like it," they can (upon such a principle) have any thing more to say?"[42]

All this may sound highly rhetorical, but at least Bentham is not fooling himself or others—he is offering no proof of his first principle, he is persuading people to accept it by showing them that they would not consider the alternatives to it to be sensible if they understood them. And this can hardly be said of G. E. Moore's famous elaboration (in his *Ethics* and in "The Nature of Moral Philosophy") of this last passage from Bentham. Moore thinks that the consequence of subjectivism pointed out by Bentham, viz., that disagreement on moral matters becomes impossible, *disproves* subjectivism, in some strict sense.

But to resume. Bentham saves for the

[40] *Introduction to the Principles of Morals and Legislation,* chap. i, § xi.

[41] Ibid., § xiv.

[42] Ibid., § xiv.

last his most telling appeal—the need for psychological realism:

> Admitting any other principle than the principle of utility to be a right principle, a principle that it is right for a man to pursue; admitting (what is not true) that the word *right* can have a meaning without reference to utility, let him say whether there is any such thing as a *motive* that a man can have to pursue the dictates of it: if there is, let him say what that motive is, and how it is to be distinguished from those which enforce the dictates of utility: if not, then lastly let him say what it is this other principle can be good for?[43]

This rhetorical question is clearly meant to have a negative answer—no other first principle sets up as good anything that anyone has any motive to seek. Bentham is, of course, assuming the truth of psychological hedonism. Besides this list (which I have here shortened) of rhetorical questions, a serious consideration of which, Bentham believes, will lead any doubter to be reconciled to the principle of utility, Bentham has one other device for making that principle appear plausible. He points out that "when a man attempts to combat the principle of utility, it is with reasons drawn, without his being aware of it, from that very principle itself."[44] Also, most men, without thinking of it, order their lives or at least found their judgments of people's actions by assuming this principle. Since this is the case, it is only being intellectually honest to accept that principle explicitly when our universal dependence upon it is pointed out to us.

But G. E. Moore, though not quite so vitriolic as he is against Mill, is inclined to believe that Bentham's case rests on a commission of the naturalistic fallacy. Here again he follows Sidgwick:

> "Bentham," says Sidgwick, "explains that his fundamental principle 'states the greatest happiness of all those whose interest is in question as being the right and proper end of human action' ": and yet "his language in other passages of the same chapter would seem to imply" that he *means* by the word "right" "conducive to the general happiness." Prof. Sidgwick sees that, if you take these two statements together, you get the absurd result that "greatest happiness is the end of human action, which is conducive to the general happiness."[45]

This absurdity is due to "the naturalistic fallacy, which is implied in Bentham's statements."[46] Now, apparently Moore does not wish to condemn Bentham's definition (on Sidgwick's authority) of "right" as "conducive to general happiness." This alone would be no commission of the naturalistic fallacy. (It must be remembered that Moore himself at the time accepted a very similar definition of "right.") What he wishes to condemn is Bentham's use (still on Sidgwick's authority) of this definition to prove that the greatest happiness is the only end of human action.

> [Bentham] applies the word "right," therefore, to the end, as such, not only to the means which are conducive to it; and, that being so, right can no longer be defined as "conducive to the general happiness," without involving the fallacy in question. For now it is obvious that the definition of right as conducive to general happiness can be used by him in support of the fundamental principle that general happiness is the right end; instead of being itself derived from that principle. . . . What I am maintaining is that the *reasons* which he actually gives for his ethical proposition are fallacious ones so far as they consist in a definition of right. What I suggest is that he did not perceive them to be fallacious; that, if he had done so, he would have been led to seek for other reasons in support of his Utilitarianism; and that, had he sought for other reasons, he *might* have found none which he thought to be sufficient. In that case he would have changed his whole system—a most important consequence.[47]

43 Ibid., § xiv, 10.

44 Ibid., § xiii.

45 Moore, op. cit., p. 17.

46 Ibid., p. 18.

47 Ibid., pp. 18–19.

It is clear here that Moore is interpreting Bentham as trying to give a strict proof of the principle of utility, by means of a definition of "right" which commits the naturalistic fallacy (since, even though right is complex, it includes a nonnatural or value component and hence cannot be identified with the referent of "conducive to the general happiness," which embraces no nonnatural property). This, however, flies directly in the face of the whole organization of chapter i, in which, as we have seen, Bentham not only disavows a strict proof of that principle but shows clearly what sort of proof is here possible.

But let us look more closely at the passages that, pulled out of their context, have led to this misinterpretation. It is quite correct that Bentham does specify the principle of utility as ". . . that principle which states the greatest happiness of all those whose interest is in question, as being the right and proper, and only right and proper and universally desirable, end of human action."[48] But where in this same chapter does he use language indicating that he means to *define* "right" as conducive to the greatest happiness? I find only two passages that could be construed in this way. The first is:

> Of an action that is conformable to the principle of utility, one may always say either that it is one that ought to be done, or at least that it is not one that ought not to be done. One may say also, that it is right it should be done; at least that it is not wrong it should be done: that it is a right action; at least that it is not a wrong action. When thus interpreted, the words *ought*, and *right* and *wrong*, and others of that stamp, have a meaning: when otherwise, they have none.[49]

The other, which I have already quoted, runs: ". . . admitting (what is not true) that the word *right* can have a meaning without reference to utility, let him say whether there is any such thing as a *motive* that a man can have to pursue the dictates of it. . . ."

If these passages are taken to mean that Bentham arbitrarily defines "right" as "conformity to general happiness," then the principle of utility follows immediately and tautologically. And Bentham is quite wrong in saying that it is an ethical first principle that cannot be proved and that all one can do is to get people to consider it honestly. But, if these passages are not to be taken thus, how are they to be interpreted? Bentham, note, does not say, "right" *means* "conformable to the greatest happiness." He says we may say of an action conformable to utility that it is right; that, when so used, "right" has a meaning, otherwise not; and again that "right" can have no meaning without reference to utility. Now this is perfectly consonant with the view that, though "right" does not refer to utility, what it does refer to is regularly related to utility, is present only when utility is. Moreover, it squares with the use of psychological realism as a test: that is, only when "right" is so used that it points out acts that do have utility does it fit with people's actual motives; thus any other first principle than utility would make "right" and other ethical terms meaningless, in the sense that these terms would no longer agree with people's actual motives and judgments. This is a perfectly plausible interpretation that has the merit of fitting these passages into Bentham's thought rather than speculating on them in isolation. But it has the consequence that the principle of utility is no tautology and does not involve the naturalistic fallacy in any of its forms. Can this be made out? I think it can, and without any forcing.

In the first place, though Bentham embraces psychological hedonism, he does not confuse this with ethical hedonism. The first three sentences of his *Principles* make this unmistakable: "Nature has

[48] Bentham, op. cit., chap. i, § in.

[49] Ibid., § x.

placed mankind under the governance of two sovereign masters, *pain* and *pleasure*. It is for them alone to point what we ought to do, as well as to determine what we shall do. On the one hand the standard of right and wrong, on the other the chain of causes and effects, are fastened to their throne."[50] It is true, he goes on to say, that "the *principle of utility* recognises the subjection, and assumes it for the foundation of that system, the object of which is to rear the fabric of felicity by the hands of reason and of law."[51] But here he is clearly speaking of his attempt to write a handbook for the judge and legislator that will square with actual human motives and thus deter from crime and encourage obedience to law. The twofold character of pleasure, as a test of what is desirable and as an object of desire, is made, as it were, the cornerstone of his whole attempt at legal codification and reform: "Pleasures then, and the avoidance of pains, are the *ends* which the legislator has in view [i.e., are the ends he should aim at]. . . . Pleasures and pains are the instruments he has to work with. . . ."[52] This distinction, between pleasure as marking the good and pleasure as controlling human action, is present throughout Bentham's whole discussion of principles of legislation: of cases unmeet for punishment, of rules governing the proper proportion between punishments and offenses, etc. His basic principle, that one is never justified in inflicting more pain (through punishment) than is necessary to deter from crime, would be meaningless without it.

Thus the principle of utility is definitely an ethical principle (a "standard of right and wrong," as he calls it). Though realistically geared to or paralleling a hedonistic law of human motivation, it is not that law, nor is it proved by that law. It is no identity statement, or definition, in nonethical terms, of basic ethical words, such as "right" or "desirable end." It is clearly a synthetic statement to the effect that the only situation desirable as an end in itself, and in terms of which human actions can be judged good or bad as they tend to promote or hinder its achievement, is that which exemplifies the greatest happiness of all concerned. This cannot be proved within the utilitarian system because that system is simply a development of it (plus an indefinite number of empirical laws connected directly or indirectly with the occurrence of happiness). But the utilitarian system is capable of the sort of "proof" open to any ethical system. It can be made to appear plausible, it can be presented so that people who try honestly to be reasonable will be led to accept it. And this is done, so Bentham thinks, by showing that it, and it alone of all ethical theories, squares with our unsophisticated moral judgments and reasonings and sets up as morally good something which, by the basic law of human motivation, actually is sought by people.

Now I can imagine an objector arguing in the following vein: Granted that you have shown that the proof of the principle of utility as formulated in Bentham and Mill does not rest on the set of fallacies traditionally ascribed to it, haven't you, on the other hand, made of it little more than a farce? You point out that it is no proof at all, it is merely an appeal to people's belief. It is just an attempt to get people to accept utilitarianism. It is reduced to so much propaganda.

This is no place for an extended statement of method in ethics. But since, as indicated at the outset, this paper was written largely from a methodological rather than a historical interest, a few concluding words on this head may not be inappropriate.

First, it seems to me that Bentham and

[50] Ibid., § i.

[51] Ibid.

[52] Ibid., chap. iv, § i.

Mill are right in saying that any ethical theory must contain at least one first principle that cannot be proved; for to prove it would involve deriving it from some more basic principle, which latter would, then, be part of the theory. And, as Mill indicates, this is true of theories in other branches of philosophy. Examples would be the correspondence theory of truth in epistemology, the tautological theory of entailment in the philosophy of logic, the nominalistic theory of existence in ontology. Though I think it proper to demand that theories in different philosophic disciplines be harmoniously fitted together to make a categorically unified metaphysics, they are not derivable from anything more basic. This is their peculiarity as philosophical. They are self-contained.

Second, proofs, both inductive and deductive, are possible within a philosophical theory or system. In fact, however, a great deal of the development of such a theory is strictly neither deductive nor inductive but involves a sort of consistency that may perhaps be designated as "fittingness" or "appropriateness." Philosophic competence in developing a theory is a curious amalgam of technical, logical and linguistic skill and philosophic insight and imagination.

Third, however competently developed, there still remains the question of the acceptability of a philosophic theory as a whole. This is in part just a matter of actual success or failure in getting people who turn their attention to such matters to accept the theory. But this is not quite all; for it must be admitted that there are good and bad ways of going about this. Appeal to authority—whether of a church, a great tradition in philosophy, the writings of a certain individual philosopher, or the tenets of a particular school of thought—is a bad way. Another bad way is through confusion as to what one is doing. An important instance is the confusion between talking within a system and about a system, which, no doubt, springs from the desire for certainty and seems to be the source of that curious delusion that there are self-evident first principles. A good way of going about gaining acceptance of a philosophic system is to show that, though clearer and more consistent, it yet squares in some overall large fashion with common sense, with those ways of organizing experience that we all adopt when not in the closet of philosophic speculation. Why is this a good way? In the first place, it is the way most likely to succeed in the long run. We humans are basically intellectually honest, I optimistically believe, and will not for long accept a philosophic theory that we cannot in any way integrate with our everyday fashion of looking at things. In the second place, common sense, so far as relevant in this matter, is itself metaphysics—only half-thought-out, full of confusions and even contradictions, yet the residue of attempts through the centuries of untold numbers of men to categorize experience. It is, then, with all its need of clarification, a more reliable basis than any one man's speculations for determining what categorial systems can and what ones cannot be permanently successful in ordering experience.

Fourth, implicit in all of the third point is a metaphysics. There are people who do accept and reject philosophic systems. There is experience that can be categorized in different ways. And so on. All this, of course, I accept in my own metaphysics. And it is consonant with my method of "proving" that metaphysics by appeal to common sense. But what of another metaphysics that might reject all this, and thus the whole method it embraces? What can I do with it? Nothing, except to say it will not be accepted for long by many, which, of course, is to bring it within my metaphysics. Yet this is the peculiar situation a metaphysical system is in. And so here we must stop.

This may seem a long way from Bentham and Mill, but I am convinced that a sympathetic reading of the "proof" of utilitarianism by these men shows that they were trying to face, in ethics, the sort of peculiar difficulty that any philosophic theory is in when questions about establishing it, as contrasted with proving things within it and by means of it, are honestly faced. And, though I do not wish to condone laxity of formulation, I do wish to condemn that sort of casuistry which fastens to another man's words and neglects his sentences or, in reading a sentence, ignores the paragraphs and chapters.

A.I. Melden / Two comments on utilitarianism

Discussions of utilitarianism are so familiar, the arguments and counterarguments so well worn, that one reasonably hesitates to enter the old lists. And yet there is need of freeing certain of the basic issues which these discussions have raised from the very special contexts in which, too often, they are placed. When utilitarianism has been attacked or defended, it has been attacked or defended as naturalistic or as hedonistic. And when, as it happens on occasion, utilitarianism has been treated as a type of intuitionism, recognition has not, in general, been accorded to the fact that it can be construed, in addition, as a type of emotivism. And in the recent discussions of the meaning of ethical terms where the merits or demerits of some type or other of the emotive theory have been explored, there is too often the failure to appreciate the fact that decisions pro or con emotivism are singularly indecisive with respect to certain more general issues in ethical theory. Indeed—and this, it seems to me, is at least a possibility that warrants consideration—such semantical decisions may have to be made only in the light of issues of a more general sort to which emotivism, naturalism, or intuitionism must address themselves if they are to compete as serious ethical theories.

What I propose to do, therefore, is to describe the main features of a type of ethical theory which I shall label "utilitarianism" and which cuts across many of the familiar lines of classification. It may be hedonistic and it may be nonhedonistic. It may be naturalistic, intuitionistic, or emotivistic. And if such labeling is in effect to broaden its generally received application, there will be at least the recognition of the pervasiveness of the issues I shall raise. I shall then proceed to comment upon the responsibilities of ethical theories in general and the extent to which utilitarianism as I shall describe it succeeds in meeting in particular two of these responsibilities.

Reprinted from THE PHILOSOPHICAL REVIEW, *vol. 60 (1951), pp. 508–524 by permission of the author and editors.*

I

Let us call any ethical theory a case of utilitarianism if it satisfies the following conditions:

a) There is some introspectible property of an experience which is a fundamental value property. This property is the property by virtue of which we may speak of the experience as an experience of liking or favoring, a satisfaction of desire or interest, a sense of well-being, a feeling of pleasure or what have you. Let us call the selected property "the value property." Corresponding remarks apply to the meanings of the "disvalue property." Depending upon the type of utilitarianism in question the familiar distinctions between intrinsic and extrinsic value properties may be usefully introduced.

b) The value property makes for, and it is the only thing that makes for, good in any distinctively ethical sense. By "makes for" I mean some one of the following relations: (i) logical identity (in which case the utilitarianism is a type of naturalism); (ii) a synthetic a priori connection which holds between the value property and a nonintrospectible but intuitable property of experience (in which case the theory is a type of intuitionism); or (iii) some causal relation such that under appropriate circumstances the value property will occasion an approval, wish, command, decision, demand, etc., which it is the characteristic and essential function of the ethical term "good" to express.[1] Corresponding remarks apply to the ethically used terms "bad" and "evil." Depending upon the type of view in question the familiar distinctions between intrinsic and extrinsic good in the ethical sense of that term may be usefully introduced.

c) Let me use the term "experience-goodness" to mean a property of an experience which is identical either with the good-making property or with the intrinsic experience property, if any, of goodness, in the ethical sense of that term, which the good-making property makes for. (For the naturalist, the experience-goodness is identical with the fundamental value property described in (*a*). For the intuitionist, the experience-goodness is an intuitable property since it, unlike the value property described in (*a*), is good in an ethical sense. For the emotivist, the experience-goodness is the value property described in (*a*) since good, in any ethical sense, is not the name of any property at all.) Correspondingly, one may speak of the "experience-badness." The locutions "experience-goods" and "experience-evils" will be experiences, namely, instances of these properties.

d) The fundamental value-property described in (*a*) has magnitude. The same thing is true of the fundamental disvalue property. And, further, the value and disvalue properties are commensurate so that we may speak of the magnitude of the net value of the net disvalue, or, indeed, of the net value neutrality of one or more experiences. Nothing like a calculus is intended since the magnitudes need only be intensive.

e) Goods in any ethical sense, whether intrinsic or instrumental, have magnitude. (That one thing may be better than another would be granted on any ethical theory, emotive no less than nonemotive.) A similar remark applies to evils in any ethical sense. Further, a complex state may be a net good (in the ethical sense), a net evil (in the ethical sense), or a net neutral

[1] For Hume, to take one currently neglected type of emotivism, the ethical term "good" is, as he puts it, an "epithet," since it expresses an approval, namely, a felt pleasure, which occurs when, under certain conditions, the pleasantness, immediate or indirect, of the object is contemplated. For Stevenson, to take a contemporary example, there is, in the experience in the speaker, a liking which occasions a wish that others share it and which it is the essential function of the ethical term "good" to express.

state. If the good or evil is instrumental, the magnitude in question will be derivative from the magnitudes of the intrinsic goods or evils produced or likely to be produced.

f) The magnitude of any unmixed good in any ethical sense is the magnitude of the relevant (i.e., thereby obtained and obtainable, or likely to be obtained) experience-goods.[2] Corresponding remarks apply to unmixed "evil" in the ethical sense. In the case of mixed goods and evils, i.e., net goods, evils, or net ethically neutral states, the magnitude in question will be the magnitude of the net experience-goods and net experience-evils. This is clear since experience-goods are either value experiences or intrinsically good (in the ethical sense) experiences, and these are commensurate with disvalue experiences and intrinsically evil experiences respectively. In any case, the magnitude of any good or evil in the ethical senses of these terms will be the magnitudes of certain properties of experiences.

g) We can now specify the necessary and sufficient conditions of the correct application of the terms "ought," "right," "duty," "obligation," etc. The necessary and sufficient condition in all cases will pertain to magnitude of experience-goodness. We offer no definitions of these ethical terms.

Suppose, for example, a moral agent confronted by several possible courses of action in a given moral situation. He ought, is obliged, or is duty bound to perform one of these, if and only if it is productive of the most net experience-goodness. It will be right to feel sympathy, for example, if and only if such feelings promote or tend to promote actions that are right, and actions are right if and only if they are productive of experience-goodness and no alternative action then performable produces or is likely to produce more net experience-goodness. And if one performs a right action from the right motives then the action will be doubly meritorious, but it will be meritorious in such cases precisely because of the experience-goodness which both motives and actions produce or tend to produce, directly or indirectly. Further, if there is any sense in which A has a right and B a correlative obligation to A, then the right and the obligation will obtain if and only if the action in question, in the context of tacitly assumed conditions, is productive of more experience-goodness than would be obtained if the action were not performed. In short, magnitude or quantity of net experience-goodness is a necessary and sufficient condition of right, ought, obligation, duty, in any moral sense or senses of these terms. And by these experience-goods we mean either value experiences, or experiences of an intuitable goodness distinct from the value property. In any case the necessary and sufficient conditions pertain to the quantity of some property found through introspection or intuition in some actual or possible individual experiences.

II

Any ethical theory purports to clarify and systematize the nature and criteria of those features of our experience to which admittedly ethical terms and statements

[2] It does not follow that except in the instrumental sense nothing other than an experience is good in any ethical sense of the term. On an emotive theory, for example, the usual instrumental-intrinsic distinction between goods in the ethical sense may disappear. Instead there will be the distinction between intrinsic values and instrumental values where "value" is used in a nonethical sense. The point is that "good" in the ethical sense is, on such a view, not the name of any property at all; hence, to say that a character trait, for example, is good, is not to say that it is good in the sense that it produces or is likely to produce the property of goodness in any ethical sense of that term.

correctly apply. In the very nature of the case the test of the relevance and competence of judgments in ethical theory can be made only by an appeal to these features of our moral experience. Analysis pursued independently of these data risks irrelevancy; theory elaborated in oblivion or disdain of the data to be explained is simply irresponsible, and this is true whatever the sense of "explanation" may be, in philosophy no less than in science. For the point is that we do make moral judgments, utter moral statements, and that our confidence *in at least some of these* is and must be far greater than our assurance concerning any philosophical theory. That pleasure is good I cannot question; but that the statement is tautological, the report of an intuition, or simply expressive is a matter on which as philosopher I may report a genuine perplexity. That it is wrong to inflict pain upon those whose preference in the colors of their ties differs from our own is a matter that no ethical theory as such can refute; nothing except the purely factual or nonnormative demonstration by any of the physical or social sciences of the consequences of such preferences which I can then morally weigh with a like unquestionable assurance could possibly lead me to alter my mind. That there are rights and obligations which arise in the special social relations in which men may stand to one another is no matter which waits upon ethical theory for proof, since any ethical theory which fails to jibe with these admitted rights and obligations is thereby disqualified. And this is by no means to deny that given all of the available factual data pertaining to any moral problem there may be genuine perplexity to which even an enlightened common sense is exposed. In part, the difficulty may be due to a characteristic vagueness of ethical terms. But vagueness is mischievous only when it goes unrecognized in discourse that professes to be precise; and precision is the most trivial of the virtues since it can be obtained by instituting definitions which succeed only in changing the subject matter. The test here, clearly, is the pertinence of our definitions and analyses to the subject matter that occasions the perplexity and the continued applicability of our terms to those cases concerning which admittedly there is no hesitation or doubt. In part, too, the difficulty may stem from the confusion between private or social bias and moral and, in this sense, reasonable preference. Or, it may be that none of these factors may serve to account for certain genuine perplexities or differences in moral judgment. What we can do, in all cases, is to attempt, by the judicious use of the familiar techniques employed in moral judgment and persuasion, to narrow the limits of our moral uncertainties and disagreements. But, unless there is *some* area of agreement and unquestioned assurance as a basis for philosophical discussion, we have no check whatsoever upon the competence of our labors as theorists. Indeed, unless ethical theories address themselves to the same admitted data, they are to that extent not competitors at all, but different theories about different subject matters. And to that extent, the disagreements to which such philosophers may be party are not philosophical but moral.

Does utilitarianism fill this bill? I propose to make two main comments about the rights of persons and the correlative obligations of moral agents. The first has to do with what we may describe as a generic obligation. As an example I take as unquestioned the moral conviction that persons as persons, all else being equal, have rights to the goods of life—experience-goods. But all else is never equal. Hence, as an example of a special right and a special obligation, I shall consider the admitted special moral situation created by the making of a promise.

III

A.

The traditional utilitarians have maintained, quite plausibly, that a world without consciousness would be a world devoid of value in any simple or underivative sense, and that a world in which experience-evils is the general rule would scarcely be the sort of world that accords with our moral ideals. And they have sometimes concluded that the necessary and sufficient conditions of "right" and "ought" is quantity of experience-goods. But if this is the inference, it is surely fallacious.

Mill maintains "that actions are right in proportion as they tend to promote happiness, wrong as they tend to produce the reverse of happiness [meaning by] happiness . . . pleasure and the absence of pain; and [meaning by] unhappiness, pain and the privation of pleasure."[3] Bentham is more circumspect. He defines "right action" as action conformable to the principle of utility, but he is careful to specify that the number of interests affected is involved in the conception of utility. In effect, therefore, "right action" is defined as action which is most conducive to the promotion of pleasure and the decrease of pain of the greatest number.[4] And it is well that he is so circumspect. For one cannot consistently assert both (a) that quantity of experience-good promoted is a sufficient condition of right action and (b) that if any action is right the quantity of experience-good must be enjoyed by the greatest number. For if the quantity of net experience-good is sufficient by (a) to make an action right but is reserved for the special privilege of a few at the expense of the many, then the action is wrong by (b). But if Bentham is not guilty of this inconsistency, Mill surely is. And that he is, is instructive. For if, as I assume it is agreed, all else being equal, persons as persons have a right to experience-goods and a right to the relief from experience-evils, then right action is action that is productive of the most experience-good and the least experience-evil provided these are distributed in the right way. The point is that utilitarianism cannot, as I have specified the theory, provide a satisfactory account of right action because it fails to take into account the right to the experience-goods and the right to the relief from experience-evils which persons have as persons. And this is true whether the utilitarianism is emotive, naturalistic, or intuitionistic, hedonistic or nonhedonistic. Let me consider a number of possible replies the utilitarian may make:

1. If the utilitarian replies that he is by no means committed to an egoistic doctrine, since experience-goodness is after all repeatable and every person is a locus of such goodness in the sense that it is capable of being exemplified in his experience, we shall retort that this latter consideration is trivial and to no avail. The premise is trivial because admittedly, experience-goodness is a property and, as property, undeniably repeatable. It is to no avail since the property may be repeated in indefinitely many ways, exemplified in the experience of one or more persons. The more experience-good, the more experience-good; but the fact that the more experience-good there is the more times experience-goodness is repeated does not entail that the more experience-goodness there is the more widely and fairly it is repeated. Indeed it is by no means necessary that the more experience-goodness

[3] *Utilitarianism,* chap. ii.

[4] *An Introduction to the Principles of Morals and Legislation,* chap. i, secs. 1, 2, 3, 10. I ignore for my purposes the discussion of the allegation that this definition involves Bentham in the Naturalistic Fallacy.

there is the more times it is repeated. For, conceivably, it need not be repeated at all but enjoyed in the continuous experience of a single individual. And there is, as far as I can see, no theoretical moral objection on utilitarian grounds to an egoistic enjoyment of goods if it should turn out to be the case that the maximizing of the net experience-good is to be obtained by allocating all experience-goods to the life of a single individual. Yes, experience-goodness is repeatable, but should it be repeated not only in the experiences of the same persons but fairly, in the right way, in the experiences of many? Stated abstractly, the question answers itself.

2. A utilitarian may retort, if he chooses, that distribution of experience-goodness makes no moral difference whatsoever. He may argue that given the same net experience-good, it makes no moral difference if all experience-evils are concentrated in the lives of one or more persons who thus function as scapegoats. If he does so, our dispute with him is no longer philosophical but moral. But the classical utilitarians have been too sensible to make this baldly absurd moral judgment; and, where they have expressed a form of the kind of philosophical theory I have called "utilitarianism" and are confronted by this issue, they tacitly or even explicitly, as in the case of Mill, involve themselves in the kind of contradiction noted above.

3. The utilitarian may argue that after all it is impossible to maximize experience-goodness and minimize experience-evils without distributing these in a manner that accords with our unquestioned moral sensibilities. But clearly he cannot mean that this is logically impossible. There is no logical necessity, given any magnitude of net experience-goodness, in supposing it to be distributed badly, wrongly. "Right" in the phrase "right distribution of net experience-goodness" is not redundant. And there is no intuitable necessary connection between these logically distinct terms. The utilitarian can only mean that human beings in all of their psychological and social respects are so constituted, or that the laws of divine legislation are so formulated, that maximizing net experience-goodness insures its fair distribution. But this natural, or divinely pre-established, harmony, is, so far, a hope. For we cannot, with the same confidence and assurance we feel concerning the desirability of certain distributions of the goods of life, assert the empirical statement that the goods of our human experience will be maximized only when they are fairly distributed. A democratic society would be preferable to a totalitarianism, according to the utilitarian, not because the rights of persons as persons to the enjoyment of the experience-goods and the relief from the experience-evils is respected in the former and ignored in the latter, but simply because, and this is his hope, the former happens to produce more net experience-goods than the latter. Indeed, there is no moral objection to the egoist that the utilitarian can offer if it should be the case, and this, however unlikely, is surely conceivable, that by furthering the egoist's interests the maximum net experience-goodness is promoted. The utilitarian's objection to egoism is not that it is a type of immoralism; it is no better and no worse than the factual judgment that egoism tends invariably or in general to inhibit the magnitude of net experience-goodness. The latter may be true but it is not the moral judgment that the egoist and those who aid him are wrong. And if, finally, the utilitarian argues that the objective of the egoist is hopeless on the ground that no man can really gain all the experience-goods, be immune to any of the experience-evils, and thus be in a continuous transport of delight, since the right of the disaffected about him will occasion disquiet and destroy the rapturous experience which the egoist foolishly seeks to gain, we can retort: (a) this may be

true but it is not logically necessary, and (b) if it is true it is because the egoist has not lost all sense of right and wrong.

4. Finally, the utilitarian may argue that it is necessary to introduce qualitative as well as quantitative factors in speaking of the greatest quantity of net experience-goods. Some goods, it may be suggested, are preferable to others, not because of quantity of good-making factors involved but rather because of the latter's intrinsic qualitative superiority. Such a view, advanced by Mill in the case of pleasure, is so far compatible with utilitarianism as we have defined it. For in that case there is an intrinsic sense of "goodness" which is not the quality of pleasantness but the quality of goodness which some pleasant experiences have to a greater degree than others. But "good" in that sense will be, none the less, an experience-goodness, even though the magnitude of the experience-goodness will not be, in general, the magnitude of the value property, namely, pleasure, that makes for that goodness. Now it may be argued, by analogy, that in considering the greatest net good, we must take into account not only the magnitude of the net experience-goodness—whatever this may be—but also the distribution of this quality. In short, the distribution of the experience-goodness will, like the magnitude of the experience-goodness itself, provide us with a dimension for the determination of the magnitude of that good which is greater in the case of right or fair distributions of experience-goodness and less in the case of the unfair distributions contemplated by, say, an egoist. Hence with this emendation, it will be argued that what makes for the rightness of any action still remains quantity of good produced.

This, however plausible, is liable to a number of objections. (a) Suppose, for example, it is better if a given experience-goodness is shared by two persons A and B than if it is enjoyed only by A. Let us make it clear that "better" here has no reference to utility in the promotion of further experience-goodness; it is just fairer or juster, all other things apart, that A and B share the experience goodness than that A enjoy it alone, and this, it is now alleged, is because there is more good in the first situation than in the latter. But in this case the goodness in question is no longer the quality of any experience at all, for it is a goodness that is not present in the experience of A and it is a goodness that is not present in the experience of B, since it is a goodness that is present in the community constituted by A and B. Hence, instead of being a case of utilitarianism, the view is quite clearly a nonutilitarian teleological ethics of some sort or other. And if we are not to succumb to the pleasant seduction of a vague but edifying use of "good," it is imperative that we remind ourselves of the specific limitations which utilitarianism in contradistinction to other types of teleological ethics places upon the uses of "good" in terms of which the conditions of rights and obligations are to be specified. Further, (b) the position now takes on a formidable degree of complexity. The persuasiveness of utilitarianism is due in a considerable measure to its simplicity, and this is an advantage which, in general, teleological ethical theories have not hesitated to claim. For it is argued against deontological views that unless some ultimate reference is made to goods present in or promoted by actions, the appeal to right and obligation as fundamental or underivative considerations introduces a hopeless degree of complexity of competing rights and obligations which can be resolved only by a questionable appeal to intuition. But this claim of utilitarianism, we have seen, turns out to be the claim of teleology in general and with respect to the latter a number of embarrassing difficulties now emerge. For the good which an admittedly right distribution of experience-goodness provides as a bonus over and above the experience-goodness itself is surely comparable with the latter, and, if so, how? No numerical indices of distribution seem at all plausible. Those who more explicitly speak of the greatest happiness of the greatest number as better than the same happiness of a much smaller number must face the prospect of explaining how it is that we may prefer on occasion, and this is the analogue of the difficulty they pose for deontologists, a smaller to a greater quantity of experience-goodness. The problem has rarely been appreciated by proponents of teleological ethical theories, utilitarians and nonutilitarians, naturalists, intuitionists, and emotivists; but on any except a simple-minded and inadequate theory it is a matter of genuine perplexity to which any responsible moral philosopher must address himself. But, finally (c), what is meant by saying that it is better to distribute goods in one way rather than in another? I should have thought that this meant that it is morally preferable or better to do so in one way than in another. And what can this mean but that it accords far more with what is right in one case than in another? The goodness bonus, it would seem, is a moral goodness that is intelligible only in terms of the right of persons as persons which desirable distribution secures. Hence it is not merely the goodness *produced* that makes one action right. Rather it is that the goodness (and this is experience-goodness) that is produced is produced or distributed in the right way. So the logical circle still remains: Right action produces a quantity of net experience-good when that good is distributed in the right way—in a way that respects the rights of persons.

My first comment, then, apropos of utilitarianism itself is that it simply leaves out of account that which in many actions, at least, would be regarded as essential to their being right—the fact that persons as persons (all other things being equal) have rights to the goods which experience does and can provide. But my second comment, to which I now turn, is that all other things are seldom equal, and that, with respect to such inequalities, special rights and obligations arise which are equally embarrassing to utilitarianism.

B.

According to the theory under discussion, obligations are necessarily and sufficiently accounted for in terms of the net quantity of experience-goodness aroused, promoted, or likely to be promoted by the relevant actions. A familiar and critical case for the utilitarian is the commonly recognized obligation to keep one's promise.

Let me make a number of observations in order to preclude some misapprehensions which the immediately preceding statement may occasion. By the obligation in question I do not necessarily mean duty, for our obligations may conflict and compete, but a conflict of duties is a moral absurdity. It is, I suggest, a simple misrepresentation of common sense that consists in attributing to it the quite questionable thesis that we have an unqualified obligation, namely, a duty, to keep every promise, or, what amounts to the same thing, that the keeping of any promise in any situation is obligatory. Common sense surely recognizes that, while a promise creates a special obligation, the duty to perform the promised action is contingent upon certain conditions being satisfied. The problem we are now to consider is whether this special obligation is accountable for on utilitarian grounds, that is, whether the conditions of duty are those specified by the theory. Again, it is unquestionable that every action by which the agent deliberately performs what he takes to be his duty is morally good, but this is not to our present point. For the moral goodness of the action is derived from the performance of a presumed duty. It would be circular to say that the obligation to keep a promise depends upon the moral goodness of the action, since the moral goodness of the action is derived from the performance of the presumed duty.[5] But, quite apart from this, the goodness, which for the utilitarian is a necessary and sufficient condition of the obligation, is not the goodness of the action *per se* but the experience-goodness brought about or likely to be brought about by the action. Finally, let us avoid another and a very important sort of misunderstanding. To deny that quantity of experience-goodness is a necessary and a sufficient condition of obligation is not to deny that we ever have an obligation to promote experience-goodness or that experience-goodness is ever a relevant condition of obligation. The contradictory of *What alone is necessary and sufficient to an obligation is quantity of net experience-goodness produced* is not *Quantity of net experience-goodness produced is always irrelevant to problems of obligation.* Unfortunately, utilitarians have committed and encouraged just this confusion when they suggest or imply that the only alternative to their doctrine is an admittedly defective Kantian formalism. And if the utilitarian challenges us to cite other possibilities surely this, if intended as an argument in favor of his own view, is a simple case of the old *argumentum ad ignorantiam.*

Let us now consider the following imaginary situation:[6] Two explorers are at the North Pole. One has been badly injured and cannot make it back to his base. For the other to attempt to bring him back is to preclude any possibility of his own admittedly extremely desirable survival. The injured person persuades his companion that he ought to be left to his fate; but, before he is left to die, he gives his partner a sum of money and makes him promise to use it, upon his return to civilization, to pay for his son's education. The survivor returns to civilization. What obligation, if any, does he have by virtue of his promise?

Now, if utilitarianism is correct, the obligation to keep one's promise is determined wholly by the experience-goods produced or likely to be produced by the action. It would seem therefore that nothing that has happened in the past and only what can be expected in the future is relevant. For the conditions of obligation are prospective, not retrospective. Hence the survivor ought (since ought is wholly determined by consequences) to ignore the promise and act in just the way he ought to act if he were suddenly to come upon the money through sheerest accident. But this does violence to our moral sensibilities. And no sensible utilitarian would recommend this course of action. Instead he will reply in some one or more of the following ways:

1. He may argue that the moral value of promise-keeping pertains not to the individual action of keeping a promise, but to the whole institution of promises, that a failure to keep a promise which would bring even unfortunate consequences in its train is frowned upon, and rightly so, because the failure weakens confidence in, and thus weakens or destroys the utility of, promises in general. Hence the utilitarian will argue that in considering the utility of the action we consider the utility of the type of action. This is, of course, the well-known kind of indirect argument which Hume has made familiar in the case of the rules of property.[7] But this will not do in the special case imagined. For the utility of keeping a promise in so far as

[5] H. A. Prichard, "Does Moral Philosophy Rest on a Mistake?" *Mind*, n. s. 21 (1912), 26 [pp. 61–72 above.].

[6] The example is Carritt's in *Ethical and Political Thinking* (Oxford: Clarendon Press, 1947), p. 64.

[7] *A Treatise of Human Nature*, Bk. III, p. II, sec. 2, p. 497 of the Selby-Bigge edition.

it promotes the confidence in, and the continued operation of, the useful system of promises is a utility that derives from the publicity accorded the act, and the harm done to the highly useful system of promises by the failure to keep a promise is a harm derived from the weakened confidence in promisers who are known to break their promises. Hence, to this indirect argument, the retort "Keep it quiet" is altogether appropriate.[8] And the safely returned explorer, reasoning in accordance with strict utilitarian principles, can now say to himself: "The utility of the system of promises will in no way be impaired if my failure to keep the promise I made is kept secret, and the utility of the money I now have will be maximized if I were to proceed intelligently in the way I ought to proceed if I had simply stumbled upon the money through the sheerest accident. Hence, if I promote no more net goods in the experience of men by keeping my promise than by assisting the Society for the Propagation of Cacti and Other Succulents, there is no reason for saying that I ought to keep my promise."

2. The utilitarian might employ a more subtle form of the indirect argument. He may appeal to the consequences upon the agent himself of his failure to keep his promise. And these consequences, he will argue, are surely harmful, for the failure to keep the promise will gnaw at his moral vitals. It will weaken his disposition to keep promises in normal situations. It will lead him to distrust others who offer their promises to him and hence help to weaken the highly useful system of promises. But this reply will not do either. For the harm that results in the character of the promiser is a harm that rests upon the promiser's presumption that he has an obligation to keep his promise, the consciousness that he ought to weigh his promise carefully, and the fear that others may be tempted, with unfortunate consequences, in like situations. And if this is the nature of the reply, the logic is manifestly unsound. For the utilitarian cannot argue that the survivor ought to keep his promise because of the effect upon him of his recognition of his obligation unless there is the recognition of an obligation. Hence the utilitarian must intend, not that there is the recognition of an obligation, but that the survivor is so disposed, that he *feels* morally bound, even though he is not morally bound at all, to keep his promise, and that this disposition or character is eminently useful on the whole. But the question of the utility *on the whole* is beside the point; it may be granted by the nonutilitarian. What is at issue is the assertion, in effect, that the survivor, in his special case, is not obligated. For this is to assert, in effect, that, if the survivor were sufficiently circumspect and free from the ordinarily useful effects of sentiment and habit, he would consider this disposition morally pernicious in the special situation in which he is placed.

But if this is the nature of the utilitarian's reply, the dispute between the utilitarian and his critic is no longer philosophical but moral. And I need hardly comment upon the hopeless a priorism of anyone who would argue that our imaginary survivor has no real obligation since his philosophical theory—utilitarianism—constrains him to this conclusion. It would be odd, to say the least, to appeal to a philosophical theory to support a moral judgment which, if valid, would be just the kind of consideration among others offered in support of the philosophical theory in question. The issue is, then, moral, not philosophical; and, concerning this issue, the parties involved can only hope that their moral judgment is not the unfortunate expression of an initial or a prioristic philosophical bias. But if, as I imagine

[8] Carritt, op. cit., p. 64, attributes this reply to utilitarianism to Mabbott, in "Punishment," *Mind* (April 1939), 155–157 [pp. 90–92 above].

we would, when we examine the conditions of moral judgment and engage in our imaginary moral experiment, we concede that our imaginary survivor does have an obligation by virtue of his promise, other and more desperate measures of defense must be adopted by the utilitarian.

3. I shall deal summarily with a familiar query: "Surely you don't believe that anyone has an obligation to keep a promise when keeping it promotes great pain, suffering, ill-being?" I need scarely comment upon the foolishness of this defense. The contradictory of "Quantity of experience-good is a necessary and sufficient condition of obligation" is not "We have obligations to act in such a way as to promote quantity of experience-evil." In order to show that quantity of net experience-good is not a necessary and sufficient condition of obligation, we need only show either that it is not a necessary, or that it is not a sufficient, condition. And in our example it clearly is not a necessary condition of obligation since the survivor would be obligated to keep his promise if he had to choose only between keeping his promise and acting in some other way which produced no more net experience-good.

4. I consider, finally, the following defense: "Surely you don't believe that one may have an obligation to keep a promise when there is no good promoted! Isn't the keeping of a promise desirable because it is desirable, even in the exceptional case of our survivor, that men abide by general rules of conduct? And isn't a firmly established set of general rules, which all respect, an indispensable condition of any ideal community of persons?" To this no one would, I trust, object. An ideal community is just such a community in which men are bound by general rules and in which their respect for these rules is manifest and quite different from an attention that springs from the fear of being caught and punished. This, so far, is consistent with the best in the Kantian philosophy of morals. But in reply to this line of defense our comments parallel precisely those made earlier in connection with the appeal to a goodness alleged to obtain in the case of the right distribution of experience-goods. For (a) the goodness thus served and promoted is not experience-goodness at all, but the goodness alleged to obtain in a community of men. At this point utilitarianism has been abandoned in favor of some presumably nonutilitarian teleological ethics; (b) there are the important problems of the commensurability of the goodness of this community with experience-goodness. For the community is good in a sense distinct from the sense in which an experience is good, and how far experience-goods may be subverted in order to insure this good of a community is a problem which teleologists in ethical theory must now face as the analogue of the difficulties they are prone to raise concerning the comparison of obligations on the familiar deontological theories. And finally (c) what is meant by saying that it is good that men honor and respect *some* general rules of conduct? I should have thought that the good thus served is a moral good. And I should have thought that the moral good in question is a good that consists precisely in the respect paid to the familiar dictum that what is right in one case is right in any similar case, that, as Kant long ago taught us, mere difference in personal identity, like many another nonmoral difference, makes no difference to our moral obligations. It seems, then, quite possible that the good that is served by one who respects the moral rule concerning the keeping of promises is a good that derives from recognizing and meeting an obligation.

My second comment, then, is that utilitarianism simply fails to account for certain special rights and obligations. The logic of the situation would remain unchanged by considering the equally famous case of the punishment of the innocent. But I have contented myself with the examination of promises. And I conclude that utilitarianism simply cannot explain the special obligation in question except by explaining it away. Hume may well have been correct when he described a promise as "a form of words," namely, a ritual. But he and the utilitarians who follow him are mistaken either in their analysis of obligation or in their account of the conditions of its occurrence. For it is the function of the form of words used "I promise, etc." to solicit the trust of the promisee and thereby to place the promiser under a special obligation to meet the promisee's special moral demand, in circumstances which cannot be specified by reference to quantity of net experience-good alone.

Stuart M. Brown, Jr. / Duty and the production of good

Utilitarians claim that any act, productive of good, is either right or dutiful, and that an act is right or dutiful only if it is productive of good. The value of any act, that is to say, is wholly instrumental or extrinsic.

The utilitarian does not deny the obvious fact that an intrinsic value is commonly claimed for moral acts. But this intrinsic value cannot according to the utilitarian be rationally justified. For, he asserts, the only reason for acting in certain ways and for refusing to act in others is the production of good and the avoidance of evil. But since an act has value only in so far as there are reasons for doing it, and since the only reason for doing any act is the production of good, an act is valuable only as good-producing.

For two centuries, nonutilitarian philosophers have been attacking this position and defending a claim to the intrinsic value of morally right and dutiful acts. They have accused the utilitarians of confusing a perfectly valid reason for doing an act with a reason for doing the act as a duty. They have charged utilitarians with failure to distinguish between right acts, which there is some reason for doing, and dutiful acts, which as right and reasonable are justified by peculiarly moral reasons. Utilitarianism, they have argued, has mistakenly identified the nonmoral usage of "ought," in statements concerning the proper and improper employment of implements and equipment, with a moral usage of "ought" in judgments justifying praise or blame, punishment or reward. But the arguments supporting these charges have left many utilitarians unconvinced. I shall attempt, therefore, by arguments somewhat different from the traditional ones, to prove the nonutilitarian's case.

My arguments compose one general thesis: utilitarians, who are not avowed moral skeptics and who seriously claim to recognize moral obligations, must affirm or assume a complete and necessary coincidence between dutiful and good-producing

Reprinted from THE PHILOSOPHICAL REVIEW, *vol. 61 (July 1952), pp. 298–311 by permission of the author and editors.*

acts; but this coincidence cannot reasonably and consistently be maintained.

This complete and necessary coincidence can be made out in one or the other of two alternative ways. Some utilitarians, like Bentham and Moore in *Principia Ethica,* have held that the terms "dutiful" and "productive of the greatest good" are precisely identical in meaning. Other utilitarians, including Moore himself in the little book entitled *Ethics,* have held that, while in one clear sense these terms do not have a precisely identical meaning, they nevertheless have an identical usage in the sense of being applicable only to one and the same act.

The alternative chosen by Bentham and by Moore in *Principia Ethica* is superficially the stronger of the two. Bentham simply denies to "ought" and "right" any meaning other than "good-producing." When interpreted as referring to acts, as conforming or not conforming to the principle of utility, "the words *ought,* and *right* and *wrong,* and others of that stamp, have a meaning: when otherwise [interpreted], they have none."[1] Simply to state a principle of conduct incompatible with those of the principle of utility is, Bentham insists, to confute it.[2] And when he comes to examine ethical theories alternative to his own, he claims that they are either forms of utilitarianism in disguise or expressions of mere sentiment and unreasoned opinion.[3] Because "dutiful" and "productive of greatest good" are identical in meaning, the utilitarian principle simply states a logically necessary relationship between these two terms. To deny this principle, as it must be denied by any nonutilitarian theory, is to formulate a self-contradiction. To try to say positively what any nonutilitarian rule affirms is only to utter nonsense, to express a sentiment irrationally protesting the unassailable rationality of utility theory.

In *Principia Ethica,* Moore's statement of this utilitarian thesis is much more precise and clear than Bentham's. It is demonstrably certain, Moore insists, that "the assertion 'I am morally bound to perform this action' is identical with the assertion 'This action will produce the greatest possible amount of good in the Universe.' "[4] In the sense, that is, in which Moore thought good to be indefinable, duty is definable. In place of the word "duty" as it occurs in any sentence, another linguistic phrase about the production of good in the Universe can be substituted without change or loss in meaning. This other phrase, identical in meaning with "duty," is the definition of "duty."

But this way of establishing the necessary coincidence is disastrous to the utilitarian position as a moral theory. It is disastrous because, by identifying the meanings of "dutiful" and "good-producing," a utilitarian cannot use the notion of "good-producing" as the reason why acts are dutiful. The reason why anything is what it is cannot be provided in any phrase that is precisely synonymous with some other word for the thing. If I ask "Why ought I to return these borrowed books?" I am given no answer when, "dutiful" and "good-producing" being synonmyms, you reply "Because returning these books will produce the greatest good under the circumstances." The assertion of different sentences, asserting exactly the same thing with exactly the same meaning, is simply the reassertion of whatever claim is made in the first statement.

This objection eliminates as a reason only the general phrase "Because this act is productive of the greatest good." It does not eliminate, as a reason, a specific prediction about the good which some par-

[1] *Principles of Morals and Legislation,* chap. i, sec. 10.

[2] Ibid., chap. ii, sec. 1.

[3] Ibid., chap. ii, sec. 14.

[4] *Principia Ethica,* chap. v, sec. 89.

ticular act is likely to produce. For there is a clear difference in meaning between the general claim "This act will produce the greatest possible good," which as identical with "This act is dutiful" cannot be a reason, and the specific factual statement "This act will produce such and such particular goods." Such a specific prediction, it may be alleged, is all a utilitarian requires as a reason in support of moral judgments and all that he is actually intending to claim.

But if this is all he is actually intending to claim, then his position is utterly paradoxical. For in holding that "dutiful" means "good-producing" and nothing else intelligible, he cannot explain how it happens that the commonest question in ordinary moral discourse has the form "Why ought I, in this instance, to do so and so?" People, who very obviously do understand what "ought" means in many, or even most moral situations, ask just this question. Understanding what "ought" means in most situations, which on this view is understanding that it means "good-producing," people nevertheless, in situations where there is moral doubt, do ask "Why ought I to do this?" and do not ask "What advantage or profit is to be gained by doing this?" A man, who understands the meaning of "ought" to be "good-producing," can only be in doubt as to where the greater profit lies. Yet instead of asking for specific information about profit and advantage, he asks "Why?" as if he were inquiring for a more general reason, like the notion "good-producing." Not only does he ask if he were inquiring for a general reason, he is, as often as not, satisfied when such general reasons are given him. But from this, it apparently follows that people, who know perfectly well what "ought" means in most cases of its use, suddenly become puzzled as to just what it means and only want to be reassured as to the correctness of their normal usage. Nevertheless, this being what they want, why do they not ask explicitly about the meaning of "ought"? Apparently, anybody who asks this question "Why?" is asking an utterly confused question and cannot be supposed to know what it is he is trying to ask. For it cannot be supposed that anyone who clearly knows what he is asking can put his question in a linguistic form which must always be interpreted in one or the other of two quite different ways and can never be interpreted as the question it appears to be. What is paradoxical in all of this is that the utilitarian should claim, on the one hand, to make ordinary moral experience intelligible and be unable, on the other, to make sense of the commonest question in ordinary moral discourse.

There is then a decisive objection to the claim that "dutiful" and "good-producing" are synonyms. This objection is not that these terms have distinct meanings, though this is true and can be shown. The decisive objection is that, assuming this synonymy, the utilitarian cannot accomplish his task as an ethical theorist. He can neither explain the questions in which we ask for moral reasons nor give us reasons for answering such questions.

But the utilitarian can deny the distinction between dutiful and good-producing acts in a somewhat different way. He may allow or even insist that "dutiful" and "good-producing" are not synonymous terms but maintain that each term, nevertheless, necessarily implies the other. Thus, the statement "All dutiful acts are productive of the greatest good" is at once informative and analytic. It cannot be denied without self-contradiction. But when it is asserted in answer to the question "Why is this a duty?" it provides information which is not given in the initial claim "This is your duty."

This is the position adopted by Moore in *Ethics.* At the time *Ethics* was written, it was quite as plain to Moore that "dutiful" and "good-producing" are not synonymous[5] as it had previously seemed demonstrably certain to him that they are synonymous.[6] The statement "It is always our duty to do what will have the best possible consequences" is not, Moore now correctly asserts, the mere tautology it would necessarily have to be if the alleged synonymy were true.[7] But the two terms, Moore holds, are logically equivalent. Despite a difference in meaning, they have exactly and necessarily the same application. Whatever act is a duty is always also productive of the greatest good, and whatever act produces the greatest good is always also a duty.[8]

Utilitarianism, on this second alternative, meets all the objections urged against the position taken by Bentham and by Moore in *Principia Ethica.* For assuming that "dutiful" and "good-producing" are not synonyms, a man who understands how to use "dutiful" may, in specific circumstances, ask for grounds supporting the claim "This is your duty." The assertion "This will produce the greatest good" is an answer. In this manner, the commonest question in ordinary moral discourse is given both an explanation as the question it appears to be and the kind of reason which seems to qualify as an answer.

Nevertheless, this way of denying the distinction between dutiful and good-producing acts is also untenable. The arguments, which show this, are equally valid against the position of Bentham.

For while it is now admitted, as it must be, that "dutiful" and "good-producing" mean somewhat different things, no effort is made to account for this difference in meaning. Different as the meanings of the two words may be, the utilitarian insists upon their logical equivalence. Against this all too casual and dogmatic utilitarian effort to make the terms either synonymous or equivalent, two distinct objections may be made.

On the one hand, it may be objected that the utilitarian's thesis fails to explain the language of moral men. By such men, it is thought that certain acts, in given circumstances, are absolutely and unconditionally dutiful. We may, for example, find Kant guilty of a gruesome error when he held, in answering the objection of Benjamin Constant, that it is our duty not to lie, even to save a friend from death. Our duty in this particular situation, we claim, is to save the friend from the murderer. But if it is our duty to do this, then under these circumstances saving the friend is right and absolutely so. We do not calculate consequences. We do not stop to inquire what good our friend will in the future be to us or to himself or to the community. And if a man, under such circumstances, were to make these calculations, we should judge him to be immoral. For reasons of this sort, Sidgwick, who as a utilitarian would have been gratified to find "dutiful" equivalent to "good-producing," was forced to deny the adequacy of the utilitarian analysis of these terms,[9] and to supplement utilitarian theory by appeals to a rational intuition.

Further, while all acts have some consequences and are in some degree productive of good and bad, it is commonly supposed that some acts are wholly lacking in moral significance. To wear a loud orange tie rather than a maroon one, to hear Wagner rather than Mozart, to cut one's salad with a knife rather than a fork—such acts, even where they offend more people than they please, pose questions of taste and manners rather than morals. To make a moral issue of such acts is to appear ridiculous, to introduce obligations into spheres of activity where esthetic criteria are funda-

[5] *Ethics* (New York: H. Holt and Co., 1912), p. 173.

[6] *Principia Ethica*, chap. v, sec. 89.

[7] *Ethics*, p. 173.

[8] Ibid., p. 172.

[9] *Methods of Ethics*, Bk. I, chap. iii, sec. 1.

mental, and so to put a discernible strain on language. Yet this is precisely what the utilitarian requires of us. For the utilitarian is just as puritanical as the strictest puritan. Because all acts have some consequences for good or evil, all acts on utility theory are of moral concern. In the absence of religious reasons for being concerned with the minutiae of life, the utilitarian nevertheless demands this concern and provides an old-age home for that honorable but pathetic figure of fun, the last puritan.

On the other hand, it may be objected that the utilitarian's thesis cannot possibly be substantiated and cannot, therefore, be other than arbitrary. For on the utilitarian account of the matter, there is no distinction between the *act* as dutiful and the *act* as productive of the greatest good. Any distinction we make must be between two different words for one and the same act or between the *meanings* of these words where meaning is psychological rather than logical. But this can be substantiated only by an appeal to usage which, as I have already shown, completely fails to support it. For example, there is no difference between the state of being married and the state of being wed, though "married" and "wed" are different words and psychologically may mean somewhat different things. But suppose that, as a fundamental thesis of a philosophical theory, I deny any difference between marriage and wedlock. On what grounds now would my thesis be dubitable; and how, if dubitable, could it be substantiated? Clearly, I think, the only reason for doubting such a thesis directly would be the failure of usage to accord with it. And the only way of supporting it, if it is doubted, is by an appeal to usage. In the case of such words as "marriage" and "wedlock," or of both of these and the phrase "united as husband and wife," the equivalence is so clear and so conclusively supported by usage that the bare assertion of it is sufficient. Far from its being mere dogmatism merely to assert it, any argument to substantiate it would be silly, because no argument could employ premises more certain than the assertion itself. In quite the same way, it would be neither dogmatic nor arbitrary simply to assert the equivalence of "dutiful" and "good-producing," if this equivalence were evident once we stopped to reflect upon it. But after serious and conscientious reflection, men of moral insight and nonutilitarian theorists deny the alleged equivalence altogether. The utilitarian principle, claimed by the utilitarian to be analytic, is dismissed by the nonutilitarian as false. This being the case, the utilitarian's continued assertion of the principle as analytic and of the key terms in it as equivalent is utterly arbitrary and dogmatic.

Should it be supposed that there are arguments by which the utilitarian can prove the alleged equivalence, it can be shown that the very same difficulty breaks out again in a different place. To show that the terms "dutiful" and "good-producing" mutually imply each other, the utilitarian must employ in the premises of any argument, notions which mutually imply each other. He may say, for example, that "right" and "good-producing" are equivalents, that any dutiful act is right, and that any dutiful act is therefore productive of good. But the nonutilitarian's reply is obvious: the premise asserting the equivalence of "right" and "good-producing" is false, for a morally right act is commonly and correctly supposed to be right, under some circumstances, irrespective of consequences.

Or, the utilitarian will say: When you assert "You ought to put an edge on your screwdriver," this is equivalent to "Putting an edge on your screwdriver will produce the greatest good." Thus, when you assert "You ought to return borrowed goods," this is equivalent to "Returning borrowed goods is productive of the greatest good." And here, the nonutilitarian replies that there are different usages of "ought," that the usage of "ought" in the premise is nonmoral whereas the usage in the conclusion is moral, and that the conclusion therefore does not follow from the premise.

But why, it may be urged, must the utilitarian take the utility principle as analytic? Why may he not admit that duty is one thing and the production of good another, but insist that *in fact* the two do for the most part coincide? Under a great many conditions, it is a duty to produce the greatest possible good. Under other conditions, the act productive of the greatest good is *at the same time* a duty. And in those rare cases where duty and interest do conflict, still one's interest is a value even if not a moral value. To adopt the utility principle, the argument concludes, is to preserve most moral goods together with the nonmoral ones.

Although it is legitimate for a utilitarian to tell us, in such a manner, what on the whole we ought to do, this is not an argument for a utilitarian theory but an argument for the use of the utilitarian principle in practice. The practical use of this principle may indeed be justified under specific historical and sociological conditions: where, that is, the members of a community are men of moral character, aware of the difference between the dutifulness of an act and its productiveness of goods; and where in fact each act tends to have both a value as dutiful and an instrumental value as good-producing. In the eighteenth century, when the universe was assumed to be a rational and systematically lawful system, such conditions were thought to prevail. Shaftesbury, Butler, Hutcheson, and Kant were among the nonutilitarians who thought this. Some of these nonutilitarians quite consistently employed the notion of "good-producing" as a reason *for doing* the dutiful *act.* But none of them employed the notion as the reason why an act is *dutiful.* The dutifulness of an act was tested on one set of criteria, and the expediency of it was tested on another and independent set. Even where they claimed that duty and expediency must necessarily coincide, the necessity was taken as *synthetic a priori* and not *analytic.* Since for all of these men the utility principle was either merely *synthetic* or at the most *synthetic a priori,* they all admitted cases where, so far as any man can know, duty and expediency either do not, or do not appear, to coincide. These were for them the crucial cases, for the way a man acts in them will attest his possession or lack of moral character. Hence as philosophers rather than counselors, the eighteenth-century nonutilitarians were preoccupied either with questions about virtue, as this was manifested in cases of real or apparent conflict between duty and expediency, or with problems in the metaphysics of morals as elucidating the grounds of *synthetic a priori* principles.

The appeal to fact, in order to maintain utilitarianism as a philosophical theory, is therefore illicit. For such an appeal can be successful only where the criterion of duty is distinct from and independent of the criterion of expediency. But to employ two independent criteria is to allow, what no utilitarian philosopher can either admit or explain, that any given act may have two distinct values and that, in any given situation, it may be impossible in practice to know how to realize both. On the one hand, then, the utility principle for a utilitarian theory cannot be *synthetic;* on the other hand, since moral usage is not in accord with it, the claim that it is *analytic* in any significant sense is false.

But the utilitarian may protest against the very notion of philosophy as I am using it to criticize his theory. He may accuse me of missing his entire point. The value of anything, he may insist, is adequately tested only by appeal to practical consequences. This must be the value of the utility principle as well as of everything else. In order to dismiss the utility principle, the nonutilitarian must show that it has bad consequences or consequences different from and less good than nonutilitarian principles.

The nonutilitarian, however, has never found this challenge particularly difficult to meet. For if the utilitarian principle is what on utility theory it must consistently be held to be, then this principle breaks down in practice and has morally absurd consequences.

It breaks down in practice, because it is impossible in the situations of ordinary life to foresee all the consequences of an act. The alternative which, in a given situation, seems likely to produce the greatest good may not in fact produce it. In fact, the alternative which seems productive of greatest evil may in the long run and in an unforeseeable future turn out to have been best. From this, one or the other of two conclusions follows. Either men have no duties, since what is a duty and what is not can never be known at the moment when we must act decisively in one way or another. Or men have the duty to do what no man possibly can do; that is, a duty to produce through action in the present, a good which turns out to be good only in an unpredictable future. The principle of utility, as a rule capable of guiding the conduct of men in specific situations, thus breaks down. For there is no practical difference between saying "I have no duties" and saying "I have duties but can neither know nor perform them."

On the utilitarian principle, taken strictly, this difficulty occurs in respect to every act. But even if it were admitted that, in practice, the difficulty occurs in serious form only in respect to some acts rather than all, the cases where it does occur are precisely those in which we have need of a moral principle. We need moral principles, in practice, only where there is a serious doubt as to which of several alternative acts is our duty. In ordinary life, there are many cases where no such serious doubt arises. We are frequently confronted, for example, with alternatives, one of which is a relatively clear case of good and the other a relatively clear case of evil. So long as the utilitarian refuses to allow the unforeseeable consequences in an unpredictable future to make a difficulty for these cases, the reason must be that no philosophical theory with practical applications is justified in imposing an arbitrary theoretical doubt upon what in practice is indubitable. The utility principle, then, is to be taken as applicable only to cases where there is serious doubt for practice and is to be justified by the guidance it gives in these cases. It is properly applicable only when we are faced with a choice between two genuine goods or two genuine evils. But these are precisely the cases which, on utility theory, are theoretically undecidable. For in these cases, good is weighted against good and evil against evil in a balance so delicate that only future and unpredictable consequences will on utility theory relevantly resolve the doubt. Far from being self-justifying as of instrumental value, the utility principle justifies coin-flipping in the only situations to which, in this version, it is applicable.

The difficulty here is not that borderline and undecidable cases arise for utilitarianism. Borderline and undecidable cases may arise for the moral rules of any ethical theory with practical application. What may arise for any ethical theory whatsoever cannot be urged as an objection to any one type of theory. The difficulty for utilitarianism is simply that for it no case is in principle decidable at the time when a decision must in practice be made.

Faced with this difficulty, many utilitarians abandon the principle altogether and appeal instead to commonly accepted moral maxims. These maxims, they allege, are the products of racial and cultural wisdom, and indicate those acts that in the long course of history have proven themselves most productive of good. Wherever, therefore, a case of genuine moral doubt arises, duty is discharged by acting in accordance with the moral laws of one's community.

But this way out of the difficulty is disastrous for utilitarian theory. First, it is disastrous because the difficulty itself is returned in the guise of its own solution. Serious cases of moral doubt never arise in a moral vacuum. A doubt that arises without moral reasons for doubting is idle. It presents no practical moral problem and no issue of interest to ethical philosophers. What we doubt, when we doubt for moral reasons, is the adequacy of commonly accepted maxims or of conditioned patterns of behavior. We are confronted with alternatives each of which is justified by some commonly accepted rule or by some culturally established pattern of action. Far from offering any pat solution to difficult moral problems, the moral rules of common sense, which are neither systematic nor precise, are the primary objects of doubt. What is in doubt, in strictly utilitarian terms, must be the utility value of customary maxims, and no such doubt can be settled by appeal simply to maxims as customary.

Secondly, if a man is dubious of the good likely to be produced by given acts in a specific circumstance, he must reasonably doubt the adequacy of any applicable moral rule justified by appeal to the production of good. The dubious case confronting him is a crucial test case for the utility value of any moral maxim. The utilitarian cannot reasonably claim both that moral maxims are justified by utility value and that this value is to be assumed in all cases where it is dubitable.

And thirdly, the definition of a dutiful act has now been radically modified. In any difficult case, it is one's duty to act in accordance with moral maxims, whether or not the act realizes good. What has primary moral value is not an act, because an act in accordance with a maxim may not in fact produce good. What has primary moral value is a maxim, action in accordance with which tends on the whole to produce good. And with this shift in the fundamental emphasis of his theory, the utilitarian is forced to retire from the field of moral philosophy. For, on the one hand, what has primary moral value is never a good rule of action, but rather the good act; and, on the other, the utilitarian has allowed the goodness of a dutiful act, which need not produce good, to be intrinsic.

Rather than lose their case in this manner, a utilitarian may take the consistent but morally absurd alternative. He may hold it a duty to produce the greatest good even where it is impossible in practice to know which of several acts will accomplish this. The intrinsic value of an act, as the moral act of a moral man, is denied, and no value can accrue to acts as done for moral reasons on moral motives. But this ruthlessly consistent and only consistent form of utilitarianism rends the delicate fabric of moral notions beyond possibility of recognition or repair. On this alternative, we should hold men responsible for the dereliction of duties which neither they nor anyone else can reasonably discharge. We should give as the reason why such acts are dutiful a reason which the agent could not employ to determine what his duty is. We should say it makes no difference to our judgment of the moral value of an act, producing great good or great evil, whether the agent acted rationally or irrationally, with good intentions or bad ones, while he was well and conscious or ill and unaware of what he was doing. We should say, in short, that the value of a good act is precisely like the value of a good ax. Just as the value of a poor ax is not increased by the excellent repute of its manufacturer or the good intentions of a hardware merchant, so the instrumental value of a human act is not modified by differences in the agency of its production. The moral absurdity of consistent utilitarianism has its source in this: moral values, unlike instrumental values, are intimately related to and in part determined by the human agency of production.

In the end, the fundamental error of utilitarianism is its excessive rationalism, its peculiar reliance upon a self-evident analytic principle and its insensitive denial of any values failing to justify themselves on the strict canons of prudential reasoning. This is simply a narrow-minded and self-consciously rationalistic form of Platonic moral philosophy. It appeals, on the one hand, to rational intuition and to the self-evidence of the theoretically fundamental principles. On the other hand, it appeals to prudence and to the profit to be gained by being moral in practice. But since utilitarianism is modeled on this pattern of Greek rationalism, its failure to account for moral obligations is understandable. For in Platonic philosophy, the notion of moral obligation is never brought into sharp focus and never becomes a fundamental problem for ethical theory.

The moral experience, out of which the notion of obligation was crystallized, is Stoic, Jewish, and Christian. It arises out of the conviction that men as individuals frequently come to stand in peculiarly noninstrumental and nonnaturalistic relationships to each other and to their gods. Where such relationships prevail, a man may claim a moral right to be treated in accordance with them and not to have himself and his acts assessed wholly as instruments. He has a moral duty to act in regard to others in a manner appropriate to this relationship. To give, under these circumstances, a reason in support of an alleged obligation is to state more fully the moral relationship out of which the specific duty arises. The Old Testament itself provides a model for such ethical reasoning. The reason why a Jew of Moses' time was obliged to act in accordance with some specific law is that the obligation to act was assumed by him as his part of a sacred covenant with God. The obligation to return a borrowed book is assumed by the borrower in the act of borrowing it. Borrowing is possible, just as covenants are possible, only between agents who stand to each other in those moral relationships of which obligations and their recognition are indispensable parts.

Henry David Aiken / Definitions, factual premises, and ethical conclusions

We have seen that the claim to infer significant ethical propositions from definitions of ethical terms, which appears to constitute the essence of the naturalistic fallacy, is a special case of a more general fallacious claim, namely the claim to deduce ethical propositions from ones which are admittedly non-ethical."[1] In these words Mr. A. N. Prior sums up—I think very fairly—a view which many philosophers have come to regard as the fundamental point of departure for any adequate analysis of moral discourse. It, or something like it, is also popular among social scientists who like to insist upon the ethical "neutrality" of their disciplines.[2]

[1] A. N. Prior, *Logic and the Basis of Ethics,* (Oxford: Clarendon Press, 1949), p. 95.

[2] For example, see Max Weber, *The Methodology of the Social Sciences,* ed. Shils and Finch (Glencoe, Ill.: Free Press, 1949), pp. 1–113. For my part Weber's prolonged discussion does little to clarify the problems at issue. In fact, I must confess that Weber's powers as methodologist seem to me generally quite overrated.

Despite the fact, however, that some of the best minds in recent philosophy have, for a variety of reasons, maintained the view, it seems to me to be correct only in certain very limited senses. And even in these senses it is, as usually formulated, seriously misleading. There are other, more important senses in which, as I shall presently try to show, the contrary position must be upheld. My reasons for this contention do not involve a defense of ethical naturalism.

Let us begin by reviewing those respects in which the view—I will henceforth refer to it as antidescriptivism—might plausibly be maintained.

Consider first the wider version, namely the thesis that the claim to deduce ethical proposition from ones admitted to be nonethical is fallacious. Now by "ethical proposition" let us here understand "any judgment containing such words as 'ought,' 'right,' and 'desirable' which is used normatively to prescribe that something is to be done or approved." And by "nonethical proposition" let us under-

Reprinted from THE PHILOSOPHICAL REVIEW, *vol. 61 (July 1952), pp. 331–348 by permission of the author and editors.*

stand "any statement of fact or of logic to which the predicates 'true,' 'false,' or 'probable' may be ascribed, and in which no sign functions essentially in the prescriptive or imperative mode." Let us agree also that the laws of logic by which alone one statement can be validly deduced from another apply only to propositions which are true or false.[3] Granted these assumptions, it is not hard to see in what sense it would be acceptable to say that ethical propositions cannot be deduced from nonethical premises. To suppose the contrary, it might plausibly be held, would be simply to involve oneself in a fundamental confusion of categories.[4]

Consider next the narrower version of antidescriptivism, namely the thesis that significant ethical propositions cannot be validly inferred from definitions of ethical terms. For present purposes let us understand roughly by "definition" "any statement in which the purely descriptive or logical meaning of an expression is stipulated, analyzed, or otherwise characterized." Here again, given the previous interpretation of "ethical propositions," it would be simply an egregious blunder to try to infer a significant ethical proposition from the definition of an ethical term—assuming, for the nonce, that it has one. The blunder would be comparable in some ways, despite evident differences, to the error of trying to infer a nonlinguistic statement of fact from the analysis of a concept.

So far, then, the contentions of antidescriptivism, in both its wider and its narrower versions, may perhaps be granted. To this extent, we can agree that at the bottom there really *are* basic categorical mistakes inherent in the "naturalistic fallacy," even though the arguments intended to show this by Moore and his followers are quite inconclusive.[5] Unless these statements are immediately qualified, however, they tend to be misleading. For they appear to convey the impression, and indeed have conveyed the impression to a generation of moral philosophers, that statements of fact provide no proper basis for the support of normative ethical propositions, and that in no sense could it be reasonably supposed that significant ethical propositions may be legitimately inferred from definitions of ethical terms.

II

Let us see how such an impression has arisen. We may begin by mentioning a number of the most influential conceptions of "definition" in moral philosophy. First the view expressed by Moore in *Principia Ethica:* "What, then, is good? How is good to be defined? Now, it may be thought that this is a verbal question. A definition does indeed often mean the expressing of one word's meaning in other words. But this is not the sort of definition I am asking for. . . . My business is solely with that object or idea, which I hold, rightly or wrongly, that the word is generally used to stand for. What I want to discover is the nature of that object or idea. . . ."[6]

[3] I am, of course, here using the terms "true" and "false" in their stricter or cognitive sense. Other looser and more figurative senses are irrelevant to the present point. In another place I will have something to say about these senses as employed in moral discourse.

[4] Careful reading of such versions of the emotive theory as that of Profesor Ayer suggests that perhaps nothing more was implied by the proponents of the theory than I have stated in this and the following paragraphs. The not entirely unjustified opposition to the view was largely due to misleading formulations. Cf. *Language, Truth and Logic* (New York: Dover Publications, 1952), pp. 105–106.

[5] Cf. William Frankena, "The Naturalistic Fallacy," *Mind* 48 (1939), pp. 472 ff. Cf. also A. N. Prior, *Logic*, pp. 1–12, 95–107.

[6] *Principia Ethica* (Cambridge: The University Press, 1903), p. 6.

And again, "definitions of the kind that I was asking for, definitions which describe the real nature of the object or notion denoted by a word, and which do not merely tell us what the word is used to mean, are only possible when the object or notion in question is something complex."[7] A similar conception is to be found in Perry's *General Theory of Value:* "No one would be disposed to deny that there is a common something in truth, goodness, legality, wealth, beauty and piety that distinguishes them from gravitation and chemical affinity. It is the express business of theory of value to discover what this something is; to define the genus, and discover the differentiae of the species. By means of such definitions and systematic connections theory of value may unify the special philosophical and social sciences enumerated above and arbitrate between them."[8] Whether either of these conceptions of definition is defensible as it stands we fortunately do not now have to consider. What is of interest to us here is that both of them are designed to serve an essentially cognitive function, whether it be that of factual knowledge, logical analysis, or linguistic transformation. Other roles of symbols are simply ignored.

We are now faced with an interesting dilemma; if, on the one hand, we insist on construing "definition" in terms of the above mentioned conceptions, it would appear that many statements occurring in moral philosophy that are normally interpreted as definitions simply are not so at all; but, if, on the other hand, we insist on construing such statements as bona fide definitions, then these theories of definition must be regarded as faulty, since they fail to characterize properly the statements in question.

In either case, however, we must conclude that the intentions of many moral philosophers who have made such statements have been radically misunderstood. And the source of the misunderstanding must be attributed to those who, like Moore, have insisted upon applying the term "definition," itself conceived in essentially cognitive or descriptive terms, to expressions whose roles are primarily noncognitive. It is these analysts who are responsible for the misleading implications of the thesis that the claim to infer an ethical conclusion from the definition of an ethical term is fallacious. For, although as we have seen, they are correct in maintaining that, in the sense considered above, ethical conclusions cannot be inferred from definitions of ethical terms, they mislead us into supposing that those charged with commission of the fallacy actually *did* claim to draw such inferences. The truth is that, in the case of most of the moral philosophers charged with this claim, what they really asserted was something utterly different. To be sure such philosophers often did draw ethical conclusions from "definitions" of ethical terms (together with other premises which were usually factual). But their definitions were not, and were never intended to be, construed as descriptive definitions in any of the senses considered above.

For purposes of illustration, let us briefly consider the doctrine known traditionally as hedonism. I shall discuss it in the form popularized by J. S. Mill and subsequently reformulated and criticized by Bradley, Moore, and their followers. By hedonism let us understand here the doctrine which holds that "happiness (or pleasure) alone is good" or that "pleasure is desirable, and is the only thing that is desirable as an end." I may say, in passing, that I have no interest here in any of the reasons that might be given or in fact were given by Mill and other writers in defense of this doctrine. Nor do I wish to suggest in any

[7] Ibid., p. 7. Cf. also pp. 8–9.

[8] R. B. Perry, *General Theory of Value* (Cambridge: Harvard University Press, 1950), pp. 4–5.

way that the doctrine, as it stands, is defensible. I have to do, at this point, only with the allegation that the hedonist is wrong when he infers from the thesis of hedonism that in particular situations we always ought to choose that alternative which will produce the most happiness or the least suffering. The thesis itself may be vulnerable; that is beside the point. What I maintain is that no fallacy whatever is involved in making the inference.

In order to show this, let us consider the status which Mill himself assigns to the thesis. First of all it is fairly clear even in *Utilitarianism* that he does *not* regard it as a theoretical statement of any sort, whether analytic or synthetic. As he says repeatedly in this work,[9] it is a "principle" or "rule" of conduct. Morality, like legislation, is a "practical art"; its rules, as distinguished from the laws of science, are "practical principles" for the conduct of life.[10] This point is elaborated with the greatest clarity in the *Logic*, a work which, in this connection, none of his critics appears to have noticed. In that work, it may be remembered, Book VI is "The Logic of the Moral Sciences," at the end of which Mill devotes a chapter to what he calls "The Logic of Practice or Art, Including Morality or Policy."[11] In this chapter, he begins by sharply distinguishing "moral science"—we would now call it "social science"—which is concerned with inquiries into "the course of nature," from that "inquiry the results of which do not express themselves in the indicative, but in the imperative mode, or in paraphrases equivalent to it; what is *called* the knowledge of duties, practical ethics, or morality."[12] So understood, he tells us, the rules of morality do not consist in assertions respecting matters of fact. "The method, therefore, of ethics can be no other than that of Art or Practice."[13] Now it is the function of Art to propose an end. This end having been proposed, it is handed to the sciences which in turn treat it as an effect. They explore its causes, and then send it back to Art with a theorem which states the circumstances and conditions under which it could be produced. Art in turn considers these and asserts on its own authority that the attainment of the end is desirable. "But though the reasonings which connect the end or purpose of every art with its means belong to the domain of Science, the *definition* of the end itself belongs exclusively to art, and forms its peculiar province."[14] And then, as clearly as can be, "Propositions of science assert a matter of fact: an existence, a coexistence, a succession, a resemblance. The Propositions now spoken of (those of art) do not assert that anything is, but enjoin or recommend that something should be. They are a class by themselves. A proposition of which the predicate is expressed by the words *ought* or *should be*, is generically different from one which is expressed by *is*, or *will be*."[15] Morality, Mill maintains, is the Art of Life, and its supreme principle, of course, is for him the thesis of hedonism. This thesis *defines* the end of conduct, and provides the basis for justifications of "secondary" moral rules that prescribe our particular duties, and through them for the justification of specific ethical propositions that prescribe our duties in particular cases.

So far, then, is Mill from committing the *real* fallacies in question, that he himself

[9] Everyman's edition, pp. 2, 11, 32, etc. [pp. 14, 21, 37 above].

[10] Ibid., p. 2. Compare also the crucial first paragraph of the much criticized fourth chapter, p. 32 [p. 37 above].

[11] *A System of Logic*, 8th ed., pp. 652–659 [pp. 1–9 above].

[12] Ibid., p. 653 (italics mine) [p. 3 above].

[13] Ibid.

[14] Ibid., p. 656 (italics mine) [p. 7 above].

[15] Ibid., pp. 656–657 (italics in text) [p. 7 above].

formulates, with the greatest clarity and elegance of language, just what they might be presumed to consist in. To be sure, he claims to infer significant ethical conclusions from that definition which identifies the end of the Art of Life; but this is because the definition itself "enunciates the object aimed at, and affirms it to be a desirable object."[16] The definition does not provide a logical analysis of "desirable" or "good"—at least as "logical analysis" is now understood. *This* analysis is provided in his general account of "The Logic of Practice." The definition itself is nothing but the statement or, better, the *enunciation* of a norm or standard of conduct. And the "inferring" of significant conclusions from it is the business not of theoretical but of practical reason.[17] A fallacy would be involved here, only if one attempted to infer an ethical conclusion from definitions concerned essentially with the explication of the descriptive meanings of symbols.

If we return now to *Utilitarianism* and interpret it as Mill appears to have intended, not as a metaethical theory or analysis of moral discourse, but as an enunciation of his doctrine of hedonism and as a defense of it against practical[18] objections, we will find that many (although not all) of the supposedly questionable or fallacious "claims" of that work involve no serious theoretical confusions whatever. On the point at issue, he is, I believe, quite consistent. To say, therefore, that for Mill the principle of hedonism constitutes a definition of the desirable, is to say in effect that it is ipso facto and by intention a practical or, if you like, a persuasive definition. But there is no confusion. Nor is there any deception. The imputation of confusion or deception arises solely from the mistaken and misleading application of descriptive definitional models in the interpretation of what plainly and explicitly is a normative ethical system. Given his own definition of desirable he is perfectly justified in inferring from it, in conjunction with the relevant "theorems" of science, those conclusions which prescribe in particular just what we ought to do. The categorial blunder, I submit, is not Mill's, but that of his critics.

Now I can imagine that certain of my readers may conclude from all this that we should have seized the first horn of our dilemma in the first place, namely, that many statements occurring in works of moral philosophy that are normally interpreted as definitions simply are not so at all. I do not agree. Acceptance of such an alternative rests upon an essential attitude toward definitions which I reject. But even if for the sake of argument we accept it, it still does not follow that any confusion is involved in Mill's doctrine on the point in question. For one cannot charge someone else with the commission of a fallacy on the ground that he claims to infer an ethical conclusion from a definition of ethical terms, when it is as plain as can be that *his* so-called "definition" was designed for a purpose very different from that which animates the preconception of definition implicit in the first horn of our dilemma. Even more to the point, one has no right to suppose that by means of such a conception of definition together with ordinary rules of logic, one can shed any light on the process involved in inferring ethical conclusions from what are *normally* interpreted as definitions in moral philosophy. Indeed, by so construing definition one thereby puts well-nigh insuperable difficulties in the way of properly interpreting what moral philosophers say and mean. By what is perhaps nothing more than a process of association of ideas one is led, when one sees the word "definition," or when one sees something that looks like a definition, to an interpretation of it which at once utterly misses the point and results in a mistaken charge of

[16] Ibid., p. 656 [p. 7 above].

[17] Cf. ibid., p. 657 [p. 7 above].

[18] Cf. *Utilitarianism*, p. 5 [p. 17 above].

logical confusion or even perhaps of downright deception.

A more profitable procedure, it seems to me, is to resist the temptation to cut the Gordian knots of meaning by essentialist definitions (they might as well be called stipulations) and to recognize instead the ambiguities and vagueness inherent in the normal use of "definition" and the variable functions of actual definitions. In this way one will approach a certain type of discourse without prior preconceptions as to the model to which it ought to conform. And perhaps, if one is lucky and manages to keep all the necessary distinctions in mind, one may be able to perform the philosopher's function of correctly interpreting a form of discourse. What is wanted is not an immediate cry of confusion, but the illumination of a normal function of language; not the implicit attribution of bad faith or of obscurantism, but the explanation of the nature of symbolic processes that answer to other needs than those of science or formal logic.

Any normal reader of Plato, Epicurus, or J. S. Mill recognizes at once that he is reading, for the most part, *in* moral philosophy, not *about* it. Such a reader, I submit, takes their "definitions" and "inferences" for what they are, namely practical definitions of norms and practical reasonings to particular moral conclusions. I agree with Professor Stevenson and with Professor Robinson, that the *Republic* is a prolonged essay in the persuasive or practical definition of "justice."[19] For better or worse, Plato was desperately concerned to defend a system of norms upon the acceptance of which, as he believed, the salvation of Athens depended. But there was nothing deceptive or illicit in what he was doing. The term "justice," no doubt, has a strong aura of emotive meaning. And like anyone else who attempts to define a norm in terms of "justice," he inevitably "traded" on its emotive meaning. But that he was proposing an "ideal," not describing a fact, in his famous definition of justice seems to me as clear as day.

I do not at all agree, therefore, with Professor Robinson's remark, "A persuasive definition, it may be urged, is at best a mistake and at worst a lie, because it consists in getting someone to alter his valuations under the false impression that he is not altering his valuations but correcting his knowledge of facts. I am tentatively inclined to accept this view, with the practical conclusion that we should not use persuasive definitions."[20] I do not say that it never happens that emotive meanings are used illicitly to modify attitudes. Of course it does. I do say that in the context of normative ethics, where it is understood that a writer is making practical proposals for the guidance of conduct, no confusion and no deception is involved.

This is why I should prefer, in discussing Plato or Mill, to use the phrase "practical definition" rather than "persuasive definition" to characterize what they are doing. The latter expression, perhaps unfortunately, appears to suggest a process which involves confusions and lies. And it does so, it should be emphasized, precisely because of the tendency of analysts to approach moral philosophers with descriptive models in mind as *the* norms for correct definition and valid inference. A

[19] Cf. Charles L. Stevenson, *Ethics and Language* (New Haven: Yale University Press, 1944), pp. 224–226. Also, Richard Robinson, *Definition* (Oxford: Clarendon Press, 1950), p. 166.

[20] Robinson, *Definition*, p. 170. It is instructive, I think, to see that in so many words Professor Robinson has drawn a "practical conclusion" from what he believes to be the statement of a fact. I applaud the inference, and, given his belief about the effects of persuasive definition, I consider it to have been his duty to have drawn it. If I do not make the inference, it is because I take a different view of the definitions in question.

practical definition, as I understand it, is explicitly and openly intended as the statement of a norm. It may, since it is stated in ethical terms, also be emotively loaded. But this cannot be avoided in any case. So long as we realize what is happening, no harm is done.

III

I wish, now, to say a word about current classifications of "ethical theories." In my judgment most of them are misleading; and they are so precisely because they appear to be set up for the purpose of classifying theories concerning the nature of ethical terms and moral judgments, whereas the doctrines so classified are abstracted from historical works in moral philosophy the purpose of which was to define the right or the good only in the normative or practical sense. Thus, for example, Professor Broad classifies "ethical theories" in accordance with certain principles that distinguish among them according to their conceptions of "ethical characteristics." Clearly his classification concerns only metaethical theories, not substantive normative systems. But then he applies his classification to such a writer as Mill who, in the only work in moral philosophy to which his critics ever refer, was *doing* ethics, not talking about it, and whose definitions were definitions of ends, not theoretical analyses of ethical "characteristics." Broad, in accordance with the standard view, says that "Mill presumably meant to be a naturalistic hedonist. But it is difficult to be sure in the case of such an extremely confused writer that he really was one."[21] And yet, if one looks at the *Logic* or at those passages in *Utilitarianism* in which he does talk briefly *about* moral judgments, it is unless I am badly mistaken quite evident that, in Broad's sense of the terms, Mill is neither a naturalist nor a hedonist in his theoretical ethics. He was, rather, primarily a noncognitivist with a strong prejudice *against* descriptivism or "naturalism." His affiliation is with the emotivists and imperativists, rather than the naturalists. Only in his normative ethics is Mill a hedonist of sorts.

Indeed I am not at all sure that one can find a clear case of naturalistic hedonist in Broad's sense, i.e., one who believes that "good" is analyzable without remainder in terms of "pleasure." A number of eighteenth-century writers do seem to have held that "good" in its "natural" use does mean the same thing as "agreeable" or "pleasant." But they were usually at pains to distinguish this use from "moral goodness" which, for them, carries with it normative or practical implications. Even Bentham, who in his downright way did say that only when applied to actions conformable to the principle of utility do the words "ought" and "right" have a meaning, is only an apparent exception.[22] For, as Mr. Stuart Hampshire has suggested, it was really Bentham's concern to replace all this fiddle-faddle of "morality" with scientific social engineering guided exclusively by the social norm of greatest happiness.[23]

But perhaps even these remarks may be indirectly misleading. For in saying that the great classical moral philosophers were not primarily interested in "the analysis of ethical terms" I may have created the impression, which I most certainly wish to avoid, that the term "analysis" should be preempted in ethics for the kind of thing that analytical ethicists generally do now-

[21] Cf. C. D. Broad, *Five Types of Ethical Theory* (New York: Harcourt, Brace and Co., 1930), p. 258.

[22] Cf. *British Moralists*, ed. L. A. Selby-Bigge (Oxford: Clarendon Press, 1897), I, 342.

[23] S. Hampshire, "Fallacies in Moral Philosophy," *Mind* 58 (1949), 473.

adays.[24] I believe, however, that it would have an altogether desirable effect if philosophers somewhat enlarged their conceptions of the roles of analysis itself, so as to acknowledge explicitly its normative and practical functions. The clarification of aims, in my judgment, is at least as important a task for analytical philosophers as is the description and elucidation of moral discourse itself. However much one may disagree with it in detail, Professor Popper's *The Open Society and Its Enemies* is a brilliant example of what the philosopher may do in the way of clarification of purposes and in sweeping away the manifold confusions which produce practical misunderstanding.

Disagreement, at the practical or moral level, frequently arises, not so much from differences of opinion about matters of fact or from well-defined and outright conflicts in interest, as from confusions of language and thought and from ambiguity and vagueness in the formulation of aims, and hence in the aims themselves. Hedonists, for example, have been called "pig philosophers" by those who, had they only understood them, might have found more perhaps to agree than disagree with. And on the other hand, as we shall see, hedonists have frequently provoked disagreement by faulty statements of their fundamental principle. The interminable disagreements in contemporary moral philosophy among those who have called themselves "hedonists," "voluntarists," "eudaemonists," and "instrumentalists" are often due not so much to well-defined differences of aim as to opposing expressions of what, if we could get clear about them, might turn out to be common aims.

The reason for this is due largely to the vagueness and the ambiguities latent in such notions as desire, will, satisfaction, pleasure, pain, end, feeling, attitude, and belief—precisely the terms, in short, in terms of which basic norms have so often been expressed. It is, or should be, the business of the moral philosopher not merely to codify and adumbrate the principles by which we are to live, but also to remove misunderstandings standing in the way of their acceptance, and to provide them with such determinateness of meaning as may enable them to function adequately as practical guides to conduct.

Only by such processes of reflection or analysis are we at last able to grasp *what* we are enjoined to accept as right or good; only so can we intelligently deliberate on the appropriate means to its realization. It is simply not true that the only function of deliberation or practical reason is to devise means to the fulfillment of already given ends-in-view. As often as not it is the means that are clear, not the end. Not knowing what you want, or confusion as to its nature, is at least as common and perhaps an even more tragic privation than not knowing how to get it. Utilitarianism, as it stands, is unquestionably inadequate as a moral philosophy. But its failure, comparatively speaking, is due mainly to a very fundamental lack of clarity with respect to its own governing purposes. Thus when Mill tells us that "human nature is so constituted as to desire nothing which is not either a part of happiness or a means to happiness,"[25] it would seem that he did not mean to assert that we desire what we desire. In such a passage, one is forced to conclude that "happiness" or "pleasure" (for him, of course, they are equivalent) are not to be understood simply as synonyms for "object of desire" or "realization of desire." Surely, one supposes, Mill, with his awareness of human ignorance and his fear of the uncorrected impulses of the mob, did not wish to assert that in our dealings with others what we

[24] Professor Karl Popper is a notable exception.

[25] *Utilitarianism*, p. 36 [p. 40 above].

should regard as intrinsically desirable is the realization of their desires *as they stand;* surely, as a consequentialist who put his emphasis not on motives but on their fruits, he did not mean to enjoin us to regard objects of desire alone as intrinsically worthy of our respect and solicitude. And yet, almost in the same breath, we find him saying, to our confusion and despair, that "desiring a thing and finding it pleasant" are not merely "two parts of the same phenomenon," but "in strictness of language, two modes of naming the same psychological fact."[26] So construed, it would seem there is no difference whatever between ethical hedonism and ethical voluntarism, and that psychological hedonism is a vacuous tautology, not a theory at all. The truth of the matter is that, by an inattention to a fundamental ambiguity in the term "pleasure" and its derivatives, Mill allowed himself to fall into a confusion which is fatal not for his metaethics but for his normative moral philosophy.

Now in one sense, of course, Mill was quite within his right in equating "desiring" and "finding pleasant"; both expressions, as Professor Ryle tells us,[27] do refer to inclination, which is a sort of proneness or readiness to do certain sorts of things on purpose. And in another sense, he is also justified in talking, as he so often does, about a "desire for pleasure." But this latter expression requires that "pleasure" and "desire" be distinguished and, indeed, contrasted. So understood, "pleasure," as opposed to "desire," does *not* refer to inclinations, but rather to certain distinctive feelings or moods which we designate by such expressions as delight, joy, contentment, the sense of well-being, and (in one sense) satisfaction. But it obviously makes a tremendous difference for moral philosophy and for those who are enjoined to base their deliberations on the assumption that pleasure alone is desirable which of these senses of "pleasure" is intended. On one interpretation we are, in effect, enjoined to contribute as much as we can to the delight, joy, contentment, well-being and satisfaction of ourselves and others. On the other interpretation we are enjoined, I suppose, to respect (or coddle) other people's inclinations and wishes, to help them to get what they happen to be aiming at. No greater ethical difference, I submit, can be imagined. For my part, it is plain that after all it is the former sort of thing toward which Mill's hedonism was fundamentally oriented.[28]

I have dwelt again on Mill merely to illustrate my contention that analysis is an indispensable tool for normative ethics itself, and that the clarification and subse-

[26] Ibid.

[27] Cf. Gilbert Ryle, *The Concept of Mind* (London, New York: Hutchinson's University Library, 1949), pp. 83 ff.

[28] Much the same sort of difficulty appears when we turn to Mill's discussion of "qualities of pleasure." If "pleasure" is construed as a feeling word, then "quality of pleasure" means one thing; if it is construed as equivalent to "desire," it means quite another. And, if "quality of pleasure" is construed as "kind of feeling," one thing is meant when some kinds of pleasure are regarded as "higher" than others; if, as Mill suggests, it means nothing more than "decided preference," then something quite different is implied when some pleasures are said to be higher than others. Again Mill is simply confused. And in any case, to promote or support other people's preferences, when well-considered, is one thing; to promote certain "higher" qualities of feeling or certain *experiences* of pleasure, such as those involving the exercise of our so-called higher faculties, is something else. All through Mill's moral and social philosophy one can find a tension which arises primarily on the fact that he had not sufficiently clarified *what* he regarded as intrinsically valuable. I do not say that the tension would automatically disappear once the ambiguities in the term "pleasure" were brought into the open. But I do say that only then could one intelligently decide, as a putative hedonist, what one was really for.

quent definition of aims is an indispensable part of successful practical deliberation. Other illustrious examples of moral confusion and of the use of analysis toward its removal come readily to mind. The history of egoism, as everyone knows, is one long history of equivocation, ambiguity, and vagueness. Its plausibility or attractiveness for many thoughtless people has depended largely, I think, upon these factors. When they are eliminated by such superb essays in clarification as the second appendix to Hume's second *Enquiry*, the business of normative moral philosophy is thereby immeasurably advanced.

IV

We have now to consider the second part of Mr. Prior's statement, namely, the wider thesis that a fallacy is involved whenever we attempt to deduce or claim to deduce moral conclusions from statements of fact. I have already indicated in what sense this seems to me to be plausible. I shall now try to show in what sense it is mistaken and misleading. Let me again emphasize that my reason for believing that moral conclusions may be inferred from statements of fact does not in the least depend upon the tacit assumption that moral conclusions are, after all, a species of factual statement, or that the ethical terms occurring in the conclusions are descriptively synonymous with descriptive or empirical predicates occurring in the premises. This is as it may be. I have already indicated elsewhere that I do think that "good" and "right" have, in certain contexts, descriptive meanings. But my present argument does not depend upon this fact. Nor do I wish, at this point, to cavil at the difficulties involved in such ill-defined expressions as "ethical terms," "ethical conclusion," "nonethical term," "empirical or natural predicate," "nonethical premise," and the like. The difficulties implicit in the ordinary use of these expressions in contemporary ethical theory I have also pointed out elsewhere.[29] Professor Morton White, in his admirable essay, "A Finitistic Approach to Philosophical Theses," has shown how tenuous is the thesis of antinaturalism in its ordinary "infinitistic" formulation.[30] There will be some naturalists who may choose to avail themselves of Frankena's and White's criticisms of the question-begging assumptions and imponderable infinitistic theses involved in the usual arguments provided by antinaturalists in their attack upon the naturalistic fallacy.[31] I do not wish to avail myself of these criticisms however, just though they are. For I do believe that, when all the question-begging assumptions and the infinitism have been removed, there really is a sense in which the naturalistic fallacy really *is* a fallacy.

Nevertheless I believe that under certain conditions it is entirely proper to infer (not deduce), ethical conclusions from factual premises. (The quotation, a few pages back, from Professor Robinson is an interesting example of this.) And the reasons why some philosophers have supposed that a fallacy is involved in such inferences are (a) the tenacious hold which descriptive models have upon all of us in our interpretation of symbols generally, and, more important, (b) the ingrained tendency to regard the processes of validation obtaining in formal logic and in inductive reasoning as the only processes in which questions of validity can ever arise. So tenacious are these assumptions that, when certain philosophers get even the vaguest

29 See "Evaluation and Obligation: Two Functions of Judgments in the Language of Conduct," *Journal of Philosophy* 47 (Jan. 5, 1950), pp. 5–7.

30 Cf. M. G. White, "A Finitistic Approach to Philosophical Theses," *Philosophical Review* 60 (July 1951), 307–311.

31 Cf. ibid.; also Frankena, "Naturalistic Fallacy," pp. 472 ff.

inkling that there may be standards of relevance in art and morals, they leap immediately to the absurd conclusion that a work of art is a deductive system or that a moral code is one of the social sciences. Perhaps the most fantastic example of this sort of thing in recent literature may be found in Professor James Feibleman's *Aesthetics.* According to him, the act of artistic creation is simply a deduction of the logical consequences implicit in the artist's initial idea.[32] The relations holding between a theme and its variations, he says in so many words, are not merely analogous (in some sense) to but identical with those which hold between the axioms and theorems of a deductive system. Such a view, you will say, is absurd. I agree. It is logicism gone mad. But nestled at the heart of the absurdity, I am convinced, is, if he only knew how to make use of it, a genuine insight. This insight, however, is concealed from its author by virtue of his unconscious addiction to the notion that validity and relevance are notions which are exemplified only in logical systems. The insight is this: there are relations of relevance—some people call them relations of "propriety" or "fittingness"—which hold between the parts of a successful work of art.[33] And in the same way, although (since here we are dealing with propositions the absurdity is less palpable) it is absurd to say that ethical conclusions can be *deduced* from factual premises, there is still an insight of sorts concealed within the absurdity. For there are conditions of relevance, which permit, in certain circumstances, the inference of significant ethical judgments from statements of fact. Some of these I will mention shortly.

Meanwhile it must be remarked that in recent years moral philosophers have been more prone to see the absurdity than the insight within it. And this is due, again, to a subtle addiction to descriptivistic attitudes implicit in the above-mentioned notion concerning validity. Thus, for example, although Professor Charles Stevenson is perhaps more sensitive than any other philosopher to the reality of persuasive definition, he himself falls into it when he refuses, for no reason sanctioned by ordinary language, to accept the possibility that there are any "rational methods" other than those of formal logic and science. Although he freely allows the right of moralists to use, *inter alia,* what he regards as rational methods when they happen to be appropriate for the purpose of "irrigating" ethical judgments, he nevertheless insists there are no criteria of validity with respect to ethical disputation as such. But why should he fear lest the notion of "validity" be extended so as to include forms of inference which are neither demonstrative nor inductive? As he himself wisely says, "When an inference does not purport to comply with the usual rules, any insistence on its failure to do so is gratuitous."[34] And yet he maintains, to my mind quite unconvincingly, that it is "wholly impracticable and injudicious" *(sic)* to sanction a definition of validity which extends its usage beyond its applications to logic and to science.[35] Apart from a tenacious desire to reserve the emotive meaning of such expressions as "rational" and "valid" for processes of reasoning involved in formal logic and inductive science, what is there to commend Stevenson's position? Again, why must it be misleading to say that "validity," not in special "philosophical" senses but in normal common-sensical applica-

[32] Cf. James F. Feibleman, *Aesthetics* (New York: Duell, Sloan, and Pearce, 1949), pp. 12 ff.

[33] Cf. my "The Concept of Relevance in Aesthetics," *Journal of Aesthetics and Art Criticism,* December 1947, pp. 152–161.

[34] C. L. Stevenson, *Ethics and Language,* p. 153.

[35] Ibid., p. 154.

tions, is a normative as well as perhaps (in some uses) a descriptive term? It is so, surely. To say that "x is invalid" is, in effect, to say "x fails to conform to certain accepted conditions; do not accept x." In the realm of logic, its function is to control and direct belief. In the realm of ethics, it is not only to control belief, but also to control and direct practical second-level attitudes.

I submit that Professor Stevenson is still, in an extremely subtle and involved way, under the spell of descriptive and logical models in his approach to nonscientific forms of *reasoning,* even though he is quite free from such models in his analysis of nonscientific *terms.* To be sure, he does not, like Perry, make the mistake of interpreting moral disputation simply as a variety of scientific and logical inference, albeit with a subject matter that cuts across the special sciences. On the contrary. Yet he does appear to regard science and logic as *the* proper models in regard to all questions of relevance and validity. And it is because of this, I believe, that he is forced to conclude that there is no such thing as validity in morals except, by accident, when purely factual or logical issues are momentarily in view.

In principle, of course, he is free, on his own view, to *disapprove* those who employ invalid arguments in the process of supporting ethical judgments. That is his privilege as a moral being. But as an analyst he is bound to regard such arguments, from the standpoint of moral discourse itself, as entirely within the proprieties. Thus although he may, as an individual, be against certain forms of irrationality in ethics, he is obliged, as an ethical theorist, to accept them as integral parts of moral persuasion and argument.

The issue, here, I realize, is exceedingly delicate, so much so, indeed, that I am not altogether sure that I also have not been unintentionally misleading. Perhaps, in the end, all one can do is to go on indefinitely correcting the misleading impressions of one's own preceding remarks. This may, in fact, be all that writing a book in philosophy amounts to. I must state my conviction, in any case, that I get the strongest sort of impression from Professor Stevenson's writings that he is almost as much concerned to protect science and logic as the only *valid* methods or argumentation as he is to free ethics itself from bondage to a false god of rationality.

Now I agree once and for all that there are no logical rules by means of which one can deduce the ethical proposition "x ought to be done" from any combination of purely factual statements. What I do maintain is that, according to ordinary usage, it is entirely permissible to *infer* ethical conclusions from factual premises. I should now like to support this contention with some examples. Suppose that it could be shown that a certain act would cause another person unnecessary hardship or suffering; I think that any normal person in our society would regard this as a good, if not sufficient, reason for inferring that, other things remaining equal, the act in question ought not to be performed. Again, suppose it could be shown that the fulfillment of a certain promise would probably cause the person to whom one made it to destroy himself; here also, I think that normal persons would, perhaps reluctantly, conclude from this that the promise ought to be broken. Other examples come immediately to mind.

I conclude from this that, however difficult they may be to specify, there are nevertheless broad rules of relevance or valid inference in moral discourse which enable us, in certain circumstances, to infer ethical conclusions from nonethical premises. But I do not in the least wish to imply by this that the ordinary laws of logic should be amended or broadened. Such laws have no immediate application to the kinds of inference in question. My contention is merely that within the universe of discourse called "moral" or "ethical," certain types of inference are permissible, others not. Nor do I wish to say that moral judgments may be "logically derived" from nonethical statements of fact.[36] Nothing is gained, I think, from such an unnecessary and really misleading extension of the expression "logical derivation." All that needs defending is the thesis that moral reasoning has its own proprieties which, while certainly not written into the starry heavens above, are at least constant and extensive enough to enable the members of a given civilization to distinguish a good reason from a bad one.

[36] Cf. Hampshire, "Fallacies," pp. 470 ff. Let me state here that, although apparently different sorts of stimuli have given rise to our respective reflections on moral philosophy, I find myself in agreement with most, although not all, of Mr. Hampshire's admirable essay. In my judgment the most stimulating thinking about ethics to be found in contemporary philosophy is being done at Oxford by Mr. Hampshire and his colleagues.

Jonathan Harrison / Utilitarianism, universalization, and our duty to be just

"In considering what common interest requires, we are, besides the immediate effects of actions, to consider what their general tendencies are, what they open the way to, and what would actually be the consequences if all were to act alike. If under the pretence of great indigence, superfluity to the owner, or intention to give to a worthier person, I may take away a man's property, or adjudge it from him in a court of justice; another or all, in the same circumstances may do so; and thus the boundaries of property would be overthrown, and general anarchy, distrust and savageness be introduced."—Richard Price.[1]

According to Utilitarianism, it is often said, an action is right if it produces at least as much good as any other action which the agent could have done in the circumstances in which he was placed. Besides being right, it is also a duty, if it produces more good than any other action that the agent could have done. When we are faced with a situation in which we have to choose between a number of actions, each of which would produce as much good or more than anything else we could do, but of none of which is it true that it would produce more good than anything else we could do, then we have not a duty to perform any particular one of these actions to the exclusion of the others. What is our duty is to do one or other of these actions; but it is a matter of indifference which of them we do, and we have done our duty, whichever one of them we perform.[2]

There are, therefore, some right actions which are not duties, and so the words "right" and "a duty" cannot mean the same thing. This fact has been regarded as unimportant,[3] because it has been supposed that the circumstances in which we

[1] Richard Price, *A Review of the Principal Questions in Morals*, ed. D. Daiches Raphael (Oxford: Clarendon Press, 1948), p. 164.

[2] *See* G. E. Moore, *Ethics* (London: Williams and Norgate, 1912), pp. 32–35. The definition of utilitarianism used here would not have satisfied Professor Moore, but it will do for our purposes.

[3] *See* W. D. Ross, *The Right and the Good* (Oxford: Clarendon Press, 1930), pp. 3–4.

Reprinted from PAS, *vol. 53 (1952–1953), pp. 105–134, courtesy of the author and editor of The Aristotelian Society.*

are faced with a choice between a number of right actions, none of which are duties, occur but seldom.

However, it seems to me that such situations, so far from being rare, are arising all the time. At any moment of the day, when I am not engaged in doing anything in particular, there are at least half a dozen actions I can think of which I could do, which it would be perfectly right for me to do, but none of which could, by any stretch of the imagination, be said to be duties. It is often supposed that, in such circumstances, I have no duties, but this is a mistake. Among the actions which I could do at this moment are some wrong ones; I might, for example, throw my muffin in my friend's face, or wantonly break the window of the cafe in which I am drinking tea with him. Since it is within my power to perform, at this very moment, some wrong actions, I must, at this very moment, have some duty incumbent upon me, namely, the duty of refraining from performing any of these wrong actions. And furthermore, a man of more ascetic temperament and sterner moral character than myself might well argue that, at this very moment, I was not doing my duty; that my money might be better employed in succouring the needy; my time in furthering the development of a noble cause; my mind in contemplating the benevolence of my Maker or the enormities of my sins.

For these reasons, it seems to me that, so far from right actions almost always being duties, right actions are hardly ever duties. What is my duty is to perform one of the number of alternative right actions which I could perform; in doing any one of them I do my duty, though I could equally well have done it in doing any other. The occasion when we can say of one particular action that it, and it alone, is a duty, occurs comparatively seldom.

Utilitarianism might, then, be defined as the theory which holds that an action is right if there is no action within the power of the agent which would produce more good than it, and that it is my duty to perform some right action or other. The circumstances in which there is only one right action within the power of the agent will fall under this principle as a special case, and, when this special case arises, that right action will also be a duty.

I will not bore my readers by citing any of the well-known objections to utilitarianism, but there is one particular difficulty in this theory which, for the purpose of this article, is of special interest. There are some actions which we think we have a duty to do, although they themselves produce no good consequences, because such actions would produce good consequences if they were generally practised. There are some actions which we think we have a duty to refrain from doing, even though they themselves produce no harmful consequences, because such actions would produce harmful consequences if the performance of them became the general rule. I think I have a duty to vote for that person whose party I think would govern the nation best, although I do not think that the addition of my vote to the total number of votes which are cast for him is going to make any difference to the result of the election, simply because I realise that, if all his other supporters were to do as I do, and fail to go to the polls, the man would not be elected. I refrain from walking on the grass of a well-kept park lawn, not because I think that my walking on the grass is going to damage the lawn to such an extent as to detract from anybody's pleasure in contemplating it, but because I realise that, if everybody else who walked in the park were to do likewise, the grass in the park would be spoilt. These two duties cannot be derived from the duty of setting a good example, or of refraining from setting a bad example, for I should still feel them incumbent upon me, even if no one were to know that I had defaced my ballot paper, and even if the park was empty of everyone but me.

Such facts, if they are facts, have not been entirely neglected by Utilitarians. Hume, for example, may have had them in mind when he distinguished between justice and benevolence. Of the social virtues of benevolence and humanity he says: "And as the good, resulting from their benign influence is in itself complete and entire, it also excites the moral sentiment of approbation, without any reflection on farther consequences, and without any more enlarged views of the concurrence or imitation of the other members of society."[4] Whereas of justice he says: "The case is not the same with the social virtues of justice and fidelity. They are highly useful, or indeed absolutely necessary to the well-being of mankind; but the benefit resulting from them is not the consequence of every individual single act; but arises from the whole scheme or system concurred in by the whole, or the greater part of the society."[5] Comparing the virtues of justice and benevolence, he says: "The happiness and prosperity of mankind, arising from the social virtue of benevolence and its subdivisions, may be compared to a wall, built by many hands, which still rises by each stone that is heaped upon it, and receives increase proportional to the diligence and care of each workman. The same happiness, raised by the social virtue of justice and its subdivisions, may be compared to the building of a vault, where each individual stone would, of itself, fall to the ground; nor is the whole fabric supported but by the mutual assistance and combination of its corresponding parts."[6]

[4] L. A. Selby-Bigge, ed., Hume's *Enquiries Concerning Human Understanding and Concerning the Principles of Morals* (Oxford: Clarendon Press, 1902), second edition, p. 304.

[5] Loc. cit.

[6] Op. cit., p. 305.

Benevolent actions, if I have interpreted Hume rightly, themselves produce good consequences, and would produce good consequences whether anybody else performed benevolent actions or not. A just action, however, would not produce good consequences if it was the only instance of its kind. Just actions only produce good consequences so long as the performance of just actions is the rule rather than the exception. This is why one may often be bound to perform a just action which has consequences which are harmful. I must perform it, even when it itself has harmful consequences, because it is an action of a kind the general performance of which is necessary to society. This is why justice is "conventional" in a way in which benevolence is not. Justice is conventional in that the benefit to be derived from it depends upon its customary observance. No benefit will be obtained from my practice of justice unless my fellows practice it too, and the same is true of them. This is not to say that I make an explicit agreement with them that we shall all behave justly in order to gain the benefits of justice. Indeed, our obligation to be just could not be derived from any such agreement, because the obligation to keep agreements is itself a subdivision of justice. Both I and my neighbors are not just because we agree to be just, but because we each realise that the common practice of justice is in the interest of all of us.

However, it is not certain that Hume did hold the view which I have just attributed to him. This view may easily be confused with another rather similar view, and Hume himself, I am afraid, failed to make the distinction. There are some actions which, besides being of a sort which would produce good consequences if generally performed, are themselves necessary to the production of these good consequences. If two men are rowing a boat, the boat will progress only so long as they both row, and will fail to progress if either of them stops rowing. In this case, the actions of either oarsman are necessary if the good which consists in the progress of the boat is to be secured. Such actions, since they are necessary conditions of the production of a certain good, do themselves produce good consequences, and so they must clearly be distinguished from those actions which, though they are of a sort the general performance of which would produce good consequences, do not produce good consequences themselves. Moreover, the good which consists in the movement of the boat cannot be split into parts, and part attributed to the actions of one oarsman, and part to the actions of the other; the whole of this good must be produced, or none of it. Hence the good in question must be considered as being equally the consequence of the actions of either man, and it is the whole of this good which each man must take into account when he is considering whether or not he has a duty to row. Now it may have been Hume's view that justice is a duty, not because just actions are of a sort which would produce good consequences if generally practiced, but because just actions are severally necessary if any good is to be produced by the general practice of justice.

There are arguments which might be used to try to show that Hume held the latter of the two views which I have just distinguished; which tend to show that Hume thought that we had a duty to be just because, if we were not just, the whole of the good consequent upon the general performance of justice would be lost; rather than that he thought that we should perform just actions because they were of a sort the general performance of which would produce good consequences, even when they themselves did not. In the first place, he sometimes speaks as if the performance of every just action is necessary if any just action is to produce good consequences. I must be just, even when it seems that the consequences of my being just are bad, because, if I am not just, the good which the general practice of justice brings about will be lost. In the second place, he thinks that, in a state of nature, it will be nobody's duty to be just, because if, in such a state, only one of us behaves justly, no good will result. Whereas what he should have said—and, perhaps, what he would have said—if he had held that a just action is made right by the fact that it is of a sort the general performance of which would produce good consequences, is, that it is our duty to be just, even in a state of nature. For it is still true, even in a state of nature, that the general performance of just actions would produce good consequences, even though individual just actions performed in that state do not produce good consequences; hence it seems, we would have a duty to be just in a state of nature, even if, by being just, we produce consequences which are indifferent, or even bad.

The fact that Hume thought that we would not have a duty to be just in a state of nature, and the fact that he sometimes speaks as if the performance of every just action is necessary if any just action is to have good consequences, seems to indicate that Hume thought that we had a duty to perform just actions because they, together with other just actions, were severally necessary to the production of the good resultant upon the practice of justice. But there are some arguments which tend to show, either that he thought that we had a duty to practice just actions because they were of a sort the general performance of which would have good consequences, or that, if he did not actually hold this, his theory is as a result a worse one than I have supposed it to be.

Firstly, the view that we must be just in this particular case, so that the good consequent upon the practice of justice as a whole should be brought about, is unrealistic. It is simply false that the performance of every just action is necesssary if the good produced by the practice of justice is to be secured. If this were true, the human race would have perished miserably many years ago. An occasional act of injustice here and there does not undermine the whole beneficial effect of the practice of justice, and, if such actions are performed in secret, they may sometimes not even produce any harmful effects at all.

Secondly, the view that we must be just, because just actions are severally necessary to the production of the good of justice, would make our duty to be just more rigid than we in fact believe it to be. Our normal view on the practice of justice in hard cases is this. We think that we should not turn aside from justice whenever it seems that an unjust action would produce some good, but, on the other hand, we do think that there are occasions on which unjust actions should be performed, because the good to be gained is considerable. But, if the whole of the good consequent upon the practice of justice were dependent upon the performance of just actions in every particular case, it is difficult to believe that the consequences of any individual unjust action, considered in itself, could ever be good enough to justify me in performing it. I must, therefore, apply rules of justice in all circumstances, however trivial, and however great the immediate good to be gained by neglecting them.

Thirdly, if Hume did hold the view that we must perform just actions because just actions are necessary if the general practice of justice is to have any value, then his theory is incapable of accounting for the difficulties with which utilitarianism is faced, and for which it was, in part, intended to account. This theory was, in part, intended to explain how we could have a duty to perform some actions the consequences of which were indifferent or positively bad, and it is one of the great merits of the view that we have a duty to perform actions because they are of a sort which would produce good consequences if generally practiced, that it does enable us to explain how it is that we have a duty to perform some actions which, in themselves, have bad or indifferent consequences. But the theory that it is our duty to perform just actions because their performance is necessary for the good of justice to be realised does not, in fact, do this. It does not, as does the other theory, admit and account for the fact that we have a duty to perform some actions which do not themselves produce good consequences, for it does not recognise that there are such duties. All that can be said, if we adopt it, is that there are some actions, which seem to produce no good consequences, or even to produce bad consequences, when we take a narrow and restricted view. When we take a more enlarged view, and consider these actions along with other actions of the same sort, it will be seen that, in actual fact, they really do produce good consequences; they produce good consequences because they are one of a set of actions the several performances of which are necessary if a certain good is to be produced. This view, therefore, does not find a place in the utilitarian scheme of duties for our duty to perform actions which do not themselves have good consequences. It merely denies that we have any such duties, and tries to explain how the illusion that we have arises.

Utilitarians—as well as moral philosophers who have not been utilitarians—have not always failed to notice the fact that we think actions are right if they are of a sort which would produce good consequences if generally practiced, or are wrong if they are of a sort which would produce bad consequences if other people did the same. Mill, for example, remarked: "In the case of abstinences—indeed of things which people forbear to do from moral considerations, though the consequences in the particular case might be beneficial—it would be unworthy of an intelligent agent not to be consciously aware that the action is of a class which, if practiced generally, would be generally injurious, and that this is the ground of the obligation to abstain from it."[7] But utilitarians have not always realised that, in admitting that the performance of such actions is a duty, they are departing from, or at least modifying, utilitarianism as it is stated above. And that they are departing from, or modifying, utilitarianism, as it is usually thought of, is clear. For actions which are permissible, according to utilitarianism as I have defined it above, might well not be permissible, according to utilitarianism in this modified form. For it may very well be true of an action, both that there is no other action within the power of the agent that would produce better consequences than it, and that it is an instance of a class of actions which would produce harmful consequences if they were to be generally performed. In this case, I should, according to utilitarianism as it is normally thought of, be acting rightly if I performed it; whereas, according to this modified form of utilitarianism, I should be acting wrongly.

But the principle that I should perform actions, if they are of a sort which would produce good consequences if generally performed, and should refrain from performing actions which would produce bad consequences, if generally performed, is not free from difficulty.

In the first place, the principle is, as it stands, insufficiently precise. An action, it says, is right if it is of a sort which would produce good consequences, if generally practiced, and wrong if it is of a sort which would produce harmful consequences, if generally practiced. But no action is an instance of just one sort of class of actions; every action is an instance of many such sorts. It may well be that among the many classes of action of which a given action is an instance, there may be some classes which would have good consequences, if generally performed, some classes which would have bad consequences, if generally performed, and yet other classes, the general performance of which would be indifferent. When we say that the consequences, for good or for ill, of the class of actions of which a given action is a member should be taken into account when we are considering whether or not that action ought to be performed, about which of the many classes, of which the action in question is an instance, are we talking? Which of these classes should be considered, when we are wondering whether such an action is a right and proper one for us to do?

Some of the classes, of which it is a member, should not be considered by us because the consequences which they would have, if generally performed, are different from the consequences their subclasses would have, if they were generally performed. Suppose, for example, that a red-headed man with one eye, a wart on his right cheek, and a mermaid tattooed on his left forearm, were to tell a lie on a Tuesday. It might be argued that it was quite permissible for him to have told this lie, because his action in telling the lie belongs to the class of actions performed on a Tuesday, and the consequences of the general performance of actions on a Tuesday is indifferent. But the class of actions performed on a Tuesday is not the sort of class which it is important to consider, when meditating upon the consequences of the general performance of certain classes of actions. For the class of actions performed on a Tuesday contains within itself a number of subclasses: deceitful actions on a Tuesday, self-sacrificing actions on a Tuesday, revengeful actions on a Tuesday, and so on. The consequences of the general performance of actions in these subclasses will

[7] John Stuart Mill, *Utilitarianism*, Everyman's Edition, pp. 17–18 [p. 26 above].

differ both from one another and from the consequences of the general performance of that wider class which is the genus. Since this is the case, it would be unreasonable for us to consider the consequences of the general performance of actions on a Tuesday. For the consequences of the general practice of lying on a Tuesday are different from those of the general practice of actions of any sort on a Tuesday, and it is the consequences of the general performance of the more specific class of actions which it is important for us to consider.

It can be important for us to consider the consequences of the general performance of a certain class of actions only if that class contains within itself no subclasses, the consequences of the general practice of which is either better or worse than the consequences of the general practice of actions belonging to it. It would be inaccurate to say that this class is of the wrong sort because it is too generic. For the class of actions performed between 3:00 p.m. and 3:01 p.m. on Tuesday is a good deal more specific than it is, and yet is of the wrong sort for precisely the same reason.

If, on the other hand—to revert to our original example—we were to consider, not the consequences of the general practice of lying, but the consequences of the general practice of lying by one-eyed, redheaded men with warts on their right cheeks and mermaids tattooed on their left forearms, then the class of actions we were considering would be a wrong one, but for a different reason. The class of actions performed on Tuesday afternoon was a wrong one to consider, because it could be "relevantly specified"; that is to say, by the addition of characteristics such as "being the telling of a lie" I could obtain a more specific class of actions, the consequences of the general performance of which would be different from the consequences of the general performance of actions belonging to it. The class of actions, "lies told by one-eyed, redheaded men with warts on their right cheeks and mermaids tattooed on their left forearms," is a wrong one because it can be "irrelevantly generalized"; that is to say, by subtracting characteristics such as "being an action performed by a one-eyed man" I can obtain more general classes of actions, the consequences of the general performance of which do not differ from the consequences of the general performance of actions belonging to it.

In the second place, the principle seems to rule out as being wrong a number of actions which everybody normally thinks to be permissible, and would make obligatory as duties many actions which people do not normally consider to be such. The principle that I should perform actions, the general practice of which would be beneficial, is often used as an argument for pacifism, and with some plausibility. If everybody were to refrain from participating in wars, there would be no wars; hence it is my duty to refrain from participating in wars, whether anybody else cooperates with me or not. But the same principle can be used to justify actions which even a pacifist would condemn. If nobody were to lay violent hands upon the persons of his neighbours, or upon their property, everyone would live in peace with his fellow men—and what a desirable state of affairs this would be! But must the policeman for this reason refrain from forcibly apprehending the criminal, the judge from sending him to prison, and the gaoler from keeping him there? Similarly, the principle that I should refrain from performing actions which would be harmful if generally performed would make it obligatory for me to refrain from performing many actions which I have, no doubt, a duty not to do. But it would also make it obligatory for me to refrain from performing many actions which we would all regard as being permissible, if not positively as duties. It would make it my duty, for example, not to become a professional philosopher, because, in a world in which everybody became professional philosophers, it would be impossible to survive. The same principle would prohibit entry into almost any trade or profession, with the possible exception of that of agricultural labourer.

But in answering the first difficulty, the means of answering this second difficulty have already been provided. It is true, for example, that if we consider violent actions generally, then, if everybody refrained from violent actions, good consequences would result. But the class of violent actions is not the class which it is important to consider when we are wondering whether an action is of a sort which would have good or bad consequences if generally performed. The class of violent actions is not the right class for us to consider because it can relevantly be made more specific. It contains within itself, as sub-classes, such species of violent actions as the violence of a parent towards a child, the violence of a policeman towards a criminal, the violence of a criminal towards a householder, the violence of one soldier to another, the violence of one small boy to another small boy. Since the consequences of the general practice of these subclasses of violent action may be, and very probably are, different from the consequences of the universal practice of violent actions in general, then it is the consequences of the general practice of the species which we should consider, not of the genus. So, too, participation in wars is a class of actions which can be made relevantly more specific, if it is limited by the addition of suitable characteristics. It contains subclasses, such as participation in wars on behalf of an aggressor, participation in wars on behalf of a country which is resisting aggression, participation in wars as a mercenary on behalf of a country of which one is not a citizen, participation in religious wars, participation in disciplinary wars on behalf of some international authority. Since the consequences of the general performance of these species will differ from the consequences of the general performance of the genus, then it is the species which should be considered, not the genus. To take the third example, if everyone were to become university lecturers, the consequences would, no doubt, be deplorable. But the entering into the profession of university lecturer is a class of actions which contains species such as that of becoming a university lecturer by men who have no aptitude for medicine, no liking for the civil service, and who have a capacity for acquiring and disseminating information which would be unsuitable for school-children, but of not much use or interest to ordinary adults. Becoming a university lecturer is a class of actions which can be relevantly specified, and, since this is so, it is the consequences of the general practice of the species which we should consider, not the consequences of the general practice of the genus.

Actions are right if they are of a sort which would produce good consequences, if generally practiced. Now being right is a property of the individual action. Being generally practiced (or seldom, or always, or never practiced, as the case may be) is a property of the sort of action this action is, or of the class of actions of which it is a member. But of what is producing good consequences a property? When actions of this sort are not generally practiced, producing good consequences will, of course, be a property of nothing. But when actions of this sort are generally practiced, of what will producing good consequences be a property? Not of the sort, because sorts or classes cannot produce good consequences, or fail to produce them, though instances of the sort or members of the class can. Producing good consequences must, then, be a property of the individual actions. But if we say that every individual action of the sort produces good consequences, then our principle does not meet the difficulty which it was introduced to meet, namely, the difficulty that there are actions which are right, although they do not produce good consequences. Whereas if we say that only some of the individual actions of the sort produce good consequences, we are faced with this perplexing situation: the rightness of some instances of the sort is derived from the good consequences produced by other instances of the sort. We are faced, too, with this further difficulty. A utilitarian, if he is to deserve the name at all, must try to derive the rightness of actions in some way from the good ends which they serve. So it may be objected that, if the general practice of a sort of action produces good consequences, even when some actions of the sort produce no good consequences, or even bad consequences, would not even better consequences be produced if people were to refrain from performing those actions of the sort which did not produce good consequences, and performed only those that did?[8] But if this is the case, then it cannot be argued that the rightness of those actions which do not produce good consequences is dependent on the fact that in some way they serve a good end, for this, so far from being a fact, is, as the preceding argument has shown, simply not true.

The argument I have just stated does not, I think, show that the man who holds that our duty to perform a certain action may be founded upon the good consequences of the general performance of similar actions cannot properly be called a utilitarian, but it does serve to elicit an important property which such classes of action must have. Consider, for example, the class of actions "drinking cocoa for breakfast." It may well be that actions of this class would have good consequences, if generally performed, and it may even be that this class of actions cannot relevantly be made more specific, in the way in which I have explained. But even so, the fact, if it is a fact, that actions of this sort would produce good consequences, if they were to be generally performed, could not possibly be an adequate reason for thinking that either I, or anybody else, has a duty to drink cocoa for breakfast. If I have a duty to drink cocoa for breakfast at all, this duty is derived from the effects of drinking cocoa on my health and temper, i.e., on the effects of the particular action to be performed, not upon the effects of the general performance of similar actions.

If this is so, then the mere fact that actions of a certain class would have good consequences if they were generally performed cannot be sufficient to make performance of such actions a duty, even when the class in question cannot relevantly be made more specific. Something more is necessary. Actions of the class in question must be so related to one another that, if they are not performed in the majority of cases, then they will not produce good consequences—or, at any rate not such good consequences—in any. They must be related to one another in such a way that the good consequences produced by those of them which do produce good consequences are dependent upon a sufficient number of those of them which do not have good consequences being performed. Mr. R. F. Harrod, in an excellent article on the subject,[9] has characterised such classes (in the way in which one would expect of an economist) thus: "There are certain acts which when performed on n similar occasions have con-

[8] *See* D. G. C. Macnabb, *David Hume: His Theory of Knowledge and Morality* (London, New York: Hutchinson's University Library, 1951), p. 182.

[9] R. F. Harrod, "Utilitarianism Revised," *Mind* 45 (April 1936) [pp. 73–87 above].

sequences more than n times as great as those resulting from one performance. And it is in this class of cases that obligations arise."[10] By obligation, apparently, Mr. Harrod does not mean just any sort of obligation. He means our obligation to perform certain actions, although we could produce better consequences by not performing them.

The difference between the view just outlined and the other theory which Hume might have held is this. According to the other theory, the performance of any action was necessary if the others were to produce good consequences. Hence the good consequences produced by the general performance of the class of actions was equally dependent upon the performance of every member of the class. According to the view just outlined, not every member of the class of actions in question must be performed if the others are to continue to have any value. I may omit to perform any one (or any two, or any three) of those actions which themselves produce no good consequences, without detracting from the value of those which do. But if we were to neglect to perform all the actions in the class which themselves had no good consequences, then the good consequences produced by the others would be seriously affected. Hence our objection is answered. Not to perform any one of the actions which themselves produce no good consequences would not detract from the good produced by the general performance of actions of the class provided that the others continued to be performed. But not to perform any at all would seriously diminish it, if not take it away altogether.

Hence we must perform certain actions, which produce no good consequences or even produce harmful consequences, because, if everybody took the liberty of infringing the rule demanding their performance in the same circumstances, its utility would be lost. But we do not think that such rules should be applied in all circumstances. We do not, it is true, think that we should fail to apply a rule, simply because one particular failure to apply it would produce no bad consequences, or even if application of the rule produced harmful consequences, provided that these consequences are not harmful beyond a certain point. But we do not think that such rules should be applied, however disastrous the consequences of applying them are. We think that, if the consequences of a certain application of a rule are disastrous, or even bad beyond a certain point, then the rule should be set aside in this particular case. In other words, when benevolence conflicts with justice, we do not, as Hume seemed to imply, think that justice should always override benevolence. In what circumstances, then, should justice prevail, and in what circumstances benevolence?

We should, I think, only apply a rule to a hard case if the gain which would result from failing to apply the rule in all cases as hard or harder exceeds the loss which would result from failure to apply the rule to those cases.To suppose that the utility of a rule must be destroyed, or even greatly diminished, by failure to apply it in certain restricted instances is a mistake. If we were only to fail to apply it to the hardest of hard cases, the rule might be neglected so rarely that its utility might be undiminished. It is only when we cease to apply the rule to cases less hard that the utility of the rule is impaired, and, even so, the gain from relieving the hard cases may be sufficient to counterbalance the loss of some of the benefit derived from the general application of the rule. If the gain from relieving the hard cases is only just sufficient to balance the loss of utility to the rule, then it is a matter of indifference whether we apply the rule or not. If the gain is insufficient to do this, then the rule should be applied. Mr.

[10] Op. cit., p. 148 [p. 81 above].

Harrod, in the article I have just mentioned, sums up the matter thus: "A lie is justified when the balance of pain or loss of pleasure is such that, if a lie was told in all circumstances when there was no less a balance of pain or loss of pleasure, the harm due to the total loss of confidence did not exceed the sum of harm due to truthfulness in every case."[11] It should be remembered that, though the gain due to failing to apply a rule to a case which is not very hard is, in respect of every individual failure to apply the rule, smaller than the gain resulting from failure to apply a rule to a case which is very hard, not very hard cases occur much more frequently than very hard cases, and, in this respect, the not very hard cases have the advantage. On the other hand, the fact that not very hard cases are frequent means that the loss of utility to the rule by failure to apply it to them will be correspondingly greater than the loss of utility caused by failure to apply it to the very hard cases.

Readers will have noticed that this modified form of utilitarianism agrees with intuitionism in the form in which it is held by Sir David Ross in that, according to both him and it, we should not break certain rules simply because the consequences of breaking them are better than the consequences of keeping them. But it is, in one important respect, superior to Sir David Ross's theory. He thinks that we should pay our debts, keep our promises, honour our agreements, and tell the truth even in circumstances when we could produce more good by failing to do so. On the other hand, he quite properly does not hold the extreme view, that these rules should be observed, however great are the advantages of breaking them. In his own language, he thinks that we have a prima facie duty to bring about as much good as we can, as well as prima facie duties to keep our promises and tell truth, and so on. When our prima facie duty to produce as much good as we can conflicts with our other duties, he thinks that sometimes it is a duty to perform the former prima facie duty, sometimes a duty to perform one of the others. But he is quite unable to provide us with any principle which will tell us when we should tell the truth, or keep the promise, and when we should tell the lie, or break the promise, in order to produce good consequences. He is quite sure that the principle by which we decide between these two conflicting rules is not what utilitarianism, as he understand it, says it is. According to the unmodified form of utilitarianism, we should tell the truth only so long as the consequences of truth-telling are better than the consequences of lying. If the consequences of truth-telling are just as good, or just as bad, as the consequences of lying, then it does not matter whether we tell the truth or not. If the consequences of lying are better than the consequences of telling the truth, then we should lie. Sir David Ross, on the other hand, thinks that we should not lie if the consequences of lying are only slightly better than the consequences of telling the truth, but that we should lie, if the consequences of lying are greatly better. But just how much better the consequences of lying must be than the consequences of telling the truth he is unable to tell us. But this modified form of utilitarianism can tell us, and it is, in this respect, if in no other, superior to Sir David Ross's view.

Utilitarianism, in its modified form, may also provide us with the solution to another of Sir David Ross's problems. What happens when, for example, my prima facie duty to tell the truth conflicts with my prima facie duty to keep my promises? Sir David Ross tells us that, when this happens, it is sometimes my duty to tell the truth, and sometimes my duty to keep my promise. But again, he is unable to

[11] Op. cit., p. 149 [p. 81 above].

provide us with any principle whereby we can decide between such conflicting prima facie duties. This, indeed, accords with his general view that, though rules can be given concerning what actions are prima facie duties, no rules can be given concerning what actions are duties.

Sir David Ross, though he thinks no principles can be given about duties, thinks that we do at least know enough about them to be able to reject the traditional utilitarian's way of solving the problem. We should not, he thinks, tell the lie and keep the promise, or tell the truth and break the promise, according to which of these two alternatives produces the most good. On this point he is probably right. But, it should be noticed, this is not the principle which the modified form of utilitarianism which we are discussing would recommend. We should not consider just the consequences of telling this lie and keeping this promise, or telling this truth and breaking this promise. We should consider what would be the consequences if everybody were to tell such lies in order to keep such promises or, what comes to the same thing, to break such promises in order to enunciate such truths. It may well be that, after reflection upon the general practice of such actions, we conclude that we should keep the promise and tell the lie, even though the consequences of breaking the promise and telling the truth would be better. It should be remembered, too, that the consequences of the general practice of keeping this sort of promise or of telling this sort of truth may differ from the consequences of the general practice of promise-keeping or truth-telling as genera.

So far, so good. But it may well be objected that we have no duty to perform an action simply because it is of a sort which would produce good consequences if performed by everybody, or to refrain from performing it because the general performance of it would be bad. Surely, it might be argued, we must be realistic about matters of duty. We should not base our conduct upon what would happen, if certain conditions, which may be unfulfilled, were realised. We should base our conduct upon what, after the fullest consideration possible in the time at our disposal, it seems most likely will happen. If, therefore, I can relieve a hard case by failing to apply a rule of justice, I should do so, even if the consequences of everybody doing the same would be bad, so long as I have reason to suppose that everybody will not do the same. Even if good consequences would be brought about by the general performance of a certain type of action, I have no duty to perform it, so long as I have good reason to believe that actions of that type will not, in fact, be generally performed. This, it might seem, is what Hobbes thought, and Hume—some of the time—because they both thought that we had not a duty to be just in a state of nature, i.e., in a state in which nobody else is just. Hume, though he thought that we had no duty to be just in a state of nature, thought that our duty to be benevolent was still incumbent upon us, for our duty to be benevolent, unlike our duty to be just, is in no way dependent upon the performance of benevolent actions by other people. Hence, in a state of nature, I have a duty to be benevolent to my fellows and to women[12] and domestic animals, though I have no duty to be just to them.

Mr. Harrod has an answer to this problem which does not seem to me to be

[12] "In many nations the female sex are reduced to like slavery, and are rendered incapable of all property, in opposition to their lordly masters. But though the males, when united, have in all countries bodily force sufficient to maintain this severe tyranny, yet such are the insinuation, address and charms of their fair companions, that women are commonly able to break the confederacy, and share with the other sex in all the rights and privileges of society." L. A. Selby-Bigge, Hume's *Enquiries*, p. 191.

satisfactory. He says: "I believe that, where the practice is not general, a second refining process is required. Will the gain due to its application by all conscientious, i.e., moral, people *only* be sufficient to offset the loss which the crude utilitarian principle registers? It may be objected that there are no moral people. To meet this, for the word moral in the second refining principle, say people sufficiently moral to act disinterestedly in this kind of case."[13]

This answer, however, cannot be accepted. It is being objected that we do not have a duty to apply the principle where nobody else applies it, and Mr. Harrod replies that we have a duty to apply it if there are enough moral people to do likewise. But wherein lies their morality? In applying the principle? But then, they cannot be moral if the principle is not moral, and it is the morality of the principle which is being called in question—and actually, by Mr. Harrod himself, set aside, in favour of the principle as doubly refined. And how many people are there moral enough to apply the principle in a state of nature? Surely, none at all, for a state of nature is defined as one in which there is nobody moral enough to apply the principle.

I think that Mr. Harrod, under the guise of defending the principle that the good or bad consequences of the general performance of a certain type of action should be considered, is really siding with its opponents. For I think that he really believes that it is important to know how many people there are sufficiently moral to apply the principle which I apply, because he thinks that it is important for me to know how likely it is that other people will apply the principle, before I can make up my mind whether I myself have a duty to apply it. But this is just what opponents of the principle think. They think that I have not a duty to be just rather than to relieve a hard case, even if the consequences which would result if everybody were to be unjust in similar cases would be bad, so long as I have reason to believe that other people will not be unjust in similar cases. They think that I have not a duty to be just in a state of nature, even though good consequences would result if everybody were to be just, because I have reason to believe that I shall be alone in my practice of justice.

To the man who objects that one may be unjust to relieve a hard case, even if such an action would have bad consequences if everybody else were to do the same, provided that I have reason to believe that nobody else will do the same, one is inclined to make the following answer. I am not in a better position to estimate what other people will do than they are to estimate what I will do and, if everybody were to relieve hard cases because they thought that it was unlikely that other people would do the same, bad consequences would result. We are inclined to say, if nobody were just in a state of nature, because they thought it unlikely that justice would also be practised by others, then we would never get out of a state of nature. If it be objected that we were never in a state of nature, it may be replied that we are all in a state of nature with regard to some things. Men may not be in a state of nature with regard to debt-paying, nor Englishmen with regard to queueing, but nations are in a state of nature with regard to international agreements, and housewives are, very likely, in a state of nature with regard to saving scrap, when they are told that, if everybody handed in their old dustbin lids, enough metal would be saved to build a battleship.

But, of course, in making these answers, we are not justifying the principle—though we are making it more plausible—for we are falling back on the very principle we are trying to justify. Nor is it

[13] Op. cit., p. 151 [p. 83 above].

possible to justify the principle. If it is true, then it must be accepted as true without reason, though this does not mean that it is irrational to accept it. In this respect it is like any fundamental moral principle, so the fact that it cannot be justified must not be held against it.

But the probability or otherwise of other people doing what I do does have a bearing on my duty to do an action (or to refrain from doing it) if it would have good (or bad) consequences if everybody else did the same. It is true that, if I only have good reason for thinking that other people will not do what I do, then my duty to be just in a hard case still applies. For other people's reasons for thinking that theirs will not be the general practice are as good as mine and, if everybody failed to apply a rule in a hard case merely because they had good reasons for thinking that others would not do the same, bad consequences would result. But if I had conclusive reasons for thinking that other people would not do the same, then it would be my duty to relieve the hard case. For only one person can have conclusive reasons for thinking that others will not relieve the hard cases he relieves, and, from one person's relieving hard cases, no disastrous consequences follow. Similarly, in a state of nature, if I only have good reasons for thinking that others will not apply the rules I apply, my duty to apply these rules remains. But if I have conclusive reasons for thinking that others will not apply the rules I apply, my duty to apply them ceases. For if everybody were to fail to apply these rules only in circumstances in which they knew that nobody else would do the same, no bad consequences would follow. If these two examples seem artificial, this is only because I have considered extreme cases. It is unlikely that I should know that nobody but I will fail to apply a rule of justice in a hard case, and it is unlikely that I should know that no one but I will be just in a state bordering upon a state of nature. But I may sometimes know that the majority of people will not apply a rule to cases as hard as the case to which I fail to apply it, or know that the majority of people are too shortsighted and unrestrained to apply a rule of justice in cases where others do not. In such cases, supposing imitation by a minority of people only is not sufficient to produce any good (or bad) effects, my duty to apply the rule ceases.

This, however, is not an exception to the principles already expounded, but a consequence of them. What I am saying, in other words, is that my knowledge of the behaviour of other people is a characteristic which relevantly specifies the class of actions the consequences of the general practice of which it is my duty to consider. I have a duty to perform a certain action, although believing that other people will not perform it, because, if everybody who believed that other people would not perform it were to do similar actions, good consequences would result. I have not a duty to perform an action, when knowing that other people will not do likewise because, if people performed similar actions only when they knew no one else would do the same, no good consequences would follow.

My duty to perform actions of a sort which would have good consequences if they were generally practiced will thus depend, in some measure, upon my ignorance of the behaviour of other people. I must not, for example, turn aside from applying a principle of justice in a hard case when I do not know that other people will not do the same, because I have every reason to believe that they will have much the same reasons for failing to apply a rule of justice to similar hard cases as I have for failing to apply it to this one, and because, if everybody were to do what I propose doing, disastrous consequences would follow. But, if I were omniscient about the behaviour of other people, then it would be my duty to do that action, which itself has good consequences. But this is not because the principle that we ought always to perform those actions which would have good consequences, if generally performed, and to refrain from performing those actions which would have bad consequences, if generally performed, is not applicable to people who have complete knowledge of the behaviour of others. It is because, to people who have complete knowledge of the behaviour of others, the two principles, that we should perform those actions which themselves have good consequences and that we should perform those actions which are of a sort which would have good consequences, if practiced generally, enjoin the same actions. If everybody having complete knowledge of the behaviour of other people were to perform those actions which themselves had good consequences, good consequences would result; whereas, if all people not having complete knowledge of the behaviour of other people were to perform those actions which themselves had good consequences, bad consequences would result. In the case of people having complete knowledge of the behaviour of others, the unmodified utilitarian principle falls under the modified principle as a special case, and an omniscient being would be justified in acting upon it, though beings like ourselves would not.[14] This does not mean, of course, that the two principles are identical. They would not be identical, even if they always enjoined identical actions, whereas they only do this in very special circumstances. Even when they enjoin identical actions, it is the modified utilitarian principle which is obligatory. The unmodified principle derives its obligatoriness from its accordance with the modified principle, and it is not obligatory in its own right.

It will not have escaped the reader, and it certainly did not escape Mr. Harrod, that there is some connection between the modified utilitarian principle and the Kantian categorical imperative. Now I do not think that the modified utilitarian principle can be deduced, as Kant thought moral principles could be deduced, from the idea of law in general. The claim that moral principles can be deduced from the idea of law in general depends, I think, upon the claim that there is only one set of principles upon which, taken singly or together, it is possible for everybody to act, coupled with a definition of "law" according to which no principle upon which everybody cannot act can properly be said to be a law. It does not seem to me that the claim that there is only one set of principles upon which everyone can act is justified. A universe in which everybody acted morally is perfectly conceivable, but so is a universe in which everybody acted morally with the exception that everybody committed suicide at the age of fifty. The fact that it is possible for everybody to commit suicide at the age of fifty (and, at the same time, to be moral in other respects) does not seem to me to show that it is obligatory, or even permissible, to do this.

Nor do I think that imperfect duties can be derived from the impossibility of one's being able to will that everybody should fail to perform an imperfect duty. First of all it is not clear to me that this is impossible. If a man were sufficiently callous to murder his own wife, might he not be sufficiently callous, supposing he had the power, to will that other men should

[14] Cf. Butler, *Works*, Gladstone's Edition, vol. II, p. 190*n*. "For instance: As we are not competent judges, what is upon the whole for the good of the world, there may be other immediate ends appointed us to pursue, besides that one of doing good, or producing happiness. Though the good of the creation be the only end of the Author of it, yet he may have laid us under particular obligations, which we may discern and feel ourselves under, quite distinct from a perception, that the observance or violation of them is for the happiness or misery of our fellow creatures." Also C. D. Broad, *Five Types of Ethical Theory* (London: K. Paul, Trench, Trubner and Co., Ltd., 1930), pp. 81–82.

murder theirs? Besides, why cannot one will that everybody should fail to perform an (imperfect) duty? Not because of the moral repugnance such general negligence would cause us; Kant is supposed to be giving our inability to will that an action should be generally performed as a reason for thinking that it is wrong, and not vice versa. Are we unable to will general neglect of a duty, because such neglect would be contrary to our interest? Kant speaks as if I cannot will that people should not help others in distress, because, in that case, no one would help me when I am in distress. But, if the fact that an action has consequences which are detrimental to my interest is a bad reason for thinking that it is wrong, surely the fact that I cannot, from self interest, will its universal performance, is a worse one.

But the modified utilitarian principle, though it is not impossible for everybody to fail to act upon it and though it is not impossible, though it may be immoral, for one to will that everybody should transgress it, does conform to some suggestions which may be found in the works of Kant. First of all, the unmodified utilitarian principle is self-defeating, whereas the modified principle is not. If everybody were to act upon the unmodified utilitarian principle, everybody would fail to apply rules of justice to certain hard cases, and bad consequences would result. But the purpose of the people who applied the unmodified utilitarian principle would be to produce good consequences, and so the general application of the rule they were practicing would defeat the ends which determined them to adopt it.

Secondly, suppose that I apply the unmodified utilitarian principle to a certain case, knowing that, if other people apply the modified principle, I can produce good consequences by doing so. In this case, my conduct, though beneficial, is in a certain sense inconsistent. It is not inconsistent in the sense that it is impossible for me to do what I do, nor in the sense that it is impossible for everybody to do what I do, nor in the sense that it is impossible for me to do what I do while others do what they do. My principle is inconsistent with theirs in the sense that both of them could not be acted upon by everybody or, for that matter, by anybody. Since my own principle would be self-defeating if universally adopted, I do not regard it as fit for application by everybody, but take the liberty of allowing myself to make an exception to the ones that I do regard as suitable. Should it be argued, on behalf of a more nearly Kantian position, that my principle is really "Apply the unmodified utilitarian formula, so long as everybody else applies the modified formula," and that this principle cannot be acted upon by everybody, I reply that this argument rests upon a confusion. A judge is applying the principle "Condemn all murderers" just as much when he frees an innocent man as when he sentences a murderer. Similarly, the rest of the world, which is applying the modified utilitarian formula, may just as much be acting on the principle "Apply the unmodified utilitarian formula so long as everybody else applies the modified formula" as am I, who apply the unmodified formula. What is impossible, is not that everybody should apply this principle but that it should ever enjoin more than one person to apply the unmodified utilitarian formula.

The result is some reconciliation between the doctrine of Kant and the teleological ethical principles which he despised. An end, we must say, stands in much the same relation to the morality of principles as do the "facts" in relation to the truth of propositions, and we can no more decide what principles are and are not moral, by means of consistency alone, without reference to ends, than we can settle what propositions are true, by means of consistency alone, without reference to "facts." But though the fitness of any principle to be a moral principle cannot be decided without some reference to an end, the principle must be such that this end is harmoniously and coherently realised by its universal application and, if it can be successfully applied only by a given individual who relies upon the methods of others being more orthodox than his own, the principle is not one which deserves to be called "moral."

In other words, the unmodified utilitarian principle is not eligible to be part of a system of universal legislation, whereas the modified principle is, though it is not the only principle which is. In this respect the modified principle does, while the unmodified principle does not, conform to one of the conditions which any principle must fulfill if it is to be regarded as a principle on which we ought to act, and this condition it is one of Kant's great merits to have emphasized. No principle is fit to be a moral principle unless it is fit that it should be universally adopted and universally applied, though a principle may be unfit for universal adoption, even where universal adoption is logically possible. Our attitude to a principle cannot be a distinctively moral one unless we are prepared to accept, and sometimes to recommend, its universal application. The unmodified utilitarian principle conforms to neither of these two conditions. It is not fit for universal adoption, because the very grounds, namely, that it serves a good end, which recommend its application by one person, prohibit its application by everybody. And our attitude to it cannot be a moral one. For we can be prepared to apply it ourselves only so long as others do not, and hence we cannot possibly be prepared to recommend that it be adopted by others besides ourselves.

J. O. Urmson / The interpretation of the moral philosophy of J. S. Mill

It is a matter which should be of great interest to those who study the psychology of philosophers that the theories of some great philosophers of the past are studied with the most patient and accurate scholarship, while those of others are so burlesqued and travestied by critics and commentators that it is hard to believe that their works are ever seriously read with a sympathetic interest, or even that they are read at all. Amongst those who suffer most in this way John Stuart Mill is an outstanding example. With the exception of a short book by Reginald Jackson,[1] there is no remotely accurate account of his views on deductive logic, so that, for example, the absurd view that the syllogism involves *petitio principii* is almost invariably fathered on him; and, as von Wright says, "A good systematic and critical monograph on Mill's Logic of Induction still remains to be written."[2]

[1] Reginald Jackson, *An Examination of the Deductive Logic of J. S. Mill* (London: Oxford University Press, H. Milford, 1941).

[2] Georg H. von Wright, *A Treatise on Induction and Probability* (London: Routledge and Paul, 1951), p. 164.

But even more perplexing is the almost universal misconstruction placed upon Mill's ethical doctrines; for his *Utilitarianism* is a work which every undergraduate is set to read and which one would therefore expect Mill's critics to have read at least once. But this, apparently, is not so; and instead of Mill's own doctrines a travesty is discussed, so that the most common criticisms of him are simply irrelevant. It will not be the thesis of this paper that Mill's views are immune to criticism, or that they are of impeccable clarity and verbal consistency; it will be maintained that, if interpreted with, say, half the sympathy automatically accorded to Plato, Leibniz, and Kant, an essentially consistent thesis can be discovered which is very superior to that usually attributed to Mill and immune to the common run of criticisms.

One further note must be made on the scope of this paper. Mill, in his *Utilitarianism* attempts to do two things; first, he attempts to state the place of the conception of a *summum bonum* in ethics, secondly, he attempts to give an account of the nature of this ultimate end. We shall

Reprinted from THE PHILOSOPHICAL QUARTERLY, *vol. 3 (January 1953), pp. 33–39 by permission of the author and editors.*

be concerned only with the first of these two parts of Mill's ethical theory; we shall not ask what Mill thought the ultimate end was, and how he thought that his view on this point could be substantiated, but only what part Mill considered that the notion of an ultimate end, whatever it be, must play in a sound ethical theory. This part of Mill's doctrine is logically independent of his account of happiness.

Two mistaken interpretations of Mill

Some of Mill's expositors and critics have thought that Mill was attempting to analyse or define the notion of right in terms of the *summum bonum.* Thus Mill is commonly adduced as an example of an ethical naturalist by those who interpret his account of happiness naturalistically, as being one who defined rightness in terms of the natural consequences of actions. Moore, for example, while criticising Mill's account of the ultimate end says: "In thus insisting that what is right must mean what produces the best possible results Utilitarianism is fully justified."[3] Others have been less favourable in their estimation of this alleged view of Mill's. But right or wrong, it seems clear to me that Mill did not hold it. Mill's only reference to this analytic problem is on page 27 (of the Everyman's edition, to which all references will be made) [p. 33 above] where he refers to a person "who sees in moral obligation a transcendent fact, an objective reality belonging to the province of 'Things in themselves'," and goes on to speak of this view as an irrelevant opinion "on this point of Ontology," as though the analysis of ethical terms was not part of ethical philosophy at all as he conceived it, but part of ontology. It seems clear that when Mill speaks of his quest being for the "criterion of right and wrong" (p. 1) [p. 13 above], "concerning the foundation of morality" (p. 1) for a "test of right and wrong" (p. 2) [p. 14 above], he is looking for a "means of ascertaining what is right or wrong" (p. 2), not for a definition of these terms. We shall not, therefore, deal further with this interpretation of Mill; if a further refutation of it is required it should be sought in the agreement of the text with the alternative exposition shortly to be given.

The other mistaken view avoids the error of this first view, and indeed is incompatible with it. It is, probably, the received view. On this interpretation Mill is looking for a test of right or wrong as the ultimate test by which one can justify the ascription of rightness or wrongness to courses of action, rightness and wrongness being taken to be words which we understand. This test is taken to be whether the course of action does or does not tend to promote the ultimate end (which Mill no doubt says is the general happiness). So far there is no cause to quarrel with the received view, for it is surely correct. But in detail the view is wrong. For it is further suggested that for Mill this ultimate test is also the immediate test; the rightness or wrongness of any particular action is to be decided by considering whether it promotes the ultimate end. We may, it might be admitted on Mill's view sometimes act, by rule of thumb or in a hurry, without actually raising this question; but the actual justification, if there is one, must be directly in terms of consequences, including the consequences of the example that we have set. On this view, then, Mill holds that an action, a particular action, is right if it promotes the ultimate end better than any alternative, and otherwise it is wrong. However we in fact make up our minds in moral situations, so far as justification goes no other factor enters

[3] *Principia Ethica* (Cambridge: The University Press, 1948), p. 106.

into the matter. It is clear that on this interpretation Mill is immediately open to two shattering objections; first, it is obviously and correctly urged, if one has, for example, promised to do something it is one's duty to do it at least partly because one has promised to do it and not merely because of consequences, even if these consequences are taken to include one's example in promise-breaking. Secondly, it is correctly pointed out that on this view a man who, *ceteris paribus*, chooses the inferior of two musical comedies for an evening's entertainment has done a moral wrong, and this is preposterous.[4] If this were in fact the view of Mill, he would indeed be fit for little more than the halting eristic of philosophical infants.

A revised interpretation of Mill

I shall now set out in a set of propositions what I take to be in fact Mill's view and substantiate them afterwards from the text. This will obscure the subtleties but will make clearer the main lines of interpretation.

A. A particular action is justified as being right by showing that it is in accord with some moral rule. It is shown to be wrong by showing that it transgresses some moral rule.
B. A moral rule is shown to be correct by showing that the recognition of that rule promotes the ultimate end.
C. Moral rules can be justified only in regard to matters in which the general welfare is more than negligibly affected.
D. Where no moral rule is applicable the question of the rightness or wrongness of particular acts does not arise, though the worth of the actions can be estimated in other ways.

As a terminological point it should be mentioned that where the phrase "moral rule" occurs above, Mill uses the phrase "secondary principle" more generally, though he sometimes says "moral law." By these terms, whichever is preferred, Mill is referring to such precepts as "Keep promises," "Do no murder," or "Tell no lies." A list of which Mill approves is to be found in *On Liberty* [London: 1859; (p. 135)].

There is, no doubt, need of further explanation of these propositions; but that, and some caveats, can best be given in the process of establishing that these are in fact Mill's views. First, then, to establish from the text that in Mill's view particular actions are shown to be right or wrong by showing that they are or are not in accord with some moral rule. (i) He says with evident approbation on p. 2: "The intuitive, no less than what may be termed the inductive, school of ethics, insists on the necessity of general laws. They both agree that the morality of an individual action is not a question of direct perception, but of the application of a law to an individual case. They recognise also, to a great extent, the same moral laws." Mill reproaches these schools only with being unable to give a unifying rationale of these laws (as he will do in proposition B). (ii) He says on page 22 [p. 29 above]: "But to consider the rules of morality as improvable is one thing; to pass over the intermediate generalisations entirely and endeavour to test each individual action directly by the first principle, is another. It is a strange notion that the acknowledgement of a first principle is inconsistent with the admission of secondary ones." He adds, with feeling: "Men really ought to leave off talking a kind of nonsense on this subject which they would neither talk nor listen to on other matters

[4] For one example of this interpretation of Mill and the first and more important objection, see Edgar F. Carritt, *The Theory of Morals*, chap. iv.

of practical concernment." (iii) Having admitted on p. 23 [p. 29 above] that "rules of conduct cannot be so framed as to require no exceptions," he adds (p. 24) [p. 29 above] "We must remember that only in these cases of conflict between secondary principles is it requisite that first principles should be appealed to. There is no case of moral obligation in which some secondary principle is not involved; and if only one, there can seldom be any real doubt which one it is, in the mind of any person by whom the principle itself is recognised." This quotation supports both propositions A and D. It shows that for Mill moral rules are not merely rules of thumb which aid the unreflective man in making up his mind, but an essential part of moral reasoning. The relevance of a moral rule is the criterion of whether we are dealing with a case of right or wrong or some other moral or prudential situation. (iv) The last passage which we shall select to establish this interpretation of Mill (it would be easy to find more) is also a joint confirmation of propositions A and D, showing that our last was not an obiter dictum on which we have placed too much weight. In the chapter entitled "On the connection between justice and utility," Mill has maintained that it is a distinguishing mark of a just act that it is one required by a specific rule or law, positive or moral, carrying also liability to penal sanctions. He then writes this important paragraph (p. 45) [pp. 46–47 above], which in view of its importance and the neglect that it has suffered must be quoted at length: "The above is, I think, a true account, as far as it goes, of the origin and progressive growth of the idea of justice. But we must observe, that it contains, as yet, nothing to distinguish that obligation from moral obligation in general. For the truth is, that the idea of penal sanction, which is the essence of law, enters not only into the conception of injustice, but into that of any kind of wrong. We do not call anything wrong, unless we mean to imply that a person ought to be punished in some way or other for doing it; if not by law, by the opinion of his fellow-creatures; if not by opinion, by the reproaches of his own conscience. This seems to be the real turning point of the distinction between morality and simple expediency. It is a part of the notion of Duty in every one of its forms, that a person may rightfully be compelled to fulfil it. Duty is a thing which may be exacted from a person, as one exacts a debt. Unless we think that it may be exacted from him. we do not call it his duty. . . . There are other things, on the contrary, which we wish that people should do, which we like or admire them for doing, perhaps dislike or despise them for not doing, but yet admit that they are not bound to do; it is not a case of moral obligation; we do not blame them, that is, we do not think that they are proper objects of punishment. . . . I think there is no doubt that this distinction lies at the bottom of the notions of right and wrong; that we call any conduct wrong, or employ, instead, some other term of dislike or disparagement, according as we think that the person ought, or ought not, to be punished for it; and we say, it would be right to do so and so, or merely that it would be desirable or laudable, according as we would wish to see the person whom it concerns, compelled, or only persuaded and exhorted, to act in that manner." How supporters of the received view have squared it with this passage I do not know; they do not mention it. If they have noticed it at all it is, presumably, regarded as an example of Mill's inconsistent eclecticism. Mill here makes it quite clear that in his view right and wrong are derived from moral rules; in other cases where the ultimate end is no doubt affected appraisal of conduct must be made in other ways. For example, if one's own participation in the ultimate end is impaired without breach of moral law, it is (*Liberty*, p. 135) imprudence or lack of self-respect, it is not wrong-doing. So much for the establishment of this interpretation of Mill, in a positive way, as regards points A and D. We must now ask whether there is anything in Mill which is inconsistent with it and in favour of the received view.

It is impossible to show positively that there is nothing in Mill which favours the received view against the interpretation here given, for it would require a complete review of everything that Mill says. We shall have to be content with examining two points which might be thought to tell in favour of the received view.

(*a*) On p. 6 [p. 18 above] Mill says: "The creed which accepts as the foundation of morals, Utility, or the Greatest Happiness Principle, holds that actions are right in proportion as they tend to promote happiness, wrong as they tend to promote the reverse of Happiness." This seems to be the well-known sentence which is at the bottom of the received interpretation. Of course, it could be taken as a loose and inaccurate statement of the received view, if the general argument required it. But note that strictly one can say that a certain action tends to produce a certain result only if one is speaking of type- rather than token-actions. Drinking alcohol may tend to promote exhilaration, but my drinking this particular glass either does or does not produce it. It seems, then, that Mill can well be interpreted here as regarding moral rules as forbidding or enjoining types of action, in fact as making the point that the right moral rules are the ones which promote the ultimate end (my proposition B), not as saying something contrary to proposition A. And this, or something like it, is the interpretation which consistency requires. Mill's reference to "tendencies of actions" at the top of p. 22 [p. 29 above] supports the stress here laid on the word "tend," and that context should be examined by those who require further conviction.

(*b*) Mill sometimes refers to moral rules as "intermediate generalisations" (e.g., p. 22) from the supreme principle, or as "corollaries" of it (also p. 22). These are probably the sort of phrases which lead people to think that they play a purely heuristic role in ethical thinking for Mill. As for the expression "intermediate generalisation," Mill undoubtedly thinks that we should, and to some extent do, arrive at and improve our moral rules by such methods as observing that a certain type of action has had bad results of a social kind in such an overwhelming majority of cases that it ought to be banned. (But this is an oversimplification; see the note on p. 58 [p. 56] on how we ought to arrive at moral rules, and the pessimistic account of how we in fact arrive at them in *Liberty*, p. 69–70.) But this account of the genesis of moral rules does not require us to interpret them as being anything but rules when once made. It really seems unnecessary to say much of the expression "corollary"; Mill obviously cannot wish it to be taken literally; in fact it is hard to state the relation of moral rules to a justifying principle with exactitude and Mill, in a popular article in *Fraser's* [*Magazine*], did not try very hard to do so.

Moral rules and the ultimate end

We have already been led in our examination of possible objections to proposition A to say something in defence of the view that Mill thought that a moral rule is shown to be correct by showing that the recognition of that rule promotes the ultimate end (proposition B). A little more may be added on this point, though it seems fairly obvious that if we are right in saying that the supreme principle is not to be evoked, in Mill's view, in the direct justification of particular right acts, it must thus come in in an indirect way in view of the importance that Mill attached to it. And it is hard to think what the indirect way is if not this. (i) On p. 3 [p. 14 above] Mill reproaches other moral philosophers with not giving a satisfactory account of moral rules in terms of a fundamental principle, though they have correctly placed moral rules as governing particular actions. It would be indeed the mark of an inconsistent philosopher if he did not try to repair the one serious omission which he ascribes to others. (ii) Mill ascribes to Kant (p. 4) [p. 15 above] the use of utilitarian arguments because, Mill alleges, he in fact supports the rules of morality by showing the evil consequences of not adopting them or adopting alternatives. Thus Mill is here regarding as distinctively utilitarian the justification or rejection of moral rules on the ground of consequences. He could hardly have wished to suggest that Kant would directly justify, even inadvertently, particular actions on such grounds. But it is perhaps not to the point to argue this matter more elaborately. If anyone has been convinced by what has gone before, he will not need much argument on this point; with others it is superfluous to make the attempt.

In what fields are moral rules of right and wrong applicable?

The applicability of moral rules is, says Mill, "the characteristic difference which marks off, not justice, but morality in general, from the remaining provinces of Expediency and Worthiness" (p. 46 [p. 47 above]. Mill says little or nothing in *Utilitarianism* about the boundary between morality and worthiness (surely it would be better to have said the boundary between right and wrong on the one hand and other forms of both moral and non-moral appraisal on the other?). It seems reasonable to suppose that he would have recognised that the use of moral rules must be confined to matters in which the kind of consequence is sufficiently invariable for there not to be too many exceptions. But this is a pragmatic limitation; Mill does have something to say about a limitation in principle in *Liberty* which I have crudely summarised in my proposition C—moral rules can be justifiably maintained in regard only to matters in which the general welfare is more than negligibly affected.

It is important to note that Mill in *Liberty* is concerned with freedom from moral sanctions as well as the sanctions of positive law. The distinction between self-regarding and other actions is regarded by him as relevant to moral as well as to political philosophy. The most noteworthy passage which bears on the scope of moral rules is on page 135. Here he mentions such things as encroachment on the rights of others as being "fit objects of moral reprobation, and, in grave cases, of moral retribution and punishment." But self-regarding faults (low tastes and the like) are "not properly immoralities and to whatever pitch they are carried, do not constitute wickedness. . . . The term duty to oneself, when it means anything more than prudence, means self-respect or self-development." Self-regarding faults render the culprit "necessarily and properly a subject of distaste, or, in extreme cases, even of contempt," but this is in the sphere of worthiness not of right and wrong.

So much then for Mill's account of the logic of moral reasoning. It must be emphasized that no more has been attempted than a skeleton plan of Mill's answer, and that Mill puts the matter more richly and more subtly in his book. Even on the question interpretation more store must be laid on the effect of a continuous reading in the light of the skeleton plan than on the effect of the few leading quotations introduced in this paper. It is emphatically not the contention of this paper that Mill has given a finally correct account of these matters which is immune to all criticism; an attempt has been made only to give a sympathetic account without any criticism favourable or unfavourable. But I certainly do maintain that the current interpretations of Mill's *Utilitarianism* are so unsympathetic and so incorrect that the majority of criticisms which have in fact been based on them are irrelevant and worthless.

John Rawls / Two concepts of rules

In this paper I want to show the importance of the distinction between justifying a practice[1] and justifying a particular action falling under it, and I want to explain the logical basis of this distinction and how it is possible to miss its significance. While the distinction has frequently been made,[2] and is now becoming commonplace, there remains the task of explaining the tendency either to overlook it altogether, or to fail to appreciate its importance.

To show the importance of the distinction I am going to defend utilitarianism

[1] I use the word "practice" throughout as a sort of technical term meaning any form of activity specified by a system of rules which defines offices, roles, moves, penalties, defenses, and so on, and which gives the activity its structure. As examples one may think of games and rituals, trials and parliaments.

[2] The distinction is central to Hume's discussion of justice in *A Treatise of Human Nature*, bk. III, pt. 2, esp. secs. 2–4. It is clearly stated by John Austin in the second lecture of *Lectures on Jurisprudence* (4th ed.; London, 1873), I, 116ff. (1st ed., 1832). Also it may be argued that J. S. Mill took it for granted in *Utilitarianism;* on this point cf. J. O. Urmson, "The Interpretation of the Moral Philosophy of J. S. Mill," *Philosophical Quarterly* 3 (January 1953) [pp. 168–174 above]. In addition to the arguments given by Urmson there are several clear statements of the distinction in *A System of Logic* (8th ed.; London, 1872), bk. VI, ch. xii pars. 2, 3, 7 [pp. 3, 4 above.]. The distinction is fundamental to J. D. Mabbott's important paper, "Punishment," *Mind* 48 (April 1939) [pp. 88–98 above]. More recently the distinction has been stated with particular emphasis by S. E. Toulmin in *The Place of Reason in Ethics* (New York: Cambridge University Press, 1950), see esp. ch. xi, where it plays a major part in his account of moral reasoning. Toulmin doesn't explain the basis of the distinction, nor how one might overlook its importance, as I try to in this paper; and in my review of his book (*Philosophical Review* 50 [October 1951]), as some of my criticisms show, I failed to understand the force of it. See also H. D. Aiken, "The Levels of Moral Discourse," *Ethics* 62 (1952); A. M. Quinton, "Punishment," *Analysis* 14 (June 1954), and P. H. Nowell-Smith, *Ethics* (London: Penguin Books, 1954), pp. 236–239, 271–273.

Reprinted from THE PHILOSOPHICAL REVIEW, *vol. 64 (January 1955), pp. 3–32 by permission of the author and editors. This article is a revision of a paper presented to the Harvard Philosophy Club on April 30, 1954.*

against those objections which have traditionally been made against it in connection with punishment and the obligation to keep promises. I hope to show that if one uses the distinction in question then one can state utilitarianism in a way which makes it a much better explication of our considered moral judgments than these traditional objections would seem to admit.[3] Thus the importance of the distinction is shown by the way it strengthens the utilitarian view regardless of whether that view is completely defensible or not.

To explain how the significance of the distinction may be overlooked, I am going to discuss two conceptions of rules. One of these conceptions conceals the importance of distinguishing between the justification of a rule or practice and the justification of a particular action falling under it. The other conception makes it clear why this distinction must be made and what is its logical basis.

I

The subject of punishment, in the sense of attaching legal penalties to the violation of legal rules, has always been a troubling moral question.[4] The trouble about it has not been that people disagree as to whether or not punishment is justifiable. Most people have held that, freed from certain abuses, it is an acceptable institution. Only a few have rejected punishment entirely, which is rather surprising when one considers all that can be said against it. The difficulty is with the justification of punishment: various arguments for it have been given by moral philosophers, but so far none of them has won any sort of general acceptance; no justification is without those who detest it. I hope to show that the use of the aforementioned distinction enables one to state the utilitarian view in a way which allows for the sound points of its critics.

For our purposes we may say that there are two justifications of punishment. What we may call the retributive view is that punishment is justified on the grounds that wrongdoing merits punishment. It is morally fitting that a person who does wrong should suffer in proportion to his wrongdoing. That a criminal should be punished follows from his guilt, and the severity of the appropriate punishment depends on the depravity of his act. The state of affairs where a wrongdoer suffers punishment is morally better than the state of affairs where he does not; and it is better irrespective of any of the consequences of punishing him.

What we may call the utilitarian view holds that on the principle that bygones are bygones and that only future consequences are material to present decisions, punishment is justifiable only by reference to the probable consequences of maintaining it as one of the devices of the social order. Wrongs committed in the past are, as such, not relevant considerations for deciding what to do. If punishment can be shown to promote effectively the interest of society it is justifiable, otherwise it is not.

I have stated these two competing views very roughly to make one feel the conflict between them: one feels the force of *both* arguments and one wonders how they can be reconciled. From my introductory remarks it is obvious that the resolution which I am going to propose is that in this case one must distinguish between justifying a practice as a system of rules to be applied and enforced, and justifying

[3] On the concept of explication see the author's paper, "Outline of a Decision Procedure for Ethics," *Philosophical Review* 60 (April 1951) 177–197.

[4] While this paper was being revised, Quinton's appeared; footnote 2 supra. There are several respects in which my remarks are similar to his. Yet as I consider some further questions and rely on somewhat different arguments, I have retained the discussion of punishment and promises together as two test cases for utilitarianism.

a particular action which falls under these rules; utilitarian arguments are appropriate with regard to questions about practices, while retributive arguments fit the application of particular rules to particular cases.

We might try to get clear about this distinction by imagining how a father might answer the question of his son. Suppose the son asks, "Why was *F* put in jail yesterday?" The father answers, "Because he robbed the bank at *B*. He was duly tried and found guilty. That's why he was put in jail yesterday." But suppose the son had asked a different question, namely, "Why do people put other people in jail?" Then the father might answer, "To protect good people from bad people" or "To stop people from doing things that would make it uneasy for all of us; for otherwise we wouldn't be able to go to bed at night and sleep in peace." There are two very different questions here. One question emphasizes the proper name: it asks why *F* was punished rather than someone else, or it asks what he was punished for. The other question asks why we have the institution of punishment: why do people punish one another rather than, say, always forgiving one another?

Thus the father says in effect that a particular man is punished, rather than some other man, because he is guilty, and he is guilty because he broke the law (past tense). In his case the law looks back, the judge looks back, the jury looks back, and a penalty is visited upon him for something he did. That a man is to be punished, and what his punishment is to be, is settled by its being shown that he broke the law and that the law assigns that penalty for the violation of it.

On the other hand we have the institution of punishment itself and recommend and accept various changes in it, because it is thought by the (ideal) legislator and by those to whom the law applies that, as a part of a system of law impartially applied from case to case arising under it, it will have the consequence, in the long run, of furthering the interests of society.

One can say, then, that the judge and the legislator stand in different positions and look in different directions: one to the past, the other to the future. The justification of what the judge does, qua judge, sounds like the retributive view; the justification of what the (ideal) legislator does, qua legislator, sounds like the utilitarian view. Thus both views have a point (this is as it should be since intelligent and sensitive persons have been on both sides of the argument); and one's initial confusion disappears once one sees that these views apply to persons holding different offices with different duties, and situated differently with respect to the system of rules that make up the criminal law.[5]

One might say, however, that the utilitarian view is more fundamental since it applies to a more fundamental office, for the judge carries out the legislator's will so far as he can determine it. Once the legislator decides to have laws and to assign penalties for their violation (as things are there must be both the law and the penalty) an institution is set up which involves a retributive conception of particular cases. It is part of the concept of the criminal law as a system of rules that the application and enforcement of these rules in particular cases should be justifiable by arguments of a retributive character. The decision whether or not to use law rather than some other mechanism of social control, and the decision as to what laws to have and what penalties to assign, may be settled by utilitarian arguments; but if one decides to have laws then one has decided on something whose working in particular cases is retributive in form.[6]

[5] Note the fact that different sorts of arguments are suited to different offices. One way of taking the differences between ethical theories is to regard them as accounts of the reasons expected in different offices.

[6] In this connection see Mabbott, op. cit., pp. 163–164 [pp. 95–96 above.].

The answer, then, to the confusion engendered by the two views of punishment is quite simple: one distinguishes two offices, that of the judge and that of the legislator, and one distinguishes their different stations with respect to the system of rules which make up the law; and then one notes that the different sorts of considerations which would usually be offered as reasons for what is done under the cover of these offices can be paired off with the competing justifications of punishment. One reconciles the two views by the time-honored device of making them apply to different situations.

But can it really be this simple? Well, this answer allows for the apparent intent of each side. Does a person who advocates the retributive view necessarily advocate, as an *institution*, legal machinery whose essential purpose is to set up and preserve a correspondence between moral turpitude and suffering? Surely not.[7] What retributionists have rightly insisted upon is that no man can be punished unless he is guilty, that is, unless he has broken the law. Their fundamental criticism of the utilitarian account is that, as they interpret it, it sanctions an innocent person's being punished (if one may call it that) for the benefit of society.

On the other hand, utilitarians agree that punishment is to be inflicted only for the violation of law. They regard this much as understood from the concept of punishment itself.[8] The point of the utilitarian account concerns the institution as a system of rules: utilitarianism seeks to limit its use by declaring it justifiable only if it can be shown to foster effectively the good of society. Historically it is a protest against the indiscriminate and ineffective use of the criminal law.[9] It seeks to dissuade us from assigning to penal institutions the improper, if not sacrilegious, task of matching suffering with moral turpitude. Like others, utilitarians want penal institutions designed so that, as far as humanly possible, only those who break the law run afoul of it. They hold that no official should have discretionary power to inflict penalties whenever he thinks it for the benefit of society; for on utilitarian grounds an institution granting such power could not be justified.[10]

[7] On this point see Sir David Ross, *The Right and the Good* (Oxford: The University Press, 1930), pp. 57–60.

[8] See Hobbes's definition of punishment in *Leviathan*, ch. xxviii; and Bentham's definition in *The Principle of Morals and Legislation*, ch. xii, par. 36, ch. xv, par. 28, and in *The Rationale of Punishment* (London, 1830), bk. I, ch. i. They could agree with Bradley that: "Punishment is punishment only when it is deserved. We pay the penalty, because we owe it, and for no other reason; and if punishment is inflicted for any other reason whatever than because it is merited by wrong, it is a gross immorality, a crying injustice, an abominable crime, and not what it pretends to be." *Ethical Studies*, 2nd ed. (Oxford: Clarendon Press, 1927), pp. 26–27. Certainly by definition it isn't what it pretends to be. The innocent can only be punished by mistake; deliberate "punishment" of the innocent necessarily involves fraud.

[9] Cf. Leon Radzinowicz, *A History of English Criminal Law: The Movement for Reform 1750–1833* (London: Stevens Press, 1948), esp. ch. xi on Bentham.

[10] Bentham discusses how corresponding to a punitory provision of a criminal law there is another provision which stands to it as an antagonist and which needs a name as much as the punitory. He calls it, as one might expect, the *anaetiosostic*, and of it he says: "The punishment of guilt is the object of the former one: the preservation of innocence that of the latter." In the same connection he asserts that it is never thought fit to give the judge the option of deciding whether a thief (that is, a person whom he believes to be a thief, for the judge's belief is what the question must always turn upon) should hang or not, and so the law writes the provision: "The judge shall not cause a thief to be hanged unless he have been duly convicted and sentenced in course of law" (*The Limits of Jurisprudence Defined*, ed. C. W. Everett [New York: Columbia University Press, 1945], pp. 238–239).

The suggested way of reconciling the retributive and the utilitarian justifications of punishment seems to account for what both sides have wanted to say. There are, however, two further questions which arise, and I shall devote the remainder of this section to them.

First, will not a difference of opinion as to the proper criterion of just law make the proposed reconciliation unacceptable to retributionists? Will they not question whether, if the utilitarian principle is used as the criterion, it follows that those who have broken the law are guilty in a way which satisfies their demand that those punished deserve to be punished? To answer this difficulty, suppose that the rules of the criminal law are justified on utilitarian grounds (it is only for laws that meet his criterion that the utilitarian can be held responsible). Then it follows that the actions which the criminal law specifies as offenses are such that, if they were tolerated, terror and alarm would spread in society. Consequently, retributionists can only deny that those who are punished deserve to be punished if they deny that such actions are wrong. This they will not want to do.

The second question is whether utilitarianism doesn't justify too much. One pictures it as an engine of justification which, if consistently adopted, could be used to justify cruel and arbitrary institutions. Retributionists may be supposed to concede that utilitarians *intend* to reform the law and to make it more humane; that utilitarians do not *wish* to justify any such thing as punishment of the innocent; and that utilitarians may appeal to the fact that punishment presupposes guilt in the sense that by punishment one understands an institution attaching penalties to the infraction of legal rules, and therefore that it is logically absurd to suppose that utilitarians in justifying *punishment* might also have justified punishment (if we may call it that) of the innocent. The real question, however, is whether the utilitarian, in justifying punishment, hasn't used arguments which commit him to accepting the infliction of suffering on innocent persons if it is for the good of society (whether or not one calls this punishment). More generally, isn't the utilitarian committed in principle to accepting many practices which he, as a morally sensitive person, wouldn't want to accept? Retributionists are inclined to hold that there is no way to stop the utilitarian principle from justifying too much except by adding to it a principle which distributes certain rights to individuals. Then the amended criterion is not the greatest benefit of society *simpliciter,* but the greatest benefit of society subject to the constraint that no one's rights may be violated. Now while I think that the classical utilitarians proposed a criterion of this more complicated sort, I do not want to argue that point here.[11] What I want to show is that there is *another* way of preventing the utilitarian principle from justifying too much, or at least of making it much less likely to do so: namely, by stating utilitarianism in a way which accounts for the distinction between the justification of an institution and the justification of a particular action falling under it.

I begin by defining the institution of punishment as follows: a person is said to suffer punishment whenever he is legally deprived of some of the normal rights of a citizen on the ground that he has violated a rule of law, the violation having been established by trial according to the due process of law, provided that the deprivation is carried out by the recognized legal authorities of the state, that the rule of law clearly specifies both the offense and the attached penalty, that the courts construe statutes strictly, and that the

[11] By the classical utilitarians I understand Hobbes, Hume, Bentham, J. S. Mill, and Sidgwick.

statute was on the books prior to the time of the offense.[12] This definition specifies what I shall understand by punishment. The question is whether utilitarian arguments may be found to justify institutions widely different from this and such as one would find cruel and arbitrary.

This question is best answered, I think, by taking up a particular accusation. Consider the following from Carritt:

> . . . the utilitarian must hold that we are justified in inflicting pain always and only to prevent worse pain or bring about greater happiness. This, then, is all we need to consider in so-called punishment, which must be purely preventive. But if some kind of very cruel crime becomes common, and none of the criminals can be caught, it might be highly expedient, as an example, to hang an innocent man, if a charge against him could be so framed that he were universally thought guilty; indeed this would only fail to be an ideal instance of utilitarian 'punishment' because the victim himself would not have been so likely as a real felon to commit such a crime in the future; in all other respects it would be perfectly deterrent and therefore felicific.[13]

Carritt is trying to show that there are occasions when a utilitarian argument would justify taking an action which would be generally condemned; and thus that utilitarianism justifies too much. But the failure of Carritt's argument lies in the fact that he makes no distinction between the justification of the general system of rules which constitutes penal institutions and the justification of particular applications of these rules to particular cases by the various officials whose job it is to administer them. This becomes perfectly clear when one asks who the "we" are of whom Carritt speaks. Who is this who has a sort of absolute authority on particular occasions to decide that an innocent man shall be "punished" if everyone can be convinced that he is guilty? Is this person the legislator, or the judge, or the body of private citizens, or what? It is utterly crucial to know who is to decide such matters, and by what authority, for all of this must be written into the rules of the institution. Until one knows these things one doesn't know what the institution is whose justification is being challenged; and as the utilitarian principle applies to the institution one doesn't know whether it is justifiable on utilitarian grounds or not.

Once this is understood it is clear what the countermove to Carritt's argument is. One must describe more carefully what the *institution* is which his example suggests, and then ask oneself whether or not it is likely that having this institution would be for the benefit of society in the long run. One must not content oneself with the vague thought that, when it's a question of *this* case, it would be a good thing if *somebody* did something even if an innocent person were to suffer.

Try to imagine, then, an institution (which we may call "telishment") which is such that the officials set up by it have authority to arrange a trial for the condemnation of an innocent man whenever they are of the opinion that doing so would be in the best interests of society. The discretion of officials is limited, however, by the rule that they may not condemn an innocent man to undergo such an ordeal unless there is, at the time, a wave of offenses similar to that with which they charge him and telish him for. We may imagine that the officials having the discretionary authority are the judges of the higher courts in consultation with the chief of police, the minister of justice, and a committee of the legislature.

Once one realizes that one is involved in setting up an *institution*, one sees that the hazards are very great. For example, what check is there on the officials? How is one to tell whether or not their actions are

12 All these features of punishment are mentioned by Hobbes; cf. *Leviathan*, ch. xxviii.

13 *Ethical and Political Thinking* (Oxford: Clarendon Press, 1947), p. 65.

authorized? How is one to limit the risks involved in allowing such systematic deception? How is one to avoid giving anything short of complete discretion to the authorities to telish anyone they like? In addition to these considerations, it is obvious that people will come to have a very different attitude towards their penal system when telishment is adjoined to it. They will be uncertain as to whether a convicted man has been punished or telished. They will wonder whether or not they should feel sorry for him. They will wonder whether the same fate won't at any time fall on them. If one pictures how such an institution would actually work, and the enormous risks involved in it, it seems clear that it would serve no useful purpose. A utilitarian justification for this institution is most unlikely.

It happens in general that as one drops off the defining features of punishment one ends up with an institution whose utilitarian justification is highly doubtful. One reason for this is that punishment works like a kind of price system: by altering the prices one has to pay for the performance of actions it supplies a motive for avoiding some actions and doing others. The defining features are essential if punishment is to work in this way; so that an institution which lacks these features, e.g., an institution which is set up to "punish" the innocent, is likely to have about as much point as a price system (if one may call it that) where the prices of things change at random from day to day and one learns the price of something after one has agreed to buy it.[14]

If one is careful to apply the utilitarian principle to the institution which is to authorize particular actions, then there is *less* danger of its justifying too much. Carritt's example gains plausibility by its indefiniteness and by its concentration on the particular case. His argument will only hold if it can be shown that there are utilitarian arguments which justify an institution whose publicly ascertainable offices and powers are such as to permit officials to exercise that kind of discretion in particular cases. But the requirement of having to build the arbitrary features of the particular decision into the institutional practice makes the justification much less likely to go through.

II

I shall now consider the question of promises. The objection to utilitarianism in connection with promises seems to be this: it is believed that on the utilitarian view when a person makes a promise the only ground upon which he should keep it, if he should keep it, is that by keeping it he

[14] The analogy with the price system suggests an answer to the question how utilitarian considerations insure that punishment is proportional to the offense. It is interesting to note that Sir David Ross, after making the distinction between justifying a penal law and justifying a particular application of it, and after stating that utilitarian considerations have a large place in determining the former, still holds back from accepting the utilitarian justification of punishment on the grounds that justice requires that punishment be proportional to the offense, and that utilitarianism is unable to account for this. Cf. *The Right and the Good* (Oxford: Clarendon Press, 1930), pp. 61–62. I do not claim that utilitarianism can account for this requirement as Sir David might wish, but it happens, nevertheless, that if utilitarian considerations are followed penalties will be proportional to offenses in this sense: the order of offenses according to seriousness can be paired off with the order of penalties according to severity. Also the absolute level of penalties will be as low as possible. This follows from the assumption that people are rational (i.e., that they are able to take into account the "prices" the state puts on actions), the utilitarian rule that a penal system should provide a motive for preferring the less serious offense, and the principle that punishment as such is an evil. All this was carefully worked out by Bentham in *The Principles of Morals and Legislation*, chs. xiii–xv.

will realize the most good on the whole. So that if one asks the question "Why should I keep *my* promise?" the utilitarian answer is understood to be that doing so in *this* case will have the best consequences. And this answer is said, quite rightly, to conflict with the way in which the obligation to keep promises is regarded.

Now of course critics of utilitarianism are not unaware that one defense sometimes attributed to utilitarians is the consideration involving the practice of promise-keeping.[15] In this connection they are supposed to argue something like this: It must be admitted that we feel strictly about keeping promises, more strictly than it might seem our view can account for. But when we consider the matter carefully it is always necessary to take into account the effect which our action will have on the practice of making promises. The promiser must weigh, not only the effects of breaking his promise on the particular case, but also the effect which his breaking his promise will have on the practice itself. Since the practice is of great utilitarian value, and since breaking one's promise always seriously damages it, one will seldom be justified in breaking one's promise. If we view our individual promises in the wider context of the practice of promising itself we can account for the strictness of the obligation to keep promises. There is always one very strong utilitarian consideration in favor of keeping them, and this will insure that when the question arises as to whether or not to keep a promise it will usually turn out that one should, even where the facts of the particular case taken by itself would seem to justify one's breaking it. In this way the strictness with which we view the obligation to keep promises is accounted for.

Ross has criticized this defense as follows:[16] However great the value of the practice of promising, on utilitarian grounds, there must be some value which is greater, and one can imagine it to be obtainable by breaking a promise. Therefore there might be a case where the promiser could argue that breaking his promise was justified as leading to a better state of affairs on the whole. And the promiser could argue in this way no matter how slight the advantage won by breaking the promise. If one were to challenge the promiser his defense would be that what he did was best on the whole in view of all the utilitarian considerations, which in this case *include* the importance of the practice. Ross feels that such a defense would be unacceptable. I think he is right insofar as he is protesting against the appeal to consequences in general and without further explanation. Yet it is extremely difficult to weigh the force of Ross's argument. The kind of case imagined seems unrealistic and one feels that it needs to be described. One is inclined to think that it would either turn out that such a case came under an exception defined by the practice itself, in which case there would not be an appeal to consequences in general on the particular case, or it would happen that the circumstances were so peculiar that the conditions which the practice presupposes no longer obtained. But certainly Ross is right in thinking that it strikes us as wrong for a person to defend breaking a promise by a general appeal to consequences. For a general utilitarian defense not open to the promiser: it

[15] Ross, *The Right and the Good*, pp. 37–39, and *Foundations of Ethics* (Oxford: Clarendon Press, 1939), pp. 92–94. I know of no utilitarian who has used this argument except W. A. Pickard-Cambridge in "Two Problems about Duty," *Mind*, n.s., 61 (April 1932), 153–157, although the argument goes with G. E. Moore's version of utilitarianism in *Principia Ethica* (Cambridge: The University Press, 1903). To my knowledge it does not appear in the classical utilitarians; and if one interprets their view correctly this is no accident.

[16] Ross, *The Right and the Good*, pp. 38–39.

is not one of the defenses allowed by the practice of making promises.

Ross gives two further counterarguments:[17] First, he holds that it overestimates the damage done to the practice of promising by a failure to keep a promise. One who breaks a promise harms his own name certainly, but it isn't clear that a broken promise always damages the practice itself sufficiently to account for the strictness of the obligation. Second, and more important, I think, he raises the question of what one is to say of a promise which isn't known to have been made except to the promiser and the promisee, as in the case of a promise a son makes to his dying father concerning the handling of the estate.[18] In this sort of case the consideration relating to the practice doesn't weigh on the promiser at all, and yet one feels that this sort of promise is as binding as other promises. The question of the effect which breaking it has on the practice seems irrelevant. The only consequence seems to be that one can break the promise without running any risk of being censured; but the obligation itself seems not the least weakened. Hence it is doubtful whether the effect on the practice ever weighs in the particular case; certainly it cannot account for the strictness of the obligation where it fails to obtain. It seems to follow that a utilitarian account of the obligation to keep promises cannot be successfully carried out.

From what I have said in connection with punishment, one can foresee what I am going to say about these arguments and counterarguments. They fail to make the distinction between the justification of a practice and the justification of a particular action falling under it, and therefore they fall into the mistake of taking it for granted that the promiser, like Carritt's official, is entitled without restriction to bring utilitarian considerations to bear in deciding whether to keep *his* promise. But if one considers what the practice of promising is, one will see, I think, that it is such as not to allow this sort of general discretion to the promiser. Indeed, the point of the practice is to abdicate one's title to act in accordance with utilitarian and prudential considerations in order that the future may be tied down and plans coordinated in advance. There are obvious utilitarian advantages in having a practice which denies to the promiser, as a defense, any general appeal to the utilitarian principle in accordance with which the practice itself may be justified. There is nothing contradictory, or surprising, in this: utilitarian (or aesthetic) reasons might properly be given in arguing that the game of chess, or baseball, is satisfactory just as it is, or in arguing that it should be changed in various respects, but a player in a game cannot properly appeal to such considerations as reasons for his making one move rather than another. It is a mistake to think that if the practice is justified on utilitarian grounds then the promiser must have complete liberty to use utilitarian arguments to decide whether or not to keep his promise. The practice forbids this general defense; and it is a purpose of the practice to do this. There-

[17] Ross, ibid., p. 39. The case of the nonpublic promise is discussed again in *Foundations of Ethics*, pp. 95–96, 104–105. It occurs also in Mabbott, "Punishment," op. cit., pp. 155–157 [pp. 91–92 above], and in A. I. Melden, "Two Comments on Utilitarianism," *Philosophical Review*, 60 (October 1951), 519–523 [pp. 117–128 above], which discusses Carritt's example in *Ethical and Political Thinking*, p. 64.

[18] Ross's example is described simply as that of two men dying alone where one makes a promise to the other. Carritt's example (cf. *n.* 17 supra) is that of two men at the North Pole. The example in the text is more realistic and is similar to Mabbott's. Another example is that of being told something in confidence by one who subsequently dies. Such cases need not be "desert-island arguments" as Nowell-Smith seems to believe (cf. his *Ethics*, pp. 239–244).

fore what the above arguments presuppose—the idea that if the utilitarian view is accepted then the promiser is bound if, and only if, the application of the utilitarian principle to his own case shows that keeping it is best on the whole—is false. The promiser is bound because he promised: weighing the case on its merits is not open to him.[19]

Is this to say that in particular cases one cannot deliberate whether or not to keep one's promise? Of course not. But to do so is deliberate whether the various excuses, exceptions and defenses, which are understood by, and which constitute an important part of, the practice, apply to one's own case.[20] Various defenses for not keeping one's promise are allowed, but among them there isn't the one that, on general utilitarian grounds, the promiser (truly) thought his action best on the whole, even though there may be the defense that the consequences of keeping one's promise would have been *extremely* severe. While there are too many complexities here to consider all the necessary details, one can see that the general defense isn't allowed if one asks the following question: What would one say of someone who, when asked why he broke his promise, replied simply that breaking it was best on the whole? Assuming that his reply is sincere, and that his belief was reasonable (i.e., one need not consider the possibility that he was mistaken), I think that one would question whether or not he knows what it means to say "I promise" (in the appropriate circumstances). It would be said of someone who used this excuse without further explanation that he didn't understand what defenses the practice, which defines a promise, allows to him. If a child were to use this excuse one would correct him; for it is part of the way one is taught the concept of a promise to be corrected if one uses this excuse. The point of having the practice would be lost if the practice did allow this excuse.

It is no doubt part of the utilitarian view that every practice should admit the defense that the consequences of abiding by it would have been extremely severe; and utilitarians would be inclined to hold that some reliance on people's good sense and some concession to hard cases is necessary. They would hold that a practice is justified by serving the interests of those who take part in it; and as with any set of rules there is understood a background of circumstances under which it is expected to be applied and which need not—indeed which cannot—be fully stated. Should these circumstances change, then even if there is no rule which provides for the case, it may still be in accordance with the practice that one be released from one's obligation. But this sort of defense allowed by a practice must not be confused with the general option to weigh each particular case on utilitarian grounds which critics of utilitarianism have thought it necessarily to involve.

The concern which utilitarianism raises by its justification of punishment is that it may justify too much. The question in connection with promises is different: it is how utilitarianism can account for the obligation to keep promises at all. One feels that the recognized obligation to keep one's promise and utilitarianism are incompatible. And to be sure, they are incompatible if one interprets the utilitarian view as necessarily holding that each person has complete liberty to weigh every particular action on general utilitarian grounds. But must one interpret utilitarianism in this way? I hope to show that, in the sorts of cases I have discussed, one cannot interpret it in this way.

[19] What I have said in this paragraph seems to me to coincide with Hume's important discussion in the *Treatise of Human Nature*, bk. III, pt. 2, sec. 5; and also sec. 6, par. 8.

[20] For a discussion of these, see H. Sidgwick, *The Methods of Ethics* (6th ed.; London: Macmillan and Co., Ltd., 1901), bk. III, ch. vi.

III

So far I have tried to show the importance of the distinction between the justification of a practice and the justification of a particular action falling under it by indicating how this distinction might be used to defend utilitarianism against two longstanding objections. One might be tempted to close the discussion at this point by saying that utilitarian considerations should be understood as applying to practices in the first instance and not to particular actions falling under them except insofar as the practices admit of it. One might say that in this modified form it is a better account of our considered moral opinions and let it go at that. But to stop here would be to neglect the interesting question as to how one can fail to appreciate the significance of this rather obvious distinction and can take it for granted that utilitarianism has the consequence that particular cases may always be decided on general utilitarian grounds.[21] I want to argue that this mistake may be connected with misconceiving the logical status of the rules of practices; and to show this I am going to examine two conceptions of rules, two ways of placing them within the utilitarian theory.

The conception which conceals from us the significance of the distinction I am going to call the summary view. It regards rules in the following way: one supposes that each person decides what he shall do in particular cases by applying the utilitarian principle; one supposes further that different people will decide the same particular case in the same way and that there will be recurrences of cases similar to those previously decided. Thus it will happen that in cases of certain kinds the same decision will be made either by the same person at different times or by different persons at the same time. If a case occurs frequently enough one supposes that a rule is formulated to cover that sort of case. I have called this conception the summary view because rules are pictured as summaries of past decisions arrived at by the *direct* application of the utilitarian principle to particular cases. Rules are regarded as reports that cases of a certain sort have been found on *other* grounds to be properly decided in a certain way (although, of course, they do not *say* this).

There are several things to notice about this way of placing rules within the utilitarian theory.[22]

[21] So far as I can see it is not until Moore that the doctrine is expressly stated in this way. See, for example, *Principia Ethica*, p. 147, where it is said that the statement "I am morally bound to perform this action" is identical with the statement "*This* action will produce the greatest possible amount of good in the Universe" (my italics). It is important to remember that those whom I have called the classical utilitarians were largely interested in social institutions. They were among the leading economists and political theorists of their day, and they were not infrequently reformers interested in practical affairs. Utilitarianism historically goes together with a coherent view of society, and is not simply an ethical theory, much less an attempt at philosophical analysis in the modern sense. The utilitarian principle was quite naturally thought of, and used, as a criterion for judging social institutions (practices) and as a basis for urging reforms. It is not clear, therefore, how far it is necessary to amend utilitarianism in its classical form. For a discussion of utilitarianism as an integral part of a theory of society, see L. Robbins, *The Theory of Economic Policy in English Classical Political Economy* (London: Macmillan, 1952).

[22] This footnote should be read after sec. 3 and presupposes what I have said there. It provides a few references to statements by leading utilitarians of the summary conception. In general it appears that when they discussed the logical features of rules the summary conception prevailed and that it was typical of the way they talked about moral rules. I cite a rather lengthy group of passages from Austin as a full illustration.

John Austin in his *Lectures on Jurisprudence* meets the objection that deciding in accordance with the utilitarian principle case by case is impractical by saying that this is a misinter-

1. The point of having rules derives from the fact that similar cases tend to recur and that one can decide cases more quickly if one records past decisions in the form of rules. If similar cases didn't recur, one would be required to apply the utilitarian principle directly, case by case, and rules reporting past decisions would be of no use.

2. The decisions made on particular cases are logically prior to rules. Since rules gain their point from the need to apply the utilitarian principle to many similar cases, it follows that a particular case (or several cases similar to it) may exist whether or not there is a rule covering that case. We are pictured as recognizing particular cases prior to there being a rule which covers them, for it is only if

---

pretation of utilitarianism. According to the utilitarian view ". . . our conduct would conform to *rules* inferred from the tendencies of actions, but would not be determined by a direct resort to the principle of general utility. Utility would be the test of our conduct, ultimately, but not immediately: the immediate test of the rules to which our conduct would conform, but not the immediate test of specific or individual actions. Our rules would be fashioned on utility; our conduct, on our rules" (vol. I, p. 116). As to how one decides on the tendency of an action he says: "If we would try the tendency of a specific or individual act, we must not contemplate the act as if it were single and insulated, but must look at the class of acts to which it belongs. We must suppose that acts of the class were generally done or omitted, and consider the probable effect upon the general happiness or good. We must guess the consequences which would follow, if the class of acts were general; and also the consequences which would follow, if they were generally omitted. We must then compare the consequences on the positive and negative sides, and determine on which of the two the *balance* of advantage lies. . . . If we truly try the tendency of a specific or individual act, we try the tendency of the class to which that act belongs. The *particular* conclusion which we draw, with regard to the single act, implies a *general* conclusion embracing all similar acts. . . . To the rules thus inferred, and lodged in the memory, our conduct would conform *immediately* if it were truly adjusted to utility" (ibid., p. 117). One might think that Austin meets the objection by stating the practice conception of rules; and perhaps he did intend to. But it is not clear that he has stated this conception. Is the generality he refers to of the statistical sort? This is suggested by the notion of tendency. Or does he refer to the utility of setting up a practice? I don't know; but what suggests the summary view is his subsequent remarks. He says: "To consider the specific consequences of single or individual acts, would *seldom* [my italics] consist with that ultimate principle" (ibid., p. 117). But would one ever do this? He continues: ". . . this being admitted, the necessity of pausing and calculating, which the objection in question supposes, is an imagined necessity. To preface each act or forbearance by a conjecture and comparison of consequences, were clearly *superfluous* [my italics] and mischievous. It were clearly superfluous, inasmuch as the *result of that process* [my italics] would be embodied in a known *rule*. It were clearly mischievous, inasmuch as the *true* result would be expressed by that rule, whilst the process would probably be faulty, if it were done on the spur of the occasion" (ibid., pp. 117–118). He goes on: "If our experience and observation of particulars were not *generalized*, our experience and observation of particulars would seldom avail us in *practice*. . . . The inferences suggested to our minds by repeated experience and observation are, therefore, drawn into *principles*, or compressed into *maxims*. These we carry about us ready for use, and apply to individual cases promptly . . . without reverting to the process by which they were obtained; or without recalling, and arraying before our minds, the numerous and intricate considerations of which they are *handy abridgments* [my italics]. . . . True theory is a *compendium* of particular truths. . . . Speaking then, generally, human conduct is inevitably *guided* [my italics] by *rules*, or by *principles* or *maxims*" (ibid., pp. 117–118). I need not trouble to show how all these remarks incline to the summary view. Further, when Austin comes to deal with cases "of comparatively rare occurrence" he holds that specific considerations may outweigh the general. "Looking at the reasons from which we had inferred the rule, it were absurd to think it inflexible. We should therefore dismiss the

we meet with a number of cases of a certain sort that we formulate a rule. Thus we are able to describe a particular case as a particular case of the requisite sort whether there is a rule regarding *that* sort of case or not. Put another way: what the *A*'s and the *B*'s refer to in rules of the form 'Whenever *A* do *B*' may be described as *A*'s and *B*'s whether or not there is the rule 'Whenever *A* do *B*,' or whether or not there is any body of rules which make up a practice of which that rule is a part.

To illustrate this consider a rule, or maxim, which could arise in this way: Suppose that a person is trying to decide whether to tell someone who is fatally ill what his illness is when he has been asked to do so. Suppose the person to reflect and then decide, on utilitarian grounds, that

---

rule; resort directly to the *principle* upon which our rules were fashioned; and calculate *specific* consequences to the best of our knowledge and ability" (ibid., pp. 120–121). Austin's view is interesting because it shows how one may come close to the practice conception and then slide away from it.

In *A System of Logic*, bk. VI, ch. xii, par. 2, Mill distinguishes clearly between the position of judge and legislator and in doing so suggests the distinction between the two concepts of rules. However, he distinguishes the two positions to illustrate the difference between cases where one is to apply a rule already established and cases where one must formulate a rule to govern subsequent conduct. It's the latter case that interests him and he takes the "maxim of policy" of a legislator as typical of rules. In par. 3 the summary conception is very clearly stated. For example, he says of rules of conduct that they should be taken provisionally, as they are made for the most numerous cases. He says that they "point out" the manner in which it is least perilous to act; they serve as an "admonition" that a certain mode of conduct has been found suited to the most common occurrences. In *Utilitarianism*, ch. ii, par. 24, the summary conception appears in Mill's answer to the same objection Austin considered. Here he speaks of rules as "corollaries" from the principle of utility; these "secondary" rules are compared to "landmarks" and "direction-posts." They are based on long experience and so make it unnecessary to apply the utilitarian principle to each case. In par. 25 Mill refers to the task of the utilitarian principle in adjudicating between competing moral rules. He talks here as if one then applies the utilitarian principle directly to the particular case. On the practice view one would rather use the principle to decide which of the ways that make the practice consistent is the best. It should be noted that while in par. 10 Mill's definition of utilitarianism makes the utilitarian principle apply to morality, i.e., to the rules and precepts of human conduct, the definition in par. 2 uses the phrase "actions are right in *proportion* as they *tend* to promote happiness" [my italics] and this inclines towards the summary view. In the last paragraph of the essay "On the Definition of Political Economy," *Westminster Review* (October 1836), Mill says that it is only in art, as distinguished from science, that one can properly speak of exceptions. In a question of practice, if something is fit to be done," in the majority of cases" then it is made the rule. "We may . . . in talking of art *unobjectionably* speak of the *rule* and the *exception,* meaning by the rule the cases in which there exists a preponderance . . . of inducements for acting in a particular way; and by the exception, the cases in which the preponderance is on the contrary side." These remarks, too, suggest the summary view.

In Moore's *Principia Ethica*, ch. v, there is a complicated and difficult discussion of moral rules. I will not examine it here except to express my suspicion that the summary conception prevails. To be sure, Moore speaks frequently of the utility of rules as generally followed, and of actions as generally practiced, but it is possible that these passages fit the statistical notion of generality which the summary conception allows. This conception is suggested by Moore's taking the utilitarian principle as applying directly to particular actions (pp. 147–148) and by his notion of a rule as something indicating which of the few alternatives likely to occur to anyone will generally produce a greater total good in the immediate future (p. 154). He talks of an "ethical law" as a prediction, and as a generalization (pp. 146, 155). The summary conception is also suggested by his discussion of exceptions (pp. 162–163) and of the force of examples of breaching a rule (pp. 163–164).

he should not answer truthfully; and suppose that on the basis of this and other like occasions he formulates a rule to the effect that when asked by someone fatally ill what his illness is, one should not tell him. The point to notice is that someone's being fatally ill and asking what his illness is, and someone's telling him, are things that can be described as such whether or not there is this rule. The performance of the action to which the rule refers doesn't require the stage-setting of a practice of which this rule is a part. This is what is meant by saying that on the summary view particular cases are logically prior to rules.

3. Each person is in principle always entitled to reconsider the correctness of a rule and to question whether or not it is proper to follow it in a particular case. As rules are guides and aids, one may ask whether in past decisions there might not have been a mistake in applying the utilitarian principle to get the rule in question, and wonder whether or not it is best in this case. The reason for rules is that people are not able to apply the utilitarian principle effortlessly and flawlessly; there is need to save time and to post a guide. On this view a society of rational utilitarians would be a society without rules in which each person applied the utilitarian principle directly and smoothly, and without error, case by case. On the other hand, ours is a society in which rules are formulated to serve as aids in reaching these ideally rational decisions on particular cases, guides which have been built up and tested by the experience of generations. If one applies this view to rules, one is interpreting them as maxims, as "rules of thumb"; and it is doubtful that anything to which the summary conception did apply would be called a *rule.* Arguing as if one regarded rules in this way is a mistake one makes while doing philosophy.

4. The concept of a *general* rule takes the following form. One is pictured as estimating on what percentage of the cases likely to arise a given rule may be relied upon to express the correct decision, that is, the decision that would be arrived at if one were to correctly apply the utilitarian principle case by case. If one estimates that by and large the rule will give the correct decision, or if one estimates that the likelihood of making a mistake by applying the utilitarian principle directly on one's own is greater than the likelihood of making a mistake by following the rule, and if these considerations held of persons generally, then one would be justified in urging its adoption as a general rule. In this way *general* rules might be accounted for on the summary view. It will still make sense, however, to speak of applying the utilitarian principle case by case, for it was by trying to foresee the results of doing this that one got the initial estimates upon which acceptance of the rule depends. That one is taking a rule in accordance with the summary conception will show itself in the naturalness with which one speaks of the rule as a guide, or as a maxim, or as a generalization from experience, and as something to be laid aside in extraordinary cases where there is no assurance that the generalization will hold and the case must therefore be treated on its merits. Thus there goes with this conception the notion of a particular exception which renders a rule suspect on a particular occasion.

The other conception of rules I will call the practice conception. On this view rules are pictured as defining a practice. Practices are set up for various reasons, but one of them is that in many areas of conduct each person's deciding what to do on utilitarian grounds case by case leads to confusion, and that the attempt to coordinate behavior by trying to foresee how others will act is bound to fail. As an alternative one realizes that what is required is the establishment of a practice, the specification of a new form of activity;

and from this one sees that a practice necessarily involves the abdication of full liberty to act on utilitarian and prudential grounds. It is the mark of a practice that being taught how to engage in it involves being instructed in the rules which define it, and that appeal is made to those rules to correct the behavior of those engaged in it. Those engaged in a practice recognize the rules as defining it. The rules cannot be taken as simply describing how those engaged in the practice in fact behave: it is not simply that they act as if they were obeying the rules. Thus it is essential to the notion of a practice that the rules are publicly known and understood as definitive; and it is essential also that the rules of a practice can be taught and can be acted upon to yield a coherent practice. On this conception, then, rules are not generalizations from the decisions of individuals applying the utilitarian principle directly and independently to recurrent particular cases. On the contrary, rules define a practice and are themselves the subject of the utilitarian principle.

To show the important differences between this way of fitting rules into the utilitarian theory and the previous way, I shall consider the differences between the two conceptions on the points previously discussed.

1. In contrast with the summary view, the rules of practices are logically prior to particular cases. This is so because there cannot be a particular case of an action falling under a rule of a practice unless there is the practice. This can be made clearer as follows: In a practice there are rules setting up offices, specifying certain forms of action appropriate to various offices, establishing penalties for the breach of rules, and so on. We may think of the rules of a practice as defining offices, moves, and offenses. Now what is meant by saying that the practice is logically prior to particular cases is this: Given any rule which specifies a form of action (a move), a particular action which would be taken as falling under this rule given that there is the practice would not be *described as* that sort of action unless there was the practice. In the case of actions specified by practices it is logically impossible to perform them outside the stage-setting provided by those practices, for unless there is the practice, and unless the requisite properties are fulfilled, whatever one does, whatever movements one makes, will fail to count as a form of action which the practice specifies. What one does will be described in some *other* way.

One may illustrate this point from the game of baseball. Many of the actions one performs in a game of baseball one can do by oneself or with others whether there is the game or not. For example, one can throw a ball, run, or swing a peculiarly shaped piece of wood. But one cannot steal base, or strike out, or draw a walk, or make an error, or balk; although one can do certain things which appear to resemble these actions such as sliding into a bag, missing a grounder and so on. Striking out, stealing a base, balking, etc., are all actions which can only happen in a game. No matter what a person did, what he did would not be described as stealing a base or striking out or drawing a walk unless he could also be described as playing baseball, and for him to be doing this presupposes the rule-like practice which constitutes the game. The practice is logically prior to particular cases: unless there is the practice the terms referring to actions specified by it lack a sense.[23]

[23] One might feel that it is a mistake to say that a practice is logically prior to the forms of action it specifies on the grounds that if there were never any instances of actions falling under a practice then we should be strongly inclined to say that there wasn't the practice either. Blue-prints for a practice do not make a practice. That there is a practice

2. The practice view leads to an entirely different conception of the authority which each person has to decide on the propriety of following a rule in particular cases. To engage in a practice, to perform those actions specified by a practice, means to follow the appropriate rules. If one wants to do an action which a certain practice specifies then there is no way to do it except to follow the rules which define it. Therefore, it doesn't make sense for a person to raise the question whether or not a rule of a practice correctly applies to *his* case where the action he contemplates is a form of action defined by a practice. If someone were to raise such a question, he would simply show that he didn't understand the situation in which he was acting. If one wants to perform an action specified by a practice, the only legitimate question concerns the nature of the practice itself ("How do I go about making a will?").

This point is illustrated by the behavior expected of a player in games. If one wants to play a game, one doesn't treat the rules of the game as guides as to what is best in particular cases. In a game of baseball if a batter were to ask "Can I have four strikes?" it would be assumed that he was asking what the rule was; and if, when told what the rule was, he were to say that he meant that on this occasion he thought it would be best on the whole for him to have four strikes rather than three, this would be most kindly taken as a joke. One might contend that baseball would be a better game if four strikes were allowed instead of three; but one cannot picture the rules as guides to what is best on the whole in particular cases, and question their applicability to particular cases as particular cases.

3 and 4. To complete the four points of comparison with the summary conception, it is clear from what has been said that rules of practices are not guides to help one decide particular cases correctly as judged by some higher ethical principle. And neither the quasi-statistical notion of generality, nor the notion of a particular exception, can apply to the rules of practices. A more or less general rule of a practice must be a rule which according to the structure of the practice applies to more or fewer of the kinds of cases arising under it; or it must be a rule which is more or less basic to the understanding of the practice. Again, a particular case cannot be an exception to a rule of a practice. An exception is rather a qualification or a further specification of the rule.

It follows from what we have said about the practice conception of rules that if a person is engaged in a practice, and if he is asked why *he* does what *he* does, or if he is asked to defend what he does, then his explanation, or defense, lies in referring the questioner to the practice. He cannot say of *his* action, if it is an action specified by a practice, that he does it rather than some other because he thinks it is best on the whole.[24] When a man engaged in a practice is queried about his action he must assume that the questioner either doesn't know that he is engaged in it ("Why are you in a hurry to pay him?" "I promised to pay him today") or doesn't know what the practice is. One doesn't so much justify one's particular action as

entails that there are instances of people having been engaged and now being engaged in it (with suitable qualifications). This is correct, but it doesn't hurt the claim that any given particular instance of a form of action specified by a practice presupposes the practice. This isn't so on the summary picture, as each instance must be "there" prior to the rules, so to speak, as something from which one gets the rule by applying the utilitarian principle to it directly.

[24] A philosophical joke (in the mouth of Jeremy Bentham): "When I run to the other wicket after my partner has struck a good ball, I do so because it is best on the whole."

explain, or show, that it is in accordance with the practice. The reason for this is that it is only against the stage-setting of the practice that one's particular action is described as it is. Only by reference to the practice can one *say* what one is doing. To explain or to defend one's own action, as a particular action, one fits it into the practice which defines it. If this is not accepted it's a sign that a different question is being raised as to whether one is justified in accepting the practice, or in tolerating it. When the challenge is to the practice, citing the rules (saying what the practice is) is naturally to no avail. But when the challenge is to the particular action defined by the practice, there is nothing one can do but refer to the rules. Concerning particular actions there is only a question for one who isn't clear as to what the practice is, or who doesn't know that it is being engaged in. This is to be contrasted with the case of a maxim which may be taken as pointing to the correct decision on the case as decided on *other* grounds, and so giving a challenge on the case a sense by having it question whether these other grounds really support the decision on this case.

If one compares the two conceptions of rules I have discussed, one can see how the summary conception misses the significance of the distinction between justifying a practice and justifying actions falling under it. On this view rules are regarded as guides whose purpose it is to indicate the ideally rational decision on the given particular case which the flawless application of the utilitarian principle would yield. One has, in principle, full option to use the guides or to discard them as the situation warrants without one's moral office being altered in any way: whether one discards the rules or not, one always holds the office of a rational person seeking case by case to realize the best on the whole. But on the practice conception, if one holds an office defined by a practice, then questions regarding one's actions in this office are settled by reference to the rules which define the practice. If one seeks to question these rules, then one's office undergoes a fundamental change: one then assumes the office of one empowered to change and criticize the rules, or the office of a reformer, and so on. The summary conception does away with the distinction of offices and the various forms of argument appropriate to each. On that conception there is one office and so no offices at all. It therefore obscures the fact that the utilitarian principle must, in the case of actions and offices defined by a practice, apply to the practice, so that general utilitarian arguments are not available to those who act in offices so defined.[25]

Some qualifications are necessary in what I have said. First, I may have talked of the summary and the practice conceptions of rules as if only one of them could be true of rules, and if true of any rules, then necessarily true of all rules. I do not, of course, mean this. (It is the critics of utilitarianism who make this mistake insofar as their arguments against utilitarianism presuppose a summary concep-

[25] How do these remarks apply to the case of the promise known only to father and son? Well, at first sight the son certainly holds the office of promiser, and so he isn't allowed by the practice to weigh the particular case on general utilitarian grounds. Suppose instead that he wishes to consider himself in the office of one empowered to criticize and change the practice, leaving aside the question as to his right to move from his previously assumed office to another. Then he may consider utilitarian arguments as applied to the practice; but once he does this he will see that there are such arguments for not allowing a general utilitarian defense in the practice for this sort of case. For to do so would make it impossible to ask for and to give a kind of promise which one often wants to be able to ask for and to give. Therefore he will not want to change the practice, and so as a promiser he has no option but to keep his promise.

tion of the rules of practices.) Some rules will fit one conception, some rules the other; and so there are rules of practices (rules in the strict sense), and maxims and "rules of thumb."

Secondly, there are further distinctions that can be made in classifying rules, distinctions which should be made if one were considering other questions. The distinctions which I have drawn are those most relevant for the rather special matter I have discussed, and are not intended to be exhaustive.

Finally, there will be many borderline cases about which it will be difficult, if not impossible, to decide which conception of rules is applicable. One expects borderline cases with any concept, and they are especially likely in connection with such involved concepts as those of a practice, institution, game, rule, and so on. Wittgenstein has shown how fluid these notions are.[26] What I have done is to emphasize and sharpen two conceptions for the limited purpose of this paper.

IV

What I have tried to show by distinguishing between two conceptions of rules is that there is a way of regarding rules which allows the option to consider particular cases on general utilitarian grounds; whereas there is another conception which does not admit of such discretion except insofar as the rules themselves authorize it. I want to suggest that the tendency while doing philosophy to picture rules in accordance with the summary conception is what may have blinded moral philosophers to the significance of the distinction between justifying a practice and justifying a particular action falling under it; and it does so by misrepresenting the logical force of the reference to the rules in the case of a challenge to a particular action falling under a practice, and by obscuring the fact that where there is a practice, it is the practice itself that must be the subject of the utilitarian principle.

It is surely no accident that two of the traditional test cases of utilitarianism, punishment and promises, are clear cases of practices. Under the influence of the summary conception it is natural to suppose that the officials of a penal system, and one who has made a promise, may decide what to do in particular cases on utilitarian grounds. One fails to see that a general discretion to decide particular cases on utilitarian grounds is incompatible with the concept of a practice; and that what discretion one does have is itself defined by the practice (e.g., a judge may have discretion to determine the penalty within certain limits). The traditional objections to utilitarianism which I have discussed presuppose the attribution to judges, and to those who have made promises, of a plentitude of moral authority to decide particular cases on utilitarian grounds. But once one fits utilitarianism together with the notion of a practice, and notes that punishment and promising are practices, then one sees that this attribution is logically precluded.

That punishment and promising are practices is beyond question. In the case of promising this is shown by the fact that the form of words "I promise" is a performative utterance which presupposes the stage-setting of the practice and the proprieties defined by it. Saying the words "I promise" will only be promising given the existence of the practice. It would be absurd to interpret the rules about promising in accordance with the summary conception. It is absurd to say, for example, that the rule that promises should be kept could have arisen from its being found in past cases to be best on the whole to keep one's promise; for unless there were al-

[26] *Philosophical Investigations* (Oxford, 1953), I, pars. 65–71, for example.

ready the understanding that one keeps one's promises as part of the practice itself there couldn't have been any cases of promising.

It must, of course, be granted that the rules defining promising are not codified, and that one's conception of what they are, necessarily depends on one's moral training. Therefore it is likely that there is considerable variation in the way people understand the practice, and room for argument as to how it is best set up. For example, differences as to how strictly various defenses are to be taken, or just what defenses are available, are likely to arise amongst persons with different backgrounds. But irrespective of these variations it belongs to the concept of the practice of promising that the general utilitarian defense is not available to the promiser. That this is so accounts for the force of the traditional objection which I have discussed. And the point I wish to make is that when one fits the utilitarian view together with the practice conception of rules, as one must in the appropriate cases, then there is nothing in that view which entails that there must be such a defense, either in the practice of promising or in any other practice.

Punishment is also a clear case. There are many actions in the sequence of events which constitute someone's being punished which presuppose a practice. One can see this by considering the definition of punishment which I gave when discussing Carritt's criticism of utilitarianism. The definition there stated refers to such things as the normal rights of a citizen, rules of law, due process of law, trials and courts of law, statutes, etc., none of which can exist outside the elaborate stage-setting of a legal system. It is also the case that many of the actions for which people are punished presuppose practices. For example, one is punished for stealing, for trespassing, and the like, which presuppose the institution of property. It is impossible to say what punishment is, or to describe a particular instance of it, without referring to offices, actions, and offenses specified by practices. Punishment is a move in an elaborate legal game and presupposes the complex of practices which make up the legal order. The same thing is true of the less formal sorts of punishment: a parent or guardian or someone in proper authority may punish a child, but no one else can.

There is one mistaken interpretation of what I have been saying which it is worthwhile to warn against. One might think that the use I am making of the distinction between justifying a practice and justifying the particular actions falling under it involves one in a definite social and political attitude in that it leads to a kind of conservatism. It might seem that I am saying that for each person the social practices of his society provide the standard of justification for his actions; therefore let each person abide by them and his conduct will be justified.

This interpretation is entirely wrong. The point I have been making is rather a logical point. To be sure, it has consequences in matters of ethical theory; but in itself it leads to no particular social or political attitude. It is simply that where a form of action is specified by a practice there is no justification possible of the particular action of a particular person save by reference to the practice. In such cases the action is what it is in virtue of the practice and to explain it is to refer to the practice. There is no inference whatsoever to be drawn with respect to whether or not one should accept the practices of one's society. One can be as radical as one likes but in the case of actions specified by practices the objects of one's radicalism must be the social practices and people's acceptance of them.

I have tried to show that when we fit the utilitarian view together with the practice conception of rules, where this conception is appropriate,[27] we can formulate it in a way which saves it from several traditional objections. I have further tried to show how the logical force of the distinction between justifying a practice and justifying an action falling under it is connected with the practice conception of rules and cannot be understood as long as one regards the rules of practices in accordance with the summary view. Why, when doing philosophy, one may be inclined to so regard them, I have not discussed. The reasons for this are evidently very deep and would require another paper.

[27] As I have already stated, it is not always easy to say where the conception is appropriate. Nor do I care to discuss at this point the general sorts of cases to which it does apply except to say that one should not take it for granted that it applies to many so-called "moral rules." It is my feeling that relatively few actions of the moral life are defined by practices and that the practice conception is more relevant to understanding legal and legal-like arguments than it is to the more complex sort of moral arguments. Utilitarianism must be fitted to different conceptions of rules depending on the case, and no doubt the failure to do this has been one source of difficulty in interpreting it correctly.

J.J.C. Smart / Extreme and restricted utilitarianism

I

Utilitarianism is the doctrine that the rightness of actions is to be judged by their consequences. What do we mean by 'actions' here? Do we mean particular actions or do we mean classes of actions? According to which way we interpret the word 'actions' we get two different theories, both of which merit the appellation 'utilitarian.'

(1) If by 'actions' we mean particular individual actions we get the sort of doctrine held by Bentham, Sidgwick, and Moore. According to this doctrine we test individual actions by their consequences, and general rules, like 'keep promises,' are mere rules of thumb which we use only to avoid the necessity of estimating the probable consequences of our actions at every step. The rightness or wrongness of keeping a promise on a particular occasion depends only on the goodness or badness of the consequences of keeping or of breaking the promise on that particular occasion. Of course part of the consequences of breaking the promise, and a part to which we will normally ascribe decisive importance, will be the weakening of faith in the institution of promising. However, if the goodness of the consequences of breaking the rule is *in toto* greater than the goodness of the consequences of keeping it, then we must break the rule, irrespective of whether the goodness of the consequences of *everybody's* obeying the rule is or is not greater than the consequences of *everybody's* breaking it. To put it shortly, rules do not matter, save *per accidens* as rules of thumb and as de facto social institutions with which the utilitarian has to reckon when estimating consequences. I shall call this doctrine 'extreme utilitarianism.'

(2) A more modest form of utilitarianism has recently become fashionable. The doctrine is to be found in Toulmin's book *The Place of Reason in Ethics*, in Nowell-Smith's *Ethics* (though I think Nowell-Smith has qualms), in John Austin's *Lec-*

Reprinted from THE PHILOSOPHICAL QUARTERLY, *vol. 6, no. 25 (October 1956) pp. 344–354 by permission of the author and editors. Based on a paper read to the Victorian Branch of the Australasian Association of Psychology and Philosophy, October 1955.*

tures on Jurisprudence (Lecture II), and even in J. S. Mill, if Urmson's interpretation of him is correct (*Philosophical Quarterly* 3 [January 1953], pp. 33–39 [pp. 168–174 above]. Part of its charm is that it appears to resolve the dispute in moral philosophy between intuitionists and utilitarians in a way which is very neat. The above philosophers hold, or seem to hold, that moral rules are more than rules of thumb. In general the rightness of an action is *not* to be tested by evaluating its consequences but only by considering whether or not it falls under a certain rule. Whether the rule is to be considered an acceptable moral rule is, however, to be decided by considering the consequences of adopting the rule. Broadly, then, actions are to be tested by rules and rules by consequences. The only cases in which we must test an individual action directly by its consequences are (*a*) when the action comes under two different rules, one of which enjoins it and one of which forbids it, and (*b*) when there is no rule whatever that governs the given case. I shall call this doctrine 'restricted utilitarianism.'

It should be noticed that the distinction I am making cuts across, and is quite different from, the distinction commonly made between hedonistic and ideal utilitarianism. Bentham was an extreme hedonistic utilitarian and Moore an extreme ideal utilitarian, and Toulmin (perhaps) could be classified as a restricted ideal utilitarian. A hedonistic utilitarian holds that the goodness of the consequences of an action is a function only of their pleasurableness and an ideal utilitarian, like Moore, holds that pleasurableness is not even a necessary condition of goodness. Mill seems, if we are to take his remarks about higher and lower pleasures seriously, to be neither a pure hedonistic nor a pure ideal utilitarian. He seems to hold that pleasureableness is a necessary condition for goodness, but that goodness is a function of other qualities of mind as well. Perhaps we can call him a quasi-ideal utilitarian. When we say that a state of mind is good I take it that we are expressing some sort of *rational preference*. When we say that it is pleasurable I take it that we are saying that it is enjoyable, and when we say that something is a higher pleasure I take it that we are saying that it is more truly, or more deeply, enjoyable. I am doubtful whether 'more deeply enjoyable' does not just mean 'more enjoyable, even though not more enjoyable on a first look,' and so I am doubtful whether quasi-ideal utilitarianism, and possibly ideal utilitarianism too, would not collapse into hedonistic utilitarianism on a closer scrutiny of the logic of words like 'preference,' 'pleasure,' 'enjoy,' 'deeply enjoy,' and so on. However, it is beside the point of the present paper to go into these questions. I am here concerned only with the issue between extreme and restricted utilitarianism and am ready to concede that both forms of utilitarianism can be either hedonistic or non-hedonistic.

The issue between extreme and restricted utilitarianism can be illustrated by considering the remark 'But suppose everyone did the same.' (Cf. A. K. Stout's article in *The Australasian Journal of Philosophy*, Vol. 32, pp. 1–29.) Stout distinguishes two forms of the universalisation principle, the causal form and the hypothetical form. To say that you ought not to do an action A because it would have bad results if everyone (or many people) did action A may be merely to point out that while the action A would otherwise be the optimific one, nevertheless when you take into account that doing A will probably cause other people to do A too, you can see that A is not, on a broad view, really optimific. If this causal influence could be avoided (as may happen in the case of a secret desert island promise) then we would disregard the universalisation principle. This is the causal form of the principle. A person who accepted the universalisation principle in its hypothetical form would be one who was concerned only with what would happen *if* everyone did the action A: he would be totally unconcerned with the question of whether in fact everyone would do the action A. That is, he might say that it would be wrong not to vote because it would have bad results if everyone took this attitude, and he would be totally unmoved by arguments purporting to show that my refusing to vote has no effect whatever on other people's propensity to vote. Making use of Stout's distinction, we can say that an extreme utilitarian would apply the universalisation principle in the causal form, while a restricted utilitarian would apply it in the hypothetical form.

How are we to decide the issue between extreme and restricted utilitarianism? I wish to repudiate at the outset that milk and water approach which describes itself sometimes as 'investigating what is implicit in the common moral consciousness' and sometimes as 'investigating how people ordinarily talk about morality.' We have only to read the newspaper correspondence about capital punishment or about what should be done with Formosa to realise that the common moral consciousness is in part made up of superstitious elements, of morally bad elements, and of logically confused elements. I address myself to good-hearted and benevolent people and so I hope that if we rid ourselves of the logical confusion the superstitious and morally bad elements will largely fall away. For even among good-hearted and benevolent people it is possible to find superstitious and morally bad reasons for moral beliefs. These superstitious and morally bad reasons hide behind the protective screen of logical confusion. With people who are not logically confused but who are openly superstitious or morally bad I can of course do nothing. That is, our ultimate pro-attitudes may be different. Nevertheless I propose to rely on *my own* moral consciousness and to appeal to *your* moral consciousness and to forget about what people ordinarily say. 'This obligation to obey a rule,' says Nowell-Smith (*Ethics*, p. 239), 'does not, *in the opinion of ordinary men*' (my italics), 'rest on the beneficial consequences of obeying it in a particular case.' What does this prove? Surely it is more than likely that ordinary men are confused here. Philosophers should be able to examine the question more rationally.

II

For an extreme utilitarian, moral rules are rules of thumb. In practice the extreme utilitarian will mostly guide his conduct by appealing to the rules ('do not lie,' 'do not break promises,' etc.) of common sense morality. This is not because there is anything sacrosanct in the rules themselves but because he can argue that probably he will most often act in an extreme utilitarian way if he does not think as a utilitarian. For one thing, actions have frequently to be done in a hurry. Imagine a man seeing a person drowning. He jumps in and rescues him. There is no time to reason the matter out, but usually this will be the course of action which an extreme utilitarian would recommend if he did reason the matter out. If, however, the man drowning had been drowning in a river near Berchtesgaden in 1938, and if he had had the well-known black forelock and moustache of Adolf Hitler, an extreme utilitarian would, if he had time, work out the probability of the man's being the villainous dictator, and if the probability were high enough he would, on extreme utilitarian grounds, leave him to drown. The rescuer, however, has not time. He trusts to his instincts and dives in and rescues the man. And this trusting to instincts and to moral rules can be justified on extreme utilitarian grounds. Furthermore, an extreme utilitarian who knew that the drowning man was Hitler would nevertheless praise the rescuer, not condemn him. For by praising the man he is strengthening a courageous and benevolent disposition of mind, and in general this disposition has great positive utility. (Next time, perhaps, it will be Winston Churchill that the man saves!) We must never forget that an extreme utilitarian may praise actions which he knows to be wrong. Saving Hitler was wrong, but it was a member of a class of actions which are generally right, and the motive to do actions of this class is in general an optimific one. In considering questions of praise and blame it is not the expediency of the praised or blamed action that is at issue, but the expediency of the praise. It can be expedient to praise an inexpedient action and inexpedient to praise an expedient one.

Lack of time is not the only reason why an extreme utilitarian may, on extreme utilitarian principles, trust to rules of common sense morality. He knows that in particular cases where his own interests are involved his calculations are likely to be biased in his own favour. Suppose that he is unhappily married and is deciding whether to get divorced. He will in all probability greatly exaggerate his own unhappiness (and possibly his wife's) and greatly underestimate the harm done to his children by the breakup of the family. He will probably also underestimate the likely harm done by the weakening of the general faith in marriage vows. So probably he will come to the correct extreme utilitarian conclusion if he does not in this instance think as an extreme utilitarian but trusts to common sense morality.

There are many more and subtle points that could be made in connection with the relation between extreme utilitarianism and the morality of common sense. All those that I have just made and many more will be found in Book IV Chapters 3–5 of Sidgwick's *Methods of Ethics.* I think that this book is the best book ever written on ethics, and that these chapters are the best chapters of the book. As they occur so near the end of a very long book they are unduly neglected. I refer the reader, then, to Sidgwick for the classical exposition of the relation between (extreme) utilitarianism and the morality of common sense. One further point raised by Sidgwick in this connection is whether an (extreme) utilitarian ought on (extreme) utilitarian principles to propagate (extreme) utilitarianism among the public. As most people are not very philosophical and not good at empirical calculations, it is probable that they will most often act in an extreme utilitarian way if they do not try to think as extreme utilitarians. We have seen how easy it would be to misapply the extreme utilitarian criterion in the case of divorce. Sidgwick seems to think it quite probable that an extreme utilitarian should not propagate his doctrine too widely. However, the great danger to humanity comes nowadays on the plane of public morality—not private morality. There is a greater danger to humanity from the hydrogen bomb than from an increase of the divorce rate, regrettable though that might be, and there seems no doubt that extreme utilitarianism makes for good sense in international relations. When France walked out of the United Nations because she did not wish Morocco discussed, she said that she was within her rights because Morocco and Algiers are part of her metropolitan territory and nothing to do with U.N. This was clearly a legalistic if not superstitious argument. We should not be concerned with the so-called 'rights' of France or any other country but with whether the cause of humanity would best be served by discussing Morocco in U.N. (I am not saying that the answer to this is 'Yes.' There are good grounds for supposing that more harm than good would come by such a discussion.) I myself have no hesitation in saying than on extreme utilitarian principles we ought to propagate extreme utilitarianism as widely as possible. But Sidgwick had respectable reasons for suspecting the opposite.

The extreme utilitarian, then, regards moral rules as rules of thumb and as sociological facts that have to be taken into account when deciding what to do, just as facts of any other sort have to be taken into account. But in themselves they do not justify any action.

III

The restricted utilitarian regards moral rules as more than rules of thumb for short-circuiting calculations of consequences. Generally, he argues, consequences are not relevant at all when we are deciding what to do in a particular case. In general, they are relevant only to deciding what rules are good reasons for acting in a certain way in particular cases. This doctrine is possibly a good account of how the modern unreflective twentieth-century Englishman often thinks about morality, but surely it is monstrous as an account of how it is most rational to think about morality. Suppose that there is a rule *R* and that in 99% of cases the best possible results are obtained by acting in accordance with *R*. Then clearly *R* is a useful rule of thumb; if we have not time or are not impartial enough to assess the consequences of an action it is an extremely good bet that the thing to do is to act in accordance with *R*. But is it not monstrous to suppose that if we *have* worked out the consequences and if we have perfect faith in the impartiality of our calculations, and if we *know* that in this instance to break *R* will have better results than to keep it, we should nevertheless obey the rule? Is it not to erect *R* into a sort of idol if we keep it when breaking it will prevent, say, some avoidable misery? Is not this a form of superstitious rule-worship (easily explicable psychologically) and not the rational thought of a philosopher?

The point may be made more clearly if we consider Mill's comparison of moral rules to the tables in the nautical almanack. (*Utilitarianism, Everyman's* Edition pp. 22–23) [p. 29 above]. This comparison of Mill's is adduced by Urmson as evidence that Mill was a restricted utilitarian but I do not think that it will bear this interpretation at all. (Though I quite agree with Urmson that many other things said by Mill are in harmony with restricted rather than extreme utilitarianism. Probably Mill had never thought very much about the distinction and was arguing for utilitarianism, restricted or extreme, against other and quite non-utilitarian forms of moral argument.) Mill says: 'Nobody argues that the art of navigation is not founded on astronomy, because sailors cannot wait to calculate the Nautical Almanack. Being rational creatures, they go out upon the sea of life with their minds made up on the common questions of right and wrong, as well as on many of the far more difficult questions of wise and foolish. . . . Whatever we adopt as the fundamental principle of morality, we require subordinate principles to apply it by.' Notice that this is, as it stands, only an argument for subordinate principles as rules of thumb. The example of the nautical almanack is misleading because the information given in the almanack is in all cases the same as the information one would get if one made a long and laborious calculation from the original astronomical data on which the almanack is founded. Suppose, however, that astronomy were different. Suppose that the behaviour of the sun, moon, and planets was very nearly as it is now, but that on rare occasions there were peculiar irregularities and discontinuities, so that the almanack gave us rules of the form 'in 99% of cases where the observations are such and such you can deduce that your position is so and so.' Furthermore, let us suppose that there were methods which enabled us, by direct and laborious calculation from the original astronomical data, not using the rough and ready tables of the almanack, to get our correct position in 100% of cases. Seafarers might use the almanack because they never had time for the long calculations and they were content with a 99% chance of success in calculating their positions. Would it not be absurd, however, if they *did* make the direct calculation, and, finding that it disagreed with the almanack calculation, nevertheless ignored it and stuck to the almanack conclusion? Of course the case would be altered if there were a high enough probability of making slips in the direct calculation: then we might stick to the almanack result, liable to error though we knew it to be, simply because the direct calculation would be open to error for a different reason, the fallibility of the computer. This would be analogous to the case of the extreme utilitarian who abides by the conventional rule against the dictates of his utilitarian calculations simply because he thinks that his calculations are probably affected by personal bias. But if the navigator were sure of his direct calculations would he not be foolish to abide by his almanack? I conclude, then, that if we change our suppositions about astronomy and the almanack (to which there are no exceptions) to bring the case into line with that of morality (to whose rules there are exceptions), Mill's example loses its appearance of supporting the restricted form of utilitarianism. Let me say once more that I am not here concerned with how ordinary men think about morality but with how they ought to think. We could quite well imagine a race of sailors who acquired a superstitious reverence for their almanack, even though it was only right in 99% of cases, and who indignantly threw overboard any man who mentioned the possibility of a direct calculation. But would this behaviour of the sailors be rational?

Let us consider a much discussed sort of case in which the extreme utilitarian might go against the conventional moral rule. I have promised to a friend, dying on a desert island from which I am subsequently rescued, that I will see that his fortune (over which I have control) is given to a jockey club. However, when I am rescued I decide that it would be better to give the money to a hospital, which can do more good with it. It may be argued that I am wrong to give the money to the hospital. But why? (*a*) The hospital can do more good with the money than the jockey club can. (*b*) The present case is unlike most cases of promising in that no one except me knows about the promise. In breaking the promise I am doing so with complete secrecy and am doing nothing to weaken the general faith in promises. That is, a factor which would normally keep the extreme utilitarian from promise breaking even in otherwise unoptimific cases does not at present operate. (*c*) There is no doubt a slight weakening in my own character as an habitual promise keeper, and moreover psychological tensions will be set up in me every time I am asked what the man made me promise him to do. For clearly I shall have to say that he made me promise to give the money to the hospital, and, since I am an habitual truth teller, this will go very much against the grain with me. Indeed I am pretty sure that in practice I myself would keep the promise. But we are not discussing what my moral habits would probably make me do; we are discussing what I ought to do. Moreover, we must not forget that even if it would be most rational of me to give the money to the hospital it would also be most rational of you to punish or condemn me if you did, most improbably, find out the truth (e.g. by finding a note washed ashore in a bottle). Furthermore, I would agree that though it was most rational of me to give the money to the hospital it would be most rational of you to condemn me for it. We revert again to Sidgwick's distinction between the utility of the action and the utility of the praise of it.

Many such issues are discussed by A. K. Stout in the article to which I have already referred. I do not wish to go over the same ground again, especially as I think that Stout's arguments support my own point of view. It will be useful, however, to consider one other example that he gives. Suppose that during hot weather there is an edict that no water must be used for watering gardens. I have a garden and I reason that most people are sure to obey the edict, and that as the amount of water that I use will be by itself negligible no harm will be done if I use the water secretly. So I do use the water, thus producing some lovely flowers which give happiness to various people. Still, you may say, though the action was perhaps optimific, it was unfair and wrong.

There are several matters to consider. Certainly my action should be condemned. We revert once more to Sidgwick's distinction. A right action may be rationally condemned. Furthermore, this sort of offence is normally found out. If I have a wonderful garden when everybody else's is dry and brown there is only one explanation. So if I water my garden I am weakening my respect for law and order, and as this leads to bad results an extreme utilitarian would agree that I was wrong to water the garden. Suppose now that the case is altered and that I can keep the thing secret: there is a secluded part of the garden where I grow flowers which I give away anonymously to a home for old ladies. Are you still so sure that I did the wrong thing by watering my garden? However, this is still a weaker case than that of the hospital and the jockey club. There will be tensions set up within myself: my secret knowledge that I have broken the rule will make it hard for me to exhort others to keep the rule. These psychological ill effects in myself may be not inconsiderable: directly and indirectly they may lead to harm which is at least of the same order as the happiness that the old ladies get from the flowers. You can see that on an extreme utilitarian view there are two sides to the question.

So far I have been considering the duty of an extreme utilitarian in a predominantly non-utilitarian society. The case is altered if we consider the extreme utilitarian who lives in a society every member, or most members, of which can be expected to reason as he does. Should he water his flowers now? (Granting, what is doubtful, that in the case already considered he would have been right to water his flowers.) As a first approximation, the answer is that he should not do so. For since the situation is a completely symmetrical one, what is rational for him is rational for others. Hence, by a reductio ad absurdum argument, it would seem that watering his garden would be rational for none. Nevertheless, a more refined analysis shows that the above argument is not quite correct, though it is correct enough for practical purposes. The argument considers each person as confronted with the choice either of watering his garden or of not watering it. However there is a third possibility, which is that each person should, with the aid of a suitable randomising device, such as throwing dice, give himself a certain probability of watering his garden. This would be to adopt what in the theory of games is called 'a mixed strategy.' If we could give numerical values to the private benefit of garden watering and to the public harm done by 1, 2, 3, etc., persons using the water in this way, we could work out a value of the probability of watering his garden that each extreme utilitarian should give himself. Let a be the value which each extreme utilitarian gets from watering his garden, and let $f(1)$, $f(2)$, $f(3)$, etc., be the public harm done by exactly 1, 2, 3, etc., persons respectively watering their gardens. Suppose that p is the probability that each person gives himself of watering his garden. Then we can easily calculate, as functions of p, the probabilities that exactly 1, 2, 3, etc., persons will water their gardens. Let these probabilities be $p_1, p_2 \ldots p_n$. Then the total net probable benefit can be expressed as

$$V = p_1 (a - f(1)) + p_2 (2a - f(2)) + \ldots p_n (na - f(n))$$

Then if we know the function $f(x)$ we can calculate the value of p for which $\frac{dV}{dp} = 0$. This gives the value of p which it would be rational for each extreme utilitarian to adopt. The present argument does of course depend on a perhaps unjustified assumption that the values in question are measurable, and in a practical case such as that of the garden watering we can doubtless assume that p will be so small that we can take it near enough as equal to zero. However, the argument is of interest for the theoretical underpinning of extreme utilitarianism, since the possibility of a mixed strategy is usually neglected by critics of utilitarianism, who wrongly assume that the only relevant and symmetrical alternatives are of the form "everybody does *X*" and "nobody does *X*."

I now pass on to a type of case which may be thought to be the trump card of restricted utilitarianism. Consider the rule of the road. It may be said that since all that matters is that everyone should do the same it is indifferent which rule we have, 'go on the left hand side' or 'go on the right hand side.' Hence the only *reason* for going on the left hand side in British countries is that this is the rule. Here the rule does seem to be a reason, in itself, for acting in a certain way. I wish to argue against this. The rule in itself is not a reason for our actions. We would be perfectly justified in going on the right hand side if (*a*) we knew that the rule was to go on the left hand side, and (*b*) we were in a country peopled by superanarchists who always on principle did the opposite of what they were told. This shows that the rule does not give us a reason for acting so much as an indication of the probable actions of others, which helps us to find out what would be our own most rational course of action. If we are in a country not peopled by anarchists, but by non-anarchist extreme Utilitarians, we expect, other things being equal, that they will keep rules laid down for them. Knowledge of the rule enables us to predict their behaviour and to harmonise our own actions with theirs. The rule 'keep to the left hand side,' then, is not a logical *reason* for action but an anthropological *datum* for planning actions.

I conclude that in every case if there is a rule *R* the keeping of which is in general optimific, but such that in a special sort of circumstances the optimific behaviour is to break *R*, then in these circumstances we should break *R*. Of course we must consider all the less obvious effects of breaking *R*, such as reducing people's faith in the moral order, before coming to the conclusion that to break *R* is right: in fact we shall rarely come to such a conclusion. Moral rules, on the extreme utilitarian view, are rules of thumb only, but they are not bad rules of thumb. But if we *do* come to the conclusion that we should break the rule and if we have weighed in the balance our own fallibility and liability to personal bias, what good reason remains for keeping the rule? I can understand 'it is optimific' as a reason for action, but why should 'it is a member of a class of actions which are usually optimific' or 'it is a member of a class of actions which as a class are more optimific than any alternative general class' to be a good reason? You might as well say that a person ought to be picked to play for Australia just because all his brothers have been, or that the Australian team should be composed entirely of the Harvey family because this would be better than composing it entirely of any other family. The extreme utilitarian does not appeal to artificial feelings, but only to our feelings of benevolence, and what better feelings can there be to appeal to? Admittedly we can have a pro-attitude to anything, even to rules, but such artificially begotten pro-attitudes smack of superstition. Let us get down to realities, human happiness and misery, and make these the objects of our pro-attitudes and anti-attitudes.

The restricted utilitarian might say that he is talking only of *morality*, not of such things as rules of the road. I am not sure how far this objection, if valid, would affect my argument, but in any case I would reply that as a philosopher I conceive of ethics as the study of how it would be *most rational* to act. If my opponent wishes to restrict the word 'morality' to a narrower use he can have the word. The fundamental question is the question of rationality of action *in general*. Similarly if the restricted utilitarian were to appeal to ordinary usage and say 'it might be most rational to leave Hitler to drown but it would surely not be *wrong* to rescue him,' I should again let him have the words 'right' and 'wrong' and should stick to 'rational' and 'irrational.' We already saw that it would be rational not to have rescued Hitler. In ordinary language, no doubt, 'right' and 'wrong' have not only the meaning 'most rational to do' and 'not most rational to do' but also have the meaning 'praiseworthy' and 'not praiseworthy.' Usually to the utility of an action corresponds utility of praise of it, but as we saw, this is not always so. Moral language could thus do with tidying up, for example by reserving 'right' for 'most rational' and 'good' as an epithet of praise for the motive from which the action sprang. It would be more becoming in a philosopher to try to iron out illogicalities in moral language and to make suggestions for its reform than to use it as a court of appeal whereby to perpetuate confusions.

One last defense of restricted utilitarianism might be as follows. 'Act optimifically' might be regarded as itself one of the rules of our system (though it would be odd to say that this rule was justified by its optimificality). According to Toulmin (*The Place of Reason in Ethics* [Cambridge: The University Press, 1950], pp. 146–48) if 'keep promises,' say, conflicts with another rule we are allowed to argue the case on its merits as if we were extreme utilitarians. If 'act optimifically' is itself one of our rules then there will always be a conflict of rules whenever to keep a rule is not itself optimific. If this is so, restricted utilitarianism collapses into extreme utilitarianism. And no one could read Toulmin's book or Urmson's article on Mill without thinking that Toulmin and Urmson are of the opinion that they have thought of a doctrine which does *not* collapse into extreme utilitarianism, but which is, on the contrary, an improvement on it.

H.J. McCloskey / An examination of restricted utilitarianism

It is my purpose in this paper to show that *restricted utilitarianism* is no more tenable as an ethical theory than is the better known *extreme utilitarianism* which it is intended to supersede.[1] According to restricted utilitarianism we justify particular actions by reference to general rules or practices and the rules by reference to the principle of utility. Hence according to this theory particular actions may be obligatory even though they are not productive of the maximum good possible.

This theory arises out of its exponents' dissatisfaction with extreme utilitarianism, according to which "it is always the duty of every agent to do that one, among all the actions which he can do on any given occasion, whose total consequence will have the greatest intrinsic value" (G. E. Moore, *Ethics* [Oxford: At the University Press, 1912]). This is evident in the writings of its contemporary exponents and sympathizers, such as J. O. Urmson and John Rawls. Urmson, for instance, argues that restricted utilitarianism is much superior to extreme utilitarianism just because it escapes the standard, fatal objections to that theory.[2] This is why he regards it as important to show that the traditional interpretation of John Stuart Mill as an extreme utilitarian is mistaken. Rawls argues along the same lines, illustrating in some detail the superiority of the restricted theory by reference to the objections that are urged against the extreme view in connection with punishment and the obligation to keep promises.[3] Rawls and Urmson in

[1] The terminology is that adopted by J. J. C. Smart in "Extreme and Restricted Utilitarianism," *Philosophical Quarterly* 6 (1956), 344 [p. 195 above]. All subsequent references to Smart's views relate to this article. [Professor McCloskey adds that the terminology "restricted utilitarianism" was used to refer to what has since come to be called "rule utilitarianism." Ed.]

[2] J. O. Urmson, "The Interpretation of the Moral Philosophy of J. S. Mill," *Philosophical Quarterly* 3 (1953), 33–39 [pp. 168–174 above].

[3] John Rawls, "Two Concepts of Rules," *Philosophical Review* 64 (1955), 3 [pp. 175–194 above]. All subsequent references to Rawls's views relate to this article.

Reprinted from THE PHILOSOPHICAL REVIEW, *vol. 66 (1957), pp. 466–485 by permission of the author and editors.*

their respective articles are simply voicing an almost general feeling among contemporary utilitarians that the simple device of treating the Principle of Utility not as a justification of particular obligations but of general practices or principles provides a general solution to the traditional objections to utilitarianism. There are some grounds for this confidence; and it is significant that J. J. C. Smart, who seeks to defend extreme against restricted utilitarianism, does so almost entirely by pointing to inadequacies in the restricted utilitarian theory. Smart does not show that extreme utilitarianism can meet the objections that are commonly urged against it and with which the restricted theory seeks to deal. Instead, he concentrates on attempting to show that the restricted theory cannot meet any objections encountered by the extreme theory and that in its attempts to do so, it involves itself in absurdities; and only to a much lesser extent does he concern himself with showing that some of the more usual, but less telling, objections to extreme utilitarianism are not real objections. The most acute difficulties encountered by the extreme theory are those involving considerations of justice—for example, punishment; and it is of note that Smart fails to consider such cases and that he gives no indication how the extreme theory might be made to cope with them. On the other hand, in spite of Smart's contention to the contrary, the restricted theory does seem to assist utilitarianism in escaping many of these difficulties; but it is not completely successful in this; and it does encounter new and serious difficulties of its own. These difficulties are as fatal to the claims of the restricted theory as are the difficulties commonly urged against utilitarianism to the claims of the extreme theory. To bring this out, it is necessary to note and examine the main varieties of restricted utilitarianism.

Pure and mixed. (a) According to what might be called the *pure* restricted theory, the principle of utility is the primary principle by reference to which the "rules in practice" are justified. It is appealed to only when considering the rules in practice and never when discussing the rightness or wrongness of actions. Urmson explains restricted utilitarianism in this way, but I know of no utilitarian who, in an undeviating way, defends pure restricted utilitarianism. It is nonetheless an important position because many exponents of restricted utilitarianism write as if this is the view they wish to defend and as if they have not succeeded in distinguishing it from the other varieties. Smart concentrates his attention on this variety, probably for these reasons. (b) Secondly, there is the *mixed* variety. According to this variety, the principle of utility is the primary principle which justifies the "rules in practice," but it is also a rule or secondary principle which competes with the other rules. Stephen Toulmin most nearly of all the restricted utilitarians espouses this version, but it seems to be that to which practically all restricted utilitarians are forced by pressure of difficulties.

Conditional and unconditional. (a) *Unconditional* restricted utilitarianism is that which treats the rules as being rules which in themselves prescribe no exceptions or spheres in which they do not hold. (b) *Conditional* restricted utilitarian theories are those according to which the practices or rules are such that they allow, as not being covered by the practice, special types of cases which might at first appear to fall under the practice. An unconditional restricted utilitarian theory might be to the effect that stealing is never right. A conditional variety of the theory might explain the "rule in practice" as being "stealing is never right except by a starving man from a wealthy one and 'in similar sorts of cases .' " Most restricted utilitarians assume the unconditional variety, although under pressure some switch to the conditional variety. Rawls suggests that the latter is the more defensible variety, but he seems half-heartedly to go on and associate it with the mixed variety. The mixed and the conditioned varieties of restricted utilitarianism are occasioned by the difficulties with which a pure unconditional theory cannot deal.

Rawls defends restricted utilitarianism by taking the activities of punishment and promise-keeping as examples which illustrate how the restricted theory can meet difficulties fatal to extreme utilitarianism. The following example brings out the nature of these difficulties as they may arise in respect to punishment.

Suppose that a sheriff were faced with the choice either of framing a Negro for a rape that had aroused hostility to the Negroes (a particular Negro generally being believed to be guilty but whom the sheriff knows not to be guilty)—and thus preventing serious anti-Negro riots which would probably lead to some loss of life and increased hatred of each other by whites and Negroes—or of hunting for the guilty person and thereby allowing the anti-Negro riots to occur, while doing the best he can to combat them. In such a case the sheriff, if he were an extreme utilitarian, would appear to be committed to framing the Negro. Stubborn, extreme utilitarians try to avoid this sort of embarrassing conclusion, but such is the dissatisfaction generally felt with their moves here that Rawls is rightly able to commend the restricted theory on the grounds that it, by contrast, offers a plausible utilitarian solution.

Rawls points out that we must distinguish between justifying a practice as a system of rules which are applied and enforced and justifying a particular action that falls under these rules. Utilitarian arguments, he contends, are appropriate with regard to questions about practices, while retributive arguments fit the application of particular rules to particular cases. As he reasons, "So firstly we should explain that *A* is put in jail because he is guilty, and that it is the practice to punish and put into jail those found guilty after a fair legal trial; and secondly, we should justify *the practice* of putting people found guilty in jail on utilitarian grounds."

This move, besides doing justice to the two important components in punishment —guilt of the punished and utility in the allocation of the punishment—seems to get over the difficulty that utilitarianism appears to involve unjust, illegitimate punishment of the innocent, because, as Rawls shows, punishing the innocent is condemned on utilitarian grounds as being contrary to a general utilitarian institution. The defense of utilitarianism on this point is not complete, however, until it is shown that the system of punishment is a better utilitarian institution than any comparable possible institution.

Arguing to this conclusion, Rawls sets out a contrast between the institution of punishment and an institution corresponding to that which critics of utilitarianism claim to be presupposed by the utilitarian theory. This institution Rawls refers to as "*telishment.*" It consists in the infliction of suffering on innocent and guilty individuals alike for the sake of the general well-being, the victims being selected by senior state officials. Rawls argues of such an institution that it does not have the utilitarian justification punishment has, and from this he moves to the more general conclusion that "it happens in general that as one drops off the defining features of punishment one ends up with an institution whose utilitarian justification is highly doubtful." Rawls's point is that the critics of utilitarianism do not seem to see that their criticisms presuppose the setting up by utilitarians of an alternative institution to that of punishment, and that once this is appreciated and once the new institution of telishment is described in detail, this institution is seen not to have the same utilitarian justification that is possessed by the institution of punishment.

Rawls's reply to criticisms of the type

urged by W. D. Ross and others of the extreme utilitarians' defense of promise-keeping is in effect that these criticisms hold only against extreme utilitarianism and not against utilitarianism as such.[4] Restricted utilitarianism acknowledges that not all promises which ought to be kept produce the best possible results. This, it is explained, is so because it is the practice and not the individual action falling under it which has a utilitarian justification. Since the practice which has this justification is one which involves the abdication of the right to weigh individual promises on the utilitarian principle, there is no difficulty over the obligation to keep particular promises which do not have the best possible consequences. Bringing out the nature of the practice of promise-keeping, Rawls writes:

> What would one say of someone who, when asked why he broke his promise, replied simply that breaking it was best on the whole? . . . It would be said of someone who used this excuse without further explanation, that he didn't understand what defenses the practice, which defines a promise, allows to him. . . . The point of having the practice would be lost if the practice did allow this excuse.

It is quite clear from the examples of promise-keeping and punishment that the restricted theory does escape some of the more usual objections urged against the extreme utilitarian theory. The former theory is able to offer reasons, within the utilitarian framework, for punishing only the guilty and for keeping those promises which it is generally felt should be kept, even when acting otherwise might produce valuable results. The restricted theory cannot deal with all the more usual objections urged against the extreme theory, however; and it itself is exposed to new objections. In brief, it fails to give reasons for keeping *all* those promises (and other obligations) which ought to be kept, but which on the extreme theory appear not to be obligatory; it implies obligations (for example, to keep promises) which in fact are not real obligations; it fails to assist the utilitarian position in meeting objections arising in respect of many activities, such as killing, the wrongness of which does not depend upon the existence of any institution; it involves a very paradoxical form of ethical relativism; and at key points the theory is vague and confused, and necessarily so. These objections may now be developed in detail.

(1) If the value of the institution or rule in practice is assessed on a utilitarian calculus, then it must be asked: Why should there not be exceptions to the institution also on utilitarian grounds in those situations in which the exception is not going to damage the institution? Exponents of the restricted theory speak as if to make exceptions on utilitarian grounds is to set up a different practice; but to punish an innocent person when and only when to do so is not to weaken the existing institution of punishment and when the consequences of doing so are valuable is not to set up what Rawls calls an institution of telishment. So even were it true that telishment is an institution that cannot be justified on utilitarian grounds—and this is by no means clear—it would still not follow that we should never telish. Similarly with promise-keeping and promise-breaking. The most that the restricted utilitarian can seriously contend is that if we knew that most people were going to treat promises as utilitarians are said to be in consistency bound to treat them, and that the general practice and all the valuable results that accrue from having a practice of promise-keeping were to be thereby endangered, then the individual promise which has bad consequences should nonetheless be kept: whereas if we know that the practice will not be endangered, that most people anyway are not

[4] See W. D. Ross, *The Right and The Good* (Oxford: Clarendon Press, 1930), esp. chs. i and ii, and *Foundations of Ethics* (Oxford: Clarendon Press, 1939), esp. ch. v.

utilitarians, and there can be a general expectation that people can be counted on to act in certain ways in the future, then surely it is unreasonable to insist that even here the utilitarian principle itself cannot be invoked and that the promise should be kept. Yet if this point is allowed it follows that in our society, or at least in a society predominantly of nonutilitarians, utilitarians should not keep promises of which the consequences on the whole are bad. The only defense for conforming with the rule when the consequences of such conformity are bad would seem to be a causal one—that lack of conformity on this occasion weakens the practice, and so on. But this defense is possible only in rare, particular cases. Hence either there must be admission that very many promises need not be kept after all and that the restricted version is little better off than the extreme theory, or we get the absurd insistence on conformity with the rule, with no good reason for this being offered. The latter absurdity can be illustrated by amending an analogy used in another context by J. D. Mabbott and applying it in the context of restricted utilitarianism. The analogy then runs:

> The following dialogue at a bridge table will illustrate the fallacy. I am the third player on the first trick; the second player has played the ace. I hold the king. I remember that I have been told that the third player should play high. I whisper to my mentor behind me (the mentor representing the restricted utilitarian), "What do I play?" He says, "The king." "But it will do no good; the ace has been played." "Never mind that. You must play your king, that is the rule and you must conform with the rule."[5]

If the restricted utilitarian nonetheless denies this absurdity and insists that the rules of a practice should be kept where a breach will not harm the practice and will produce good results—that is, if he insists firmly that utility is a first principle and not a rule or secondary principle and that decisions must be reached by reference to secondary principles, then it follows from the pure variety of the restricted theory that all promises should be kept, that the truth should always be told, and that the consequences are irrelevant simply because the first principle is irrelevant. And this conclusion is as objectionable as the other; the more especially as it seems also to imply that there are no duties where there are no rules in practice.

What seems to have happened in the development of restricted utilitarianism is that the restricted utilitarians have become confused between what are *in fact* accepted as good reasons in morals and what on their theory *should be* accepted as such. This is an important point and an important criticism. It is quite true, as the restricted utilitarians suggest, that we do regard it as giving a good reason for an action to point out that it is an instance of a general practice; but it does not follow from this that these same reasons should be regarded on the utilitarian theory as good reasons. Clearly on the utilitarian theory—the extreme or restricted version —to point to the fact that an action is an instance of a general moral practice is not always to give a good moral reason.

These various arguments which make up this first general objection to restricted utilitarianism would seem to be fatal to the claims of all varieties of the restricted theory.

(2) There are, of course, conflicts even between rules in practice. Even the restricted utilitarian has to face the conflicts of duties so commonly supposed to be fatal to the Kantian theory. There are either of two possible courses open to him. One is to argue that we should judge between the conflicting duties in particular situations on the grounds of the value of the consequences of the respective *actions*.

[5] Mabbott, "Interpretations of Mill's Utilitarianism," *Philosophical Quarterly* 6 (1956), 115.

But this either amounts to the extreme utilitarian position, or at least exposes it to extension along the lines of making the consequences always relevant, as after all they really are. Alternatively, the restricted utilitarian could choose between the practices on the basis of the value of the practices. This would seem to be the consistent move; but it leads to the absurdity of always preferring one practice to another. For example, if it were determined that truth-telling is socially more valuable as a practice than promise-keeping, then in any conflict between these two activities it would always be obligatory to tell the truth and break a promise. This clearly is absurd, and no serious moral philosopher, utilitarian or otherwise, would be happy to accept a theory which led to this sort of conclusion. Further, there would remain the problem of what happens when two instances of the one rule conflict; for example, when two promises are in opposition, or when the truth at one level is incompatible with the truth at another level.

(3) This problem concerning the resolution of conflicts of duties brings to our notice another difficulty for restricted utilitarianism, namely, the problem of how one is to determine the utilitarian value of the various alternative practices. Take punishment, for example. Is it clear, as Rawls assumes, that an institution of telishment would be bad on utilitarian grounds? Something of the sort appears to have been the prevailing institution in Russia since the Revolution, and it is not clear that it has been contrary to the public good. While I am no admirer of the U.S.S.R.—on moral grounds—I am nevertheless disposed to believe that the very great advances in that country since the Revolution and the alleviation of human misery over such vast areas of the world would not have been possible without the aid of some such institutions. Its utilitarian justification seems now to be diminishing, and the Russians appear to be acting as good utilitarians should, modifying the institution as the principle of utility requires. I may be wrong in this belief that such an institution had a utilitarian justification in the U.S.S.R.; at least it is arguable, but it is not seriously arguable that such an institution was morally unjustifiable in Russia whatever the empirical facts prove to be.

Further, we do not have to go to Russia to see that a system like telishment is possible, and possibly justifiable on utilitarian grounds. The people of Australia, guided by their prime minister, the Rt. Hon. R. G. Menzies, came very close to approving the introduction of a significant body of retrospective legislation. Punishment under retrospective legislation is punishment under quite a different institution to that in which one is punished only for offenses which are offenses at the time of the act. Punishment under retrospective legislation is a possible institution. The prime minister of Australia thought that it was a socially valuable institution. I am not qualified to judge whether he was right; but I suspect that he was right on the point of utility. Whether he was right on the point of utility or not, however, he was not so clearly right on the question of morals. But this is something a restricted utilitarian cannot afford to admit.

Similarly, laws such as those relating to punishment of habitual criminals, as well as those forbidding loitering with intent, alter the system from the kind which Rawls describes and which he suggests that we can justify on utilitarian grounds. The same sort of arguments would seem to be applicable concerning the institution of slavery in ancient Greece. The latter institution, for the greater part of the time it prevailed, seems to have had a utilitarian justification; but it did not have a moral justification.

What it is important to stress here, however, is the difficulty of settling a dispute of the following kind: Is punishment or telishment the more valuable institution? Such a question is not an a priori question but an empirical one for which apparently there are considerations supporting each alternative. I am quite uncertain as to the solution of the empirical question, and I suggest that if we are honest with ourselves we all must admit to such uncertainty; yet I, and I suspect most other people, am not uncertain in the same way about the moral wrongness of telishment, and this surely is significant. It suggests a direct insight into the obligatoriness and disobligatoriness of certain kinds of activities—direct insight that can give us the assurance in our moral judgments that we have, but which we could not have if they were dependent upon the findings of an empirical enquiry. Ross and other intuitionists have been accused of being dogmatists by utilitarian writers; but the charge is totally unwarranted in most cases and is much more appropriate when directed against the restricted utilitarian philosophers themselves, for they are dogmatic about empirical matters concerning which they have very little evidence. It is an amazing thing, when one considers the importance of morality, to find that restricted utilitarians do virtually nothing toward defending their assumption that the current moral conventions are, in terms of utility, the morally best conventions; and further that these same moral philosophers do nothing toward entering into a general empirical enquiry in this sphere. (Mill would be an almost isolated exception if he could properly be regarded as a restricted utilitarian.)

So much for our third objection. It would hold equally well against all varieties of restricted utilitarianism.

(4) A fourth criticism relates to the vagueness of the key concept in the restricted utilitarian theory—the concept which is variously designated "social practice," "rule in practice," "institution," "principle," or simply "rule." This vagueness is an important feature of the theory, and once it is eliminated the theory becomes much less plausible.

Rawls explains the notion of "a rule in practice" thus:

> In the case of actions specified by practices it is logically impossible to perform them outside the stage-setting provided by those practices for unless there is the practice, and unless the requisite properties are fulfilled whatever one does, whatever movements one makes will fail to count as a form of action which the practice specifies. What one does will be described in some *other* way.
>
> One may illustrate this point from the game of baseball. . . . No matter what a person did, what he did would not be described as stealing a base or striking out or drawing a walk unless he could also be described as playing baseball, and for him to be doing this presupposes the rule-like practice which constitutes the game. *The practice is logically prior to particular cases; unless there is the practice, the terms referring to actions specified by it lack a sense.*

Rawls is here giving a correct account of one of the concepts of a "rule" required by the restricted utilitarian theory. One of the telling arguments of the restricted utilitarians is that various moral activities have their possibility and reality only in the context of a practice. Hence the need arises to ensure that there is a practice by conforming with it, at least on the whole.

Now, if Rawls is right—that the concept of "rules in practice" makes the practice logically prior to the action specified by it—then restricted utilitarianism is of assistance to the general utilitarian position in overcoming only some of the difficulties which beset extreme utilitarianism. Clearly not all of the activities claimed to be obligatory in their own right are such that they presuppose a general practice *to exist* as activities of a certain kind; and certainly they do not presuppose a general practice to be obligatory. Restricted utilitarianism arose out of an attempt to deal with the difficulties associated with the obligations relating to promise-keeping, truth-telling, repayment of debts, stealing, and punishment, and these are the difficulties the theory does appear to help to resolve. But there are other difficulties for extreme utilitarianism—difficulties associated with the obligations to perfect one's talents, to treat others as ends and not as means, not to kill, and so on. Whether or not there is a practice of not killing others whenever we wish to do so, it is still prima facie wrong to kill, although where there is widespread disregard of the obligation, it may be permissible to kill more often than in a society in which the established practice is to not kill others. Further, murder and abstinence from murder are activities *logically prior* to a general practice and have a reality independent of a general practice in a way that promise-keeping does not. The same is true respecting the duty not to treat others as mere means and also the duty to perfect our talents. These do not depend for their moral bindingness on their consequences, nor upon there being a general practice; hence if we are to treat others as means—and it is frequently necessary to do so—we need to have good reasons for doing so. The model of "rules" talk is promise-keeping and contracts generally. The "rules" talk is less effective with other prima facie duties, and with others again quite irrelevant.

The concept of a "rule in practice" elucidated by Rawls, while appropriate to a great deal of restricted utilitarian theory, is inappropriate for other parts of the writings of its exponents. A much vaguer concept is used. Clearly the sense in which the principle of utility can be thought of as a rule among rules cannot be the sense outlined by Rawls. The games analogy, popular with restricted utilitarians, brings out this confusion in the concept. It is a rule of football that if the ball is kicked between the center two posts at the end of the field it counts as a goal; and that a goal equals six behinds; that it is permissible to bump an opponent in the side but not in the back; that when a player is injured, and only when he is injured, he may be replaced by a reserve; and so on. It is a rule in practice, however, that a losing side replaces its weakest players in the last quarter, whether they are injured or not; that a team has a mascot; and so on. Now a careful consideration of the writings of restricted utilitarians brings out that there is an alternation between senses of rules corresponding roughly to these two senses of rule in football. For example, promise-keeping is a rule in practice in one sense; the next of kin caring for the aged is a rule in another sense of "rule"; and evading tax within the limits allowed by the law is a rule in practice in perhaps another sense again. Some points require one sense, some the other, and some, other senses again; but the theory requires a consistent sense.

Another sense of "rule" to be noted here is such that a rule is simply equated with the principle of an action. Some utilitarians talk as if the practice aspect of the "rule in practice" is unimportant—that it is the principle of the action that is the relevant consideration, and further that there are some principles which on utilitarian grounds, should be universalized. Hence, irrespective of the empirical fact as to whether an activity is practised or not, there are some principles, so it is argued, which, if they were generally practised, would be justifiable on utilitarian grounds, and these are those with which we should conform. The sole virtue of this contention is that it escapes the absurdity of implying that what is right or wrong and what is a good or a bad reason depends on the prevailing customs. To establish this kind of view—that it is the principle which counts, where the principle is one which would have utilitarian justification if it were a principle in practice—it has to be shown that conformity with the principle will help to bring about its general adoption and that the value of the act on this account is greater than the value of the consequences of a breach of the principle. This will not be the case very often, however; certainly it will not be the case often enough to permit a utilitarian theory to be established along these lines.

This means that the practice is what counts; *and it means that what constitutes a valid moral reason in support of an action depends on the cultural practice*; although it is true that it also means that what constitutes a valid reason in support of the practice itself is universal, unchanging, and objective. But the first conclusion is plainly false. The Spartan youths surely, while not morally blameworthy, were certainly mistaken in their moral conduct; and so too is the Soviet official who, in accord with the institution of "punishment" that prevails in Russia, frames an innocent individual; and so too were the Greek slave owners, the recent Nazi concentration-camp officers, and the contemporary Russian slave masters. To point to the practice is not to give a valid moral reason for holding another man in slavery.

The logic of the expression "valid moral reason" needs to be noted here. On the restricted utilitarian theory its logic would appear to run as follows: "X was a valid moral reason for owning a slave in the fourth century B.C., but it is not a valid moral reason today." In fact the logic appears to be: "X was *thought to constitute a valid moral reason* for owning a slave by the Greeks of the fourth century B.C., but we see now that it was not a valid moral reason and that the Greeks were mistaken in the matter."

This point draws attention to a general difficulty for restricted utilitarianism, a difficulty which its exponents seem not to have considered because it has been concealed from them by the vagueness of their formulations of their theories. The difficulty springs from the fact that not all rules in practice are good utilitarian rules in practice nor the best utilitarian rules that could be rules in practice. What does the restricted utilitarian say about our duty in a society in which the rules in practice are not the best possible utilitarian rules, and perhaps not even rules justifiable at all on utilitarian grounds? The restricted utilitarian in fact seems to say nothing because he appears to have assumed that the rules in practice of Anglo-Saxon societies are the only rules that matter, and that these are good utilitarian rules in practice. On the whole they do seem to be good utilitarian rules, although many of them are by no means the best possible rules in practice. Examples of the latter probably include the prevailing rules relating to marriage, divorce, and sexual behavior generally; rules concerning the care of the aged by relations, if these may be called rules in practice; many systems of "punishment" in Anglo-Saxon countries; and the like. In any case, not all societies are Anglo-Saxon societies. Russia has its institutions of slave labor and "telishment"; Japan and the East their unutilitarian rules in practice. What is the moral agent's duty in these societies? The impression one gets from the writings of restricted utilitarians very strongly suggests conformity with the practice; and, after all, this is the impact this general account of ethics does have. Two answers are possible in terms of restricted utilitarianism, however, and both may be considered here.

We may consider first societies in which there are both rules in practice which have no utilitarian justification and other rules which should positively be condemned on utilitarian grounds. To suggest that there should be conformity with such rules in practice and that to indicate the rule in practice is to give a good moral reason for one's behavior would in most of these cases be to advocate blatant immorality. The Nazi rule in practice relating to treatment of Jews is a case in point; the Japanese practice of committing suicide to avoid dishonorable capture by the enemy is another case in point; and the many sacrificial practices of primitive religious groups are other examples. To point to the fact that one's action is in conformity with a rule in practice of one or other of these kinds is not to give an excuse or explanation which may exonerate the agent. Yet if it is suggested that the moral agent should not conform with these practices, what is the moral agent's duty in such a society? Should he be guided simply by the principle of utility itself, justifying his individual actions directly by reference to it? This is not an unreasonable answer, but it means that in such a society restricted utilitarianism is incapable of saving the general utilitarian position from attack along the lines indicated by critics such as Ross. Further, it means that it is up to the individual moral agent in each society to determine whether the various practices are justifiable utilitarian practices. Different conclusions will no doubt be reached by different agents about some of these practices.

Where the rules in practice are rules which have positive utilitarian justification but are nonetheless not the best rules in practice possible, the position is less clear. Some rules in practice are so much inferior to other possible rules in practice, even where the former have some utilitarian justification, that it is often positively immoral to condone the practice by conforming with it. Here the examples would depend on the sense of "rules in practice" used by the theory. On any usage examples are possible, but if the looser usage is adopted such that a rule in practice includes how people in fact behave and believe it to be clever to behave, then a multitude of examples becomes available. But quite apart from these cases, it is clear that conformity with the rule in practice, even where it is a good utilitarian rule or institution, such as telishment, is not necessarily the morally best action possible. If on the other hand it is maintained that conformity with the practice is only morally right where the rule in practice is the best possible utilitarian rule, then this same criticism may still be urged. In addition, two other criticisms become relevant. If we should be right in conforming only when the practice is the best possible utilitarian practice, we should not often be able, in order to have a good moral reason, to point to the fact that we are conforming with a practice. That is to say, the move that characterizes restricted utilitarianism could seldom be made; and equally important, it could rarely be known that it could be made. It is unlikely, however, that any restricted utilitarian would maintain that we should conform only with the best possible practices.

Most of the points made here as our fourth objection to restricted utilitarianism may be well illustrated by reference to sexual morality. In the sphere of sexual behavior we find a clear distinction between the moral rule in practice and the behavior in practice. Further, we find, as modern investigators such as Kinsey have confirmed, that within one community there are different moral codes, or in the language of restricted utilitarianism, different rules in practice. The state in terms of its laws and sanctions recognizes one system of rules in practice; but this system may not coincide with those of any one group within the state. Which of these various practices is the restricted utilitarian's rule in practice? To which does one have to point to have a good moral reason for one's behavior? Some of these rules in practice have a better utilitarian justification than others; some have little utilitarian justification by contrast with others; but all have some utilitarian justification, because practically any code of sexual behavior is better than none. Is conformity the right thing, and does it or does it not matter which of these rules or set of rules is the set of rules in practice?

These objections apply with equal force against all varieties of the restricted theory, although the objection relating to the equivocation in the use of the expression "rule" is of special importance in respect to the mixed restricted utilitarian theories.

(5) Finally, it needs to be noted that it is difficult, in terms of the criterion used by restricted utilitarians, to distinguish in the way in which we do between *nonmoral* and *moral* practices. The test of a moral practice—that it is a *moral* practice and therefore a basis for valid moral reasons—would seem to be either that it is conducive to good consequences or that it is thought so to be. If the former is the test, then many so-called nonmoral and even immoral practices, for example keeping to the left and possibly even slavery in the U.S.S.R., should be regarded as moral; and some so-called moral practices should perhaps be denied the name. If on the other hand the criterion is that the practice is generally thought to be productive of good consequences, then many important, genuinely moral practices would not qualify for the title, and some nonmoral practices would qualify. If we make the fact the criterion, we can seldom be sure that a practice is a moral practice; if we make the belief the criterion, then it would be surprising if many practices qualified. People just do not think or have opinions about the utilitarian value of institutions like promise-keeping, truth-telling, and so on. Further, it would seem to follow from the theory that many principles—the so-called prudential maxims—should be elevated to the level of moral practices; but clearly whether so elevated or not, prudential maxims would remain of a significantly different moral status from the principles of promise-keeping, truth-telling, and so on.

Many other objections could be urged against restricted utilitarianism; but the objections already developed are sufficient to bring out that the distinction between justifying a practice and justifying an action falling under the practice will not do for utilitarianism what the exponents of restricted utilitarianism claim that it will do. It does not provide a means of saving utilitarianism as a tenable ethical theory.

As we have seen, most of the objections indicated above are fatal not only to the claims of the pure version but of all versions of restricted utilitarianism. It is worthwhile, however, to examine briefly the more complex varieties, since it may be thought that they have special merits which enable them to provide a more sure basis for utilitarianism.

The mixed version, as we have seen, admits the principle of utility as a secondary principle while putting it up also as the primary principle which provides the justification of the secondary principles. It will at once be noticed that this complicates the account of the relation between the primary and secondary principles and obscures the concept of "rule" in the way already indicated. Clearly the sense in which promises are dependent for their reality upon the existence of the practice is different from the sense in which we can have a rule or practice of producing good. It is a theoretically possible version of utilitarianism, however, and one which escapes two absurdities to which the pure restricted theory leads, namely, that we should always conform with the rule and that we have no duties except those falling under the rules (in Rawls's sense of "rule"). Further, it is a version of which John Austin appears to have been an unwilling adherent and of which Toulmin is a lukewarm exponent.

Toulmin's lukewarmness consists in the fact that while he is prepared to insist on the relevance of the principle of utility in all situations involving moral obligations, thereby treating it as a secondary as well as the primary principle, he is unwilling to treat it as a secondary principle of *duty*. Thus his particular theory is exposed to one of the absurdities of the pure theory—that there are no duties where there are no rules in Rawls's sense of "rule"—and also to the difficulties which are encountered by the mixed theory. These include the difficulties relating to the concept of rule and to the relation between the primary principle and the secondary rules. Toulmin suggests that this is the variety of utilitarianism he is adopting in various places, including the section in which he discusses the issue of conflicts of duties.[6]

It is difficult to argue against this variety of the theory except in terms of the general objections to restricted utilitarianism already noted. This is not because of any special virtue of this variety, nor for the reason wrongly advanced by Smart—that this version represents a collapse of restricted utilitarianism into the extreme theory—but simply because of its indefiniteness. In theory mixed restricted utilitarianism does represent a different theory from extreme utilitarianism. In practice it is difficult to determine whether the two have been assimilated. Unless we are told how to weigh the practice against the consequences and how much weight to attribute to the practice qua practice, it is difficult to know how the mixed version works out in detail and whether its exponent has or has not fallen back into the outmoded extreme utilitarian calculus. Toulmin gives us no help in this matter, and the same seems to have been true of Austin. This means that no new objections relating specifically to this variety of utilitarianism can be developed here. Of those objections already indicated, however, 1, 3, 4, and 5 may effectively be pressed against it.

The conditional varieties of restricted utilitarianism are also difficult to appraise. This is because they too are so vaguely stated that they could imply anything at all. My impression is that if all the exceptions and conditions hinted at by some utilitarians as being part of the practice are indeed part of the practice, then there is little left of the practice at all. It is difficult to see that we can do justice to the special cases in which we break promises with justification on utilitarian grounds by saying, as is suggested by exponents of these varieties, that we are really not going against the practice. We *are* going against the practice. When we make a promise we are not accepting an obligation to act in a certain way except where there are good consequences resulting from an alternative action; and where we do break a promise on this sort of ground we think of ourselves as having and facing a conflict, and not of puzzling over what the practice is. The conditional amendment of the theory seems to detract from all that is introduced into utilitarianism by restricted utilitarianism, namely, by the admission of the moral significance of promises (and the like) which have no direct utilitarian justification and which would appear to be overridden by utilitarian considerations. These varieties are too vague and elusive to discuss in detail, however, and their rejection must be based on the general objections to restricted utilitarianism already noted. Nevertheless, once they are made more precise, additional specific objections could be urged against them. It is worth recording here that it is probably not without significance that the most notable

[6] Stephen Toulmin, *The Place of Reason in Ethics* (Cambridge: The University Press, 1950), pp. 147–148.

utilitarians have not only not adopted the conditional variety but have in fact positively denied its central thesis.

It is now necessary simply to point out that some sort of synthesis of restricted and extreme utilitarianism will not provide a solution to the difficulties which appear to be fatal to the claims of each theory. Extreme utilitarianism breaks down at points at which the restricted theory is unable to offer any assistance, for example, in respect to the duty to refrain from killing; and further, restricted utilitarianism, besides having fatal intrinsic defects, also has the defects of relating only to some duties and only to some societies, and then not to all the rules in practice in these societies. Utilitarianism therefore breaks down as an account of our moral obligations; and it breaks down because it is unsuccessful in accounting for the obligatoriness of those activities singled out by Ross as activities which are intrinsically obligatory.

S.I. Benn / An approach to the problems of punishment

I shall develop in this article certain distinctions suggested by recent contributions to the philosophical discussion of punishment, which help to clarify the issues involved. Having separated out what I consider the four central philosophical questions, I shall suggest an approach to them, which, while mainly utilitarian, takes due account, I believe, of the retributivist case where it is strongest, and meets the main retributivist objections.

I make three key distinctions:

(1) Between justifying punishment in general (i.e. as an institution), and justifying particular penal decisions as applications of it;
(2) Between what is implied in postulating guilt as a necessary, and as a sufficient, condition for punishment;
(3) Between postulating guilt in law and guilt in morals, as a condition for punishment.

I distinguish, further, four philosophical questions, to which a complete and coherent approach to punishment would have to provide answers:

What formal criteria must be satisfied in justifying:

(1) Punishment in general, i.e. as an institution?
(2) Any particular operation of the institution?
(3) The degrees of punishment attached to different classes of offence?
(4) The particular penalty awarded to a given offender?

Preliminaries

A. *"Punishment" defined*

Prof. Flew[1] has suggested five criteria for the use of "punishment" in its primary sense, i.e., five conditions satisfied by a

[1] A. Flew: "The Justification of Punishment," in *Philosophy* 29 (1954), 291–307.

Reprinted from PHILOSOPHY, *vol. 33, no. 127 (October 1958), pp. 325–341 by permission of the author and editors.*

standard case to which the word would be applied:

(i) It must involve an "evil, an unpleasantness, to the victim";
(ii) It must be for an offence (actual or supposed);
(iii) It must be of an offender (actual or supposed);
(iv) It must be the work of personal agencies (i.e. not merely the natural consequences of an action);
(v) It must be imposed by authority (real or supposed), conferred by the system of rules (hereafter referred to as "law") against which the offence has been committed.

It is not a misuse to talk, for example, of "punishing the innocent," or of a boxer "punishing his opponent"; but since these usages, though related to the primary one, disregard one or more of the criteria ordinarily satisfied, they are extensions, or secondary usages. In considering the justification for punishment, I shall confine the word to the primary sense, unless I indicate otherwise.

B. *The distinction between justifying punishment in general, and justifying the particular application*

There would seem, on the face of it, to be a real difference between utilitarian and retributivist approaches to the justification of punishment, the former looking to its beneficient consequences, the latter exclusively to the wrongful act. It remains to be seen whether the gulf can be bridged. The first step is to distinguish between a rule, or an institution constituted by rules, and some particular application thereof. To ask what can justify punishment in general, is to ask why we should have the sort of rules that provide that those who contravene them should be made to suffer; and this is different from asking for a justification of a particular application of them, in punishing a given individual. Retributivist and utilitarian have tried to furnish answers to both questions, each in his own terms; the strength of the former's case rests on his answer to the second, of the latter's on his answer to the first. Their difficulties arise from attempting to make one answer do for both.

I. *What formal criteria must be satisfied in justifying punishment in general, as an institution?*

The retributivist refusal to look to consequences for justification makes it impossible to answer this question within his terms. Appeals to authority apart, we can provide ultimate justification for rules and institutions, only by showing that they yield advantages.[2] Consequently, what

[2] Admittedly, a rule might be justified *in the first place* by reference to one more general, under which it is subsumed as a particular application—e.g. "It is wrong to pick flowers from public gardens because it is wrong to steal—and this is a special case of stealing." But this would not be conclusive. It could be countered by making a distinction between private and public property, such that while the more general rule prohibits stealing the former, it does not extend to the latter. Whether the distinction can be accepted as relevant must depend on the reasons for the more general rule, understood in terms of its expected advantages, and on whether to allow the exception would tend to defeat them. Consider "Euthanasia is wrong because it is wrong to kill." It could be argued that the latter does not require the former; that a proper distinction can be made between killings generally, and those satisfying the conditions: i. that the patient wants to be killed; ii. that the purpose is to put him out of pain; iii. that there is no hope for his recovery. Suppose the reason for the general prohibition is to ensure that the life of man shall not be "solitary, poor, nasty, brutish, and short"; then exceptions satisfying the above criteria might be admissible, on the grounds that not only would they not defeat the objectives of the rule, but that advantages would follow from distinguishing on the basis of these criteria, that

pass for retributivist justifications of punishment in general, can be shown to be either denials of the need to justify it, or mere reiterations of the principle to be justified, or disguised utilitarianism.

Assertions of the type "it is fitting (or justice requires) that the guilty suffer" only reiterate the principle to be justified—for "it is fitting" means only that it ought to be the case, which is precisely the point at issue. Similarly, since justification must be in terms of something other than the thing in question, to say that punishment is a good in itself is to deny the need for justification. For those who feel the need, this is no answer at all. Given that punishment would not be justified for the breach of *any* rule, but only of legal rules, what is the peculiar virtue of law that makes it particularly fitting for breaches of just this type of rule? Even if we make punishment a definitional characteristic of "a legal system," so that "law" entails "punishment," we are still entitled to ask why we should have rule systems of precisely this sort.

Some retributivists argue that while punishment is a prima facie evil, and thus in need of justification, it is less objectionable than that the wicked should prosper. This is to subsume the rule "Crimes ought to be punished" under a more general rule: either "The wicked ought to be less well off than the virtuous" or "The wicked ought not to profit from their crimes." Now "wickedness" involves assessment of character; we do not punish men for their wickedness, but for particular breaches of law. There may be some ignoble but prudent characters who have never broken a law, and never been punished, and noble ones who have—our system of punishment is not necessarily the worse for that. We may have to answer for our characters on the Day of Judgment, but not at Quarter Sessions. The state is not an agent of cosmic justice; it punishes only such acts as are contrary to legal rules, conformity to which, even from unworthy motives like fear, is considered of public importance. And if we offer the narrower ground, that the wicked ought not to profit from their *crimes*, we are bound to justify the distinction between crimes and offences against morals in general. What is the special virtue of legal rules, that a breach of them alone warrants punishment? It seems that the wicked are to be prevented from prospering only if their wickedness manifests itself in selected ways; but how is the selection made, unless in terms of its consequences? In any case, if we permit the subsumption of "Crime ought to be punished" under the more general "The wicked ought not to prosper," it would still be proper to seek justification for the latter. It would not help to say "Justice requires it," for this would only deny the right to ask for justification. I see no answer possible except that in a universe in which the wicked prospered, there would be no inducement to virtue. The subsumption, if allowed, would defer the utilitarian stage of justification; it would not render it superfluous.

A veiled utilitarianism underlies Hegel's treatment of punishment, as annulling a wrong. For if punishment could annul the wrong, it would be justified by the betterment of the victim of the crime or of society in general. Not indeed that the argument is a good one; for the only way to annul a wrong is by restitution or compensation, and neither of these is punishment. A man may be sent to prison for assault, and *also* be liable for damages. Similarly with the argument that punish-

---

would otherwise be missed. On the other hand, it might be said that it is *absolutely* wrong to kill—which is to deny the need for justification in terms of purpose or consequences, but is also to deny the need for *any* moral (as opposed to authoritative) justification. But in that case, how are we to decide whether "Thou shalt not kill" does, or does not, extend to a duty "officiously to keep alive"?

ment reaffirms the right. Why should a reaffirmation of right take precisely the form of punishment? Would not a formal declaration suffice? And even if the reaffirmation necessarily involved a need, right, or duty to punish, the justification would be utilitarian, for why should it be necessary to reaffirm the right, if not to uphold law for the general advantage?[3]

Others have treated punishment as a sort of reflex, a reaction of the social order to the crime following in the nature of things, like a hangover.[4] This is to confuse rules with scientific laws. The penal consequences of a breach of a rule follow only because men have decided to have rules of precisely this sort. Laws of nature, unlike rules, need no justification (except perhaps in theology) because they are independent of human choice. To treat punishment as a natural unwilled response to a breach of law is to deny the need for justification, not to justify[5]. Once we agree to have penal rules, any particular punishment might be justified (though not necessarily sufficiently justified) by reference to a rule. But this is to answer a different question from that at present under consideration.

For Bosanquet, punishment was retributive in the sense that, ideally at least, it was the returning upon the offender of "his own will, implied in the maintenance of a system to which he is a party," in the form of pain. It tends to "a recognition of the end by the person punished;" it is "his right, of which he must not be defrauded."[6] Now while a criminal may not seek to destroy the entire social order, and may even agree in principle that lawbreakers should be punished, his efforts to elude the police are evidence that he does not will his own punishment in any ordinary sense. He may be unreasonable and immoral in making exceptions in his own favour—but we cannot therefore construct a theory of punishment on a hypothetical will that would be his were he reasonable and moral, for then he might not be a criminal. To say that punishment is his "right" is to disregard one of the usual criteria for the use of that word, namely, that it is something which will be enforced only if its subject so chooses, the corollary being that it operates to his advantage. Only by pretending that punishment is self-imposed can we think of the criminal as exercising choice; and only by treating it as reformative can we regard it as to his advantage. By claiming that punishment tends "to a recognition of the end by the person punished," Bosanquet introduces such a reformative justification; but to that extent the argument is utilitarian.

To sum up: retributive justifications of punishment in general are unsatisfactory

[3] Cf. Lord Justice Denning, in evidence to the Royal Commission on Capital Punishment: "The ultimate justification of any punishment is not that it is a deterrent but that it is the emphatic denunciation by the community of a crime." Cmd. 8932, §53 (1953). But "denunciation" does not imply the deliberate imposition of suffering, which is the feature of punishment usually felt to need justification.

[4] Cf. Sir Ernest Barker, in *Principles of Social and Political Theory* (Oxford: Clarendon Press, 1951), p. 182: "the mental rule of law which pays back a violation of itself by a violent return, much as the natural rules of health pay back a violation of themselves by a violent return."

[5] For J. D. Mabbott, too, punishment is a kind of automatic response, though in a different sense. "Punishment is a corollary not of law but of law-breaking. Legislators do not *choose* to punish. They hope no punishment will be needed. The criminal makes the essential choice; he 'brings it on himself.' " ("Punishment," in *Mind* 48 [1939], 161 [p. 95 above]. He reaffirms the position in "Freewill and Punishment," in *Contemporary British Philosophy*, 3rd series, ed. H. D. Lewis [1956], p. 303.) But legislators choose to make *penal* rules, and it is this choice that needs justification.

[6] *The Philosophical Theory of the State*, 4th edn. (London, New York: The Macmillan Co., 1923), p. 211.

for the very reason that they refuse to look to the consequences of a rule, thereby denying a necessary part of the procedure for justifying it. To look to the consequences does not entail treating the criminal merely as a means to a social end, as critics have asserted; for in weighing advantages and disadvantages, the criminal, too, must "count for one." But equally, he must count "for no more than one." While we must not lose sight of his welfare altogether, we are not bound to treat him as our sole legitimate concern.

Bentham's case is that punishment is a technique of social control, justified so long as it prevents more mischief than it produces. At the point where damage to criminals outweighs the expected advantage to society, it loses that justification. It operates by reforming the criminal, by preventing a repetition of the offence, and by deterring others from imitating it. (These need not exhaust the possibilities of advantage—Bentham included the satisfaction of vengeance for the injured party.)

Not all theories dealing with the reform of criminals are theories of punishment. Prison reformers concerned with moral reeducation offer theories of punishment only if they expect the suffering involved in loss of liberty, etc., itself to lead to reformation. Reformative treatment might cure criminal inclinations by relaxing the rigours of punishment; it might nevertheless defeat its purpose by reducing the deterrent effect for others. "Reformation" is in any case ambiguous. A man would be "a reformed character" only if he showed remorse for his past misdeeds, and determined not to repeat them, not through fear of further punishment, but simply because they were wrong. A criminal who decides that "crime does not pay" is merely deterred by his own experience which is as much "an example" to himself as to others.

Sentences of preventive detention, transportation, deportation, and the death penalty, may all be examples of punishment operating as a preventive. Punishment might be aimed at preventing repetitions of an offence by the criminal himself where there are good grounds (e.g. a long criminal record) for supposing him undeterrable.

The strongest utilitarian argument for punishment in general is that it serves to deter potential offenders by inflicting suffering on actual ones. On this view, punishment is not the main thing; the technique works by threat. Every act of punishment is to that extent an admission of failure; we punish only that the technique may retain a limited effectiveness for the future. Thus the problem of justifying punishment arises only because it is not completely effective; if it were, there would be no suffering to justify.

Retributivists do not deny that punishment may act in these ways, nor that it has these advantages. They maintain only that they are incidental; that a system of punishment constructed entirely on these principles would lead to monstrous injustices. These I consider below. It is evident, however, that while *some* sort of justification can be offered within the utilitarian framework, the retributivist is at best denying the need for justification, or offering utilitarianism in disguise. I conclude, therefore, that any justification for punishment in general must satisfy the formal condition that the consequences for everyone concerned of adopting the technique shall be preferable to the consequences of not doing so. If the main advantage arises from a lower incidence of crime (by way of reform, prevention, deterrence, or otherwise), this must be weighed against the penal suffering actually inflicted, and these together must be preferable to a higher incidence of crime, but with no additional suffering inflicted as punishment. This is a frankly utilitarian conclusion. The strength of the retributivist position lies in its answer to the second question, to which I now turn.

II. *What formal criteria must be satisfied in justifying any particular application of the technique of punishment?*

Critics of the utilitarian approach contend that a justification of punishment in terms of deterrence, prevention, and reform could be extended to justify (i) punishing the innocent, providing they were widely believed to be guilty (in the interest of deterrence); (ii) making a show of punishment, without actually inflicting it (again, deterrence, but this time on the cheap); (iii) punishment in anticipation of the offence (in the interests of prevention or reform). These criticisms, if just, would surely be conclusive. They are based, however, on a misconception of what the utilitarian theory is about. "Punishment" implies, in its primary sense, inflicting suffering only under specified conditions, of which one is that it must be for a breach of a rule. Now if we insist on this criterion for the word, "punishment of the innocent" is a logical impossibility, for by definition, suffering inflicted on the innocent, or in anticipation of a breach of the rule, cannot be "punishment." It is not a question of what is morally justified, but of what is logically possible. (An analogous relation between "guilt" and "pardon" accounts for the oddity of granting "a free pardon" to a convicted man, later found to be innocent.) When we speak of "punishing the innocent," we may mean: (i) "pretending to punish," in the sense of manufacturing evidence, or otherwise imputing guilt, while knowing a man to be innocent. This would be to treat him *as if* he were guilty, and involve the lying assertion that he was. It is objectionable, not only as a lie, but also because it involves treating an innocent person differently from others without justification, or for an irrelevant reason, the reason offered being falsely grounded.[7] (ii) We may mean, by "punish," simply "cause to suffer," i.e., guilt may not be imputed. This would be a secondary use of the word. In that case, it could not be said that, as a matter of logical necessity, it is either impossible or wrong to punish the innocent. To imprison members of a subversive party (e.g. under Defence Regulation 18B) treating them *in that respect* like criminals, though no offence is even charged, would not necessarily be immoral. Critics might describe it as "punishing the innocent," but they would be illegitimately borrowing implications of the primary sense to attack a type of action to which these did not apply. It is only necessarily improper to "punish the innocent" if we pretend they are guilty, i.e., if we accept all the primary usage criteria; in any looser sense, there need be nothing wrong in any given case. For in exceptional conditions it may be legitimate to deprive people of their liberty as part of a control technique, without reference to an offence (e.g. the detention of lunatics or enemy aliens). Similar arguments apply in the case of the show of punishment. A utilitarian justification of punishment cannot be extended to cover lies, or the making of distinctions where there are no relevant differences; it would be impossible merely to pretend to punish *every* criminal—and unless a relevant criterion could be found, there could be no grounds for treating some differently from others.

The short answer to the critics of utilitarian theories of punishment, is that they are theories of *punishment,* not of *any* sort of technique involving suffering.

We may now turn to the retributivist position itself. F. H. Bradley asserted "the

[7] Cf. A. Quinton: "On Punishment," in *Analysis* 14, no. 6 (June 1954); reprinted in *Philosophy, Politics, and Society,* ed. P. Laslett (New York: Macmillan, 1956).

necessary connection of punishment and guilt. Punishment is punishment, only where it is deserved . . . if punishment is inflicted for any other reason whatever than because it is merited by wrong, it is a gross immorality, a crying injustice, an abominable crime, and not what it pretends to be."[8] Now, we must distinguish between legal and moral guilt. If the necessary connection asserted is between punishment and legal guilt, then this is a definition of "punishment" masquerading as a moral judgment. It would be more accurate to write "Punishment is 'punishment' only when it is deserved," for the sentence is then about the use of a word, not about the rightness of the act. "The infliction of suffering on a person is only properly described as punishment if that person is guilty. The retributivist thesis, therefore, is not a moral doctrine, but an account of the meaning of the word 'punishment.' "[9]

But this is not the only form of retributive thesis. There are at least four possibilities:

(i) That guilt (i.e. a breach of law) is a *necessary* condition of punishment (this is the position just examined);
(ii) That guilt (i.e. a breach of a *moral* rule) is a *necessary* condition of punishment;
(iii) That guilt (*legal*) is a *sufficient* condition of punishment;
(iv) That guilt (*moral*) is a *sufficient* condition of punishment.

Position (iii) is *not* logically necessary, for it does not follow from the definition of punishment; we *cannot* "punish" where there has been no breach, but we can, and often do, let off with a caution where there has. Other conditions besides guilt may have to be satisfied before punishment is wholly justified in a given case.

The introduction, in (ii) and (iv), of moral guilt puts a new complexion on retributive theory. A person who is morally guilty deserves blame, and the conditions for blameworthiness could be listed. But it is in no sense necessary that a person who is blameworthy should also be punishable. We may blame liars, but unless, e.g., they make false tax returns, or lie to a court of law, we should not feel bound to punish them. If the conditions of blameworthiness cannot be assimilated completely to the conditions for punishment, moral guilt cannot be a sufficient condition for punishment.

Position (ii) might be supported in two ways:

(*a*) A prima facie moral duty to obey law may yield, in the case of an immoral law, to a stronger duty; a breach of law would not then entail moral guilt, and we should question the justice of the punishment.[10]

(*b*) Certain conditions, like unavoidable ignorance or mistake of fact, lunacy, infancy, and irresistible duress, would exonerate from blame; offences committed under these conditions should not be punishable—and are not in fact punished, though the deterrent effects of the punishment would be no less in these cases than in others. Therefore, in a negative sense at least, the criteria of blameworthiness must be satisfied, if the necessary conditions for punishment are to be satisfied. Punishment is retribution for such moral lapses as the law recognizes.

[8] *Ethical Studies*, 2nd edn. (Oxford: Clarendon Press, 1927) pp. 26–27.

[9] A. Quinton: op. cit., in *Analysis*, p. 137, in *Philosophy, Politics, and Society*, p. 86.

[10] Cf. C. W. K. Mundle, "Punishment and Desert," in *Philosophical Quarterly* 4 (1954): "the retributive theory implies that punishment of a person by the state is morally justifiable if, and only if he has done something which is both a legal and moral offence, and only if the penalty is proportionate to the moral gravity of his offence," p. 227.

The first argument (*a*) might be met in two ways. From the judge's standpoint, so long as he continued in office, it would be his duty to enforce the law, whatever his opinion of it.[11] For him, at least, the absence of moral guilt would not be a bar to punishment. Secondly, criticism of a rule is only indirectly criticism of the justice of a punishment inflicted for a breach of it. The utilitarian could argue that a law that is itself mischievous (in Bentham's sense of "mischief") cannot justify the further mischief of punishment; no good can come of it any way. This is not, therefore, a defence of a retributive theory of punishment, so much as a statement of conditions that a rule must satisfy if punishment is properly to attach to it.

The second argument (*b*) is inconclusive. If the technique of punishment operates primarily by deterrence, it can serve its purposes only in respect of deliberate acts. No act committed under any of the above conditions would be deliberate. If, therefore, offences of these types are left unpunished, the threat in relation to other offences remains unimpaired, for the sane potential murderer gets no comfort from mercy extended to the homicidal maniac, and other homicidal maniacs will be unaffected either way. Consequently to punish in such cases would be a pointless mischief. In any case, because some of the conditions for blame and punishment coincide, it does not follow that the satisfaction of the former is a necessary condition for the satisfaction of the latter.[12] I shall return to this point later in relation to motive.

Of the four possible interpretations of the retributivist relation of guilt to punishment, it is the first only, whereby guilt in law is a necessary condition for punishment, that is completely persuasive; and this is precisely because it is a definition and not a justification. Consequently, it need not conflict with a utilitarian view.

For a utilitarian to require, for every case of punishment, that it be justified in terms of preventing more mischief than it causes, would be to miss the point of punishment as an institution. Indeed, any rule would be pointless if every decision still was required to be justified in the light of its expected consequences. But this is particularly true of penal rules; for the effectiveness of punishment as a deterrent depends on its regular application, save under conditions sufficiently well understood for them not to constitute a source of uncertainty. Legal guilt once established, then, the initial utilitarian presumption against causing deliberate suffering has been overcome, and a case for a penalty has been made out. But it may still be defeated; for since guilt is not a sufficient condition, there may well be other relevant considerations (e.g. that this is a first offence). The following formal criterion may be postulated, however, which any such consideration must satisfy, namely, that to recognize it as a general ground for waiving the penalty would not involve an otherwise avoidable mischief to society *greater* than the mischief of punishing the offender.

One of the criticisms levelled against utilitarianism is that by relating the justi-

[11] This is roughly Mabbott's view ("Punishment," in *Mind* 48 [1939], p. 162 [p. 95 above]. He is a rare example of a retributivist who dissociates punishment and moral guilt.

[12] A man who had broken a law (say, an import regulation), of the existence of which he was ignorant (but avoidably so), would be liable to punishment. It would be to counsel perfection to say that everyone has a moral duty to know of *every* law that might affect him. I should say, in this case, that the offender had been imprudent, but not immoral, in not ascertaining his legal position. I should impute no moral guilt either for his ignorance or for his breach of the rule; but I should not feel, on that account, that he was an injured innocent entitled to complain that he had been wrongly punished.

fication of punishment to its expected consequences, rather than to the crime itself, it would justify penalties divorced from the relative seriousness of crimes, permitting severe penalties for trivial offenses, if that were the only way to reduce their number. A serious but easily detected crime might warrant lesser penalties than a minor but secret one. This conclusion being intolerable, the retributivist contends that to escape it we must seek the measure of the penalty in the crime itself, according to the degree of wickedness involved in committing it.

Again, I distinguish the justification of rules from the justification of particular applications. To ask "How much punishment is appropriate to a given offence?" is ambiguous: it may refer either to the punishment allotted by a rule to a *class* of acts, or to a particular award for a given act within that class. The distinction is pointed by the practice of laying down only maximum (and sometimes minimum) penalties in the rule, leaving particular determinations to judicial discretion.

III. *What formal criteria must be satisfied in justifying the degrees of punishment attached to different classes of offence?*

"The only case" (said Kant) "in which the offender cannot complain that he is being treated unjustly is if his crime recoils upon himself and he suffers what he has inflicted on another, if not in a literal sense, at any rate according to the spirit of the law." "It is only *the right of requital* (*jus talionis*) which can fix definitely the quality and the quantity of the punishment." This is the most extreme retributive position; its essential weakness is present, however, in more moderate attempts to seek the determinants of punishment exclusively in the offence itself.

If retaliatory punishment is not to be effected "in a literal sense" (which might well be intolerably cruel, and in some cases physically impossible), but rather "according to the spirit of the law," it involves a sort of arithmetical equation of suffering as impracticable as the hedonistic calculus. Suffering of one sort cannot be *equated* with another, though it may be possible to prefer one to another (or to be indifferent as between one and another). I can certainly say that I would rather see A suffer in one way, than B in another, or that there is really nothing to choose between the two. But this is quite different from saying that A ought to be made to suffer in exactly the same degree as B, whom he has injured; for this involves not a preference enunciated by some third person, but a quasi-quantitative comparison of the sufferings of two different people, treated as objective facts. And there is no way of making this comparison, even though the external features of their suffering may be identical. It is even more evidently impossible when the suffering of one is occasioned by, say, blackmail, and of the other by imprisonment.[13]

The difficulty remains in the compromise between a utilitarian and retaliatory position attempted by W. D. Ross. While admitting that the legislator must consider the deterrent ends of punishment in assessing penalties, he maintains that the injury inflicted by the criminal sets an upper limit to the injury that can legitimately be inflicted on him. "For he has lost his prima facie rights to life, liberty, or property, only in so far as these rested on an explicit or implicit undertaking to respect the corresponding rights in others, and in so far as he has failed to respect

[13] Hegel virtually admits the impossibility of answering this question rationally (*Philosophy of Right*, § 101) but insists nevertheless that there must be a right answer (§ 214) to which we must try empirically to approximate. But by what test shall we judge whether our shots at justice are approaching or receding from the target?

those rights."[14] But how are we to make this equation between the rights invaded and consequently sacrificed, and the amount of suffering so justified—unless there is already available a scale, or rule, fixing the relation? But then how is the scale to be justified?

J. D. Mabbott admits there can be no direct relation between offence and penalty, but seeks, by comparing one crime with another, to make an estimate of the penalties *relatively* appropriate. "We can grade crimes in a rough scale and penalties in a rough scale, and keep our heaviest penalties for what are socially the most serious wrongs regardless of whether these penalties . . . are exactly what deterrence would require."[15] But what are we to understand by "socially the most serious wrongs"? On the one hand, they might be those that shock us most deeply—we could then construct a shock scale, and punish accordingly. There are some shocking acts, however, that we should not want to punish at all (e.g. some sexual offences against morality); at the same time, we should be hard put to it to know what penalties to attach to new offences against, say, currency control regulations, where the intial shock reaction is either negligible, because the rule is unsupported by a specific rule of conventional morality, or where it is of a standard mild variety accompanying any offence against the law as such, irrespective of its particular quality. On the other hand, "the most serious wrongs" may be simply those we are least ready to tolerate. That, however, would be to introduce utilitarian considerations into our criteria of "seriousness." For to say that we are not prepared to tolerate an offence is to say that we should feel justified in imposing heavy penalties to deter people from committing it. But in making deterrent considerations secondary to the degree of "seriousness," M. Mabbott implicitly excludes this interpretation.

The retributivists' difficulties arise from seeking the measure of the penalty in the crime, without first assuming a scale or a rule relating the two. Given the scale, any given penalty would require justification in terms of it; but the scale itself, like any rule, must in the end be justified in utilitarian terms. It remains to be seen whether this necessarily opens the way to severe penalties for trivial offences.

For the utilitarian, arguing in deterrent terms, it is the threat rather than the punishment itself which is primary. Could we rely on the threat being completely effective, there could be no objection to the death penalty for every offence, since *ex hypothesi* it would never be inflicted. Unhappily, we must reckon to inflict some penalties, for there will always be some offenders, no matter what the threatened punishment. We must suppose, then, for every class of crime, a scale of possible penalties, to each of which corresponds a probable number of offences, and therefore of occasions for punishment, the number probably diminishing as the severity increases. Ultimately, however, we should almost certainly arrive at a hard core of undeterrables. We should then choose, for each class of offence, that penalty at which the marginal increment of mischief inflicted on offenders would be just preferable to the extra mischief from which the community is protected by this increment of punishment. To inflict any heavier penalty would do more harm than it would prevent. (This is Bentham's principle of "frugality".)[16]

This involves not a quasi-quantitative comparison of suffering by the community and the offender, but only a preference. We might say something like this: To

[14] *The Right and the Good*, 1930, pp. 62–63.

[15] "Punishment," p. 162.

[16] *Introduction to the Principles of Morals and Legislation*, chap. xv, §§ 11–12.

increase the penalty for parking offences to life imprisonment would reduce congestion on the roads; nevertheless the inconvenience of a large number of offences would not be serious enough to justify disregarding in so great a measure, the prima facie case for liberty, even of a very few offenders. With blackmail, or murder, the possibility of averting further instances defeats to a far greater extent the claims of the offender. One parking offence more or less is not of great moment; one murder more or less is.

In retaliatory theory we are asked to estimate the damage done by the crime, and to inflict just that amount (or no more than that amount) on the criminal; here we are required only to choose between one combination of circumstances and another. The choice may not always be easy; but it is not impossible, or even unusual. For we are well accustomed to choosing between things incapable of quantitative comparison; what is impossible is to assess what one man has suffered from blackmail, and then to impose its equivalent on the blackmailer in terms of a prison sentence. The difference is between a prescription and a description. To say, as I do above, that the right penality is that at which the marginal increment of mischief inflicted is just preferable to the mischief thereby avoided, is to invite the critic to choose (or prescribe) one state of affairs rather than another. But to say that the penalty should equal (or should not exceed) the suffering of the victim of the crime is to invite him to prescribe a course dependent not on his own preferences, but on a factual comparison of incomparables, on an equation of objective conditions.

The utilitarian case as I have now put it is not open to the objection that it would justify serious penalties for trivial offences. For to call an offence "trivial" is to say that we care less if this one is committed than if others are, i.e., we should be unwilling to inflict so much suffering to prevent it, as to prevent others. "Relatively serious crimes" are those relatively less tolerable, i.e., we prefer to inflict severer penalties rather than to suffer additional offences. If this is so, "Trivial crimes do not deserve severe penalties" is analytic; consequently a utilitarian justification could not be extended to cover a contrary principle.[17]

Some penalties we are unwilling to inflict whatever their deterrent force. We are less ready to torture offenders than to suffer their offences. And there are people who would rather risk murders than inflict the death penalty, even supposing it to be "the unique deterrent." To kill, they say, is absolutely wrong. Now this may mean only that no circumstances are imaginable in which its probable consequences would make it right, i.e., in which the mischief done would not outweigh the mischief prevented—not that it could *never* be right, only that in any imaginable conditions it would not be. This would not exclude justification by consequences, and is therefore compatible with the view of punishment I am advancing. On the other hand, if the absolutist denies altogether the relevance of consequences, he is making an ultimate judgment for which, in the nature of the case, justification can be neither sought nor offered and which is therefore undiscussible.

I conclude, from this discussion, that

[17] We could say "Some trivial crimes deserve serious penalties" if we wished to imply that some crimes are a good deal more serious than they are generally held to be. But the sentence would be better punctuated: "Some 'trivial' crimes . . . ," for they are "trivial" in the view of others, not of the speaker. Consider, in this connection, the difference of opinion between pedestrians' and motorists' associations on the gravity of driving offences—and on the penalties appropriate. A pedestrian might not think a prison sentence too severe a penalty for speeding—but neither is it, for him, a trivial offence.

any justification for the nature and degree of punishment attached to a given class of offence must satisfy the following formal criterion: that the marginal increment of mischief inflicted should be preferable to the mischief avoided by fixing that penalty rather than one slightly lower. Assuming that the advantages of punishment derive mainly from upholding rules, this means that the conformity secured, weighed against the suffering inflicted, should be preferable to a lower level of conformity, weighed against the suffering inflicted by imposing a lesser penalty. (This entails neither that a very few offenders suffering heavy penalties must be preferred to a larger number of offenders suffering lighter penalties, nor the converse; preferences are not settled by multiplication.)

IV. *What formal criteria must be satisfied in justifying the particular penalty awarded to a given offender?*

Two men guilty of what is technically the same offence (i.e., who have broken the same rule) are not necessarily punished alike. This could be justified only by reference to relevant criteria, other than simple guilt, by which their cases are distinguished. Provocation, temptation, duress, and a clean record may all make a difference. But these are also relevant to the determination of blame. From these considerations arise two possible objections to the view I am advancing:

(*a*) Is it consistent with utilitarianism that in determining the sentence, we should look to the particular conditions of the crime, rather than to the consequences of the penalty? Should we not look forward to the exemplary advantages of the maximum penalty, rather than backward to extenuating circumstances?

(*b*) Since we do look backwards, and assess the penalty in the light of criteria also relevant to an assessment of blameworthiness, can we not say that men deserve punishment only in the measure that they deserve blame?

As to (*a*): a rule once accepted, there is no need to justify every application in terms of its consequences; it is necessary to justify in utilitarian terms only the criteria of extenuation, not every application of them. Now precisely because an offence has been committed under exceptional circumstances (e.g., severe temptation, provocation, duress), leniency would not seriously weaken the threat, since offenders would expect similar leniency only in similar circumstances, which are such, in any case, that a man would be unlikely to consider rationally the penal consequences of his act. Given that, the full measure of the penalty would be unjustifiable.[18]

As to (*b*); while some criteria tend to mitigate both blame and punishment, the latter need not depend on the degree of the former. The question of motive is crucial. We generally regard a man as less blameworthy if he breaks a rule "from the highest motives," rather than selfishly or maliciously. A traitor from conscientious conviction may be blamed for wrongheadedness, but, if we respect his integrity, we blame him less than a merely mercenary one. But honest motives will not always mitigate punishment. It may be vital for the effectiveness of government that conscientious recalcitrants (e.g., potential fifth columnists acting from polit-

[18] Grading sentences according to the number of previous convictions might be justified by the failure, *ex hypothesi*, of lesser penalties on earlier occasions, to act as deterrents. Possible imitators with similar records may possibly require a similarly severe deterrent example. For most of the rest of us, with little criminal experience, lighter penalties awarded to less hardened offenders are sufficient deterrents. A case can therefore be made for reserving the severest penalties for the class of criminals least easily deterred.

ical conviction) be deterred from action. But since strong moral convictions are often less amenable to threats than other motives, they could scarcely be admitted in such cases in extenuation of punishment. On the other hand, if the mischief of the penalty needed for a high degree of conformity exceeds its advantages, it may be reasonable to give up punishing conscientious offenders altogether, provided they can be discerned from the fakes.[19] We no longer punish conscientious objectors to military service, having found by experience that they are rarely amenable to threats, that they are unsatisfactory soldiers if coerced, and that, given a rigorous test of conscientiousness, their numbers are not likely to be so great as to impair the community purpose.

The considerable overlapping of the factors tending to mitigate blame and punishment nevertheless demands explanation. Morality and law are alike rule systems for controlling behaviour, and what blame is to one, punishment is to the other. Since they are closely analogous as techniques for discouraging undesirable conduct, by making its consequences in different ways disagreeable, the principles for awarding them largely coincide. But it does not follow that because we usually also blame the man we punish, we should punish in the light of the criteria determining moral guilt. Morality operates as a control not only by prescribing or prohibiting acts, but also by conditioning character (and therefore conduct in general). We blame men for being bad tempered; we punish them only for assault. Furthermore, punishment is administered through formal machinery of investigation, proof, conviction, sentence, and execution; blame by informal and personal procedures which may well take account of evidence of character that might nevertheless be rightly inadmissible in a court of law. To the extent that the techniques are analogous, they may be expected to employ similar criteria; but the analogy cannot be pushed all the way.

Conclusion

The quarrel between retributivist and utilitarian is primarily about procedures of justification, about how to go about defending or attacking punishment, in general or in particular, about the formal criteria that together form a schema to which any justification must conform. I have maintained that when what is wanted is a justification of a rule, or an institution, of punishment in general, or of the scale of punishments assigned to different classes of offence, it must be sought in terms of the net advantages gained or mischiefs avoided. When the particular sentence is a question, the first consideration is guilt, without which punishment in a strict sense is impossible, but which once established constitutes a prima facie case for it. The second consideration must be the legally prescribed limits, within which the penalty must fall. Beyond that, decision must be made in the light of criteria tending to mitigate if not totally defeat the presumption in favour of the

[19] Consider, in this connection, the difficulty of distinguishing the genuine survivor of a suicide pact, who has been unable to carry out his side of the bargain, from the cheat who relies on a counterfeit pact to evade the maximum penalty for murder. (See the Report on Capital Punishment, referred to above, §§ 163–176.) The same applies to "mercy-killing": "How, for example, were the jury to decide whether a daughter had killed her invalid father from compassion, from a desire for material gain, from a natural wish to bring to an end a trying period of her life, or from a combination of motives?" (Ibid., § 179). Nevertheless, where we feel reasonably sure that the motive was merciful, we expect leniency. A mercy-killing is not in the same class as a brutal murder for profit, and we may feel justified in tolerating a few examples rather than inflict the maximum penalty on this type of offender.

maximum penalty. These criteria must themselves be justified in terms of the net advantages, or mischief avoided, in adopting them as general principles.

These are formal principles only. To make out a substantial justification, we must postulate first the sort of advantages we expect from punishment as an institution. I have assumed that its principal advantage is that it secures conformity to rules (though others might conceivably be offered, e.g., that it reformed criminal characters, which could be regarded as a good thing in itself; or that it gave the injured person the satisfaction of being revenged). Further, I have assumed that it operates primarily by way of deterrence. These are in part assumptions of fact, in part moral judgments. I maintain that these being given, the criteria by which the prima facie case for punishment may be defeated, wholly or in part, are generally justifiable in utilitarian terms; that they do not weaken the deterrent threat, that they avoid inflicting suffering which would not be justified by the resultant additional degree of conformity. Further, the total assimilation to the system of punishment of criteria tending to defeat or mitigate blameworthiness, is unjustifiable in theory and is not made in practice. We do not punish men because they are morally guilty, nor must we *necessarily* refrain because they are morally guiltless, nor mitigate the punishment in the same degree for all the same reasons that we mitigate blame. This is not to say that the justifications sought are not *moral* justifications; it is simply that they must be made in the light of criteria different from those governing blame, since however close the analogy may be between the two techniques of control, there are still significant differences between them.

Norman Kretzmann / Desire as proof of desirability

There are some very familiar passages in Mill's *Utilitarianism* in which he attempts to show the extent to which and the way in which the principle of utility can be proved. The familiarity of those passages is almost solely a result of their so often having served as targets for criticism and even ridicule. One brief analogical argument within those passages outstrips everything else in them for notoriety. Students of elementary logic have it held up to them as a pellucid instance of the fallacy of "figure of speech" and of the human frailty to which even the finest minds are subject; F. H. Bradley is "ashamed to have to examine such reasoning";[1] G. E. Moore finds it "as naive and artless a use of the naturalistic fallacy as anybody could desire."[2]

The argument is indeed filled with difficulties. But, I want to maintain, it is neither shameful nor naive nor, even for anti-naturalists, fallacious. Nor is it in any way embarrassing for utilitarians or for other kinds of democrats. Instead it offers us, under the interpretation I want to place upon it, a suggestive principle in social and political ethics, a completely consistent and pre-eminently important version of the principle of utility.

In order to maintain this I am willing if need be to give up the defence of the historical Mill, and in any case I have to avoid involving in the discussion any other parts of Mill's defence of utilitarianism than that analogical argument. Other parts of it may or may not be fallacious or otherwise objectionable; but, thanks to Professor Everett W. Hall's broader investigations in "The 'Proof' of Utility in Bentham and Mill,"[3] we may forgo those other parts here without feeling that they go undefended. I am completely in sym-

[1] *Ethical Studies* (Oxford: Clarendon Press, 1927), p. 115*n*.

[2] *Principia Ethica* (Cambridge: The University Press, 1903), p. 66.

[3] *Ethics* 60 (October 1949), pp. 1–18 [pp. 99–116 above].

Reprinted from THE PHILOSOPHICAL QUARTERLY, *vol. 8, no. 32 (July 1958), pp. 246–258 by permission of the author and editors.*

pathy with Professor Hall's attitude in that excellent paper, but, as this paper will show, my defence of Mill and my development of the particular point in question is more sanguine than his and is otherwise oriented. Since my interest in this topic is almost exclusively constructive rather than historical, I have not felt limited to explicating Mill's text or obliged to reproduce what are demonstrably his own views.

I am going to quote Mill's analogical argument, to introduce some of the outcries that have recently been raised against it, to introduce (and mainly reject) some recently attempted salvagings of it, and finally to discuss it with a view to laying down an interpretation that will make good sense of it while remaining plausibly true to Mill's intent.

I

> Questions about ends are, in other words, questions about what things are desirable. The utilitarian doctrine is, that happiness is desirable, and the only thing desirable, as an end; all other things being only desirable as means to that end. What ought to be required of this doctrine—what conditions is it requisite that the doctrine should fulfil—to make good its claim to be believed?
>
> *The only proof capable of being given that a thing is visible, is that people actually see it. The only proof that a sound is audible, is that people hear it: and so of the other sources of our experience. In like manner, I apprehend, the sole evidence it is possible to produce that anything is desirable, is that people do actually desire it.*[4]

If any interpretation of the argument indicated by italics in this passage can compete with G. E. Moore's for widest acceptance, I suppose it is H. W. B. Joseph's. In his *Introduction to Logic* he lights upon it as "an excellent example" of the fallacy of "figure of speech," which, he says, "arises through the ambiguous force of some verbal inflexion, which is wrongly alleged to imply in one case what it really implies in others." He sets forth his case against Mill's reasoning in this way: "He is trying to prove that the chief good, or one thing desirable, is pleasure. [That step of Mill's argument really *follows* the quoted passage, in which he endeavours only to lead into his further proof that happiness, or pleasure, is *a* good, one genuine desirable.] . . . But *visible, audible* mean what *can* be seen or heard; whereas Mill is trying to prove that happiness *ought to be* desired, or is the thing *worth* desiring. Yet the termination *-able* or *-ible* must be taken to have the same force in the words *desirable* as in *audible* or *visible* if the argument is to have any force at all; and the only thing shown is that men can desire happiness: which was never in question."[5]

We may for the present take this as the paradigm of one kind of attack upon Mill's argument—the kind depending upon finding within it an informal logical fallacy. That is a charge of such seriousness that it must really be accounted a scandal. Mill, himself expert in the traditional logic and therefore also in the traditional theory of fallacies, having come to what Joseph correctly recognizes as "a critical point of his argument," is supposed to fall into the kind of trap a competent beginner should know how to avoid. Or, as Moore puts it when he, too, finds a fallacy less special than the one he chose to call "naturalistic," "Well, the fallacy in this step is so obvious, that it is quite wonderful how Mill failed to see it. The fact is that 'desirable' does not mean 'able to be desired' as 'visible' means 'able to be seen,'" etc., etc.[6]

Critics who take this tack must find a farcical irony in Mill's citing a remarkably

[4] *Utilitarianism*, ch. IV, p. 32 (Everyman's ed.) [p. 37 above]; italics added.

[5] Ch. XXVII, sect. 6.

[6] *Principia Ethica*, p. 67.

similar instance in his own discussion of the *Fallacia Figurae Dictionis:*

> The following is a Stoical argument taken from Cicero, *De Finibus*, book the third: "Quod est bonum, omne laudabile est. Quod autem laudabile est, omne honestum est. Bonum igitur quod est, honestum est." Here the ambiguous word is *laudabile*, which in the minor premise means anything which mankind are accustomed, on good grounds, to admire or value; as beauty, for instance, or good fortune; but in the major it denotes exclusively moral qualities.[7]

So far, then, the evidence against accepting a condemnation of the argument on the ground that it contains an elementary logical fallacy is of the puniest, but still worth noting. Mill *was* at a critical point of his argument and cannot have been unaware of it, and he was, or had been, quite conscious of the kind of error he is accused of committing. These considerations ought at least to lead us to investigate the supposed error more thoroughly.

Since around the turn of the century, when Mill was held up to scorn on this point and others in the logic of his ethics by Bradley, Moore, and Joseph, the tendency has, however, been to take the fallacious character of the argument more and more for granted. Professor Karl Britton in his recent study of Mill's philosophy, apparently agrees with Joseph and with Moore in imputing to him a fallacy of ambiguity; and he does so without condescending to a careful analysis of the argument. A sense of history, and presumably also of fair play, compels him, however, to explain Mill's failing in this matter as inherited.

> It is not enough to see that Mill confuses 'can be desired' with 'ought to be desired.' There is at least a hundred years of history behind this blunder. Mill confused the two because he was brought up in a tradition which never was quite willing to distinguish them. He is speaking for Bentham, Hume, and Locke, in this argument: he is moved by the conviction that the good must arouse desire, and that the only absolutely authentic natural desires are the simple organic desires for pleasure or relief from pain.[8]

That Mill may be taken as summing up for classic British empiricism on this point is quite possibly true; but what is really important in this passage is mostly false. It is not *correct* to see that Mill confuses "can be desired" with "ought to be desired." And that so puerile a "blunder" could have escaped the notice not only of Mill but of four generations of his philosophical ancestors as well is an allegation even more wonderful, even more serious, and consequently perhaps even more deserving of concern than are those so often directed simply against Mill. But to confine our attention to him, has Professor Britton read him correctly when he attributes to him the conviction that the good must arouse desire? Without stopping just now to discuss this at length we may remark that it seems at any rate superficially odd that Mill's saying, in effect, that if anything is actually desired by people it is desirable should be viewed as evidence of a belief on his part that if anything is desirable it must actually be desired. But we shall return to this point.

As will be clear from what has already been said, Moore readily attacks this argument from at least two standpoints. It is hard to keep them quite distinct, however, since in Moore's view both lines of attack converge upon a supposed ambiguity. In the first place he would agree with Joseph and with Britton that Mill has been taken in by an ambiguity that should not really have been one at all, that would never have fooled almost anyone else for a moment. (For no one ever really uses the word "desirable" as synonymous with

[7] *A System of Logic*, Bk. V, ch. vii.

[8] Karl Britton, *John Stuart Mill* (London, Baltimore: Penguin, 1953), p. 50.

"capable of being desired"; it is not easy to think of any use that might be served by a word with that meaning, since almost anything at all, I suppose, *can* be desired.)

But in the second place and more predictably Moore condemns it, or exults over it, as a classic case of the "naturalistic fallacy."

> . . . the commonest of all views with regard to the meaning of the word 'good,' is that to call a thing good is to say that it is desired, or desired for its own sake; and curiously enough this view has been used as an argument in favour of [utilitarianism] . . .; on the ground that no man ever desires (or desires for its own sake) anything at all except *pleasure* (or *his own* pleasure), and that hence, since 'good' means 'desired,' any set of effects which contains more pleasure *must* always be better than one which contains less.[9]

Mill is beyond any question a naturalist in ethics, at least as regards his self-conscious official pronouncements. And if naturalism thus implied is fallacious, then plainly Mill is a fallacy-monger and among the princes of them as far as ethics is concerned. But once that much has been allowed, I find it difficult to interpret some of what Moore has to say in this passage about Mill's naturalism. For what Mill is offering us in the argument in question is the one *proof* that anything is desirable, or good—not a *definition* of the word "desirable" or of its usual synonym "good." A definition would require an if-and-only-if formulation, and Mill's proof will not translate accurately into such a formulation. This will be seen more easily in the discussion below of the analogy itself.

The ease with which his commentators transform what are clearly antecedent and consequent propositions for Mill and the frequent reference they make to *meaning* rather than to *proof* as the relation between the desired and the desirable indicate, I think, the prevalence of Moore's influence. Since Mill is a naturalist in ethics it is supposed that when he speaks of the desired and the good he must mean to define the good in terms of the desired, since that is the essence of the "naturalistic fallacy." That Mill commits this "fallacy" elsewhere—as for example when he reduces the principle of utility to the recognition that " 'happiness' and 'desirable' are synonymous terms"[10]—is perfectly well-known. He could not be even an *heretical* utilitarian otherwise. But it is a mistake to find an instance of the naturalistic fallacy—or as Professor Frankena more descriptively puts it, a variety of the "definist" fallacy—in this proof of desirability; and though it may seem a trifling mistake in view of the fact that the "fallacy" does occur repeatedly in his *Utilitarianism*, still it has led to a great deal of unwarranted ridicule of Mill on this point and to the missing of what seems to be an otherwise little-emphasized aspect of his thinking about ethics, as I hope to show.

II

There is a reference on page 51 of Professor Britton's book to a "defence of Mill" by J. Wisdom in his *Philosophy and Psycho-Analysis*. If what Professor Wisdom has to say in this matter can be considered a defence at all, it surely is one that Mill himself would have found exotic.

According to Professor Wisdom,

> Mill said that the desirable is the desired [did he?] and he didn't mean all the nonsense he's been said to mean. He didn't mean that the desirable is what happens to be consciously desired at the moment. He meant that it is what is really desired. What is really desired is what is desired when *all* our inclinations towards it are faced and

[9] *Ethics* (New York: H. Holt and Co., 1912), p. 99. Mill is not mentioned, but the intended reference is pretty clear.

[10] *Utilitarianism*, p. 58*n* [p. 56*n* above].

> not some ignored, including desires not to have a desire for such a thing; in other words, our desire for X is a real desire when all our desires for all that is for us in X have been 'owned' and 'sifted.'[11]

Explanations of "owned" and "sifted" follow this passage in Professor Wisdom's text. But it may be easier for now and not altogether incorrect to gain a clearer notion of what he intends by comparing this passage with another near the end of the same essay.

> . . . on page 39 [of his book *Science and Ethics*, Dr. C. H. Waddington] . . . says he means 'if the ethical system is to be derived from the nature of the experimental [world] . . . one of the most important data is the scientifically ascertained course of evolution.' If it were not for the words 'scientifically ascertained' this might easily mean '*One* of the criteria as to what a man or people really want is what they tend to get hold of in the end' and then it would be right though not easily applicable except in simple matters like wine and cars.[12]

I take Professor Wisdom to be urging in Mill's behalf the inadequacy of such desires as receive overt or, more particularly, conscious expression to stand alone as evidence for desirability. Such a position, as will appear, was almost certainly not held by Mill. Yet there are aspects of these remarks—like the criterion for genuine desire suggested in the second passage—that would have lent strength to Mill's position as I interpret it. But this, too, can be made clearer in what follows.

The defence of Mill offered by Professor Hall in the article cited above is of course far more thorough and systematic than that suggested by Professor Wisdom. Hall divides Mill's proof into three steps, which he calls 1*A*, 1*B*, and 2. Only the first of these concerns us at present. Regarding that first step Professor Hall states it as "final and quite unassailable" that it cannot be interpreted as an attempt at a strict deduction. The use of the analogy should have made that much obvious, but the criticisms of Moore, Bradley, and the rest have shown how far from clear is even the obvious in Mill for preconvinced anti-utilitarians. In general, Professor Hall's strictures against Mill's critics seem to be perfectly correct, and what he says in Mill's favour is also correct, I think, though it is not nearly so strong or far-reaching as he might have made it. His version of Mill's intent in step 1*A*, the analogical argument, is phrased as follows:

> A theory that sets up, as ends desirable in themselves (i.e., good, *not* simply capable of being desired), states of affairs that nobody ever desires is just being academic and unrealistic.[13]

That is true, as far as it goes. But I am sure that there is a great deal more to be found in that argument, just as true and much more interesting.

III

Since Mill's argument is analogical, we may take the seemingly strongest point made against it to be that the sameness supposed to warrant the analogy is linguistic, or perhaps even orthographic, only. The analogy as Mill gives it is founded upon sketches of the proofs for visibility and for audibility, but we may confine ourselves to the first of these without imparing the argument.

"The only proof capable of being given that an object is visible, is that people actually see it." In other words, If anything is actually seen by people, it is visible; *not* If anything is visible, it is actually seen by people. For, transposing the first version we obtain, If anything is invisible, it is not actually seen by people,

[11] John Wisdom, *Philosophy and Psycho-Analysis* (New York: Philosophical Library, 1953), p. 107.

[12] Wisdom, pp. 110–111.

[13] Hall, p. 9 [p. 107 above].

which is clearly true; whereas the transposition of the second reads, If anything is not actually seen by people, it is invisible, which is at best a very unusual doctrine.

In this as in the analogous formulae about the desired and the desirable the key words are "people" and "actually." Momentarily disregarding its role in Mill's argument, let us examine this formula about the seen and the visible in order to determine the meaning of "people" in its occurrence there.

Obviously "people" does not mean *all* people.

Can it indifferently denote any one person? Can it, that is to say, be considered synonymous with "someone"? But that includes the hallucinator, for example; and while for some purposes we might want to group his visual experiences too under the term "seeing," we should hardly take his visually altogether unverifiable report as a "proof" that some object is visible.

Presumably, then, we are safe in saying that neither all people nor merely any given individual person is what is meant by "people" in this formula.

It is much more likely that it is the majority of seeing persons that is meant. For the sake of convenience we may abbreviate "majority of seeing persons" to "normal observer." It seems plain that when, for example, it is said that Sirius is visible in the night sky of the Northern Hemisphere in winter, what is meant is that it is actually seen then and there by most people who know how to look for it and who do so. The normal observer, given a star-chart and a clear northern winter night, sees Sirius if he wants to. It may be, then, that it is the *interested* normal observer that is meant.

But might the word "people" in the formula possibly mean the acutest observer? If we are asked how many visible stars there are in the Pleiades the answer might be that it depends upon the observer, though the same sense is conveyed by an answer of this sort: "Six or seven; but some exceptionally keen-sighted person claims to have seen eight or even nine." Of course the visual experiences of the acutest observer also furnish problems of verification to the normal observer; but what the acutest observer sees, unlike what is seen by the hallucinator, is almost always sooner or later available for the normal observer's sight as well. He may require special instruments, or he may need to take the time to move closer to the object, or to learn just what it is he's to look for, but the eventual coincidence of his report on the visible object with the previous report of the acutest observer is, after all, just what distinguishes the keen-sighted from the hallucinators. The usual course, or, at any rate, a cautious course, would be to take as proven to be visible those objects that are actually seen both by the normal observer and by the acutest observer, where "acutest" *need* mean no more than does "abnormal" until such corroboration takes place.

What meaning could be attached to the designation "least acute observer" is not clear; and in any case the notion of the least acute observer is not of much use in proving that an object is visible in any ordinary sense.

Our results so far might then give us the following reading of the formula: If anything is actually seen both by the normal observer and by the acutest observer, it is visible; or, less conservatively: If anything is actually seen by the normal observer, it is visible.

Now, what is meant here by "actually seen"? Since it is a proof that is at issue, we should certainly expect the data to be characterized by some kind of public availability, to constitute evidence in the usual sense. This does not limit the seeing to seeing that is conscious to the extent that it might be the subject of a report—"I see a red patch on the left and a blue one on the right"—but *some* overt action on the observer's part is called for if a proof is to result. When we look for our pen and fail to find it in a place where, we are later told by others, it lay in "plain sight," we seem perfectly justified in saying that we did not actually see it. No doubt light reflected from it did strike our retina, and there may be ready psychological explanations of just why we only saw it and did not recognize it, why we failed to see it actually. But whatever "actually seen" does mean, it must be other than this unrecognized encountering if it is to serve as the index of visibility. And while other forms of overt behaviour than speech or the deliberate grasping or avoidance of an object are easy to imagine and would surely do as well as they, the modification of "see" by "actually" must convey overtness of reaction, whatever else.

What of mistakes? We have already mentioned the hallucinator's error—deeming something visible that is not in fact so —but what of our reaching for the rose we see and grasping a nettle instead? Can that overt act be considered a proof that the nettle was as visible as the rose? Or more fundamentally, more fairly, does it indicate that the nettle was actually seen? If the reaching after the rose was preceded by an exclamation of delight and the touching of the nettle followed by a cry of pain, we put it down to subnormal eyesight or unusually poor eye-hand coordination. And if the admiring child reaches out to stroke the flame, he shows that he sees the moving colours and feels the warmth and appreciates all that, and he shows just as plainly that he does not *fore*see the pains of being burnt and reprimanded. Surely in such cases we do not want to have to say that it was the nettle, not the rose, that was actually seen, since it was what was grasped; or that searing and scolding were visible to the child because that was what he got. In the first case the thing seen was through inadvertence not the thing reacted to; and in the second case the character of the thing seen was misjudged, so that the reaction to it was abnormal.

It is perhaps needless to say, but, for the purposes of appreciating the analogical argument, essential to bear in mind that considerations very similar to these apply in certain cases involving desiring and the desirable.

A final formulation of the relation between seeing and the visible can now be proposed: If anything is seen in such a way as to occasion some overt reaction on the part of the normal observer, and that reaction later proves to have been normal for the thing in question, then that thing is visible. This, it is hoped, is an accurate analysis of the visibility-criterion offered by Mill in the basis for this analogical argument.

If it is so, and if Mill's argument is framed on a reasonably close analogy, then the following formulation of his desirability-criterion is mutatis mutandis, also correct: If anything is desired in such a way as to occasion some overt reaction on the part of the normal desirer, and that reaction proves to have been normal for the thing in question, then that thing is desirable.

Certainly it cannot surprise anyone to find in Mill this staunchest kind of support for democracy. The principle of utility, he says,

> is a mere form of words without rational signification, unless one person's happiness, supposed equal in degree (and with the proper allowance made for kind), is counted for exactly as much as another's. Those conditions being supplied, Bentham's dictum, "everybody to count for one, nobody for more than one," might be written under the principle of utility as an explanatory commentary.[14]

In the present formula, as similarly in the one about the seen and the visible, the

[14] *Utilitarianism*, p. 58 [pp. 55–56 above].

crucial questions are how to determine that actual desiring is taking place and how to determine the content of the actual desires of the normal desirer. Ideally, both questions are answered simultaneously in the democratic process—in votes, in newspaper circulations, in letters to governmental representatives, in purchases, in vocational choices, etc. Almost all of these and other occasions for overt registration of desire are instances of more or less forced choice, but, again ideally, over the long run the democratic process broadly conceived allows for the registration of desires at least for different alternatives in the forced choices, if not very often for less stringent conditions of choice.

The further the analogues are compared in different respects, the more striking becomes the analogy. Just as there are many kinds of visible objects, so are there many kinds of desirables:

> Utilitarians are quite aware that there are other desirable possessions and qualities besides virtue, and are perfectly willing to allow to all of them their full worth.[15]

> . . . desirable things . . . are as numerous in the utilitarian as in any other scheme. . . .[16]

So it is not quite right to think of Mill's argument as applying only to the desirable as identifiable with the good, unless in the broadest sense of "good."

The role of the radicals of the political right or left, the role of the avant-garde in the arts, of the teacher, of the moral or religious hero, of the intellectual—of any of society's recalcitrants—is similar in the case of desire and the desirable to the role of the keen-sighted (or of the hallucinator) in the case of sight and the visible, one possible difference of major importance being that the democratic thesis demands a constantly ongoing selective adoption by the normal desirer of the goals of his more volatile, more gifted fellows. That is to say, a belief in genuine progress is a prerequisite for acceptance of Mill's argument here. He himself shows this in another context in the opening pages of *Utilitarianism:*

> A being of higher faculties . . . can never *really* wish to sink into what he feels to be a lower grade of existence.[17]

But without proceeding further in the enjoyable work of following out the ramifications of the analogy we may summarize for a moment what we take to be Mill's position in this way: There is no means of determining what is good or beautiful or right except by consulting people's desires. It makes no sense to say that there can be anything good or beautiful or right that would over the longest conceivable run not come to be desired by the normal desirer; but it is something altogether different, and almost certainly true, to say that there are at any given moment desirables that the normal desirer fails to desire—or even that are not desired by anyone. This needs emphasis. It is easy to misinterpret Mill on this point when, for example, he says that

> if human nature is so constituted as to desire nothing which is either not a part of happiness or a mean of happiness, we can have no other proof, and we require no other, that these are the only things desirable.[18]

It might look as if he were saying here that the desirable *is* what is desired and nothing more. But what he says in fact is, of course, that if nothing *can* be desired other than happiness, then happiness is the only possible good, the only possible desirable. To be capable of being desired is a necessary though certainly not a sufficient condition of desirability. To be desired is neither a necessary nor a sufficient

[15] Ibid., p. 18 [p. 26 above].

[16] Ibid., p. 6 [p. 18 above].

[17] Ibid., p. 8 [p. 19 above], italics added.

[18] Ibid., p. 36 [p. 40 above].

condition of desirability, unless the desire is on the part of the normal desirer, in which case the desire is sufficient, is evidential, for desirability. But even this is true strictly only over the longest possible run. The infinite series of actual desires converges on the desirable.

As Peirce was later to say of the truth that it was the "opinion which is fated to be ultimately agreed to by all who investigate," so Mill might consistently be made to say that the good, or the desirable, is the object or set of objects that are fated to be ultimately desired in common by all who have desires—is what the whole community of desirers, or the normal desirer, will come eventually to desire. The likelihood is, of course, that in both cases we shall have to content ourselves with an approach that turns out to be asymptotic, an approximation to a standard.

The identification of the good, or the desirable, in the preceding paragraph raises a question about the status of a non-hedonistic—in this case what might be called a "conatistic"—utilitarianism. Professor Albert Hammond states this question in a recent paper entitled "Euthyphro, Mill, and Mr. Lewis":

> However often mistakenly, men presume a reason, a differentiation in the object when they strive, wish, long for, desire. . . . Desire may in part be caused, as thirst is caused by inner dryness. But normally desire is in part the outcome of the discernment of a state of affairs, inner or outer, and of another imagined state of affairs as desirable. If desire be kept in its purely descriptive role, then an ethics founded on it will be, for all its "relativism," an "absolute" doctrine. As in the case of all absolute doctrines it will confront the other Socratic question, "Why is this good?" If knowledge be admitted into the ground of desire, then that which is discerned in the object as ground of the desire must be allowed to be good as differentiated from that which might have been discerned as the ground of aversion.[19]

In a conatistic utilitarianism (which is of course not Mill's) *anything* is admissible into the ground of desire, for the nature of the ground of desire is not at issue. No definition of "desirability" or of "goodness" is offered. That something is desirable can be proved, if only provisionally. What it is for something to be desirable, what in it or in desirers produces the desire for it, is a question that may or may not admit of a single answer. But even if it should be a decidable question, still the business of making ever more efficient responses to *that* question need not be the concern of ethics as a science of practice. Perhaps this amounts to what Professor Hammond calls keeping desire "in its purely descriptive role."

In the light of the discussion so far let us take a last look at the classic objection to the logic of Mill's argument, this time in a statement of it by G. E. Moore:

> If 'desirable' is to be identical with 'good,' then it must bear one sense; and if it is to be identical with 'desired,' then it must bear quite another sense. And yet to Mill's contention that the desired is necessarily good, it is quite essential that these two senses of 'desirable' should be the same. If he holds they are the same, then he has contradicted himself elsewhere; if he holds they are not the same, then the first step in his proof of Hedonism is absolutely worthless.[20]

There is no question but that Mill's usage of "desirable" is synonymous for him with "good" (although, as we have remarked, there is nothing in his argument that depends upon our acceptance of this usage)—"for what is the principle of utility, if it be not that 'happiness' and 'desirable' are synonymous terms?" But it seems strange that the question should even be raised as to whether or not "desirable" is synonymous with "desired" in that same formula. Of course it is not. He is no more defining "desirable" than he was defining "visible" but is instead, as

[19] *Journal of Philosophy* 49 (1952), p. 384.

[20] *Principia Ethica*, pp. 67–68.

he plainly says, offering the only proof that anything is desirable, or, on his view, good. And it certainly is not essential to Mill's contention that "desired" and "good" should have their meanings united under "desirable." Far from it; for if that were the case, his formula would be either trivially true or empirically a patent falsehood, and nothing like a proof.

At the end of the passage just cited Moore correctly refers to the argument under consideration as "the first step in [Mill's] . . . proof of Hedonism." But this first step is not itself connected except accidentally with traditional hedonism. It is possible to take human desires and aversions as criteria for right and wrong without finding oneself committed to the further thesis that it is always pleasure (or anything else) that is desired and always pain (or anything else) that is shunned. A purely conatistic utilitarianism is a perfectly consistent position and the one I am concerned with exploring in a preliminary fashion in this paper.

It seems very likely that Moore's scorn of Mill's efforts in this argument is closely akin to his feeling about Bradley's "Time is unreal." In the 1917 paper "The Conception of Reality" Moore was to say:

> I do think it is possible that *part* of what Mr. Bradley is asserting may be something which no unsophisticated person would think of expressing in the same way, and I will admit, therefore, that he does not, very likely, mean by "Time is unreal" *merely* what other people would mean by this phrase, but something else *as well.* What, however, I cannot help thinking is that, even if he means something more, he *does* mean what ordinary people would mean *as well:* that what they would mean is at least a *part* of his meaning.[21]

The mixture of technical and ordinary usages in a single formula, or even the compression of them in a single word, is, as Mr. Paul has pointed out in his discussion of Moore in *The Revolution in Philosophy,* useful "in starting metaphysics," but is furthermore "the very curse which analytic discrimination had originally been brought in to cure."[22]

But the merits of that case, however considerable, need not be considered now; for in the passage in question Mill is guiltless of that kind of mixture or compression. The word "desirable" is being used in one sense only, and that one its ordinary sense.

But Moore raises another, possibly more serious, objection, on page 102 of his *Ethics,* in connection with his supposed discovery of the naturalistic fallacy in the argument.

"Of course," he says, "it may be held . . . that, as a matter of fact anything whatever which is desired, always is intrinsically good."

Yes, this is, with minor but significant alterations, what we have to claim for Mill —that if anything is, as a matter of fact, desired in such a way as to occasion some overt reaction on the part of the normal desirer, and if that reaction proves to have been normal for the thing in question, then that thing is desirable. Whether or not we should want to go on to say that that thing is then as well intrinsically good is a further question not really here at issue and probably to be answered negatively if at all.

"But," Moore goes on, "that is not the question. We are not disputing for the moment that this may be so *as a matter of fact.* All that we are trying to show is that, even if it is so, yet, to say that a thing is intrinsically good is not *the same thing* as to say that it is desired: and this follows absolutely if, even in a single case,

[21] G. E. Moore, *Philosophical Studies* (New York: Harcourt, Brace and Co., Inc., 1942), p. 208.

[22] G. A. Paul, "G. E. Moore: Analysis, Common Usage, and Common Sense," in *The Revolution in Philosophy,* Gilbert Ryle, ed. (London: Macmillan, 1956), pp. 64–65.

a man believes that a thing *is* desired and yet does *not* believe that it is intrinsically good."

While we do not say that "intrinsically good," or, preferably, "desirable," is synonymous with "desired," having maintained a contrary position throughout this discussion, what Moore says at the end of that passage may nevertheless at first seem damaging even to that contrary position. But if we are consistent supporters of the democratic thesis implied in Mill's argument and stated in this paper, we shall have no recourse other than to state that it is strictly incredible that a thing be desired by the human majority (we cannot limit the community of desirers in this case any more than we do the community of observers in the analogue) and be at the same time undesirable, or even indifferent. Whether or not in determining this majority we ought as well to count the votes of the dead, as Santayana suggests is really an academic question. We always do so to varying large extents, whether we know it or not. And I think that surprisingly often the same can be said of the votes of the yet-to-be-born. But in any case we cannot consistently with the democratic thesis disenfranchise any segment of the contemporary human population. The voice of any given people at any moment of time is not to be confused with the voice of the god that is all peoples throughout all times.

I know that in defending Mill I have also extended him and even departed from him, but not, I hope, in ways that he might not himself have gone, was not already going. There are, moreover, traditionally important questions of ethics other than the social-political ones alluded to in this paper that are fitted by Mill into his utilitarianism. I do not now want to assume the responsibility of defending Mill's analogical argument in applications to cases that call for relatively private value-judgments on the part of relatively isolated individuals. I doubt that such cases can be fitted under the formula given here without considerable further elaboration and development of a sort that might very well take us even further from the actual position held by Mill. But that historical consideration is unimportant in this context, and such elaboration and development should not yet be dismissed from possibility.

What I believe I have extracted from the difficulties of Mill's argument is a hard saying but a true one; the one on which developments in social and political ethics will have to proceed until self-government is no longer what Santayana calls "the tragedy of those who do as they wish, but do not get what they want."

John Rawls / Justice as reciprocity

I

It might seem at first sight that the concepts of justice and fairness are the same, and that there is no reason to distinguish between them. To be sure, there may be occasions in ordinary speech when the phrases expressing these notions are not readily interchangeable, but it may appear that this is a matter of style and not a sign of important conceptual differences. I think that this impression is mistaken, yet there is, at the same time, some foundation for it. Justice and fairness are, indeed, different concepts, but they share a fundamental element in common, which I shall call the concept of reciprocity. They represent this concept as applied to two distinct cases: very roughly, justice to a practice in which there is no option whether to engage in it or not, and one must play; fairness to a practice in which there is such an option, and one may decline the invitation. In this paper I shall present an analytic construction of the concept of justice from this point of view, and I shall refer to this analysis as the analysis of justice as reciprocity.

Throughout I consider justice as a virtue of social institutions only, or of what I have called practices.[1] Justice as a virtue of particular actions or of persons comes in at but one place, where I discuss the prima facie duty of fair play (sec. 4). Further, the concept of justice is to be understood in its customary way as representing but one of the many virtues of social institutions; for these institutions may be antiquated, inefficient, or degrading, or any number of other things, without being unjust. Justice is not to be confused with an all-inclusive vision of a good society, or thought of as identical with the concept of right. It is only one part of any such conception, and it is but one species of right. I shall focus attention, then, on the usual sense of justice in which it means essentially the elimination of arbitrary distinctions and the establishment within the structure of a practice of a proper share,

[1] I use the word "practice" throughout as a sort of technical term meaning any form of activity specified by a system of rules which defines offices and roles, rights and duties, penalties and defenses, and so on, and which gives the activity its structure. As examples one may think of games and rituals, trials and parliaments, markets and systems of property.

balance, or equilibrium between competing claims. The principles of justice serve to specify the application of "arbitrary" and "proper," and they do this by formulating restrictions as to how practices may define positions and offices, and assign thereto powers and liabilities, rights and duties. While the definition of the sense of justice is sufficient to distinguish justice as a virtue of institutions from other such virtues as efficiency and humanity, it does not provide a complete conception of justice. For this the associated principles are needed. The major problem in the analysis of the concept of justice is how these principles are derived and connected with this moral concept, and what is their logical basis; and further, what principles, if any, have a special place and may properly be called the principles of justice? The argument is designed to lay the groundwork for answering these questions.

I shall proceed in the following way. In section 2 I formulate a conception of justice by stating and commenting upon the two principles associated with it. While it is possible to argue that a case can be made for calling these principles *the* principles of justice, there is, for the moment, no need to regard them in this way. It is sufficient that they are typical of a family of principles which are normally associated with the concept of justice in the sense that a declaration that an institution is unjust would normally be supported, and would normally be expected to be supported, by reference to principles in this family. I am assuming, then, that an intuitive sense of the principles comprising this family is part of one's everyday understanding of the notion of justice. The way in which the principles of this family resemble one another, and the manner in which they are associated with the concept of justice, is shown by the background against which they may be thought to arise. How this is so the subsequent argument is designed to make clear.

In section 3 I attempt to demonstrate how the two principles of section 2, which are typical of those associated with the concept of justice, can be viewed as those principles which mutually self-interested and rational persons, when similarly situated and when required to make a firm commitment in advance, would acknowledge as restrictions governing the assignment of rights and duties in their common practices, and would thereby accept as limiting their rights against one another. The principles of justice are those required once the constraints of having a morality are applied to what can be mutually acknowledged on those occasions when questions of justice arise. One can say: The principles normally associated with the concept of justice are generated by applying these constraints to persons as situated on these occasions. In this fact the principles of justice find their philosophical derivation as part of a moral concept; and the manner in which they are associated with and complete the sense of justice is explained.

Sections 2 and 3 contain the main elements of the argument. In section 4 I have included a number of supplementary remarks to eliminate certain misunderstandings and to place the analysis of sections 2 and 3 in its proper perspective in relation to various other views to which it is in some ways related; and in section 5 the concept of reciprocity as the common element in the concepts of justice and fairness is isolated and discussed together with the prima facie duty of fair play. With these sections the main part of the analytic construction is completed.

In order, however, to bring out the special force of the analysis of justice as reciprocity, I shall argue in sections 6 and 7 that it is this aspect of justice for which utilitarianism, in its classical form as represented by Bentham and Sidgwick, is unable to account; but that this aspect is expressed, and allowed for, even if in a misleading way, by the idea of the social contract. There is, indeed, irony in this conclusion; for utilitarians attacked the notion of the social contract not only as a historical fiction, but as a superfluous hypothesis.[2] They thought that utility alone provides sufficient grounds for all social obligations, and that it is in any case the real basis of contractual obligations. But this is not so, I hope to show, unless one's conception of social utility embodies within it restrictions the basis of which can only be understood if one makes reference to those aspects of contractarian thought which express the concept of justice as reciprocity: namely, that persons must be regarded as possessing an original and equal liberty, and their common practices are unjust (or alternatively, unfair, depending on the options allowed) unless they accord with principles which persons so circumstanced and related could be reasonably expected to acknowledge and freely accept before one another. I hope that the comparison with classical utilitarianism will serve to bring out the distinctive features of the conception of justice as reciprocity, and thereby give substance and content to what is, I am afraid, a somewhat formal and abstract discussion.

II

The conception of justice which I want to consider has two principles associated with it. Both of them, and so the conception itself, are extremely familiar; and, indeed, this is as it should be, since one would hope eventually to make a case for regarding them as the principles of justice. It is unlikely that novel principles could be candidates for this position. It may be possible, however, by using the concept of reciprocity as a framework, to assemble these principles against a different background and to look at them in a new way. I shall now state them and then provide a brief commentary to clarify their meaning.

First, each person participating in a practice, or affected by it, has an equal right to the most extensive liberty compatible with a like liberty for all; and second, inequalities are arbitrary unless it is reasonable to expect that they will work out to everyone's advantage, and provided that the positions and offices to which they attach, or from which they may be gained, are open to all. These principles express justice as a complex of three ideas: liberty, equality, and reward for services contributing to the common good.[3]

[2] See Hume *Of the Original Contract* (1748), and Bentham *A Fragment of Government* (1776), ch. 1, pars. 36–48.

[3] These principles are, of course, well known in one form or another. They are commonly appealed to in daily life to support judgments regarding social arrangements and they appear in many analyses of justice even where the writers differ widely on other matters. Thus if the principle of equal liberty is commonly associated with Kant (see *The Philosophy of Law*, W. Hastie, trans. [Edinburgh, 1887], pp. 56f), it can also be found in works so different as J. S. Mill's *On Liberty* (1859) and Herbert Spencer's *Justice* (pt. IV of *Principles of Ethics*) (London, 1891). Recently H. L. A. Hart has argued for something like it in his paper "Are There Any Natural Rights?" *Philosophical Review*, 64 (1955), 175–191. The injustice of inequalities which are not won in return for a contribution to the common advantage is, of course, a frequent topic in political writings of all sorts. If the conception of justice developed here is distinctive at all, it is only in selecting these two principles in this form; but for another similar analysis, see W. D. Lamont, *The Principles of Moral Judgment*; (Oxford: Clarendon Press, 1946), ch. V. Moreover, the essential elements could, I think, be found in St. Thomas Aquinas and other medieval writers, even though they failed to draw out the implicit equalitarianism of their premises. See Ewart Lewis *Medieval Political Ideas* (London: Routledge and Paul, 1954), vol. I, the introduction to ch. IV, especially pp. 220f. Obviously the important thing is not simply the an-

A word about the term "person." This expression is to be construed variously depending on the circumstances. On some occasions it will mean human individuals, but in others it may refer to nations, provinces, business firms, churches, teams, and so on. The principles of justice apply to conflicting claims made by persons of all of these separate kinds. There is, perhaps, a certain logical priority to the case of human individuals: it may be possible to analyze the actions of so-called artificial persons as logical constructions of the actions of human persons, and it is plausible to maintain that the worth of institutions is derived solely from the benefits they bring to human individuals. Nevertheless an analysis of justice should not begin by making either of these assumptions, or by restricting itself to the case of human persons; and it can gain considerably from not doing so. As I shall use the term "person," then, it will be ambiguous in the manner indicated.

The first principle holds, of course, only if other things are equal: that is, while there must always be a justification for departing from the initial position of equal liberty (liberty being defined by reference to the pattern of rights and duties, powers and liabilities, established by a practice), and the burden of proof is placed on him who would depart from it, nevertheless, there can be, and often there is, a justification for doing so. Now, that similar particular cases, as defined by a practice, should be treated similarly as they arise, is part of the very concept of a practice; in accordance with the analysis of justice as regularity, it is involved in the notion of an activity in accordance with rules, and expresses the concept of equality in one of its forms: that is, equality as the impartial and equitable administration and application of the rules whatever they are, which define a practice. The first principle expresses the concept of equality in another form, namely, as applied to the definition and initial specification of the structure of practices themselves. It holds, for example, that there is a presumption against the distinctions and classifications made by legal systems and other practices to the extent that they infringe on the original and equal liberty of the persons participating in them, or affected by them. The second principle defines how this presumption may be rebutted.

It might be argued at this point that justice requires only that there be an equal liberty. If, however, a more extensive liberty were possible for all without loss or conflict, then it would be irrational to settle upon a lesser liberty. There is no reason for circumscribing rights unless their exercise would be incompatible, or would render the practice defining them less effective. Where such a limitation of liberty seems to have occurred, there must be some special explanation. It may have arisen from a mistake or misapprehension; or perhaps it persists from a time past when it had a rational basis, but does so no longer. Otherwise, such a limitation would be inexplicable; the acceptance of it would conflict with the premise that the persons engaged in the practice want the things which a more extensive liberty would make possible. Therefore no serious distortion of the concept of justice is likely to follow from associating with it a principle requiring the greatest equal liberty. This association is necessary once it is supposed, as I shall suppose, that the persons engaged in the practices to which the principles of justice apply are rational.

The second principle defines what sorts of inequalities are permissible; it specifies how the presumption laid down by the first principle may be put aside. Now by inequalities it is best to understand not any differences between offices and positions,

---

nouncement of these principles, but their interpretation and application, and the way they are related to one's conception of justice as a whole.

but differences in the benefits and burdens attached to them either directly or indirectly, such as prestige and wealth, or liability to taxation and compulsory services. Players in a game do not protest against there being different positions, such as that of batter, pitcher, catcher, and the like, nor to there being various privileges and powers specified by the rules. Nor do citizens of a country object to there being the different offices of government such as that of president, senator, governor, judge, and so on, each with its special rights and duties. It is not differences of this kind that are normally thought of as inequalities, but differences in the resulting distribution established by a practice, or made possible by it, of the things men strive to attain or to avoid. Thus they may complain about the pattern of honors and rewards set up by a practice (e.g., the privileges and salaries of government officials) or they may object to the distribution of power and wealth which results from the various ways in which men avail themselves of the opportunities allowed by it (e.g., the concentration of wealth which may develop in a free price system allowing large entrepreneurial or speculative gains).

It should be noted that the second principle holds an inequality is allowed only if there is a reason to believe that the practice with the inequality, or resulting in it, will work for the advantage of *every* person engaging in it. Here it is important to stress that every person must gain from the inequality. Since the principle applies to practices, it implies then that the representative man in every office or position defined by a practice, when he views it as a going concern, must find it reasonable to prefer his condition and prospects with the inequality to what they would be under the practice without it. The principles exclude, therefore, the justification of inequalities on the grounds that the disadvantages of those in one position are outweighed by the greater advantages of those in another position. This rather simple restriction is the main modification I wish to make in the utilitarian principle as usually understood. When coupled with the notion of a practice, it is a restriction of consequence, and one which some utilitarians, notably Hume and Mill, have used in their discussions of justice without realizing apparently its significance, or at least without calling attention to it.[4]

Further, it is also necessary that the various offices to which special benefits or burdens attach are open to all. It may be, for example, to the common advantage, as just defined, to attach special benefits to certain offices. Perhaps by doing so the requisite talent can be attracted to them and encouraged to give its best efforts. But any offices having special benefits must be won in a fair competition in which contestants are judged on their merits. If some offices were not open, those excluded would normally be justified in feeling unjustly treated, even if they benefited from the greater efforts of those who were allowed to compete for them. Moreover, they would be justified in their complaint

[4] It might seem as if J. S. Mill, in paragraph 36 of chapter V of *Utilitarianism*, expressed the utilitarian principle in this form, but in the remaining two paragraphs of the chapter, and elsewhere in the essay, he would appear not to grasp the significance of the change. Hume often emphasizes that every man must benefit. For example, in discussing the utility of general rules, he holds that they are requisite to the "well-being" of every individual; from a stable system of property "every individual person must find himself a gainer in balancing the account. . . ." "Every member of society is sensible of this interest; everyone expresses this sense to his fellows along with the resolution he has taken of squaring his actions by it, on the condition that others will do the same." (*A Treatise of Human Nature*, bk. III, pt. II, sect. II, par. 22.) Since in the discussion of the common good, I draw upon another aspect of Hume's account of justice, the logical importance of general rules, the conception of justice which I set out is perhaps closer to Hume's view than to any other. On the other hand, see footnote 27.

not only because they were excluded from certain external emoluments of office, but because they were barred from attaining the great intrinsic goods which the skillful and devoted exercise of some offices represents, and so they would be deprived, from the start, of one of the leading ways to achieve a full human life.

Now if one can assume that offices are open, it is necessary only to consider the design and structure of practices themselves and how they jointly, as a system, work together. It will be a mistake to focus attention on the varying relative positions of particular persons, who may be known to us by their proper names, and to require that each such change, as a once and for all transaction viewed in isolation, must be in itself just. It is the practice, or the system of practices, which is to be judged, and judged from a general point of view: unless one is prepared to criticize it from the standpoint of a representative man holding some particular office, one has no complaint against it. Thus, as one watches players in a game and is moved by the changing fortunes of the teams one may be downcast by the final outcome; one may say to oneself that the losing team deserved to win on the basis of its skill, endurance, and pluck under adverse circumstances. But it will not follow from this that one thinks the game itself, as defined by its rules, is unfair. Again, as one observes the course of a free price system over time one witnesses the rise of one particular group of firms and the decline of another. Some entrepreneurs make profits, others have to take losses; and these profits and losses are not always correlated with their foresight and ability, or with their efforts to turn out worthwhile products. The fate of entrepreneurs is often the outcome of chance, or determined by changes in tastes and demand which no one could have foreseen; it is not always, by any means, founded on their deserts. But it does not follow from this that such an economic system is unjust. That the relative positions of particular entrepreneurs should be determined in this way is a consequence of the rules of the capitalist game. If one wishes to challenge it, one must do so, not from the changing relative positions of this or that entrepreneur, in this or that particular turn of fortune, but from the standpoint of the representative entrepreneur and his legitimate expectations in the system as a working institution, also, of course, keeping in mind the relation of this institution to the other practices of society.

Nothing is more natural than for those who suffer from the particular changes taking place in accordance with a practice to resent it as unjust, especially when there is no obvious correlation between these changes and ordinary conceptions of merit. This is as natural as that those who gain from inequities should overlook them, and even in time come to regard them as their due. Yet since the principles apply to the form and structure of practices as such, and not to particular transactions, the conception of justice they express requires one to appraise a practice from a general point of view, and thus from that of a representative man holding the various offices and positions defined by it. One is required to take a reasonably long view, and to ascertain how the practice will work out when regarded as a continuing system. At a later point I shall argue that unless persons are prepared to take up this standpoint in their social criticism, agreement on questions of justice is hardly possible; and that once they are prepared to do so, an argument can be given for taking these principles as the principles of justice.

III

Given these principles one might try to derive them from a priori principles of reason, or claim that they were known by intuition. These are familiar enough steps and, at least in the case of the first principle, might be made with some success. Of all principles of justice that of equality in its several forms is undoubtedly the one most susceptible to a priori argument. But it is obvious that the second principle, while certainly a common one, cannot be claimed as acceptable on these grounds. Indeed, to many persons it will surely seem overly restrictive; to others it may seem too weak. Some will want to hold that there are cases where it is just to balance the gains of some against the losses of others, and that the principle as stated contains an exaggerated bias in the direction of equality; while there are bound to be those to whom it will seem an insufficient basis upon which to found an account of justice. These opinions are certainly of considerable force, and it is only by a study of the background of the principle and by an examination of its intended applications that one can hope to establish its merits. In any case, a priori and intuitive arguments, made at this point, are unconvincing. They are not likely to lead to an understanding of the basis of the principles of justice, not at least as principles of justice: for what one wants to know is the way in which these principles complete the sense of justice, and why they are associated with this moral concept, and not with some other. I wish, therefore, to look at the principles in a different way; I want to bring out how they are generated by imposing the constraints of having a morality upon persons who confront one another on those occasions when questions of justice arise.

In order to do this, it seems simplest to present a conjectural account of the derivation of these principles as follows. Imagine a society of persons amongst whom a certain system of practices is already well established. Now suppose that by and large they are mutually self-interested; their allegiance to their established practices is normally founded on the prospect of their own advantage. One need not, and indeed ought not, to assume that, in all senses of the term "person," the persons in this society are mutually self-interested. If this characterization holds when the line of division is the family, it is nevertheless likely to be true that members of families are bound by ties of sentiment and affection and willingly acknowledge duties in contradiction to self-interest. Mutual self-interestedness in the relations between families, nations, churches, and the like, is commonly associated with loyalty and devotion on the part of individual members. If this were not so the conflicts between these forms of association would not be pursued with such intensity and would not have such tragic consequences. If Hobbes' description of relations between persons seems unreal as applied to human individuals, it is often true enough of the relations between artificial persons; and these relations may assume their Hobbesian character largely in consequence of that element which that description professedly leaves out, the loyalty and devotion of individuals. Therefore, one can form a more realistic conception of this society if one thinks of it as consisting of mutually self-interested families, or some other association. Taking the term "person" widely from the start prepares one for doing this. It is not necessary to suppose, however, that these persons are mutually self-interested under all circumstances, but only in the usual situations in which they participate in their common practices concerning which the question of justice arises.

Now suppose further that these persons are rational: they know their own interests more or less accurately; they realize that the several ends they pursue may conflict with each other, and they are able to decide what level of attainment of one they are willing to sacrifice for a given level of attainment of another; they are capable of tracing out the likely consequences of adopting one practice rather than another, and of adhering to a course of action once they have decided upon it; they can resist present temptations and the enticements of immediate gain; and the bare knowledge or perception of the difference between their condition and that of others is not, within certain limits and in itself, a source of great dissatisfaction. Only the very last point adds anything to the standard definition of rationality as it appears say in the theory of price; and there is no need to question the propriety of this definition given the purposes for which it is customarily used. But the notion of rationality, if it is to play a part in the analysis of justice should allow, I think, that a rational man will resent or will be dejected by differences of condition between himself and others only where there is an accompanying explanation: that is, if they are thought to derive from injustice, or from some other fault of institutions, or to be the consequence of letting chance work itself out for no useful common purpose. At any rate, I shall include this trait of character in the notion of rationality for the purpose of analyzing the concept of justice. The legitimacy of doing so will, I think, become clear as the analysis proceeds. So if these persons strike us as unpleasantly egoistic in their relations with one another, they are at least free in some degree from the fault of envy.[5]

Finally, assume that these persons have roughly similar needs, interests, and capacities, or needs, interests, and capacities in various ways complementary, so that fruitful cooperation amongst them is possible; and suppose that they are sufficiently equal in power and the instruments thereof to guarantee that in normal circumstances none is able to dominate the others. This condition (as well as the other conditions) may seem excessively vague; but in view of the conception of justice to which the argument leads, there seems to be no reason for making it more exact at this point.[6]

Since these persons are conceived as engaging in their common practices, which are already established, there is no question of our supposing them to come together to deliberate as to how they will set up these practices for the first time. Yet we can imagine that from time to time they discuss with one another whether any of them has a legitimate complaint against their established institutions. This is only natural in any normal society. Now suppose that they have settled on doing this in the following way. They first try to arrive at the principles by which complaints and so practices themselves are to be judged. That is, they do not begin by complaining; they begin instead by establishing the criteria by which a complaint is to be counted legitimate. Their procedure for this is to let each person propose the principles upon which he wishes his complaints to be tried with the understanding that, if acknowledged, the complaints of others will be similarly tried; and moreover, that no complaints will be heard at all until everyone is roughly of

[5] There is no need to discuss here this addition to the usual conception of rationality. The reason for it will become clear as the argument proceeds, for it is analogous to, and is connected with, the modification of the utilitarian principle which the argument as a whole is designed to explain and to justify. In the same way that the satisfaction of interests, the representative claims of which violate the principles of justice, is not a reason for having a practice (see below, section 7), unfounded envy, within limits, need not be taken into account. One could, of course, have another reason for this addition, namely, to see what conception of justice results when it is made. This alone would not be without interest.

[6] In this description of the situation of the persons, I have drawn on Hume's account of the circumstances in which justice arises, see *A Treatise of Human Nature*, bk. III, pt. II, sec. II, and *An Enquiry Concerning the Principles of Morals*, sec. III, pt. I. It is, in particular, the scarcity of good things and the lack of mutual benevolence that leads to conflicting claims, and which gives rise to the "cautious, jealous virtue of justice," a phrase from the *Enquiry*, ibid., par. 3.

one mind as to how complaints are to be judged. Thus while each person has a chance to propose the standards he wishes, these standards must prove acceptable to the others before his charges can be given a hearing. They all understand further that the principles proposed and acknowledged on this occasion are binding on future occasions. So each will be wary of proposing a principle which would give him a peculiar advantage in his present circumstances, supposing it to be accepted (which is, perhaps, in most cases unlikely). Each person knows that he will be bound by it in future circumstances the peculiarities of which cannot be known, and which might well be such that the principle is then to his disadvantage. The basic idea in this procedure is that everyone should be required to make in advance a firm commitment to acknowledge certain principles as applying to his own case and such that others also may reasonably be expected to acknowledge them; and that no one be given the opportunity to tailor the canons of a legitimate complaint to fit his own special conditions, and then to discard them when they no longer suit his purpose.[7] Hence each person will propose principles of a general kind which will, to a large degree, gain their sense from the various applications to be made of them, the particular circumstances of these applications being as yet unknown. These principles will express the conditions in accordance with which each person is the least unwilling to have his interests limited in the design of practices, given the competing interests of the others, on the supposition that the interests of others will be limited likewise. The restriction which would so arise might be thought of as those a person would keep in mind if he were designing a practice in which his enemy were to assign him his place.

The elements of this conjectural account can be divided into two main parts so that each part has a definite significance. Thus the character and respective situations of the parties, that is, their rationality and mutual self-interestedness, and their being of roughly similar needs, interests and capacities, and their having needs, interests and capacities in various ways complementary, so that fruitful forms of cooperation are possible, can be taken to represent the typical circumstances in which questions of justice arise. For questions of justice are involved when conflicting claims are made upon the design of a practice and where it is taken for granted that each person will insist, so far as possible, on what he considers his rights. It is typical of cases of justice to involve persons who are pressing on one another their claims, between which a fair balance or equilibrium must be found. So much is expressed by the sense of the concept.

On the other hand, the procedure whereby principles are proposed and ac-

[7] Thus everyone is, so far as possible, prevented from acting on the kind of advice which Aristotle summarizes in the *Rhetoric*, k. I, ch. 15. There he describes a number of ways in which a man may argue his case, and which are, he observes, especially characteristic of forensic oratory. For example, if the written law tells against his case, a man must appeal to the universal law and insist on its greater equity and justice; he must argue that the juror's oath "I will give my verdict according to my honest opinion" means that one will not simply follow the letter of the unwritten law. On the other hand, if the law supports his case, he must argue that not to apply the law is as bad as to have no laws at all, or that less harm comes from an occasional mistake than from the growing habit of disobedience; and he must contend that the juror's oath is not meant to make the judges give a verdict contrary to law, but to save them from the guilt of perjury if they do not understand what the law really means. Cf. 1375a25–1372b25. Such tactics are, of course, common in arguments of all kinds; the notion of a considered judgment, and Adam Smith's and Hume's idea of an impartial spectator, is in part derived from the conception of a person so placed that he has no incentive to make these manoeuvers.

knowledged can be taken to represent the constraints of having a morality; it is these constraints which require rational and mutually self-interested persons to act reasonably, in this case, to acknowledge familiar principles of justice. (The condition that the parties be sufficiently equal in power and the instruments thereof to guarantee that in normal circumstances none is able to dominate the others is to make the adoption of such a procedure seem more realistic; but the argument is not affected if we do without this condition, and imagine that the procedure is simply laid down.) Once the procedure is adopted and carried through each person is committed to acknowledge principles as impartially applying to his own conduct and claims as well as to another's, and he is committed moreover to principles which may constitute a constraint, or limitation, upon the pursuit of his own interests. Now a person's having a morality is analogous to having made a firm commitment in advance to acknowledge principles having these consequences for one's own conduct. A man whose moral judgments always coincided with his interests could be suspected of having no morality at all. There are, of course, other aspects to having a morality: the acknowledgment of moral principles must not only show itself in accepting a reference to them as reasons for limiting one's claims, but also in acknowledging the burden of providing a special explanation, or excuse, when one acts contrary to them, or else in showing shame and remorse (although not on purpose!), and (sincerely) indicating a desire to make amends, and so on. These aspects of having a morality and, more particularly, the place of moral feelings such as shame and remorse cannot be considered here. For the present it is sufficient to remark that the procedure of the conjectural account expresses an essential aspect of having a morality: namely, the acknowledgment of principles as impartially applying to one's own claims as well as to others, and the consequent constraint upon the pursuit of one's own interests.[8]

The two parts into which the foregoing account may be divided are intended, then, to represent the kinds of circumstances in which questions of justice arise (as expressed by the sense of the concept of justice) and the constraints which having a morality would impose upon persons so situated. By imposing these constraints on persons in the occasions of justice one can see how certain principles are generated, and one understands why these principles, and not others, come to be associated with the concept of justice; for given all the conditions as described in the conjectural account, it would be natural if the two principles of justice were to be jointly acknowledged. Since there is no way for anyone to win special advantages for himself, each would consider it reasonable to acknowledge equality as an initial principle. There is, however, no reason why they should regard this position as final. If there are inequalities which satisfy the conditions of the second principle, the immediate gain which equality would allow can be considered as intelligently invested in view of its future return. If, as is quite likely, these inequalities work as incentives to draw out better efforts, the members of this society may look upon them as concessions to human nature: they, like us, may think that people

[8] The idea that accepting a principle as a moral principle implies that one generally acts on it, failing a special explanation, has been stressed by R. M. Hare, *The Language of Morals* (Oxford: The University Press, 1952). His formulation of it needs to be modified, however, along the lines suggested by P. L. Gardiner, "On Assenting to a Moral Principle," *Proceedings of the Aristotelian Society*, n.s. 55 (1955), 23–44. See also C. K. Grant, "Akrasia and the Criteria of Assent to Practical Principles," *Mind* 65 (1956), 400–407, where the complexity of the criteria for assent is discussed. That having a morality at all involves acknowledging and acting on principles which may be contrary to one's self-interest is mentioned below, see section 5.

ideally should want to serve one another. But as they are mutually self-interested, their acceptance of these inequalities is merely the acceptance of the relations in which they actually stand, and a recognition of the motives which lead them to engage in their common practices. Being themselves self-interested, they have no title to complain of one another. And so provided the conditions of the principle are met, there is no reason why they should not allow such inequalities. Indeed, it would be short-sighted of them not to do so, and could result, in most cases, only from their being dejected by the bare knowledge, or perception, that others are better situated. Each person will, however, insist on an advantage to himself, and so on a common advantage, for none is willing to sacrifice anything for the others.[9]

These remarks are not offered as a rigorous proof that persons conceived and situated as the conjectural account supposes, and required to adopt the procedure described, would settle on the two principles of justice stated and commented upon in section 2. For this a much more elaborate and formal argument would have to be given. I shall not undertake a proof in this sense. In a weaker sense, however, the argument may be considered a proof, or as a sketch of a proof, although there still remain certain details to be filled in, and various alternatives to be ruled out. These I shall take up in later lectures. For the moment the essential point is simply that the proposition I seek to establish is a necessary one, or better, it is a kind of theorem: namely, that when mutually self-interested and rational persons confront one another in the typical circumstances of justice, and when they are required by a procedure expressing the constraints of having a morality to jointly acknowledge principles by which their claims on the design of their common practices are to be judged, they will settle upon these two principles as restrictions governing the assignment of rights and duties, and thereby accept them as limiting their rights against one another. It is this theorem which accounts for these principles as principles of justice, and explains how they come to be associated with this moral concept. Moreover it is analogous to theorems about human conduct in other branches of social thought. That is, a simplified situation is described in which rational persons, pursuing certain ends and related to one another in a definite way, are required to act, subject to certain limitations. Then, given this situation, it is shown that they will act in a certain manner. The failure so to act would only mean that one or more of the conditions did not obtain. The proposition we are interested in is not, then, an empirical hypothesis. This is, of course, as it should be; for this proposition is to play a part in an analysis of the concept of justice. Its point is to bring out how the principles associated with the concept derive from its sense, and to show the basis for saying that the principles of justice may be regarded as those principles which arise when the constraints of having a morality are imposed upon persons in typical circumstances of justice.

IV

This conception of justice is, of course, connected with a familiar way of thinking which goes back at least to the Greek Sophists, and which regards the acceptance of the principles of justice as a compromise between persons of roughly equal power who would enforce their will on each other if they could, but who, in view of the equality of forces amongst them and for the sake of their own peace and security, acknowledge certain forms of conduct in-

[9] A similar argument is given by F. Y. Edgeworth in "The Pure Theory of Taxation," *Economic Journal* 7 (1897). Reprinted in *Classics in the Theory of Public Finance*, ed. Musgrave and Peacock (New York: St. Martin's, 1958), pp. 120f.

sofar as prudence seems to require. Justice is thought of as a pact between rational egoists, the stability of which pact is dependent on a balance of power and a similarity of circumstances.[10] While the analytic construction of the two previous sections is connected with this tradition, and with its most recent variant, the theory of games,[11] it differs from it in several important respects. To forestall misinterpretations, and to help clarify the argument already given, I shall set out some of these differences at this point.

First, I wish to use the previous conjectural account of the derivation of the principles of justice as a way of analyzing the concept. Therefore I do not want to be interpreted as assuming a general theory of human motivation. When it is supposed that the parties are mutually self-interested, and are not willing to have their interests sacrificed to the others, I am referring to their conduct and motives as they are taken for granted in cases where questions of justice ordinarily arise. Justice is the virtue of practices where there are assumed to be competing interests and conflicting claims, and where it is supposed that persons will press their rights against one another. That persons are mutually self-interested in certain situations and for certain purposes, is what gives rise to the question of justice in practices covering those circumstances. Amongst an association of saints, if such a community could really exist, disputes about justice could hardly occur; for they would all work selflessly together for one end, the glory of God as defined by their common religion. Reference to this end would settle every question of right. The justice of practices does not arise until there are several different parties (whether we think of these as individuals, associations, or nations, and so on, makes no difference) who do press their claims on one another and who do regard themselves as representatives of interests which deserve to be considered. These conditions can obtain under the most varied circumstances and from any number of motives. The claims which nations press upon one another have mixed and various interests behind them. The same is true of social and personal conflicts in general. The conjectural account involves, then, no particular theory of human motivation; and it obviously does not imply that persons as human individuals are rational (or irra-

[10] Perhaps the best known statement of this conception is that given by Glaucon at the beginning of book II of Plato's *Republic*. Presumably it was, in various forms, a common view among the Sophists; but that Plato gives a fair representation of it is doubtful. See K. R. Popper, *The Open Society and Its Enemies*, rev. ed. (Princeton, N. J.: Princeton University Press, 1950), pp. 112–118. Certainly Plato usually attributes to it a quality of manic egoism which one feels must be an exaggeration; on the other hand, see the Melian Debate in Thucydides, *The Peloponnesian War*, book V, ch. VII, although it is impossible to say to what extent the views expressed there reveal any current philosophical opinion. Also in this tradition are the remarks of Epicurus on justice in *Principal Doctrines*, XXXI–XXXVIII. In modern times elements of the conception appear in a more sophisticated form in Hobbes *The Leviathan* and in Hume *A Treatise of Human Nature*, book III, pt. II, as well as in the writings of the school of natural law such as Pufendorf's *De jure nature et gentium*. Hobbes and Hume are especially instructive. For Hobbes's argument see Howard Warrender's *The Political Philosophy of Hobbes* (Oxford: The University Press, 1957). W. J. Baumol's *Welfare Economics and the Theory of the State* (Cambridge, Mass.: Harvard University Press, 1952), is valuable in showing the wide applicability of Hobbes's fundamental idea (interpreting his natural law as principles of prudence), although in this book it is traced back only to Hume's *Treatise*.

[11] See J. von Neumann and O. Morgenstern, *The Theory of Games and Economic Behavior*, 2nd ed. (Princeton, N. J.: Princeton University Press, 1947). For a comprehensive and not too technical discussion of the developments since, see R. Duncan Luce and Howard Raiffa, *Games and Decisions: Introduction and Critical Survey* (New York: John Wiley & Sons, 1957). Chapters VI and XIV discuss the developments most obviously related to the analysis of justice.

tional) egoists. What it does is simply incorporate into the conception of justice the relations between persons which set the stage for questions of justice. This the conjectural account must do if it is to be a proper analysis. How wide or general these relations are and from what interests and motives they may be brought about on different occasions, are not matters that need to be discussed. They have no direct bearing on the analysis of justice.

Again, in contrast to the various conceptions of the social contract, the several parties do not establish any particular society or practice; nor do they covenant to obey a particular sovereign or to accept a given constitution.[12] They do not, as in the theory of games (in certain respects a marvelously sophisticated development of this tradition), decide on individual strategies adjusted to their respective circumstances in the game. What the parties do is to jointly acknowledge certain principles of appraisal applicable to their common practices either as already established or as merely proposed. They accede to standards of judgment, not to a given practice; they do not make any specific agreement, or bargain, or adopt a particular strategy. The subject of their acknowledgment is then very general. It is simply the acknowledgment of certain principles of judgment, fulfilling certain conditions, to be used in criticizing the arrangement of their common affairs. Now, as we have seen, the relations of mutual self-interest between the parties who are similarly circumstanced mirror the condition under which questions of justice arise, and the procedure by which the principles of judgment are proposed and acknowledged reflects the constraints of having a morality. Each aspect, then, of the hypothetical description serves to emphasize a feature of the notion of justice. One could, if one liked, view the principles of justice as the "solution" of this highest order "game" of adopting, subject to the procedure described, principles of argument for all coming particular "games" the peculiarities of which one can in no way foresee. Or one could say the principles of justice represent the just or fair solution of this highest order "bargaining problem." The comparison is no doubt helpful; but it must not obscure the fact that this highest order "game," or "bargaining problem," is of a special sort.[13] Its significance is that

[12] For a general survey see Otto von Gierke, *The Development of Political Theory*, B. Freyd, trans. (London, 1939) pt. II, ch. II, and J. W. Gough, *Social Contract*, 2nd. edition (Oxford: The University Press, 1957).

[13] The difficulty one gets into by a mechanical application of the theory of games to moral philosophy can be brought out by considering among several possible examples, R. B. Braithwaite's study, *Theory of Games as a Tool for the Moral Philosopher* (Cambridge: The University Press, 1955). On the analysis there given, it turns out that the fair division of playing time between Matthew and Luke depends on their preferences, and these in turn are connected with the instruments they wish to play. Since Matthew has a threat advantage over Luke, arising purely from the fact that Matthew, the trumpeter, prefers both of them playing at once to neither of them playing, whereas Luke, the pianist, prefers silence to cacophony, Matthew is allotted 26 evenings of play to Luke's 17. If the situation were reversed, the threat advantage would be with Luke. See pp. 36f. But now we have only to suppose that Matthew is a jazz enthusiast who plays the drums, and Luke a violinist who plays sonatas, in which case it will be fair, on this analysis, for Matthew to play whenever and as often as he likes, assuming, of course, as it is plausible to assume, that he does not care whether Luke plays or not. Certainly something has gone wrong. To each according to his threat advantage is hardly the principle of fairness. What is lacking is the concept of morality, and it must be brought into the conjectural account in some way or other. In the text this is done by the form of the procedure whereby principles are proposed and acknowledged (section 3). If one starts directly with the particular case as known, and if one accepts as given and definitive the preferences and relative positions of the parties, whatever they are, it is impossible to give an analysis of

its various pieces represent aspects of the concept of justice.

Finally, I do not, of course, conceive the several parties as necessarily coming together to establish their common practices for the first time. Some institutions may, to be sure, be set up de nuovo. But the hypothetical scheme has been so framed that it will apply when the full complement of social institutions already exists and represents the result of a long period of development. On the other hand, the account is not merely conjectural. In any society where people reflect upon their institutions (and this must include practically all societies), they will have some idea of what principles would be acknowledged under the conditions described, and there will be occasions when questions of justice are actually discussed in this way. Therefore if their practices do not accord with these principles, or better, if their practices grossly depart from them, there will be a noticeable effect seen in the quality of their social relations. For in this case there will be some recognized situations in which persons are mutually aware that one of them is being forced to accept what the other would concede is unjust, at least as applied to himself. One of them is, then, either claiming a special status for himself, or openly taking advantage of his position. He thus invites the other either to retaliate, when and in whatever way he can, or to acknowledge that he is inferior. But where persons mutually acknowledge the principles upon which their arrangements are founded as just or fair, the situation is necessarily different. For this mutual acknowledgment must show itself in an absence of resentment and in a sense of being fairly or justly treated. The conjectural account displays, then, the elements which determine the way in which participants in a practice will feel and react to one another. In this sense it is not simply a fiction, nor a purely abstract model. Since with due qualifications moral beliefs manifest themselves in conduct, an analysis of these, and of the concept of justice in particular, must connect up eventually with an explanation of human action and social institutions.

V

That the principles of justice may be regarded as associated with the sense of justice in the manner described illustrates some important facts about them. For one thing it suggests the thought that justice is the first moral virtue in the sense that it arises once the concept of morality is imposed on mutually self-interested persons who are similarly situated; it is the first moral concept to be generated when one steps outside the bounds of rational self-interest. More relevant at the moment, the conjectural derivation emphasizes that fundamental to both justice and fairness is the concept of reciprocity. In the sense in which I shall use this concept, the question of reciprocity arises when free persons, who have no moral authority over one another and who are engaging in or who find themselves participating in a joint activity, are amongst themselves settling upon or acknowledging the rules which define it and which determine their respective shares in its benefits and bur-

the moral concept of fairness. Braithwaite's use of the theory of games, insofar as it is intended to analyze the concept of fairness, is, I think, mistaken. This is not, of course, to criticize in any way the theory of games as a mathematical theory, to which Braithwaite's book certainly contributes, nor as an analysis of how rational (and amoral) egoists might behave (and so as an analysis of how people sometimes actually do behave). But it is to say that if the theory of games is to be used to analyze the concept of justice, its formal structure must be interpreted in a special and general manner as indicated in the text. Once we do this, though, we are in touch with a much older tradition.

dens. The principle of reciprocity requires of a practice that it satisfy those principles which the persons who participate in it could reasonably propose for mutual acceptance under the circumstances and conditions of the hypothetical account. Persons engaged in a practice meeting this principle can then face one another openly and support their respective positions, should they appear questionable, by reference to principles which it is reasonable to expect each to accept. A practice will strike the parties as conforming to the notion of reciprocity if none feels that, by participating in it, he or any of the others are taken advantage of or forced to give in to claims which they do not accept as legitimate. But if they are prepared to complain this implies that each has a conception of legitimate claims which he thinks it reasonable for all to acknowledge. If one thinks of the principles of justice as arising in the manner described, then they specify just this sort of conception.

It is this requirement of the possibility of mutual acknowledgment of principles by free and equal persons who have not authority over one another which makes the concept of reciprocity fundamental to both justice and fairness. Only if such acknowledgment is possible can there be true community between persons in their common practices; otherwise their relations will appear to them as founded to some degree on force and circumstance. Now, in ordinary speech, the concepts of justice and fairness are distinguished roughly in this way: Fairness applies to practices where persons are cooperating with or competing against one another and which allow a choice whether or not to do so. Thus one speaks of fair games, fair trade, and fair procedures of collective bargaining. No one has to play games, or to be in business in any particular industry; and if the rules of collective bargaining allow one party to demand certain things of the other, on any given occasion one of them must have taken the initiative. In the long run, the initiative is expected to be shared more or less evenly between them. On the other hand, justice applies to practices in which there is no choice whether or not to participate. It applies to those institutions which are either so pervasive that people find themselves enmeshed in them and made to conduct their affairs as they specify, as with systems of property and forms of government; or to those practices which, while limited to certain segments of society, nevertheless give no option to those caught in them, such as slavery and serfdom, and exclusion from the franchise and subjection to special forms of taxation. The element of necessity in justice does not render the conception of mutual acknowledgment any less applicable than in cases where there is choice, although it does, other things being equal, make it more urgent to change unjust than unfair institutions. One activity in which persons participating in a practice can always engage is that of proposing and acknowledging principles to one another supposing each to be similarly circumstanced. To judge practices by the principles so arrived at is to apply to them the principle of reciprocity.

Now if the participants in a practice acknowledge that it satisfies the principle of reciprocity, and so accept its rules as just or fair (as the case requires), then, from the standpoint of justice, they have no complaint to lodge against it. Moreover, their engaging in it gives rise to a prima facie duty (and a corresponding prima facie right) of the parties to each other to act in accordance with the practice when it falls upon them to comply. When any number of persons engage in a practice or conduct a joint undertaking according to rules, and thereby restrict their liberty, those who have submitted to these restrictions when required have a right to a similar acquiescence on the part of those who have benefited by their submission. These conditions will obtain if a practice is correctly acknowledged to be just or fair, for in this case all who participate in it will benefit from it. The rights and duties so arising are special rights and duties in the sense that they depend on previous actions voluntarily undertaken, in this case in the parties having engaged in a common practice and knowingly accepted its benefits.[14] It is not, however, an obligation which presupposes a deliberate performative act in the sense of a promise, or contract, and the like.[15] An unfortunate mistake of the idea of the social contract was to suppose that political obligation does require some such act, or at least, to use language which suggests it.[16] It is sufficient that one has knowingly participated in and accepted the benefits of a practice acknowledged to be fair. This prima facie obligation may, of course, be overridden: it may happen, when it comes one's turn to follow a rule, that other considerations will justify not doing so. But one cannot, in general, be released from this obligation by denying the justice or fairness of the practice only when it falls upon one to obey. If a person rejects a practice, he should, so far as possible, declare his intention in advance and avoid participating in it or enjoying its benefits.

This duty I have called that of fair play, but it should be admitted that to refer to it in this way is, perhaps, to extend the ordinary notion of fairness. Usually acting unfairly is not so much the breaking of any particular rule, even if the infraction is difficult to detect (cheating), but taking advantage of loopholes or ambiguities in rules, availing oneself of unexpected or special circumstances which make it impossible to enforce them, insisting that rules be enforced to one's advantage when they should be suspended, and more generally, acting contrary to the intention of a practice. It is for this reason that one speaks of the sense of fair play: acting fairly requires more than simply being able to follow rules; what is fair must often be felt, or perceived, one wants to say. It is not, however, an unnatural extension of the duty of fair play to have it include the obligation which participants who have knowingly accepted the benefits of their common practice owe to each

14 For the definition of this prima facie duty, and for the idea that it is an important and distinct special duty, I am indebted to H. L. A. Hart. See his paper "Are There Any Natural Rights?", p. 185f. The concept of this duty has certain affinities to Hume's concept of convention, see the *Treatise*, bk. III, pt. II, sec. II, par. 9f, and the *Enquiry*, appendix III, pars. 7f, and 11; but Hume, concerned with origins, expressed the idea somewhat differently. For the relation with Locke's concept of tacit consent, see footnote 16 below.

15 The sense of "performative" here is to be derived from J. L. Austin's paper in the symposium, "Other Minds," *Proceedings of the Aristotelian Society*, Supplementary Volume (1946), pp. 170–174.

16 Thus Locke, in pars. 117–122 of *The Second Treatise of Government*, makes a distinction between express and tacit consent and asserts that it is only expressed consent which makes one fully a member of a commonwealth. He certainly means to refer to some explicit performative act, although I am unclear as to what act he has in mind. In contrast, he speaks of tacit consent which, while it does bind one to obeying the laws of a commonwealth, does not make one a full member of it. This is misleading since tacit consent, as ordinarily understood, is as much consent and binds as far as express consent. Its being tacit refers to the manner in which it is given. What Locke means by tacit consent is analogous to the duty of fair play, if not identical with it. This is shown by the definition of it in par. 119. (It may have other meanings, however, elsewhere in the *Treatise*). Even for Locke, then, an obligation to obey the rules laid down by a legitimate political authority can arise independently of a performative act, whether express or tacit, although not without a prior voluntary act. At least he mentions no such obligations, assuming a person possessed of full reason and without fail. The duty to honor one's parents, par. 66, for example, is not of this description.

other to act in accordance with it when their performance falls due; for it is usually considered unfair if someone accepts the benefits of a practice but refuses to do his part in maintaining it. Thus one might say of the tax-dodger that he violates the duty of fair play: he accepts the benefits of government but will not do his part in releasing resources to it; and members of labor unions often say that fellow workers who refuse to join are being unfair: they refer to them as "free riders," as persons who enjoy what are the supposed benefits of unionism, higher wages, shorter hours, job security, and the like, but who refuse to share in its burdens in the form of paying dues, and so on.

The duty of fair play stands beside other prima facie duties such as fidelity and gratitude as a basic moral notion; yet it is not to be confused with them.[17] These duties are all clearly distinct, as would be obvious from their definitions. As with any moral duty, that of fair play implies a constraint on self-interest in particular cases; on occasion it enjoins conduct which a rational egoist strictly defined would not decide upon. So while justice does not require of anyone that he sacrifice his interests in that general position and procedure whereby the principles of justice are proposed and acknowledged, it may happen that in particular situations arising in the context of engaging in a practice, the duty of fair play will often cross his interests in the sense that he will be required to forego particular advantages which the peculiarities of his circumstances might permit him to take. There is, of course, nothing surprising in this. It is simply the consequence of the firm commitment which the parties may be supposed to have made or which they would make in the general position, together with the fact that they have participated in and accepted the benefits of a practice which they regard as fair.

Now the acknowledgment of this constraint in particular cases, which is manifested in acting fairly or wishing to make amends, feeling ashamed, and the like, when one has evaded it, is one of the forms of conduct by which participants in a common practice exhibit their recognition of each other as persons with similar interests and capacities. In the same way that, failing a special explanation, a criterion for the recognition of suffering is helping one who suffers, acknowledging the duty of fair play is a necessary part of the criterion for recognizing another as a person with interests and feelings similar to one's own.[18] A person who never under any circumstances showed a wish to help others in pain would show, at the same time, that he did not recognize that they were in pain; nor could he have any feelings of affection or friendship for anyone; for having these feelings implies, failing

[17] This, however, commonly happens. Hobbes, for example, when invoking the notion of a "tacit covenant," appeals not to the natural law that promises should be kept but to his fourth law of nature, that of gratitude. On Hobbes's shift from fidelity to gratitude, see Warrender, op. cit., pp. 51–52, 233–237. While it is not a serious criticism of Hobbes, it would have improved his argument had he appealed to the duty of fair play. On his premises he is perfectly entitled to do so. Similarly Sidgwick thought that a principle of justice, such as every man ought to receive adequate requital for his labor, is like gratitude universalized. See *Methods of Ethics*, bk. III, ch. V, sec. 5. There is a gap in the stock of moral concepts used by philosophers into which the concept of the duty of fair play fits quite naturally.

[18] I am using the concept of criterion here in what I take to be Wittgenstein's sense. See *Philosophical Investigations* (Oxford: B. Blackwell, 1953); and Norman Malcolm's review, "Wittgenstein's *Philosophical Investigations*," *Philosophical Review* 63 (1954), 543–547. That the response of compassion, under appropriate circumstances, is part of the criterion for whether or not a person understands what "pain" means, is, I think, in the *Philosophical Investigations*. The view in the text is simply an extension of this idea.

special circumstances, that he comes to their aid when they are suffering. Recognition that another is a person in pain shows itself in sympathetic action; this primitive natural response of compassion is one of those responses upon which the various forms of moral conduct are built.

Similarly, the acceptance of the duty of fair play by participants in a common practice is a reflection in each person of the recognition of the aspirations and interests of the others to be realized by their joint activity. Failing a special explanation, their acceptance of it is a necessary part of the criterion for their recognizing one another as persons with similar interests and capacities, as the conception of their relations in the general position supposes them to be. Otherwise they would show no recognition of one another as persons with similar capacities and interests, and indeed, in some cases, perhaps hypothetical, they would not recognize one another as persons at all, but as complicated objects involved in a complicated activity. To recognize another as a person one must respond to him and act towards him in certain ways; and these ways are intimately connected with the various prima facie duties. Acknowledging these duties in some degree, and so having the elements of morality, is not a matter of choice or of intuiting moral qualities or a matter of the expression of feelings or attitudes (the three interpretations between which philosophical opinion frequently oscillates); it is simply the pursuance of one of the forms of conduct in which the recognition of others as persons is manifested.

The remarks in the last two paragraphs are unhappily somewhat obscure. The thesis they sketch, however, need not be argued here. Their main purpose is simply to forestall, together with the remarks in section 4, a misinterpretation of the view presented, and to indicate in advance the manner in which the concept of justice is connected with human conduct and enters into an explanation of it. If in the conjectural account one emphasizes the condition of equality of power between the parties, it might seem that the argument implied that the acceptance of justice and the acknowledgment of the duty of fair play depends in everyday life solely on their being a de facto balance of forces between the parties. It would indeed be unwise to underestimate the importance of such a balance in securing justice; but it is not the only basis thereof. In the conjectural account it was stated that the condition of equality of power was unnecessary for the argument, and that the procedure expressing the constraints of having a morality could be regarded as simply laid down. The place of the condition of equal power was to indicate circumstances in which such a procedure might be adopted, or, if already in existence, might continue in use. But now one must ask, what is the basis of the procedure beyond that of the condition of equal power? In establishing the fundamental proposition about the concept of justice it may be satisfactory to suppose that it is simply laid down. But the concept of justice is embedded in the thoughts, feelings, and actions of real persons; in studying the concept of justice one is studying something abstracted from a certain form of life. Now what is the basis of the procedure in this form of life? The answer, sketched above, is that the recognition of one another as persons with similar interests and capacities must show itself, failing a special explanation, in the acceptance of the principles of justice and in the acknowledgment of the duty of fair play in particular cases. The procedure is not strictly speaking "imposed" by anything; it is involved in the notion of persons recognizing one another as persons with similar interests and capacities and engaged in common undertakings. Thus even if a person is in a position to insist that the design of a practice give him an unjust advantage over another, or even if, in a particular situation, he can with impunity reap a gain which is disallowed, he will, failing a special explanation, not do so. This conduct is what expresses his recognition of others as persons with interests and capacities similar to his own. Or put a bit differently: since practices to which fairness applies differ from those to which justice applies in that they allow a certain freedom of choice to the parties of participating or not participating, there is a tendency, other things being equal, for the former practices to be more in accordance with the principle of reciprocity than the latter. The greater freedom of maneuver of the parties tends to pull these practices in line with what this principle requires. (Who can be gotten to play unfair games?) One could say, then, that the recognition of others as persons leads people to view one another as if each always possessed the freedom of choice and maneuver which holds when fairness applies. It leads them to view justice as fairness. It is this recognition of one another as persons, and the conditions of it, which explains the way in which the concept of justice may be worked into an account of human action.

It may be helpful to conclude this section by a brief summary of the conception of justice contained in this and the preceding sections. The conception at which we have arrived is that the principles of justice may be thought of as associated with the concept of justice in virtue of the possibility of their being derived once the constraints of having a morality are imposed upon rational and mutually self-interested parties who are related and situated in a special way. A practice is just or fair (depending on the case) if it is in accordance with the principles which all who participate in it might reasonably be expected to propose or to acknowledge before one another when they are similarly circumstanced and required to make a firm commitment in advance without knowledge of what will be their peculiar condition, and thus when it satisfies the principle of reciprocity and its rules are those which the parties could accept as just should occasion arise for them to debate its merits. Regarding the participants themselves, once persons knowingly engage in a practice which they acknowledge to be just and accept the benefits of doing so, they are bound by the duty of fair play to follow the rules when it comes their turn to do so, and this implies a limitation on their pursuit of self-interest in particular cases.

VI

The argument so far has been excessively abstract. While this is perhaps unavoidable, I should now like to bring out some of the special features of the conception of justice as reciprocity by comparing it with the conception of justice in classical utilitarianism as represented by Bentham and Sidgwick, and with its counterpart in welfare economics.

In order to do this, the following consequence of the conception of justice as reciprocity must first be noted, namely, that where it applies, there is no moral value in the satisfaction of a claim incompatible with it. Such a claim violates the conditions of reciprocity and community amongst persons, and he who presses it, not being willing to acknowledge it when pressed by another, has no grounds for complaint when it is denied; whereas he against whom it is pressed can complain. As it cannot be mutually acknowledged it is a resort to coercion—granting the claim is possible only if one party can compel acceptance of what the other will not admit. But it makes no sense to concede claims the denial of which cannot be complained of in preference to claims the denial of which can be objected to. Thus in deciding on the justice of a practice it is not enough to ascertain that it answers to wants and interests in the fullest and most effective manner. For if any of these conflict with justice, they should not be counted, as their satisfaction is no reason at all for having a practice. It would be irrelevant to say, even if true, that it resulted in the greatest satisfaction of desire. In tallying up the merits of a practice one must toss out the satisfaction of interests the claims of which are incompatible with the principles of justice.

The conception of justice in classical utilitarianism conflicts, then, with the conception of justice as reciprocity. For on the utilitarian view justice is assimilated to benevolence and the latter in turn to the most effective design of institutions to promote the general welfare. Justice is a kind of efficiency.[19] Now it is said occasionally that this form of utilitarianism puts no restrictions on what might be a just assignment of rights and duties in that there might be circumstances which, on utilitarian grounds, would justify institutions highly offensive to our ordinary sense of justice. But the classical utilitarian conception is not totally unprepared for this objection. Beginning with the notion that the general happiness can be represented by a social utility function consisting of a sum of individual utility functions with identical weights (this being the meaning of the maxim that each counts for one and no more than one),[20] it is commonly assumed that the utility functions of individuals are similar in all essential respects. Differences between individuals are ascribed to accidents of education and upbringing, and they should not be taken into account. This assumption, coupled with that of diminishing marginal utility, results in a prima facie case for equality, e.g., of equality in the distribution of income during any given period of time, laying aside indirect effects on the future. Equality can easily be seen to follow by reflecting that if one person A has more income say than another B, it must be possible, given the assumptions, to increase the total utility shared by A and B by transferring units of income

[19] While this assimilation is implicit in Bentham's and Sidgwick's moral theory, explicit statements of it as applied to justice are relatively rare. One clear instance in *The Principles of Morals and Legislation* occurs in ch. X, footnote 2 to section XL: ". . . justice, in the only sense in which it has a meaning, is an imaginary personage, feigned for the convenience of discourse, whose dictates are the dictates of utility, applied to certain particular cases. Justice, then, is nothing more than an imaginary instrument, employed to forward on certain occasions, and by certain means, the purposes of benevolence. The dictates of justice are nothing more than a part of the dictates of benevolence, which, on certain occasions, are applied to certain subjects. . . ." Likewise in *The Limits of Jurisprudence Defined*, ed. by C. W. Everett (New York: Columbia University Press, 1945), pp. 117f., Bentham criticizes Grotius for denying that justice derives from utility; and in *The Theory of Legislation*, ed. by C. K. Ogden (New York: Harcourt, Brace and Co., 1931), p. 3, he says that he uses the words "just" and "unjust" along with other words "simply as collective terms including the ideas of certain pains or pleasures." That Sidgwick's conception of justice is similar to Bentham's is admittedly not evident from his discussion of justice in Book III, ch. V of *Methods of Ethics*. But it follows, I think, from the moral theory he accepts. Hence C. D. Broad's criticisms of Sidgwick in the matter of distributive justice in *Five Types of Ethical Theory* (New York: Harcourt, Brace and Co., 1930), pp. 249–253, do not rest on a misinterpretation.

[20] This maxim is attributed to Bentham by J. S. Mill in *Utilitarianism*, ch. V, par. 36. I have not found it in Bentham's writings, nor seen such a reference. Similarly James Bonar, *Philosophy and Political Economy* (London, 1893), p. 23*n*. But it accords perfectly with Bentham's ideas. See the hitherto unpublished manuscript in David Baumgardt, *Bentham and the Ethics of Today* (Princeton, N. J.: Princeton University Press, 1952), Appendix IV. For example, "the total value of the stock of pleasure belonging to the whole community is to be obtained by multiplying the number expressing the value of it as respecting any one person, by the number expressing the multitude of such individuals" (p. 556).

from A to B. For that the utility functions are the same means that x units to A gives the same utility as x units to B; and diminishing marginal utility implies that in general the $(n + 1)^{th}$ unit yields less utility than the nth.

Yet even if utilitarianism is interpreted as having such restrictions built into the utility function, and even if it is supposed that these restrictions have in practice much the same result as the application of the principles of justice (and appear perhaps to be ways of expressing these principles in the language of mathematics and psychology), the fundamental idea is very different from the conception of justice as reciprocity. For one thing, that the principles of justice should be accepted is interpreted as the contingent result of a higher order administrative decision. The form of this decision is regarded as being similar to that of an entrepreneur deciding how much to produce of this or that commodity in view of its marginal revenue, or to that of someone distributing goods to needy persons according to the relative urgency of their wants. The choice between practices is thought of as being made on the basis of the allocation of benefits and burdens to individuals (these being measured by the present capitalized value of their utility over the full period of the practice's existence), which results from the distribution of rights and duties established by a practice.

Moreover, the individuals receiving these benefits are not conceived as being related in any way: they represent so many different directions in which limited resources may be allocated. The value of assigning resources to one direction rather than another depends solely on the preferences and interests of individuals as individuals. The satisfaction of desire has its value irrespective of the moral relations between persons, say as members of a joint undertaking, and of the claims which, in the name of these interests, they are prepared to make on one another;[21] and it is this value which is to be taken

[21] An idea essential to the classical utilitarian conception of justice. Bentham is firm in his statement of it: "It is only upon that principle [the principle of asceticism], and not from the principle of utility, that the most abominable pleasure which the vilest of malefactors ever reaped from his crime would be reprobated, if it stood alone. The case is, that it never does stand alone; but is necessarily followed by such a quantity of pain (or, what comes to the same thing, such a chance for a certain quantity of pain) that the pleasure in comparison of it, is as nothing: and this is the true and sole, but perfectly sufficient, reason for making it a ground for punishment." (*The Principles of Morals and Legislation*, ch. II, sec. IV. See also ch. X, sec. X, footnote 1.) The same point is made in *The Limits of Jurisprudence Defined*, pp. 115f. Although much recent welfare economics, as found in such important works as I. M. D. Little, *A Critique of Welfare Economics*, 2nd edition (Oxford: The University Press, 1957) and K. J. Arrow, *Social Choice and Individual Values* (New York: Wiley, 1951), dispenses with the idea of cardinal utility and uses instead the theory of ordinal utility as stated by J. R. Hicks, *Value and Capital*, 2nd ed. (Oxford: The University Press, 1946), pt. I, it assumes with utilitarianism that individual preferences have value as such and so accepts the idea being criticized here. The same is true of those writers who, following von Neumann's lead, hold on to the notion of cardinal utility. See, for example, J. C. Harsanyi, "Cardinal Welfare, Individual Ethics, and Interpersonal Comparisons of Utility," *Journal of Political Economy*, 63 (1955), 309–321. Indeed, the same must apply here because the cardinal utility is generated by applying the notion of a probability mixture to a set of preferences having value as they stand. I hasten to add, however, that this is no objection to it as a means of analyzing economic policy, and for that purpose it may, indeed, be a necessary simplifying assumption. Nevertheless it is an assumption which cannot be made in so far as one is trying to analyze moral concepts, especially the concept of justice, as economists would, I think, agree. Justice is usually regarded as a separate and distinct part of any comprehensive criterion of economic policy. See, for example, Tibor Scitovsky, *Welfare and Competition* (London: Unwin University Books, 1963), pp. 59–69, and Little, *Welfare Economics*, ch. VII.

into account by the (ideal) legislator who is conceived as adjusting the rules of the system from the center so as to maximize the value of the social utility function.[22]

It is thought that the principles of justice will not be violated by a legal system so conceived provided these executive decisions are correctly made. In this fact the principles of justice are said to have their derivation and explanation; they simply express the most important general features of social institutions in which the administrative problem is solved in the best way. These principles have, indeed, a special urgency because, given the facts of human nature, so much depends on them; and this explains the peculiar quality of the moral feelings associated with justice.[23] This assimilation of justice to a higher order executive decision, certainly a striking conception, is central to classical utilitarianism; and it also brings out its profound individualism, in one sense of this ambiguous word. It regards persons as so many separate directions in which benefits and burdens may be assigned; and the value of the satisfaction or dissatisfaction of desire is not thought to depend in any way on the moral relations in which individuals stand, or on the kinds of claims which they are willing, in the pursuit of their interests, to press on each other.

VII

Many social decisions are, of course, of an administrative nature. Certainly this is so when it is a matter of social utility in what one may call its ordinary sense: that is, when it is a question of the efficient design of social institutions for the use of common means to achieve common ends. In this case either the benefits and burdens may be assumed to be impartially distributed, or the question of distribution is misplaced, as in the instance of maintaining public order and security or national defense. Nevertheless it is a fundamental mistake to use the notion of a higher order executive decision as the basis for interpreting the principles of justice and their derivation. In this section I shall try to show why classical utilitarianism is wrong in doing so. Throughout I shall use the example of slavery; it has the advantage of being a clear case regarding which men, both unreasonable and reasonable, may be expected to agree.

[22] The force of the word "ideal," which I have put in parentheses, is to take account of the fact that Bentham did not, of course, believe that there should be an actual administrator or legislator with full power to adjust the rules of the system from the center. But he did think, as a principle of justification, that one institution is better than another if, in the course of the way in which it could be expected to work, it is reasonable to suppose that on the whole it will have better consequences from the standpoint of an ideal legislator so defined. Representative institutions are to be preferred to monarchy and aristocracy because, human nature being what it is, democracy will in the long run give results more in accord with the principle of utility as an ideal legislator would apply it. See his *Plan of Parliamentary Reform* in *The Works of Jeremy Bentham,* ed. John Bowring (London, 1843), vol. III. One might say, further, in view of the argument in the first two chapters of *The Principles of Morals and Legislation,* that Bentham thought that the principle of utility was the only one that could be consistently recommended and the only one that could be mutually acknowledged. He says, for example: "When a man attempts to combat the principle of utility, it is with reasons drawn, without his being aware of it, from the very principle itself." Ch. I, par. 13. In the footnote to par. 14 of ch. II he would appear to say that the principle of utility is the only one by which a man can justify his opinions not only when he reflects within himself, but when he addresses the community. If, however, the argument of the previous sections is correct, these notions properly interpreted require a modification in the conception of the principle of utility as Bentham stated it.

[23] See J. S. Mill's argument in *Utilitarianism,* ch. V, pars. 16–25.

One may begin by noticing that classical utilitarianism permits one to argue that slavery is unjust on the grounds that the advantages to the slaveholder as slaveholder do not counterbalance the disadvantages to the slave and to society at large, burdened by a comparatively inefficient system of labor. Now the conception of justice as reciprocity, when applied to the practice of slavery with its offices of slaveholder and slave, would not allow one to consider the advantages of the slaveholder in the first place. As that office is not in accordance with principles which could be mutually acknowledged, the gains accruing to the slaveholder, assuming them to exist, cannot be counted as in any way mitigating the injustice of the practice. The question whether these gains outweigh the disadvantages to the slave and to society cannot arise, since in considering the justice of slavery these gains have no weight at all which requires that they be overridden. Where the conception of justice as reciprocity applies, slavery is always unjust.

I am not, of course, suggesting the absurdity that the classical utilitarians approved of slavery.[24] I am only rejecting a type of argument which their view allows them to use in support of their disapproval of it. The conception of justice as derivative from efficiency implies that judging the justice of a practice is always, in principle at least, a matter of weighing up advantages and disadvantages, each having an intrinsic value or disvalue as the satisfaction of interests, irrespective of whether or not these interests necessarily involve acquiescence in principles which could not mutually be acknowledged. Utilitarianism cannot account for the fact that slavery is always unjust, nor for the fact that it would be recognized as irrelevant in defeating the accusation of injustice for one person to say to another, engaged with him in a common practice and debating its merits, that nevertheless it allowed of the greatest satisfaction of desire. The charge of injustice cannot be rebutted in this way. If justice were derivative from a higher order executive efficiency, this would not be so.

But now, even if it is taken as established that, so far as the ordinary conception of justice goes, slavery is always unjust (that is, slavery by definition violates commonly recognized principles of justice), the classical utilitarian would surely reply that these principles, like other moral principles subordinate to that of utility, are only generally correct. It is simply for the most part true that slavery is less efficient than other institutions; and while common sense may define the concept of justice in such a way that slavery is proved unjust, nevertheless, where slavery would lead to the greatest satisfaction of desire, it is not wrong. Indeed, it is then right, and for the very same reason that justice, as ordinarily understood, is usually right. If, as ordinarily understood, slavery is always unjust, to this extent the utilitarian conception of justice might be admitted to differ from that of moral opinion. Still the utilitarian would want to hold that, as a matter of moral principle, his view is correct in giving no special weight to considerations of justice beyond that allowed for by the general presumption of effectiveness. And this, he claims, is as it should be. The everyday opinion is morally in error, although, indeed, it is a useful error, since it protects rules of generally high utility.

The question, then, relates not simply to the analysis of the concept of justice as common sense defines it, but the analysis of it in the wider sense as to how much weight considerations of justice, as de-

[24] To the contrary, Bentham argued very powerfully against it. See *A Fragment of Government*, ch. II, par. 34, footnote 2, *The Principles of Morals and Legislation*, ch. XVI, par. 44, footnote, ch. XVII, par. 4 footnote, *The Theory of Legislation*, pt. III, ch. II.

fined, are to have when laid against other kinds of moral considerations. Here again I wish to argue that reasons of justice have a special weight for which only the conception of justice as reciprocity can account. Moreover, it belongs to the concept of justice that they do have this special weight. While Mill recognized that this was so, he thought that it could be accounted for by the special urgency of the moral feelings which naturally support principles of such high utility. But it is a mistake to resort to the urgency of feeling; as with the appeal to intuition, it manifests a failure to pursue the question far enough. The special weight of considerations of justice can be explained from the conception of justice as reciprocity. It is only necessary to elaborate a bit what has already been said, as follows.

If one examines the circumstances in which a certain tolerance of slavery is justified, or perhaps better, excused, it turns out that these are of a rather special sort. Perhaps slavery exists as an inheritance from the past and it proves necessary to dismantle it piece by piece; at times slavery may conceivably be an advance on previous institutions. Now while there may be some excuse for slavery in special conditions, it is never an excuse for it that it is sufficiently advantageous to the slaveholder to outweigh the disadvantages to the slave and to society. A person who argues in this way is not perhaps making a wildly irrelevant remark; but he is guilty of a moral fallacy. There is disorder in his conception of the ranking of moral principles. For the slaveholder, by his own admission, has no moral title to the advantages which he receives as a slaveholder. He is no more prepared than the slave to acknowledge the principle upon which is founded the respective positions in which they both stand. Since slavery does not accord with principles which they could mutually acknowledge, they each may be supposed to agree that it is unjust: it grants claims which it ought not to grant and in doing so denies claims which it ought not to deny. Amongst persons in a general position who are debating the form of their common practices, it cannot, therefore, be offered as a reason for a practice that, in conceding these very claims that ought to be denied, it nevertheless meets existing interests more effectively. By their very nature the satisfaction of these claims is without weight and cannot enter into any tabulation of advantages and disadvantages.

Furthermore, it follows from the concept of morality that, to the extent that the slaveholder recognizes his position vis-à-vis the slave to be unjust, he would not choose to press his claims. His not wanting to receive his special advantages is one of the ways in which he shows that he thinks slavery is unjust. It would be fallacious for the legislator to suppose, then, that it is a ground for having a practice that it brings advantages greater than disadvantages, if those for whom the practice is designed and to whom the advantages flow, acknowledge that they have no moral title to them and do not wish to receive them.

For these reasons the principles of justice have a special weight; and with respect to the principle of the greatest satisfaction of desire, as cited in the general position amongst those discussing the merits of their common practices, the principles of justice have an absolute weight. In this sense they are not contingent; and this is why their force is greater than can be accounted for by the general presumption (assuming that there is one) of the effectiveness, in the utilitarian sense, of practices which in fact satisfy them.

If one wants to continue using the concepts of classical utilitarianism, one will have to say, to meet this criticism, that at least the individual or social utility functions must be so defined that no value is given to the satisfaction of interests the representative claims of which violate the principles of justice. In this way it is no doubt possible to include these principles within the form of the utilitarian conception; but to do so is, of course, to change its inspiration altogether as a moral conception. For it is to incorporate within it principles which cannot be understood on the basis of a higher order executive decision aiming at the greatest satisfaction of desire.

It is worth remarking, perhaps, that this criticism of utilitarianism does not depend on whether or not the two assumptions, that of individuals having similar utility functions and that of diminishing marginal utility, are interpreted as psychological propositions to be supported or refuted by experience or as moral and political principles expressed in a somewhat technical language. There are, certainly, several advantages in taking them in the latter fashion.[25] For one thing, one might say that this is what Bentham and others really meant by them, at least as shown by how they were used in arguments for social reform. More importantly, one could hold that the best way to defend the classical utilitarian view is to interpret these assumptions as moral and political principles. It is doubtful whether, taken as psychological propositions, they are true of men in general as we know them under normal conditions. On the other hand, utilitarians would not have wanted to propose them merely as practical working principles of legislation, or as expedient maxims to guide reform, given the egalitarian sentiments of modern society.[26] When pressed they might well have invoked the idea of a more or less equal capacity of men in relevant respects if given an equal chance in a just society.

If, however, the argument above regarding slavery is correct, granting these assumptions as moral and political principles makes no difference. To view individuals as equally fruitful lines for the allocation of benefits, even as a matter of moral principle, still leaves the mistaken notion that the satisfaction of desire has value in itself irrespective of the relations between persons as members of a common practice, and irrespective of the claims upon one another which the satisfaction of interests represents. To see the error of this idea one must give up the conception of justice as an executive decision altogether and refer to the notion of justice as fairness: that participants in a common practice be regarded as having an original and equal liberty and that their common practices be considered unjust unless they accord with principles which persons so circumstanced and related could freely acknowledge before one another, and so could accept as fair. Once the emphasis is put upon the concept of the mutual recognition of principles by participants in a common practice the rules of which are to define their several relations and give form to their claims on one another, then it is clear that the granting of a claim the principle of which could not be acknowledged by each in the general position (that is, in the position in which the parties propose and acknowledge principles before one another) is not a reason for adopting a practice. Viewed in this way, the background of the claim is seen to exclude it from consideration; that it can represent

[25] See D. G. Ritchie, *Natural Rights* (London, 1894), pp. 95ff., 249ff. Lionel Robbins has insisted on this point on several occasions. See *An Essay on the Nature and Significance of Economic Science*, 2nd ed. (London: Macmillan & Co., 1935), pp. 134–143; "Interpersonal Comparisons of Utility: A Comment," *Economic Journal* 48 (1938), 635–641, and more recently, "The Theory of Economic Policy," in *English Classical Political Economy* (London: Macmillan & Co., 1952), pp. 179ff.

[26] As Sir Henry Maine suggested Bentham may have regarded them. See *The Early History of Institutions* (London, 1875), pp. 398ff.

a value in itself arises from the conception of individuals as separate lines for the assignment of benefits, as isolated persons who stand as claimants on an administrative or benevolent largesse. Occasionally persons do so stand to one another; but this is not the general case, nor, more importantly, is it the case when it is a matter of the justice of practices themselves in which participants stand in various relations to be appraised in accordance with standards which they may be expected to acknowledge before one another. Thus, however mistaken the notion of the social contract may be as history, and however far it may overreach itself as a general theory of social and political obligation, it does express, suitably interpreted, an essential part of the concept of justice.[27]

VIII

The framework of the analysis of the concept of justice is now complete, and some of its special features have been brought out by comparing it with the conception of justice in classical utilitarianism. It should be remarked, though, that the original modification of the utilitarian principle (that it require of practices that the offices and positions defined by them be equal unless it is reasonable to suppose that the representative man in every office would find the inequality to his advantage), slight as it may seem at first sight, actually has a different conception of justice behind it. The argument has been intended to show how this is so by developing the concept of justice as reciprocity and by indicating how this notion, which involves the mutual acceptance from a general position of the principles on which a practice is founded, is the common element in the concepts of justice and fairness, and how the conception of justice so framed requires the exclusion from consideration of claims violating the principles of justice. The slight alteration of principle reveals another family of notions, another way of looking at the concept of justice.

Again, I should like to emphasize that I have been dealing with the concept of justice. The analytic construction is directed at setting out the kinds of principles upon which judgments concerning the justice of practices may be said to stand and the manner in which these principles are associated with the concept of justice in view of its sense. The analysis will be successful to the degree that it expresses the principles involved in these judgments when made by competent persons upon deliberation and reflection, or, more personally, to the extent that it clarifies for any particular individual his reflections about matters of justice. Moreover, the analysis is pointed toward a universal moral idea, for every people may be supposed to have the concept of justice. In the life of every society there must be at least some relations in which the parties consider themselves to be circumstanced and related as the concept of justice as reciprocity requires. Societies will differ from one another not in having or in failing to have this notion but in the

[27] Thus Kant took the right step when he interpreted the original contract as an "Idea of Reason," and so in effect, as an ethical principle applicable to social arrangements irrespective of the question of origins. See the second part of the essay, "On the Saying 'That may be right in theory but has no value in practice' " (1793), in *Kant's Principle of Politics*, trans. W. Hastie (Edinburgh, 1891). All the elements of the analysis of justice as reciprocity is stated as the meaning of the second formulation of the categorical imperative in the *Grundlegung*. See *The Groundwork of the Metaphysic of Morals*, trans. H. J. Paton (London, New York: Hutchinson's University Library, 1948), pp. 95ff. I should like to stress this tie with Kant's moral theory as well as that with Hume and utilitarianism generally, for I think it can be shown that the conflict between them is not of the sort often supposed.

range of cases to which they apply it and in the emphasis which they give to it as compared with other moral concepts.

A comprehensive understanding of the concept of justice is necessary if these variations and the reasons for them are to be intelligible. No study of the development of moral ideas and of their influence in society is more sound than an analysis of the fundamental moral concepts upon which it must depend. I have tried, therefore, to give an analysis of the concept of justice which will apply generally, however large a part the concept may have in a given morality, and which can be used in explaining the course of men's thoughts about justice and its relation to other moral concepts.

J.H. Burns / Utilitarianism and democracy

This discussion arises out of Mr. Norman Kretzmann's article "Desire as Proof of Desirability."[1] I do not wish to take issue on Mr. Kretzmann's defence of John Stuart Mill against the common charge that his argument about desire and desirability rests on an elementary confusion. But some of Mr. Kretzmann's incidental remarks about democracy and Mill's attitude to it seem to call for further consideration. (It should be emphasized that my interest here, unlike Mr. Kretzmann's, is primarily "historical" rather than "constructive.")

Mr. Kretzmann suggests [p. 240 above] the following reformulation of Mill's essential argument:

> If anything is desired in such a way as to occasion some overt reaction on the part of the normal desirer, and that reaction proves to have been normal for the thing in question, then that thing is desirable.

[1] *The Philosophical Quarterly*, vol. 8, no. 32 (July 1958), pp. 246–258 [pp. 231–241 above].

He then continues:

> Certainly it cannot surprise anyone to find in Mill this staunchest kind of support for democracy.

He quotes Mill's endorsement of Bentham's principle, "everybody to count for one, nobody for more than one," and goes on to indicate the means of determining "the actual desires of the normal desirer"; these means are found "ideally" in "the democratic process broadly conceived." Subsequent passages, particularly towards the end of the article, confirm the impression that Mr. Kretzmann sees a close connection between Mill's kind of utilitarianism and "the democratic thesis" (cf. p. 258) [p. 241 above].

For light on this point it may be useful to look at some aspects of Mill's explicit discussions of political themes. Thereafter it may be possible to come back to *Utilitarianism* and say something further about its doctrine.

Throughout a lifetime of political reflec-

Reprinted from THE PHILOSOPHICAL QUARTERLY, *vol. 9, no. 35 (April 1959), pp. 168–171 by permission of the author and editors.*

tion Mill's attitude towards democracy remained in some degree ambivalent.[2] He was never able to assent without reservations to the straightforward democratic principle of majority rule. This was because he remained convinced that men were not in fact equally endowed with the qualities which make for sound political judgment. He feared the consequences of simple majority rule while acknowledging the justice of the majority's claim to some kind of ultimate control in society. To resolve this dilemma he turned, with varying degrees of enthusiasm and lasting faith, to a number of institutional devices. First among these must be ranked the expert guidance of a professionally trained administrative service. Second, no doubt, in Mill's mature thought, came Thomas Hare's scheme for "Personal Representation," a proportional system ensuring adequate representation for minority groups in the deliberative assembly. But among other devices considered by Mill—second chambers, rejection of voting by ballot, the establishment of an expert Legislative Commission—one is especially significant here. This is his scheme for plural voting based on grades of presumed intelligence. Such a scheme was first put forward by Mill in 1859 (*Thoughts on Parliamentary Reform*): it was retained, with careful deliberation, in the *Representative Government* of 1861. Mill was well aware that plural voting was scandalous in the eyes of radical democrats—just because it violated the principle that everybody should count for one, nobody for more than one, because it violated the alleged equal right of all individuals to the franchise. But, Mill argued, the franchise involved a share in power over others, and "there is no such thing in morals as a right to power over others." So far, then, from there being an equal right to vote, there was no *right* to vote at all. The power of voting was a trust, to be conferred in proportion to the individual's fitness to exercise it. Mill did not deny that in a properly educated society *every* adult individual would be fit for some share in that power. He did deny that every individual either was or would be entitled to an equal share.

All this, then, is to be found in Mill's political theory. His denial, in that context, of the principle, "Everybody to count for one, nobody for more than one," need not entail a similar denial in the ethical theory of *Utilitarianism.* There he does indeed endorse the principle as "an explanatory commentary" on the principle of utility itself. And it is a commentary which is, of course, by no means politically irrelevant. It would be quite possible to hold—Mill himself clearly did hold—that a government, however chosen, however constituted, ought not, in determining its policies, to "respect persons," but should rather, in order to promote the greatest happiness, give equal consideration to the happiness of each and every individual. But the word "equal" is notoriously ambiguous; and to add nothing to what has just been said would still be to concede too much to the view that there is a simple and a straightforward relationship between Mill's utilitarianism and democracy in an equally simple and straightforward sense. In fact, what may be termed the non-democratic element in Mill's thought penetrates his ethical doctrine as well as his political theory.

In a passage of *Utilitarianism* no less famous than that to which Mr. Kretzmann primarily directs his attention, Mill upholds the view that it is perfectly compatible with utilitarian principles to maintain that some pleasures are intrinsically more desirable and more valuable than others. Then, in an argument closely resembling that examined by Mr. Kretz-

[2] I may perhaps refer here to an article in which I have examined this point in some detail for the period down to the publication of *Considerations on Representative Government:* "J. S. Mill and Democracy 1829–1861," *Political Studies*, vol. 5, nos. 2 and 3 (June and October 1957), 158–175 and 281–294.

mann, Mill suggests that the criterion for determining the value of various pleasures is to be found in the preferences of those who are "equally acquainted with, and equally capable of appreciating and enjoying" the pleasures in question.[3] The difficulties of this argument are not our concern here. What is important is the corollary: that the preferences of "intelligent human beings," "instructed persons," "beings of higher faculties," and so on, are to be decisive. In the light of this, the passage in which Mill accepts the Benthamite principle of equality needs to be re-examined. The Greatest Happiness Principle, Mill says,

> is a mere form of words without rational signification unless one person's happiness, supposed equal in degree (with the proper allowance made for kind) is counted for exactly as much as another's.[4]

The parenthetical phrase is surely crucial. Taken together with the earlier passage just referred to, it can mean only that the kinds of happiness preferred by "beings of higher faculties" and the like are, in the final reckoning, to count for more than those preferred by more ordinary mortals. It may still make sense to go on, as Mill does, and talk about the "equal claim of everybody to happiness in the estimation of the moralist and of the legislator" or about "a *right* to equality of treatment."[5] But the sense is not what it was for Bentham, and the "democratic" implications are not nearly so simple.[6] Some of the complications are perhaps apparent in Mr. Kretzmann's obiter dicta about the (never formulated) "democratic thesis." Thus we are told that this thesis

> demands a constantly ongoing selective adoption by the normal desirer of the goals of his more volatile, more gifted fellows (p. 255) [p. 238 above].

It is not clear why or in what sense "the democratic thesis" should "demand" anything of the kind. Again, we are told that

> The infinite series of actual desires converges on the desirable. . . . Mill might consistently be made to say that the good, or the desirable, is the object or set of objects that are fated to be ultimately desired in common by all who have desires—is what the whole community of desirers, or the normal desirer, will come eventually to desire (ibid.).

Perhaps he might; but he would scarcely have regarded such a view as having much to do with democracy. Certainly Mill's argument, in this as in other contexts, depends upon belief in progress. But Mill (perhaps unlike Mr. Kretzmann) was not sure about the relation between progress and democracy. Early in his development he learned from de Tocqueville to fear "Chinese stationariness" in democratic societies. He knew, of course, that there were dangers on the other side; the development of Comte's thought reinforced all the caution he had derived from the teaching of Bentham and his father in regard to the rule of irresponsible élites. But if the arguments of *Utilitarianism*, *Liberty*, and *Representative Government* converge, as I believe they do, it is not towards any simple "democratic thesis" but rather toward some such view as the following.

There are certain tasks in society, including those of government and legislation, for which some men are manifestly better equipped than others. There are certain forms of power for which some men are fitter than others. There are certain valuable things in human life whose value is appreciated by some men but not by

[3] *Utilitarianism* . . . etc., Everyman's Library edition, pp. 7–10 [pp. 19–21 above].

[4] Ibid., p. 58 [p. 55 above].

[5] Ibid., pp. 58, 59 [pp. 56 above]; italics in original.

[6] As to the sense in which these phrases must be understood in Mill's usage, a useful clue is provided by Mr. R. P. Anschutz (*The Philosophy of J. S. Mill* [Oxford: At the University Press, 1953], p. 26), when he says of Mill's "principle of individuality" that it asserts "that all men should be respected as ends in themselves."

others. In any simple form of "democratic" society, those tasks will be botched, that power will be abused, those values will be swamped by the mass. On the other hand, some form of the principle of utility remains the only acceptable moral and political standard; and the aim of society is thus to maximize the happiness of the greatest possible number of its members. The wishes of the majority, accordingly, must not only be consulted: they must in the end prevail. But those wishes must not rule unrestrained and uncriticized. They must, wherever possible, be checked and balanced by the freely formed and freely expressed views of the enlightened few. The reasonableness and practicability of Mill's "ideal state" are not here under discussion. The conclusion I wish to suggest is that a political ideal in which universal suffrage is combined with "personal representation" and plural voting based on educational qualifications, with the administration by a skilled bureaucracy of laws drafted by a commission of experts, and with the austere principles of governmental (and social) non-intervention laid down in the *Liberty*, is one to which the term "democratic" has only the vaguest and most unhelpful application.

Morton A. Kaplan / Some problems of the extreme utilitarian position

Utilitarianism is a familiar position among philosophers in the British Isles and has lately been presented in perhaps its most extreme form by J. J. C. Smart.[1] Smart argues vigorously against those he regards as holding an inferior and illogical view of utilitarianism, namely, the restricted utilitarians. The advocates of restricted utilitarianism, Smart says, hold that certain rules of thumb, which are good rules for a great majority of cases, ought to be followed generally, even in those cases in which they do not produce the best result. This, Smart contends, is an untenable position. I should like to show, to the contrary, that no rational man can in practice exclusively follow the extreme utilitarian doctrine, that is, choose the most advantageous action in a set of circumstances regardless of rules to the contrary, any more than any society could tolerate the doctrine as the exclusive basis for social action. The arguments I employ may raise some questions about utilitarianism in any form, but I do not wish at this time to push the argument that far.

Smart argues that restricted utilitarianism—in which the consequences of the rule for action determine the action to be taken in any circumstance—either collapses into extreme utilitarianism or produces an irrational result. He cites an example designed to prove this contention. Consider, he says, the case of a weather almanac that is right in 99 per cent of the cases. Smart admits that its predictions might serve as a good rule of thumb for sailors if it is too difficult or too costly to make individual calculations, but he denies the rationality of blind adherence to the rule. "We could well imagine," he says, "a race of sailors who acquired a superstitious reverence for their almanac, even though it was right in only 99 per cent of the cases, and who indignantly threw overboard any man who mentioned the possi-

[1] J. C. C. Smart, "Extreme and Restricted Utilitarianism," *Philosophical Quarterly* 6 (October 1956), 344–354 [pp. 195–203 above].

Reprinted from ETHICS, *vol. 70, no. 3 (April 1960), pp. 228–232 by permission of the author and the University of Chicago Press.*

bility of a direct calculation.[2] But would this behavior of the sailors be rational?"

In the example he chooses, it is difficult to disagree with Smart, for his logic is irrefutable. Why follow a rule of thumb that would produce a bad result in a particular case if an easy and cheap calculation can establish a better course of action? However, I believe that there are cases in which the calculation of the consequences of individual acts is undesirable and, therefore, in which it is desirable to follow the rule despite the fact that the calculation might lead to a "better" decision in the individual instance. In such cases, it may indeed be desirable to "throw overboard" someone who suggests a "direct calculation." I do not deny that there is always some sense in which only the decision with the best consequences ought to be made but hope to show that this sense coincides with the extreme utilitarian standard in only a trivial way.

Direct calculation may be permissible in individual cases if specific instrumental relationships are involved, provided that the costs of calculation are not too high; but such calculations are highly undesirable in social situations which are dependent upon diffuse[3] and non-specific attitudes on the parts of the role holders. In the example of the sailors and the almanac the only issue is that of getting the ship safely to port. In such a case the rational criteria are those of efficiency, and the sailors are or ought to be oriented toward each other in terms of strict achievement criteria which are the most appropriate criteria for achieving the task at hand, the *common* purpose for all of them. In such cases more efficient methods for achieving the same end are to be applauded and, if this involves a "direct calculation" rather than the application of a rule of thumb, so much the worse for the rule.

Where, however, there is no common purpose or where achievement criteria are not involved, Smart's calculus may not be the best. There are social circumstances in which the worth of an arrangement depends precisely upon the fact that criteria of efficiency are not applied and in which the role holders look to each other for diffuse, affective support, in short, for love rather than for efficiency. Consider the stability of a marriage if husband and wife coldly calculated each day whether it were possible to find a prettier or richer mate, or if each had to fear that the other would leave if the first became ill. Suppose one did become ill and the other suggested a discussion to calculate the possible course

[2] By a direct calculation, Smart would seem to mean something of the following. Suppose the almanac asserts that storms follow coronas around the moon. If one sailor has access to a barometer and it indicates no storm, then this would be the direct calculation that Smart advocates in opposition to following the rule of thumb given by the almanac. We can get a better example from another area of activity. Suppose we know that left-handed batters hit right-handed pitchers better than right-handed batters in games of baseball and that a manager must decide whether to substitute a left-handed pinch-hitter for a right-handed regular against a right-handed pitcher at a crucial moment. He would do better, according to Smart, to find out whether this particular right-handed batter hits better against right-handed pitchers than the potential pinch-hitter. In fact, many managers overlook this and do act—unwisely—on the basis of the rule. In cases like this, Smart is correct.

[3] A diffuse attitude is one not confined to particular role relationships. Thus family relationships are diffuse; we expect to be supported by our families in all our activities. Most business relationships, on the contrary, are specific. Thus workers in an assembly line have a right to expect support from each other in carrying out the specific task of manufacture but cannot normally expect support in unrelated activities. Thus, in some contexts, diffuse support is required; in others, specific support. In fact, diffuse support within the firm would interfere with the profit or production orientation and with economic survival. On the other hand, specific attitudes within the family would interfere with the maintenance of the family.

of the illness and whether he ought to get a divorce on the basis of a probability estimate of the various outcomes.

I am not trying to prejudice the case by using examples which, I admit, will stir the moral sensibility of the reader. I use these examples because they seem to me at least to indicate that certain relationships which are very important to human beings require attitudes that are diffuse and non-instrumental if they are to achieve their purpose.[4]

If my arguments are admitted, it may be pointed out in rebuttal that they establish only the disadvantage of acting contrary to the general rule in the particular case and that therefore they still collapse into the extreme utilitarian position. There is a sense in which this argument is correct, but, to the extent that extreme utilitarianism insists upon the calculation of consequences in the individual cases, I think the argument fails to hold. Thus, I do not contend that the bonds of matrimony may never be broken rationally but merely that the consideration of a decision to break them can rationally occur only after the consequences of the marriage are clearly undesirable rather than every time an opportunity to change for the possible better offers itself. And I think even the admissible calculation applies only to the timing and specific object of the change rather than to the decision to change.

Calculation of advantage with respect to individual actions therefore may be inconsistent with the maintenance of relationships that are much more important than the advantage that could be gained from individual decisions contrary to the rule. The rules of the society often perform the function of stabilizing these relationships and thus are validated by their consequences. If such rules did not exist, the specific instrumental attitude toward individual actions might then become optimal, but this would be a generally less desirable situation.

I do not think desirable behavior could be achieved even in principle, let alone in fact, by Smart's rational calculators. Smart uses an example to claim the contrary. Let us imagine, he says, a community where each man has a garden but where there is a water shortage. If water is used by most men to water the lawn, there will not be enough water for drinking and cooking. Suppose further that each man can water his garden secretly from the others, but does not do so because of his desire for the good of the community. Now suppose that there is a sick old lady in the hospital who loves flowers. Will one of the householders—out of his beneficent desire for her happiness—water his garden to grow flowers for her? Smart says that he will not because by a reductio ad absurdum he sees that if everyone behaves this way (presumably each will have a little old lady he wants to aid), no one will have water. I shall use the simpler but traditional game theoretic example of the prisoners' dilemma to establish that Smart is logically mistaken and that his extreme utilitarian calculus will lead to the result he wishes to avoid.

Two prisoners are held in separate cells by the sheriff. They have committed a major crime but the sheriff lacks proof. He therefore tells each prisoner in turn: "If neither confesses, you both will be convicted of a misdemeanor and receive very light sentences; if both confess, both will receive very heavy sentences; if one confesses and the other does not, the one who confesses will be freed and the other will receive the heaviest possible sentence." Assume that each prisoner values the pen-

[4] It may even be, although I do not propose to pursue this point, that the concept of the self and of its identity may be shattered by a completely instrumental attitude. One may experience the world as an "alien" and "cold" place. Dissociation and mental disturbance may result if all human relationships are subordinated to manipulation for advantage.

alties he must pay inversely to their length, that he is indifferent to the fate of the other prisoner, and that he makes his decision in isolation. On Smart's reasoning, both prisoners should remain silent. Each will see that in this way each will receive a very light sentence whereas if each talks each will receive a heavy sentence. Since the prisoners are both rational men and will act the same way, both will necessarily decide that they must keep silent.

Unfortunately, the reasoning is defective. Let us consider the matter from the standpoint of prisoner A, who mentally constructs a matrix for the problem and considers his alternatives. If prisoner B confesses, A avoids the heaviest penalty by confessing also. If B does not confess, A gets off free by confessing and therefore must do so. Therefore A rationally must confess regardless of B's decision. Since the same reasoning holds for B, both rationally must confess and receive very heavy sentences, although obviously there is a preferable co-operative solution if there were only some way to reach it. I may point out as an aside that the strategic criterion here is that of dominance[5] which, in game theoretic analysis, is much stronger than the minimax principle of von Neumann.

The same dilemma occurs in the case of the lawns and water shortage. Watering is dominant over non-watering. That is, if someone else waters his lawn, it is better to water one's own lawn; and if no one else waters his lawn, it is still preferable to water one's own lawn. Since, however, the water may be used up, the sooner one waters his lawn the better. Even where each wishes the good of the community, if he also desires some private good or some good for some other private person (the sick lady), each will water the lawn if there are many individuals with lawns, for in this case no individual use will diminish appreciably the supply of water. But the use of water by all—as specified by the extreme utilitarian calculus—will do grave harm. Individual rationality, in Smart's sense, produces bad results for all. Only moral inhibitions or a desire to live by the rules will protect the community from this result.

This is not true where each desires the good of the community, the number of individuals and lawns is small, and each individual use of water, therefore, appreciably diminishes the supply. In this case so much harm may be done to the community by any individual use that this harm will outweigh considerations of private good, whether egoistic or beneficent. One is hard put, however, to explain beneficent motivation on extreme utilitarian grounds, and it is a commonplace observation that humans are not motivated entirely on beneficent grounds. In any event, even assuming community-oriented beneficence, if there is any element of egoism or private beneficent motivation, there will always be examples in which the cost to the community of any particular individual's acting contrary to the rule is outweighed by the private gain although the result to the community of all acting contrary to the rule—as they must according to the extreme utilitarian standard—will be undesirable and possibly disastrous.

On the basis of reasonable assumptions concerning the nature of social problems and human motivation in present-day society, the acceptance of extreme utilitarian principles would be likely to turn society into a Hobbesian war of all against all. Unless all can agree to observe some rules of behavior and to punish those who do not, this war probably cannot be moder-

[5] One strategy is said to be dominant over another when, for any strategy chosen by the opponent, it produces a better result. This is clearly a stronger criterion than minimax which merely guarantees a minimal expected outcome but does not preclude the possibility that, for certain strategies of an opponent, one might do better than the outcome given by the minimax criterion.

ated. Even where all agree to observe these rules, the situation would remain precarious until the rules were internalized and thereby modified the desires of individuals, that is, until individuals refused to break the rules even to secure their advantage in individual cases.

One may regard such a development as an implicit maximization over time and thereby hold that it is merely another example of the extreme utilitarian principle. But, if so, one is maximizing whatever he regards as good by accepting the consequences of the rule, which, according to Smart's explanation, is the restricted utilitarian position. I think there is a difference. One might well want to throw overboard someone who suggested calculating advantage in individual cases. One can follow the rule to advantage only if assured that others will not calculate the possible advantages of breaking the rule. For the most desirable standards to be observed, men must have confidence in each other's behavior.

If a norm is accepted conditionally (that is, only for those cases in which it is not advantageous to break it), it will not motivate anyone at any time except in those cases where the rule coincides with the action that would be taken in the individual case in the absence of the rule. This coincidence does not occur in the prisoners' dilemma or the lawn watering.

Where it is known or suspected that the rule does not correspond to the action that would be best in the case of "direct calculation," or where it is thought that other individuals might believe they did not correspond even when they did, it will become more difficult for others to observe the rule. In a lawless community, lawless behavior may be the most appropriate response. Therefore, in order to avoid this kind of situation, it is desirable for some rules to be followed automatically by all without calculation and therefore without the attempt to do better than the rule allows in some particular cases. This permits all to do well in a way not possible in the absence of such rules. Rules of this kind may be reinforced by secondary gains, that is, by the approval gained as a reward for being good and offered either by the community or by that internalized watchman, the conscience. Conscience permits the individual to live in a better society than would be possible otherwise.

The extreme utilitarian calculus would undercut the establishment of such desirable norms and therefore is to be condemned. It is hardly legitimate to save the principle by turning the rule or norm itself into something desirable, for, on extreme utilitarian standards, the rule is only a rule of thumb and not to be followed unless it produces the best results. But, clearly, in many individual cases, provided only secrecy can be maintained, better results will be achieved by breaking the rule.

I recognize that Smart wants to talk about the beneficent calculators rather than egoistic ones. But it seems to me that this is merely another form of following a rule or moral standard of decency and thus begs the question. If we build into the desires of men the desire for the good of society, we automatically exclude many problems. I would not deny that if each marriage partner valued the happiness of the other more than his own, the calculation of advantage for the other would not upset the marriage, although in real marriages it might produce a cloying stickiness that would undermine the marriage. If, in the prisoners' dilemma, each prisoner values the other's freedom more than his own, clearly neither will talk. In the lawn watering if each prefers to have his neighbor use the water, none will use it. This may still not be maximal, for it would be less satisfactory than if someone used it but undoubtedly would be better than if everyone used it.

However, the moment even a small egoistic element or even some element of private beneficence is built into the problem in addition to the desire for society's gain —except in that case in which the individual use of water would exhaust or have a marked effect upon the supply—it generally becomes rational for each to use the small amount for the reasons of strategy dominance cited in the prisoners' dilemma. In any real society the egoistic element will be strong enough to establish, in my opinion, the undesirability of living in a community where all behave according to the extreme utilitarian position. It is a rare situation in which the individual's breaking of the rule has sufficient influence upon the total action of the society to outweigh the value of his dereliction. But, since this is true for all, the individual can live in a desirable society only if some rules are regarded by all as moral imperatives.

The extreme utilitarian may agree that he favors rules for society but not for himself; he may attempt to rise above the ordinary life of the community. In this case he must hope that others do not copy his behavior for, if they did, he would get the same undesirable result as the prisoners in the prisoners' dilemma. Therefore even the extreme utilitarian would have to favor social rules which penalize violators, and training, at least for others, which in the form of conscience provides an internal check upon action. But one can hardly isolate himself from his society's form of training. Smart may then rejoin that, if both sanctions are operative, extreme utilitarianism prescribes following the rule. I do not doubt this, but he then would save the doctrine by giving up the game. One may call this society's revenge on the extreme utilitarian who now so values the rule that he does not desire to break it or who has established so many social constraints that it now costs too much to break it. It is, therefore, practically impossible to be an extreme utilitarian.

Unlike, in Aristotle's terms, beasts or gods, men are socially oriented with respect to many relationships, and participants in these relationships will find it a disadvantage to have a calculating turn of mind. It is better for the husband to refuse to cheat on his wife because of consideration of long-run satisfaction than because of the fear of discovery. But I suggest that it is even better to be spontaneous and not to have such thoughts in the first place. In short, even restricted utilitarianism may be a better standard for the philosopher evaluating different societies and their rules than for the active man in his life.

If so, perhaps it is better to discuss utilitarianism (except in those cases where criteria of efficiency are the relevant criteria) as an evaluative yardstick for the observer trying to determine which moral rules are best for society rather than as a doctrine for real men. And then perhaps we can regard restricted utilitarianism as stating that in cases in which diffuse affective relationships are involved and in cases in which long-run maximization is desirable, rules of action are preferable to decisions based upon the specific conditions of individual cases. In other circumstances the appropriate criteria may be those of efficiency. Perhaps therefore it is better to refuse to regard either utilitarian standard as a dogma but to examine the conditions of life in which each is appropriate either as a guide for action or as a standard for evaluating actions.

Jan Narveson / The desert island problem

I

One of the difficulties traditionally confronting the would-be utilitarian is presented by offbeat situations such as occasionally might occur on desert islands and the like. Actually, if we confine the term "utilitarian" to those who follow Mill, the argument embarrasses not only utilitarians but anyone who holds that the moral value of an act lies in its consequences, so long as he includes the satisfaction of interests among those consequences. Let us call such a view "consequentialism." The "consequentialist," then, must try to hold that the value of any act lies in its consequences; and the would-be non-consequentialist attempts to maroon him upon the desert island of the desert island problem.

A typical version of the desert island problem is as follows[1]: You and Jones are marooned on a desert island, and Jones takes to cultivating flowers, which he does with splendid results. You have no particular taste in flowers, and also no particular affection for Jones. Jones then becomes fatally ill and, in his final moments of life, he requests you to tend his flowers for him for a while after he dies—until, let us say for definiteness, the nasturtiums cease to bloom. You promise him to do this—though just exactly why is not at all clear. It is stipulated that neither you nor Jones has any belief in immortality or in special religious doctrines which have the consequence that you are in any way obliged to tend the flowers. Jones then dies. So now the question arises: Do you or don't you have to admit that there is some moral value in tending Jones's flowers until the nasturtiums cease to bloom? And thus the dilemma looms for the consequentialist: Either he does not admit any moral value in tending the flowers, in which case his view is radically at variance with the common moral consciousness; or he does admit it, in which case he ap-

[1] This example is derived, with some modification, from one supplied by Professor Roderick Firth of Harvard.

Reprinted from ANALYSIS, *vol. 23, no. 3 (January 1963), pp. 63–67 by permission of the author and editors and Basil Blackwell, publisher, Oxford, England.*

pears to have on his hands a case in which something has moral value but not on account of its consequences.

II

Four comments need to be made before I propose my answer to this type of problem.

1. It has always bothered me *why* you made that promise. Did you *have* to make that promise? Or didn't you? A consequentialist might, certainly, toy with the following argument: If you were morally obligated to make the promise, what could account for that? Surely we are not normally obliged to *make* promises. *If* we make them, then we are obliged to keep them, but that is something else. Now perhaps the only answer to the question why you ought to make the promise, or at any rate why there is moral value in making the promise, is to spare Jones any further mental anguish on that score, which would be a consequentialist reason of sorts. However, this would only delay the issue, for one certainly has the option of not keeping the promise, and in that case the consequentialist's problem arises again.

On the other hand, one might simply argue that there is no obligation whatever, nor any moral value whatever, in making the promise. One might argue that if Jones is asking you to make yourself uncomfortable by working away in his garden when you would rather be lolling about on the beach, then he has no right to ask that of you; and you, far from being obliged to make the promise, ought as a good utilitarian to rebuke him kindly for making this unkind request. If you do not have any moral obligation to make the promise, however, then you can argue that if you *do* make it, it will have been simply out of affection, or out of a kind of aesthetic attitude which you have towards the dead —irrational, perhaps, but nevertheless an interest, and hence one which you would be satisfying by tending Jones's garden. True, you can say, the average man might feel some kind of obligation to make the promise: but in fact, he is just wrong and there is no such obligation.

I must confess that I do not see how the non-consequentialist can reply to this suggestion. For it seems to me that the ordinary moral consciousness, though it might offhand be inclined to pronounce a morally favourable judgment on making the promise, is not very definite on the point. It seems to me that it would be swayed by this argument, and might even be swayed to the point of suggesting that you ought not to make the promise in this situation. And if you cannot be shown to have a moral obligation of any sort to make the promise in the first place, then the question of whether you ought to keep it if you make it becomes uninteresting.

2. It might be thought that John Rawls's influential article "Two Concepts of Rules"[2] provides the solution to this problem. But, it seems to me, the Rawls's "amendment" to utilitarianism does not radically alter the picture, though it might first be thought to do so. It seems to me that it would merely be the basis for the utilitarian's handling of the question in the preceding manner. The upshot of Rawls's article, I think, is that the notion that you are morally obliged to keep a promise is a part of the notion of promising in the first place. As I understand him, his view holds that to say that you promise to do x is essentially equivalent to your saying "I hereby declare myself morally obligated to do x." If that is what you mean when you promise to do something, of course it is nonsense for you to ask yourself whether you are morally obligated to *keep* a promise once made, unless something morally important has arisen in the mean-

[2] *Philosophical Review* 64 (1955) [pp. 175–194 above].

time which overrides the obligation to keep the promise. But this does *not* have the consequence that utilitarianism, construed as the view that the values of acts stem from the consequences of those particular acts, is false—as some, I believe, have supposed. Quite the contrary: it means that for a utilitarian, one ought not to make a promise unless there is some good to be derived from making that particular promise. And, in effect, this merely means that the estimation of consequences must occur prior to making the promise and not subsequently. The justification for keeping the promise simply is made identical by definition with the justification for making it in the first place.

3. Nowell-Smith has taken the view that we cannot be bothered with questions about what would be our obligations under unforeseeable circumstances.

He argues that probably we wouldn't have such a duty as is here under discussion but he also says[3] that our moral language just wasn't built for such cases and so it is impossible to say what one would or would not say under those circumstances. If that is his view, it seems to me a mistaken one: mistaken, however, for reasons which are in the end too involved to discuss here at length. But in any case, I do not understand why the circumstances of the case do not make for a clear issue. If we cannot decide what the right conclusion would be prior to actually experiencing the situation, I do not see how our actually being in the situation could help; for all of the morally relevant features of the case are presently in full daylight. Now, if ever, is surely the time to find out what ought or ought not to be done in those exceptional cases.

4. Finally, it should be clear, I hope, that no amount of fishing for consequences is of any use in a problem of this type. With ingenuity, one can often discover consequences which would very likely arise in this sort of case. But in order to be able to appeal to those, it would be necessary to show that the case cannot happen without such hidden consequences, and this is clearly impossible to show. It is always conceivable that there will be such consequences, but it is equally conceivable that there will not. Appeal to possible consequences for one's conscience if one does not tend the flowers after having promised to do so are of no avail, since they presuppose the moral judgment that the flowers ought to be tended if you have promised to tend them. This type of solution, then, which appears to be the sort that early discussion of this subject by utilitarians tended to assume, is irrelevant.

III

What, then, is the solution to the desert island problem? Half of the solution, I believe, has been given in II, 1 above. But I wish to go further and suggest that a consequentialist could even consistently *make* the promise. Let us see how this is.

The utilitarian's principle is that what makes an act morally good is that its consequence is to satisfy some interest or interests (or to tend to do so). The solution to the desert island problem lies in the uncovering of an ambiguity in the concept of satisfying an interest.

1. We tend to suppose that an interest is satisfied when satisfaction is produced in the person whose interest it is. And since this is normally the case when an interest is satisfied, this is not surprising and not, for that matter, in any way erroneous. The utilitarians are quite plainly thinking along these lines when they tend to equate "doing it because you want to" with "getting pleasure out of it." But whatever their view about the equivalence of "pleasure" with "satisfaction,"

[3] Nowell-Smith, *Ethics* (New Orleans: Pelican, 1954), p. 241.

their theory's essential thrust is certainly to identify the moral goodness of an act with its *experienced* consequences for the interested person. And when they hold that the "greatest happiness for the greatest number" is the goal of moral action, they are plainly relying on this identification.

2. But it is possible to read the phrase "x satisfies an interest" in a different way. In order to bring this home, I take a case from the novel *Man's Fate*, by André Malreaux. In this novel, one of the characters devotes a good portion of his life to the project of assassinating Chiang Kai-shek. He ends up by throwing himself with a bomb on his person in front of a car which he takes to be that of Chiang Kai-shek, killing himself and all of the occupants of the car. Now, as it happens, Chiang is not actually in the car, it having been advertised as containing him precisely in order to avoid Chiang's assassination in that manner. Because we know that his project is not going to attain its purpose, we feel a sense of tragedy as the incident is related. Why? After all, the character who sacrificed himself *believes* that he has at last succeeded, and so might be said, in a sense, to have died happy. But the fact is, it is precisely because his interest, which happens to be a very important one to him, has gone unsatisfied that we feel the sense of tragedy. We feel, in fact, that it is yet more tragic because he does not know—because his efforts are in vain, he has been fooled.

We may say, if we like, that our feeling stems from the fact that if he *had* known about the miscarriage of his efforts, he *would have* felt very miserable. That is, indeed, undoubtedly true. But of course he doesn't and can't feel miserable, since the person formerly denoted by "he" now fails to exist. However you care to phrase it, it is perfectly plain that he has died unsatisfied, and that *that* is what the tragedy consists in.

Similarly, if Jones dies and you do not tend his flowers, then your feeling is that Jones is not getting what he wanted. This will not cut any ice with you if you have not promised him to tend them, although you will doubtless feel somewhat sorry for him when you watch his flowers withering on the vine for lack of attention. But then, it is precisely because you feel that he is not getting his interests satisfied that makes you promise him to tend his nasturtiums in the first place, if you do. And if this is so, then it is still true that it is because of the *consequences* of this particular act of tending the flowers—namely, that Jones has now got what he wanted (though he is no longer capable of knowing this or deriving any pleasure from it) —that gives your act of tending them whatever moral value it may have.

The question still remains whether there is really any moral value in the satisfying of interests when they do not produce any feelings of satisfaction. In my opinion, there really isn't, and we ought to treat all matters pertaining to the dead on the level of personal feelings and preferences. We cannot *morally* blame a person for refusing to perform services for the dead. Nevertheless, we must certainly permit people to perform them if they are so inclined, and I am inclined to think that I would be so inclined myself.

Our question, however, is whether the consequentialist or the non-consequentialist was right on this matter. I think it is now clear that the consequentialist is right: for it is on account of the consequences of the act of tending the nasturtiums that it has any moral value, *if* it does have any. Whatever moral value it has can only be accounted for by the consequentialist view. And if you share the view stated in the last paragraph, then you will also agree that even classical utilitarianism needs no amending to take care of this particular problem.

James Cargile / Utilitarianism and the desert island problem

Some writers, in relating Ethics and Epistemology, have discussed the ethics of belief: What ought a man to believe on the given evidence? Belief is here treated as voluntary, as when we speak of "suspending belief." But belief is not always considered a matter entirely within the agent's control, and in this light, genuinely ethical questions arise.

For example, it is not uncommon in religious communities for a member of the community who becomes an atheist to be considered ethically bad. Why should this be so, if "desertion of the faith" is not a matter within the agent's control? It is not enough to say that the community is just wrong. The naturalness of their condemnation, even when they themselves would recognize that the agent's unbelief was involuntary, should be explained. I think that one element which may be important is that the people may regard unbelief in one of their own as a lack of feeling for the tradition of the community which is a sign of bad character. This attitude relates to the "Desert Island Problem."

This is a case which has been put forward as constituting a special problem for a Utilitarian Ethics.[1] The story is as follows: Smith and Jones, marooned for years on a desert island, have become close friends. Smith loves flowers and has managed to raise a little garden. Jones finds flowers uninteresting. Smith is taken ill, and soon the unhappy Jones is waiting at his friend's deathbed. Smith says "Jones old friend." "Yes, Smith?" Jones replies. "Jones, I would rest easier if you could grant me one last wish." "Anything," answers Jones. "Will you water my flowers when I'm gone? The thought of anything happening to them fills me with anguish." Jones warmly assures Smith that he will water his flowers, and Smith dies happy. Shortly after burying Smith, Jones tears up the garden to make a salad.

This story is supposed to constitute a difficulty for Utilitarianism because this ethical theory is not supposed to condemn

[1] Jan Narveson, "The Desert Island Problem," *Analysis* 23 (January 1963) [pp. 279–282 above].

Reprinted from ANALYSIS, *vol. 25, no. 1 (October 1964), pp. 23–24 by permission of the author and editors.*

Jones for breaking his promise, since no bad consequences follow this action. But our moral sensibilities are supposed to be outraged at Jones's action. Good ethical judgment is supposed to condemn him for breaking his promise. Utilitarians are caught in this emotion-packed situation endorsing Jones's salad. It is obviously the useful thing.

This is not really a difficulty for the Utilitarian Theory. What we censure Jones for is being able to be so detached. The theory, on the other hand, only tells Jones that *if* he is able to act unemotionally, then the salad is the right thing. Common ethical intuition censures Jones for being able to act unemotionally.

Similarly, when the court in the Camus novel *The Stranger* takes it as a mark against the defendant that he did not feel grief at his mother's death, it is taking this lack of feeling as a sign of bad character, rather than supposing that the defendant, in failing to feel grief, was failing to do something he could have done if he tried.

Utilitarianism judges actions and not men. But it need not conflict with an ethics that judges men. It can approve of Jones's action without approving of Jones's being able to do it.

The following sort of examples are often troublesome in thinking about ethics: A vitally important scientist passes a burning house in which a derelict is calling for help (in an obviously uneducated accent). The scientist doesn't try to save the man, though the chances were fair. We want to disapprove despite the hedonistic calculus. A sailor clinging to a raft doesn't extend his arm when his brother is swept by, because it is clear that this action would only lose them both. Again there is a conflict.

It is perfectly possible consistently to insist that if a person is rational he ought to do a certain thing, and yet censure him for doing that thing. The justifiability of censuring an agent for being unemotional may be questioned, depending on the case, but the fact that it is done is worth recognizing. If a case is considered in which a momentary lapse of rationality would be expected of a good man, and the reason for approving is not recognized, you may be led to endorse a silly action even when there is time for deliberation, just because you thought you endorsed it in the case when there was not time for deliberation. We need a new double standard; one for men and one for actions, of course with various complex interconnections.

Richard A. Wasserstrom / The obligation to obey the law

The question of what is the nature and extent of one's obligation to obey the law is one of those relatively rare philosophic questions which can never produce doubts about the importance of theory for practice. To ask under what circumstances, if any, one is justified in disobeying the law, is to direct attention to problems which all would acknowledge to be substantial. Concrete, truly problematic situations are as old as civil society.

The general question was posed—though surely not for the first time—well over two thousand years ago in Athens when Crito revealed to Socrates that Socrates' escape from prison could be easily and successfully accomplished. The issue was made a compelling one—though once again surely not for the first time—by Crito's insistence that escape was not only possible but also *desirable*, and that disobedience to law was in *this* case at least, surely justified. And the problem received at the hand of Socrates—here perhaps for the first time—a sustained theoretical analysis and resolution.

Just as the question of what is the nature and extent of one's obligation to obey the law demanded attention then—as it has throughout man's life in the body politic—it is no less with us today in equally vexing and perplexing forms. Freedom rides and sit-ins have raised the question of whether the immorality of segregation may justify disobeying the law. The all too awesome horrors of a nuclear war have seemed to some to require responsive action, including, if need be, deliberate but peaceful trespasses upon government-owned atomic testing grounds. And the rightness of disobedience to law in the face of court-ordered school integration

This essay is an expanded and substantially revised version of a paper, "Disobeying the Law," which was presented at the December 1961 meeting of the Eastern Division of the American Philosophical Society and which was published in Journal of Philosophy *58 (1961), 641.*

This revision has been benefitted by the helpful comments and suggestions of my colleagues, Professors Herbert Packer and Gerald Gunther; and especially of Professor Arnold Kaufman of the Department of Philosophy of the University of Michigan, presently a Fellow at the Center for Advanced Study in the Behavioral Sciences. R.A.W.

Reprinted from the UCLA LAW REVIEW, *vol. 10 (May 1963), pp. 780–807 by permission of the author and the Regents of the University of California.*

has been insisted upon by the citizens of several states and acted upon by the governor of at least one.[1]

The problem is one of present concern and the questions it necessarily raises are real. But even if the exigencies of contemporary life were not such as to make this topic a compelling one, it is one which would still be peculiarly ripe for critical inquiry. In part this is so because despite their significance many of the central issues have been relatively neglected by legal or political philosophers and critics. Many of the important questions which bear upon the nature and extent of one's obligation to obey the law have been dealt with summarily and uncritically; distinguishable issues have been indiscriminately blurred and debatable conclusions gratuitously assumed.

More important is the fact that historically the topic has generally been examined from only one very special aspect of the problem. Those philosophers who have seriously considered questions relating to one's obligation to obey the law have considered them only in the context of revolution. They have identified the conditions under which one would, if ever, be justified in disobeying the law with the conditions under which revolution would, if ever, be justified; and they have, perhaps not surprisingly, tended thereby to conclude that one would be justified in disobeying the law if, and only if, revolution itself would in that case be justified.[2]

To view the problem in a setting of obedience or revolution is surely to misconstrue it. It is to neglect, among other things, something that is obviously true—that most people who disobey the law are not revolutionaries and that most acts of disobedience of the law are not acts of revolution. Many who disobey the law are, of course, ordinary criminals: burglars, kidnappers, embezzlers, and the like. But even of those who disobey the law under a claim of justification, most are neither advocates nor practitioners of revolution.[3]

If the traditional, philosophical treatment of this subject is unduly simplistic and restrictive, contemporary legal thought is seldom more instructive. It is distressing, for one thing, that those whose daily intellectual concern is the legal system have said so little on this subject. And it is disturbing that many of those who have said anything at all appear so readily to embrace the view that justified disobedience of the law is a rare, if not impossible, occurrence. What is so disturbing is not the fact that this view is held—although I think it a mistaken one—but rather that such a conclusion is so summarily reached or assumed.[4]

I must make it clear at the outset that it is not my purpose to devote the remain-

[1] This is to say nothing of the stronger claim, involved in many of the war crimes prosecutions, that one does have a duty to disobey the law and, therefore, that one can be properly punished for having obeyed the law.

[2] See, e.g., Austin, *The Province of Jurisprudence Determined* (New York: Noonday Press, 1954), 53–55; Hume, *A Treatise of Human Nature*, bk. III, §§ 9, 10; Locke, *The Second Treatise of Government*, chs. 18, 19.

[3] A subject which has surely not received the philosophical attention it deserves is that of the nature of revolution. What, for instance, are the characteristics of a revolution? Must the procedures by which laws are made or the criteria of validity be altered? Or is it sufficient that the people who occupy certain crucial offices be removed in a manner inconsistent with existing rules? Must force or resistance accompany whatever changes or alterations are made? Whatever the answers may be to questions such as these, it is, I think, plain that particular laws may be disobeyed under a claim of justification without any of these features being present. One can *argue* that for one reason or another, any act of disobedience must necessarily lead to revolution or the overthrow of the government. But then this is an argument which must be demonstrated.

[4] Professor Henry Hart, for example, in his extremely stimulating analysis of the aims of the criminal law seems to hold such a view. Professor Hart believes that the criminal law ought only be concerned with that conduct

der of this article to a documentation of the claims just made concerning either historical or contemporary thought. I do not wish to demonstrate that people in fact do believe what they appear to believe about the possibility of justified disobedience to law. Nor do I wish to show why it is that people have come to believe what they appear to believe. Rather, in very general terms I am concerned here with *arguments*—with those arguments which have been or which might be given in support of the claim that because one does have an obligation to obey the law, one ought not ever disobey the law.

To describe the focus of the article in this manner is, however, to leave several crucial matters highly ambiguous. And thus, before the arguments can be considered properly, the following matters must be clarified.

A. There are several different views which could be held concerning the nature of the stringency of one's obligation to obey the law. One such view, and the one which I shall be most concerned to show to be false, can be characterized as holding that one has an *absolute* obligation to obey the law. I take this to mean that a person is never justified in disobeying the law; to know that a proposed action is illegal is to know all one needs to know in order to conclude that the action ought not to be done;[5] to cite the illegality of an action is to give a sufficient reason for not having done it. A view such as this is far from uncommon. President Kennedy expressed the thoughts of many quite reflective people when he said not too long ago:

> . . . [O]ur nation is founded on the principle that observance of the law is the eternal safeguard of liberty and defiance of the law is the surest road to tyranny.
>
> The law which we obey includes the final rulings of the courts as well as the enactments of our legislative bodies. Even among law-abiding men few laws are universally loved.
>
> But they are universally respected and not resisted.
>
> Americans are free, in short, to disagree with the law, but not to disobey it. For in a government of laws and not of men, no man, however prominent or powerful, and no mob, however unruly or boisterous, is entitled to defy a court of law.
>
> If this country should ever reach the point where any man or group of men, by force or threat of force, could long deny the commands of our court and our Constitution, then no law would stand free from doubt, no judge would be sure of his writ and no citizen would be safe from his neighbors.[6]

A more moderate or weaker view would be that which holds that, while one does have an obligation to obey the law, the obligation is a prima facie rather than absolute one. If one knows that a pro-

which is morally blameworthy. From this he infers that no real problem can ever be presented by laws which make knowledge of the illegality of an action one of the elements of the offense. And this is so because the "knowing or reckless disregard of legal obligation affords an independent basis of blameworthiness *justifying the actor's condemnation as a criminal*, even when his conduct was not intrinsically antisocial." (Emphasis added.) Hart, "The Aims of the Criminal Law," 23 *Law and Contemporary Problems* 401, 418 (1958). Some such view can also be plausibly attributed to, among others, Professor Lon Fuller, see text at section II, and Professor Herbert Wechsler, see text at section IV. Of course, all of these scholars, or any other person holding such a view, might well insist that the position is tenable only if an important qualification is made, namely, that the legal system in question be that of an essentially democratic society. For a discussion of this more restricted claim, see text at section IV.

[5] Because I am concerned with the question of whether one is ever *morally justified* in acting illegally, I purposely make the actor's knowledge of the illegality of the action part of the description of the act. I am not concerned with the question of whether ignorance of the illegality of the action ought to excuse one from moral blame.

[6] N. Y. Times, Oct. 1, 1962, p. 22, col. 6. The same qualification must be made here as was made in note 4 supra—President Kennedy may well have meant his remarks to be applicable only to the legal system which is a part of the set of political institutions of the United States.

posed course of conduct is illegal then one has a good—but not necessarily a sufficient—reason for refraining from engaging in that course of conduct. Under this view, a person may be justified in disobeying the law, but an act which is in disobedience of the law does have to be justified, whereas an act in obedience of the law does not have to be justified.

It is important to observe that there is an ambiguity in this notion of a prima facie obligation. For the claim that one has a prima facie obligation to obey the law can come to one of two different things. On the one hand, the claim can be this: The fact that an action is an act of disobedience is something which always does count against the performance of the action. If one has a prima facie obligation to obey the law, one always has that obligation—although, of course, it may be overridden by other obligations in any particular case. Thus the fact that an action is illegal is a relevant consideration in every case and it is a consideration which must be outweighed by other considerations before the performance of an illegal action can be justified.

On the other hand, the claim can be weaker still. The assertion of a prima facie obligation to obey the law can be nothing more than the claim that as a matter of fact it is *generally* right or obligatory to obey the law. As a rule the fact that an action is illegal is a relevant circumstance. But in any particular case, after deliberation, it might very well turn out that the illegality of the action was not truly relevant. For in any particular case the circumstances might be such that there simply was nothing in the fact of illegality which required overriding—*e.g.*, there were no bad consequences at all which would flow from disobeying the law in this case.

The distinction can be made more vivid in the following fashion. One person, *A*, might hold the view that any action in disobedience of the law is intrinsically bad. Some other person, *B*, might hold the view that no action is intrinsically bad unless it has the property, *P*, and that not all actions in disobedience of the law have that property. Now for *A*, the fact of disobedience is *always* a relevant consideration,[7] for *B*, the fact of disobedience may always be initially relevant because of the existence of some well-established hypothesis which asserts that the occurrence of any action of disobedience is correlated highly with the occurrence of *P*. But if in any particular case disobedience does not turn out to have the property, *P*, then, upon reflection, it can be concluded by *B* that the fact that disobedience is involved is not a reason which weighs against the performance of the act in question. To understand *B*'s position it is necessary to distinguish the relevance of *considering* the fact of disobedience from the relevance of the fact of disobedience. The former must always be relevant, the latter is not.

Thus there are at least three different positions which might be taken concerning the character of the obligation to obey the law or the rightness of disobedience to the law. They are: (1) One has an absolute obligation to obey the law; disobedience is never justified. (2) One has an obligation to obey the law but this obligation can be overridden by conflicting obligations; disobedience can be justified, but only by the presence of outweighing circumstances. (3) One does not have a special obligation to obey the law, but it is in fact usually obligatory, on other grounds, to do so; disobedience to law often does turn out to be unjustified.

B. It must also be made clear that when I talk about the obligation to obey the law

[7] To repeat, though, it surely is not necessarily conclusive, or sufficient, since an action in obedience to the law may under some other description be worse, or less justifiable, than disobedience.

or the possibility of actions which are both illegal and justified, I am concerned solely with *moral obligations* and *morally justified* actions. I shall be concerned solely with arguments which seek to demonstrate that there is some sort of a connection between the legality or illegality of an action and its morality or immorality. Concentration on this general topic necessarily renders a number of interesting problems irrelevant. Thus, I am not at all concerned with the question of why, in fact, so many people do obey the law. Nor, concomitantly, am I concerned with the nonmoral reasons which might and do justify obedience to law—of these, the most pertinent, is the fact that highly unpleasant consequences of one form or another are typically inflicted upon those who disobey the law. Finally there are many actions which are immoral irrespective of whether they also happen to be illegal. And I am not, except in one very special sense, concerned with this fact either. I am not concerned with the fact that the immorality of the action itself may be a sufficient reason for condemning it regardless of its possible illegality.

C. My last preliminary clarification relates to the fact that there is a variety of kinds of legal rules or laws and that there is a variety of ways in which actions can be related to these rules. This is an important point because many moral philosophers, in particular, have tended to assimilate all legal rules to the model of a typical law or legal order which is enforced through the direct threat of the infliction by the government of severe sanctions, and have thereby tended to assume that all laws and all legal obligations can be broken or disobeyed only in the manner in which penal laws can be broken or disobeyed. That this assimilation is a mistake can be demonstrated quite readily. There are many laws that, unlike the typical penal law, do not require or prohibit the performance of any acts at all. They cannot, therefore, be disobeyed. There are laws, for example, that make testamentary dispositions of property ineffective, unenforceable, or invalid, if the written instrument was not witnessed by the requisite number of disinterested witnesses. Yet a law of this kind obviously does not impose an obligation upon anyone to make a will. Nor, more significantly, could a person who executed a will without the requisite number of witnesses be said to have disobeyed the law. Such a person has simply failed to execute a valid will.[8]

The foregoing observations are relevant largely because it is important to realize that to talk about disobeying the law or about one's obligation to obey the law is usually to refer to a rather special kind of activity, namely, that which is exemplified

[8] See Hart, *The Concept of Law* (Oxford: Clarendon Press, 1961), 27–48, particularly for the clearest and fullest extant philosophical analysis of the important distinguishing characteristics of different kinds of legal rules.

In this connection a stronger point than the one made above can be made. It is that there are many laws which, if they can be disobeyed at all, cannot be disobeyed in the way in which the typical criminal law can be disobeyed. For there are many laws that either impose or permit one to impose upon oneself any number of different legal obligations. And with many of these legal obligations, regardless of how created, it seems correct to say that one can breach or fail to perform them without thereby acting illegally or in disobedience of the law. One's obligation to obey the law may not, therefore, be coextensive with one's legal obligations. In the typical case of a breach of contract, for example, the failure to perform one's contractual obligations is clearly a breach of a legal obligation. Yet one can breach a contract and, hence, a legal obligation without necessarily acting illegally. This last assertion is open to question. And arguments for its correctness would not here be germane. It is sufficient to recognize only that failing to honor or perform some types of legal obligations may be a quite different kind of activity from violating or disobeying a law or order which is backed up, in some very direct fashion, by a governmentally threatened severe sanction.

by, among other things, actions in violation or disobedience of a penal law. It is this special type of activity which alone is the concern of this article.

II

One kind of argument in support of the proposition that one cannot be justified in disobeying the law is that which asserts the existence of some sort of *logical* or conceptual relationship between disobeying the law and acting immorally.[9] If the notion of illegality entails that of immorality then one is never justified in acting illegally just because part of the meaning of *illegal* is *immoral;* just because describing an action as illegal is—among other things—to describe it as unjustified.[10]

A claim such as this is extremely difficult to evaluate. For one has great difficulty in knowing what is to count as truly relevant—let alone decisive—evidence of its correctness. There is, nevertheless, a supporting argument of sorts which can be made. It might go something like this:

It is a fact which is surely worth noticing that people generally justify action that *seems to be* illegal by claiming that the action *is not really* illegal. Typically an actor who is accused of having done something illegal will not defend himself by pointing out that, while illegal, his conduct was nevertheless morally justified. Instead, he will endeavor to show in one way or another that it is really inaccurate to call his conduct illegal at all. Now it looks as though this phenomenon can be readily accounted for. People try to resist the accusation of illegality, it might be argued, for the simple reason that they wish to avoid being punished. But what is interesting and persuasive is the fact that people try just as hard to evade a charge of illegality even in those situations where the threat of punishment is simply not an important or even relevant consideration.

The cases of the recent sit-ins or freedom rides are apt. To be sure, the claim was that the preservation of segregated lunchcounters, waiting rooms, and the like was morally indefensible. But an important justification for the rightness of the

[9] It is worth emphasizing that I am not at all interested in the claim—which in many ways is an odd one to belabor—that there is a logical relationship between disobeying the law and acting illegally. See, e.g., Carnes, "Why Should I Obey the Law?" 71 *Ethics* 14 (1960).

[10] Professor Fuller may hold to some version of this view in his article, "Positivism and Fidelity to Law—A Reply to Professor Hart," 71 *Harv. L. Rev.* 630, 656 (1958), where, after characterizing the position of legal positivism as one which says that "On the one hand, we have an amoral datum called law, which has the peculiar quality of creating a moral duty to obey it. On the other hand, we have a moral duty to do what we think is right and decent." Professor Fuller goes on to criticize this bifurcation of law and morality on the grounds that "The 'dilemma' it states has the verbal formulation of a problem, but the problem it states makes no sense. It is like saying I have to choose between giving food to a starving man and being mimsey with the borogroves. I do not think it unfair to the positivistic philosophy to say that it never gives any coherent meaning to the moral obligation of fidelity to law."

Others who at least suggest adherence to such a position are: Kurt Baier, *The Moral Point of View* (Ithaca: Cornell University Press, 1965), 134; P. Nowell-Smith, *Ethics* (New Orleans: Pelican, 1959), 236–237; and Thomas D. Weldon, *The Vocabulary of Politics* (Melbourne, London: Penguin Books, 1953), 57, 62, 66–67. And there are surely passages in Hobbes that could also be read in this way. See, e.g., Hobbes, *Leviathan,* chs. XIII, XVIII. The claim that *illegal* entails *immoral* is closely related to, but surely distinguishable from, the position that Professor Fuller, among many others, may also hold, namely, that there are certain minimum "moral" requirements that must be met before any rule can be a law.

actions employed in integrating these facilities in the fashion selected rested upon the insistence that the perpetuation of segregation in these circumstances was itself illegal. One primary claim for the rightness of freedom rides was that these were not instances of disobeying the law. They were instead attempts to invoke judicial and executive protection of legal, indeed constitutional, rights. While there were some, no doubt, who might have insisted upon the rightness of sit-ins even if they were clearly illegal, most people were confident of the blamelessness of the participants just because it was plain that their actions were not, in the last analysis, illegal. Were it evident that sit-ins were truly illegal many might hold a different view about the rightness of sitting-in as a means to bring about integrated facilities.

Language commonly invoked in the course of disputes between nations furnishes another equally graphic illustration of the same point. In the continuing controversy over the status of Berlin, for instance, both the United States and Russia have relied upon claims of legality and have been sensitive to charges of illegality, to an appreciably greater extent than one would otherwise have supposed. And much the same can be said of the more recent dispute between India and China. Now if nations which have little to fear in the way of the imposition of sanctions for acting illegally are nevertheless extraordinarily sensitive to charges of illegal conduct, this also may be taken as evidence of the fact that *illegality* implies *immorality*.

Wholly apt, too, was the controversy over the Eichmann trial. To some, the fact that the seizure and trial of Eichmann by Israel was illegal was sufficient to cast grave doubts upon the justifiability of the proceedings. To others, the charge of illegality made it necessary to demonstrate that nothing really illegal had occurred. What is significant about all this is the fact that all of the disputants implicitly acknowledged that illegality was something which did have to be worried about.

Such in brief is the argument which might be advanced and the "evidence" which might be adduced to support it. I think that such an argument is not persuasive, and I can best show this to be so in the following fashion.

Consider the case of a law that makes it a felony to perform an abortion upon a woman unless the abortion is necessary to preserve *her* life. Suppose a teenager, the daughter of a local minister, has been raped on her way home from school by an escapee from a state institution for mental defectives. Suppose further that the girl has become pregnant and has been brought to a reputable doctor who is asked to perform an abortion. And suppose, finally, that the doctor concludes after examining the girl that her life will not be endangered by giving birth to the child.[11] An abortion under these circumstances is, it seems fair to say, illegal.[12] Yet, we would surely find both intelligible and appealing the doctor's claim that he was nonetheless justified in disobeying the law by performing an abortion on the girl. I at least can see nothing logically odd or inconsistent about recognizing both that there is a law prohibiting this conduct and that further questions concerning the rightness of obedience would be relevant and, perhaps, decisive. Thus I can see nothing logically odd about describing this as a case in which the

[11] These facts are taken from Packer & Gampell, *Therapeutic Abortion: A Problem in Law and Medicine*, 11 *Stan. L. Rev.* 417 (1959), where they are introduced in a different context.

[12] Such would seem to be the case in California, for example, where *Cal. Pen. Code* § 274 makes the performance of an abortion a felony unless the abortion is necessary to preserve the life of the pregnant woman.

performance of the abortion could be both illegal and morally justified.[13]

There is, no doubt, a heroic defense which can be made to the above. It would consist of the insistence that the activity just described simply cannot be both illegal and justified. Two alternatives are possible. First, one might argue that the commission of the abortion would indeed have been justified if it were not proscribed by the law. But since it is so prohibited, the abortion is wrong. Now if this is a point about the appropriateness of kinds of reasons, I can only note that referring the action to a valid law does not seem to preclude asking meaningful questions about the obligatoriness of the action. If this is a point about language or concepts it does seem to be perfectly intelligible to say that the conduct is both illegal and morally justified. And if this is, instead, an *argument* for the immorality of ever disobeying a valid law, then it surely requires appreciable substantiation and not mere assertion.

Second, one might take a different line and agree that other questions can be asked about the conduct, but that is because the commission of the abortion under these circumstances simply cannot be illegal. The difficulty here, however, is that it is hard to understand what is now meant by *illegal.* Of course, I am not claiming that in the case as I have described it, it is clear that the performance of the abortion must be illegal. It might not be. But it might be. Were we to satisfy all the usual tests that we do invoke when we determine that a given course of conduct is illegal, and were someone still to maintain that because the performance of the abortion is here morally justified it cannot be illegal, then the burden is on the proponent of this view to make clear how we are to decide when conduct is illegal. And it would further be incumbent upon him to demonstrate what seems to be highly dubious, namely, that greater clarity and insight could somehow be attained through a radical change in our present terminology. It appears to be a virtually conclusive refutation to observe that there has never been a legal system whose criteria of validity—no matter how sophisticated, how rational and how well defined—themselves guaranteed that morally justified action would never be illegal.

Thus an argument as strong as any of the above must fail. There is, of course, a weaker version which may be more appealing. If it is true that there is something disturbing about justifying actions that are conceded to be illegal, then one way to account for this is to insist that there is a logical connection between the concepts involved, but it is something less than the kind of implication already discussed. Perhaps it is correct that *illegal* does not entail *immoral; illegal* might nevertheless entail *prima facie immoral.* The evidence adduced tends to show that among one's moral obligations is the prima facie duty to obey the law.[14]

Once again, it is somewhat difficult to know precisely what to make of such a claim. It is hard to see how one would decide what was to count as evidence or

[13] I am supposing, of course, that one would regard the performance of the abortion—in the absence of the relevant penal law—as clearly morally justified. If one disagrees with this assessment of the morality of the case, then some other example ought to be substituted. One likely candidate, drawn from our own history, is that of the inherent rightness in refusing to return an escaped Negro slave to his "owner." If one believes that refusing to do so would be clearly justifiable, then consider whether the existence of the fugitive slave laws necessarily rendered a continued refusal unjustified.

[14] Sir W. David Ross, for example, suggests that the obligation to obey the law is a prima facie obligation which is a compound of three more simple prima facie duties. Ross, *The Right and the Good* (Oxford: Clarendon Press, 1930), 27–28.

whether the evidence was persuasive. At a minimum, it is not difficult to imagine several equally plausible alternative explanations of the disturbing character of accusations of illegal activity. In addition, to know only that one has a prima facie duty to obey the law is not to know a great deal. In particular, one does not know how or when that obligation can be overridden. And, of course, even if it is correct that acting illegally logically implies acting prima facie immorally, this in no way shows that people may not often be morally justified in acting illegally. At most, it demands that they have some good reason for acting illegally; at best, it requires what has already been hypothesized, namely, that the action in question, while illegal, be morally justified.

Thus, it is clear that if the case against ever acting illegally is to be made out, conceptual analysis alone cannot do it. Indeed, arguments of quite another sort must be forthcoming. And it is to these that I now turn.

III

One such argument, and the most common argument advanced, goes something like this: The reason why one ought never to disobey the law is simply that the consequences would be disastrous if everybody disobeyed the law. The reason why disobedience is never right becomes apparent once we ask the question "But what if everyone did that?"

Consider again the case of the doctor who has to decide whether he is justified in performing an illegal abortion. If he only has a prima facie duty to obey the law it looks as though he might justifiably decide that in this case his prima facie obligation is overridden by more stringent conflicting obligations. Or, if he is simply a utilitarian, it appears that he might rightly conclude that the consequences of disobeying the abortion law would be on the whole and in the long run less deleterious than those of obeying. But this is simply a mistake. The doctor would inevitably be neglecting the most crucial factor of all, namely, that in performing the abortion he was disobeying the law. And imagine what would happen if everyone went around disobeying the law. The alternatives are obeying the law and general disobedience. The choice is between any social order and chaos. As President Kennedy correctly observed, if any law is disobeyed, then no law can be free from doubt, no citizen safe from his neighbor.

Such an argument, while perhaps overdrawn, is by no means uncommon.[15] Yet, as it stands, it is an essentially confused one. Its respective claims, if they are to be fairly evaluated, must be delineated with some care.

At a minimum, the foregoing attack upon the possibility of justified disobedience might be either one or both of two radically different kinds of objection. The first, which relates to the consequences of an act of disobedience, is essentially a *causal* argument. The second questions the *principle* that any proponent of justified disobedience invokes. As to the causal argument, it is always relevant to point out that any act of disobedience may have certain consequences simply because it is an act of disobedience. Once the occurrence of the act is known, for example, ex-

[15] Socrates, for instance, supposes that were he to escape he might properly be asked: "[W]hat are you about? Are you going by an act of yours to overturn us—the laws and the whole state, as far as in you lies? Do you imagine that a state can subsist and not be overthrown, in which the decisions of law have no power, but are set aside and overthrown by individuals?" Plato, *Crito*. Analogous arguments can be found in, for example: John Austin, *The Province of Jurisprudence Determined*, 52–53; Hobbes, *Leviathan*, ch. XV; Hume, *A Treatise of Human Nature*, bk. III, pt. II, 3, 6, 8, 9; Toulmin, *An Examination of the Place of Reason in Ethics* (Cambridge: The University Press, 1950), 151.

penditure of the state's resources may become necessary. The time and energy of the police will probably be turned to the task of discovering who it was who did the illegal act and of gathering evidence relevant to the offense. And other resources might be expended in the prosecution and adjudication of the case against the perpetrator of the illegal act. Illustrations of this sort could be multiplied, no doubt, but I do not think either that considerations of this sort are very persuasive or that they have been uppermost in the minds of those who make the argument now under examination. Indeed, if the argument is a causal one at all, it consists largely of the claim that any act of disobedience will itself cause, to some degree or other, general disobedience of all laws; it will cause or help to cause the overthrow or dissolution of the state. And while it is possible to assert that any act of disobedience will tend to further social disintegration or revolution, it is much more difficult to see why this must be so.

The most plausible argument would locate this causal efficacy in the kind of example set by any act of disobedience. But how plausible is this argument? It is undeniable, of course, that the kind of example that will be set is surely a relevant factor. Yet, there is nothing that precludes any proponent of justified disobedience from taking this into account. If, for example, others will somehow infer from the doctor's disobedience of the abortion law that they are justified in disobeying *any* law under *any* circumstances, then the doctor ought to consider this fact. This is a consequence—albeit a lamentable one—of his act of disobedience. Similarly, if others will extract the proper criterion from the act of disobedience, but will be apt to misapply it in practice, then this too ought to give the doctor pause. It, too, is a consequence of acting.[16] But if the argument is that disobedience would be wrong even if no bad example were set and no other deleterious consequences likely, then the argument must be directed against the principle the doctor appeals to in disobeying the law, and not against the consequences of his disobedience at all.

As to the attack upon a principle of justified disobedience, as a principle, the response "But what if everyone disobeyed the law?" does appear to be a good way to point up both the inherent inconsistency of almost any principle of justified disobedience and the manifest undesirability of adopting such a principle. Even if one need not worry about what others will be led to do by one's disobedience, there is surely something amiss if one cannot consistently defend his right to do what one is claiming he is right in doing.

In large measure, such an objection is unreal. The appeal to "But what if everyone did that?" loses much, if not all, of its persuasiveness once we become clearer about what precisely the "did that" refers to. If the question "But what if everyone did that?" is simply another way of asking "But what if everybody disobeyed the law?" or "But what if people generally disobeyed the laws?" then the question is surely quasi-rhetorical. To urge general or indiscriminate disobedience to laws is to invoke a principle that, if coherent, is manifestly indefensible. It is equally plain, however, that with few exceptions such a principle has never been seriously espoused. Anyone who claims that there are actions that are both illegal and justified surely need not be thereby asserting that it is right generally to disobey all laws or even any particular law. It is surely not inconsistent to assert both that indiscriminate disobedience is indefensible and that discriminate disobedience is morally right and proper conduct. Nor, analogously, is it at all evident that a person who claims to be justified in performing an illegal action is thereby committed to or giving endorsement to the principle that the en-

[16] For a very special and related version of this argument, see text at section V.

tire legal system ought to be overthrown or renounced. At a minimum, therefore, the appeal to "But what if everyone did that?" cannot by itself support the claim that one has an absolute obligation to obey the law—that disobeying the law can never be truly justified.

There is, however, a distinguishable but related claim which merits very careful attention—if for no other reason than the fact that it is so widely invoked today by moral philosophers. The claim is simply this: While it may very well be true that there are situations in which a person will be justified in disobeying the law, it is surely not true that disobedience can ever be justified solely on the grounds that the consequences of disobeying the particular law were in that case on the whole less deleterious than those of obedience.[17]

This claim is particularly relevant at this juncture because one of the arguments most often given to substantiate it consists of the purported demonstration of the fact that any principle which contained a proviso permitting a general appeal to consequences must itself be incoherent. One of the most complete statements of the argument is found in Marcus Singer's provocative book, *Generalization in Ethics:*

> Suppose, . . . that I am contemplating evading the payment of income taxes. I might reason that I need the money more than the government does, that the amount I have to pay is so small in comparison with the total amount to be collected that the government will never miss it. Now I surely know perfectly well that if I evade the payment of taxes this will not cause others to do so as well. For one thing, I am certainly not so foolish as to publicize my action. But even if I were, and the fact became known, this would still not cause others to do the same, unless it also became known that I was being allowed to get away with it. In the latter case the practice might tend to become widespread, but this would be a consequence, not of my action, but of the failure of the government to take action against me. Thus there is no question of my act being wrong because it would set a bad example. It would set no such example, and to suppose that it must, because it would be wrong, is simply a confusion. . . . Given all this, then if the reasons mentioned would justify me in evading the payment of taxes, they would justify everyone whatsoever in doing the same thing. For everyone can argue in the same way—everyone can argue that if he breaks the law this will not cause others to do the same. The supposition that this is a justification, therefore, leads to a contradiction.
>
> I conclude from this that, just as the reply "Not everyone will do it" is irrelevant to the generalization argument, so is the fact that one knows or believes that not everyone will do the same; and that, in particular, the characteristic of knowing or believing that one's act will remain exceptional cannot be used to define a class of exceptions to the rule. One's knowledge or belief that not everyone will act in the same way in similar circumstances cannot therefore be regarded as part of the circumstances of one's action. One's belief that not everyone will do the same does not make one's circumstances relevantly different from the circumstances of others, or relevantly different from those in which the act is wrong. Indeed, on the supposition that it does, one's circumstances could never be specified, for the specification would involve an infinite regress.[18]

[17] This is a particular illustration of the more general claim that for one reason or another utilitarianism cannot be a defensible or intelligible moral theory when construed as permitting one's moral obligation to do any particular action to be overridden by a direct appeal to the consequences of performing that particular action. For recent statements of the claim see, e.g., Nowell-Smith, op. cit. supra note 10; John Rawls, "Two Concepts of Rules," 64 *Philosophical Rev.* 3 (1955) [pp. 175–194 above], in Fred Olafson, ed., *Society, Law, and Morality* (Englewood Cliffs, N. J.: Prentice-Hall, 1961), 420; Singer, *Generalization in Ethics* (New York: Knopf, 1961), 61–138, 178–216; Toulmin, op. cit. supra note 15, at 144–165; Harrison, "Utilitarianism, Universalization, and Our Duty To Be Just," 53 *PAS* 105 (1952–1953) [pp. 151–167 above].

For some criticisms of this restriction on utilitarianism see, e.g., Wasserstrom, *The Judicial Decision* (Stanford, Calif.: The Stanford University Press, 1961), 118–137. But see Hart, "Book Review," 14 *Stan. L. Rev.* 919, 924–926 (1962).

[18] Singer, op. cit. supra note 17, at 149–150.

Singer's argument is open to at least two different interpretations. One quite weak interpretation is this: A person cannot be morally justified in acting as he does unless he is prepared to acknowledge that everyone else in the identical circumstances would also be right in acting the same way. If the person insists that he is justified in performing a certain action because the consequences of acting in that way are more desirable than those of acting in any alternative fashion, then he must be prepared to acknowledge that anyone else would also be justified in doing that action whenever the consequences of doing that action were more desirable than those of acting in any alternative fashion. To take Singer's own example: A person, *A*, could not be morally justified in evading the payment of his taxes on the grounds that the consequences of nonpayment were *in his case* more beneficial, all things considered, than those of payment, unless *A* were prepared to acknowledge that any other person, *X*, would also be justified in evading his, *i.e.*, *X's* taxes, if it is the case that the consequences of *X*'s nonpayment would in *X*'s case be more beneficial, all things considered, than those of payment. If this is Singer's point, it is, for reasons already elaborated, unobjectionable.[19]

But Singer seems to want to make a stronger point as well. He seems to believe that even a willingness to generalize in this fashion could not justify acting in this way. In part his argument appears to be that this somehow will permit everyone to justify nonpayment of taxes; and in part his argument appears to be that there is a logical absurdity involved in attempting to make the likelihood of other people's behavior part of the specification of the relevant consequences of a particular act. Both of these points are wrong. To begin with, on a common sense level it is surely true that the effect which one's action will have on other people's behavior is a relevant consideration. For as was pointed out earlier, if *A* determines that other people will be, or may be, led to evade *their* taxes even when the consequences of nonpayment will in their cases be less beneficial than those of payment, then this is a consequence of *A*'s action which he must take into account and attempt to balance against the benefits which would accrue to society from his nonpayment. Conversely, if for one reason or another *A* can determine that his act of nonpayment will not have this consequence, this, too, must be relevant. In this sense, at least, other people's prospective behavior is a relevant consideration.

More importantly, perhaps, it is surely a mistake—although a very prevalent one in recent moral philosophy—to suppose that permitting a general appeal to consequences would enable everyone to argue convincingly that he is justified in evading his taxes. Even if I adopt the principle that everyone is justified in evading his taxes whenever the consequences of evasion are on the whole less deleterious than those of payment, this in no way entails that I or anyone else will always, or ever, be justified in evading my taxes. It surely need not turn out to be the case—even if no one else will evade his taxes—that the consequences will on the whole be beneficial if I succeed in evading mine. It might surely be the case that I will spend

[19] Neither Singer nor I have adequately refuted the confirmed ethical egoist who insists that he is prepared to generalize but only in the sense that *X*'s nonpayment is justified if, and only if, the consequences of *X*'s nonpayment would in *X*'s case be more beneficial *to A* than those of payment. This is a problem which surely requires more careful attention than it typically receives. It will not do simply to insist that the egoist does not understand ordinary moral discourse. Instead, what must be demonstrated are the respects in which the egoist's position is an inherently unjust one. But to make this showing is beyond the scope of this article.

the money saved improvidently or foolishly; it might very well be true that the government will make much better use of the money. Indeed, the crucial condition which must not be ignored and which Singer does ignore is the condition which stipulates that the avoidance of one's taxes in fact be optimific, that is, more desirable than any other course of conduct.

The general point is simply that it is an empirical question—at least in theory—what the consequences of any action will be. And it would surely be a mistake for me or anyone else to suppose that that action whose consequences are most pleasing to me—in either the short or long run—will in fact be identical with that action whose consequences are on the whole most beneficial to society. Where the demands of self-interest are strong, as in the case of the performance of an unpleasant task like paying taxes, there are particular reasons for being skeptical of one's conclusion that the consequences of nonpayment would in one's own case truly be beneficial. But once again there is no reason why there might not be cases in which evasion of taxes would be truly justified, nor is there any reason why someone could not consistently and defensibly endorse nonpayment whenever these circumstances were in fact present.

There is one final point which Singer's discussion suggests and which does appear to create something of a puzzle. Suppose that I believe that I am justified in deliberately trespassing on an atomic test site, and thereby disobeying the law, because I conclude that this is the best way to call attention to the possible consequences of continued atmospheric testing or nuclear war. I conclude that the consequences of trespassing will on the whole be more beneficial than any alternative action I can take. But suppose I also concede—what very well may be the case—that if everyone were to trespass, even for this same reason and in the same way, the consequences would be extremely deleterious. Does it follow that there is something logically incoherent about my principle of action? It looks as though there is, for it appears that I am here denying others the right to do precisely what I claim I am right in doing. I seem to be claiming, in effect, that it is right for me to trespass on government property in order to protest atomic testing only if it is the case that others, even under identical circumstances, will not trespass. Thus, it might be argued, I appear to be unwilling or unable to generalize my principle of conduct.

This argument is unsound, for there is a perfectly good sense in which I am acting on a principle which is coherent and which is open to anyone to adopt. It is simply the principle that one is justified in trespassing on government property whenever—among other things—it happens to be the case that one can say accurately that others will not in fact act on that same principle. Whether anyone else will at any given time act on any particular principle is an empirical question. It is, to repeat what has already been said, one of the possible circumstances which can be part of the description of a class of situations. There is, in short, nothing logically self-contradictory or absurd about making the likelihood of even identical action one of the relevant justifying considerations. And there is, therefore, no reason why the justifiability of any particular act of disobedience cannot depend, among other things, upon the probable conduct of others.

IV

It would not be at all surprising if at this stage one were to feel considerable dissatisfaction with the entire cast of the discussion so far. In particular, one might well believe that the proverbial dead horse has received still another flaying for the simple reason that no one has ever seriously argued that people are never justified in disobeying the law. One might insist, for instance, that neither Socrates nor President Kennedy was talking about all law in all legal systems everywhere. And one might urge, instead, that their claims concerning the unjustifiability of any act of disobedience rest covertly, if not overtly, on the assumption that the disobedience in question was to take place in a society in which the lawmaking procedures and other political institutions were those which are characteristic of an essentially democratic, or free, society. This is, of course, an important and plausible restriction upon the original claim, and the arguments which might support it must now be considered.

While there are several things about a liberal, democratic or free society which might be thought to preclude the possibility of justified disobedience, it is evident that the presence of all the important constitutive institutions *cannot* guarantee that unjust or immoral laws will not be enacted. For the strictest adherence to principles of representative government, majority rule, frequent and open elections and, indeed, the realization of all of the other characteristics of such a society, in no way can insure that laws of manifest immorality will not be passed and enforced. And if even the ideal democratic society might enact unjust laws, no existing society can plausibly claim as much. Thus, if the case against the possibility of justified disobedience is to depend upon the democratic nature of the society in question, the case cannot rest simply on the claim that the only actions which will be made illegal are those which are already immoral.

What then are the arguments which might plausibly be advanced? One very common argument goes like this: It is, of course, true that even democratically selected and democratically constituted legislatures can and do make mistakes. Nevertheless, a person is never justified in disobeying the law as long as there exist alternative, "peaceful" procedures by which to bring about the amendment or repeal of undesirable or oppressive laws. The genuine possibility that rational persuasion and argument can bring a majority to favor any one of a variety of competing views, both requires that disapproval always be permitted and forbids that disobedience ever be allowed. This is so for several reasons.

First, it is clearly unfair and obviously inequitable to accept the results of any social decision-procedure only in those cases in which the decision reached was one of which one approves, and to refuse to accept those decisions which are not personally satisfying. If there is one thing which participation, and especially voluntary participation, in a decision-procedure entails, it is that all of the participants must abide by the decision regardless of what it happens to be. If the decision-procedure is that of majority rule, then this means that any person must abide by those decisions in which he was in a minority abide when he is a member of the majority.

As familiar as the argument is, its plausibility is far from assured. On one reading, at least, it appears to be one version of the universalization argument. As such, it goes like this. Imagine any person, *A*, who has voted with the majority to pass a law making a particular kind of conduct illegal. *A* surely would not and could not acknowledge the right of any person voting with the minority justifiably to disobey that law. But, if *A* will not and cannot recognize a right of justified disobedience here, then *A* certainly cannot consistently or fairly claim any right of justified disobedience on his part in those cases in which he, *A*, happened to end up being in a minority. Thus, justified disobedience can never be defensible.

This argument is fallacious. For a person who would insist that justified disobedience was possible even after majoritarian decision-making could very plausibly and consistently acknowledge the right of any person to disobey the law under appropriate circumstances regardless of how that person had voted on any particular law. Consider, once again, the case already put of the doctor and the pregnant girl. The doctor can surely be consistent in claiming both that circumstances make the performance of the illegal abortion justified and that any comparable action would also be right irrespective of how the actor, or the doctor, or anyone else, happened to have voted on the abortion law, or any other law. The point is simply that there is no reason why any person cannot consistently: (1) hold the view that majority decision-making is the best of all forms of decision-making; (2) participate voluntarily in the decision-making process; and (3) believe that it is right for *anyone* to disobey majority decisions whenever the relevant moral circumstances obtain, *e.g.*, whenever the consequence of obedience to that law at that time would on the whole be more deleterious than those of obedience.

But this may be deemed too facile an answer; it also may be thought to miss the point. For it might be argued that there is a serious logical inconsistency of a different sort which must arise whenever a voluntary participant in a social decision-procedure claims that not all the decisions reached in accordance with that procedure need be obeyed. Take the case of majority rule. It is inconsistent for anyone voluntarily to participate in the decision-process and yet at the same time to reserve the right to refuse to abide by the decision reached in any particular case. The problem is not an inability to universalize a principle of action. The problem is rather that of making any sense at all out of the notion of having a majority decide anything—of having a procedure by which to make group decisions. The problem is, in addition, that of making any sense at all out of the fact of voluntary participation in the decision-procedure—in knowing what this participation can come to if it does not mean that every participant is bound by all of the decisions which are reached. What can their participation mean if it is not an implicit promise to abide by all decisions reached? And even if the point is not a logical one, it is surely a practical one. What good could there possibly be to a scheme, an institutional means for making social decisions, which did not bind even the participants to anything?

The answer to this argument—or set of arguments—is wholly analogous to that which has been given earlier. But because of the importance and prevalence of the argument some repetition is in order.

One can simply assert that the notion of any social decision-making procedure is intelligible only if it entails that all participants always abide by all of the decisions which are made, no matter what those decisions are. Concomitantly, one can simply insist that any voluntary participant in the decision-process must be consenting or promising to abide by all decisions which are reached. But one cannot give as a plausible reason for this assertion the fact that the notion of group decision-making becomes incoherent if anything less in the way of adherence is required of all participants. And one cannot cite as a plausible reason for this assertion the fact that the notion of voluntary participation loses all meaning if anything less than a promise of absolute obedience is inferred.

It is true that the notion of a group

decision-making procedure would be a meaningless notion if there were no respects in which a group decision was in any way binding upon each of the participants. Decisions which in no way bind anyone to do anything are simply not decisions. And it is also true that voluntary participation is an idle, if not a vicious, act if it does not commit each participant to something. If any voluntary participant properly can wholly ignore the decisions which are reached, then something is surely amiss.

But to say all this is not to say very much. Group decision-making can have a point just because it does preclude any participant from taking some actions which in the absence of the decision, he might have been justified in performing. And voluntary participation can still constitute a promise of sorts that one will not perform actions which, in the absence of voluntary participation, might have been justifiable. If the fact of participation in a set of liberal political institutions does constitute a promise of sorts, it can surely be a promise that the participant will not disobey a law just because obedience would be inconvenient or deleterious to him. And if this is the scope of the promise, then the fact of voluntary participation does make a difference. For in the absence of the participation in the decision to make this conduct illegal, inconvenience to the actor might well have been a good reason for acting in a certain way. Thus, participation can create new obligations to behave in certain ways without constituting a promise not to disobey the law under any circumstances. And if this is the case, adherence to a principle of justified disobedience is not inconsistent with voluntary participation in the decision-making process.

Indeed, a strong point can be made. The notion of making laws through voluntary participation in democratic institutions is not even inconsistent with the insistence that disobedience is justified whenever the consequences of disobedience are on the whole more beneficial than those of obedience. This is so because a promise can be a meaningful promise even if an appeal to the consequences of performing the promise can count as a sufficient reason for not performing the promise.[20] And if this is the case for

[20] The point here is analogous to that made in the discussion of Singer's argument. Moral philosophers have often argued that one cannot appeal simply to the consequences of performing or not performing a particular promise as a reason for not performing that promise. And the reason why this is so is that the notion of having promised to do something would be unintelligible if the promisor could always, when the time came for performance, be excused if it were the case that the consequences of nonperformance were more beneficial than those of performance. This would make promising unintelligible, so the argument goes, because promising entails or means obligating oneself to do something. But if the appeal to consequences is what is to be determinative of one's obligations, then the promise becomes a wholly superfluous, meaningless act. Rawls, for instance, puts the point this way: "Various defenses for not keeping one's promise are allowed, but among them there isn't the one that, on general utilitarian grounds, the promiser (truly) thought his action best on the whole, even though there may be the defense that the consequences of keeping one's promise would have been *extremely* severe. While there are too many complexities here to consider all the necessary details, one can see that the general defense isn't allowed if one asks the following question: What would one say of someone who, when asked why he broke his promise, replied simply that breaking it was best on the whole? Assuming that his reply is sincere, and that his belief was reasonable (i.e., one need not consider the possibility that he was mistaken), I think that one would question whether or not he knows what it means to say 'I promise' (in the appropriate circumstances). It would be said of someone who used this excuse without further explanation that he didn't understand what defenses the practice, which defines a promise, allows to him. If a child were to use this excuse one would correct him, for it is part of the way one is taught the concept of

promises generally, it can be no less the case for the supposed promise to obey the law.

Finally, even if it were correct that voluntary participation implied a promise to obey, and even if it were the case that the promise must be a promise not to disobey on consequential grounds, all of this would still not justify the conclusion that one ought never to disobey the law. It would, instead, only demonstrate that disobeying the law must be prima facie wrong, that everyone has a prima facie obligation to obey the law. This is so just because it is sometimes right even to break one's own promises. And if this, too, is a characteristic of promises generally, it is, again, no less a characteristic of the promise to obey the law.

The notions of promise, consent, or voluntary participation do not, however, exhaust the possible sources of the obligation to obey the laws of a democracy. In particular, there is another set of arguments which remains to be considered. It is that which locates the rightness of obedience in the way in which any act of disobedience improperly distributes certain burdens and benefits among the citizenry. Professor Wechsler, for example, sees any act of disobedience to the laws of the United States as "the ultimate negation of all neutral principles, to take the benefits accorded by the constitutional system, including the national market and common defense, while denying it allegiance when a special burden is imposed. That certainly is the antithesis of law."[21]

On the surface, at least, Professor Wechsler's claim seems overly simple; it appears to be the blanket assertion that the receipt by any citizen, through continued, voluntary presence of benefits of this character necessarily implies that no act of disobedience could be justified. To disobey any law after having voluntarily received these benefits would be, he seems to suggest, so unjust that there could never be overriding considerations. This surely is both to claim too much for the benefits of personal and commercial security and to say too little for the character of all types of disobedience. For even if the receipt of benefits such as these did simply impose an obligation to obey the law, it is implausible to suppose that the obligation

---

a promise to be corrected if one uses this excuse. The point of having the practice would be lost if the practice did allow this excuse." Rawls, in Olafson, op cit. supra note 17, 429–430.

Now I am not concerned to dispute Rawls's remark if taken as descriptive of our institution of promising. For what I am here concerned with is the claim, implicit throughout, that promising would be a meaningless or pointless activity if the excuse were permitted. I should say though that the passage quoted from Rawls is not, I think, central to his main argument. I think I can show this to be a mistake through the following two examples.

(1) *A* has promised *B* that he will mow *B*'s lawn for *B* on Sunday. On Sunday, *A* is feeling lazy and so he refuses to mow the lawn.

(2) *A* is sitting home on Sunday, feeling lazy, when *B* calls him up and asks him to come over and mow *B*'s lawn. *A* refuses to mow the lawn.

Ceteris paribus, it would be the case that *A* is wrong in refusing to mow *B*'s lawn in example (1) but not blamable for refusing to mow *B*'s lawn in example (2). Why is this so? Because *A*'s promise to mow *B*'s lawn creates an obligation which in the absence of such a promise is nonexistent. If this is so, then permitting the general utilitarian defense does not make a promise a meaningless gesture. This is so because there are many situations in which, in the absence of having promised to do so, we are not, for example, obligated to inconvenience ourselves simply for another's convenience. Personal inconvenience then might be one excuse which must be inconsistent with the practice of promising, even if the general appeal to consequences is not. Thus, promising would and could have a real point even if the general appeal to consequences were a good defense.

[21] Wechsler, "Toward Neutral Principles of Constitutional Law," 73 *Harv. L. Rev.* 1, 35 (1959).

thereby imposed would be one that stringent.

But there is a more involved aspect of Professor Wechsler's thesis—particularly in his insistence that disobedience of the law, where benefits of this kind have been received, is the negation of all neutral principles. I am not at all certain that I understand precisely what this means, but there are at least two possible interpretations: (1) Unless everyone always obeyed the law no one would receive these obviously valuable benefits. (2) Since the benefits one receives depend upon the prevalence of conditions of uniform obedience, it follows that no one who willingly receives these benefits can justly claim them without himself obeying. The first has already been sufficiently considered.[22] The second, while not unfamiliar, merits some further attention.

In somewhat expanded form, the argument is simply this. What makes it possible for any particular person to receive and enjoy the benefits of general, personal and economic security is the fact that everyone else obeys the law. Now, if injustice is to be avoided, it is surely the case that any other person is equally entitled to these same benefits. But he will have this security only if everyone else obeys the law. Hence the receipt of benefits at others' expense requires repayment in kind. And this means universal obedience to the law.[23]

There are two features of this argument which are puzzling. First, it is far from clear that the benefits of security received by anyone necessarily depend upon absolute obedience on the part of everyone else. It just might be the case that an even greater quantum of security would have accrued from something less than total obedience. But even if I am wrong here, there is a more important point at issue. For reasons already discussed, it is undeniable that even in a democracy a price would be paid, for instance, were the doctor to refuse to perform the abortion because it was illegal. If this is so, then the fact that a person received benefits from

[22] See text at section III.

[23] For a somewhat related characterization of the source of the obligation to obey the law, see Hart, "Are There Any Natural Rights?," 64 *Philosophical Rev.* 175, 185 (1955), in Olafson, *Law, Society, and Morality* 173, 180–181 (1961): "A third very important source of special rights and obligations which we recognize in many spheres of life is what may be termed mutuality of restrictions. . . . In its bare schematic outline it is this: When a number of persons conduct any joint enterprise according to rules and thus restrict their liberty, those who have submitted to these restrictions when required have a right to a similar submission from those who have benefited by their submission. The rules may provide that officials should have authority to enforce obedience and make further rules, and this will create a structure of legal rights and duties, but the moral obligation to obey the rules in such circumstances is *due to* the cooperating members of the society, and they have the correlative moral right to obedience. In social situations of this sort (of which political society is the most complex example) the obligation to obey the rules is something distinct from whatever other moral obligations there may be for obedience in terms of good consequences (e.g., the prevention of suffering); the obligation is due to the cooperating members of the society as such and not because they are human beings on whom it would be wrong to inflict suffering."

I would point out only two things. First, as Professor Hart himself asserts—in a passage not quoted—the existence of this right in no way implies that one is never justified in disobeying the law. The right which any participating member has in others' obedience can justifiably be infringed in appropriate circumstances. Second, and here perhaps Professor Hart disagrees for reasons already elaborated, there is no reason that I can see why an appeal to the consequences of disobeying a particular law cannot be a sufficient justification for infringing upon that right. It is surely conceivable, at least, that this is all the submission to rules which anyone ought to have given, and hence all the submission which anyone is entitled to expect from others.

everyone else's obedience does not necessarily entail that it is unjust for him to fail to reciprocate in kind. The benefit of general security might not have been worth the cost. A greater degree of flexibility on the part of others, a general course of obedience except where disobedience was justified, might have yielded a greater benefit. People may, in short, have done more or less than they should have. And if they did, the fact that anyone or everyone benefited to some degree in no way requires that injustice can only be avoided through like and reciprocal conduct. If it is better, in at least some circumstances, to disobey a law than to obey it, there is surely nothing unjust about increasing the beneficial consequences to all through acts of *discriminate* disobedience.

If the argument based upon the effect of receipt of certain benefits is therefore not very persuasive, neither in most cases is the argument which is derived from the way in which any act of disobedience is thought to distribute burdens unfairly among the citizenry. The argument can be put very briefly: If there is one thing which any act of disobedience inevitably does, it is to increase the burdens which fall on all the law-abiding citizens. If someone disobeys the law even for what seems to be the best of reasons, he inevitably makes it harder—in some quite concrete sense—on everyone else. Hence, at a minimum this is a good reason not to disobey the law, and perhaps a sufficient reason as well.

This argument is appealing because there is at least one kind of case it fits very well. It is the case of taxation. For suppose the following, only somewhat unreal, conditions: that the government is determined to raise a specified sum of money through taxation, and that, in the long, if not the short, run it will do so by adjusting the tax rate to whatever percentage is necessary to produce the desired governmental income. Under such circumstances it could plausibly be argued that one of the truly inevitable results of a successfully executed decision to evade the payment of one's taxes—a decision made, moreover, on ostensibly justifiable grounds—is that every other member of society will thereby be required to pay a greater tax than would otherwise have been the case. Thus in some reasonably direct and obvious fashion any act of disobedience—particularly if undetected—does add to the burdens of everyone else. And surely this is to make out at least a strong case of prima facie injustice.

Now, for reasons already elaborated, it would be improper to conclude that evasion of one's taxes could never be justified. But the argument is persuasive in its insistence that it does provide a very good reason why evasion always must be justified and why it will seldom be justifiable. But even this feature of disobedience is not present in many cases. Tax evasion, as opposed to other kinds of potentially justified disobedience, is a special, far from typical case. And what is peculiar to it is precisely the fact that any act of disobedience to the tax laws arguably shifts or increases the burden upon others. Such is simply not true of most types of acts of disobedience because most laws do not prohibit or require actions which affect the distribution of resources in any very direct fashion.

Thus, if we take once again the case of the doctor who has decided that he is justified in performing an illegal abortion on the pregnant girl, it is extremely difficult, if not impossible, to locate the analogue of the shifting of burdens involved in tax evasion. How does the performance of the abortion thereby increase the "costs" to anyone else? The only suggestion which seems at all plausible is that which was noted earlier in a somewhat different context. Someone might argue that it is the occurrence of illegal actions which increase the cost of maintaining a police force, a judiciary and suitable correctional institutions. This cost is a burden which is borne by the citizenry as a whole. And hence, the doctor's illegal acts increase their burdens—albeit very slightly. The difficulty here is threefold. First, if the doctor's act is performed in secret and if it remains undetected, then it is hard to see how there is any shift of economic burden at all. Second, given the fact that police forces, courts and prisons will always be necessary as long as unjustified acts of disobedience are a feature of social existence, it is by no means apparent that the additional cost is anything but truly de minimus.[24] And third, the added costs, if any, are in the doctor's case assumed by the doctor *qua* member of the citizenry. He is not avoiding a burden; at most he adds something to everyone's—including his own—existing financial obligations. Thus, in cases such as these, it is not at all evident that disobedience need even be prima facie unjust and hence unjustified.

V

There is one final argument which requires brief elucidation and analysis. It is in certain respects a peculiarly instructive one both in its own right and in respect to the thesis of this article.

It may be true that on some particular occasions the consequences of disobeying a law will in fact be less deleterious on the whole than those of obeying it—even in a democracy. It may even be true that on some particular occasions disobeying a law will be just whereas obeying it would be unjust. Nevertheless, the reason why a person is never justified in disobeying a law—in a democracy—is simply this: The chances are so slight that he will disobey only those laws in only those cases in which he is in fact justified in doing so, that the consequences will on the whole be less deleterious if he never disobeys any law. Furthermore, since anyone must concede the right to everyone to disobey the law when the circumstances so demand it, the situation is made still worse. For once we entrust this right to everyone we can be sure that many laws will be disobeyed in a multitude of cases in which there was no real justification for disobedience. Thus, given what we know of the possibilities of human error and the actualities of human frailty, and given the tendency of democratic societies to make illegal only those actions which would, even in the absence of a law, be unjustified, we can confidently conclude that the consequences will on the whole and in the long run be best if no one ever takes it upon himself to "second-guess" the laws and to conclude that in his case his disobedience is justified.[25]

The argument is, in part, not very different from those previously considered. And thus, what is to be said about it is not very different either. Nonetheless, upon pain of being overly repetitive, I would insist that there is a weak sense in which the argument is quite persuasive and a strong sense in which it is not. For the argument makes, on one reading, too strong an empirical claim—the claim that the consequences will in the long run always in fact be better if no one in a democracy ever tries to decide when he is justified in disobeying the law. As it stands, there is no reason to believe that the claim is or must be true, that the consequences will always be better. Indeed, it

24 Curiously, perhaps, given a legal system in which laws are in general good and hence in which the possibility of justified disobedience is rare, the special or added cost of an occasional act of justified disobedience is diminished still further.

25 For fuller analyses and assessments of this argument in different contexts see, e.g., Rawls, supra note 17; Wasserstrom, op. cit. supra note 17, at 118–171.

is very hard to see why, despite the hypothesis, someone might still not be justified in some particular case in disobeying a law. Yet, viewed as a weaker claim, as a summary rule, it does embody a good deal that is worth remembering. It can, on this level, be understood to be a persuasive reminder of much that is relevant to disobedience: that in a democracy the chances of having to live under bad laws are reduced; that in a democracy there are typically less costly means available by which to bring about changes in the law; that in a democracy—as in life in general—a justified action may always be both inaptly and ineptly emulated; and that in a democracy—as in life in general—people often do make mistakes as to which of their own actions are truly justified. These are some of the lessons of human experience which are easy to forget and painful to relearn.

But there are other lessons, and they are worth remembering too. What is especially troubling about the claim that disobedience of the law is never justified, what is even disturbing about the claim that disobedience of the law is never justified in a democratic or liberal society, is the facility with which its acceptance can lead to the neglect of important moral issues. If no one is justified in disobeying the Supreme Court's decision in *Brown v. Board of Educ.*[26] this is so because, among other things there is much that is wrong with segregation. If there was much that was peculiarly wrong in Mississippi this fall, this was due to the fact, among other facts, that a mob howled and a governor raged when a court held that a person whose skin was black could go to a white university. Disobeying the law is often—even usually—wrong; but this is so largely because the illegal is usually restricted to the immoral and because morally right conduct is still less often illegal. But we must always be sensitive to the fact that this has not always been the case, is not now always the case and need not always be the case in the future. And undue concentration upon what is wrong with disobeying the law rather than upon the wrong which the law seeks to prevent can seriously weaken and misdirect that awareness.

[26] 347 U.S. 483 (1954).

B. J. Diggs / Rules and utilitarianism

Although moral rules have had a prominent place in recent moral philosophy, their character is not clear. One reason for this is the vagueness and ambiguity which infect the use of the term "rule": Philosophers tend to conceive of moral rules on some particular model, sometimes in a confused way, often innocently and without a clear view of the alternatives. J. Rawls called attention to one important instance of this: He pointed out that the tendency to regard rules as convenient guides, or as summaries of earlier experiences, seems to have blinded some philosophers ". . . to the significance of the distinction between justifying a practice and justifying a particular action falling under it. . . ."[1]

Partly as a consequence, utilitarianism has been interpreted in a special way as asserting that the rightness and wrongness of particular acts is decidable on general utilitarian grounds. This form of utilitarianism, so-called "act utilitarianism," is open to serious and well-known objections.[2]

The appeal of the recently more popular "rule utilitarianism" is that it is able to meet some of these objections and still retain the tie between morality and "the general welfare," which is one of the most attractive characteristics of utilitarianism. I shall argue in this paper, however, that rule utilitarians (and some of their critics, and many others who view moral rules in the same general way) have also tended unwittingly to adopt a particular kind of rule as the model of a moral rule. When this kind of rule has been delineated and alternatives noted, I think rule utilitarianism loses much of its initial appeal.

My object in this paper, however, is not so much to refute rule utilitarianism as to contribute to the clarification of moral rules. By distinguishing two kinds of rules I shall try to illuminate one of the fundamental options (as well as one of the

[1] "Two Concepts of Rules," *Philosophical Review* 64 (1955), 29–30 [pp. 192–193 above].

[2] Cf. e.g., R. B. Brandt, *Ethical Theory* (Englewood Cliffs, N.J.: Prentice-Hall, 1959), ch. 15.

Reprinted from the AMERICAN PHILOSOPHICAL QUARTERLY, *vol. 1, no. 1 (January 1964), pp. 32–44 by permission of the author and editors.*

fundamental confusions) open to moral theory. (1) The first kind of rule is exemplified by the rules which workers follow as part of their jobs; these rules may be used to describe a job. (2) The other kind of rule characterizes such common games as baseball, chess, and the like. Both kinds of rule define "practices," but the practices are very different. I think the easy tendency to confuse them may have blinded moral philosophers to significant distinctions between justifying a system of rules designed to contribute to some goal or product, justifying a system of rules which defines a "form of life" and justifying moral rules. Marking these distinctions should help clarify certain steps taken in recent moral philosophy: One should be able to appreciate more fully the point of Baier's assertion that although moral rules are "for the good of everyone alike," they are not designed to promote the greatest good of everyone.[3] One should also be able to see more clearly why Rawls maintains that the decision on the rules of justice is not properly conceived on the utilitarian model as an administrative decision on how to promote the greatest happiness.[4] The analysis of rules is illuminating, moreover, not only because it helps mark major differences of this kind, but also because it shows what is behind some of the twists and turns of moral theory.

I

1.0 The first kind of rule which I shall describe belongs to a large class of rules which I call "instrumental." All rules in this large class are adopted or followed as a means to an end, in order to "accomplish a purpose" or "get a job done." The simplest of these rules is the "practical maxim" which one ordinarily follows at his own pleasure, such as "Be sure the surface to be painted is thoroughly dry" or "Do not plant tomatoes until after the last frost."[5]

The instrumental rule to which I call attention is more complex. On many occasions when one wants a job done, either he is not in a position or not able or not willing to do the job himself. If he is in a position of power or authority or if he has money, he may simply order or hire others to "do the job" and leave it to them. In numerous cases, however, he himself lays down rules of procedure, and establishes "jobs" or "roles" in the institutional sense. A "job" in this latter sense is not a job to be "done," but a job to be "offered to" or "given" to a person. If a person "takes" or is "assigned" "the job" then we often think of him as under an obligation to "do his job," and this partly consists in his following rules. Instrumental rules of this kind, unlike practical maxims, have a social dimension: It *makes sense* to ask whether a job-holder (or role-taker) is *obligated* to follow a particular rule, or whether this is one of his *duties*, and the penalty attaching to a breach of the rules does not consist simply in his not "getting the job done."

Rules of this kind are found in very different institutions. Some are rules of a "job" in the ordinary sense. Others apply to anyone who voluntarily assumes a "role," such as "automobile driver." Others characterize a position which one is obliged to take by law, for example, that of private in the army. The goals which the rules are designed to serve may be ordinary products of labor, such as houses,

[3] Kurt Baier, *The Moral Point of View* (Ithaca, N.Y.: Cornell University Press, 1958), 200–204.

[4] "Justice as Fairness," *Philosophical Review* 67 (April 1958), 164–194. It will be clear that Rawls's analysis in "Two Concepts of Rules" does not support a utilitarian theory.

[5] Cf. Max Black, "Notes on the Meaning of 'Rule'," *Theoria* 24 (1958), 107–126, 139–161; reprinted in his *Models and Metaphors* (Ithaca, N.Y.: Cornell University Press, 1962), 95–139.

steel beams, etc.; or fairly specific goals such as "getting vehicles to their destinations safely and expeditiously"; or goals as general as "the national defense." In some cases the rules, differing from job to job, mark a division of labor, as the rules which say what factory workers, or the members of a platoon, are to do. In other cases, the same rules apply more or less equally to all, as in the case of (at least some) rules regulating traffic.

Notwithstanding their variety, these rules can be classified together because they share two fundamental characteristics: (1) The rules prescribe action which is thought to contribute to the attainment of a goal. This is the "design" of such rules, at least in the sense that if the prescribed action does not effectively contribute to the attainment of the goal, for the most part, then the rule itself is subject to criticism. (2) The rules are "laid down" or "legislated" or "made the rule" by a party which has power or authority of some kind; one cannot learn "what the rules are" simply by determining what general procedures most effectively promote the goal. This latter characteristic sharply differentiates these rules from what I have called practical maxims, although both share the first characteristic and are "instrumental."[6]

I shall now consider each of these two characteristics in turn.

1.1 Since rules of this kind are designed to serve a goal, the "best" set of rules is that set, *other things equal,* which is most effective in promoting the goal. The qualification is important: One ordinarily asks the question, "Is this a good rule?" in order to determine whether or not the action to be prescribed by the rule, together with other acts, will most efficiently produce the goal, without violating certain other rules, and in a way that harmonizes best with other aims, assuming persons can be persuaded to follow the rule.[7]

Consider a factory planner designing an assembly line, or an army officer considering platoon reorganization, or a traffic planning commission trying to decide whether a street should be made a throughway. In each case rules are proposed, but there is no contradiction in saying that action on the rules will not contribute to the goal. Within its context the question "Is this a good rule?" is one of practical fact and experience. This indicates one sense in saying that the goal is "over and beyond" the action and the rules.

[6] Practical maxims should not be dismissed, however, as "mere rules of thumb" on the one hand, or as "simply stating relations between means and ends" on the other. When one follows a maxim the rule *directs* action and is a *criterion* of certain kinds of rightness and wrongness in acting.

In passing, note that Rawls's "summary conception," as a whole, does not properly apply to practical maxims, although several features of this conception do apply. Rawls's analysis, admirable as it is, is very apt to mislead. For the "summary view," as he calls it, is a blend of two quite distinct conceptions: In part it is a confused conception or a misconception of a rule, as a summary or report. In other respects it is an accurate conception of what I have called a practical maxim. This may account for an ambivalence in Rawls's article: Cf. ". . . it is doubtful that anything to which the summary conception did apply would be called a *rule.*" p. 23 [p. 188 above]; "Two Concepts . . . ," with "Some rules will fit one conception, some rules the other; and so there are rules of practices (rules in the strict sense), and maxims and 'rules of thumb' " (p. 29). The point is that maxims are rules in a *different* sense from other kinds of rules, whereas no rule, *qua rule,* is a summary or report.

The importance of this point is that there are two possible confusions here, not one: A person may conceive moral rules as summaries or reports, or he may conceive moral rules on the model of maxims. The texts of Austin and Mill, which Rawls cites, together with Rawls's discussion, suggest that the latter, more than the former, was their mistake. *V.,* however, note 13 below.

[7] Cf. my "Technical Ought," *Mind* 69 (July 1960).

There is another sense in saying this: In practice a goal is often described in terms of rules or procedures which are thought to produce it (when, for example, a beam is to be built according to procedural specifications). Moreover, at the time of action one may not be able to say just what he wants in other terms. Nevertheless, there is no contradiction, explicit or implied, in saying that this person got the goal (in the sense that he can truthfully say "This has all the desirable features of what I wanted") without anyone's having laid down or followed rules. Although the beam was not constructed according to specifications, tests may now show that it is as strong as one could have wished for. In this sense it is *logically* possible for one to attain the goal which a set of instrumental rules is designed to serve without these rules having been followed. I shall refer to this characteristic by saying that the goal of any set of instrumental rules is "logically independent" of these rules.

Although an instrumental action is *properly* described in many ways, depending on the context, it can always be *truthfully* described in terms of a goal, as a "trying to get or produce G." For a goal is essential to such action, and to the rules which guide it. Nevertheless, it is clear that it is logically possible to act and follow instrumental rules without attaining the goal, and to attain the goal without following rules.

Moreover, although obviously one cannot act *on* a rule of any kind if there is no rule, one can act *in the way* specified by a set of instrumental rules (as well as attain a desired result) without *these* rules having been adopted. A group of workers, for example, may hit upon certain procedures which are so effective that they are made "the rule"; in such a case we may say, somewhat misleadingly, that one discovered a good rule by observing the actual results of a line of action. In complex cases it is very unlikely that men will act in the way rules would prescribe if the rules have not in fact been enacted. Nevertheless, there is no contradiction in saying that men acted in this way but there were no rules prescribing this course of action.[8]

Thus in the case of instrumental rules the action as well as the goal may be said to be logically independent of the rules.

1.2 Now consider the second major characteristic of rules of this kind, namely, that they are "laid down," "legislated," "made," or "adopted."

It is clear enough that an employer, for example, who "informs" his employee of the rules, is not simply "giving information." Moreover, this act or performance is very different from one's "adopting" a practical maxim or making a rule "a rule for himself." Note that in the case of a maxim the adoption of the rule is "incomplete" so long as one simply resolves to follow it. Rules of the present kind, however, are normally made for others to follow: To make their adoption complete, one must get at least some of these others "to agree," in some sense to follow the rules.

This is so in spite of our sometimes speaking, in the sense indicated earlier, of one's "discovering a good rule" of this kind. We also speak of an administrator's "thinking of a good rule," "deciding on a rule," and "informing an employee of the rules decided on." It is quite clear, however, that "thinking of a rule" and "deciding on it" are steps taken *in the direction of* adopting a rule; the latter corresponds roughly to the stage of "resolution" in the case of a maxim. They are only steps; the rule will not become effective, and strictly speaking, will not *be* a rule, until it is "put in force" or "made a rule."

Legislation is one way of putting such a rule in force. In this case parents and guardians "teach" their children what the laws are; they do not ask for consent. In

[8] Cf. Rawls, ibid., p. 22 [pp. 186–187 above].

other cases the members of a group, working co-operatively, "decide on the rules," or an employer or a sergeant "tells one the rules." By such an act those subject to the rules are "directed to follow them," and the rules are then "in force." The rules serve on the one hand as guides to action —they tell one what to do—and on the other as criteria of correctness of action—acts in accord with them are said to be *right* and breaches of them are said to be *wrong*. The rules thus tell one both *what* to do, and *that* he should do it. They are useful just on this account: One may lay down rules of this kind to make use of unskilled labor, or to gain the benefits of a division of labor, or simply to coordinate activity as in the case of an efficient traffic system.

The analysis of what the various cases of adopting a rule have in common and what it is to be subject to rules, takes one to the difficult problem of what constitutes an authority. For our purpose the following will suffice: A party seems to be constituted as a *de facto* authority when one accepts the fact that this party prescribes an act, as a *reason* for following the prescription (a rule of the present kind being one form of prescription). This indicates the somewhat technical sense of saying that the rule follower "agrees to" follow the rules.[9] In the case of rules of the present kind authority is ordinarily constituted and agreement to follow the rules obtained by contract, law, convention, or the like. Some such arrangement is necessary to induce a person to follow rules of this kind, since persons other than the rule-follower "are interested in" the goal, and normally he himself does not get (more than a share of) the product of his labor. The contract, law, or convention both promises some reward to the rule-follower, and at the same time converts others' "being interested in" the goal to their "having an interest in it"—in a legal or quasi-legal sense. This, of course, is why one who follows rules of this kind, unlike one who adopts a maxim as his guide, is not free to alter or follow the rules "at his pleasure."

The point which needs particular emphasis here, however, is that the contract, law, or convention is essential to the rule's being a rule; it is not "external" to the rule, since without it one's "laying down the rules" would be only so much rhetoric. When a contract is simply "to do a job," notice that the criterion of correctness is simply "getting the job done." If I hire a person to paint a house, he has done what he is supposed to do when the house is painted. On the other hand, to the extent to which a contract lays down rules specifying how the job is to be done, the rules are the criterion. If a painter contracts to follow certain procedures, and then fails to follow them, he has not done what he is supposed to do. This should make it quite clear that it is the contract, law, or convention which determines in a given case that rules will be the criterion of correctness. The "agreement" secured by contract, law, or convention thus makes a rule a rule, and without something like it there could be no rules of this kind.

1.3 The discussion of the two major characteristics of these rules reveals two criteria of correctness. On the one hand, there is a criterion of a "good" rule. On the other, there are rules *in force* constituting a criterion in certain respects of the *right thing to do*. In the case of these rules there is thus a clear distinction between the justification of a rule or practice and the justification of a particular action falling under it. Perhaps on this very account

[9] Cf. Black, *Theoria* 24, pp. 120–121. Black's analysis of the "laying down of rules" in terms of "promulgator activities" and "subject activities" (pp. 139–164) is illuminating, as is H. L. A. Hart's recent analysis of the complex idea of "acceptance" in the case of the law. *The Concept of Law* (Oxford: Clarendon Press, 1961), chs. IV–VI, esp. pp. 107–114.

some have been led to view moral rules as rules of this kind.

1.3.1 Before going on to moral rules let us notice that this distinction is not important simply because acts are judged by rules which are judged in turn in another manner, in this case by reference to a goal. The significance of the distinction derives more from the fact that the two criteria are "independent" in the following way: One may do the thing which most contributes to the goal, yet violate the rules in force; and one may act according to the rule in force when the rule is a poor one.

Moreover, the rules *in force,* not the rules which are *best,* constitute (at least under certain conditions) the criterion of right and wrong acts. This is evident in practice: A worker who does his job is *entitled* to his pay, whether or not the rules he follows in doing his job are *good* rules. This question, whether or not the rules in force are "good," ordinarily does not have to be settled for them to serve as a criterion of right action. Normally it does not even arise.

Of course, one might criticize the rules *in force* as "illegitimate" or as laid down by one who lacks rightful or proper authority, and *on this account* argue that they are not the "true" criterion of right action. However, the question of the "legitimacy" of the rules is not settled by determining which rules are best. To try to have it this way would be to invite disagreement concerning which rules *are* best, and to have no effective rule at all.[10] It would be wholly impractical to accept as authoritative or binding and as the criterion of right action only "the rules which are best." Who, for example, would lay down or contract to follow under penalty rules characterized only in this way?

[10] Cf. Hume's remarks on the need of a "determinate rule of conduct," or "general rules," in his discussions of justice, both in the *Treatise* and *Inquiry.* Hume, however, does not make precisely the same point.

Thus, even though rules of the present kind are explicitly designed to promote a goal, the rule follower is not generally at liberty to use the goal as his criterion of the right thing to do. The distinction between the two criteria so far remains firm.

1.3.2 Nevertheless, the independence of these two criteria can be overemphasized. For one thing, the criterion of a good rule, in virtue of its being used by those who adopt rules, is an indirect criterion of right action. The rules which are the criterion of right and wrong action do not prescribe action which just *as a matter of fact* contributes or fails to contribute to the goal; the rules are *criticizable* if they are not good rules. Thus it does not "just so happen" that the right act *tends* to contribute to the goal. If it did not generally do this it would not be called "right," for there would be no such rules.

Second, no statement of a rule includes reference to all conditions pertinent to its application; one would not wish so to encumber it, even if every contingency could be foreseen. This implies that every rule follower is expected to know "what he is doing" in a sense larger than "following the rules"; and if the rules are instrumental he is often expected to know the goal to which his rule-directed action supposedly contributes—to know "what he is doing" in this sense. Not always, to be sure, but often he could not make a sound judgment of when and how to apply the rule without this knowledge.

For both of these reasons it is a mistake to say, in a pedestrian and casuistical way, that "the criterion of right acts is the rules." It is a mistake to think of *every* exception and *every* case as somehow included in the rule. The motive for doing so, presumably to preserve the authority of rules, is mistaken: There is an important difference between interpreting a rule, or violating it *in special circumstances,* and deciding each individual case just as if there were no rules. A person subject to rules who follows the latter course merits a special kind of criticism. Although it is difficult to specify conditions in which the violation of an instrumental rule is proper, surely the bare fact "that by doing so one can better promote the goal" is not sufficient. The rule follower is not the sole or final authority on the propriety of breaking a rule, even when it is for the benefit of the other party.

This brings us back to the independence of the two criteria. However, it should now be clear that these criteria are interrelated and operate together. Moreover, since there are two criteria in the case of rules of the present kind, it always *makes sense* to ask if an action right by the rules is also right in the respect that it is good that a rule prescribes it. It not only *makes sense* to speak of its being proper to violate a rule: "successful violations" tend to be commended.

II

2.0 As soon as rules of the foregoing kind have been described it is rather obvious that many moral theorists, intentionally or not, have cut moral rules to their pattern. Anyone who regards the standard of morally right action as itself a means to an end will have this tendency, and this is typically true of rule utilitarians: The distinctive characteristic of their theory is that a system of rules is the criterion of morally right action, and these rules in turn are to be judged good or bad according to the consequences which action on the rules either generally produces as a matter of fact, or would produce if people could be persuaded to follow them.[11] The consequence which has been thought to be critical in assessing the soundness of a system of rules has been variously identified, as "the happiness of all," "public utility," "security," "the general welfare," etc. Nevertheless, in spite of the difference in name and even in conception, this has been taken to be a consequence, real or possible, and as an end or goal which a good system of rules would first promote and then ensure. The question of which system of rules will be most successful in this respect generally has been thought to be, at least broadly speaking, empirical: Fact and practical experience will decide which system is best. The theory thus implies that the goal and goal promoting action, both, in senses indicated earlier, are *logically* independent of any system of rules. This fundamentally instrumental and telic character of the system of rules, and indirectly of rule-directed action as well, is a distinctive feature of utilitarian-

[11] See, for example, J. O. Urmson's "The Interpretation of the Moral Philosophy of J. S. Mill," *Philosophical Quarterly*, vol. 3 (1953), pp. 33–39 [pp. 168–174 above]. By and large I agree with this interpretation of Mill, although Mill showed other tendencies, not only toward a more radical utilitarianism but, in the opposite direction, toward the ethics of Bradley. John Austin is sometimes said to be a good representative of this point of view, but his conception of moral rules as commands, learned in the way we learn practical maxims, is a hodgepodge (see *The Province of Jurisprudence Determined*, Lectures I–III). In *some* respects Hume's discussion of the artificial virtues, especially justice, is a much better (and perhaps the best) classical example of this type of theory.

Among contemporaries (and apart from useful textbook presentations) see Brandt, *Ethical Theory*, and J. Hospers, *Human Conduct*. S. Toulmin in *The Place of Reason in Ethics* and P. H. Nowell-Smith in *Ethics* have come closest to an explicit statement of the theory.

An examination of actual cases of this kind of theory, with all the proper qualifications, especially if the theory is extended beyond utilitarianism, would require considerable space. I do not undertake the historical investigation here. In my judgment the theory has a popularity which exceeds its merit, and some tendencies which are pernicious (see Section IV below). By isolating the germ, the disease may be better understood—its valuable antibodies notwithstanding.

ism.[12] Moreover, as I pointed out above, it is an essential feature of rules of the foregoing kind that persons other than the rule follower are "interested" in the product; this "interest" is expressed in some kind of contract, convention, or law which gives the rules authority. In utilitarian theory the "party-in-authority" tends to be "the people"; directly or indirectly they enter conventions, "adopt" rules, then enforce them, so that all may share the fruits of the rule-directed action. The product is shared, the goal is the good of all.

2.1 Moral rules on the rule utilitarian view thus have the basic characteristics of the rules which I discussed in (1). When the two are compared, and the analysis in (1) is brought to bear, it quickly reveals that rule utilitarianism is faced with a fundamental problem. If the position is to have the advantage over act utilitarianism that is claimed for it, then the criterion of right action must be a system of rules and not general utility. Rules are a criterion of right action, however, only on condition that they are "rules-in-force" and in some sense "agreed to." But obviously the rules which are "in force" or "agreed to" may or may not be the rules which maximize utility; and to the extent that they are not, then the "best rules" by the utilitarian standard, not having been "adopted," are not the criterion of right action. The best rules may not even be known. The "rules" and the "utilitarianism" in "rule utilitarianism" thus constitute two independent criteria, and they may not be in much accord.

2.1.1 The analysis in (1) not only clearly shows the nature of this difficulty, but also helps one to understand some of the directions in which utilitarianism has moved in an effort to avoid it. Some good utilitarians, mindful of evil in ordinary conventions, tend to say that just as men *ought* to adopt a rule only if it maximizes utility, so one is *obligated* to follow a rule only if it maximizes utility. This doctrine implies that one may freely disregard a rule if ever he discovers that action on the rule is not maximally felicific, and in this respect makes moral rules like "practical maxims." It deprives social and moral rules of their authority and naturally is in sharp conflict with practice. On this alternative rule utilitarianism collapses into act utilitarianism.[13]

2.1.2 Other rule utilitarians, equally concerned to avoid an ethical conventionalism, either close their eyes to the difficulty or else overlook it. They either just declare an ideal set of rules to be the criterion, or else say that the criterion of right action is the system of rules which, *if* adopted, *would* maximize utility, or something of the sort. Such a formulation clearly does not acknowledge that rules must be adopted if they are to be rules: The "if adopted" is only a way of describing the ideal and actually obscures the necessity of a rule's being adopted.

The fact that it is commonly the case that some moral principles and rules to which a person subscribes are not "in force" in his society raises important issues for *any* moral philosophy of rules. I cannot even try to do them justice here. Nevertheless, surely it is a mistake to maintain that a set of rules, thought to be ideally utilitarian or felicific, is the criterion of right action. If the rules are simply described in this way and are not

[12] It would be a mistake to say that utilitarians maintained this deliberately, after considering alternatives, or even that they did so consistently. John Stuart Mill, in Chapter IV of *Utilitarianism,* seems to have been unaware of the issue when he discussed happiness as "a concrete whole" and virtue as one of its "parts." Cf. below 4.5.

[13] For a clear recent statement of this position, see J. J. C. Smart, "Extreme and Restricted Utilitarianism," *Philosophical Quarterly* 6 (1956), 344–354 [pp. 195–203 above]. Notice that Smart argues explicitly that moral rules are "rules of thumb."

enumerated, we so far do not have any rules and are not likely to get any.[14] On the other hand, if we are presented with a list, but these are not rules in practice, the most one could reasonably do is to try to get them adopted. A manager in the quiet of his office may dream of a system of rules which will maximize production, and a utilitarian may build a theory around the set of rules which will maximize utility. Surely the latter would be as foolish as the former if he said that these ideal rules are the criterion of right and wrong acts. As previous analysis has shown, acts are not judged by proposed rules, ideal rules, and rules-in-theory: for these do not fully qualify as rules.[15]

2.1.3 Other rule utilitarians show a finer appreciation of the logic of their position: They interpret moral rules on analogy with the rules in (1), even if it forces them to admit that the criterion of right action is not the set of rules which maximizes utility. This alternative seems to be popular with those whose primary allegiance is to a "morality of rules," and who are utilitarian only because they suppose that "welfare" *must* have something to do with morality. (After all, what else *can* serve as a criterion of rules?)

On this alternative it always makes sense to ask whether or not a "moral or social convention" subscribed to in practice is best, and this gives sense to the question, sometimes asked, whether a people who follow their conventions act in the best way they could. At the same time the question whether an individual ought to do something in particular—for example, repay money borrowed—is quite a different question, to be answered by referring, at least in part, to the practices and conventions of that society. Such a view does not make the blunder of taking an ideal system of rules as the criterion of which particular acts are right, and yet it does not endorse conventions which are obviously questionable. One may seek earnestly to reform the moral conventions of a people, and yet insist that these conventions, some of which are in need of reform, are the general criterion by which a man must decide what in particular he ought to do, and by which his acts are to be judged. At the same time, such a view need not dichotomize the two criteria. As we found above, rules of this kind have an open texture which permits the criterion of the rules to enter into their proper interpretation. I think we may presume, moreover, that there are instances in which one should violate the letter of a moral rule when following it would clearly be to the detriment of the general welfare or the welfare of all parties concerned. Rule utilitarians could no doubt take instances of this sort to support their theory. As we also found above, one may admit this without depriving rules of their authority.[16]

[14] Cf. above, *1.3.1.*

[15] See *1.2* and *1.3.1* above. Since utilitarianism is rather often associated with reform, it tends to be formulated in ideal terms. See, for example, J. S. Mill's most explicit statement of his position in ch. II, paragraph 10 of *Utilitarianism*" . . . the standard of morality, which may accordingly be defined 'the rules and precepts for human conduct,' by the observance of which an existence such as has been described might be, to the greatest extent possible, secured to all mankind. . . ." In this passage, how is "possible" to be taken? Does it mean "possible, within the framework of existing institutions?" For one attempt to avoid in this way the difficulties inherent in an ideal formulation, see R. B. Brandt, op. cit., pp. 396–400. This attempt goes only part of the way in meeting the difficulty. On the difficulty itself cf. H. J. McCloskey, "An Examination of Restricted Utilitarianism," *Philosophical Review* 66 (1957), esp. pp. 475–481 [pp. 204–216 above]; and J. Austin, op. cit., Lecture III.

[16] I think this is the most favorable interpretation which can be given to the utilitarianism of the nineteenth-century reformers: They framed a theory which would make sense of reform, but at the same time had too much practical (if not always philosophical) sense

III

3.0 A careful development and criticism of rule utilitarianism, as just outlined, would be worth while, but it is outside the range of this paper. Even without this development, however, it can be shown that rule utilitarians, by using the kind of rule in (1) as a model, have exercised a definite option, and I want to indicate the general character of this option. To do this, I shall first consider briefly the rules of certain kinds of games.[17]

3.1 Rules of common competitive games, such as baseball, chess, and the like, say how a game is to be played. They state the "object of the game," "the moves," "how the counting should go," etc. Often they are stated in "rule books," and sometimes they are enforced by referees appointed by an acknowledged authority. These formalities, however, are not at all necessary. The rules must be "laid down" or "adopted" in some sense, but all that is required (in the case of those games being discussed) is that a group of players "agree" on a set of rules. This agreement may consist simply in their following and enforcing rules which they all have learned: Think, for example, of a group of small boys playing baseball, and think of the difference between one's knowing the rules and playing the game. In such cases there is no formally agreed-upon authority; each player —in principle—is both rule-follower and rule-enforcer. No player has the authority to modify the rules at will, but the players together can change them in any way they see fit. As one should expect, there are many variations.

In the latter respects game rules of this kind are quite like the rules in (1). These game rules, however, noticeably lack the first major characteristic of those rules: They are not designed to yield a product. More precisely, they are not adopted to promote the attainment of a goal which, in the senses indicated earlier, is "over and beyond" the rules.[18] They do not serve a goal which is "logically independent" of the game which they define.

3.1.1 Of course people who play games do so with various motives, and some of the goals which motivate them are logically independent of the game; for example, exercise, recreation, the opportunity to talk to friends or make a conquest. Undoubtedly games are popular because they serve so many ends. Nevertheless, motives and goals of this kind are not essential. Many players participate (so far as can be determined without psychoanalyzing them) "just because they want to" or simply "from love of the game." Actually this kind of motive, even if it is not typical, is that which is most distinctive of

---

to advocate the use of the criterion of rules as the criterion of acts. It is as if they perceived the importance of moral rules and practices but were unable fully to accommodate these to their theory. I think that the presence of the two criteria, which the analysis of the rules in (1) clearly reveals, explains for example the "tension" between chapter two of Mill's *Utilitarianism* on the one hand, and chapters three and five on the other.

[17] I can be brief because rules of this kind have been discussed by others. I shall mostly confine myself to points not previously mentioned, or at least not emphasized. I am perhaps most indebted to Rawls's acute analysis of what he calls the "practice conception," and on the whole agree with it. The name is misleading since very many "practices," as we ordinarily think of them, are defined by rules (e.g. by job rules) which are quite unlike those to which his "practice conception of rules" properly applies. Although unimportant in itself, it is just this kind of thing, I suspect, which has led moral philosophers into serious error. One can sympathize since it is almost impossible to find a conventional expression which is not misleading in some important respect.

[18] Some games have become instruments to such a considerable degree, and some instrumental activities have become so much like games, that no description will prevent the intrusion of dubious and borderline cases.

players: One who "loves a game" commonly regards another, who lacks the motive, as poorly appreciating "the quality of the game." This is apt to be missed just because games have been turned into instruments for exercise, diversion, etc., to such a great degree. The point is, they *need* not be.

Moreover, games *qua* games do not seem to have a design or goal *different* from the motives of the rule-followers, in the way rules of jobs commonly do. What is this goal? One who most appreciates a game speaks about it rather as if it were an aesthetic object, worth playing on its own account and apart from any product or result; and if he is asked to justify his claim that it is good, he seems to have a problem analogous to that of justifying an aesthetic judgment.[19] Sometimes, to be sure, the rules of games are changed, and in particular instances violated, in order to change the consequences. Many official rules, for example, have been changed in order to lessen player injuries; and particular persons may find a game played by the official rules too strenuous, or pursuit of the ball after a bad drive too troublesome. These facts, however, do not imply that the rules are designed to produce consequences, such as the right amount of exercise or exertion or the good health of the players. Changes of the kind mentioned simply indicate that the rules of a game, like the rules of a job, are adopted in a context by persons who have many desires and many obligations other than "to play the game" and "follow its rules." Games are often altered to make them harmonize better with such contextual features. It is true, of course, that persons who have turned games into instruments change or violate the rules more readily. As we say, these people do not take the game as seriously.

Some philosophers are inclined to say that even when one plays a game "just because he wants to" or "for love of the game," the game is still an instrument—to "his enjoyment" or "pleasure." This stand depends for its cogency on our being able to describe this pleasure or enjoyment without referring to the game, which should be possible if the pleasure or enjoyment really were something separate from playing the game. However, although it is clearly possible to play a game and not enjoy it, the converse does not appear plausible. To be sure, one sometimes says that he gets about the same enjoyment from one game as another, especially when the two are similar. But this is apt to mean that he has no strong preference for one game over another, that he likes one as well as the other, not that there is a kind of pleasurable feeling which in fact results from both, more or less equally, and which *conceivably* could be had from very different activities or even from being acted *on* in some way. (Similarly, when one says that he "likes to talk to one person about as much as another," this clearly does not mean that talking to the two persons produces the same kind of pleasure in him.) Moreover, when we speak of getting about the same enjoyment from two games, sometimes the "enjoyment" does not appear to be, strictly speaking, the enjoyment "of playing the game," but rather the enjoyment of exercising, talking to friends, etc. I do not deny, however, that games can become instruments. I want to argue that they need not be, often are not, and that in calling them games we do not imply that they are instruments.

The kind of goal the pursuit of which to some degree *is* essential to the playing of

[19] This reminds one of the ancient distinction between "doing" and "making," and between (what the medievals called) "immanent" and "transitive" activity. I do not mean to deny that some jobs are worth doing "on their own account," but even when "one enjoys a job," there is a discernible purpose which it is designed to promote.

the game is the "object of the game," as defined by the rules, and the various subgoals which promote this object according to the rules. Such goals as these, for example, "to score the most runs," "to get the batter out at second base," obviously are not logically independent of the rules of the game—if there were no rules it would be logically impossible to try to do these things. It is just nonsense to speak of changing the rules so that one can better attain the object of the game.

3.1.2 Since the action within a game is designed to attain goals defined by the rules, the action as well as the goal logically depends on the rules: In important respects a move in the game has the consequences it has because the rules say it has; *in these respects* the rules define the consequences and determine the character of the action.[20] Since the character of instrumental action is fixed at least partly by the goal which the action is designed to serve, the action can be described in this essential respect, as a "trying to get the goal," without referring to or presupposing rules. In the case of play in a game, unless the game has become an instrument, this is not possible; if one describes the action in a game apart from the rules, as a "trying to catch a ball," he leaves out the design. On account of this difference one may feel inclined to say that whereas rules of the kind described in (1) *may* be used to describe an action, game rules by defining new kinds of action just constitute "forms of life."[21]

3.2 However, this is but one side of the story, and if it were the only one it is not likely that the two kinds of rules would be confused. To see the other side, which is equally important, one should attend to the fact that the play in a game is not wholly defined by the rules of the game. "The kind of game he plays" ordinarily does not refer to the game as defined by the rules; "to play a game" ordinarily means more than following the rules. The point is that although the object of the game is defined by the rules, since the action in a game normally consists in "trying to attain that object" and since the game rules do not determine success in this respect, the action in *this* respect is instrumental. Players often develop tactics and strategies and skills in playing. Sometimes they follow what I have called practical maxims, and at other times they follow team rules agreed on among themselves or laid down by the "manager." The latter are, of course, examples of the rules described in (1). Obviously they should not be confused with rules of games, as I have described them. For one can be said to play a game without his following any particular set of instrumental rules.

The point of greatest importance here is that although game rules are not themselves instruments, they support, as it were, a considerable amount of instrumental activity, much of which logically could not be carried on without them. To play a game is typically to follow the rules of the game *and* engage in this instrumental activity; a "good player" does more than just follow the rules. Even one who "loves the game for its own sake" derives his satisfaction from the kind of *instrumental* activity which the rules of the game make possible. Games make new goals, new pursuits, and new skills available to men.

In this situation it is not surprising that some should regard games themselves as instruments. To regard them in this way, however, would be to confuse their function.

IV

4.0 The rules of games just considered differ most significantly from the rules de-

[20] This is the point which Rawls emphasized.

[21] Cf. A. I. Melden, "Action," *Philosophical Review* 65 (1956), 523–541.

scribed in (1) because they are, by our criterion, "non-instrumental." This point of difference between the two kinds of rules is one of the most important to be found. I have been concerned to mark it here to focus attention on the thesis, maintained by many utilitarians, that moral rules and social institutions are instruments designed to promote a goal logically independent of the rules and institutions. The thesis is only rarely discussed, and I think that failure to discuss it helps account for the recurrent popularity of utilitarianism. However, morality is obviously not a game, and if the thesis is to be fully assessed, moral rules must be carefully analyzed and alternatives considered. This is out of the question here. In the remainder of this paper I shall note a complexity which is too often overlooked, and just indicate the critical force of certain recently developed lines of argument. However, the fundamental issue here is not at all new.[22]

4.1 Consider the rule "Do not cheat." Often it is taught in the context of a game, and it acquires a rather specific sense in this context. The rule in this use can be paraphrased as "Do not violate the rules of the game in order to gain an advantage for yourself." In this use the rule logically presupposes games as social institutions; if there were no games, the rule could not have this use and this meaning.

The same general point applies to many other moral rules, such as "Keep your promises," "Do not steal," and "Do not lie." Each of these logically presupposes institutions and practices, such as "promising," "a system of property," "a language." Since these moral rules presuppose such practices, they cannot be understood apart from them; the practice, constituted by its own rules, makes the moral rule meaningful. Philosophical analyses which have attempted to clarify moral rules apart from institutionalized practices have surrounded them with theoretical perplexities and

[22] Historically one perhaps first senses the issue in his reading of Plato and Aristotle. Is man's end somehow "writ in his nature" in such a way that it can be determined apart from a determination of virtue? If so, it might be reasonable to regard virtue as a *means* to the end, and instruction in virtue as a matter of learning from practical experience the best means. On the other hand, if man's end cannot be determined without the determination of virtue—if man's end is properly defined in terms of virtue, as activity in accordance with it, and man's nature is defined as potentialities for this end—then virtue is not a means and its discovery in practical experience must be understood differently. Although the second interpretation is the sounder, there were tendencies in medieval thought to favor the first—undoubtedly deriving from the fact that God, who is certainly different from man, was said to be man's end. Moreover, the desire of God was said to be implanted in man's nature. This inclination was said to be a natural participation of the eternal law, and natural virtue was said to be an insufficient means to God. I think myself, however, that the second interpretation gives a sounder account of the ethics not only of Augustine but also of Aquinas. Yet it is not surprising that out of this tradition there should have come the contrary (Lockian) doctrine that natural law applies to man in a "state of nature," and that man by compact makes societies as a remedy for natural evils and as a means to natural goals. This doctrine in turn, by way of reaction, stimulated theories according to which the distinction of right and wrong is not founded in nature, but in contract, convention, or rules. In the nineteenth century the opposition between the two general points of view assumed more of its original form when idealists worked out their own interpretation of the social contract, and opposed utilitarianism. (See, for example, Bradley's "Pleasure for Pleasure's Sake" in *Ethical Studies* and Bosanquet's *Philosophical Theory of the State.*) Very recent philosophy in some respects strongly resembles idealism, undoubtedly because it itself is a reaction to a kind of philosophy which arose in reaction to idealism. For one example, cf. Bosanquet, op. cit., with A. I. Melden, *Rights and Right Conduct* (Oxford, 1959).

This is, of course, only a fragmentary account of the historical origins of the issue.

turned them into "mere forms" of morality.[23]

However, the fact that these moral rules presuppose institutions or practices does not *in itself* decide the question whether or not they are instrumental and utilitarian. In some respects the rules "Do not cheat," "Do not lie," etc., are like the rules "Do not violate traffic lights," "Do not drive on the wrong side," etc. These rules obviously presuppose practices, and the rules and practices appear to be primarily instrumental and utilitarian. We can easily conceive of the practices being changed in order to provide a more effective system of traffic control.

On the utilitarian view moral rules and the institutions which they presuppose are rather like a system of this kind. The assumption is that men have various destinations which they want to reach and the social aim is to provide the system of institutions which will be most effective in helping them along. As men together devise such public instruments as roads and bridges, which no one alone could construct, and then regulate the use of these instruments for the "public good," so on this view men together have developed such institutions as "promising," "a system of property," etc. These institutions may not have arisen through deliberate design, although (there often seems to be the assumption that) if an institution or practice has arisen, then it *must* have been rewarding, and consequently *must* have served some purpose. The instrumental character of these institutions is evidenced more directly, however, by the fact that persons hold and dispose of property, make promises, and, quite generally, engage in the life of their institutions with goals in mind. If these reasons are decisive, moreover, one's language, too, should be viewed as a social tool.[24] Certainly men have purposes in speaking.

As in the case of a traffic system, however, on occasion it is to a person's advantage to break the rules of their institutions. Men must be taught not to; they must be made to realize that temporary advantage is far outweighed by the more permanent benefits to be gained if all can be depended on to follow the rules. Moral rules, such as "Keep your promises," "Do not steal," "Do not lie," like the rules "Always obey traffic signals," "Do not drive on the wrong side," seem to be conceived as deriving from the occasional but recurrent conflict between private advantage and public institutions. Utilitarians commonly make the point that if a person in his own interest is sometimes led to violate a rule, he will nevertheless insist, also in his own interest, that others follow the rule: The "security" which derives from a system of public institutions is given an important place in moral theory. Moral rules of this kind thus seem to be conceived as supports for and ancillary to the public institutions which they presuppose. If these rules could only be made to serve a system of truly *rational* (i.e., utilitarian) institutions, the aforementioned conflict would be minimized, as the happiness of all was promoted. The negative morality of rules would be lost in liberal affection for the general welfare.

4.2 Moral rules of this kind in a sense do *tend* to support the institutions and practices which they presuppose: They *tend* to receive their effective interpretation from the character of the institutions, and they are both taught and reaffirmed most vigorously when persons from self-interest show an inclination to violate the

[23] This misinterpretation accounts for some criticisms of a morality of rules. Cf. A. Macbeath, *Experiments in Living* (London, 1952), Lecture XIII.

[24] Cf. Hume's *Treatise*, III, II, II. Esp. p. 490 in Selby-Bigge edition.

rules of the institutions. As a consequence (and for an additional reason which will soon be apparent[25]) these institutions and practices have, as it were, a "moral dimension" or a "moral part." Nevertheless, in assessing rule utilitarianism it is important to distinguish moral rules on the one hand from other rules which also define and characterize the underlying institutions and practices. For it is possible to learn the rules of a game, and to play the game, without being tempted to cheat, without grasping the concept of "cheating," and without learning the moral rule "Do not cheat." It is not uncommon for children to do this. Children ordinarily also learn to speak correctly, in the sense of learning many rules of the language, without learning the rule "Do not lie," thus without grasping the moral concept of a lie. It may not be so evident, but it is also the case that one can learn many rules governing property, can learn to make a promise, etc., without grasping the moral force of the rules "Do not steal," "Keep your promises," etc. There are surely legal experts on property and contract who have, as we say, very little moral understanding.[26]

[25] See 4.5 below.

[26] Although an adequate description of property and promising in a sense implies that theft and promise-breaking are morally wrong, a person may fail to "see" the implication. When we teach a child what property and promising are, we commonly say that it is wrong for him to take what belongs to another and wrong for him not to do what he has promised to do. So far, however, the child is not guilty of theft or promise-breaking, and until he has witnessed them, or an inclination thereto, in himself or another (since he has not yet had occasion to *use* the rules "Do not steal" and "Keep your promises"), he will have little practical understanding of these rules. Before he reaches this point, however, he may have learned enough of the underlying rules to exchange property, make promises, etc. Growth in moral understanding is long and complex and participation in ordinary practices does not wait upon it.

In considering the soundness of rule utilitarianism, there are thus two interrelated questions. The first is whether or not the institutions of promising, property, language, etc., are instruments serving goals logically independent of these institutions. This bears on the question of the soundness of utilitarianism not only as a *moral* but as a *social* theory. Then there is the more restricted question whether rule utilitarianism offers a sound account of moral rules.

4.3.1 Several lines of thought, some recently developed, bear on these questions. To take one example, primarily as it applies to the first of the questions: Utilitarians, as already indicated, have put considerable emphasis on "security," if not as *the* goal, nevertheless as an important "part" of the goal. A person cannot be "secure," however, without being able to *count on* others to act and refrain from acting in a variety of ways. His counting on others, moreover, is in a great many cases not "an expectation" based on an ordinary induction. For most often the expectation involved in one's counting on another is based on the fact that the action or restraint in question is governed by rules which define rights, obligations, duties, etc.: One can count on another because the other (presumably) is acting on such rules.[27] For this reason the expression "counting on another" in many occasions of its use makes no more sense apart from rules than "deciding to act" or "acting" makes apart from reasons for acting. There is also the related point that the action which one counts on another to do, itself, in many cases presupposes rules; for example, just as one could not count on a person to "play first base" if there were no game of baseball, so one could not count on another to "keep his promise" or "respect property" if there were no practice of promising or institu-

[27] Cf. Hart, op. cit., pp. 54–57.

tion of property.[28] Although "security" is an ambiguous term, in the sense in which it refers to a significant social goal it could not mean what it does without rules which define institutions and practices.

For both these reasons "security" just does not appear to be a goal which is logically independent of the rules of institutions and practices like property, promising, language, etc. Moreover, it would seem very strange to think of the greatest number having the greatest happiness or pleasure or welfare without being fairly secure. The utilitarian position thus appears to be quite vulnerable, even apart from the fact that its proponents have notoriously failed to give "happiness," "pleasure," "welfare," and the like clarity of meaning which they must have to function as goals.

4.3.2 Furthermore, as the earlier analysis of games revealed, the fact that one does many things as a means to an end when engaging in a practice gives no support to the claim that the practice itself is a means. The fact that one uses various devices to win a game does not imply that the game is an instrument, and similarly, the fact that one uses words as tools, or makes a promise or deals in property for some purpose, does not support the view that institutions and practices such as language, promising, and property are instruments for the promotion of goals logically independent of these institutions and practices. Nor does this appear plausible: It seems rather to be the case that institutions and practices create or establish most of the goals which men pursue, in the sense that these goals, like the object of a game, would be logically impossible without the institutions and practices. It also appears that persons who engage in business, or make speeches, or follow intellectual pursuits ultimately because "they just enjoy doing these things" are rather like players who enjoy a game for its own sake—in the respect that they derive their enjoyment from instrumental activity which is also made possible by institutions and practices.

At this point, however, it becomes apparent that much requires to be worked out before one can replace the utilitarian view of social institutions with another which is more adequate.

4.4 When one turns to consider utilitarianism as a theory of moral rules, *to some extent* the same arguments apply. For some moral rules *are* in some respects ancillary to the practices and institutions which they presuppose, and in so far as this is the case, then generally speaking moral rules are just as utilitarian as, and no more utilitarian than, these practices and institutions. Notice that the most common uses of the moral rules "Do not lie," "Do not steal," and the like presuppose not only underlying institutions and practices, but also, as suggested above, a tendency or inclination of some persons at some times not to conform to the institutions and practices. This seems to explain why persons living in a law-abiding community use these moral rules so little. This in turn suggests that moral rules are "protective devices," rather like a police system, which also is little used in a law-abiding community and which also presupposes both institutions and an inclination on the part of some persons to violate them. The "police" view of moral rules is partial, but it is also partly true: It helps one see why moral rules are so often conceived as "external" to an individual, imposing restraints on him (and why some philosophers tend to pattern moral rules on rules in a prison!) At the same time it helps one understand why some people "internalize" moral rules in the way they do. For some insist on the importance of following moral rules only because they value a system of institutions and the

[28] Cf. Hume, loc. cit. Black and many others make the same point.

"happiness and security" which the institutions afford. Seeing that valued institutions would cease to exist if people generally did not act in the way moral rules prescribe, they teach these rules—although morality for them is primarily a matter of promoting individual or public welfare, and it would be better if moral rules had little use. This interest in morality is epitomized in the person who regards moral rules as a protector of life, liberty, and property; breaking the rules breeds fear, ruins business, and disrupts the game. This is the internalization of moral rules as ancillary to institutions; it tends to characterize utilitarians past and present.

4.5 Moral rules, however, may be internalized in quite another way, and on this account utilitarianism as a *moral* theory is open to an additional criticism specific to itself.

For a person who values an institution constituted by rules may come to see that rules by nature apply to all members of a class. One who sees this may then be led to look upon the rules which characterize some particular institutions and practices not simply as "applying to all," but at the same time as constituting "a common standard of correctness." And in this way one may be led to the abstract but practical conception of "a community of men living under the idea of law," of which particular institutions afford so many possible examples. In so far as one thinks that others as well as himself act under this conception, he will no doubt value a particular game or language or any other such institution not only *qua* game, *qua* language, etc., but also as a particular instance and a particular form of such a community.

When the idea of such a community is attained and made to govern practice (as it seems to have been, for example, by the Socrates of the *Crito*) then the moral rules "Do not lie," "Do not steal," etc., will appear in a new light. One who acts under such an idea will teach these rules neither as primarily negative and restraining, nor primarily as supports or protections for particular institutions. For although he may view the rules in these ways, he will regard them primarily as affirming in so many different ways the fundamental principle "Live under the idea of law." The principle may be stated negatively, in the form "Do not make an exception of oneself," but his primary aim in teaching the rules will be to raise one to the conception of a moral community. Since such a community potentially includes all men, part of the challenge may be to find particular institutions in which the conception can be realized.

Moral rules regarded in this way of course still presuppose particular institutions and practices. However, they are no longer, properly speaking, "ancillary to" the institutions and practices: They now "add something" to the institutions and practices which they presuppose; the institutions and practices now have a new dimension. Cheating comes to be deplored not primarily because it tends to disrupt a game but because it detracts from the quality which a game can have. If there is cheating, one may simply prefer not to play. In a similar way, lying may be deplored because it detracts from the quality of speech, theft because it detracts from the quality of exchange, etc. Put affirmatively, the idea of a moral community is realizable analogically—only in a variety of forms—in sportsmanship, morally mature speech, honest argument, etc. It should be evident that common institutions and practices are often not in fact logically independent of morality; one has to form a limited or abstract conception of them to make them so.

When moral rules are regarded in this way,[29] then obviously they do not serve

[29] Cf. K. Baier, op. cit., pp. 200–204, and W. D. Falk's comments on "natural obligation" and "mature moral thinking" in "Morality and Convention," *Journal of Philosophy* 57 (1960), 675–685.

a goal logically independent of themselves. In the language of Mill, virtue has now become a "part" of the end, a "part of happiness." Only it is clear that when Mill said this, with his usual willingness to sacrifice theory to good sense, he deserted utilitarianism. The instrumental and utilitarian pattern just will not fit.

V

Further discussion of moral rules is beyond the aim of this paper. My primary purpose has been to contribute to the clarification of moral rules by clarifying a fundamental option open to moral theory. To this end I have both analyzed the general utilitarian view of social rules and practices, along with some variations, and I have tried to lay bare the (largely implicit) utilitarian view of moral rules. I have analyzed moral rules, however, only to the point where the character and significance of the option, and the force of some of the arguments which apply, will be fairly clear. I do not want to suggest that all moral rules are like those which I have considered. The analysis of games, in distinguishing the moral player from the good player, may remind one that there are two traditions in the history of ethics, one emphasizing an exoteric ethic and a moral law known to all, the other an esoteric ethic and a virtue reserved for the wise. I have been concerned, almost exclusively, with the former, and not all of that.

In the course of the discussion attention has been called to the fact that moral rules can be (and thus tend to be) conceived as summaries, reports, practical maxims, rules designed to promote a goal, rules which define institutions, rules which protect institutions, and as particular forms of the fundamental principle of justice.[30] Marking the important differences between these alternatives should remove more than one confusion and at the same time provide *some* of the subtlety which will be needed if the discussion of moral rules is to make genuine advances in the future.

[30] The list is not meant to be exhaustive. Cf. e.g., D. S. Shwayder, "Moral Rules and Moral Maxims," *Ethics* 67 (1957), 269–285.

R. B. Brandt / Some merits of one form of rule utilitarianism

Utilitarianism is the thesis that the moral predicates of an act—at least its objective rightness or wrongness, and sometimes also its moral praiseworthiness or blameworthiness—are functions in some way, direct or indirect, of consequences for the welfare of sentient creatures, and of nothing else. Utilitarians differ about what precise function they are; and they differ about what constitutes welfare and how it is to be measured. But they agree that all one needs to know, in order to make moral appraisals correctly, is the consequences of certain things for welfare.

Utilitarianism is thus a normative ethical thesis and not, at least not necessarily, a meta-ethical position—that is, a position about the meaning and justification of ethical statements. It is true that some utilitarians have declared that the truth of the normative thesis follows, given the ordinary, or proper, meaning of moral terms such as "right." I shall ignore this further, meta-ethical claim. More recently some writers have suggested something very similar, to the effect that our concept of "morality" is such that we could not call a system of rules a "moral system" unless it were utilitarian in some sense.

This latter suggestion is of special interest to us, since the general topic of the present conference is "the concept of morality," and I wish to comment on it very briefly. It is true that there is a connection between utilitarianism and the concept of morality; at least I believe—and shall spell out the contention later—that utilitarianism cannot be explained, at least in its most plausible form, without making use of the concept of "morality" and, furthermore, without making use of an analysis of this concept. But the reverse relationship does not hold: it is not true that the concept "morality" is such that we cannot properly call a system of rules a morality unless it is a thoroughly utilitarian system, although possibly we would not call a system of rules a "morality" if it did not regulate at all the forms of conduct which may be expected to do good or harm to

Reprinted from the UNIVERSITY OF COLORADO STUDIES SERIES IN PHILOSOPHY, NO. 3 *by permission of the author and the University of Colorado Press. This essay is a revised version of a paper presented to a conference on moral philosophy held at the University of Colorado in October 1965.*

sentient persons. One reason why it is implausible to hold that any morality is necessarily utilitarian is that any plausible form of utilitarianism will be a rather complex thesis, and it seems that the concept of morality is hardly subtle enough to entail anything so complex—although, of course, such reasoning does not exclude the possibility of the concept of morality entailing some simple and unconvincing form of utilitarianism. A more decisive reason, however, is that we so use the term "morality" that we can say consistently that the morality of a society contains some prohibitions which considerations of utility do not support, or are not even thought to support: for example, some restrictions on sexual behavior. (Other examples are mentioned later.) Thus there is no reason to think that only a utilitarian code could properly be called a "moral code" or a "morality," as these terms are ordinarily used.

In any case, even if "nonutilitarian morality" (or "right, but harmful") were a contradiction in terms, utilitarianism as a normative thesis would not yet be established; for it would be open to a nonutilitarian to advocate changing the meaning of "morality" (or "right") in order to allow for his normative views. There is, of course, the other face of the coin: even if, as we actually use the term "morality" (or "right"), the above expressions are not contradictions in terms, it might be a good and justifiable thing for people to be taught to use words so that these expressions would become self-contradictory. But if there are good reasons for doing the last, presumably there are good and convincing reasons for adopting utilitarianism as a normative thesis, without undertaking such a roundabout route to the goal. I shall, therefore, discuss utilitarianism as a normative thesis, without supposing that it can be supported by arguing that a nonutilitarian morality is a contradiction in terms.

II

If an analysis of concepts like "morally wrong" and "morality" and "moral code" does not enable us to establish the truth of the utilitarian thesis, the question arises what standard a normative theory like utilitarianism has to meet in order for a reasonable presumption to be established in its favor. It is well known that the identity and justification of any such standard can be debated at length. In order to set bounds to the present discussion, I shall state briefly the standard I shall take for granted for purposes of the present discussion. Approximately this standard would be acceptable to a good many writers on normative ethics. However this may be, it would be agreed that it is worth knowing whether some form of utilitarianism meets this standard better than any other form of utilitarian theory, and it is this question which I shall discuss.

The standard which I suggest an acceptable normative moral theory has to meet is this: The theory must contain no unintelligible concepts or internal inconsistencies; it must not be inconsistent with known facts; it must be capable of precise formulation so that its implications for action can be determined; and—most important—its implications must be acceptable to thoughtful persons who have had reasonably wide experience, when taken in the light of supporting remarks that can be made and when compared with the implications of other clearly statable normative theories. It is not required that the implications of a satisfactory theory be consonant with the uncriticized moral intuitions of intelligent and experienced people, but only with those intuitions which stand in the light of supporting remarks, etc. Furthermore, it is not required of an acceptable theory that the best consequences would be produced by people adopting that theory, in contrast to other theories by which they might be convinced. (The theory might be so complex that it would be a good thing if most people did not try their hand at applying it to concrete situations!) It may be a moving *ad hominem* argument, if one can persuade an act-utilitarian that it would have bad consequences for people to try to determine the right act according to that theory, and to live by their conclusions; but such a showing would not be a reasonable ground for rejecting that normative theory.

III

Before turning to the details of various types of utilitarian theory, it may be helpful to offer some "supporting remarks" which will explain some reasons why some philosophers are favorably disposed toward a utilitarian type of normative theory.

(a) The utilitarian principle provides a clear and definite procedure for determining which acts are right or wrong (praiseworthy or blameworthy), by observation and the methods of science alone and without the use of any supplementary intuitions (assuming that empirical procedures can determine when something maximizes utility), for all cases, including the complex ones about which intuitions are apt to be mute, such as whether kleptomanic behavior is blameworthy or whether it is right to break a confidence in certain circumstances. The utilitarian presumably frames his thesis so as to conform with enlightened intuitions which are clear, but his thesis, being general, has implications for all cases, including those about which his intuitions are not clear. The utilitarian principle is like a general scientific theory, which checks with observations at many points, but can also be used as a guide to beliefs on matters inaccessible to observation (like the behavior of matter at absolute zero temperature).

Utilitarianism is not the only normative theory with this desirable property; egoism is another, and, with some qualifications, so is Kant's theory.

(b) Any reasonably plausible normative theory will give a large place to consequences for welfare in the moral assessment of actions, for this consideration enters continuously and substantially into ordinary moral thinking. Theories which ostensibly make no appeal of this sort either admit utilitarian considerations by the back door or have counterintuitive consequences. Therefore the ideal of simplicity leads us to hope for the possibility of a pure utilitarian theory. Moreover, utilitarianism avoids the necessity of weighing disparate things such as justice and utility.

(c) If a proposed course of action does not raise moral questions, it is generally regarded as rational, and its agent well-advised to perform it, if and only if it will maximize expectable utility for the agent. In a similar vein, it can be argued that society's "choice" of an institution of morality is rational and well-advised if and only if having it will maximize expectable social utility—raise the expectable level of the average "utility curve" of the population. If morality is a system of traditional and arbitrary constraints on behavior, it cannot be viewed as a rational institution. But it can be, if the system of morality is utilitarian. In that case the institution of morality can be recommended to a person of broad human sympathies as an institution which maximizes the expectation of general welfare; and to a selfish person, as an institution which, in the absence of particular evidence about his own case, may be expected to maximize his own expectation of welfare (his own welfare being viewed as a random sample from the population). To put it in other words, a utilitarian morality can be "vindicated" by appeal either to the humanity or to the selfishness of human beings.

To say this is not to deny that non-utilitarian moral principles may be capable of vindication in a rather similar way. For instance, to depict morality as an institution which fosters human equality is to recommend it by appeal to something which is perhaps as deep in man as his sympathy or humanity.[1]

IV

The type of utilitarianism on which I wish to focus is a form of rule utilitarianism, as contrasted with act utilitarianism. According to the latter type of theory (espoused by Sidgwick and Moore), an act is objectively right if no other act the agent could perform would produce better consequences. (On this view, an act is blameworthy if and only if it is right to perform the act of blaming or condemning it; the principles of blameworthiness are a special case of the principle of objectively right actions.) Act utilitarianism is hence a rather atomistic theory: the rightness of a single act is fixed by its effects on the world. Rule utilitarianism, in contrast, is the view that the rightness of an act is fixed, not by its relative utility, but by the utility of having a relevant moral rule or of most or all members of a certain class of acts being performed.

The implications of act utilitarianism are seriously counterintuitive, and I shall ignore it except to consider whether some ostensibly different theories really are different.

[1] It would not be impossible to combine a restricted principle of utility with a morality of justice or equality. For instance, it might be said that an act is right only if it meets a certain condition of justice, and also if it is one which, among all the just actions open to the agent, meets a requirement of utility as well as any other.

V

Rule utilitarianisms may be divided into two main groups, according as the rightness of a particular act is made a function of ideal rules in some sense, or of the actual and recognized rules of a society. The variety of theory I shall explain more fully is of the former type.

According to the latter type of theory, a person's moral duties or obligations in a particular situation are determined, with some exceptions, solely by the moral rules, or institutions or practices prevalent in the society, and not by what rules (etc.) it would ideally be best to have in the society. (It is sometimes held that actual moral rules, practices, etc., are only a necessary condition of an act's being morally obligatory or wrong.) Views roughly of this sort have been held in recent years by A. Macbeath, Stephen Toulmin, John Rawls, P. F. Strawson, J. O. Urmson, and B. J. Diggs. Indeed, Strawson says in effect that for there to be a moral obligation on one is just for there to be a socially sanctioned demand on him, in a situation where he has an interest in the system of demands which his society is wont to impose on its members, and where such demands are generally acknowledged and respected by members of his society.[2] And Toulmin asserts that when a person asks, "Is this the right thing to do?" what he is normally asking is whether a proposed action "conforms to the moral code" of his group, "whether the action in question belongs to a class of actions generally approved of in the agent's community."

[2] P. F. Strawson, "Social Morality and Individual Ideal," *Philosophy* 36 (1961), 1–17.

In deliberating about the question what is right to do, he says, "there is no more general 'reason' to be given beyond one which related the action . . . to an accepted social practice."[3]

So far the proposal does not appear to be a form of utilitarianism at all. The theory is utilitarian, however, in the following way: it is thought that what is relevant for a decision whether to try to change moral codes, institutions, etc., or for a justification of them, is the relative utility of the code, practice, etc. The recognized code or practice determines the individual's moral obligations in a particular case; utility of the code or practice determines whether it is justified or ought to be changed. Furthermore, it is sometimes held that utilitarian considerations have some relevance to the rightness of a particular action. For instance, Toulmin thinks that in case the requirements of the recognized code or practice conflict in a particular case, the individual ought (although strictly, he is not morally obligated) to do what will maximize utility in the situation, and that in case an individual can relieve the distress of another, he ought (strictly, is not morally obligated) to do so, even if the recognized code does not require him to.[4]

This theory, at least in some of its forms or parts, has such conspicuously counterintuitive implications that it fails to meet the standard for a satisfactory normative theory. In general, we do not believe that an act's being prohibited by the moral code of one's society is sufficient to make it morally wrong. Moral codes have prohibited such things as work on the Sabbath, marriage to a divorced person, medically necessary abortion, and suicide; but we do not believe it was really wrong for persons living in a society with such prohibitions, to do these things.[5]

Neither do we think it a necessary condition of an act's being wrong that it be prohibited by the code of the agent's society, or of an act's being obligatory that it be required by the code of his society. A society may permit a man to have his wife put to death for infidelity or to have a child put to death for almost any reason; but we still think such actions wrong. Moreover, a society may permit a man absolute freedom in divorcing his wife and recognize no obligations on his part toward her; but we think, I believe, that a man has some obligations for the welfare of a wife of thirty years' standing

[3] Stephen Toulmin, *An Examination of the Place of Reason in Ethics* (Cambridge: The University Press, 1950), pp. 144–145. See various acute criticisms, with which I mostly agree, in Rawls's review, *Philos. Rev.* 60 (1951): 572–580.

[4] Toulmin and Rawls sometimes go further and suggest that a person is morally free to do something which the actual code or practice of his society prohibits, if he is convinced that the society would be better off if the code or practice were rewritten so as to permit that sort of thing, and he is prepared to live according to the ideally revised code. If their theory were developed in this direction, it need not be different from some "ideal" forms of rule utilitarianism, although, as stated, the theory makes the recognized code the standard for moral obligations, with exceptions granted to individuals who hold certain moral opinions. See Toulmin, *Reason in Ethics*, pp. 151–152, and Rawls, "Two Concepts of Rules," *Philos. Rev.* 64 (1955), pp. 28–29 [pp. 191–192 above], especially ftnt. 25. It should be noticed that Rawls's proposal is different from Toulmin's in an important way. He is concerned with only a segment of the moral code, the part which can be viewed as the rules of practices. As he observes, this may be only a small part of the moral code.

[5] Does a stranger living in a society have a moral obligation to conform to its moral code? I suggest we think that he does not, unless it is the right moral code or perhaps at least he thinks it is, although we think that the offense he might give to the feelings of others should be taken into account, as well as the result his nonconformity might have in weakening regard for moral rules in general.

(with some qualifications), whatever his society may think.[6]

Some parts of the theory in some of its forms, however, appear to be correct. In particular, the theory in some forms implies that, if a person has a certain recognized obligation in an institution or practice (e.g., a child to support his aged parent, a citizen to pay his taxes), then he morally does have this obligation, with some exceptions, irrespective of whether in an ideal institution he would or would not have. This we do roughly believe, although we need not at the same time accept the reasoning which has been offered to explain how the fact of a practice or institution leads to the moral obligation. The fact that the theory seems right in this would be a strong point in its favor if charges were correct that "ideal" forms of rule utilitarianism necessarily differ at this point. B. J. Diggs, for instance, has charged that the "ideal" theories imply that:

> "one may freely disregard a rule if ever he discovers that action on the rule is not maximally felicific, and in this respect makes moral rules like 'practical maxims.' . . . It deprives social and moral rules of their authority and naturally is in sharp conflict with practice. On this alternative rule utilitarianism collapses into act utilitarianism. Surely it is a mistake to maintain that a set of rules, thought to be ideally utilitarian or felicific, is the criterion of right action . . . If we are presented with a list [of rules], but these are not rules in practice, the most one could reasonably do is to try to get them adopted."[7]

I believe, however, and shall explain in detail later that this charge is without foundation.

[6] It is a different question whether we should hold offenders in such societies seriously morally blameworthy. People cannot be expected to rise much above the level of recognized morality, and we condemn them little when they do not.

[7] "Rules and Utilitarianism," *American Philosophical Quarterly* 1 (1964), 32–44 [pp. 306–323 above].

VI

Let us turn now to "ideal" forms of rule utilitarianism, which affirm that whether it is morally obligatory or morally right to do a certain thing in a particular situation is fixed not by the actual code or practice of the society (these may be indirectly relevant, as forming part of the situation) but by some "ideal" rule—that is, by the utility of having a certain general moral rule or by the utility of all or most actions being performed which are members of a relevant class of actions.

If the rightness of an act is fixed by the utility of a relevant rule (class), are we to say that the rule (class) which qualifies must be the optimific rule (class), the one which maximizes utility, or must the rule (class) meet only some less stringent requirement (e.g., be better than the absence of any rule regulating the type of conduct in question)? And, if it is to be of the optimific type, are all utilities to be counted, or perhaps only "negative" utilities, as is done when it is suggested that the rule (class) must be the one which minimizes suffering?[8]

The simplest proposal—that the rule (class) which qualifies is the one that maximizes utility, with all utilities, whether "positive" or "negative," being counted—also seems to me to be the best, and it is the one I shall shortly explain more fully. Among the several possible theories different from this one I shall discuss briefly only one which seems the most plausible

[8] In a footnote to Chapter 9 of *The Open Society*, Professor Karl R. Popper suggested that utilitarianism would be more acceptable if its test were minimizing suffering rather than maximizing welfare, to which J. J. C. Smart replied (*Mind* (1958), pp. 542–543) that the proposal implies that we ought to destroy all living beings, as the surest way to eliminate suffering. It appears, however, that Professor Popper does not seriously advocate what seemed to be the position of the earlier footnote (Addendum to fourth edition, p. 386).

of its kind and is at least closely similar to the view defended by Professor Marcus Singer.

According to this theory, an action (or inaction) at time *t* in circumstances *C* is wrong if and only if, were everyone in circumstances *C* to perform a relevantly similar action, harm would be done—meaning by "doing harm" that affected persons would be made worse off by the action (or inaction) than they already were at time *t*. (I think it is not meant that the persons must be put in a state of "negative welfare" in some sense, but simply made worse off than they otherwise would have been.) Let us suppose a person is deciding whether to do *A* in circumstances *C* at *t*. The theory, then, implies the following: (1) If everyone doing *A* in circumstances *C* would make people worse off than they already were at *t* (*A* can be inaction, such as failing to pull a drowning man from the water) whereas some other act would not make them so, then it is wrong for anyone to do *A*. (2) If everyone doing *A* would not make people worse off, then even if everyone doing something else would make them better off, it is not wrong to do *A*. (3) If everyone doing *A* would make people worse off, but if there is no alternative act, the performance of which by everyone would avoid making people worse off, then it is right to do *A*, even though doing *A* would make people relatively much worse off than they would have been made by the performance of some other action instead. The "optimific rule" theory, roughly, would accept (1) but reject (2) and (3).

Implication (3) of the theory strikes me as clearly objectionable; I am unable to imagine circumstances in which we should think it not morally incumbent on one to avoid very bad avoidable consequences for others, even though a situation somewhat worse than the status quo could not be avoided. Implication (2) is less obviously dubious. But I should think we do have obligations to do things for others when we are not merely avoiding being in the position of making them worse off. For instance, if one sees another person at a cocktail party standing by himself and looking unhappy, I should suppose one has some obligation to make an effort to put him at his ease, even though doing nothing would hardly make him worse off than he already is.

Why do proponents of this view, like Professor Singer, prefer his view to the simpler, "maximize utility" form of rule-utilitarianism? This is not clear. One objection sometimes raised is that an optimific theory implies that every act is morally weighty and none morally indifferent. And one may concede that this is a consequence of some forms of utilitarianism, even rule-utilitarianism of the optimific variety; but we shall see that it is by no means a consequence of the type of proposal described below. For the theory below will urge that an action is not morally indifferent only if it falls under some prescription of an optimific moral code, and, since there are disadvantages in a moral code regulating actions, optimific moral codes will prohibit or require actions of a certain type only when there are significant utilitarian reasons for it. As a consequence, a great many types of action are morally indifferent, according to the theory. Professor Singer also suggests that optimific-type theories have objectionable consequences for state-of-nature situations;[9] we may postpone judgment on this until we have examined these consequences of the theory here proposed, at a later stage. Other objections to the optimizing type of rule-utilitarianism with which I am familiar either confuse rule-utilitarianism with act-utilitarianism, or do not distinguish among the several possible forms of optimizing rule-utilitarianisms.

[9] M. G. Singer, *Generalization in Ethics* (New York: A. A. Knopf, Inc., 1961), p. 192.

VII

I propose, then, that we tentatively opt for an "ideal" rule utilitarianism, of the "maximizing utility" variety. This decision, however, leaves various choices still to be made between theories better or worse fitted to meet various problems. Rather than attempt to list alternatives and explain why one choice rather than another between them would work out better, I propose to describe in some detail the type of theory which seems most plausible. I shall later show how this theory meets the one problem to which the "actual rule" type theories seemed to have a nice solution; and I shall discuss its merits, as compared with another quite similar type of theory which has been suggested by Jonathan Harrison and others.

The theory I wish to describe is rather similar to one proposed by J. D. Mabbott in his 1953 British Academy lecture, "Moral Rules." It is also very similar to the view defended by J. S. Mill in *Utilitarianism,* although Mill's formulation is ambiguous at some points and he apparently did not draw some distinctions he should have drawn. (I shall revert to this historical point.)

For convenience I shall refer to the theory as the "ideal moral code" theory. The essence of it is as follows. Let us first say that a moral code is "ideal" if its currency in a particular society would produce at least as much good per person (the total divided by the number of persons) as the currency of any other moral code. (Two different codes might meet this condition, but, in order to avoid complicated formulations, the following discussion will ignore this possibility.) Given this stipulation for the meaning of "ideal," the Ideal Moral Code theory consists in the assertion of the following thesis: *An act is right if and only if it would not be prohibited by the moral code ideal for the society; and an agent is morally blameworthy (praiseworthy) for an act if, and to the degree that, the moral code ideal in that society would condemn (praise) him for it.* It is a virtue of this theory that it is a theory both about objective rightness and about moral blameworthiness (praiseworthiness) of actions, but the assertion about blameworthiness will be virtually ignored in what follows.

VIII

In order to have a clear proposal before us, however, the foregoing summary statement must be filled out in three ways: (1) by explaining what it is for a moral code to have currency; (2) by making clear what is the difference between the rules of a society's moral code and the rules of its institutions; and (3) by describing how the relative utility of a moral code is to be estimated.

First, then, the notion of a moral code having currency in a society.

For a moral code to have currency in a society, two things must be true. First, a high proportion of the adults in the society must subscribe to the moral principles, or have the moral opinions, constitutive of the code. Exactly how high the proportion should be, we can hardly decide on the basis of the ordinary meaning of "the moral code"; but probably it would not be wrong to require at least ninety percent agreement. Thus, if at least 90 percent of the adults subscribe to principle *A,* and 90 percent to principle *B,* etc., we may say that a code consisting of *A* and *B* (etc.) has currency in the society, provided the second condition is met. Second, we want to say that certain principles *A, B,* etc., belong to the moral code of a society only if they are recognized as such. That is, it must be that a large proportion of the adults of the society would respond correctly if asked, with respect to *A* and

B, whether most members of the society subscribed to them. (It need not be required that adults base their judgments on such good evidence as recollection of moral discussions; it is enough if for some reason the correct opinion about what is accepted is widespread.) It is of course possible for certain principles to constitute a moral code with currency in a society even if some persons in the society have no moral opinions at all, or if there is disagreement, e.g., if everyone in the society disagrees with every other person with respect to at least one principle.

The more difficult question is what it is for an individual to subscribe to a moral principle or to have a moral opinion. What is it, then, for someone to think sincerely that any action of the kind *F* is wrong? (1) He is to some extent motivated to avoid actions which he thinks are *F*, and often, if asked why he does not perform such an action when it appears to be to his advantage, offers, as one of his reasons, that it is *F*. In addition, the person's motivation to avoid *F*-actions does not derive entirely from his belief that *F*-actions on his part are likely to be harmful to him or to persons to whom he is somehow attached. (2) If he thinks he has just performed an *F*-action, he feels guilty or remorseful or uncomfortable about it, unless he thinks he has some excuse—unless, for instance, he knows that at the time of action he did not think his action would be an *F*-action. "Guilt" (etc.) is not to be understood as implying some special origin such as interiorization of parental prohibitions, or as being a vestige of anxiety about punishment. It is left open that it might be an unlearned emotional response to the thought of being the cause of the suffering of another person. Any feeling which must be viewed simply as anxiety about anticipated consequences, for one's self or person to whom one is attached, is not, however, to count as a "guilt" feeling. (3) If he believes that someone has performed an *F*-action, he will tend to admire him less as a person, unless he thinks that the individual has a good excuse. He thinks that action of this sort, without excuse, reflects on character—this being spelled out, in part, by reference to traits like honesty, respect for the rights of others, and so on. (4) He thinks that these attitudes of his are correct or well justified, in some sense, but with one restriction: it is not enough if he thinks that what justifies them is simply the fact that they are shared by all or most members of his society. This restriction corresponds with our distinction between a moral conviction and something else. For instance, we are inclined to think no moral attitude is involved if an Englishman disapproves of something but says that his disapproval is justified by the fact that it is shared by "well-bred Englishmen." In such cases we are inclined to say that the individual subscribes only to a custom or to a rule of etiquette or manners. On the other hand, if the individual thinks that what justifies his attitude unfavorable to *F*-actions is that *F*-actions are contrary to the will of God (and the individual's attitude is not merely a prudential one), or inconsistent with the welfare of mankind, or contrary to human nature, we are disposed to say the attitude is a moral attitude and the opinions expressed a moral one. And the same if he thinks his attitude justified, but can give no reason. There are perhaps other restrictions we should make on acceptable justifications (perhaps to distinguish a moral code from a code of honor), and other types of justification we should wish to list as clearly acceptable (perhaps an appeal to human equality).

IX

It is important to distinguish between the moral code of a society and its institutions, or the rules of its institutions. It is especially important for the Ideal Moral Code theory, for this theory involves the conception of a moral code ideal for a society in the context of its institutions, so that it is necessary to distinguish the moral code which a society does or might have from its institutions and their rules. The distinction is also one we actually do make in our thinking, although it is blurred in some cases. (For instance, is "Honor thy father and thy mother" a moral rule, or a rule of the family institution, in our society?)[10]

An institution is a set of positions or statuses, with which certain privileges and jobs are associated. (We can speak of these as "rights" and "duties" if we are careful to explain that we do not mean moral rights and duties.) That is, there are certain, usually nameable, positions which consist in the fact that anyone who is assigned to the position is expected to do certain things, and at the same time is expected to have certain things done for him. The individuals occupying these positions are a group of cooperating agents in a system which as a whole is thought to have the aim of serving certain ends. (E.g., a university is thought to serve the ends of education, research, etc.) The rules of the system concern jobs that must be done in order that the goals of the institution be achieved; they allocate the necessary jobs to different positions. Take, for instance, a university. There are various positions in it: the presidency, the professorial ranks, the registrars, librarians, etc. It is understood that one who occupies a certain post has certain duties, say teaching a specified number of classes or spending time working on research in the case of the instructing staff. Obviously the university cannot achieve its ends unless certain persons do the teaching, some tend to the administration, some to certain jobs in the library, and so on. Another such system is the family. We need not speculate on the "purpose" of the family, whether it is primarily a device for producing a new generation, etc. But it is clear that when a man enters marriage, he takes a position to which certain jobs are attached, such as providing support for the family to the best of his ability, and to which also certain rights are attached, such as exclusive sexual rights with his wife and the right to be cared for should he become incapacitated.

If an "institution" is defined in this way, it is clear that the moral code of a society cannot itself be construed as an institution, nor its rules as rules of an institution. The moral code is society-wide, so if we were to identify its rules as institutional rules, we should presumably have to say that everyone belongs to this institution. But what is the "purpose" of society as a whole? Are there any distinctions of status, with rights and duties attached, which we could identify as the "positions" in the moral system? Can we say that moral rules consist in the assignment of jobs in such a way that the aims of the institution may be achieved? It is true that there is a certain analogy: society as a whole might be said to be aiming at the good life for all, and the moral rules of the society might be viewed as the rules with which all must conform in order to achieve this end. But the analogy is feeble. Society as a whole is obviously not an organization like a university, an educational system, the church, General Motors, etc.; there is

[10] The confusion is compounded by the fact that terms like "obligation" and "duty" are used sometimes to speak about moral obligations and duties, and sometimes not. The fact that persons have a certain legal duty in certain situations is a rule of the legal institutions of the society; a person may not have a moral duty to do what is his legal duty. The fact that a person has an obligation to invite a certain individual to dinner is a matter of manners or etiquette, and at least may not be a matter of moral obligation. See R. B. Brandt, "The Concepts of Duty and Obligation," *Mind* 73 (1964), especially pp. 380–384.

no specific goal in the achievement of which each position has a designated role to play. Our answer to the above questions must be in the negative: morality is not an institution in the explained sense; nor are moral rules institutional expectations or rules.

The moral code of a society may, of course, have implications that bear on institutional rules. For one thing, the moral code may imply that an institutional system is morally wrong and ought to be changed. Moreover, the moral code may imply that a person has also a moral duty to do something which is his institutional job. For instance, it may be a moral rule that a person ought to do whatever he has undertaken to do, or that he ought not to accept the benefits of a position without performing its duties. Take for instance the rules, "A professor should meet his classes" or "Wives ought to make the beds." Since the professor has undertaken to do what pertains to his office, and the same for a wife, and since these tasks are known to pertain to the respective offices, the moral rules that a person is morally bound (with certain qualifications) to do what he has undertaken to do implies, in context, that the professor is morally bound to meet his classes and the wife to make the beds, other things being equal (viz., there being no contrary moral obligations in the situation). But these implications are not themselves part of the moral code. No one would say that a parent had neglected to teach his child the moral code of the society if he had neglected to teach him that professors must meet classes, and that wives must make the beds. A person becomes obligated to do these things only by participating in an institution, by taking on the status of professor or wife. Parents do not teach children to have guilt feelings about missing classes or making beds. The moral code consists only of more general rules, defining what is to be done in certain types of situations in which practically everyone will find himself. ("Do what you have promised!")

Admittedly some rules can be both moral and institutional: "Take care of your father in his old age" might be both an institutional rule of the family organization and also a part of the moral code of a society. (In this situation, one can still raise the question whether this moral rule is optimific in a society with that institutional rule; the answer could be negative.)

It is an interesting question whether "Keep your promises" is a moral rule, an institutional rule (a rule of an "institution" of promises), or both. Obviously it is part of the moral code of western societies. But is it also a rule of an institution? There are difficulties in the way of affirming that it is. There is no structure of cooperating individuals with special functions, which serves to promote certain aims. Nor, when one steps into the "role" of a promiser, does one commit one's self to any specific duties; one fixes one's own duties by what one promises. Nor, in order to understand what one is committing one's self to by promising, need one have any knowledge of any system of expectations prevalent in the society. A three-year-old, who has never heard of any duties incumbent on promisers, can tell his friends, who wish to play baseball that afternoon, that he will bring the ball and bat, and that they need give no thought to the availability of these items. His invitation to rely on him for something needed for their common enjoyment and his assurance that he will do something and his encouraging them thereby to set their minds at rest, *is* to make a promise. No one need suppose that the promiser is stepping into a socially recognized position, with all the rights and duties attendant on the same, although it is true he has placed himself in a position where he will properly be held responsible for the disappointment if he fails, and where inferences about his reliability as a person will properly be drawn if he forgets, or worse, if it turns out he was never in a position to perform. The bindingness of a promise is no more dependent on a set of expectations connected with an institution, than is the wrongness of striking another person without justifying reason.

Nevertheless, if one thinks it helpful to speak of a promise as an institution or a practice, in view of certain analogies (promiser and promisee may be said to have rights and duties like the occupants of roles in an institution, and there is the ritual-word "promise" the utterance of which commits the speaker to certain performances), there is no harm in this. The similarities and dissimilarities are what they are, and as long as these are understood it seems to make little difference what we say. Nevertheless, even if making a promise is participating in a practice or institution, there is still the *moral* question whether one is morally bound to perform, and in what conditions, and for what reasons. This question is left open, given the institution is whatever it is—as is the case with all rules of institutions.

X

It has been proposed above that an action is right if and only if it would not be prohibited by the moral code ideal for the society in which it occurs, where a moral code is taken to be "ideal" if and only if its currency would produce at least as much good per person as the currency of any other moral code.[11] We must now give more attention to the conception of an ideal moral code, and how it may be decided when a given moral code will produce as much good per person as any other. We may, however, reasonably bypass the familiar problems of judgments of comparative utilities, especially when different persons are involved, since these problems are faced by all moral theories that have any plausibility. We shall simply assume that rough judgments of this sort are made and can be justified.

(a) We should first notice that, as "currency" has been explained above, a moral code could not be current in a society if it were too complex to be learned or applied. We may therefore confine our consideration to codes simple enough to be absorbed by human beings, roughly in the way in which people learn actual moral codes.

(b) We have already distinguished the concept of an institution and its rules from the concept of a moral rule, or a rule of the moral code. (We have however, pointed out that in some cases a moral rule may prescribe the same thing that is also an institutional expectation. But this is not a necessary situation, and a moral code could condemn an institutional expectation.) Therefore, in deciding how much good the currency of a specific moral system would do, we consider the institutional setting as it is, as part of the situation. We are asking which moral code would produce the most good in the long run in this setting. One good to be reckoned, of course, might be that the currency of a given moral code would tend to change the institutional system.

(c) In deciding which moral code will produce the most per person good, we must take into account the probability that certain types of situation will arise in the society. For instance, we must take for granted that people will make promises and subsequently want to break them, that people will sometimes assault other persons in order to achieve their own ends,

[11] Some utilitarians have suggested that the right act is determined by the total net intrinsic good produced. This view can have embarrassing consequences for problems of population control. The view here advocated is that the right act is determined by the per person, average, net intrinsic good produced.

that people will be in distress and need the assistance of others, and so on. We may not suppose that, because an ideal moral code might have certain features, it need not have other features because they will not be required; for instance, we may not suppose, on the ground that an ideal moral system would forbid everyone to purchase a gun, that such a moral system needs no provisions about the possession and use of guns—just as our present moral and legal codes have provisions about self-defense, which would be unnecessary if everyone obeyed the provision never to assault anyone.

It is true that the currency of a moral code with certain provisions might bring about a reduction in certain types of situation, e.g., the number of assaults or cases of dishonesty. And the reduction might be substantial, if the moral code were current which prohibited these offenses very strongly. (We must remember that an ideal moral code might differ from the actual one not only in what it prohibits or enjoins, but also in how strongly it prohibits or enjoins.) But it is consistent to suppose that a moral code prohibits a certain form of behavior very severely, and yet that the behavior will occur, since the "currency" of a moral code requires only 90 percent subscription to it, and a "strong" subscription, on the average, permits a great range from person to person. In any case there must be doubt whether the best moral code will prohibit many things very severely, since there are serious human costs in severe prohibitions: the burden of guilt feelings, the traumas caused by the severe criticism by others which is a part of having a strong injunction in a code, the risks of any training process which would succeed in interiorizing a severe prohibition, and so on.

(d) It would be a great oversimplification if, in assessing the comparative utility of various codes, we confined ourselves merely to counting the benefits of people doing (refraining from doing) certain things, as a result of subscribing to a certain code. To consider only this would be as absurd as estimating the utility of some feature of a legal system by attending only to the utility of people behaving in the way the law aims to make them behave—and overlooking the fact that the law only reduces and does not eliminate misbehavior, as well as the disutility of punishment to the convicted, and the cost of the administration of criminal law. In the case of morals, we must weigh the benefit of the improvement in behavior as a result of the restriction built into conscience, against the cost of the restriction—the burden of guilt feelings, the effects of the training process, etc. There is a further necessary refinement. In both law and morals we must adjust our estimates of utility by taking into account the envisaged system of excuses. That *mens rea* is required as a condition of guilt in the case of most legal offenses is most important, and it is highly important for the utility of a moral system whether accident, intent, and motives are taken into account in deciding a person's liability to moral criticism. A description of a moral code is incomplete until we have specified the severity of condemnation (by conscience or the criticism of others) to be attached to various actions, along with the excuses to be allowed as exculpating or mitigating.

XI

Philosophers have taken considerable interest in the question what implications forms of rule utilitarianism have for the moral relevance of the behavior of persons other than the agent. Such implications, it is thought, bring into focus the effective difference between any form of rule utilitarianism, and act utilitarianism. In particular, it has been thought that the implications for rule utilitarianisms for two types of situation are especially significant: (a) for situations in which persons are generally violating the recognized moral code, or some feature of it; and (b) for situations in which, because the moral code is generally respected, maximum utility would be produced by violation of the code by the agent. An example of the former situation (sometimes called a "state of nature" situation) would be widespread perjury in making out income-tax declarations. An example of the latter situation would be widespread conformity to the rule forbidding walking on the grass in a park.

What are the implications of the suggested form of rule utilitarianism for these types of situations? Will it prescribe conduct which is not utility-maximizing in these situations? If it does, it will clearly have implications discrepant with those of act utilitarianism—but perhaps unpalatable to some people.

It is easy to see how to go about determining what is right or wrong in such situations, on the above-described form of rule utilitarianism—it is a question of what an "ideal" moral code would prescribe. But it is by no means easy to see where a reasonable person would come out, after going through such an investigation. Our form of rule utilitarianism does not rule out, as morally irrelevant, reference to the behavior of other persons; it implies that the behavior of others is morally relevant precisely to the extent to which an optimific moral code (the one the currency of which is optimific) would take it into account. How far, then, we might ask, would an optimific moral code take into account the behavior of other persons, and what would its specific prescriptions be for the two types of situations outlined?

It might be thought, and it has been suggested, that an ideal moral code could take no cognizance of the behavior of other persons, and in particular of the possibility that many persons are ignoring some prohibitions of the code, sometimes for the reason, apparently, that it is supposed that a code of behavior would be self-defeating if it prescribed for situations of its own breach, on a wide scale. It is a sufficient answer to this suggestion, to point out that our actual moral code appears to contain some such prescriptions. For instance, our present code seems to permit, for the case in which almost everyone is understating his income, that others do the same, on the ground that otherwise they will be paying more than their fair share. It is, of course, true that a code simple enough to be learned and applied cannot include prescriptions for all possible types of situation involving the behavior of other persons; but it can contain some prescriptions pertinent to some general features of the behavior of others.

Granted, then, that an ideal moral code may contain some special prescriptions which pay attention to the behavior of other persons, how in particular will it legislate for special situations such as the examples cited above? The proper answer to this question is that there would apparently be no blanket provision for all cases of these general types and that a moral agent faced with such a concrete situation would have to think out what an ideal moral code would imply for his type of concrete situation. Some things do seem clear. An ideal moral code would not provide that a person is permitted to be cruel in a society where most other persons are cruel; there could only be loss of utility in any special provision permitting that. On the other hand, if there is some form of cooperative activity which enhances utility only if most persons cooperate, and in which nonparticipation does not reduce utility when most persons are not cooperating, utility would seem to be maximized if the moral code somehow permitted all to abstain—perhaps by an abstract formula stating this very condition. (This is on the assumption that the participation by some would not, by example, eventually bring about the participation of most or all.) Will there be any types of situation for which an ideal moral code would prescribe infringement of a generally respected moral code, by a few, when a few infringements (provided there are not many) would maximize utility? The possibility of this is not ruled out. Obviously there will be some regulations for emergencies: one may cut across park grass in order to rush a heart-attack victim to a hospital. And there will be rules making special exceptions when considerable utility is involved: the boy with no other place to play may use the grass in the park. But, when an agent has no special claim which others could not make, it is certainly not clear that ideal moral rules will make him an exception on the ground that some benefit will come to him, and that restraint by him is unnecessary in view of the cooperation of others.

The implications of the above form of rule utilitarianism for these situations are evidently different from those of act utilitarianism.[12]

XII

The Ideal Moral Code theory is very similar to the view put forward by J. S. Mill in *Utilitarianism.*

Mill wrote that his creed held that "actions are right in proportion as they tend to promote happiness; wrong as they tend to produce the reverse of happiness." Mill apparently did not intend by this any form of act utilitarianism. He was—doubtless with much less than full awareness—writing of act-*types,* and what he meant was that an act of a certain type is morally obligatory (wrong) if and only if acts of that type tend to promote happiness (the reverse). Mill supposed that it is known that certain kinds of acts, e.g., murder and theft, promote unhappiness, and that therefore we can say, with exceptions only for very special circumstances, that murder and theft are wrong. Mill recognized that there can be a discrepancy between the tendency of an act-type, and the probable effects, in context, of an individual act. He wrote: "In the case of abstinences, indeed—of things which people forbear to do from moral considerations, though the consequences in the particular case might be beneficial—, it would be unworthy of an intelligent agent not to be consciously aware that the action is of a class which, if practiced generally, would be generally injurious, and that this is the ground of the obligation to abstain from it."[13] Moreover, he specifically denied that one is morally obligated to perform (avoid) an act just on the ground that it can be expected to produce good consequences; he says that "there is no case of moral obligation in which some secondary principle is not involved." *(op. cit.,* p. 33).

It appears, however, that Mill did not quite think that it is morally obligatory to perform (avoid) an act according as its general performance would promote (reduce) happiness in the world. For he said (p. 60) that "We do not call anything wrong unless we mean to imply that a

[12] The above proposal is different in various respects from that set forth in the writer's "Toward a Credible Form of Utilitarianism," in Castaneda and Nakhnikian, *Morality and the Language of Conduct,* 1963. The former paper did not make a distinction between institutional rules and moral rules. (The present paper, of course, allows that both may contain a common prescription.) A result of these differences is that the present theory is very much simpler, and avoids some counter-intuitive consequences which some writers have pointed out in criticism of the earlier proposal.

[13] *Utilitarianism* (New York: Library of Liberal Arts, 1957), p. 25 [p. 26 above].

person ought to be punished in some way or other for doing it—if not by law, by the opinion of his fellow creatures; if not by opinion, by the reproaches of his own conscience. This seems the real turning point of the distinction between morality and simple expediency." The suggestion here is that it is morally obligatory to perform (avoid) an act according as it is beneficial to have a system of sanctions (with what this promises in way of performance), whether formal, informal (criticism by others), or internal (one's own conscience), for enforcing the performance (avoidance) of the type of act in question. This is very substantially the Ideal Moral Code theory.

Not that there are no differences. Mill is not explicit about details, and the theory outlined above fills out what he actually said. Moreover, Mill noticed that an act can fall under more than one secondary principle and that the relevant principles may give conflicting rulings about what is morally obligatory. In such a case, Mill thought, what one ought to do (but it is doubtful whether he believed there is a strict moral obligation in this situation) is what will maximize utility in the concrete situation. This proposal for conflicts of "ideal moral rules" is not a necessary part of the Ideal Moral Code theory as outlined above.

XIII

It is sometimes thought that a rule utilitarianism rather like Mill's cannot differ in its implication about what is right or wrong from the act utilitarian theory. This is a mistake.

The contention would be correct if two dubious assumptions happened to be true. The first is that one of the rules of an optimific moral code will be that a person ought always to do whatever will maximize utility. The second is that when there is a conflict between the rules of an optimific code, what a person ought to do is to maximize utility. For then, either the utilitarian rule is the only one that applies (and it always will be relevant), in which case the person ought to do what the act utilitarian directs; or if there is a conflict among the relevant rules, the conflict-resolving principle takes over, and this, of course, prescribes exactly what act utilitarianism prescribes. Either way, we come out where the act utilitarian comes out.

But there is no reason at all to suppose that there will be a utilitarian rule in an optimific moral code. In fact, obviously there will not be. It is true that there should be a directive to relieve the distress of others, when this can be done, say, at relatively low personal cost; and there should be a directive not to injure other persons except in special situations. And so on. But none of this amounts to a straight directive to do the most good possible. Life would be chaotic if people tried to observe any such moral requirement.

The second assumption was apparently acceptable to Mill. But a utilitarian principle is by no means the only possible conflict-resolving principle. For if we say, with the Ideal Moral Code theory, that what is right is fixed by the content of the moral system with maximum utility, the possibility is open that the utility-maximizing moral system will contain some rather different device for resolving conflicts between lowest-level moral rules. The ideal system might contain several higher-level conflict-resolving principles, all different from Mill's. Or, if there is a single one, it could be a directive to maximize utility; it could be a directive to do what an intelligent person who had fully interiorized the rest of the ideal moral system would feel best satisfied with doing; and so on. But the final court of appeal need not be an appeal to direct utilities. Hence the argument that Mill-like rule utilitarianism must collapse into direct utilitarianism is doubly at fault.[14]

In fact, far from "collapsing" into act utilitarianism, the Ideal Moral Code theory appears to avoid the serious objections which have been leveled at direct utilitarianism. One objection to the latter view is that it implies that various immoral actions (murdering one's elderly father, breaking solemn promises) are right or even obligatory if only they can be kept secret. The Ideal Moral Code theory has no such implication. For it obviously would not maximize utility to have a moral code which condoned secret murders or breaches of promise. W. D. Ross criticized act utilitarianism on the ground that it ignored the personal relations important in ordinary morality, and he listed a half-dozen types of moral rule which he thought captured the main themes of thoughtful morality: obligations of fidelity, obligations of gratitude, obligations to make restitution for injuries, obligations to help other persons, to avoid injuring them, to improve one's self, and to bring about a just distribution of good things in life. An ideal moral code, however, would presumably contain substantially such rules in any society, doubtless not precisely as Ross stated them. So the rule utilitarian need not fail to recognize the personal character of morality.

XIV

In contrast to the type of theory put forward by Toulmin and others, the Ideal Moral Code theory has the advantage of implying that the moral rules recognized in a given society are not necessarily morally binding. They are binding only in so far as they maximize welfare, as contrasted with other possible moral rules. Thus if, in a given society, it is thought wrong to work on the Sabbath, to perform socially desirable abortions, or to commit suicide, it does not follow, on the Ideal Moral Code theory, that these things are necessarily wrong. The question is whether a code containing such prohibitions would maximize welfare. Similarly, according to this theory, a person may act wrongly in doing certain things which are condoned by his society.

A serious appeal of theories like Toulmin's is, however, their implications for institutional obligations. For instance, if in society *A* it is a recognized obligation to care for one's aged father, Toulmin's theory implies that it really is a moral obligation for a child in that society to care for his aged parent (with some qualifications); whereas if in society *B* it is one's recognized obligation not to care for one's aged father, but instead for one's aged maternal uncle, his theory implies that it really is the moral obligation of a person in that society to care for his aged maternal uncle—even if a better institutional system would put the responsibilities in different places. This seems approximately what we do believe.

The Ideal Moral Code theory, however, has much the same implications. According to it, an institutional system forms the setting within which the best (utility-maximizing) moral code is to be applied, and one's obligation is to follow the best moral rules in that institutional setting—not to do what the best moral rules would require for some other, more ideal, setting.

[14] Could some moral problems be so unique that they would not be provided for by the set of rules it is best for the society to have? If so, how should they be appraised morally? Must there be some appeal to rules covering cases most closely analogous, as seems to be the procedure in law? If so, should we say that an act is right if it is not prohibited, either explicitly or by close analogy, by an ideal moral code? I shall not attempt to answer these questions.

Let us examine the implications of the Ideal Moral Code theory by considering a typical example. Among the Hopi Indians, a child is not expected to care for his father (he is always in a different clan), whereas he is expected to care for his mother, maternal aunt, and maternal uncle, and so on up the female line (all in the same clan). It would be agreed by observers that this system does not work very well. The trouble with it is that the lines of institutional obligation and the lines of natural affection do not coincide, and, as a result, an elderly male is apt not to be cared for by anyone.

Can we show that an "ideal moral code" would call on a young person to take care of his maternal uncle in a system of this sort? (It might also imply he should try to change the system, but that is another point.) One important feature of the situation of the young man considering whether he should care for his maternal uncle is that, the situation including the expectations of others being what it is, if he does nothing to relieve the distress of his maternal uncle, it is probable that it will not be relieved. His situation is very like that of the sole observer of an automobile accident; he is a mere innocent bystander, but the fact is that if he does nothing, the injured persons will die. So the question for us is whether an ideal moral code will contain a rule that, if someone is in a position where he can relieve serious distress, and where it is known that in all probability it will not be relieved if he does not do so, he should relieve the distress. The answer seems to be that it will contain such a rule: we might call it an "obligation of humanity." But there is a second, and more important point. Failure of the young person to provide for his maternal uncle would be a case of unfairness or free-riding. For the family system operates like a system of insurance; it provides one with various sorts of privileges or protections, in return for which one is expected to make certain payments or accept the risk of making certain payments. Our young man has already benefited by the system and stands to benefit further; he has received care and education as a child, and later on his own problems of illness and old age will be provided for. On the other hand, the old man, who has (we assume) paid such premiums as the system calls on him to pay in life, is now properly expecting, in accordance with the system, certain services from a particular person whom the system designates as the one to take care of him. Will the ideal moral code require such a person to pay the premium in such a system? I suggest that it will, and we can call the rule in question an "obligation of fairness."[15] So, we may

[15] See John Rawls, in "Justice as Fairness," *Philosophical Review* 67 (1958), 164–194, especially pp. 179–184.

It seems to be held by some philosophers that an ideal moral code would contain no rule of fairness. The line of argument seems to be as follows: Assume we have an institution involving cooperative behavior for an end which will necessarily be of benefit to all in the institution. Assume further that the cooperative behavior required is burdensome. Assume finally that the good results will be produced even if fewer than all cooperate—perhaps 90 percent is sufficient. It will then be to an individual's advantage to shirk making his contribution, since he will continue to enjoy the benefits. Shirking on the part of some actually maximizes utility, since the work is burdensome, and the burdensome effort of those who shirk (provided there are not too many) is useless.

I imagine that it would be agreed that, in this sort of system, there should be an agreed and known rule for exempting individuals from useless work. (E.g., someone who is ill would be excused.) In the absence of this, a person should feel free to excuse himself for good and special reason. Otherwise, I think we suppose everyone should do his share, and that it is not a sufficient reason for shirking, to know that enough are cooperating to produce the desired benefits. Let us call this requirement of working except for special reason (etc.) a "rule of fairness."

Would an ideal moral code contain a rule of

infer that our young man will have a moral obligation to care for his maternal uncle on grounds both of humanity and fairness.

We need not go so far as to say that such considerations mean that an ideal moral code will underwrite morally every institutional obligation. An institution may be grossly inequitable; or some part of it may serve no purpose at all but rather be injurious (as some legal prohibitions may be). But I believe we can be fairly sure that Professor Diggs went too far in saying that a system of this sort "deprives social and moral rules of their authority and naturally is in sharp conflict with practice" and that it "collapses into act utilitarianism."

XV

It may be helpful to contrast the Ideal Moral Code theory with a rather similar type of rule utilitarianism, which in some ways is simpler than the Ideal Moral Code theory and which seems to be the only form of rule utilitarianism recognized by some philosophers. This other type of theory is suggested in the writings of R. F. Harrod, Jonathan Harrison, perhaps John Hospers and Marcus Singer, although, as I shall describe it, it differs from the exact theory proposed by any of these individuals in more or less important ways.

The theory is a combination of act utilitarianism with a Kantian universalizability requirement for moral action. It denies that an act is necessarily right if it will produce consequences no worse than would any other action the agent might perform; rather, it affirms that an act is right if and only if universal action on the "maxim" of the act would not produce worse consequences than universal action on some other maxim on which the agent could act. Or, instead of talking of universal action on the "maxim" of the act in question, we can speak of all members of the class of relevantly similar actions being performed; then the proposal is that an action is right if and only if universal performance of the class of relevantly similar acts would not have worse consequences than universal performance of the class of acts relevantly similar to some alternative action the agent might perform. Evidently it is important how we identify the "maxim" of an act or the class of "relevantly similar" acts.

One proceeds as follows. One may begin with the class specified by the properties one thinks are the morally significant ones of the act in question. (One could as well start with the class defined by all properties of the act, if one practically could do this!) One then enlarges the class by omitting from its definition those properties which would not affect the average utility which would result for all the acts in the class being performed. (The total utility might be affected simply by enlarging the size of the class; merely enlarging the class does not affect the average utility.) Conversely, one must also narrow any proposed class of "relevantly similar" acts if it is found that properties have

---

fairness? At least, there could hardly be a public rule permitting people to shirk while a sufficient number of others work. For what would the rule be? It would be all too easy for most people to believe that a sufficient number of others were working (like the well-known difficulty in farm-planning, that if one plants what sold at a good price the preceding year, one is apt to find that prices for that product will drop, since most other farmers have the same idea). Would it even be a good idea to have a rule to the effect that if one absolutely knows that enough others are working, one may shirk? This seems highly doubtful.

Critics of rule utilitarianism seem to have passed from the fact that the best system would combine the largest product with the least effort, to the conclusion that the best moral code would contain a rule advising not to work when there are enough workers already. This is a *non sequitur.*

been omitted from the specification of it, the presence of which would affect the average utility which would result if all the acts in the class were performed. The relevant class must not be too large because of omission of features which define subclasses with different utilities, or too small because of the presence of features which make no difference to the utilities.

An obvious example of an irrelevant property is that of the agent having a certain name (in most situations) or being a certain person. On the other hand, the fact that the agent wants (does not want) to perform a certain act normally is relevant to the utility of the performance of that act.

So much by way of exposition of the theory.

For many cases this theory and the Ideal Moral Code theory have identical implications. For, when it is better for action of type *A* to be performed in a certain situation than for actions of any other type to be performed, it will often be a good thing to have type *A* actions prescribed by the moral code, directly or indirectly.

The theory also appears more simple than the Ideal Moral Code theory. In order to decide whether a given act is right or wrong we are not asked to do anything as grand as decide what some part of an ideal moral code would be like, but merely whether it would be better or worse for all in a relevant class of acts to be performed, as compared with some other relevant class. Thus it offers simple answers to questions such as whether one should vote ("What if nobody did?"), pick wildflowers along the road ("What if everyone did?") join the army in wartime, or walk on the grass in a park.[16] Furthermore, the theory has a simple way of dealing with conflicts of rules: one determines whether it would be better or worse for all members of the more complex class (about which the rules conflict) of actions to be performed (e.g., promises broken in the situation where the breach would save a life).

In one crucial respect, however, the two theories are totally different. For, in contrast with the Ideal Moral Code theory, this theory implies that exactly those acts are objectively right which are objectively right on the act utilitarian theory. Hence the implications of this theory for action include the very counterintuitive ones which led its proponents to seek an improvement over act utilitarianism.

It must be conceded that this assessment of the implications of the theory is not yet a matter of general agreement,[17] and depends on a rather complex argument. In an earlier paper (*loc. cit.*) I argued that the theory does have these consequences, although my statement of the theory was rather misleading. More recently Professor

[16] One should not, however, overemphasize the simplicity. Whether one should vote in these circumstances is not decided by determining that it would have bad consequences if no one voted at all. It is a question whether it would be the best thing for all those people to vote (or not vote) in the class of situations relevantly similar to this one. It should be added, however, that if I am correct in my (below) assessment of the identity of this theory with act utilitarianism, in the end it is simple, on the theory, to answer these questions.

It hardly seems that an ideal moral code would contain prescriptions as specific as rules about these matters. But the implications for such matters would be fairly direct if, as suggested above, an ideal moral code would contain a principle enjoining fairness, i.e., commanding persons to do their share in common enterprises (or restraints), when everyone benefits if most persons do their share, when persons find doing their share a burden, and when it is not essential that everyone do his share although it is essential that most do so, for the common benefit to be realized.

[17] See, for instance, the interesting paper by Michael A. G. Stocker, "Consistency in Ethics," *Analysis* supplement, vol. 25 (January 1965), pp. 116–122.

David Lyons has come to the same conclusion, after an extensive discussion in which he urges that the illusion of a difference between the consequences of this theory of those of act utilitarianism arises because of failure to notice certain important features of the context of actions, primarily the relative frequency of similar actions at about the same time, and "threshold effects" which an action may have on account of these features.[18]

It may be worthwhile to draw attention to the features of the Ideal Moral Code theory which avoid this particular result. In the first place, the Ideal Moral Code theory sets a limit to the number and complexity of the properties which define a class of morally similar actions. For, on this theory, properties of an act make a difference to its rightness, only if a moral principle referring to them (directly or indirectly) can be learned as part of the optimific moral code. Actual persons, with their emotional and intellectual limitations, are unable to learn a moral code which incorporates all the distinctions the other theory can recognize as morally relevant; and even if they could learn it, it would not be utility-maximizing for them to try to apply it. In the second place, we noted that to be part of a moral code a proscription must be public, believed to be part of what is morally disapproved of by most adults. Thus whereas some actions (e.g., some performed in secret) would be utility-maximizing, the Ideal Moral Code theory may imply that they are wrong, because it would be a bad thing for it to be generally recognized that a person is free to do that sort of thing.

[18] David Lyons, *Forms and Limits of Utilitarianism* (Oxford: Clarendon Press, 1965).

XVI

I do not know of any reason to think that the Ideal Moral Code theory is a less plausible normative moral theory than any other form of utilitarianism. Other types of rule utilitiarianism are sufficiently like it, however, that it might be that relatively minor changes in formulation would make their implications for conduct indistinguishable from those of the Ideal Moral Code theory.

Two questions have not here been discussed. One is whether the Ideal Moral Code theory is open to the charge that it implies that some actions are right which are unjust in such an important way that they cannot be right. The second question is one a person would naturally wish to explore if he concluded that the right answer to the first question is affirmative: it is whether a rule utilitarian view could be combined with some other principles like a principle of justice in a plausible way, without loss of all the features which make utilitarianism attractive. The foregoing discussion has not been intended to provide an answer to these questions.

C. L. Ten / Mill on self-regarding actions

In the essay *On Liberty,* Mill put forward his famous principle that society may only interfere with those actions of an individual which concern others and not with actions which merely concern himself.[1] The validity of this principle depends on there being a distinction between self-regarding and other-regarding actions. But the concept of self-regarding actions has been severely criticised on the ground that all actions affect others in some way and are therefore other-regarding. The notion of self-regarding actions appears to be completely discredited. Very recently, however, there has been some dissatisfaction with the traditional debunking of Mill on this score. Two serious and important attempts to reinterpret the principle were made by Mr. J. C. Rees in an article entitled "A Re-Reading of Mill on Liberty,"[2] and by Mr. Alan Ryan in two brief but extremely useful contributions.[3] My aim is to discuss these reinterpretations of Mill, and on the basis of this, build up what I think is the correct account of Mill's notion of self-regarding actions.

I

After lucidly documenting the traditional interpretation of Mill's notion of self-regarding actions, Mr. J. C. Rees proceeds to show why this interpretation is mistaken and to give his own version of Mill's doctrine. According to the traditional interpretation, self-regarding actions are actions which affect only the agent and have no effect on others. Against this Mr. Rees argues that self-regarding actions are those actions which do not affect the *interests* of others. His case for this reinter-

[1] *On Liberty* (Everyman's Library) pp. 72–73. All references to the essay are to this edition.
[2] *Political Studies,* vol. 8 (1960), pp. 113–129.

[3] "Mr. McCloskey on Mill's Liberalism," *Philosophical Quarterly* 14 (1964), 253–260 and "John Stuart Mill's Art of Living," *The Listener,* October 21, 1965, pp. 620–622.

Reprinted from PHILOSOPHY, *vol. 43, no. 163 (January 1968), pp. 29–37, by permission of the author and editors.*

pretation is based on the following claims: (a) that there is an important difference between just "affecting others" and "affecting the interests of others," and that at crucial stages when he is stating his principle Mill brings in the word "interests"; and (b) that Mill could not be thinking of "effects" when he put forward his principle for he freely admitted that self-regarding actions affected others.

With respect to (a) it is of course true that Mill often used the word "interests" in stating his case for liberty, but what is not readily conceded is that Mill saw any distinction between "interests" and "effects" in the way that Mr. Rees does. Mr. Rees writes: ". . . [Interests] depend for their existence on social recognition and are closely connected with prevailing standards about the sort of behaviour a man can legitimately expect from others. A claim that something should be recognised as an interest is one we should require to be supported by reasons and one capable of being made the subject of discussion. On the other hand I could be very seriously affected by the action of another person merely because I had an extraordinarily sensitive nature and no claim to have others respect these tender spots would be recognised as amounting to an interest. How one is affected by a theatrical performance depends partly on one's tastes, but the interests of a businessman would be affected by a tax on business property no matter what his tastes or susceptibilities; just as the interests of a university are affected by a scheme to establish a research institute in the same area (in a common subject of course) whether the university authorities welcome the idea or not.[4] However, in *Utilitarianism* Mill explicitly stated what he meant by "interests": ". . . laws and social arrangements should place the happiness, or (as speaking practically it may be called) the interest, of every individual, as nearly as possible with the interest of the whole; . . ."[5] "Interest" then is for him synonymous with "happiness." This being the case, Mr. Rees's attempt to drive a wedge between "affecting others" and "affecting the interests of others" fails. For the latter expression turns out to mean no more than "affecting the happiness of others" and does not now appear to differ in any important sense from merely "affecting others." The fact that Mill seems to use these two expressions, together with other expressions like "conduct which concerns only himself," without distinguishing between them should then present no real difficulty. Whenever such expressions are used, they all refer to actions which do not affect the happiness of others. Mill assumed that whatever "affects" others or "concerns others" will only do so through its influence on their happiness. There is no need to accept Mr. Rees's suggestion that ". . . the ambiguity of the word 'concerns' is responsible for concealing a coherent theory based on 'interests' rather than 'effects' . . ."[6] Mr. Rees's distinction between "interests" and "effects" is not one which Mill subscribed to, and any problem arising therefrom would be nonexistent for him.

But we are still left with Mr. Rees's second argument. If Mill did not distinguish between interests and effects, was he not guilty of a blatant contradiction in admitting that self-regarding actions affected others? I do not think so. Mill's principle did not necessarily depend on there being an area of human actions which had absolutely no effect on others. This is quite clear from a passage to which Mr. Rees himself draws attention as presenting some difficulties for his reinterpretation of Mill: "But there is a sphere of action in which society, as distinguished

[4] Rees, p. 119.

[5] *Utilitarianism* (Everyman's Library), p. 16 [p. 24 above].

[6] Rees, p. 120.

from the individual, has, if any, only an *indirect interest;* comprehending all that portion of a person's life and conduct which affects only himself, or if it also affects others, only with their free, voluntary, and undeceived consent and participation. *When I say only himself, I mean directly, and in the first instance;* for whatever affects himself, may affect others through himself; . . ."[7] All the evidence which Mr. Rees presents to show that Mill was aware that self-regarding actions could affect others can be explained in the light of this passage. Mill merely meant that these self-regarding actions affected others *indirectly,* even if sometimes seriously. Mill's admissions can be accounted for in terms of a distinction which he clearly made between direct and indirect interests or direct and indirect effects, and need not depend on an alleged distinction which Mr. Rees attributes to him between interests and effects.

According to Mill, an action indirectly affects others or, what amounts to the same thing, the interests of others, if it affects their happiness simply because they dislike it or find it repugnant or immoral. Soon after stating his principle, he picked out three areas of self-regarding actions in which individual liberty should prevail. The difference between other-regarding and self-regarding actions in the area of "tastes and pursuits" is expressed in terms of actions which "harm" our fellow creatures on the one hand, and actions which do not harm them "even though they should think our conduct foolish, perverse or wrong" on the other.[8] Again, before he put forward his own principle he considered certain attitudes which he thought had worked against the cause of freedom. He criticised those who "have occupied themselves rather in inquiring what things society ought to like or dislike, than in questioning whether their likings or dislikings should be a law to individuals."[9] His principle was meant to oppose such attitudes. He was clearly aware that self-regarding actions could be disliked by others or regarded with abhorrence by them.

Sometimes these feelings of abhorrence and dislike can be intense and genuine. I think that when Mill spoke of self-regarding actions "seriously affecting" others, he had such cases in mind. He deplored a state of affairs in which punishment and severe social pressures were brought to bear on actions which merely aroused society's intense dislike and repugnance. Thus he pointed out that, "wherever the sentiment of the majority is still genuine and intense, it is found to have abated little of its claim to be obeyed."[10] We have such a situation if a society consisting of a majority of Muslims prohibited the eating of pork. Mill pointed out that the practice is "really revolting" to such a people who "also sincerely think that it is forbidden and abhorred by the Deity."[11] He said that the only tenable ground we could have for condemning such a prohibition would be that "with the personal tastes and self-regarding concerns of individuals the public has no business to interfere."[12] In other words, only by adopting the principle he put forward in the essay could we have a reason for ruling out the appeal to the majority's genuine feelings of repugnance and revulsion as a ground for interfering with individual liberty. Mill's essay *On Liberty* was a protest against the appeal which he felt was so often made to such feelings of the majority as relevant and good reasons for restricting the actions of individuals. According to him they are in themselves

[7] *On Liberty*, p. 75. (My italics.)

[8] Ibid.

[9] Ibid., pp. 70–71.

[10] Ibid., p. 71.

[11] Ibid., p. 142.

[12] Ibid.

never relevant or good reasons for interference. If the only reason that can be given for wishing to restrict an individual's freedom is an appeal to such feelings, then that individual's action is a self-regarding one. If, however, the action violates "a distinct and assignable obligation" then an additional factor appears which takes it out of the self-regarding class.[13] But even so Mill insisted that we should give the proper reason for interference: "If, for example, a man, through intemperance or extravagance, becomes unable to pay his debts, or having undertaken the moral responsibility of a family, becomes from some cause incapable of supporting or educating them, he is deservedly reprobated and might be justly punished; but it is for the breach of duty to his family or creditors, not for the extravagance."[14] He wanted to revise the framework within which questions about individual liberty and society's right of interference are raised and answered. He tried to do this by limiting the type of reasons that could legitimately be given for interference with liberty. There are certain reasons, like the majority's feelings of repugnance, which by themselves are irrelevant and should not be given as a basis for restricting the freedom of the individual.

II

But what has the notion of self-regarding actions to do with utilitarianism? Mill said that his case for liberty was based on an appeal to "utility in the largest sense, grounded on the permanent interests of a man as a progressive being."[15] What does he mean by this? I do not think that we can fully understand the nature of his defence of individual liberty unless we find an answer to this.

Mr. Ryan has argued that *On Liberty* is not inconsistent with utilitarianism, but on the contrary it is the working out of the consequences of a utilitarian doctrine which runs through many of Mill's writings. Mill distinguished between law and morality on the one hand, and prudence and aesthetics on the other. The area of law and morality is other-regarding and only in this area can sanctions or punishment be applied. Law and morality differ only in the type of sanction that is used. The sanction behind morality is that of public opinion or social disapproval. To say that an action is wrong or immoral is to say that it must be stopped by society, at least through the pressure of public opinion. Mill's famous principle may, according to Mr. Ryan, be regarded as a limitation of morality to the other-regarding sphere. Self-regarding actions do not belong to the area of morality and we cannot therefore apply sanctions to them.

I find all this extremely valuable and Mr. Ryan has presented his case with great cogency. But he takes for granted that a utilitarian morality is other-regarding, and hence an action can only be said to be immoral when it harms persons other than the agent. The notion of "harm to others" is, however, a complex one, and Mill interpreted it in a way that is radically different from Bentham. *On Liberty* may be a utilitarian tract, but if it is, there is still a world of difference between Mill's utilitarianism and Bentham's. Mill's essay may indeed be fruitfully regarded as a rebellion against Benthamite utilitarianism. I shall first discuss some of the relevant features of Benthamite utilitarianism, and then show why Mill could not go all the way with it.

For Bentham the aim of both moral and legal rules is to achieve the greatest happiness of the greatest number, each person counting as one. Bentham's utili-

[13] Ibid.
[14] Ibid.
[15] Ibid., p. 74.

tarianism, however, contains one other feature which is of great importance. All pleasures and pains are relevant no matter what their nature or what the context may be. Any two lots of pleasures and pains which are of the same "value" as measured by his "felicific calculus" are of equal relevance. It is this feature which Mr. John Rawls so vividly drew attention to in his well-known article, "Justice as Fairness": ". . . the individuals receiving these benefits are not conceived as being related in any way: they represent so many different directions in which limited resources may be allocated. The value of assigning resources to one direction rather than another depends solely on the preferences and interest of individuals as individuals. The satisfaction of desire has its value irrespective of the moral relations between persons, say as members of a joint undertaking, and of the claims which, in the name of these interests, they are prepared to make on one another: and it is this value which is to be taken into account by the (ideal) legislator who is conceived as adjusting the rules of the system from the centre so as to maximise the value of the social utility function."[16] Thus if we are deciding whether the institution of slavery is just, we must treat at the same level both the pleasures of the slave-holder on the one hand and the miseries of the slaves on the other.[17] And if we are deciding whether or not to prohibit murder, incendiarism and robbery it is as relevant to cite the pleasure enjoyed by the offenders as it is to cite the pain suffered by the victims.[18] All pleasures and pains are to be weighed on the same scale, and none may be given a privileged status over the others.

Among the pleasures and pains to be taken into account are those of malevolence. Bentham defined the pleasures of malevolence as "the pleasures resulting from the view of any pain supposed to be suffered by the beings who may become the objects of malevolence. . . .[19] But even these pleasures are in themselves good because every pleasure is as such good, and as good as the same quantity of any other pleasure. This being the case there is no reason why morality and the law should be other-regarding as Mill understood the term. Consider the case of homosexuality between consenting adults in private. In a society where the majority regards such behaviour with repugnance, it may well be that pleasures of malevolence are aroused by the prospect of homosexuals being punished for their conduct. These pleasures may not be sufficient to outweigh the pain inflicted through the punishment of homosexuals, but they are always relevant and are to be weighed on the same scale as the suffering caused by punishment. It is also possible that under certain circumstances there are pleasures of malevolence which would exceed the pain inflicted by the punishment of "private immoralities." We may approach such a situation when the overwhelming majority in a society feels very strongly about the private conduct of a very small group of people, and demands that the latter be fined or imprisoned for a short spell. There would then be a good utilitarian reason for punishing that private conduct.

It is precisely the introduction of this type of reason that Mill tried to rule out with his principle. He realised that individual liberty is insecure so long as reasons like this are regarded as relevant. In the example of the prohibition on the eating of pork which I have already alluded to and in other similar examples, he

[16] *Philosophy, Politics and Society*, 2nd series, ed. Peter Laslett and W. G. Runciman (New York: Barnes & Noble, 1962), pp. 150–151.

[17] Ibid., pp. 152f.

[18] *Mill on Bentham*, ed. F. R. Leavis, pp. 48–49.

[19] *The Principles of Morals and Legislation*, ch. V, sec. XI.

pointed out how futile the case for liberty would be if the majority's genuine feelings of horror and repugnance are recognised as having a claim for serious consideration. Mill clearly rejected Benthamite utilitarianism when he said that ". . . there is no parity between the feeling of a person for his own opinion, and the feeling of another who is offended at his holding it; no more than between the desire of a thief to take a purse, and the desire of the right owner to keep it."[20] He refused to treat the resentment of the religious bigot towards another person's religious observances which he finds abominable on the same level as the latter's regard for his own form of worship.

I think that we are now in a position to understand Mill's sense of utility "grounded in the permanent interest of a man as a progressive being." Liberty is necessary for "the free development of individuality," and without liberty "there is wanting one of the principal ingredients of human happiness, and quite the chief ingredient of individual and social progress."[21] Thus Mill is still appealing to utility or the promotion of human happiness as the standard for appraising the value of liberty. He also argued that because of the diversity of the sources of human pleasures and pains and their different effects on different human beings, men will "neither obtain their fair share of happiness, nor grow up to the mental, moral and aesthetic stature of which their nature is capable" unless they are allowed freedom to pursue their own modes of life.[22]

It looks as if Mill was claiming that the sum of human happiness would increase where there was liberty. But it becomes clear as the argument proceeds that the goal is not really happiness in any sense that is detachable from "development" or "progress," and these are equated with the growth of "individuality." This is what "utility in the largest sense" means. Liberty is not to be valued because it increases the sum total of human happiness, for this implies that the connection between the two is a contingent one, but because it is a logically necessary condition for the growth of individuality. It allows men to cultivate pleasures of a particular type, namely, "native pleasures" or pleasures of "home-growth."[23] Mill strongly attacked "the despotism of custom" and men's blind and mechanical conformity to its dictates. Men must be allowed to choose for themselves not because this will lead to an increase in their happiness, but because this is in itself the most important ingredient of happiness. The sort of happiness Mill wanted to promote is logically tied up with liberty as it is involved in the very act of rational and independent choice. Men who choose in conformity with custom not because they independently agree with it, but blindly and without thought or because they are pressured to do so, cannot by definition be happier than those who choose freely and in independence. Happiness is not what Bentham conceived —a goal that is distinct from individual liberty, and as a matter of fact achievable through it. For Mill, happiness is not something that can be got through any means: "It really is of importance, not only what men do, but also what manner of men they are that do it."[24] It is not just what men believe or how they feel which is important; the manner in which they come to have certain beliefs and feelings is also important. He also said that, "If a person possesses any tolerable amount of common sense and experience, his own mode of laying down his existence is the

[20] *On Liberty*, p. 140.

[21] Ibid., p. 115.

[22] Ibid., p. 125.

[23] Ibid., p. 149.

[24] Ibid., p. 117.

best, not because it is best in itself, but because it is his own mode."[25] The importance of choosing and acting independently and in a rational manner was further emphasised by the use of expressions like "an intellectually active people" and "the dignity of thinking beings." Rational choice, as Mill's arguments in the chapter on freedom of thought and discussion make clear, implies that one knows the correct grounds for believing something and that one is prepared to listen to conflicting views whenever they arise. It thus implies the existence of freedom for those who may disagree with us.

The appeal to "utility in the largest sense" is therefore very different from any simple appeal to utility. Though Mill still appealed to human happiness, the concept of human happiness that he uses is so different from that used by Bentham that it would be misleading to say simply that *On Liberty* provides a utilitarian defence of freedom. But if one still insists on calling Mill a utilitarian, then it is important to remember that he was a utilitarian who wanted to limit the type of utilitarian considerations which can be brought in. There are some pleasures and pains which are irrelevant and should not be appealed to as a basis for restricting individual liberty.

[25] Ibid., p. 125.

III

I shall now draw together the different parts of my analysis of Mill's notion of self-regarding actions. Self-regarding actions are those actions which, if they affect others, do so only indirectly. This means that they affect others only because they are disliked or found to be immoral or repugnant. Mill claimed that the individual's freedom with respect to such actions should not be restricted because he ruled out certain reasons for interfering with liberty as irrelevant. Unless we are prepared to reject appeals to society's feelings of repugnance and dislike and similar feelings toward certain actions, individual liberty can never be secure from the "tyranny of the majority." In thus restricting the types of reasons which may be taken into account, Mill was not strictly a utilitarian because the gratification through punishment of those feelings he regarded as irrelevant could be treated as the gratification of the pleasures of malevolence, which on strictly utilitarian grounds are in themselves as good as any other type of pleasure of the same quantity. Mill's reason for allowing liberty in self-regarding actions was not that human happiness would thereby be increased, but that without such liberty there can be no "individuality." His defence of freedom is not in terms of utility, but of "utility in the largest sense," i.e. individuality.

Jan Narveson / Utilitarianism and new generations

I

One of the stock objections to utilitarianism goes like this: "If utilitarianism is correct, then we must be obliged to produce as many children as possible, so long as their happiness would exceed their misery." It has always seemed to me that there is a certain air of sophistry about this argument, and in this paper I shall endeavor to demonstrate this by exposing the fallacies upon which it is founded. I shall also consider in its own right the question of the nature and extent of our duties in the line of procreation, if any, on the utilitarian principle. To this end, three preliminary matters must be explained.

To begin with, there are two radically different questions here, of which the first is the crucial one. On the one hand, there is the question of whether we should produce person X because X would be happy if produced. Let us call this the question of the "direct effects" upon the general happiness; clearly, it is what is in point. The other question is this: should we produce person X, if we can foresee that X's existence will have a favorable effect on the happiness of other people besides X, e.g., his parents, or people who might benefit from his activities. Later on, I shall suggest that the appearance of plausibility to the objection probably stems from a subtle confusion between these two different questions. I shall spend most of my time on the first question, reserving the second until the final section of the paper.

In the second place, there is some difference of opinion about the way in which the utilitarian theory is to be formulated. Those who have put the objection are assuming that according to the utilitarian, there is a certain sort of mental state called "pleasure" or "happiness," of which it is our obligation to produce as much as possible, by whatever means. Let us call this the "greatest total happiness" formulation. But it is obviously not the one which Bentham and Mill had in mind. Their formulations, as everybody

Reprinted from MIND, *vol. 76, no. 301 (January 1967), pp. 62–72 by permission of the author and editors.*

knows, have it that the "greatest happiness of the greatest number" is the end of morality. This view Smart and Flew call the "greatest average happiness" view, though, as I shall show below, this characterization is somewhat misleading. Now, it supposedly follows directly from the "total" view that we have a duty to produce children if they would be happy; though I am inclined to think that the view involves a further confusion which, if taken account of, might clear even it of this charge to some extent. But at any rate, it is much less clear that the classical view has any such implication. For that we are to aim at the greatest happiness *of* the greatest number, does not imply that we are to aim at the greatest happiness *and* the greatest number. In order to make this perfectly clear, note that the classical utilitarians' view may be put this way: Everyone should be as happy as possible. Cast into modern logical form, this reads, "For all persons x, x should be as happy as possible," and this is equivalent to, "if a person exists, he should be as happy as possible." This last shows clearly that the classical formulation does not imply that as many happy people as possible should be brought into existence.

The third point is to be clear about the general idea of the utilitarian theory about morality. It is often thought that according to that theory, if we like jam, then we have a duty to eat jam. This is nonsense. The whole point of the utilitarian theory is that people should be permitted, in so far as possible, to do as they please. As in all moral theories, utilitarianism picks out as duties those acts which you should be constrained to do. You may or may not like doing your duty, but if you do not, that is irrelevant. Now, it makes sense to say that you have a duty to do something which you happen to enjoy doing anyway; but it does not make sense to say that you have a duty to do something *on the ground that* you like it. To assert a duty is to deny the permissibility of the opposite. Consequently, if you say that I have a duty to do whatever I like, there is nothing whose permissibility I am denying: if I liked doing A, I still could not have a duty to do A, since I could also do not-A if I liked.

What *is* true is that for the classical utilitarian, the sole ground of duty is the effects of our action on other people, and from this it follows that whenever one has a duty, it *must* be possible to say on whose account the duty arises—i.e., *whose* happiness is in question, in deciding what we are to do, the only consideration which is morally relevant, according to utilitarianism, is how others would be affected. If we cannot envisage effects on certain people which would ensue from our acts, then we have no moral material to work on and we can do as we like.

II

We are now in a position to throw light on the problem before us. The oddity in this kind of question, of course, consists in the fact that if a person is not born, he does not exist. I am neglecting the question about the point at which a person comes into existence. Those who would wish to consider embryos as a kind of person may simply replace "born" and "birth" with "conceived" and "conception" throughout. And as we all know, non-existent people are not just a special kind of people; therefore, unborn people are also not just a special kind of people. Further, "people" are among the things you can point to, see, hear, and so forth. There is no such thing as an "abstract person," though we may indeed talk in the abstract about people (concrete).

Consider now the sentential form, "if x were born, x would be happy; therefore, x ought to be born." We assume the utilitarian principle as the suppressed major premiss. Now, there are two types of logical expression which can be substituted for "x" in such an argument, namely, proper names and descriptions. Let us examine each in turn. To begin with, no sensible proposition can be formed of the consequent in the minor premiss of an argument of this form, by replacing the blanks (x's) with proper names, since, for example, "Hiram Jones ought to be born" makes no sense. If "Hiram Jones" refers, then he already is born and there is no open question left as to whether he "ought to be born"; and if, on the other hand, it does not refer, then it is not (logically) a proper name, there being nothing for it to name.

Notice, incidentally, that the point just made does not depend upon the temporality of personal existence. The name "Hiram Jones" refers, logically speaking, no matter when Jones is alive. But whether or not Jones lives in the future, it is still true of him, whenever he may live, that he was born, and consequently it is in any case nonsense to say that he ought to be born.

Nor am I denying that we may sensibly ask, once he *is* born, whether he *should have been* born. This is in many cases an interesting question, though not a very practical one under the circumstances. Some people should not have been born; and as there are other people whose existence is a good thing, we may say of them that they, in the same sense, "should have been born"; though of course they *were*, and it is not a point of much practical importance so far as it concerns the individual the desirability of whose birth is in question. Hitler should not have been born, Churchill should have been born, and there are other cases where it is debatable—though I admit that all such questions are, as we say, "purely theoretical." What I am claiming is that, if we regard "Hitler" and "Churchill" as proper names, Hitler's mother and Churchill's mother could not have presented themselves, prior to their conceptions, with sensible questions of the form "Ought we to give birth to Hitler?" "Ought we to give birth to Churchill?" The latter appear to be parallel to "Ought I to spank Adolph?" "Ought I to spank Winston?"; but they plainly are not.

Suppose, on the other hand, that we complete the argument-forms by replacing our "x" with descriptions. Thus we might say, "Someone should be born who would bring peace to the world"; and supposing that we could know that *our* boy, if born, would bring peace to the world, we might argue that this is a good reason for bringing him into existence. As indeed it is, but we have shifted our question here, and are no longer answering the one we set out to discuss. For we began by resolving to discuss the question, whether the *direct* effects of bringing someone into the world could be a reason for so doing, and "bringing peace into the world" is not of this kind. I said at the outset that the distinction between direct and indirect effects in reference to this question was a vital one, and I am about to show why. So far, then, the question is whether we could argue as follows: "Our boy, if born, would be very happy; therefore we ought to produce him." In order to show why this argument is not sanctioned by the principle of utility, whereas the former perhaps is, we must turn again to the third point argued above.

III

Three possible outcomes of an act are of interest from the utilitarian point of view. The act either will (1) increase the general happiness, (2) decrease the general happiness, or (3) have no effect on the general happiness. Neglecting such interesting but here irrelevant questions as how you decide which in fact will result, there is an important question as to just which of the three is such as to give rise to a duty, if any; but let us say for purposes of the present discussion that, in cases where the different things we can do would some of them eventuate x in (1), others in (2), and others in (3), it is our duty to avoid (2) and prefer (1). In other words, it is only with increases and decreases in the general happiness that we are morally concerned if we are utilitarians. And this means that when we specify the individuals who would be affected by our actions, as we must on the utilitarian view, the characteristic about those people with which we are morally concerned is whether their happiness will be increased or decreased. If an action would have no effects whatever on the general happiness, then it would be morally *indifferent:* we could do it or not, just as we pleased. Hence whether to do it or not would be a non-moral question, which could only be solved by non-moral considerations. If I were to have a candy bar, this would normally have no effect on the happiness of others; hence whether I am to do it or not is entirely a question, according to the utilitarians, of whether I want to or not, which is not a question about what I morally ought to do but rather one about what I *like* to do. Now, to which of these types does our present question belong: is it a moral or a non-moral one? I will show that it is ordinarily a *non-moral* one, and that in the case where it is a moral one, then it is because of its indirect effects. "Direct effects," I shall show, can only give rise to the duty *not* to have children and can never give rise to a duty to have them. Having children, in other words, is normally a matter of moral indifference. Let us see why this is so.

In order to show that the general happiness would be increased by our having a child, the argument would have to go as follows. Imagine that the total number of people is N, and that the total happiness is H, the average happiness therefore being $N/H = 1$. Now suppose that we have good evidence that any child produced by us would be twice as happy as that, giving him a value of 2. Then the average happiness after he is born will be $\frac{N+2}{N+1}$, which would be somewhat larger, therefore, than before. Does this give us a moral reason to produce children? No. We have committed a fallacy.

Suppose that we live in a certain country, say, Fervia, and we are told by our king that something is about to happen which will greatly increase the general happiness of the Fervians: namely that a certain city on Mars, populated by extremely happy Martians will shortly become a part of Fervia. Since these new Fervians are very happy, the average happiness, hence the "general happiness" of the Fervians will be greatly increased. Balderdash. If you were a Fervian, would you be impressed by this reasoning? Obviously not. What has happened, of course, is simply that the base upon which the average was calculated has been shifted. When the Fervians are told that their happiness will be affected by something, they assume that the happiness of those presently understood by them as being Fervians will be increased. The king has pulled the wool over their eyes by using, in effect, a fallacy of four terms: "Fervians" refers to one group of people on one occasion—"The general happiness of the Fervians_1 will be increased"—and another on another occasion—"Hence, the general happiness of the Fervians_2 has been increased." Because the Fervians_2 are a different group from the Fervians_1, although including the latter, it is a mere piece of sophistry to say that an increase in the happiness of the Fervians has come about as a result of this new acquisition of Martian citizenry. The fraud lies in the fact that no *particular* Fervian's happiness has been increased; whereas the principle of utility requires that before we have a moral reason for doing something, it must be because of a change in the happiness of some of the affected persons.

The argument that an increase in the general happiness will result from our having a happy child involves precisely the same fallacy. If you ask, "Whose happiness has been increased as a result of his being born?" the answer is that nobody's has. Of course, his being born might have indirect effects on the general happiness, but that is quite another matter. The "general populace" is just as happy as it was before; now, what of our new personnel? Remember that the question we must ask about *him* is not whether he is happy, but whether he is happier as a result of being born. And if put this way, we see that again we have a piece of nonsense on our hands if we suppose that the answer is either "yes" or "no." For if it is, then with whom, or with what, are we comparing his new state of bliss? Is the child, perhaps, happier than he used to be before he was born? Or happier, perhaps, than his alter ego? Obviously, there can be no sensible answer here. The child cannot be happi*er* as a result of being born, since we would than have a relative term lacking one relatum. The child's happiness has not been increased, in any intelligible sense, as a result of his being born; and since nobody else's has either, directly, there is no moral reason for bringing him into existence.

IV

But, you say, would not the world be better off than it was before, even though in your sense the general happiness has not been increased as a result of his being born? As Smart has put it,

> . . . would you be quite indifferent between (a) a universe containing only one million happy sentient beings, all equally happy, and (b) a universe containing two million happy beings, each neither more or less happy than any in the first universe? Or would you, as a humane and sympathetic person, give a preference to the second universe? I myself cannot help feeling a preference for the second universe. But if someone feels the other way I do not know how to argue with him. It looks as though we have yet another possibility of disagreement within a general utilitarian framework.[1]

This being the remark of one of the few thorough-going proponents of the utilitarian theory extant, it is in order to point out what is wrong here. It is true, of course, that utilitarianism is supposed to appeal to "sympathetic and benevolent" men (—as well as everyone else!). And no doubt a person who was sympathetic and benevolent by nature might be inclined to prefer Smart's second universe to his first. But I suggest that if he does, the inclination is morally irrelevant; and the reason Smart would not know how to argue with a person preferring the first or being indifferent, is that there is no moral argument at issue here. How large a population you like is purely a matter of taste, except in cases where a larger population would, due to indirect effects, be happier than the first, the latter possibility to be discussed below. And having children is also purely a matter of taste, for the same reason, and with the same exception.

Consider what a person who would claim that the larger universe is the better "because there is more happiness in it," is asserting. According to utilitarianism, as I pointed out earlier, all obligations and indeed all moral reasons for doing anything must be grounded upon the existence of persons who would benefit or be injured by the effects of our actions. From this it follows that a man's objective moral goodness is a function of the number of people

[1] J. J. C. Smart, *Outline of a System of Utilitarian Ethics* (Carlton: Melbourne University Press, 1961), p. 18.

whom he benefits or injures, for any given population of the universe. But the man who says "the more happiness, the better" is going far beyond this view. For he is saying that if the universe does not contain the possibility of your doing good or harm, then it is your duty to go out of your way to create situations in which you *could* do good (or harm). To put it another way: the existence of duties and of moral reasons for doing things depends, in the utilitarian conception, upon the existence of people. Consequently, one can increase the number of situations in which one has duties and moral reasons, as opposed to merely personal reasons, for doing things by increasing the population. But on whose view of morality is it our duty to go out of the way to create duties for ourselves? We believe that it is our duty to keep promises; must we also insist that, as a corollary, we must make as many promises as possible?

Such a view, incidentally, might lead to some weird consequences. Imagine a universe in which everyone is perfectly happy on account of his own efforts, so that nobody ever has a moral reason to do anything therein. Our so-called "utilitarian" who argues that we must increase the population for moral reasons, would have to say that such a universe is less desirable than one in which many people could be made happier by the efforts of others, and this in turn would, I suppose, have to be reckoned a worse one than one in which there were some sufferers whose suffering could be relieved by others! But that such is not the utilitarian view should, I think, be perfectly evident. Quite the contrary: given a universe, it follows from utilitarianism, at least as Mill and Bentham construed it, that it would be best off if everyone in it were perfectly happy by his own efforts, and worse off if people had to constrain themselves from self-seeking by assisting others.

It must always be borne in mind that I am not arguing that there is no reason of *any* kind for preferring larger to smaller universes or vice versa. In the first place, within suitable limits, a larger population has a better chance for securing happiness to all than a smaller one owing to the necessities of industrialization and economic organization, and other such things. And in the second place, there is no reason on earth why people cannot *like* larger universes better than smaller ones. I am only pointing out that we must not confuse matters of taste with matters of morality. Those who argue that they like larger populations better than small ones and therefore have a moral duty to make the population as large as possible, are in fact saying that they have a duty to make *themselves* happier: for the reason they must give for their actions is that the effect of them is to get something that they like. And this, as argued earlier, is wrong. There can be no question, on utilitarian principles, of a "duty" to do what one likes.

V

On the other hand, however, I now wish to argue that it does follow from utilitarian principles that, if we could predict that a child would be miserable if born, then it is our duty *not* to have it. This result, I admit, will look rather peculiar in view of my preceding argument; but the peculiarity can be overcome if we consider certain logical points about duty-fulfilling and duty-transgressing.

As is generally accepted today, every statement describing a particular duty on a particular occasion must be backed up by a general principle of some kind, from which the particular one follows by application. Such is certainly the case with utilitarianism, at any rate. Now let us suppose, as is plausible, that two of our utilitarian duties are to avoid inflicting misery on people, and to reduce misery where it exists. The first of these is a general principle which might be put into logically precise form in some such manner as this: "Each person x is such that for each person y, x should not inflict suffering on y," while the second would be, "Each person x is such that for each person y, if y is suffering, then x should reduce y's suffering." Now, as we know, all general statements of a hypothetical form "(x) (Fx ⊃ Gx)," are equivalent to universal disjunctions, "(x) (— Fx v Gx)." And this means that there are two ways of acting in accordance with either of these duties: either there is no person x upon whom to inflict suffering, or if there is, then to avoid inflicting it on him, in the first case; and in the second, either x is not suffering, or we reduce his suffering. I am, of course, neglecting complications such as supervening duties; also I am assuming that a duty to reduce suffering is a duty to *try* to reduce it.

On the other hand, there is only one way in which such a principle may be infringed, and that is by the occurrence of a state of affairs described by a true existentially qualified statement. Thus, I can infringe the first duty if the following statement is true: "there is someone on whom I have inflicted misery," and in the other case, "someone$_x$ is suffering and someone$_y$ has failed to reduce x's suffering."

From this analysis, it will again be evident that we cannot have a duty to produce children just because the latter would be happy. For even if it were our duty to make everyone as happy as possible, we would be guilty of no transgression of it if we were not to add to the population, though we would transgress it by making somebody less happy than he otherwise might have been. In other words, the duty being "each y is such that for each x, y should make x as happy as possible"; and if, say, "the son of Jones" does not exist, then it is not the case that Jones is failing to make his son as happy as possible. Or, to sum it up: true affirmative existential statements are not necessary to fulfil duties, but *are* necessary to *infringe* them.

Now let us suppose that we are contemplating having a child, who would, we know, be miserable. For example, suppose that we know he would have a hereditarily-acquired painful disease all his life; or that we are poverty-stricken unemployables living in a slum. In both these cases, we can reasonably predict that any child of ours would be miserable. Now, these miseries will be unavoidable if we produce the child; and consequently, a counter-instance to a duty statement will be true, namely: "a child of Smith's is miserable and the Smiths could have prevented this." This would violate the second duty. But quite likely it would violate the first too, for although one does not inflict pain on someone by giving birth to him even though he is in pain ever after, since if you cannot make someone happy by bearing him, you also cannot make him miserable by doing so, nevertheless in many such cases, e.g., the slum-dwelling case, you will actually have inflicted misery on the child by underfeeding him, exposing him to disease, filth, and ugliness, making him associate with equally wretched persons, and so forth, and thus you will also have transgressed the first duty. And in both cases, you could have avoided these evils by not having the child in question.

If, therefore, it is our duty to prevent suffering and relieve it, it is also our duty not to bring children into the world if we know that they would suffer or that we would inflict suffering upon them. And incidentally, I think this also is a strong argument against those who think that it is our *duty* to make everyone as happy as possible. For this is a duty we could infringe by having a child who we know would not be as happy as possible. And of how many people can't *this* be foreseen? Frankly, I do not think there is any such duty on utilitarian principles, but it is something to think about for those who do.

VI

Finally, we may briefly consider the moral relevance of indirect effects on the "general happiness." Clearly, it will often be the case that we can foresee good or bad effects on the existing population by the production of new people. If we assume, as seems reasonable enough to me, that an advanced civilization is likely to be happier than a primitive one, and that industrialization is necessary to advanced civilization, then it is obvious that a fairly substantial population will be necessary to achieve these desirable ends. On the other hand, as we also know, too large a population tends to have adverse effects from the agricultural point of view. With too much pressure on food supply, inferior lands have to be put into cultivation, and yield per man-hour tends to go down; withal, if the pressure is too severe, as it is in some parts of the world today, one of two evils will set in: either some people will starve or be severely shorted in their diets while others have enough, so that the various evils resulting from inequality will set in, or everyone will have less than enough. In all likelihood, there is an optimum population for any particular piece of land at a given state of advancement in agricultural technology, as the economists tell us. A further consideration is the aesthetic effects of over- or under-population. If population is very dense, people will be crowded together, and will have little solitude. Further, little land will be available for parks and natural scenery. If it is too thin, on the other hand, human intercourse is much reduced, and the interesting by-products of cities, such as the ability to maintain art galleries and concert halls, and the support of architecturally interesting buildings, will be missed.

Now it seems to me clear that all of these considerations are of the sort which will provide what, in the narrowest sense, may be called "utilitarian" reasons for changing the sizes of populations. The only question of interest is which of these would give rise to genuine duties, and which merely to something less. My final suggestions, which the reader may take or leave, follow here.

Many critics of utilitarianism will object that according to this latest turn, we have a right to increase slave populations in order to benefit the rest. This is false, I believe, but the discussion of it would occupy too much space to be included here. Other objections of the same kind also seem to me misguided.

It is obvious that there can be good reasons for producing children, and also that there can be good ones for not producing them. But when are these sufficiently stringent to give rise to a duty rather than merely to a moral inducement? My own answer, which I cannot defend here, would be that whenever the production of new children would either result in misery for them, or would result in substantial decreases in the happiness of other people, it is one's duty not to have them. If, for example, one's child would be a burden upon the public, then it seems to me one has no right to produce him. It therefore seems to me that the public has the right to prohibit the having of children in such cases.

Is it *ever* one's duty to have children? I can think of only one case where it might be. If it can be shown that the populace will suffer if its size is not increased, then it seems to me that one could perhaps require efforts in that direction, and punish those who could comply but do not. But I am inclined to think that such a situation is exceedingly rare.

There is one final question which might bring the whole issue into a sort of focus. This is: is there any *moral* point in the existence of a human race, as such? That is to say, would a universe containing people be morally better off than one containing no people? It seems to me that it would not be, as such, at any rate on utilitarian grounds. We might *prefer,* like Smart, a universe containing people to one that does not contain them, particularly since we presumably would not be able to occupy the second one ourselves; but is this, then, a moral preference? It seems to me, again, that it is not, and that the effort to make it one is a mistake. Given people to have them toward, there will be duties: but if we are not given them, questions of duty will not arise. And it is not a question of duty whether we should create new duties. Our duty is to fulfil them, once they are raised.

A. J. McCloskey / Utilitarian and retributive punishment

In this paper I wish to strengthen the arguments which I have elsewhere[1] urged against utilitarian accounts of the morality of punishment, by offering replies to a number of criticisms that have been pressed against them, in particular to various of those urged by T. L. S. Sprigge,[2] and by pressing in more detail and more explicitly than before, certain types of cases of useful, but unjust, punishment. I shall then attempt to state in greater detail and less equivocally, the retributive theory that I suggest accords with the facts of the morality of punishment as they emerge from our consideration of the shortcomings of the utilitarian accounts and from a consideration of other areas of justice. The metaethic presupposed by my argument is an intuitionist one, but, as I have noted elsewhere and as a critic such as J. J. C. Smart has noted,[3] my appeals to moral insights are readily reinterpreted as appeals to moral feelings and attitudes which are relevant considerations for those who hold emotivist, prescriptivist, and such metaethical theories, although I should, of course, wish to insist that they are more and other than this.

The burden of my argument against utilitarian theories of punishment is that utilitarianism involves accepting, as morally right and obligatory, punishment that is gravely unjust and morally objectionable. *To be just, punishment must be of an offender for an offence and not in excess of what is commensurate with the offence,* where "offence" and "offender" are to be interpreted in the morally relevant senses

[1] "An Examination of Restricted Utilitarianism," *Philosophical Review*, vol. 66, no. 4 (October 1957), 466–485 [pp. 204–216 above]; "The Complexity of the Concepts of Punishment," *Philosophy*, vol. 37, no. 142 (October 1962), 307–325; and "A Non-utilitarian Approach to Punishment," *Inquiry*, vol. 8, no. 3 (Autumn 1965), 249–263.

[2] T. L. S. Sprigge, "A Utilitarian Reply to Dr. McCloskey," *Inquiry*, vol. 8, no. 3 (Autumn 1965), 264–291; parenthetical page references are to this essay, unless otherwise noted.

[3] J. J. C. Smart, "The Methods of Science and the Methods of Ethics," *Journal of Philosophy*, vol. 62, no. 13 (June 24, 1965), 344.

Reprinted from THE JOURNAL OF PHILOSOPHY, *vol. 64, no. 3 (February 1967), pp. 91–110 by permission of the author and editors.*

of those expressions. *To be morally justified, unjust punishment must not simply be useful; rather, the good it achieves must be so great that it outweighs the evil of the injustice involved.* Although most of the examples of unjust punishment cited here as objections can be pressed against both act and rule utilitarianism (depending on whether they are viewed as isolated, useful punishments or as results of the operation of unjust institutions of punishment), I shall be primarily concerned with act utilitarianism, and this because what I regard to be major objections to rule utilitarianism have been fully set out elsewhere by J. J. C. Smart, myself, and others.[4]

It would seem to be possible to argue against utilitarianism by reference to actual cases and also in terms of merely possible cases of useful, unjust punishment. In "A Note on Utilitarian Punishment"[5] and again in "A Non-utilitarian Approach to Punishment" I argued from the logical possibility of such useful unjust punishments and unjust systems of punishment, i.e., of the kinds that involve punishment of innocent people, of persons not responsible for their actions, and excessive punishment. As a number of critics have objected to this mode of argument, their objections might first be considered before proceeding to an examination of empirically possible and actual examples. J. J. C. Smart has accepted the argument as an important one which merits reply, observing:

> . . . to be consistent the utilitarian must accept McCloskey's challenge. Let us hope that the sort of possibility he envisages will always be no more than a logical possibility, and will never become an actuality. At any rate, even though I suggest that in ethics we should test particular feelings by reference to general attitudes, McCloskey's example makes me somewhat sympathetic to the opposite view.[6]

Smart then suggests that some of the implications of any ethical theory will be "unsatisfactory" and goes on to commend utilitarianism as more satisfactory than other theories; i.e., he accepts the propriety of the appeal to merely logically possible examples but argues that *in fact* they are not decisive against utilitarianism. I should agree that all ethical theories have at least some implications that their exponents find hard to accept—and this, as will be evident from my later discussion, includes the retributive theory—but I should disagree with Smart concerning the conclusions to be drawn from these awkward implications. D. F. Thompson, in "Retribution and the Distribution of Punishment,"[7] also takes issue with me on the

[4] See J. J. C. Smart, "Extreme and Restricted Utilitarianism," *Philosophical Quarterly*, vol. 6, no. 25 (July 1956) [pp. 195–203 above], and my "An Examination of Restricted Utilitarianism" cited above. Rule utilitarianism, in so far as it diverges from act utilitarianism, involves an abandonment of utilitarianism in favor of rule worship. In so far as it avoids the charge of sacrificing utility for the sake of a pointless conformity with a rule, it comes to be more exposed to the difficulties of act utilitarianism. If "rule" is construed as it is by Toulmin (*The Place of Reason in Ethics* [New York: Cambridge University Press, 1953], pp. 150–151) and Nowell-Smith (*Ethics* [Baltimore: Penguin, 1954], p. 230) as an actual rule of a community, rule utilitarianism comes to be a relativist ethic with all its difficulties. If "rule" is construed as it is by Hare (in his attempt to show that, because of the universality of moral principles, act and rule utilitarianism do not diverge as much as is commonly supposed—see *Freedom and Reason* [New York: Oxford University Press, 1965], pp. 130–136), as a principle on which it would be useful for all to act, the relativism is avoided, but at the cost of greater rule worship (i.e., conformity with rules when such conformity causes harm and when we know that other people do not and are unlikely to come to act on the principles upon which we act). It also involves greater uncertainty concerning the rules on the basis of which we ought to act.

[5] *Mind*, vol. 72, no. 288 (October 1963), 599.

[6] J. J. C. Smart, "Methods," p. 348.

[7] *Philosophical Quarterly*, vol. 16, no. 62 (January 1966), 61–62.

question of logically possible cases of unjust punishment. However, he appears to misconstrue my thesis. I am concerned to argue not that unjust punishment is never morally right, but simply that utilitarianism does not take account of the relevance of the claims of justice when determining whether a punishment is morally right. For the utilitarian, the utility of the punishment is the only morally relevant consideration, whereas I have been concerned to argue that its justice or injustice is equally relevant and that a consideration of logically possible examples of useful, unjust punishments brings out utilitarianism's failure to take note of one of the important relevant considerations. Sprigge (272–275) approaches the argument from logically possible, unjust punishments along different lines, but lines which may well be acceptable to other utilitarians. He argues by reference to a distinction between actual and "fanciful" examples, the latter including the merely logically possible, the empirically impossible, and the empirically very unlikely examples, Sprigge contending that such examples, and the appeal to how our moral consciousness would view them, do not count against utilitarianism because our moral consciousness has developed as it has on the basis of the world as it is. There is some force in Sprigge's contention. Certainly, if we make our examples bizarre enough we may find it difficult to form any sort of moral judgment, let alone a confident one, about them. However, it is not true that moral attitudes have developed only in respect of the physical world as we know it. They have long been applied to gods who inhabit worlds of varying sorts—and this without any sense of strain or awkwardness in those who have pressed the moral judgments. That Christians acknowledge the problem of evil to be such a real problem shows that moral attitudes are not based simply on a consideration of the physical world peopled by moral agents with the sorts of human natures we know them to have. That we can enter into a serious moral appraisal of Christ's reported use of his miraculous powers further confirms this. I therefore wish to reject the substance of Sprigge's objection but nonetheless to qualify my contention and now argue that all empirically possible, no matter how unlikely, examples of useful unjust punishment tell against utilitarianism and that many empirically impossible, but logically possible cases, e.g., those involving omniscience, miraculous powers, and the like, also tell against utilitarianism. With other logically possible but empirically impossible examples, e.g., those involving radically new concepts of human nature and of human beings, it would seem to be necessary to judge the example on its merits, and it may be the case that some such examples do not count against utilitarianism. That some logically possible but empirically impossible examples count is confirmed by considering imaginary examples involving omniscient utilitarians. It is an adequate test of whether utilitarianism can in principle take account of the claims of justice that, if an omniscient utilitarian judge knew that greater total good would come by declaring an innocent man to be guilty, he ought to do so, the injustice of the decision not being a relevant consideration for him as a utilitarian. I suggest, therefore, that we may properly argue from merely logically possible cases and that at least some such cases are fatal to the claims of utilitarian accounts of the morality of punishment.

We may also argue from possible, probable, and actual cases, and this I have in the past sought to do. As various of these examples have come in for thorough, thoughtful, critical examination—for example, by T. L. S. Sprigge—we may usefully consider the sorts of replies a utilitarian may offer. Sprigge's general line of reply is of the form: "Either utilitarianism does not dictate that the punishment be inflicted—and this is usually the case—because, given the facts about the situation, the world, and human nature as they usually are, there are other, better, more sure ways of achieving the goods sought, ways that do not involve the blunting of sensibilities, the loss of respect for useful practices, and the like, or, if the case is tightened up so that it really is true that utilitarianism does dictate that punishment be inflicted, the conclusion is to be accepted." He suggests that in the latter event it is even reasonably plausible to claim that ordinary people would accept such punishment as justified, even though they may feel regret at having to make such decisions (275–286).

Sprigge presses this general line of argument against my original example of the sheriff who frames an *innocent* Negro in order to prevent race riots developing in a race-torn community in which a white woman has been raped by a Negro, and more fully against my restatement of the example (a restatement entered into in order to simplify the example rather than to strengthen it) according to which the punishment of the innocent Negro results from a conscientious utilitarian's deliberately giving false witness. I argued that a situation may arise such that a utilitarian may rightly judge that it is useful for him to bear false witness against an innocent person. In reply, Sprigge notes a number of considerations, including (a) the improbability of the whole situation and of the manner of approaching it; (b) the fact that utilitarianism bases its judgments on foreseeable consequences that rest on well-established generalizations, whereas the person contemplating bearing false witness would be acting on a hunch; (c) that it is dangerous for people to act on such hunches; (d) the certainty of the misery of the convicted man (all the worse for his being innocent) and the uncertainty of the evils the false witness is designed to prevent; and (e) the harmful effects on the agent's character. Sprigge suggests that, once note is taken of these various factors, it will become evident that there are more effective ways of advancing racial harmony, but he does allow that it is possible to deal with each specific point by imagining a situation in which it would not arise, so that it may not be out of the question that situations may arise where a reasonable utilitarian would think it right to bear false witness. He argues that in such situations it is not clear that the plain man would reject the utilitarian conclusion and that in fact he would accept it but feel regret about the situation. Some of these points can be accepted, subject to qualification, but others must be rejected. It is true that the whole situation would be an extraordinary one, that people do not go around asking themselves "How can I promote good by bearing false witness?" and the like (although I do wish to raise the question whether, if they are utilitarians, they ought to do so). It is also true that it would be dangerous and undesirable if people generally did go around asking themselves this sort of question. However, extraordinary situations that call for desperate actions do arise such that there is no difficulty in envisaging this sort of situation's presenting itself to a utilitarian as one that poses an agonizing moral dilemma. Further, although it is true that we do act and ought as a general rule to act on the basis of well-founded generalizations, there are occasions on which we ought and must act on hunches and against the evidence of generalizations. The great general, the skillful detective, the brilliant barrister often act in this way; and there are university teachers who have a flair for predicting future achievements of individuals where generalizations would mislead. One who has this sort of flair would be acting wrongly in not acting on it. Similarly, if the reference in the example to the person who bears the false witness being a visitor to the community is dropped (it was included to make it unlikely that he would encounter the situation again) and if the person be imagined to be one who had lived in the one small town all his life and who had seen trouble-makers at work and race tensions develop into riots and lynchings, then he may well reasonably be confident that, if a victim is not immediately found, violence will break out. Acting on the basis of such a hunch in such a God-like way is or can be dangerous, but it need not always be so. Our utilitarian may approach his decision with the greatest of reluctance, with humility, and from a sense of duty. He may, too, be one who has worked all his life for better race relations and who is concerned only because he cares deeply for his fellow man. If he is the sincere and thoughtful utilitarian I represent him as being, he will name as the guilty man someone whose conviction will not distress others and who himself is a shiftless, unhappy person, for example, one who is a bachelor, orphan, unemployed, and the town bum. I suggest, therefore, that it is not difficult to fill out the example and qualify it so that we have a case where unjust punishment may promote greater good.

In an interesting discussion Sprigge suggests that, if the case is really one where a sensible utilitarian would rightly bring about such punishment, it would be accepted by the plain man, but with regret. Whether it was so accepted would depend on how much good is promoted and evil prevented by the injustice, and also on the character and nature of the victim. However, the important point is that, whether or not it is accepted by the plain man, its injustice would be a factor of which the plain man would and ought to take account. If he accepted it, it would be *in spite of* its injustice. The regret he would experience if he did accept such punishment would be at having to override the claims of justice; on the other hand, it is also true that if the plain man rejected the punishment because of its injustice, he would experience regret at being unfree to prevent suffering. It is hard to see how, on the utilitarian theory, there is any room for the former regret, for it is regret at having to do something that is evil of its nature and not by virtue of its consequences. Sprigge, in a very sketchy discussion, suggests that the utilitarian can explain just and unjust actions in terms of their increasing or decreasing certain kinds of goods and evils, and hence, presumably, that regret at unjust actions would be reasonable for the utilitarian (269, 282). However, his account is very sketchy and prima facie unplausible; for unjust institutions as well as just ones may promote various of these so-called "goods of justice" (e.g., the good of being able to plan and control one's future).

The same general moves and countermoves, especially concerning the real utility of apparently useful, unjust punishment of innocent people, for example, scapegoat punishment, punishment of parents for offences of their children, collective punishments, and the like, are possible. With each example a critic such as Sprigge can point to the complexity of the relevant factors, and I can reply by writing in more and more details. And again, ultimately, the dispute would resolve itself into whether the injustice of useful punishment of the innocent person was a factor that counted and ought to count with the ordinary moral agent who was considering its morality. However, because there is another kind of case of unjust, useful punishment which presents even greater difficulties for utilitarianism and because it is possible to cite an actual case to illustrate and document the argument, no attempt will be made here to set out further examples of unjust, useful punishment of innocent people.

Punishment of the insane and of those not responsible for their "crimes" may be useful and, hence, for the utilitarian, morally right and obligatory; yet it is gravely unjust. Utilitarian attempts to deal with this difficulty are typically unconvincing. Sprigge, for instance, argues that, if workable criteria for distinguishing the sane from the insane are applicable, nonpunishment of the insane will not encourage the sane to think that they can get away with their crimes. He suggests, more generally, that the utilitarian answer to the question "Why not punish the insane?" is "Because it does no good or no good not attainable at the expense of less evil." It is not clear what would count here as "workable criteria." What we have available today are reasonably workable criteria, although they are rather rough and ready and such as to be open to abuse. Further, they are not always fully acknowledged by the law. However, the use of them, where they are used, especially in cases involving brutal murders, sex crimes, and the like, where the person involved is not fully sane (and here I should not wish to deny that some who commit such crimes are fully sane), brings the law into disrepute with a large and important section of the community, in such a way as to encourage some criminals who are sane to hope that they will escape their just deserts if they are caught, by having a skillful lawyer and a tame psychiatrist prove they are not sane. Clearly, the way to educate the general public about sanity and insanity, responsible and nonresponsible behavior, is not by bringing the law into disrepute but by direct education. Until the general public accepts the criteria of insanity used by the law, there must be a great loss of the good which most utilitarians, including Sprigge, stress, namely, respect for the law which is itself a useful institution.

"The Tait Case," now famous in recent Victorian political and legal history, reveals how such unjust punishment of those not responsible for their crimes (but who are generally believed and who so often even believe themselves to be fully responsible and deserving of punishment) may be useful and how utilitarianism is committed to a relativism geared to the psychological beliefs of the community in respect of such punishment.[8] The case concerns a man Tait, who, after pleading not guilty (his counsel basing his defence on the grounds that Tait was insane), was found guilty of the murder of an 82-year-old woman. The crime was a particularly revolting one, the woman, apparently surprising a thief, being "beaten to death, half-stripped of her clothes, crudely handled by a sexual sadist, dragged into her bedroom and thrown on the bed" (6) and a "torch had been thrust into the vagina though death was not attributed to this" (7). Tait, a known alcoholic, had only recently been released from prison on parole, a condition being that he not drink. In fact he had been drinking steadily and heavily. Further, as Burns reports, "the psychiatric witnesses for both the Crown and the defence agreed that Tait was an alcoholic and a sexual psychopath, that he was a transvestite with homosexual, sadistic and masochistic tendencies" (26). For 11 years prior to Tait's conviction Victoria had retained the death penalty in law but not in fact, judges formally sentencing murderers to death, and the government having the sentence commuted. At least partly to check the alarming apparent increase in murders (police that year reported 61 in Victoria, population about 3 million, the figure later proving to be much smaller) and also to appease a widespread public belief that Tait was a person responsible for an abominable crime of a kind that should be discouraged as effectively as possible by making the criminal pay fully for it, the State government chose to allow the sentence to stand, and, after a number

[8] The case is reported in Creighton Burns, *The Tait Case* (Melbourne: University Press, 1962). The murder occurred in August 1961, the trial in December 1961, and the "case" finally ended in November 1962.

of legal appeals had failed, proceeded to set a date for Tait's execution, Tait of all those found guilty of murder that year being singled out for hanging.[9] This was at least in part because the death penalty was judged to be a better deterrent than life imprisonment and because it was thought that there would be less political opposition to its reintroduction if Tait was made the first victim. (It is also true that some hard-headed retributionists believed that Tait's crime was so vile that it merited the supreme penalty, they, like the jury and many of the general public, rejecting the psychological evidence that Tait was insane and not responsible for his crime.) In the final event, as a result of a public campaign against the reintroduction of capital punishment, the forcing of repeated postponements of the execution by a series of legal moves directed toward having Tait declared insane (none succeeded), and because of growing public disgust at the government's inept and callous handling of the affair (a court deemed it necessary to issue an order restraining the state officials from proceeding with the execution until the hearing before it was completed), the government decided not to go on with the execution, and, instead, Tait was certified insane, and his papers marked "Never to be released." It was not announced whether the government's change of front was due to a new law's coming into operation which made it easier for Tait to be certified insane, or whether it was thought that he had come to be insane (as a result of being under threat of execution for so long?).

What is important about this case is that it brings out how the utilitarian, even the enlightened utilitarian who is clear about what constitutes responsible behavior, is committed to taking full note of the beliefs of the members of his community about responsibility when determining what constitutes useful deterrent punishment. Punishment which would have no utility in a community of enlightened people and which would shock as callous, pointless inhumanity, may in a less enlightened community be very useful punishment. Victoria in 1962 was probably as enlightened in this respect as most advanced communities of the world; yet even so the prevailing belief as revealed in the jury's verdict and by the fact that the campaign was directed against capital punishment, not punishment, was that Tait was responsible for his crime. Because of this general belief, punishing Tait (by imprisonment or hanging, whichever is the more useful deterrent) would have been as useful, or more useful, a deterrent punishment as punishing a murderer who was fully responsible for his crime but whose crime had aroused less notice. The State government in this matter acted as utilitarians ought. They probably were wrong in believing that capital punishment was a better deterrent than life imprisonment, but they were right, if it is utility and not justice that is aimed at, to seek to punish Tait with the most effective deterrent punishment.

The just and appropriate treatment for individuals such as Tait is for them to be humanely confined, treated and made well if this be possible, and released when well. Had the State government announced that it was not going to punish Tait, but rather to have him treated sympathetically and kindly as a sick person and confined only until made well, there would have been a public outcry and a loss of respect for the law. Even many who opposed his execution would have objected to Tait's not being punished at all. That there was no organized protest at Tait's papers' being marked "Never to be released"—presumably no matter whether treated and made well or not—confirms this. No doubt some

[9] The execution was fixed for 8/22/62, postponed to 9/24/62, 10/22/62, 11/1/62, with a promise, unfulfilled, of yet another date.

who acquiesced in Tait's being confined for life did so because they believed—surely somewhat dogmatically in view of the remarkable advances made in this area in the past quarter of a century—that he could never successfully be treated, but many acquiesced in Victoria, as do peoples in most advanced societies when this sort of case arises, because in their hearts they did not fully accept the experts' testimony—and this because this sort of crime is so revolting and of a kind which offends against all sorts of latent prejudices and which arouses dark fears that make it difficult for the ordinary person impartially to assess the evidence. It is because of this that even enlightened utilitarians must often condone and even enjoin the punishing of people whom they know not to be responsible for their actions. The utilitarian, in determining whether a person ought to be punished, must determine the utility of the punishment and the disutility of not punishing. His answer will depend in important ways on whether the person is responsible for his crime, whether he is generally believed to be responsible, and, if the community's views in this matter are mistaken, on the ease or difficulty of changing the community's views.

Here I have concentrated on the sort of "offence" illustrated by the Tait case; for sex-perversion crimes seem to be those which arouse irrational responses even in otherwise enlightened communities. It would, however, have been equally illuminating—and as damaging to utilitarianism—to have looked at the "crimes" and punishments of kleptomaniacs and at what happens when an attempt is made to exempt genuine kleptomaniacs from punishment.

A third type of unjust, useful punishment that poses difficulties for utilitarianism is that of *excessive punishment*, i.e., punishment disproportionate with the offence. Here again we have an interesting recent actual example of excessive punishment imposed in the belief that it was useful deterrent punishment, namely the punishment administered to the Great Train Robbers. That the punishment of 30 years imprisonment for the crime committed is excessive would, I think, be generally conceded. The punishment generally judged to be appropriate for crimes of this sort—thefts of large sums of money, bank robberies, pay-roll snatches, and the like, with violence but no loss of life—is 5 to 10 years imprisonment. Considering the stakes involved, there was relatively little violence (only what was necessary for the execution of the theft), and the only feature that distinguished this from similar crimes was the amount of money involved. The amount stolen is relevant to the issue of the gravity of a theft—a theft of £1,000 is, other things being equal, more serious that a theft of £1—but there is neither a geometrical nor an arithmetical relationship between the amount and the gravity of the crime. A theft of £10,000 clearly does not merit a penalty 10,000 times as severe as that awarded for a theft of £1. There is a range of penalties for each kind of offence, the more serious instances meriting the more severe penalties within the range. What happened with the punishment of the Great Train robbers was that they were awarded penalties inappropriate to robbery, and appropriate only to vastly graver crimes. The punishment was awarded presumably because it was thought by the judge to be necessary, useful punishment. (Had the money been recovered he might well have thought a lesser penalty would have been equally useful.) Whether the judge was right or not is not easy to determine—it is difficult to form anything approaching a reasoned opinion on this question. People may reasonably disagree, have doubts, be without an opinion on this question—but without being uncertain about the injustice of the sentence. This is because the question of the justice of a punishment is distinct from that of its utility.

Other examples could be cited where the question of what punishment is useful is seen to depend on such factors as the number of police available, their efficiency, the attitude of the public to the crime, and the like, where the issue of the just punishment does not vary with these considerations. If there is an inadequate, inefficient, understaffed police force, and an uncooperative public, very severe penalties may be more useful than mild ones. If others are unlikely to report us and if we are unlikely to be caught, a mild punishment will not be a significant deterrent, whereas a very severe penalty will be more of a deterrent. It is true that there is more to determining the utility of a punishment than simply determining whether it is an effective deterrent punishment, but these considerations confirm how different are the questions "Is this punishment useful?" and "Is this punishment just?" To answer the former we have to look at a vast range of facts; to determine the latter, it is only the crime—and the person's responsibility—that have to be considered.

Thus, to sum up this negative part of the paper, punishment may be useful but unjust because it involves punishing innocent people, people not responsible for their actions, and because it is disproportionate with the crime.

Punishment as Retribution. These criticisms of utilitarian punishment turn on and support the contention that punishment to be just must be of an offender, for an offence, in a morally relevant sense of "offence," and be such as not to exceed what is commensurate with the offence. To be just, punishment must be deserved. The objections to utilitarian punishment are an important part of the case for a retributive theory of justice in punishment—but not because, by showing that the utilitarian account is unsatisfactory, they suggest that some other account such as the retributive theory is more likely to be satisfactory—but rather because of the nature of the reasons why the utilitarian account is unsatisfactory. The utilitarian theory fails, according to the above arguments, because it cannot take note of those features of punishment which constitute the retributive theory. Thus a consideration of the case against utilitarianism is one way of bringing out the intuitive insights upon which the retributive theory rests.

It is important, now, that an attempt be made to state the retributive theory in a more positive, unequivocal way. In "A Non-utilitarian Approach to Punishment" I distinguished between punishment that was dictated by justice and punishment that was morally permissible. The point I was concerned to make was that the claims of justice are simply one sort among prima facie claims and that they may on occasion be overridden, so that it may be morally right, even though unjust, to inflict various of the punishments noted above as unjust but useful punishments. The rejection of utilitarian punishment rests on its failure to take account of the relevance of the injustice of certain punishments when determining whether they are permissible or even obligatory. Sprigge very properly takes me up on my use of the expression "morally permissible." Clearly, if the ground of my contention that unjust punishment may, under certain circumstances, be morally permissible is that there may be a clash of prima facie duties such that the claims of justice are overridden, the infliction of unjust punishment must then be obligatory and not simply permissible. This I accept. Unjust punishment may become obligatory in special circumstances, and what I have been concerned to urge, as against the utilitarian, is that, to be justified, the utility of the unjust punishment must be sufficiently great to override the stringent demands of the duty of justice which rests on the intrinsic character of the act. Further, I have spoken of just punishment also as being morally permissible; yet I have argued that retributive punishment falls into the sphere of justice and that typically the demands of justice are demands that create positive obligations. It may be the case that, when there is a clash between the prima facie duties of justice in punishment and of the promotion of good, the clash is between the duty not to be unjust and the duty to promote good. However, since the duties of justice are usually conceived of more positively, as duties to do, not simply as duties to refrain from doing, it might be argued that, when the claims of utility and justice clash in the area of punishment, the clash is between the duty to impose the deserved punishment (as opposed to the duty not to impose undeserved punishment) and the duty to promote good or to prevent evil.

It is necessary here to acknowledge that I find myself as reluctant to contend that there is a duty positively to inflict the deserved retributive punishment as utilitarians such as Smart and Sprigge have been to insist that we ought to punish innocent people to promote greater good. Both sorts of view seem to be harsh and inhumane. Rather, I have sought to argue, but not always consistently, for the more negative conclusion that the infliction of undeserved punishment is unjust and, unless dictated by an overriding prima facie duty, wrong. I have also sought to argue that, if the deserved punishment is inflicted when it serves no useful purpose, the person punished cannot legitimately complain. The judge who imposes the punishment commensurate with the offence cannot be condemned by the man punished as acting unjustly or wrongly on the grounds that, although the punishment harms no one but the guilty man, it is useless. To such an objection the judge has what I suggest is a completely adequate defence, namely, that the punishment was deserved. We may come to consider such a judge a harsh man if he always imposes the maximum punishment that is just. This is true too of the just man who insists on strict justice elsewhere—for example, in enforcing a just contract that brings about the ruin of another person. We may dislike him because of his harshness, but we cannot condemn him as having acted unjustly. At most, we should say that justice was not everything, that there is a case in humanity for mercy, kindness, leniency. However, I find myself reluctant to go further and say of the judge who has imposed the just sentence that is useless but causes no harm other than that intended to the offender, that he has acted wrongly, immorally; that he has done what he ought not to have done.

I have sought to reconcile the more negative thesis: that unjust punishment is morally wrong unless dictated by a more stringent duty than that of justice and that the man justly punished cannot legitimately complain that he is being wrongly treated simply because the deserved punishment is useless, by looking at other areas of justice. On a superficial look it appears that no injustice is involved in awarding more than is deserved where it is good that is deserved. Closer examination, however, suggests, as I shall be concerned to bring out, that it may be wrong and unjust to give more good than is deserved and, similarly, to withhold deserved evil.

Retributive punishment is an aspect or element of justice. Justice involves treating equals equally, unequals unequally, giving to each his due, and this, the giving to each of what he deserves. Sprigge objects that the injunction "Treat equals equally" says nothing, because anything can count as a ground for claiming an inequality. Certainly the rule "Treat equals equally" is vague and open to many interpretations, and it is particularly exposed to deliberate, dishonest misinterpretations. All rules allow this to some extent, even such relatively determinate rules as "Keep your promises," "Do not bear false witness." People can sincerely argue about what is a real promise, what is a bearing of false witness, whether telling the truth about seeing the milkman leaving the schoolmistress's house (where one knows that he has been doing a good-Samaritan act of changing the washer on a tap) in a leering, suggestive way likely to cause false beliefs, is a bearing of false witness, a mode of lying, etc. Sincerely and honestly applied and used, the rule "Treat equals equally" is important and significant, even though there will be more disagreements among those who hold it as to its import than among those who hold rules such as "Keep your promises," "Do not bear false witness." At the very least it rules out the treating of those we judge to be equals, unequally. If we want to be dishonest we will easily find a ground for attributing an inequality wherever we wish to find one, but most people most of the time want to be honest, and, for them, it is an important and often inconvenient rule that they ought to treat equals equally. Men who believe that men and women are equal in the relevant respects often find it awkward to accord to women the same rights as to men, and women equally often find it unpleasing to them to be expected to forego privileges that were accorded to them on the basis of their supposed inequality.

It is of course true that the determining of who are equals and unequals is as vitally important a part of the rule of justice, as is the determining of what is or is not an agreement a vital part of the rule "Keep your agreements" and of what is a lie with the rule "Never lie." In the area of retributive justice the relevant inequality seems to be obvious—the committing of a crime, with the seriousness of the crime determining the degree of inequality involved. The criminal is one who has made himself unequal in the relevant respect. My own view is that all are committed to some sort of intuitionist view, or at least practice, in the area of justice, in determining what are relevant differences. (Consider how we come to see that race is not a relevant difference but that cleanliness is in determining whom one may justly decline to have as a boarder in one's house.) So too, the issue of the seriousness of the crime, like that of the degree of goodness of an intrinsic good, impresses me as a matter of intuitive insight. However, this point need not be pressed here, for the point of importance for this inquiry is that the committing of a crime constitutes a relevant difference when the question of punishment is involved. Further, for reasons I developed at some length in "The Complexity of the Concepts of Punishment," this is not because punishment is conceptually tied to the fact that the person punished is an offender. There are lots of arguments that can be urged to show that there is no such conceptual connection.

There is a further difficulty in giving contempt to the injunction "Treat equals equally," namely that of determining whether it enjoins more than abstaining from treating equals unequally, when they are equal in the relevant respect. There is one sense in which the demands of justice are more positive than simply enjoining abstaining from injustice, namely, that where an injustice can without impropriety be very easily prevented by us, it may become a duty on us to prevent or to rectify that injustice. This is not the sense of positive duty that is of interest to us here. Rather, it is whether the duty is that of giving to those of equal deserts what they deserve, neither better nor worse than is deserved. This duty is variously explained as giving people their deserts and as treating similars similarly in respect of their deserts. The former formulation is compatible with the interpretation that the duty to award the deserved punishment is as serious a duty as that of giving the deserved reward, whereas the latter formulation implies only that people of similar deserts be treated similarly and without arbitrary discrimination between those of equal desert—that is to say, where it is a good that is deserved, giving more than is deserved equally to similars would not on this formulation be an injustice; so too, where it is an evil that is deserved, giving less to similars than they deserve, provided they are treated similarly, would also be just. I suggest that, if we look further into what the two formulations imply, we find that the differences are less than these comments suggest, for "Treat similars similarly in respect of desert" involves the duty to punish at least to some extent—and to an extent that brings its practical injunctions close to those of "Treat equals equally and unequals unequally." That the former involves the duty to administer some punishment may be brought out by looking at examples of acts of justice and injustice in other areas.

Consider rewards in the sense of honors. To withhold a reward from one of two equally deserving cases is unjust because of the inequality toward equals involved. To reward an undeserving person, for example, the son of a general, a friend of the Prime Minister, a member of the Royal Family, etc., with a decoration such as the Victoria Cross, is unjust even though it is a conferring of a good and even though no harm may result and even though much good may come from a false belief in the occurrence of heroism by those in high places. (It may also be wrong as involving deceit, but my point is that there is an element of injustice about the awarding of unearned rewards, just as there is an injustice in withholding an earned reward.) Similarly, treating equals equally and awarding all those who merit a lesser reward, for example, the Military Cross, the Victoria Cross, would be unjust (and—unfortunately because it complicates the example—harmful or at least detrimental to the utility of such rewards). However, the injustice would consist in the MCs', who are similars, being treated similarly with dissimilars, the true VC winners. The latter could properly complain that dissimilars were being treated similarly. These cases *suggest*, but only suggest, that the duty is to give what is due, neither more nor less, even when it is to the advantage of the recipient to receive a benefit over and above what he is due.

Another relevant example is provided by the parable of the laborers in the vineyard (Matthew 20: i to xvi), those who had labored from early morning receiving the same payment as those who had labored only from the eleventh hour. The parable rests on an assumption that no injustice is involved, yet it has impressed many as being morally objectionable precisely because of the arbitrary injustice involved. If we look further at the parable, the injustice seems to lie in the employer's sharing a certain amount of money disproportionately among his laborers—the criterion of who is to receive any money being labor. ("So when even was come, the lord of the vineyard saith unto his steward, Call the labourers, and pay them their hire, beginning from the last unto the first." viii.) It is by virtue of their labor that they are rewarded at all—hence the sense of injustice at the disproportion between the rewards of those who labored all day and those who labored only an hour. The suggestion, of course, is that, if those who were hired last had received what was due to them, the lord of the vineyard would properly have kept for himself what was in fact given to them. There is nonetheless a sense of shock at the undeserving benefiting equally with the deserving, where the desert is based on labor, even though the deserving receive what they deserve. The parable would shock less if the lord of the vineyard had distributed his money equally between those who had labored and those who begged along the highways, for this would lessen the suggestion that the reward was based on labor. There would, however, remain a sense that an injustice had been done, and this because the deserving were being treated similarly with the less deserving and with the undeserving.

If we consider wages generally this seems to be confirmed. Would it be unjust for some to receive more than others for exactly comparable work, where the talents of the people involved are the same and where those who receive more do not benefit at the cost of others? For example, would it be unjust for lecturers at Kent to receive a bonus of £500 this year that lecturers at other British universities do not receive? Here the example is of a nonrecurring wage rise, where the higher pay could not come to be justified in terms of better and more deserving people being attracted to the university concerned. I suggest that many would claim, with good reason, that an injustice was being done and that it consisted in people of similar deserts being treated dissimilarly, and this even though all others were receiving their deserts. (Other examples do not always suggest this, but this is chiefly because they hold of areas of labor and the wage market where the enforcement of justice is too difficult even approximately to implement, to be very relevant.)

Similarly, a head of a department may worry about the justice of recommending for promotion to a senior lectureship a man whom he believes does not deserve such promotion but who is miserable at not getting it and who could usefully spend the additional salary. Here, as in some of the other situations, we feel that a competitive situation is involved and that others may be harmed or handicapped by the act thought to be unjust. However, it is not clear that this need be so. Another case of a similar receiving more than his deserts which arouses uneasiness is that of the father who leaves both of his sons well off but to one £100,000 and to the other £900,000, where both have been kind, loyal, virtuous sons. If he had left the same amount of £100,000 to each son and the rest to a worthy charity, the case would cause less feeling of unease.

What these cases suggest is not simply that injustice is involved in people's benefiting beyond their deserts, but that this is because similars must still be treated with similars. If everyone were to benefit, for example, if all lecturers at all universities were to receive the £500 bonus this year and if, as a result of some "miraculous" prosperity through the discovery of vast oil, gold, and mineral reserves, all wage-earners in Britain could gain proportional bonuses, the notion of unjust rewards would get a grip only when British workers were considered in the context of the workers of the world. It is not clear that, if the workers of the world received more than was demanded by justice, there would be any injustice. With other rewards—titles, medals, decorations, status—the multiplying of them would be self-defeating, and so would open the way to new claims in justice for recognition of unacknowledged desert.

These examples suggest that the benefiting of equals (similars) beyond their deserts is not contrary to justice provided that similars are still treated similarly. However, where the benefiting of some class or group beyond their deserts leads to their being treated in a way similar to that in which those of greater desert are treated, we begin to be uneasy that justice is not being fully done, that there should be some acknowledgment of the dissimilarity, namely a proportional one, where this is possible. If everyone could be rewarded beyond his deserts, and all proportionately so, it is hard to see that justice would not fully be done. Yet, as we shall see, there are impressive reasons for having doubts about even this.

To consider punishment more explicitly: The above discussion suggests that it is not contrary to justice to benefit people beyond their deserts (in the case of punishment, by imposing less than the deserved evil), provided similars are treated similarly. Arbitrarily to show mercy to one and not to others exactly like him in all relevant respects, appears unjust precisely because it involves a treating of similars dissimilarly. The above consideration of rewards suggests—how strongly is not clear—that when the benefiting of similars beyond their deserts brings them to being treated on a par with those of greater desert, there is a case in justice for conferring a benefit on their superiors or, if this is not possible, for sharing the benefit proportionally, and, if this too is not possible, even for withholding the benefit from the inferiors. The same seems to be true in respect of deserved punishment and mercy. If mercy is to be shown to a murderer, equal mercy ought to be shown to those who are similar in all relevant respects. If this leads to murderers receiving the punishments commensurate with the crime of shoplifting, there is a case for proportional mercy in respect of desert to shoplifters. This suggests that, if we are to retain any sort of proportion between the innocent and the guilty and between those guilty of different kinds of offences, there is a limit to the extent of mercy compatible with justice. This suggests that there is at least a duty to punish, although not necessarily to the full extent deserved.

There are two considerations which suggest the stronger conclusion that there is a duty to impose the full deserved punishment, that mercy without good reason is a form of immorality. The first harmonizes with the foregoing discussion of the demand of justice that there be a proportion in the discrimination between dissimilars. It is a consideration that suggests itself if we reflect concerning a god who rewarded the virtuous and did not punish the vicious (e.g., where the vicious intend but never succeed in causing harm to others) in the afterlife. My own feeling is that there would be a moral fault in such a god, that he would be allowing a morally evil state of affairs to prevail, not because punishment plus the crime is an organic good but because there is an evilness about unpunished crime. It would seem from a consideration of this sort of case—and here I wish to enlarge upon and qualify the example so that it is of useless, just, retributive punishment of those who are guilty of grave offences, but who have reformed their ways, or who can do no harm, or who can be reformed without such punishment and who would not be reformed by it—that there must be a reason for mercy if it is to be morally justified, quite apart from the suffering involved in the punishment itself. An illuminating example here is to be found by imagining that Eichmann had eluded his enemies and lived a happy, prosperous life, feeling no remorse for his crimes. If, in an afterlife, a god allowed him to enjoy the same bliss as was enjoyed by the most virtuous of men, there would be an undesirable and an unjust state of affairs, at least in part because Eichmann would be being treated similarly with people very dissimilar to him. This sort of thinking, that there must be a reason for mercy quite apart from the evil of the punishment itself, harmonizes with our thinking in other spheres of justice, if the brief examination of these entered into above was well directed.

In this sort of imaginary (and for many theists, possible) example, we have something that approaches being a test of the retributive theory; for the retributive theory in any except emaciated forms implies both that punishment may be useless but just and that punishment may be obligatory but useless. I suggest that a god who administered punishment to an Eichmann in the afterlife, even if the punishment was useless, could not fairly be charged with acting unjustly, nor even with doing what he ought not to do. Equally important, this sort of imaginary example brings out, as against utilitarian theories of punishment, how clearly distinct are the judgments concerning the justice and utility of punishments. There is no paradox in the contention that a divine punishment was just but useless. Further, the utilitarian would have to argue that, if God could reform an Eichmann in the afterlife either by administering punishment or by extending to him the same goods as are given to the virtuous as rewards, God ought to allow the Eichmann to enjoy the "rewards" (which in his case would not be called such). Such favorable similar treatment of individuals so very dissimilar in respect of desert is surely gravely unjust.

The second consideration that supports this positive interpretation of the retributive theory is that mentioned by Sprigge, namely, that there are presumably occasions on which just punishment is not simply permissible but obligatory. There seems to be something very unsatisfactory about the common retributionist's reply that just punishment is obligatory "when it is useful," for this is according the dictates of justice a very negative role, a role of a much more negative character than is accorded to the demands of justice elsewhere. The duties of justice are typically more positive than merely abstaining from acts of injustice.

The foregoing is of course greatly complicated by the relevance of duties other than that of justice, for instance, that of respecting persons. To show mercy may be to show respect, but it is often also to show lack of respect for the person concerned. It seems probable that we sometimes unconsciously move from what is dictated by justice to what is dictated by respect for persons. This general discussion is also qualified by the fact that its conclusions hold of ideal societies, and of actual imperfect societies only with considerable, substantial modifications.

Joseph Margolis / Mill's

Utilitarianism *again*

Mill's proof of the principle of utility has had a notorious career. But, as far as I know, it has not been forcefully argued that Mill actually does not avail himself of the alleged proof and says a great many things which conclusively show that he never subscribed to it, on any of the alternative readings that have been advanced. "The sole evidence," Mill says, in *Utilitarianism* (chapter iv), "it is possible to produce that anything is desirable is that people do actually desire it." Now, what I think can be demonstrated is that Mill held that desirability, in any sense offered for this remark, is neither a necessary nor a sufficient condition of goodness. And since this flies in the face of the received doctrine, it may be worth considering.

Mill holds (again in chapter iv) that "happiness has made out its title as *one* of the ends of conduct, and consequently one of the criteria of morality" (in that people actually do desire happiness). But he admits that the utilitarian principle requires "not only that people desire happiness, but that they never desire anything else." This explains why he spends the time he does reconciling "the desire of virtue" with "the desire of happiness" and why (in chapter v) he spends a disproportionate amount of time reconciling justice and utility. In principle, it would be sufficient to defeat Mill to demonstrate that virtue or justice or similar "desirable" ends are not conceptually dependent on the goal of happiness. I think this may be plausibly argued, at least to a stalemate, in the sense in which "what is right" does not mean "what is conducive to what is good."[1] I am not interested in pursuing this particular line of argument here, merely in noting that it is a proper strategy by which to undermine utilitarianism. There is, however, a much more powerful way to topple Mill's utilitarianism (and, therefore, to challenge more recent versions of the doctrine): that is to demon-

[1] I am aware of J. O. Urmson's suggestions regarding construing Mill accurately. Cf. "The Interpretation of the Moral Philosophy of J. S. Mill," *The Philosophical Quarterly* 3 (1953), 33–39 [pp. 168–174 above].

Reprinted from the AUSTRALASIAN JOURNAL OF PHILOSOPHY, *vol. 45, no. 2 (August 1967), pp. 179–184 by permission of the author and editors.*

strate that the greatest happiness principle is espoused by Mill *without regard to, and even contrary to, the promptings of desire.* This, at any rate, is the thesis I should like to defend.

Consider the following remark (chapter iv):

> . . . will, in the beginning, is entirely produced by desire; including in that term the repelling influence of pain as well as the attractive one of pleasure. . . . How can the will to be virtuous, where it does not exist in sufficient force, be implanted or awakened? Only by making the person *desire* virtue—by making him think of it in a pleasurable light, or of its absence in a painful one. It is by associating the doing right with pleasure, or the doing wrong with pain, or by eliciting and impressing and bringing home to the person's experience the pleasure naturally involved in the one or the pain in the other, that it is possible to call forth that will to be virtuous which, when confirmed, acts without any thought of either pleasure or pain.

Mill is here concerned, to some extent, with the psychology of influence and education: a man may be induced to behave virtuously in so far as he may be made to associate the presence (or absence) of virtue with pleasure (or pain). But beyond this, Mill obviously *knows antecedently that virtue is good* and therefore that a man *ought* to be induced to construe virtue as pleasant. The essential paradox of utilitarianism, that it "maintains not only that virtue is to be desired, but that it is to be desired disinterestedly, for itself" (chapter iv) is resolvable only on this view. For Mill admits that virtue is to be desired "even although, in the individual instance, it should not produce those other desirable consequences which it tends to produce, and on account of which it is held to be virtue" (chapter iv). In fact, he says, "Virtue, according to the utilitarian doctrine, is not naturally and originally part of the end, but it is capable of becoming so. . . ." (chapter iv). Now, Mill nowhere means that it is psychologically impossible to view vice with pleasure (think of the Marquis de Sade). He must therefore know not only that virtue *can* be associated with pleasure but that it *ought* to be so associated. It follows that Mill does not construe virtue to be a criterion of morality on the grounds of desire, though *any* would-be criterion must be psychologically compatible with desire. Virtue must be capable of being desired, but Mill everywhere insists that the wrong things are often desired.

These considerations oblige us to examine more closely the central manoeuver in Mill's reconciliation of justice and utility. "That a feeling is bestowed on us by nature," Mill declares (chapter v), "does not necessarily legitimate all its promptings." Now, the "feeling" of justice Mill construes rather as originating with an "instinct," what he sometimes characterizes as a "natural feeling of resentment." He means by this, obviously, since he speaks of "promptings" produced by this feeling, that, by nature, we have a persistent desire to revenge ourselves for hurts suffered. The feeling of justice itself Mill holds to be this "animal desire to repel or retaliate a hurt or damage to oneself or to those with whom one sympathizes . . . moralized by being made coextensive with the demands of social good." Now, it may well be that justice, *so* construed, is compatible with utilitarianism; it is also conceivable that Mill has provided a correct analysis of what justice is—though to defeat the account is to defeat Mill along those lines sketched at the outset that I wished to disregard. But Mill has surely admitted that, by nature, men desire revenge for hurts suffered and that not all of the "promptings" of this natural feeling are morally legitimate. Consequently, desirability is not a sufficient condition of the moral goodness of revenge; and the correction of that "instinct" in accord "with the demands of social good" must be vindicated on the grounds of knowledge of what one ought to desire. If it is conceivable that a race of men be so depraved as not to desire "the greatest happiness," Mill would appear ready to correct, and (he thinks) be justified in correcting, their behaviour. If this is so, then desirability is not even a necessary condition of goodness—though, to be sure, any *effective* moral program must be capable of engaging desire.

The main feature of Mill's account is that desire is capable of being, and ought to be, *morally* trained. But of course, if this is so, then desirability, in any sense compatible with Mill's original proof of the utilitarian principle, cannot possibly serve as the criterion of morality. We desire revenge *by nature,* but we ought to desire justice (and we can be trained to). We desire virtue, Mill thinks, and though it "is not as universal . . . it is as authentic a fact as the desire of happiness" (chapter iv). Even if this be granted, Mill insists that "not only" is it "to be desired, but . . . it is to be desired disinterestedly, for itself," that anything less would not be compatible with utilitarianism. Once again, then, an established desire ought to be adjusted in the interests of morality.

Of course, a very important and honest concession has been made here by Mill. Though virtue is desired, it is not universally desired; nevertheless, we know that virtue is desirable. It is easy to see that Mill would not, and could not, hold that the desirability of virtue is determined by its actually being desired. Some things are desired, he has admitted, that are not adequately moral; and some things are moral that men, by nature, are not inclined to desire—but may be trained to desire. Think of a predominantly, or entirely, depraved race: Would virtue, or justice, on Mill's grounds, be the same or different for this race? I think there can be no question that Mill looked to a science of value (chapter i) and believed his discoveries would be binding on all men. But there is no way in which he could support his view on the strength of the original proof. The depraved society clearly would not desire the greatest happiness or disinterested virtue or justice. Nevertheless, these things are known to be the criteria of morality, to be morally worth desiring.

Again, Mill's concessions regarding the greatest happiness principle are considerable. He says quite frankly that "the ultimate sanction . . . of all morality (external motives apart) [is] a subjective feeling in our minds . . . the conscientious feelings of mankind" (chapter iii). But he admits at once that "this feeling in most individuals is much inferior in strength to their selfish feelings, and is often wanting altogether." Nevertheless, "to those who have it, it possesses all the characters of a natural feeling"; and this "conviction," Mill declares, "is the ultimate sanction of the greatest happiness morality."

We must be careful here, because, in speaking of sanctions, Mill is speaking not primarily of what justifies the principle of utility but rather of what must make the utilitarian program (as any would-be moral program) effective. Still, in speaking of sanctions, he concedes that selfish desires dominate over "conscientious" desires, that in some natures "the conscientious feelings of mankind" are altogether lacking. Apart from the educative possibilities we have already seen Mill is encouraged by, he admits that these deficient souls could only be made to respond to external sanctions. Perhaps so. But has he not, in the process, admitted that the disinterested desire of the happiness of "the aggregate of all persons" (chapter iv) is not actually felt by all and is known to be good regardless of this fact? So it is that Mill positively rejoices in insisting that "the powerful natural sentiment" of "the social feelings of mankind . . . will constitute the strength of the utilitarian morality . . . *once the general happiness is recognized as the ethical standard*" (chapter iii).[2] Clearly, Mill does not draw

[2] Italics mine.

his principle from the actual desires of men, but is concerned rather to plan to use the patterns of human psychology to further his moral program.

This, I think, is the sense of Mill's otherwise puzzling remark, that, though "the moral feelings are not innate but acquired, they are not for that reason the less natural" (chapter iii). So he speaks of "properly cultivated moral natures" (chapter iii), "every rightly brought up human being" (chapter ii). The paradox of the proof of the principle of utility is nowhere more evident than here. For Mill, in his effort to maintain that "neither pains nor pleasures are homogeneous" (chapter ii), that "some kinds of pleasure are more desirable and more valuable than others" (chapter ii), is inevitably driven to disregard the actual desires of men as a guide to the criteria of morality. "It may be objected," Mill considers,

> that many who are capable of the higher pleasures occasionally, under the influence of temptation, postpone them to the lower. But this is quite compatible with a full appreciation of the intrinsic superiority of the higher. Men often, from infirmity of character, make their election for the nearer good, though they know it to be the less valuable. . . . But I do not believe that those who undergo this very common change voluntarily choose the lower . . . pleasures in preference to the higher. I believe that, before they devote themselves exclusively to the one, they have already become incapable of the other. (chapter ii)

Quite so. But then, precisely, Mill has the knowledge of the higher good in his back pocket all the time and never needs to consult actual desires. Those who prefer the lower to the higher cannot have chosen of their own volition. "Human beings have faculties more elevated than the animal appetites and, when once made conscious of them," Mill declares, "do not regard anything as happiness which does not include their gratification" (chapter ii). Anyone who does not subscribe to this view has not been "made conscious of them." "And if the fool, or the pig," he continues, "are of a different opinion, it is because they only know their own side of the question" (chapter ii). So it must be misleading to consult the desire of mankind at large, and it is superfluous to consult the desires of those who know what is good. "Better to be Socrates dissatisfied than a fool satisfied" (chapter ii); but *to be Socrates is to know what is good for human nature,* what it is human beings *ought* to, though unreliably now, desire.

I shall not attempt to discuss here the puzzles connected with construing human happiness as the concern of moral science.[3] But it is sufficient in support of the thesis here defended, to notice that Mill is essentially a eudaemonist, who claims to know what the desires of men ought to be and therefore can well afford to be critical of their actual desires. But to say that this is the sense in which Mill offers his proof of the principle of utility in terms of desire is to change defeat into victory by an act of christening and to disregard utterly Mill's own very deep mistrust of the recognizable desires of the run of mankind. I have tried to show that, on Mill's own arguments, desirability is neither a necessary nor a sufficient condition of moral goodness and that no consultation of men's actual desires is, for him, ever in the least decisive regarding what is good. The only thing remotely relevant to the proof that he employs is the fact that people are known to desire happiness, virtue, and justice and that there are important educative possibilities available for enlarging and reinforcing our commitment to morality. But as far as I can see, apart from the internal curiosity of the alleged proof of the principle of utility, Mill's proposal of *any* proof based on desire is, given his account, an absolute anomaly.

[3] Cf. Joseph Margolis, *Psychotherapy and Morality* (New York: Random House, 1966).

Maurice Mandelbaum / On interpreting Mill's Utilitarianism

It is doubtful whether any text in the history of ethical thought is better known to contemporary British and American philosophers than John Stuart Mill's *Utilitarianism.* Nevertheless, those who discuss Mill's views have usually been content to isolate and analyze particular positions, rather than offering an interpretation of the essay as a whole. Among the propositions most often discussed are those connected with Mill's introduction of the notion of higher and lower pleasures, and those connected with his proof of the principle of utility. To the various questions associated with these passages, there has recently been added the further issue of whether Mill is to be classified as a "rule utilitarian," or whether he holds the classic position of unrestricted utilitarianism.

I do not believe that, on the whole, this method of fragmentary criticism has been particularly unfair, nor that it has led to distorted interpretations of Mill's doctrine on those issues with which most critics and commentators have been concerned. However, many passages have been left needlessly obscure, and in fact baffling. Consider, for example, the manner in which Mill uses the term "virtue" and its cognates. In a passage which immediately succeeds his discussion of the proof of the principle of utility, Mill acknowledges the distinction which is made in common language between a desire for happiness and a desire for virtue.[1] Rather surprisingly, he then goes on to say that the utilitarian doctrine "maintains not only that virtue is to be desired, but that it is to be desired disinterestedly, for itself."[2] This thesis, he claims, is in no way incompatible with holding that "actions and dispositions are only virtuous because they promote another end than virtue." The method by

[1] *Utilitarianism,* chap. iv, para. 4 (Everyman's edition, p. 33) [p. 38 above].

[In citing Mill's *Utilitarianism* I shall make use of Mill's paragraphing, so that the reader may readily find the passage regardless of the edition he uses. However, in each case I shall also add the pagination of the Everyman edition.]

[2] Chap. iv, para. 5 (p. 33) [p. 38 above].

Reprinted from the JOURNAL OF THE HISTORY OF PHILOSOPHY, *vol. 6, no. 1 (January 1968), pp. 35–46 by permission of the author and editors.*

means of which Mill can reconcile these two apparently contradictory statements is an important aspect of his ethical theory, but it is not an aspect which can easily be understood without reference to some of his generally neglected ethical writings, nor without relating it to a number of other views which he held. A similar claim can be made with respect to the issue of whether Mill should or should not be classed as a rule utilitarian, but I shall not deal with that issue in the present paper.[3] In what follows I shall draw on the whole corpus of Mill's writings, rather than attempt to deal with *Utilitarianism* in isolation. By this means, I believe, one can best explicate what is otherwise obscure in that work.[4]

[3] I discuss it at length in an article entitled "Two Moot Issues in Mill's *Utilitarianism*," published in *Modern Studies in Philosophy: John Stuart Mill*, ed. Jerome B. Schneewind (New York: Doubleday & Company, Inc., 1968).

The question of whether Mill is to be regarded as a rule utilitarian was first raised in its present influential form by J. O. Urmson. His essay, "The Interpretation of the Moral Philosophy of J. S. Mill," was originally published in *Philosophical Quarterly* (January 1953); it too appears in the volume edited by Schneewind [See pp. 168–174 above.]

[4] In what follows I shall make every effort to interpret Mill's thought as a carefully expounded and consistent position. While I am prepared to acknowledge that his style does not lend itself to that degree of explicitness and precision which contemporary modes of thought demand, it seems to me a mistake to assume, as has sometimes been assumed (e.g., by Sidgwick in *Methods of Ethics* [7th ed.], p. 93, n. 1; and by Urmson, *Phil. Quarterly*, p. 38), that since *Utilitarianism* was originally published in *Fraser's Magazine* it can be considered as merely a "popular" exposition, in which looseness of phraseology and of presentation are to be expected. Such a suggestion presupposes a dichotomy between popular and technical writing which did not exist for Mill. It also fails to take into account the consistency between *Utilitarianism* and every other exposition of Mill's ethical views, as well as its consistency with the relevant statements in his *Autobiography*.

I. *Mill on Bentham*

I suppose it will be granted that if we are to understand Mill's ethical theory we must keep in mind its relationship to the thought of Bentham. It will be recalled that in speaking of the time when he first read Bentham, Mill said: "The feeling rushed upon me, that all previous moralists were superseded, and that here indeed was the commencement of a new era of thought."[5] Even when, after his mental crisis, his own views began to diverge from those of Bentham (and of his father), he never abandoned the conviction that, in its most essential aspects, Benthamism was true. In his *Autobiography* he referred to the fact that although he found the fabric of his old opinions giving way in many places, he never allowed it to fall wholly to pieces;[6] and if one examines the series of articles which contain Mill's discussions of Bentham, dating from 1833 through an essay on John Austin published thirty years later, one finds no reason to doubt this self-estimate on his part.[7]

[5] *Autobiography*, chap. iii, para. 3. (Cf. *The Early Draft of John Stuart Mill's "Autobiography,"* ed. Jack Stillinger [Urbana, University of Illinois Press, 1961], pp. 74f.)

In citing from the *Autobiography* I shall quote from the text as given in the Columbia University Press edition, referring to that text by chapter, and by the paragraphing it follows. However, the *Early Draft*, as edited by Stillinger, is in many respects so valuable that I shall refer to it by page.

[6] Cf. *Autobiography*, chap. v, para. 14 (*Early Draft*, p. 133).

[7] The articles in question are: an anonymous essay entitled "Remarks on Bentham's Philosophy," published in 1833 as an Appendix to E. L. Bulwer's *England and the English*; his essay "Professor Sedgwick's Discourse on the Status of the University of Cambridge" (1835); his essay "Bentham," *London Review* (1838); his attack on Whewell's moral philosophy (1852); and his essay on Austin, which postdates the publication of *Utilitarianism*. (All but the first of these are to be found in

Nonetheless, as every reader of *Utilitarianism* knows, the differences between Mill's position and Bentham's are striking. One may in fact view each of the chapters of that work, except the first, as being, in part, an attempt to correct what Mill took to be either errors or lacunae in the position of Bentham. For example, the emphasis in chapter ii is placed upon rebutting what Mill took to be the most serious charge against Benthamism: its failure to acknowledge distinctions in value among various types of pleasurable experiences.[8] The relation of chapter iii of *Utilitarianism* to Bentham's views is equally obvious: it provides a supplement to the Benthamite doctrine of external sanctions by adding the internal sanction of a feeling, the feeling of obligation. In so doing it also remedies what Mill took to be a distorted picture of man which came from Bentham's emphasis on the role of a calculation of consequences in determining human action.[9] Mill's fourth chapter, which is concerned with the question of how the principle of utility is to be proved, remedies what he regarded as a flaw in Bentham's system: the failure of that system to provide any positive argument for utilitarianism, relying instead on a rejection—through what was almost a caricature—of

---

Mill's *Dissertations and Discussions*, hereafter cited as *Dissertations*. In quoting from that collection, I shall use the five-volume New York edition of 1874 [Henry Holt and Co.].)

It is worth remarking that the anonymous essay on Bentham contains Mill's most explicit account of some of the points on which he disagrees with Bentham. It is strange that the essay is not better known, for Mill mentions it in the *Autobiography*, chap. vi, para. 7 (*Early Draft*, p. 157). One can now also find references to it in the *Early Letters of John Stuart Mill* (*Collected Works*, vol. xii, [Toronto: University of Toronto Press, 1963—], p. 152, n. 12 and p. 236. Fortunately, J. B. Schneewind has included this essay in his recent edition of *Mill's Ethical Writings* (New York: Collier Books, 1965). I shall refer to this essay as "Remarks," to avoid confusion with the more celebrated later essay entitled "Bentham"; page references to it will be those of the fourth edition of Bulwer's *England and the English* (Paris, 1836), followed by reference to the Schneewind anthology.

[8] Mill attributed this deficiency in Bentham's system to Bentham's own personal limitations, not to his basic philosophic insights. He rightly saw Bentham as a person who lacked imagination and did not learn from others, and whose own range of experience was exceedingly narrow (cf. *Dissertations*, I, 378). As a consequence of these personal limitations, the concrete moral standard to be found in Bentham seemed to Mill to "do nothing for the conduct of the individual, beyond prescribing some of the more obvious dictates of worldly prudence, and outward probity and beneficence. There is no need [Mill continues] to expatiate on the deficiency of a system of ethics which does not pretend to aid individuals in the formation of their own character; which recognizes no such wish as that of self-culture" (ibid., p. 388). This complaint is echoed in *Utilitarianism*, chap. ii, para. 4 (p. 7), when Mill says that "utilitarian writers in general have placed the superiority of mental over bodily pleasures chiefly in the greater permanency, safety, uncostliness, etc., of the former—that is, in their circumstantial advantages rather than in their intrinsic nature." Mill's objection to the portrait of human nature which utilitarians had thus painted was, no doubt, founded on moral conviction—and moral conviction which *may* not have been consonant with any form of utilitarianism. Nonetheless, it should be noted that he was here also rebelling against a psychological theory: as we shall see immediately below, one of his objections to Bentham was that the Benthamite psychology overstressed the intellectual calculation of consequences as a motive for human action, and failed to acknowledge the plurality of human ends.

[9] This criticism, implicit in the paragraphs cited in the preceding note from Mill's "Bentham," is even clearer in his anonymous essay, where he says: "The prevailing error of Mr. Bentham's views of human nature appears to me to be this—he supposes mankind to be swayed by only a part of the inducements which really actuate them; but of that part he imagines them to be much cooler and more thoughtful calculators than they really are" ("Remarks," p. 325; in Schneewind, p. 60).

alternative principles.[10] With respect to the fifth chapter, which was originally begun as the draft of an independent essay on Justice,[11] the connection between *Utilitarianism* and the need to correct Bentham's system is less immediately obvious, but there are in fact even more points at which it may be seen as offering a corrective. For example, in other writings Mill had criticized Bentham for having failed to distinguish between benevolence and justice —a failure which this chapter can be seen as correcting.[12] In addition, justice provides a case, consistent with utilitarianism, in which one can safely appeal to a secondary principle or rule, and need not calculate the consequences of an action in the cumbersome way which the Benthamite formula would seem to demand.[13] And, finally, in this chapter Mill is able to explain why the secondary principle of justice could truly appear to men as being "incomparably the most sacred and binding part of all morality;"[14] thus showing, in the particular case most often cited as an objection to the principle of utility,[15] that utilitarianism could acknowledge the strength and the justification of precisely the same moral sentiments as those to which Bentham's opponents appealed.

It is usually assumed that when Mill departs from Bentham's system, enlarging the scope of what is to be regarded as humanly important, he is making concessions to the opponents of the utilitarian school, rather than building a positive moral theory of his own. Typical of this interpretation, and ably expressing it, are remarks made by A. D. Lindsay:

> We find him in all his books enunciating with firmness the Utilitarian principles, then compelled by his fairness and openness of mind to admit exceptions and insert qualifications which the older Utilitarianism, complete but narrow, had never recognized. The resultant picture is much fairer to the facts, but presents much less of a consistent doctrine, and the critical reader is always wondering why, if Mill admits this or that, he persists in maintaining general principles with which the facts admitted are clearly inconsistent.[16]

However, it is also possible to view most (though not all)[17] of the changes which

[10] Mill expressed this point strongly in "Remarks," pp. 315–316 (Schneewind, pp. 46–47). (Though later, in his unusually bitter and polemical essay on Whewell, he defended Bentham against the same charge: cf. *Dissertations*, III, 146–155.) In "Bentham" he also pointed out the latter's failure to appreciate the positions of those who did not accept the principle of utility (cf. *Dissertations*, I, 370, 375). What he found to be original in Bentham was a *method* of handling moral questions, not the discovery of any new moral principle (*ibid.*, pp. 370–372). Thus, one may infer that Mill felt that it was left to him to establish the truth of the principle of utility, and it would seem to be a fair reading of the last two paragraphs of the introductory chapter to say that it was primarily for the sake of filling this lacuna that *Utilitarianism* was written.

[11] Cf. the remark of Helen Taylor in her preface to *Three Essays on Religion* (London, 1874).

[12] For Mill's criticism of Bentham in this respect, cf. "Remarks," p. 322 (Schneewind, p. 56), and *Dissertations*, I, 384 and note. The relation of these remarks to chapter v of *Utilitarianism* is to be seen if the reader will consult Mill's comment in his edition of James Mill's *Analysis of the Phenomena of the Human Mind*, vol. 2, 2nd ed. (London, 1878), 324.

[13] While Mill strongly criticizes Bentham for overlooking the importance of secondary principles (cf. *Dissertations*, I, 409–410), his own treatment of such secondary principles (including justice) should not, in my opinion, lead one to interpret him as a rule utilitarian.

[14] Chap. v, para. 32 (p. 55) [p. 54 above].

[15] Cf. chap. v, para. 1 (p. 38) [p. 42 above].

[16] Preface to Everyman's edition of Mill: *Utilitarianism, On Liberty*, p. viii.

[17] I find the chief exception to be his introduction of the notion of higher and lower pleasures; that innovation can, I believe, be regarded as a case in which his own moral and aesthetic judgments forced him to a conclusion inconsistent with his basic theory. I might add,

Mill incorporated into utilitarianism as attempts to offer a moral theory more in line with a careful psychological account of human motivation: a theory which was to be based on Hartley and James Mill, not on the crude form of psychological hedonism which Bentham espoused. On the whole, I would stress the second of these alternative interpretations. And if we now consider Mill's early criticisms of Bentham's psychology, one can (I hope) see reason for doing so.

In his "Remarks," Mill summarized Bentham's psychological assumptions in the following propositions:

> . . . that happiness, meaning by that term pleasure and exemption from pain, is the only thing desirable in itself; that all other things are desirable solely as means to that end . . . and moreover, that pleasure and pain are the sole agencies by which the conduct of mankind is in fact governed, whatever circumstances the individual may be placed in, and whether he is aware of it or not.

And continued:

> Mr. Bentham does not appear to have entered very deeply into the metaphysical grounds of these doctrines; he seems to have taken those grounds very much upon the showing of the metaphysicians who preceded him.[18]

Now, it is clear that Mill is here using the term "metaphysical" as equivalent to what we should designate as "psychological," the noun "metaphysics" having frequently been used by Adam Smith and Hamilton, and by others, to refer to "Pneumatology" as contrasted with "Physics."[19] The general criticism which Mill levelled against Bentham's psychology was its attempt to explain human action in terms of the notion of self-interest, and its failure to see that motives not originally part of man's endowment could arise through the associative process. In an argument reminiscent of Bishop Butler, Mill pointed out that the view that self-interest dominates men is only plausible because it involves an ambiguity in terms.[20] Furthermore, he rejected Bentham's assumption that men always act for *future* pleasures or the avoidance of *future* pains. According to Mill, this form of hedonism makes it impossible to explain so-called "disinterested actions," for example, actions which spring from patriotism, benevolence, or conscience.[21]

The hedonistic theory which, in these passages, Mill himself explicitly accepts (and which he seems never to have aban-

---

however, that he probably could have argued for at least *some* of those values which he linked with the higher or nobler pleasures on grounds consistent with his other views. That he did not attempt to do so suggests that in this case Lindsay's characterization is correct.

18 "Remarks," p. 315 (Schneewind, p. 46).

19 Cf. *Oxford English Dictionary*, "Metaphysics," entry 1c.

For other instances of Mill's use of "metaphysician" and "metaphysics" in this sense, cf. his characterizations both of his father and of Helvetius as metaphysicians in "Bentham" (*Dissertations*, I (New York: Henry Holt and Co., 1874–75), 360, 408, respectively); also his remark that the relation between the question of whether moral feelings are simple or complex (and whether, if they are complex, of what simple feelings they are composed) "is a metaphysical question," "Professor Sedgwick's Discourse" (*Dissertations*, I, 149).

Among the many other references which might be cited are the following: *Utilitarianism*, chap. iv, para. 10 (p. 36) [p. 40 above]; *Dissertations*, III, 164; and the concluding paragraphs of the Introduction to the *System of Logic*.

The importance of noting that "metaphysical" is to be taken as meaning "psychological" can be seen from the fact that as able a critic as Mary Warnock holds that Mill viewed it as *logically* contradictory that we should desire anything but pleasure, and she cites his use of "metaphysical" in support of that contention (cf. Preface to the Meridian edition of Mill's *Utilitarianism*, p. 26).

20 "Remarks," pp. 322–323 (Schneewind, p. 57).

21 Cf. "Remarks," pp. 321, 323 (Schneewind, pp. 55, 58).

doned) states that men act in accordance with the pleasantness or unpleasantness of their *present* ideas. To explain how ideas of particular actions take on pleasantness or unpleasantness, Mill invokes associations dependent upon past experience. And by this means he materially enlarges the range of motives which Bentham had attributed to men.[22] As he says in this essay:

> The attempt to enumerate motives, that is, human desires and aversions, seems to me to be in its very conception an error. Motives are innumerable: there is nothing whatever which may not become an object of desire or of dislike by association.[23]

In this connection it is important to note that Mill cites Hartley against Bentham, praising Hartley on the ground that "although he considers the moral sentiments to be wholly the result of association, [he] does not therefore deny them a place in his system, but includes the feelings of 'the moral sense' as one of the six classes into which he divides pleasures and pains."[24] This passage is suggestive of Mill's own positive views, for (as we shall see) he insists on the emergence of an effective moral sense through what we should now term "functional autonomy."[25] It will be my contention that this departure from Bentham's psychological views constitutes a crucial factor in Mill's ethical theory.

The second point of criticism of Bentham which it is important to note for the sake of interpreting *Utilitarianism* as a positive and consistent formulation of a utilitarian position is Mill's rejection of the view that the rightness or wrongness of an action is to be calculated in terms of its "specific consequences." Mill states his criticism as follows:

> Now, the great fault I have to find with Mr. Bentham as a moral philosopher, and the source of the chief part of the temporary mischief which in that character, along with

[22] Unlike many later commentators, Mill notes that Bentham admitted sympathy to be an underived motive in man (cf. "Remarks," p. 322 [Schneewind, p. 56]. Also, *Dissertations*, I, 383). However, he criticized Bentham for failing to account for benevolence as "a steady principle of action" (cf. "Remarks," p. 323 [Schneewind, p. 58]). Without taking into account the results of the associative process, sympathy (according to Mill) can only explain those cases of benevolent action in which it is actually felt.

In both of his essays on Bentham, Mill stresses the importance—and the inadequacy—of Bentham's "Table of the Springs of Action" (cf. "Remarks," p. 321 [Schneewind, p. 54]. Also, *Dissertations*, I, 383).

[23] "Remarks," p. 321 (Schneewind, p. 55). The clearest expression of Mill's views on this point are to be found much later, in a context in which he is not discussing Bentham. One finds that expression in notes added to his father's *Analysis of the Phenomena of the Human Mind*, II, 233–234, 307–309.

[24] "Remarks," p. 322 (Schneewind, p. 56). Mill's criticism of Bentham's psychology in his later essay, "Bentham," follows the same general lines as those laid down in his anonymous essay, even though the later exposition is less detailed. For example, it contains an equivalent reference to Hartley (*Dissertations*, I, 387); it also contains a criticism of Bentham's failure to include motives which are not original, but are derived through the effects of association:

> Man is never recognized by him as a being capable of pursuing spiritual perfection as an end; of desiring, for its own sake, the conformity of his own character to his standard of excellence, without hope of good or fear of evil from other sources than his own inward consciousness. Even in the more limited form of conscience, this great fact of human nature escapes him. Nothing is more curious than the absence of recognition in any of his writings of the existence of conscience, as a thing distinct from philanthropy, from affection for God or man, and from self-interest in this world or in the next (*Dissertations*, I, 384).

In interpreting Mill on association it is of course necessary to bear in mind that the principle of association, as he used that term, was not only applicable to memory but was at the same time "the law of imagination, of belief, of reasoning, of the affections, of the will." (From "Blakey's History of Moral Science," *The Monthly Repository*, n. s., VII [1833], 664. Also, *Dissertations*, IV, 112–113.)

[25] This term was apparently coined by Gordon W. Allport and first used by him in *Personality: A Psychological Interpretation* (New York: Henry Holt and Co., 1937), pp. 191ff.

> a vastly greater amount of permanent good, he must be allowed to have produced is this: that he has practically, to a very great extent, confounded the principle of Utility with the principle of specific consequences, and has habitually made up his estimate of the approbation or blame due to a particular kind of action, from a calculation of the consequences to which that very action, if practiced generally, would itself lead.[26]

Now, what we must note is the additional factor, other than "specific consequences," which Mill holds must be taken into account if the utilitarian doctrine is to be acceptable. This type of factor is *not* the more remote consequences: Bentham, after all, had taken such consequences into account, as is evident in the roles played by purity, fecundity, and extent, in his felicific calculus. Instead, what Mill holds to have been neglected by Bentham is the sort of "consequence" which lies in the effect of an action on the agent's own character. The thesis that such effects are themselves relevant to the moral judgment of actions is an aspect of Mill's moral theory which, as we shall see, is of sufficient importance for quoting at length from the passage in his anonymous essay on Bentham:

> He [Bentham] has largely exemplified, and contributed very widely to diffuse, a tone of thinking according to which any kind of action or any habit, which in its own specific consequences cannot be proved to be necessarily or probably productive of unhappiness to the agent himself or to others, is supposed to be fully justified; and any disapprobation or aversion entertained towards the individual by reason of it, is set down from that time forward as prejudice and superstition. It is not considered (at least, not habitually considered), whether the act or habit in question, though not in itself pernicious, may not form part of a *character* essentially pernicious, or at least essentially deficient in some quality eminently conducive to the "greatest happiness." To apply such a standard as this, would indeed often require a much deeper insight into the formation of character, and knowledge of the internal workings of human nature, than Mr. Bentham possessed. But, in a greater or less degree, he, and every one else, judges by this standard.[27]

This appeal to the effects of an action, or type of action, upon the agent's own character (and, presumably, also upon the characters of those who might emulate the agent) is an aspect of Mill's theory which has not—so far as I can recall—been duly noted. That its expression in this anonymous essay was not an isolated instance of an ephemeral view can be seen in its repetition in Mill's attack on Sedgwick, where he says:

> In estimating the consequences of actions, in order to obtain a measure of their morality, there are always two sets of considerations involved—the consequences to the outward interests of the parties concerned (including the agent himself); and the consequences to the characters of the same persons, and to their outward interests so far as dependent upon their characters. . . . It often happens that an essential part of the morality or immorality of an action or a rule of action consists in its influence upon the agent's own mind; upon his susceptibilities of pleasure or pain; upon the general direction of his thoughts, feelings, and imagination; or upon some particular association.[28]

As we shall see, if we take this doctrine seriously, accepting the view that we are to count among the consequences of an act the effects of the performance of that act on the agent's own character, we shall be in a better position to interpret some of the more baffling aspects of *Utilitarianism*.[29]

[26] "Remarks," p. 317 (Schneewind, p. 49).

[27] "Remarks," pp. 317–318 (Schneewind, pp. 49–50). This passage follows, without interruption, upon the passage which was quoted immediately above.

[28] *Dissertations*, I, 156–157.

[29] How important Mill regarded the consequences of an action on the agent's own char-

II. *On Virtue and Utility*

The preceding discussion places us in a better position to understand why Mill considered it justifiable to claim that even though utility is the standard of morality, the concept of virtue possesses a meaning distinct from that of utility. His use of the psychological principle of functional autonomy enabled him to explain how men come to act for ends other than those included among their original desires. Furthermore, a recognition of the functional autonomy of these new motives is reconciled with psychological hedonism through Mill's insistence that human action is to be explained through the pleasantness-unpleasantness of *present* ideas, not through the calculation of future pleasures and pains. Finally, in including among the consequences of an action the effects of that action on the agent's own character, Mill was able to show that the principle of utility did not regard the morality of an action as solely dependent upon its overt consequences: the motives and the character of an agent were no less to be considered by the utilitarian than by his opponents. Bearing these points in mind, it is clear how Mill could answer the question that we originally raised: whether it is possible to say that virtue "is to be desired disinterestedly, for itself," and yet consistently hold that actions and dispositions "are only virtuous because they promote another end than virtue." That Mill's answer depends upon his adoption of a particular set of psychological assumptions is clear in the following passage:

> Whatever may be the opinion of utilitarian moralists as to the original conditions by which virtue is made virtue, however they may believe (as they do) that actions and dispositions are only virtuous because they promote another end than virtue, yet this being granted, and it having been decided from considerations of this description what *is* virtuous, they not only place virtue at the very head of the things which are good as means to the ultimate end, but they also recognize as a psychological fact the possibility of its being, to an individual, a good in itself, without looking to any end beyond it.[30]

Up to this point, then, the interpretation of Mill's doctrine of virtue poses no obstacles which cannot be overcome by looking to his other works for the relevant psychological assumptions which he accepts. However, neither in *Utilitarianism* nor elsewhere do I find an explicit characterization of the specific nature of that which he calls "virtue." In order to determine the substantive content designated by that term, we must examine in context the passages in which he uses it, its cognates, or their antonyms.

Following this method, it would seem that virtue is to be regarded as a dispositional property of persons, and that anything which is to be described as "virtuous" is connected with the existence of this property in human agents. (Thus, for example, I find no occasions on which Mill designates an action as "virtuous" because its specific consequences are good.) As examples of instances in which he uses the term as I suggest, one may note that he twice speaks of "a person of confirmed virtue,"[31] and he remarks that in conflicts of obligation the conflict can only be partially overcome through "the intellect and

---

acter can be suggested by the following psychological assertion:

> It may be affirmed with few exceptions, that any act whatever has a tendency to fix and perpetuate the state or character of mind in which it itself has originated ("Remarks," p. 318 [Schneewind, p. 50]).

I find no evidence that Mill ever broke with this assumption.

[30] *Utilitarianism*, chap. iv, para. 5 (p. 33) [p. 38 above].

[31] Ibid., para. 11 (pp. 36, 37) [p. 40 above].

virtue of the individual."[32] He also says of the readiness of a person to make an absolute sacrifice of his own happiness for the sake of the happiness of others, that this readiness—which is clearly a dispositional trait—is the highest virtue which one can find in man.[33] Furthermore, this remark reveals what Mill actually took to be the substantive character of that dispositional trait which he designated as virtue: it was a readiness to act for the greatest good of mankind, in place of acting for one's personal good. That this is an accurate interpretation of Mill's position can perhaps be seen most clearly in a passage from *On Liberty.* In that passage Mill lists those objects which deserve the strongest moral reprobation. These objects include not only acts in which one person injures another, but the dispositions which lead men to perform such acts; these dispositions, Mill says, "are moral vices and constitute a bad and odious moral character."[34] This being so, one may justifiably infer that virtue, or a virtuous character, consists in a readiness to respond to the needs of others, a disposition to act not out of self-interest but for the happiness of others. Obviously, praise of such a disposition is wholly in conformity with an acceptance of the utilitarian principle, since nothing can in the long run better serve to promote the happiness of mankind than fostering that trait of character which involves a readiness to respond sensitively to the needs of others, placing their needs above one's own. And thus Mill was wholly justified in insisting—as we noted in his criticism of Bentham—that it is not only the "specific consequences" of an action, but the effects of that action on the character of the agent himself, that a utilitarian must take into account.

Now, the trait of character which leads an agent to place the good of others ahead of his own pleasure was a trait which Mill held to be both a proper and a possible object for the individual to desire for himself. To be sure, if virtue failed to afford pleasure, we would not seek it; but it *does* afford pleasure—not through the specific consequences which it brings us, but in the idea which we have of *being* virtuous. (And by the pain which would be occasioned by the realization that we were not.) Thus, through functional autonomy, virtue—which would not be "virtue" if it did not foster happiness—becomes for an agent a goal sought for itself. If one were to object and say that a man is not truly virtuous, but is self-righteous and a prig, if he seeks virtue because the idea of his virtue is agreeable to him, one would have misunderstood how, according to Mill, the functional autonomy of motives comes about. The only reason that pleasure can be derived from a consciousness that one has acted virtuously is that there was an original bond between pleasure for ourselves and the happiness of others. This bond is depen-

[32] *Utilitarianism*, chap. ii, concl. para. (p. 24) [p. 30 above].

[33] Ibid., para. 16 (p. 15) [p. 24 above].

[34] The complete passage, which deals with acts which are injurious to others, reads as follows:

> Encroachment on their rights; infliction on them of any loss or damage not justified by his own rights; falsehood or duplicity in dealing with them; unfair or ungenerous use of advantages over them; even selfish abstinence from defending them against injury—these are fit objects of moral reprobation, and, in grave cases, of moral retribution, and punishment. And not only these acts, but the dispositions which lead to them, are properly immoral, and fit subjects of disapprobation which may rise to abhorrence. Cruelty of disposition; malice and ill-nature; that most anti-social and odious of all passions, envy; dissimulation and insincerity, irascibility on insufficient cause, and resentment disproportioned to the provocation; the love of domineering over others; the desire to engross more than one's share of advantages . . . the pride which derives gratification from the abasement of others; the egotism which thinks self and its concerns more important than everything else, and decides all doubtful questions in its own favour;—these are moral vices, and constitute a bad and odious moral character (*On Liberty*, chap. iv, para. 6 [Everyman's ed. of *Utilitarianism*, p. 135]).

dent upon our original possession of feelings of sympathy, of love, and of all those other-regarding tendencies which Mill refers to as "the social feelings."[35] Thus, unless one were first interested in others, one could not derive pleasure from the thought of acting virtuously. In short, while it is compatible with functional autonomy that the attempt to be virtuous may *eventually* lead some men to become prigs, Mill's analysis makes it clear that the pursuit of virtue originally springs from the existence in us of other-regarding sentiments, and not from a concern with our own self-image. In other words, the pursuit of virtue for its own sake is possible only for those whose social feelings have rendered them sensitive to the needs of others; for them it can be among the strongest of motives; and it can impart an immediate happiness, independent of the future. In this connection Mill says:

> Virtue, according to the utilitarian doctrine, is not naturally and originally part of the end, but it is capable of becoming so; and in those who love it disinterestedly it has become so and is desired and cherished, not as a means to happiness, but as a part of their happiness.[36]

Assuming the accuracy of the foregoing account of Mill's use of the term "virtue," one can see why—apart from all reasons of composition[37]—his treatment of justice proceeds independently of his remarks concerning virtue. In the first place, Mill apparently recognized that the concept of justice, unlike that of virtue, does not have at its root a reference to the dispositional properties of persons: in its primary meaning, he tells us, it is a characteristic attributable to certain "modes of action" or "arrangements of human affairs."[38] This being so, an analysis of the concept of justice, and of its relation to the standard of utility, would not follow a path like that involved in the analysis of virtue. In the second place, we may note that in his account of justice, unlike his account of virtue, Mill distinguishes sharply between what constitutes the *standard* of justice and what constitutes the *origin* of the sentiment which attaches to it.[39] Furthermore, we may note that in his account of the origins of the sentiment attaching to justice Mill does not make use of the principle of functional autonomy, as he did in the case of the origin of our idea of virtue. Instead, he placed reliance upon a recognition of self-interest as bound up with the recognition of rights, as well as upon a basic impulse to retaliate against injuries.

In spite of these differences, however, there is one basic similarity between Mill's account of virtue and his account of justice: he recognizes each as capable of being pursued as an end in itself, even though the moral legitimacy of each depends wholly upon its relation to the principle of utility. That this is the case with respect to virtue, we have already shown; that it is Mill's view with respect to justice is (so far as I know) universally acknowledged. And it is at this point that we can see why it is frequently held that Mill is to be regarded as a rule utilitarian. However, it is not with that complex issue with which I am here concerned. My aim in this paper has been to show the very great extent to which a careful interpretation of Mill's *Utilitarianism* presupposes that we

[35] *Utilitarianism*, chap. iii, para. 10 (p. 29) [p. 34 above].

[36] *Utilitarianism*, chap. iv, para. 5 (p. 34) [p. 38 above].

[37] Cf. note 11, above.

[38] *Utilitarianism*, chap. v, para. 4 (p. 40) [p. 43 above]. Also, cf. paras. 2 and 3 (p. 39) [pp. 42–43 above] for instances in which Mill speaks only of modes of action in connection with justice.

[39] For a crucial passage in which the distinction stands out clearly, cf. *Utilitarianism*, chap. v, paras. 21, 23 (pp. 48, 49) [p. 49 above].

take seriously those psychological doctrines which most commentators neglect.

Now, it should not be surprising to find that Mill's ultimate conclusions in the theory of morals rest upon psychological principles, and that in establishing these conclusions his associationism played a particularly important part. One thinks immediately of his *System of Logic* and of his *Examination of Sir William Hamilton's Philosophy* as two other instances of a similar sort. And if, in interpreting *Utilitarianism* we bear in mind Mill's treatment of axioms in the *Logic,* and his treatment of our belief in an external world in the *Examination,* we shall derive more assistance than by looking only to those works of political philosophy from which critics generally seek help in their interpretations of his moral theory.[40] Axioms, one will recall, have their sources in the total, cumulative effect of experiences, but it is not necessary for us to refer them back to these sources in order to understand their mathematical or logical import and to use them. Similarly, in our conception of independent, external objects, and in that paradigmatic case to which Mill often refers—our ability to judge distances—we rely in these cases on the effects of a congeries of past sensations, but our practical judgments do not demand that we refer back to these ultimate sources before we actually judge. Such examples suggest that even though the ultimate *source* of our moral notions is in all cases to be found in simple experiences of pleasure and pain, the shapes which morality can assume are highly complex, and in many cases appear as wholly independent of that in which they had their origin. Thus, the ideas and feelings connected with morality possess characteristics which one would not expect to find associated with so humble a source.[41] It is, then, not necessarily an inconsistency on the part of Mill to recognize that there are (in some sense) "nobler" or "higher" feelings and states of character than those leading us to view every action in terms of the future effects it will have on our own pleasures and pains.[42] To recognize the emergence of new forms of action is not, however, to deny that pleasure and pain lie at their base. It was for the sake of showing how Mill thought that he could derive the nobler sentiments from their primitive source in experience that we have examined his criticism of Bentham, and have analyzed his use of the concept of virtue.

40 It is worth noting that in his essay "Bain's Psychology," Mill explicitly classes Duty and Virtue with Extension, Solidity, Time and Space, as notions which "are not exact copies of any impressions on our senses." In his contrast between a priori and a posteriori theories of knowledge, he is insisting that in his view (and Bain's) it is necessary to seek to give an account of the origin of such ideas (*Dissertations,* IV, 108).

41 This can be taken as an example of what Mill called "chemical" composition, distinguishing it from "mechanical" composition (*System of Logic,* Bk. III, chap. vi, "The Composition of Causes"). In other words, it would be an example of what we, following G. H. Lewes, call "emergence."

There are two points at which Mill is relatively explicit in using this conception in connection with the results of associations: *Dissertations,* IV, 114–115, and a note which he added in his edition of his father's *Analysis of the Phenomena of the Human Mind,* II, 321.

42 Mill says:

> The cultivation of an ideal of nobleness of will and conduct, should be to individual human beings an end, to which the specific pursuit either of their own happiness or of that of others (except so far as included in that idea) should, in any case of conflict, give way. But I hold that the very question, what constitutes this elevation of character, is itself to be decided by a reference to happiness as the standard (*System of Logic,* Bk. VI, chap. xii, sec. 7). [p. 9 above]

This passage is not present in the first edition; however, it is to be found in the third edition (1851).

Duncan MacRae, Jr. / Utilitarian ethics and social change

Social change, in at least one important aspect, is change in social norms or rules.[1] Though we may observe changes over time in frequencies of behavior alone—migration or divorce, entry into new occupations, the use of machines or contraceptives—closely linked to this behavior there are usually internalized moral beliefs about its rightness or wrongness. And, as the behavior changes, prevalent characterizations of right and wrong conduct change with it.

Those who study contemporary social change may wish not merely to describe it but also to evaluate it. They may have undertaken to study change in order to speed it, retard it, or alter its direction. Or they may have become involved in controversy by sponsors of research, by persons whom they study, or by proponents of alternative social orders. In either case, the investigator may seek reasoned grounds for choosing or justifying his position. To avoid the futility of relativism, he must seek these grounds outside the old and new orders themselves. This type of inquiry combines sociology and philosophy.

The grounds for evaluating alternative degrees and directions of social change include factual assessment of its consequences, together with ethical principles by which these consequences may be judged. There will be disagreement as to consequences, but presumably this can be reduced by scientific and scholarly methods. There will be greater disagreement on the principles that hold given consequences to be good or bad, and some have questioned whether reason can reduce it. The difficulty of resolving ethical disagreement has led to a stress on factual matters

[1] The relation between norms and social structure is presented in the work of Talcott Parsons; see, e.g., *The Structure of Social Action* (New York: McGraw-Hill Book Co., 1937), pp. 697–726, and "The Superego and the Theory of Social Systems" in Parsons, R. F. Bales, and E. A. Shils, *Working Papers in the Theory of Action* (Glencoe, Ill.: Free Press, 1953). The earlier writers whose work Parsons analyzes, including particularly Durkheim and Freud, expressed this relation in their work.

Reprinted from ETHICS, *vol. 78, no. 3 (April 1968), pp. 188–198 by permission of the author and the University of Chicago Press.*

in the social sciences; valuative or ethical assertions, on the other hand, have at times been dismissed as meaningless expressions of individual emotion, not amenable to rational justification.

Recent philosophical discussion, however, has moved away from the positivistic notion that only factual statements are meaningful. Increasing attention has been devoted to the relations between reason and ethics. In this view, ethical judgments can be supported or criticized by rational argument and need not be regarded as mere expressions of individual emotion. Following this trend, students of social and political change may find rational argument relevant to ethical choices that they confront.

These developments in philosophy are not only of potential value to sociologists but can themselves be illuminated by parallels in sociological research. One point at which sociology is relevant to philosophy concerns an issue that has arisen in the discussion of utilitarian ethics—the distinction between "act utilitarianism" and "rule utilitarianism." In this argument, the notion of a "rule" assumes importance, and the concept is similar to the sociologist's "norm." The latter concept involves not merely a rule or principle of action but also observable distributions of conformity, expectations, and internalization of that rule and sanctions for deviance from it.[2]

A second philosophic issue for which sociological information is relevant concerns "generalization," or the statement of principles on which particular ethical choices are based.[3] A given act may conceivably be generalized in innumerable ways, but this range of choice is sharply limited when we consider the normative structure of the society in question, as it restricts the classification of any act by members of the society. Sociological concepts and research can aid in description of this structure and in consideration of its relevance. The situations in which conformity to a rule or norm is problematical and where research is needed to reveal possible bases of generalization are especially important when we study social change.

Thus, we are brought full circle. The evaluation of social change requires reasoned ethical standards as well as factual research. But the development of such reasoned standards may be furthered by certain types of sociological research, and this research is particularly likely to emerge from careful description of the normative aspects of social change. The purpose of this paper is to show these reciprocal relations between sociology and philosophy and to indicate the types of investigation in each field that will contribute most to them.

Utilitarianism

One type of ethics is especially consonant with social science: the type that considers the expected[4] consequences of acts as the basis for choosing rightly among alternatives. One of the main justifications for social science is that it can

[2] See J. P. Gibbs, "Norms: The Problem of Definition and Classification," *American Journal of Sociology*, 70 (March 1965), 586–594. These aspects of rules are also considered in H. L. A. Hart, *The Concept of Law* (Oxford: Clarendon Press, 1961). While this book is part of the philosophical (and legal) literature, Hart writes that it may also be regarded as an essay in descriptive sociology (see Preface).

[3] See M. G. Singer, *Generalization in Ethics* (New York: Alfred A. Knopf, Inc., 1961). We refer to his discussion of the "generalization principle" rather than to the "generalization argument" (see chap. i). He states the principle: "What is right (or wrong) for one person must be right (or wrong) for any similar person in similar circumstances" (p. 5).

[4] In the statistical, not the sociological, sense.

enable people to act more rightly by anticipating the consequences of their acts.[5] This justification is most relevant if our notions of right acts depend on consequences—if our ethics are of the type that Weber called "ethics of responsibility" as against "ethics of ultimate ends."[6] This distinction, in philosophical terms, corresponds roughly to that between teleological and deontological theories, though the latter can combine considerations of consequences and of ultimate rightness. If we considered the rightness of acts to depend on the actor's good intentions alone, or on conformity of the acts to formal rules irrespective of consequences, or on the pronouncements of authorities, there would be less reason for us to do research concerning their consequences. Thus, there is a close relation between sociology, or science in general—if it is to guide us to right acts—and the type or aspect of ethics that judges acts by their consequences.

Among the various ethical systems that consider consequences, some are likely to be simpler in formulation than others. These are the systems which, like scientific theories, have only a single implication as to what is a right act in a given situation.[7] They consist either of a single principle or of a set of principles with precise rules as to when one takes precedence over another. One such principle is that of maximizing happiness, in Bentham's sense. But for our present purposes we need not restrict our view so narrowly; "utilitarianism" may be considered a shorthand for those ethical systems that order alternative acts unambiguously in terms of their consequences, when those consequences are known. Considerable discussion has centered about this aspect of utilitarianism, apart from the particular criteria to be applied in judging consequences.

While emphasis on this aspect of utilitarianism is familiar to philosophers, the term sometimes has additional connotations with which we are not concerned. First, the Benthamite notion that men seek their own happiness has no necessary connection with utilitarianism as an ethical principle. Second, the view of society as atomistic and composed of individuals whose goals are random—a view referred to by Parsons as "utilitarianism"[8]—is also irrelevant here. A principal point of this paper will be that the normative structure of society and the interrelations of its members' goals through the existence of social norms *should* be considered in ethical formulations. If anything of this individualistic "utilitarianism" remains in the view presented here, it is only in the focus on decisions as between particular alternative acts and perhaps in the summation over equal individuals implied by an ethic of maximization.

Utilitarian ethics has been widely criticized, however. A major line of critical argument[9] has been that ethical theories

[5] This anticipation of consequences is nearly inseparable from the identification of significant alternative acts; for in defining a set of alternatives we necessarily engage in selection, and this selection can be influenced by a preliminary assessment of possible consequences.

[6] H. H. Gerth and C. W. Mills (trans. and eds.), *From Max Weber: Essays in Sociology* (New York: Oxford University Press, 1946), p. 120.

[7] By a "given" situation we mean one in which the relevant facts, including the alternatives and their differences in consequences, are known.

[8] Op. cit. (n. 1 above), pp. 51–60.

[9] Another line of criticism, which we shall not consider in detail, is that, if rational utilitarian calculations became prevalent, they would encourage justification in terms of near and visible consequences at the expense of the uncertain and remote, and undermine necessary rules (see M. A. Kaplan, "Some Problems of the Extreme Utilitarian Position," *Ethics* 70 [April 1960], 228–232). But this argument can be met in part by emphasizing the role of impartial expert decision as to the consequences of acts—a role that social science can pre-

or systems should correspond as far as possible with our moral convictions,[10] which tell us sometimes to base our actions on grounds other than consequences. Braybrooke and Lindblom have summarized a number of these critical arguments:

> There are some moral judgments . . . that seem to have force independent of utilitarian considerations and that seem capable of withstanding utilitarianism in cases of conflict. . . . The judgments in question are all peremptory ones. . . . Among them are peremptory rules such as these: that one should keep promises, even when the consequences of doing so in a particular instance would be less happy than the consequences of breaking them; that however superior any person's capacity for happiness it would not be right to make the rest of the community miserable in order to make him happy; that one should not deliberately sacrifice the lives of some members of the community . . . in order to make gratuitous contributions to the happiness of other members; that the products of individual members of the community should not be taken from them without compensation, when these have been produced on their own time with resources that either belong to them or were hitherto free for the taking; that people should not be incarcerated or executed for crimes they have not committed; that people should not be convicted of crimes and punished on the basis of *ex post facto* legislation.[11]

These "peremptory rules"—concerning promises, equality, murder, property, justice—are nearer to Weber's "ethic of ultimate ends" than to utilitarianism. Some are very relevant to planned social change, as they have served as grounds of criticism against political leaders or social movements that have pushed them aside while claiming to accomplish a greater good through changes in society.

The problem thus posed is whether expected consequences should indeed be the only criterion of the rightness of acts. These criticisms have led some to reject the construction of ethical theories based solely on consequences. But another response has been to compromise, retaining a concern for consequences by applying it (in unqualified form) only to rules or classes of acts rather than to acts in general. For, while Bentham applied it to acts,[12] the compromise view is that some of these difficulties can be met by changing its range of application.

This compromise, which has come to be called "rule utilitarianism,"[13] derives from the fact that utilitarianism applied universally to acts ("act utilitarianism") may specify certain choices as right that many members of our society would consider wrong. These choices involve deviance from peremptory rules on the ground that the overall consequences of such deviance in particular cases would be better than those of conformity. But while examples where conscience conflicts with consequences can easily be imagined for particular acts, they seem less likely when we consider changes in the rules themselves; the general prescription that prom-

---

sumably play. Moreover, it is not the same to argue for a particular ethics and to advocate its continuous application by everyone (see H. Sidgwick, *The Methods of Ethics*, 7th ed. [New York: Dover Publications, 1966], p. 490).

[10] See, e.g., J. Rawls, "Two Concepts of Rules," *Philosophical Review* 64 (January 1955), 15 [p. 175 above], where he argues against act utilitarianism on the grounds that "it cannot account for the strictness of [an] obligation" that we feel to keep promises.

[11] D. Braybrooke and C. E. Lindblom, *A Strategy of Decision* (New York: Free Press, 1963), pp. 212–213.

[12] J. Bentham, *Principles of Morals and Legislation* (New York: Hafner Publishing Co., 1948), p. 2.

[13] The literature in which this distinction has been developed includes S. E. Toulmin, *The Place of Reason in Ethics* (Cambridge: Cambridge University Press, 1950), chap. xi; J. O. Urmson, "The Interpretation of the Philosophy of J. S. Mill," *Philosophical Quarterly* 3 (January 1953), 33–40 [pp. 168–174 above]; and Rawls (n. 10 above), who also traces the earlier antecedents of the distinction.

ises be kept or that murder not be committed would seem easily justifiable in terms of its consequences. Thus, if we chose only among rules, the dictates of our pre-existing moral convictions would agree with calculation of consequences, and conscience would be permitted to prevail over consequences when we chose among individual acts.

Rule utilitarianism thus rests on a fundamental distinction between choices that concern acts falling under existing rules and choices that concern rules themselves. In the first type of choice, one might say that the act should be judged as to whether it fits the rule while the rule itself is taken for granted. In the second type of choice, one may consider whether having one rule or another would be good in its consequences. I shall argue that this distinction is a very difficult one to make in practice.[14]

In applying rule utilitarianism, how do we distinguish acts that change norms from those that simply fall within the scope of existing norms? One example, suggested by Rawls, is the difference between the roles of legislator and judge.[15] The legislator's role is set above the existing laws he changes; voting for a new law does not constitute disobedience to the old. Rawls extends this notion of a distinct rule-making "office" to choices between rules more generally. On the one hand, someone who is simply a participant in a practice is not entitled to change it; for someone in this role the rules defining the practice take precedence in particular cases. On the other hand, one can challenge a practice, and in this case "citing the rules (saying what the practice is) is naturally to no avail."[16] One must then assume another role: "If one seeks to question . . . rules, then one's office undergoes a fundamental change: one then assumes the office of one empowered to change and criticize the rules, or the office of a reformer, and so on.[17] When one does so, he may consider utilitarian arguments as applied to the practice.

This distinction between roles seems to have resolved the problem that gave rise to it, that is, the contradiction between ordinary (or act-) utilitarianism and certain peremptory rules. However, if it is applied in other realms, the new distinction itself gives rise to difficulties. I shall contend that its range of applicability is limited, as it fails to apply to some of the most significant choices between norms that we are called upon to make—choices that are central to the evaluation of social change.

It may be useful to pause and see what sorts of argumentative tactics we are following. The proponents of rule utilitarianism have observed that act utilitarianism contradicts certain prevalent moral judgments and have correctly considered this a point against act utilitarianism. But, insofar as they are arguing within a utilitarian framework, they should consider whether better alternatives are available. Perhaps their own alternative can be criticized on similar grounds; it may even be that no consistent ethical system which applies to all potential choice situations is immune from such criticisms.

We wish to show, therefore, that rule utilitarianism itself leads to conclusions that may conflict with other common ethical beliefs or convictions and, moreover, that it fails to apply to certain types of choices that involve anomie, social dis-

14 This argument will be developed from the viewpoint of act utilitarianism; but needless to say, criticism of a compromise position might induce persons to move toward either of the original extremes.

15 Rawls, *Two Concepts*, p. 7 [p. 177 above].

16 Ibid., p. 27 [p. 191 above].

17 Ibid., p. 28 [p. 191 above]. Toulmin makes a similar distinction, *Reason in Ethics* (n. 13 above), pp. 150 ff.

organization, multiple social subsystems with different norms, and the like. These actual alternatives, which confront us when we study modern social change—as well as a sociological perspective on the character of norms and variations possible among them—lead us to consider a wider range of alternatives.

One difficulty with the distinction made by rule utilitarianism is that norms can be changed in degree; a particular rule or norm can be more or less established or institutionalized.[18] When we compare alternative rules or norms, we ordinarily have a wider range of choice than the simple choice between two norms; we may have to choose between a higher and a lower degree of social integration or the counterpart of this difference as it is reflected in a single norm or rule.[19] The degree of institutionalization of a norm can be reflected in the distribution of conformity and deviance, the expectations of members of the social system, or the attitudes of members about the rightness and wrongness of the corresponding acts.

Our choices about rules, therefore, cannot be restricted to the case of complete institutionalization without eliminating many important alternatives. If we are to assess the consequences of having a given rule, we must predict them in a way that would allow them to be observed in an actual social system. To do this—rather than simply to conduct an imaginary philosophical experiment—requires us to consider the complications that go with partial institutionalization. And this, in turn, leads us to consider particular acts as affecting rules quantitatively rather than discretely.

A serious effort to observe and predict the consequences of alternative normative arrangements must therefore lead us beyond mere speculation about "what would happen if everybody did that?" Such speculation is admittedly an important ingredient of much moral and philosophical discourse,[20] but it does not seem to do justice to the implications of utilitarianism, even if that system is restricted to judgments about rules.

The fact that norms can vary in degree is connected with a second difficulty in the distinction made by rule-utilitarianism: it is hard to make a neat separation between choices among acts and choices among rules.[21] The choices that affect rules are, after all, choices among acts. And while some such acts are set apart by definition of roles such as that of the legislator, others are not. A declaration of one's intention to act as a reformer, or to create a test case,[22] may affect the way in which an act is viewed and in turn affect its consequences. But any public deviant act can

[18] For this usage of the term "institutionalized," see T. Parsons and E. A. Shils (eds.), *Toward a General Theory of Action* (Cambridge, Mass.: Harvard University Press, 1951), pp. 20*n.*, 40.

[19] This choice is of course constrained by the interrelations among norms in the structure of social systems.

[20] See C. D. Broad, "On the Function of False Hypotheses in Ethics," *Ethics* 26 (April 5, 1916), 377–397. A critique of the adequacy of considering only the actual effects of our acts on norms is also presented in Rawls, "Two Concepts" (n. 10 above), pp. 13–16 [pp. 181–184]. Such consideration is also explicitly rejected in Singer, *Generalization* (n. 3 above). But one important type of act that is used as an example of such considerations is that in which a large number of persons must choose in similar situations, with interrelated consequences, simultaneously or without knowing one another's choices; this falls into the category in which the consequences of acts are not strictly known.

[21] A similar problem arises, it must be recognized, in the separation between ethics and meta-ethics, e.g., between judging acts in terms of happiness and rationality.

[22] As in Toulmin, *Reason in Ethics* (n. 13 above), p. 151.

be expected to affect one or more norms, whether it is intended to do so or not, and the same can be said of acts that reaffirm or strengthen norms, such as rituals, sanctions, or education of the young. Whether we like it or not, we are constantly engaged in choices that may affect norms. But the actor's definition of his act should not impose a mandatory and exclusive classification of that act on the observer who judges it. An act aimed at changing one rule or norm may affect others as well; a civil rights demonstration may support the norm of equal treatment of citizens of different races while undermining the norm of proceeding through representative institutions.

The difficulty of separating the two types of acts derives in part from the fact that any act that affects rules is likely also to have direct consequences that do not work through the change of rules—or at least not through the change of rules that is primarily intended. If those acts that are intended to change rules are evaluated exclusively in terms of the effects of the intended change, many of their important consequences may be ignored; a reckless neglect of means, relative to ends, might even result. The general problem, which no version of utilitarianism can ignore, is to weigh indirect consequences operating through changes in norms against direct consequences.[23]

It might be argued that, when important rules are at stake, the indirect consequences so outweigh the direct that only the effects of changing the rules need be considered. But, when we consider the smaller incremental changes in rules that may occur—changes in degree of institutionalization—and the various mixtures of direct and indirect consequences that exist, the distinction seems inadequate.[24] Choices affecting rules, if they are to be weighed in terms of their consequences, can be made more universal and more consistent within the larger framework of act utilitarianism.

Generalization

Another issue in contemporary ethical discussion for which a sociological perspective is useful is that of generalization. It has often been pointed out that ethical statements are necessarily general; if they are to be supported by reasons, they must exemplify the general principles which are those reasons.[25] But not just any general principle will do. One can always construct fanciful categories within which an act falls, placing it in some class that avoids embarrassing counterexamples. The mere requirement that justifications must be general is not sufficient.

Further indication of this indeterminacy as to what general rule corresponds to a particular act deemed to be ethical is also given by Hare's interpretation of rule utilitarianism.[26] He contends that, since all "ought" statements are universalizable (they have to exemplify general rules), the choice of right acts is *equivalent* to a choice among rules. Thus, any deviant act which the actor believes *ought* to be done must have a corresponding general rule.

The possibility of an actor's defining

[23] A similar combination of "primary" and "secondary" consequences was assumed by Bentham, *Principles of Morals* (n. 12 above), chap. xii. This approach was also followed by Sidgwick, *Ethics* (n. 9 above), pp. 475–495.

[24] We here use a characteristic pattern of argument in favor of act utilitarianism against alternative pluralistic ethics: to call attention to situations in which the pluralistic principles may conflict or which they fail to cover.

[25] Singer, *Generalization* (n. 3 above), p. 25.

[26] R. M. Hare, *Freedom and Reason* (New York: Oxford University Press, 1965), pp. 130–131.

such a rule is quite similar to his declaring himself a reformer and stating the new rule that he wishes to institute. But we have already indicated that the actor's intention as to what rules or norms he will affect by his act cannot be the last word for an observer who evaluates the act. When leaders in the new nations create political parties, for example, they may do so as means to national or personal power; but an important effect may concern national integration. Thus, there is some indeterminacy as to *how* an act should be generalized.

Singer has proposed to reduce this indeterminacy by requiring that the principle be a *relevant* one.[27] He gives examples relating to employment, in which universalistic standards determine relevance, and to sexual relations, in which the monogamous husband-wife relation determines it.[28] But implicitly he is saying that the normative structure of our society defines relevance. These norms would not be the same in every society, and therefore an argument or generalization that was relevant in one society would not be relevant in another.

"Relevance," then, centers about the norms of the society[29] and the relations among them. It is socially defined, and its definition is largely provided by the normative structure of the society. A principle that can be used for serious justification is thus one that already exists in a given society or that can be developed from other such principles. And, while some of these principles are not purely ethical (e.g., the principles of logic), any argument involving justification must be based on *some* ethical or normative principles.

But if we define legitimate justifications in terms of the existing normative structure of a society, we limit our capacity to criticize that structure. In evaluating social change, we are appealing to an audience that places itself outside a changing society. We take this external stance even if our grounds of criticism are not utilitarian; as Gewirth has pointed out, relevance and moral propriety are not identical when we criticize a society that engages in discrimination.[30]

The normative structure of an existing society, while it must not limit us in our justifying principles, *is* relevant to our prediction of the consequences of acts. For as we have seen, the classification of acts depends in part on that structure; acts are relevant, in this sense, to some norms more than to others, and they are certainly more easily related to existing normative categories than to categories that do not currently exist. The question of which norms will be influenced is thus not entirely within the actor's choice, and it is still further beyond the discretion of an observer who might contemplate classifying an act one way or another. The classification is made by the society in which the actor is involved, in two senses: (a) the act is classified according to a pre-existing array of normative categories; and (b) its further consequences affect a *system* of norms, a social *structure*, in which it is unlikely that one norm can be altered without affecting others. Thus, the accurate description of social *structure* in these two senses is a necessary adjunct to predicting the consequences of acts.

Moreover, an existing normative structure need not be regarded as fixed; it can itself provide the basis for change. The norms of a society typically include partly

[27] *Generalization* (n. 3 above), p. 23 *et passim*.

[28] Ibid., pp. 29, 32.

[29] More generally, this reasoning extends to any social system with an organized set of norms—formal organizations, ethnic groups, primary groups, etc.

[30] A. Gewirth, "The Generalization Principle," *Philosophical Review* 73 (April 1964), 237–238. The same question might also be raised about using the set of linguistic categories of a given society as a fundamental test of proper justifications.

institutionalized and conflicting principles. The actor retains some freedom to choose which of several social categories will be used by spectators to classify his act; its staging, its justification, and the manner in which it is carried out influence this classification. One of the most important modes of influencing categorization is the successful persuasion of the audience that a new category should be created.[31]

In this sense, a major type of norm-changing act is that of the charismatic leader. Weber characterized this type of authority by Christ's words: "It is written . . . , but I say unto you. . . ."[32] The charismatic leader is thus a giver of norms. The structure of norms that he enunciates, however, is not simply an assortment of disconnected principles. It derives from the pre-existing normative structure of the society, from the specific grievances and strains[33] that contributed to the charismatic movement, and from the personal characteristics of the leader. The problem here—one not stressed in Weber's work[34] —is one of ideological dynamics: How can these new ideological systems arise from previous structures?

But while it is of central importance for the sociologist to try to predict changes in norms and their structures, we must remember that the related philosophical problem is to evaluate these changes. Our predictions, if they are accurate, set limits on our alternatives, but they do not alone provide a basis for evaluation. For this purpose, the standard of "relevance" can no longer serve us.

The arguments by which we evaluate social change must therefore be distinguished from justification in terms of accepted norms. The status of these arguments thus rests on discussion among qualified persons, including philosophers. Any arguments that are intended to provide an external point from which to view social change must look beyond the specific norms of a particular society for their justification. If they are to provide this sort of external point, they should presumably be derivable from a variety of prior ethical structures that differed considerably from one another.[35] In this sense, the general principles that we advocate as criteria of judgment and those that are expressed in the norms of a particular society must be seen as distinct.

We therefore suggest that act utilitarianism is in some respects preferable to the generalization principle, if the "similar circumstances" of that principle are culture-bound. In these terms, acts should be appraised solely in terms of their consequences; among these consequences should be considered the effects that work through changes in social norms; and these changes should be predicted not simply on logical grounds but on grounds of the expected perception of the act in question by members of a social system and its ramifications in that system. For this purpose, the generalizations of a given act that were "relevant" in one society might not be relevant in another; and the ob-

[31] This is analogous to de Jouvenel's assertion that the power to found new social aggregates is a major aspect of political influence (see B. de Jouvenel, *Sovereignty* [Chicago: University of Chicago Press, 1957], p. 21).

[32] Max Weber, *The Theory of Social and Economic Organization*, trans. A. M. Henderson and Talcott Parsons (New York: Oxford University Press, 1947), p. 361.

[33] See also R. K. Merton, *Social Theory and Social Structure*, rev. ed. (Glencoe, Ill.: Free Press, 1957), chaps. iv and v.

[34] P. M. Blau contends that Weber had no theory of revolution (see his "Critical Remarks on Weber's Theory of Authority," *American Political Science Review*, 57 [June 1963], 309).

[35] For this reason, as well as because of the internal contradictions in most such ethical structures when they are viewed in the literal perspective of scientific discourse, it is difficult to "account for" all the detailed ethical prescriptions of a society by a general ethical system that stands outside that society.

server's perspective as to how an act should be classified—for example, his imposition of a universalistic frame of reference on a particularistic society—would be set aside in favor of an effort at objective assessment of the effects of acts on norm structures. But, while making use of a kind of ethical relativism in seeking to understand the diverse structures of justification in different societies, the observer would maintain the "absolutism" of imposing a utilitarian criterion on the consequences of alternative acts.

Implications for sociological research

We have presented a critique of two contemporary philosophical views—rule utilitarianism and the generalization principle—from a sociological perspective. The interrelations between acts and norms and the possibility of altering norms in degree as well as in kind were the basis of our critique of rule utilitarianism; the existing structures of norms were the basis of our re-examination of "relevance" for the generalization principle. And both of these arguments found their place in an unqualified act utilitarianism which judges the direct effects of acts together with those indirect effects that operate through norms and their structures.

But to say that acts affect norms and that these effects are channeled by the normative structure of society is not the same as specification of these effects in particular cases. What, for example, have been the effects in recent years of the decisions of the United States Supreme Court or of social movements aimed at racial equality? What other norms have been affected besides the one most clearly under consideration? Or, in the independence movements and their continuation in the government of the new nations, what norms have been strengthened or weakened? National integration, identification of party with nation, the development of representative institutions[36] are among the normative changes that have been widely recognized as worthy of study.

It is here that sociological research is needed.[37] The problems that demand our attention are those of describing the normative structures of social systems and of assessing the conditions for their change. From the observation of historical change to the deliberate creation of norms in experimental settings, a wide range of possible researches is potentially relevant. Some of the most important aspects and consequences of social change remain to be characterized, and this description is necessary for any attempt to evaluate those changes more accurately.

The first task is the systematic characterization of norms.[38] Distributions of degrees of conformity, expectations, internalization, and sanctions need to be traced over time or to be inferred when these data are not all available. Their interrelations need to be traced—perhaps by examining the diverse results of efforts that have been made to change particular norms.

Then a systematic body of literature on the effects of norm-changing acts needs to be developed. Studies of actual conformity and of the actual effects of laws and administrative acts on informal norms will be relevant. Experimentation might even be possible, for example, with moral education in home and school and with the

[36] See, e.g., E. A. Shils, "Political Development in the New States," *Comparative Studies in Society and History*, 2 (April-July 1960), 265–292, 379–411; A. R. Zolberg, *Creating Political Order* (Chicago: Rand McNally, 1966).

[37] A point made by Sidgwick in *The Methods of Ethics*, in an edition originally published in 1907 (see n. 9 above), p. 477.

[38] See J. Jackson, "A Conceptual and Measurement Model for Norms and Roles," *Pacific Sociological Review* 9 (Spring 1966), 35–47.

public acts and communications of law-enforcement officials.

Finally, the valuative consequences of systems of norms and their institutionalization must be examined, insofar as researchers can agree on measuring them. What is the price of social change in terms of social disorganization, and how long is it likely to last? How valuable is the calculability that results from a high degree of institutionalization of norms? What is the cost, on the other hand, of a system of norms that is excessively rigid and incapable of adaptation to changing circumstances?

If research of this kind can be increased and directed to problems chosen through systematic ethical reflection, sociology will become more relevant to the ethical problems of social change. Conversely, if the ethical concepts and principles used for judgment are made more consistent with sociological concepts and information, philosophical discussion of ethics can serve more readily as a guide to sociologists.

Selected bibliography

The bibliography here is divided into six sections. These deal with Mill's major works, background on British Utilitarianism, early reactions to *Utilitarianism*, comments by major philosophers, recent relevant books, and recent relevant articles. Readers with an interest in more extensive bibliographical materials, as well as those with a continuing interest in Mill, should refer to *The Mill Newsletter*, edited by J. M. Robson, and published by the University of Toronto Press. This twice yearly periodical regularly contains an extremely thorough bibliographical section relating to all aspects of Mill scholarship. It also provides information about forthcoming works on Mill. (At present the Newsletter is available without charge to interested subscribers.) An excellent bibliography also appears in *Distributive Justice* by Nicholas Rescher (Indianapolis: Bobbs-Merrill, 1966). Rescher's bibliography, some thirty pages in length, has the advantage of being divided topically, and thus includes such sections as "Act Versus Rule Utilitarianism" and "Utilitarianism and Economic Policy: Welfare Economics." Finally, *The Life of John Stuart Mill*, by Michael S. J. Packe (New York: Macmillan, 1954), has a substantial relevant bibliography.

Mill's major writings

A System of Logic. 2 vols. London, 1843; 9th ed., 1875.
Principles of Political Economy. 2 vols. London, 1848; 7th ed., 1871.
Essays on Some Unsettled Questions of Political Economy. London, 1844.
On Liberty. London, 1859.

Thoughts on Parliamentary Reform. London, 1859.
Dissertations and Discussions. 2 vols. London, 1859; 3 vols., 1867; 4 vols., 1875.
Considerations on Representative Government. London, 1861.
Utilitarianism. London, 1863.
An Examination of Sir William Hamilton's Philosophy. London, 1865; 3rd ed., 1867.
Auguste Comte and Positivism. London, 1865.
The Subjection of Women. London, 1869.

POSTHUMOUSLY PUBLISHED

Autobiography. Edited by Helen Taylor. London, 1873.
Nature, the Utility of Religion, Theism, Being Three Essays on Religion. London, 1874.
Socialism. Edited by W. D. P. Bliss. New York, 1891.
Letters of John Stuart Mill. Edited by Hugh Elliott. 2 vols. London, 1910.
On Social Freedom, New York, 1941. (Mill's authorship in doubt.)

The Collected Works of John Stuart Mill, *in excess of twenty volumes, is currently in the process of being published by the University of Toronto Press under the general editorship of F. E. L. Priestly. Several volumes are currently available, many more shortly forthcoming, and the rest in various stages of planning.*

Background on British Utilitarianism

Abel, H. "John Stuart Mill and Socialism." *Fortnightly Review,* September 1938, pp. 343–348.
Adams, K. "How the Benthamites Became Democrats." *Journal of Social Philosophy* 7 (January 1942): 161–171.
Albee, E. *A History of English Utilitarianism.* London: Swan Sonnenschein & Co., Ltd., 1902.
Bladen, V. "Centenary of Marx and Mill." *Journal of Economic History,* 8th Supplement (1948): 32–41.
Dunning, W. "English Political Philosophy." *Political Science Quarterly* 15 (1900): 318–320.
Grote, J. *An Examination of the Utilitarian Philosophy.* Cambridge: Eighton, Bell & Co., 1870.
Irvine, W. "Shaw, the Fabians, and the Utilitarians." *Journal of the History of Ideas* 8 (1947): 218–231.
Mack, M. "Fabians and Utilitarianism," *Journal of the History of Ideas* 16 (1955): 76–88.
Palmer, P. "Benthamism in England and America." *American Political Science Review* 35 (1941): 855–871.

Pankhurst, R. *The Saint-Simonians, Mill, and Carlyle.* London: Lalibella Books, Sidgwick and Jackson, 1957.
Plamenatz, J. *The English Utilitarians.* Oxford: Basil Blackwell, 1949.
Stephan, L. *The English Utilitarians.* 3 vols. New York: G. P. Putnam's Sons, 1900.
Viner, J. "Bentham and J. S. Mill: The Utilitarian Background." *American Economy Review* 39 (1940): 360–382.
Ward, W. "English Utilitarians." *Nation,* December 11, 1915, pp. 383–385.

Some early reactions to Utilitarianism

Gurney, E. "The Utilitarian 'Ought'." *Mind* 7 (1882): 349–365.
Hodder, A. "Utilitarianism." *Ethics* 3 (1892): 90–112.
Jones, E. "Rational Hedonism." *Ethics* 5 (1894): 79–97.
———. "The Rationality of Hedonism." *Proceedings of the Aristotelian Society* 3(1) (1895): 29–45.
Rashdall, H. "Can There Be a Sum of Pleasures?" *Mind* NS8 (1899): 357–382.
Seth, J. "Is Pleasure the Summum Bonum?" *Ethics* 6 (1896): 409–424.
Sidgwick, H. "The Establishment of Ethical First Principles." *Mind* 4 (1879): 106–111.
Sutherland, J. "An Alleged Gap in Mill's Utilitarianism." *Mind* 11 (1886): 597–599.
———. "On the Utilitarian Formula." *Mind* 15 (1890): 590–592.
Woodbridge, F. "The Place of Pleasure in a System of Ethics." *Ethics* 7 (1897): 475–486.
———. "Mr. Mill on Utilitarianism." *Westminster Review* 80 (1863): 20–31.

Major philosophers on Mill and Utilitarianism

Ayer, A. "Freedom and Happiness." *New Statesman* Supplement 18, 68 (1964): 390–392.
———. *Philosophical Essays.* London: Macmillan and Company, Ltd., 1954.
Bradley, F. H. *Ethical Studies.* New York: G. E. Stechert & Company, 1904 (Reprint of 1876), Essay 3.
Broad, C. D. *Five Types of Ethical Theory.* London: Routledge & Keagan Paul, 1930.
Dewey, J. *Human Nature and Conduct.* New York: Henry Holt & Company, 1922.
———. *Outline of a Critical Theory of Ethics.* Ann Arbor: Registrar Publishing Company, 1891.
Dewey, J. and Tufts, J. *Ethics.* New York: Henry Holt & Company, 1908.
Ewing, A. *Ethics,* London: English Universities Press, 1890.
Green, T. *Prolegomena to Ethics.* Oxford: Clarendon Press, 1890.
Hartman, N. *Ethics.* Vol. 1. New York: The Macmillan Company, 1932.
Moore, G. E. *Ethics.* Oxford University Press, 1912.

———. *Principia Ethica.* Cambridge: The University Press, 1903.

Rashdall, H. *The Theory of Good and Evil.* Oxford: Clarendon Press, 1907.

Ross, W. D. *Foundations of Ethics.* Oxford: Clarendon Press, 1939.

———. *The Right and the Good.* Oxford: Clarendon Press, 1930.

Schlick, M. *The Problems of Ethics.* New York: Prentice-Hall, Inc., 1939.

Sidgwick, H. *The Methods of Ethics.* 7th Ed. Chicago: University of Chicago Press, 1907.

Sidgwick, H. *Outlines of the History of Ethics.* London: Macmillan and Company, Ltd., 1906.

Recent articles

Abraham, J. "J. S. Mill and 'Utilitarianism.'" *Listener,* June 20, 1963, 69:1031–1032.

Aiken, H. "The Levels of Moral Discourse." *Ethics* 62 (1952): 235–248.

Armstrong, K. "The Retributivist Hits Back." *Mind* NS70 (1961): 471–490.

Atkinson, R. "J. S. Mill's 'Proof' of the Principle of Utility." *Philosophy* (April 1957): 158–167.

Brandt, R. "In Search of a Credible Form of Rule-Utilitarianism." *Morality and the Language of Conduct.* Nahknikian and Castaneda, eds. Detroit: Wayne State University Press, 1953.

Braybrooke, D. "The Choice Between Utilitarians." *American Philosophical Quarterly* 4 (1967): 28–38.

Britton, K. "The Earlier Letters of John Stuart Mill." *Philosophy,* April 1, 1966, 41:174–179.

———. "Utilitarianism: the Appeal to a First Principle." *Proceedings of the Aristotelian Society,* NS60 (1959–60): 141–154.

Broiles, R. "Is Rule Utilitarianism Too Restricted?" *Southern Journal of Philosophy* 2 (1964): 180–187.

Chopra, P. "The Consequences of Human Action." *Proceedings of the Aristotelian Society* NS65 (1964–65): 147–166.

Clark, G. "Mill's 'Notorious Analogy.'" *Journal of Philosophy* 56 (1959): 652–656.

Clark, P. "Some Difficulties in Utilitarianism." *Philosophy* (July 1954): 244–252.

Cohen, B. "Some Ambiguities in the Form 'Hedonism.'" *Philosophical Quarterly* 12 (1962): 239–247.

Crombie, I. "Societal Clockwork and Utilitarian Morality." *Christian Faith and Communist Faith.* D. M. Mackinnon, ed. London: Macmillan, 1953.

Downie, R. "Mill on Pleasure and Self-development." *Philosophical Quarterly* 16 (1966): 69–71.

Duncan-Jones, A. "Utilitarianism and Rules." *Philosophical Quarterly* 7 (1957): 364–367.

Dworkin, G. "Marx and Mill: a Dialogue." *Philosophy and Phenomenological Research* 26 (1966): 403–414.

Emmons, D. "Justice Reassessed." *American Philosophical Quarterly* 4 (1967): 144–151.

Ewing, A. "Utilitarianism." *Ethics* 58 (1948): 100–111.

———. "What Would Happen if Everybody Acted Like Me?" *Philosophy* 28 (1953): 16–29.

Ezorsky, G. "Utilitarianism and Rules." *Australasian Journal of Philosophy* 43 (August 1965): 225–229.

Feinberg, J. "The Forms and Limits of Utilitarianism." *Philosophical Review* 76: 368–381.

Flathman, R. "Forms and Limits of Utilitarianism." *Ethics* 76 (1966): 309–317.

Foot, P. "Moral Beliefs." *Proceedings of the Aristotelian Society* NS59 (1958–59): 83–104.

Garvin, L. "Normative Utilitarianism and Naturalism." *Ethics* 60 (1949): 49–54.

Gauthier, D. "Rule-utilitarianism and Randomisation." *Analysis* 25 (1964–65): 68–69.

Gibbard, A. "Rule-utilitarianism: Merely an Illusory Alternative?" *Australasian Journal of Philosophy* 43 (August 1965): 211–220.

Ginsberg, M. "The Concept of Justice." *Philosophy* 38 (1963): 91–116.

Griffin, J. "Consequences." *Proceedings of the Aristotelian Society* NS65 (1964–65): 167–182.

Griffiths, A. "Justifying Moral Principles." *Proceedings of the Aristotelian Society* NS58 (1957–58): 103–124.

Haezrahi, P. "The Desired and the Desirable." *Analysis* 10 (1949): 40–48.

Hamlyn, D. "The Obligation to Keep a Promise." *Proceedings of the Aristotelian Society* NS62 (1961–62): 179–194.

Hammond, A. "Euthyphro, Mill, and Mr. Lewis." *Journal of Philosophy* 49 (1952): 377–392.

Hancock, R. "Ethics and History in Kant and Mill." *Ethics* 68 (1957): 56–60.

Harris, A. "John Stuart Mill's Theory of Progress." *Ethics* 66 (1956): 157–175.

Harsanyi, J. "Ethics in Terms of Hypothetical Imperatives." *Mind* NS67 (1958): 305–316.

Hart, H. "Prolegomenon to the Principles of Punishment." *Proceedings of the Aristotelian Society* NS60 (1959–60): 1–26.

Hughes, G. "The Ethical Relevance of Consequences." *Proceedings of the Aristotelian Society* NS48 (1947–48): 59–74.

Landesman, C. "Note on Act Utilitarianism." *Philosophical Review* 73 (1964): 243–247.

———. "Promises and Practices." *Mind* 75 (1966): 239–243.

Levi, A. "The 'Mental Crisis' of John Stuart Mill." *Psychoanalytic Review* 32 (1945): 86–101.

Long, W. "The Legend of Mill's 'Proofs.'" *Southern Journal of Philosophy* 5 (1967): 36–47.

Loring, L. "Moore's Criticism of Mill." *Ratio* 9 (1967): 84–90.

Mabbott, J. "Moral Rules." *Proceedings of the British Academy* 39 (1953): 97–117.

———. "Interpretations of Mill's *Utilitarianism*." *Philosophical Quarterly* 6 (1956): 115–120.

Margolis, J. "Rule Utilitarianism." *Australasian Journal of Philosophy* 43 (1965): 220–225.

McCloskey, H. "A Note on Utilitarian Punishment." *Mind* NS72 (1963): 599.

———. "Suppose Everyone Did the Same." *Mind* 75 (1966): 422–423.

McGreal, I. "Naturalistic Utilitarianism." *Journal of Philosophy* 47 (1950): 520–526.

Monro, D. "In Defense of Hedonism." *Ethics* 60 (1950): 285–291.

Moser, S. "A Comment on Mill's Argument for Utilitarianism." *Inquiry* 6 (1963): 308–318.

———. "Utilitarian Theories of Punishment and Moral Judgments." *Philosophical Studies* 8 (1957): 15–19.

Mothersill, M. "Hedonism and the 'Lower' Pleasures." *Journal of Philosophy* 54 (1957): 788–789.

Nakhnikian, G. "Value and Obligation in Mill." *Ethics* 62 (1951): 33–40.

Narveson, J. "Utilitarianism and Formalism." *Australasian Journal of Philosophy* 43 (1965): 58–72.

Nowell-Smith, P. "Utilitarianism and Treating Others as Ends." *Nous* 1 (1967): 81–90.

Penelhum, T. "The Logic of Pleasure." *Philosophy and Phenomenological Research* 17 (1957): 488–503.

Popkin, R. "Note on the Proof of Utility in J. S. Mill." *Ethics* 61 (1950): 66–68.

Rawls, J. "Justice as Fairness." *Philosophical Review* 67 (1958): 164–194.

———. "The Sense of Justice." *Philosophical Review* 72 (1963): 281–305.

———. Review of *The Place of Reason in Ethics*. *Philosophical Review* 60 (1951): 572–580.

Ryan, A. "Mill and the Naturalistic Fallacy." *Mind* 75 (1966): 422–425.

Sampson, R. "J. S. Mill: An Interpretation." *Cambridge Journal* (January 1950): 232–239.

Sartorius, R. "Utilitarianism and Obligation." *Journal of Philosophy*, vol. 66, no. 3, February 13, 1969, 67–81.

Singer, M. "Moral Rules and Principles." *Essays in Moral Philosophy*, Melden, ed. Seattle: University of Washington Press, 1958.

Smart, J. "The Methods of Ethics and the Methods of Science." *Journal of Philosophy* 62 (1965): 344–349.

Smart, R. "Negative Utilitarianism." *Mind*, vol. 67, no. 268 (October 1958): 542–543.

Sprigge, T. "A Utilitarian Reply to McCloskey." *Inquiry* 8 (1965): 264–291.

Stevenson, C. "Moore's Arguments against Certain Forms of Ethical Naturalism." *The Philosophy of G. E. Moore*, Schilpp, ed. Evanston and Chicago: Northwestern University Press, 1942.

Stout, A. "Suppose Everybody Did the Same?" *Australasian Journal of Philosophy*. 32 (1954): 1–29.

Strawson, P. "Social Morality and Individual Ideal." *Philosophy* 36 (1961): 1–17.

Stroll, A. "Mill's Fallacy." *Dialogue* 3 (1965): 385–404.

Thompson, D. "Retribution and the Distribution of Punishment." *Philosophical Quarterly* 16 (1966): 59–63.

Toulmin, S. "Principles of Morality." *Philosophy* 31 (1956): 142–153.

Wallace, J. "Pleasure as an End of Action." *American Philosophical Quarterly* 3 (1966): 312–316.

Wellman, C. "Reinterpretation of Mill's Proof." *Ethics* 69 (1959): 268–276.

White, R. "John Stuart Mill." *Cambridge Journal* (November 1951): 86–96.

Williams, G. "The Moral Insignificance of the Total of All Value" *Ethics* 55 (1945): 216–221.

Zinkernagel, P. "Revaluation of J. S. Mill's Ethical Proof." *Theoria* 18: 70–77.

SYMPOSIA

Mabbot, J., and Russell, L. "Is Anthropology Relevant to Ethics?" *Proceedings of the Aristotelian Society, Supplement*, 20 (1946): 61–93.

Brown, S.; Schneider, H.; Ladd, J.; and Baylis, C. "Utilitarianism and Moral Obligation." *The Philosophical Review* 61 (1952): 299–330.

Hall, E., and Rawls, J. "Justice as Fairness." *Journal of Philosophy* 54 (1957): 653–670.

Acton, H., and Watkins, J. "Negative Utilitarianism." *Proceedings of the Aristotelian Society, Supplement*, 37 (1963): 83–114.

Recent books

Hare, R. M. *Freedom and Reason*. Oxford: Clarendon Press, 1963.

Hodgson, D. *Consequences of Utilitarianism*. Oxford: Oxford University Press, 1967.

Lyons, D. *Forms and Limits of Utilitarianism*. Oxford: Oxford University Press, 1965.

MacIntyre, A. *A Short History of Ethics*. New York: The Macmillan Company, 1966.

Narveson, J. *Morality and Utility*. Baltimore: The Johns Hopkins University Press, 1967.

Rescher, N. *Distributive Justice: a Constructive Critique of the Utilitarian Theory of Distribution.* Indianapolis: Bobbs-Merrill Company, Inc., 1966.

Singer, M. G. *Generalization in Ethics.* New York: Alfred A. Knopf, 1961.

Smart, J. *An Outline of a System of Utilitarian Ethics.* Carlton: Melbourne University Press, 1961.

Toulmin, S. E. *An Examination of the Place of Reason in Ethics.* Cambridge: Cambridge University Press, 1950.

Text and Commentary Series

BERKELEY, *Principles of Human Knowledge,* Colin Murray Turbayne, editor. **2**

HUME, *Dialogues Concerning Natural Religion,* Nelson Pike, editor. **6**

KANT, *Foundations of the Metaphysics of Morals,* Robert Paul Wolff, editor. **1**

MILL, *Utilitarianism,* Samuel Gorovitz, editor. **7**

PLATO, *Meno,* Malcolm Brown, editor. **10**